EUROPE BETWEEN THE OCEANS

Author of over twenty books, including *The Ancient Celts* (1997), *Facing the Ocean* (2001) and *The Extraordinary Voyage of Pytheas the Greek* (2001), Barry Cunliffe is one of the most important and distinguished archaeologists in Europe. He has served on a variety of public bodies, including the Ancient Monuments Board, the Museum of London, the British Museum, and the Council for British Archaeology, and is currently a Commissioner of English Heritage. Knighted in 2006, his archaeological career has spanned over thirty years. He is Emeritus Professor of European Archaeology at the University of Oxford.

EUROPE BETWEEN THE OCEANS

Themes and Variations: 9000 BC–AD 1000

Barry Cunliffe

YALE UNIVERSITY PRESS
NEW HAVEN AND LONDON

For information about this and other Yale University Press publications, please contact:
U.S. Office: sales.press@yale.edu   www.yalebooks.com
Europe Office: sales@yaleup.co.uk   www.yaleup.co.uk

Set in Adobe Caslon
Designed by Peter Ward
Printed in China by Worldprint

Library of Congress Cataloguing-in-Publication Data

Cunliffe, Barry W.
      Europe between the oceans, 9000 BC–AD 1000 / Barry Cunliffe.
         p. cm.
      Includes bibliographical references and index.
      ISBN 978–0–300–11923-7 (alk. paper)
         1. Civilization, Western—History. 2. Europe—Civilization. 3. Europe—History—To 476.
         4. Europe—History—476-1492. I. Title.
      CB245.C85 2008
      940—DC22 2007038236

A catalogue record for this book is available from the British Library.

ISBN 978–0–300–17086–3 (pbk)

10 9 8 7 6 5 4 3 2 1

Contents

Preface

The westerly excrescence of the continent of Asia, which we call Europe, came to dominate the world during the course of the second millennium AD. It was here that arts and sciences flourished in the hothouse of the Renaissance and were forged into practical use during the Industrial Revolution. What made Europe so influential was the restlessness of its people: it was almost as though they were hard-wired to be mobile – and the seas that washed the peninsula facilitated that mobility. In the great voyages of exploration, which began in earnest at the end of the fifteenth century, the world was opened up. Entrepreneurs took to the sea to establish trading networks: land-grabbing and colonization followed. Within a few centuries most parts of the world had come under the influence of European culture, though some, like China and Japan, worked hard to retain their remoteness.

Humanity had evolved in Africa and from there had spread to all inhabitable parts of the earth. Why was it, then, that Europe above all other regions managed to achieve such dominance? There are no easy answers. As always it was the interplay of a number of different factors – but dominant among them was geography. Europe enjoyed a range of congenial ecozones closely spaced between the deserts of North Africa and the ice sheets of the Arctic. Moreover, its climate was moderated by the surrounding oceans and by the beneficial effects of the Gulf Stream. Communities therefore had the choice of a wide variety of ecological niches in which to develop their distinctive economies. But besides being ecologically varied, Europe was also resource-rich. Everything that was required was within comparatively easy reach – wood, stone, metals, furs – and could be distributed to all parts through intricate networks of exchange. The congenial environment and abundant resources encouraged population growth which, in turn, led to the development of complex societies hierarchically structured and controlled by elites. Competition for land, for resources and for luxury goods energized society, creating a dynamic that drove forward production, innovation and exploration.

Peninsular Europe's long and involuted interface with the sea offered a unique advantage. Not only was the littoral exceptionally resource-rich, but the sea aided – indeed, encouraged – mobility. The maritime interfaces became zones of innovation linked by networks of cross-peninsular routes. Its Atlantic façade was particularly favoured since it looked outwards: it was from there that entrepreneurs set out to explore the wider world, driven on by an innate restless energy.

European history of the second millennium AD is comparatively familiar through a number of excellent books and through the rather more narrow perspectives favoured by television, but of the formative ten thousand years before that there is surprisingly little to read by way of synthesis. Favoured subjects, like Romans and Greeks, are generously treated, as are the activities of the leading personalities of protohistory. But how these brief episodes fit together in the *longue durée* of European history is seldom considered.

This book is an attempt to present such a perspective – the long march of Europe from its recolonization following the Last Glacial Maximum around 10,000 BC to the end of the first millennium AD, when the states of Europe familiar to us now had begun to emerge.

I need hardly stress that in writing a book of this kind I have had to be selective. The literature is enormous and increases exponentially as thousands of new studies are published each year in an ever-increasing number of journals and monographs. Simply to scan the titles is to appreciate the vibrancy of archaeology in all its many manifestations.

Such is the growing complexity of the subject that there will be as many very different early histories of Europe as there are authors prepared to write them. I have chosen to emphasize what seems to me to be the underlying drive – the determining effect that the geography of the peninsula has had on the way in which the human population has developed. Geography provides the stage with all its constraints and opportunities. The human actors, too, are constrained by their innate chemistry. They are gregarious but competitive; they have a dangerous curiosity but are dynamically conservative. The complex interaction of human groups with their environment, and with each other, provides the main plot.

In focusing on these issues, which I believe to be the essential basis for understanding history, I have, of necessity, downplayed other remarkable aspects of the human achievement – the philosophies and belief systems, the delight in the visual arts and the varied responses to the charisma of leadership. There are other histories of early Europe to be written with these matters centre stage. All I can hope is that the personal overview offered in the pages to follow will provide a structure helpful to those eager to begin exploring the deeply fascinating story of our early European ancestors.

* * *

This book has grown out of a series of lectures – The Rhind Lectures – which I was invited to give in Edinburgh in 2002. The subject I chose, 'Peoples between the Oceans', looked at the significance of the sea in the early development of western European society.

I am much indebted to the Rhind Committee not only for the honour of the invitation but also for the stimulus that it gave me to explore the subject matter further. I am also indebted to two guardian angels: Lynda Smithson, who turned my illegible scrawl into an immaculate text; and Heather McCallum of Yale University Press, without whose gentle intervention this book would have been very much longer.

Barry Cunliffe
Oxford
May 2007

CHAPTER ONE

Ways of Seeing: Space, Time and People

In November 1888 two artists painted the famous walk through the cemetery of Les Alyscamps at Arles. Their visions were strikingly different. It was the tortuous rhythms of the trees and the shadows on the dead leaves covering the path that fascinated Van Gogh. Gauguin was more concerned to capture the essence of the place in slabs of sharply contrasting colours. The same scene, the same time of year and two men who were, at this stage, friends sharing the same accommodation – yet their ways of seeing and interpreting what they saw could not have been more different. So it is with us all. And the more so when we are dealing with the past, relying on the detritus left by humanity – what we are pleased to call the archaeological record – and fragmentary written texts, at best anecdotal, at worst misleading. It is hardly surprising, then, that perceptions of the past may well be conflicting – and are constantly changing.

Concepts of Space

Even geography is not what it seems. Many years ago, standing on the harbour-side at Kirkwall on the island of Orkney, north of the mainland of Scotland, I got into conversation with an island farmer and, curious about the local economy, I asked him what he did with his cattle as winter approached. He shipped a proportion of his herd south, he said. Asked where exactly, he volunteered that it was 'far south – to Aberdeen [pause] or even, sometimes, to the English plain beyond'. Our cognitive geography, like that of the Orkney farmer, is conditioned by our daily lives and by our own personal experiences of space and distance. This is nowhere more evident than with a child who, asked to draw a map of his town, will emphasize the familiar and personally important – home, school, friends' houses, playgrounds – and will inevitably distort sizes and distances between them, depending on their perceived desirability. While familiarity with satellite images and the relative times taken in air travel between major cities today enables us to conjure up a tolerably acceptable map of the world, most of our constructs will still include errors, distortions and omissions. But a real sense of space, however imperfect, is a modern phenomenon. Even in the recent past most people would have had only a very partial cognitive geography, even of their immediate world. Each community lived in a confined territory surrounded by an unknown that was both mysterious and dangerous, inhabited by people who were 'other' – different from us. Many were content with this isolation, but there have always been more enterprising individuals whose curiosity has driven them to enquire and explore. In deep prehistory we can know little of these remarkable people but in the early literate societies of the Mediterranean their strivings become discernible as they worked to build up a picture of the wider world.

Investigative geography in Europe began in the Ionian and Dorian colonies scattered along the south-east coasts of Asia Minor. Prominent among them was Miletos, surrounded by fine harbours, jutting out into a wide bay fed by the river Menderes. Today the city is a gaunt ruin, isolated by the marshlands that have crept relentlessly seawards, a victim partly of changing sea levels and partly of erosion from the flanking hills left bare by overgrazing.

From the early second millennium BC the promontory of Miletos was the home of traders closely linked to the Minoan and, later, the Mycenaean world. Later foundation myths tell of Ionian Greeks from Athens settling there,

1.1 The city of Miletos, founded by the Greeks and flourishing during the Roman period, was once a great port but the gradual silting of the wide inlet on which it stood has left it isolated amid marshes now some 6 km (3½ miles) from the sea.

probably as early as 1000 BC. By 700 BC a thriving Archaic city spread across the headland, soon to be adorned with temples to Dionysos, Artemis and Aphrodite, Demeter and Athena, and protected by a city wall. The prosperity of the city was based partly on a hinterland productive of wool and oil, but more on its highly favoured location as a route node linking the long overland trek from the east, via the valley of the river Menderes, to the coastal shipping lanes which embraced the east Mediterranean and extended northwards into the Black Sea and to the Pontic steppe. Through the port of Miletos goods and people flowed, and with the sailors and traders came knowledge. For those anxious to learn of the world there could hardly have been a better place to sit and listen.

From about 600 BC, Miletos became a centre of vibrant scholarship – a place where thinkers attempted to counter the colourful mythical view of the world revolving around a pantheon of deities with a new rationalism based partly on observational science and partly on philosophy. The earliest of these remarkable men to whom we can give a name was Thales, active in the early decades of the sixth century. He is said to have visited and studied in Egypt and is credited with developing the belief that the world originated from water and would eventually return to water. His pupil Anaximander (c.610–545) further developed this idea of a primordial element. For him it was not water but *apeiron*, probably best interpreted as that which is spatially unlimited or boundless. The products of this matter – such as wetness, dryness, heat, cold – in paired opposites gave rise to the many worlds of the universe. Anaximander is also credited with producing the first map of the world, which he envisaged to be a disc standing on a column suspended in space in the centre of the universe. The third of this remarkable group was Anaximenes (c.600–526), who may have been a pupil of Anaximander. His view of cosmogony was that everything derived from air either by rarefaction, giving rise to fire, or by condensation, leading successively to wind, cloud, water, earth and stone. He was also the first philosopher to envisage a human soul, which he believed to be a component of air.

The three Milesian philosophers brought about a profound change in thought in the early part of the sixth century – a revolution that was to set the scene for the growth of philosophy in Athens in the following centuries. While one can discern there the influences of Babylonian and Egyptian thought, what emerged at Miletos was truly revolutionary. It attempted to replace myths dependent on the machinations of the gods with rational thought.

In this cradle of intellectual excitement, some time about 530 BC, Hecataeus was born. His two works, *Histories* and *Journey Round the World*, justify the claim that he was father of both history and geography. Neither

3

1.2 About 500 BC the Greek geographer Hecataeus of Miletos attempted to describe the world. The map gives some idea of how he conceived it to be.

work survives but several hundred fragments of the latter are quoted in the writings of his successors. The *Journey* was composed of itineraries through Europe and Asia along the shores of the Mediterranean and the Black Sea, but it also included additional material on Scythia and India. From the surviving scraps it is possible to reconstruct a map sketching the world as Hecataeus envisaged it. His sources were various. He appears to have made journeys of his own, but from his favoured position at Miletos he would also have been able to draw on the knowledge of travellers coming from far afield. According to Pliny the Elder, Miletos had been responsible for founding ninety colonies, many of them around the shores of the Black Sea. Southern Italy and Sicily were by now heavily settled by Greeks and by 600 BC colonial foundations had been established around the Golfe du Lion, at Massalia (Marseille), Agathe (Agde) and Emporion (Ampurias), whence knowledge of the west Mediterranean and its barbarian hinterland was readily forthcoming. He will also have had access to Egyptian records, including the story of the Phoenician circumnavigation of Africa in about 600 BC. His knowledge of the east is most likely to have come from traders who used the overland routes to Miletos from Syria and beyond.

For Hecataeus there was a degree of symmetry about the world, arranged as he saw it on either side of an axis through the Mediterranean. For this reason he conceived it, much as Anaximander had done, as a disc surrounded by an ocean. The Mediterranean shores of Europe and the Black Sea would have been reasonably well known. There was some direct knowledge of the Ister (Danube). Scythians lived around the north shores of the Black Sea, as he would have learnt from visitors from the many Greek colonies occupying the Black Sea littoral, while in the west there were Celts, near-neighbours of the Massaliots. Beyond this, to the west and north, his Europe faded into fog and mystery, whence came vague stories of wild Hyperboreans, Tin Islands and rivers along which the much-prized amber was transported. But Hecataeus was careful to avoid anything that sounded like myth, priding himself that 'What I write here is the account that I believe to be true. For the stories told by the Greeks are many, and in my opinion ridiculous.'

To the south of Miletos, on the south-west coast of Caria, was another great coastal town, Halicarnassus. Here, in 484 BC, probably about the time of Hecataeus's death, the historian Herodotus was born. He left the city at an early age to settle for a while on the island of Samos, less than a day's sail from Miletos, using it as a base from which to travel extensively in Europe, Asia and

Africa. His expeditions took him down the Nile, as far south as Elephantine, eastwards through Syria to Babylon and Susa, and north probably to the Black Sea to observe the Scythians and the Thracians. Eventually, in 443 BC, he joined an expedition to found a colony at Thurii in southern Italy and remained there for the rest of his life. It was probably at Thurii that he wrote his celebrated *Histories*. This was designed to give an account of the conflict between Persia and the Greeks between 490 and 470 BC, but two-thirds of the book provide a magnificent sweeping background to the history, geography and anthropology of the world as he knew it.

He would have been familiar with the works of Hecataeus but was more circumspect about evidence and the limits of reasonable deduction that could be made from it:

> For my part I cannot but laugh when I see numbers of persons
> drawing maps of the world without having any reason to guide them;
> making, as they do, the Ocean-stream to run all around the earth,
> and the earth itself to be an exact circle as if described by a pair of
> compasses. (*Hist.* IV, 36)

It is a theme he takes up again when summing up his limited knowledge of northern Europe:

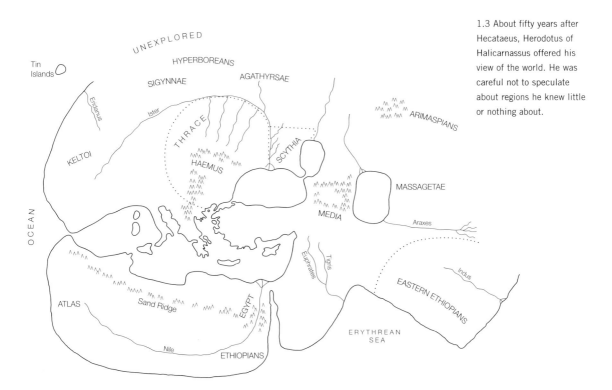

1.3 About fifty years after Hecataeus, Herodotus of Halicarnassus offered his view of the world. He was careful not to speculate about regions he knew little or nothing about.

5

Of the extreme tracts of Europe towards the west I cannot speak with any certainty, for I do not allow that there is any river, to which the barbarians give the name Eridanus, emptying itself into the northern sea whence amber is procured; nor do I know of any islands called Cassiterides whence the tin comes which we use. For in the first place the name Eridanus is manifestly not a barbarian word at all, but a Greek name invented by some poet or other; and secondly, though I have taken vast pains I have never been able to get an assurance from an eyewitness that there is any sea on the further side of Europe. Nevertheless, tin and amber do certainly come to us from the ends of the earth. (*Hist.* III, 115)

Here is a careful scholar at work, critical of his predecessors' apparent gullibility and exasperated by the idle ramblings of poets. Yet the northern parts of Europe still retained a fascination for him and he could not resist one last story. These regions, he believed, are 'very much richer in gold than any other region but how it is procured I have no certain knowledge. The story goes that the one-eyed Arimaspi purloin it from griffins, but here too I am incredulous' (*Hist.* III, 116). It is clear from what Herodotus chose to report that rare commodities like gold, tin and amber, procured in distant barbarian lands, were finding their way through exchange networks to Mediterranean ports along with garbled travellers' tales about the lands from which they came: there was also some knowledge of a mysterious outer ocean. To exploit the resources of the metal-rich west, the Phoenicians had sailed through the Pillars of Hercules (the Straits of Gibraltar) and established a permanent Atlantic port on the island of Gadir (Cadiz) by about 800 BC. From here trading posts and colonies were established north along the coast of Iberia probably as far as the river Mondego and south down the African coast to Essaouria. Surviving scraps of travellers' tales leave little doubt that more enterprising journeys were made from time to time. One Phoenician explorer, Hanno, may have got as far as Cameroon in West Africa, while another, Himilco, sailed out into the ocean 'beyond Europe', though without making any significant discoveries.

The Mediterranean port on the receiving end of the trade routes from the barbarian regions of north-western Europe was the Greek colony of Massalia (Marseille), founded around 600 BC. Two principal routes converged here, one from the north following the valleys of the Saône and the Rhône, the other from the west using the Garonne, the Carcassonne Gap and the river Aude to reach the Mediterranean at the native port of Narbo whence goods were shipped onwards to Massalia. Hardly surprising, therefore, that Massalia was to provide the first known explorer of the north-western extremities of Europe – the enterprising traveller and accomplished scientist Pytheas. Pytheas made his epic journey some time about 320 BC, returning to Massalia to write of his

1.4 Modern Marseille (centre towards bottom) has grown from the Greek trading colony of Massalia, founded by the Phocaean Greeks about 600 BC. It was carefully sited on a fine, sheltered harbour commanding the major trade route along the river Rhône which gave access to the heart of west central Europe. The mouth of the Rhône is just beyond the left margin of the picture west of the large lake, the Etang de Berre. In this infrared satellite image natural vegetation is red and forests are brown.

experiences in a book, *On the Ocean*. The text no longer survives but is known to us from fragments quoted by others. As he progressed through barbarian Europe he took measurements enabling him to estimate the height of the sun at midday on the midsummer solstice. Relating these to a reading taken at his home town, he was able to work out the distance he had travelled northwards. Longitude measurements were more difficult to judge: these could only be estimated on the basis of the time taken to make a particular journey. The first stage of his travels took him along the Aude/Garonne/Gironde, following the long-established route along which tin was transported to the Mediterranean. From here he seems to have taken to local shipping, exploring first the Armorican peninsula (Brittany), which he realized was a massive westerly projection from the land he knew as Celticā (modern France), before crossing the Channel to the tin-producing region of Cornwall. Then followed a circumnavigation of Britain which allowed him to visualize the island as triangular and to give remarkably accurate estimated lengths for its three sides. His most likely route was northwards from Cornwall through the Irish Sea and the North Channel to the Northern Isles, taking sun-height measurements on the islands of Man, Lewis and Shetland. The return route would have led southwards down the east coast to the Straits of Dover and then along the south coast, before he made for Armorica and retraced his steps back to Massalia.

This much is tolerably certain, but there are details in the surviving texts that suggest that other regions may also have been explored. At one point he describes an island called Thule lying six days' sail north of Britain where, at a certain time of year, the sun moved along the horizon but did not set and the sea was frozen. This sounds remarkably like Iceland. Elsewhere he describes the 'great estuary' from which came amber – a reference that would seem to be to the east coast of Jutland and the German Bight. In both cases he could have picked up knowledge of these places from local traders but there is no reason to suppose that he did not explore them for himself.

On the Ocean must have stunned those Mediterranean-bound scholars who read it. In many ways it was directly addressing with new evidence the uncertainties and reservations expressed by Herodotus over a hundred years before – the shape of Europe was now becoming much clearer. Pytheas was quoted with approval by near-contemporary scholars like Dicaearchus, Timaeus and Eratosthenes who were keen to welcome the new science, but two later writers, Polybius and Strabo, reviled him as a charlatan and a downright liar. Both men had their reasons – Polybius was making a bid to be an Atlantic explorer in his own right, while the far more sedentary Strabo was enamoured of his own preconceptions of the shape of Europe's Atlantic coast and the northern limit of human habitation which could not be made to fit with the observations recorded by Pytheas. According to Strabo therefore, Pytheas must have made it up.

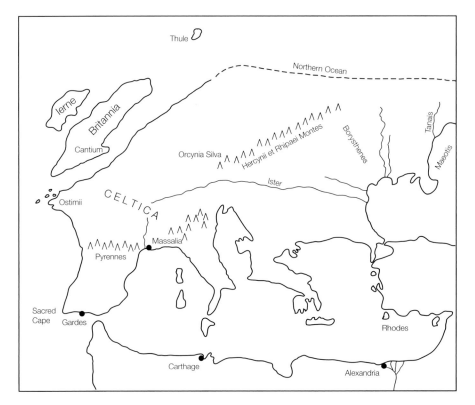

1.5 As the Greeks learned more of the world through trading ventures and exploration, so the concept of the shape of Europe, and in particular its Atlantic interface and its offshore islands, began to improve. Eratosthenes (upper map) writing at the end of the third century BC relied on information brought back by the Atlantic explorer Pytheas. Strabo's conception (lower map) at the end of the first century BC was less accurate because he rejected Pytheas as an imposter and insisted on his own preconceptions.

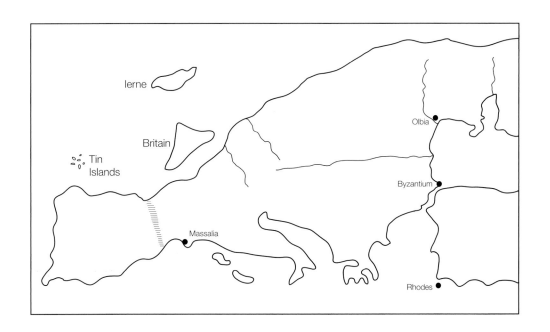

In fact, Strabo's views were already obsolete by the time his books were published at the very beginning of the first century AD. Fifty years before, Julius Caesar had explored the coastal regions of Gaul and had crossed to south-eastern Britain. He had also discovered the Rhine and had bridged it, penetrating for the first time to the edge of the great North European Plain – the homeland of the Germans. In a vivid section of his commentary on his Gallic Wars – *De bello gallico* – he sets out to describe these newly discovered barbarians to his eager audience: 'The greatest glory for a German tribe is to lay waste as much land as possible around its own territory and keep it uninhabited. They consider it a mark of valour to have driven their neighbours from their land so that no one dares to settle near them' (*BG* VI, 23). Wild generalizations, of course, but enough to present the Germans as 'other' and thus as a potential threat to Rome.

Although Caesar's penetration into German territory was limited, he was, as a military commander, keenly interested in geography. In one passage he describes, with evident wonder, the vast expanses of the forested North European Plain:

> The Hercynian forest . . . is so wide that it would take a man travelling light nine days to cross it. . . . [It] starts on the frontiers of the Helvetii, the Nemetes and the Raurici and runs straight along the line of the Danube to the country of the Dacians. . . . At this point it turns away from the river north-eastwards and is of such enormous length that it touches the territories of many different peoples. No one in western Germany would claim to have reached the eastern edge of the forest even after travelling 60 days, or to have discovered where it ends.
> (*BG* VI, 25)

He goes on to excite his readers with accounts of strange beasts said to inhabit the forest – an ox shaped like a deer with a single horn in the middle of its forehead, creatures called elks with no leg joints so that they have to lean against trees to sleep, and great aurochs only slightly smaller than an elephant. Even to pragmatists like Caesar the edges of the world disappeared into a mist of myth.

The civil war that followed Caesar's assassination in 44 BC brought to an end the exploration of the north until Augustus, the first emperor of Rome, had sufficiently stabilized his power base to move forward. The Alpine tribes were quickly subdued and in 12 BC a new forward policy beyond the Rhine could be instituted. In that year Drusus sailed along the Frisian coast to the mouth of the river Ems and coastal exploration was taken further in AD 5 by Tiberius, who reached the estuary of the Elbe, but in AD 16 the Roman armies decided to abandon Germany and to create a frontier on the Rhine–Danube line: the difficulties of the alien terrain of the North European Plain had defeated them.

From safe bases along the frontier zone Roman entrepreneurs penetrated the barbarian territories. One man travelled through Germania and brought back quantities of amber to decorate the amphitheatre for Nero's gladiatorial shows. His journey would have taken him to the Baltic coast where he was evidently successful in procuring an impressive haul of the fossilized resin. It was an epic journey but he would not have been the only entrepreneur to explore the northern regions, bringing back to Rome rare commodities such as furs and wild beasts for the arena, and with them stories of strange barbarian peoples and the land in which they lived.

At the end of the first century AD the historian Tacitus had at his disposal an array of information about northern Europe beyond the Roman frontier. In his book *Germania* he sets out to offer a comprehensive account of this alien world. Tribe after tribe is described in fascinating detail, enlivened by the odd acerbic one-liner. The Sithones, for example, 'are ruled by a woman. To this extent they have fallen lower not merely than free men but than slaves' (*Germania* 45). He ends with a brief conspectus of the peoples living along the east shores of 'the Suebian Sea' (the Baltic), the last of whom were the Fenni, occupying the coastal region of Estonia. These are 'remarkably savage and wretchedly poor . . . they feed on wild plants, wear skins and sleep on the ground'. For Tacitus this was the end of the known world: 'Everything after this point is in the realm of fable. The Hellusii and Oxiones are said to have human faces and features, the bodies and limbs of animals. As this has not been confirmed, I shall leave the matter open' (*Germania* 46). The Roman conquest of Britain in the decades following the invasion of AD 43 and Trajan's annexation of Dacia in the early second century extended the known geography of Europe still further. By the middle of the second century the broad outlines of the peninsula were familiar from the Atlantic to the Caspian Sea and from the Mediterranean to the Baltic.

A comprehensive account was produced by Marinus of Tyre some time around AD 110. His work does not survive but was extensively used by his more famous successor Claudius Ptolemaeus (Ptolemy), who worked in Alexandria. Ptolemy was both an astronomer and a geographer. In the 140s he produced his *System of Astronomy*, followed a few years later by his *Geography*, published in eight books. In the *Geography* he derides previous writers who 'chatter about the ways of peoples'. There is nothing here on the trivialities of anthropology, landscape or history. The first book sets out the principles and methods to be used in mapmaking. Every place is to be fixed using astronomical measurements on the face of a globe divided by parallels and meridians, but since accurate measurements are rare one must also resort to distances estimated by travellers. The subsequent books are largely made up of lists of places – altogether about eight thousand of them, each identified by latitude and longitude – which provide the raw materials for mapmaking. As a prime meridian for longitude he takes the line running through the Fortunate Islands (the Canaries). The last meridian he draws through Sinae (China) at 180° W.

Although Ptolemy's measurements contain many errors, coming not least from his transcription of data, quite tolerable maps can be constructed from them. The vast corpus of observational data he was able to compile firmly established the shape and size of the European peninsula.

Roman knowledge of Scandinavia was, however, strictly limited. The tribes of what is now Denmark were known by name and there was some knowledge of southern Sweden, but beyond that the map was blank. Yet it was from this broad region more than four hundred years after the collapse of Roman central government that a new wave of explorers was to emerge. These Northmen,

1.6 The Vikings, or Northmen, emanating from Norway, Denmark and Sweden, spread throughout Europe in the eighth to tenth centuries AD, using the seaways and the river routes. They were the first Europeans to sail on all of Europe's oceans.

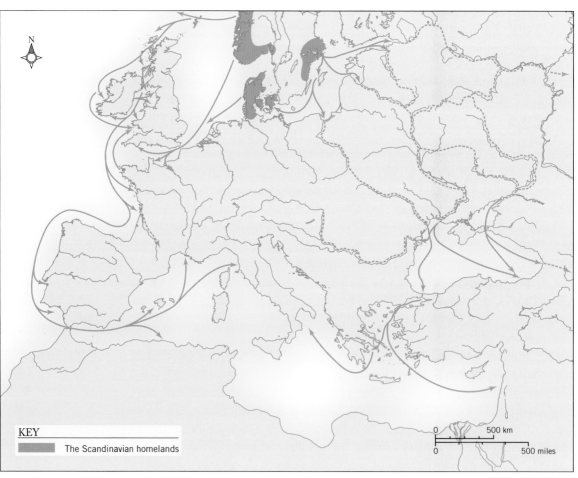

KEY

The Scandinavian homelands

0   500 km

0   500 miles

Norsemen or Vikings, as they are popularly called, came from the coasts of southern Norway, from Jutland and Zeland and from the Baltic coast of Sweden. By sea and river, over a period of three centuries, they embraced the

1.7 The Varpsund rune-stone in Uppland, Sweden records the death of a ship's captain who sailed with the explorer Ingvar in the early eleventh century AD from Sweden, via the rivers of Russia, to the Black Sea and probably to the Caspian.

whole of Europe as raiders, traders, settlers and mercenaries. Much of the land that received them was already familiar to the civilized world, but the more adventurous among them forced the boundaries into the unknown. From the Norwegian coasts shiploads of settlers reached the Faeroe Islands about AD 825 and Iceland by about AD 860, finding that Irish monks had already settled there. By about AD 1000 the Icelandic settlers had established a base in southern Greenland. Others journeyed northwards, rounding the northern extremity of Scandinavia at North Cape to reach the White Sea where walrus ivory, furs and hides were to be had. Even more remarkable were the men who left the region of Mälaren in western Sweden to explore the east, travelling along the great rivers to the Black Sea, or to the Caspian Sea, some striking off eastwards into the depths of Asia. In this way the northern extremities of Europe, hitherto unknown except to those who lived there, were drawn into the consciousness of the rest of Europe.

The names of some of the pioneers are known: Gardar the Swede, who was blown off course to the Hebrides and ended up on a remote North Atlantic island; Floki Vilgerdarson, who followed up the discovery and named the island Iceland; and Erik the Red, who gave the optimistic name Greenland to an icebound enclave in the far west. One of the most adventurous of all was Ingvar, a young Swede of about twenty-five, who set off from central Sweden with a small fleet of ships in 1036 on a journey that was to last five years. The exact details are uncertain but his route took him via the Gulf of Finland and the city of Novgorod and thence to the river Dnepr leading to the Black Sea and Byzantium. From here he crossed by way of Tbilisi to the Caspian Sea and, reaching its eastern shore, he took off eastwards into Asia where, according to the Icelandic sagas, he and his men met disaster: only a few of his followers returned home to the Mälaren region to tell the tale. Thirty memorial stones put up by grieving relatives still survive. Those who died included Ingvar's brother Harald, ships' captains, a navigator and a steersman. Ingvar justly earned the soubriquet 'the Widefarer'.

If Hecataeus's attempts to map the world he knew in 540 BC were the first faltering steps in conceptualizing the European peninsula, Ingvar's epic journey 1500 years later symbolizes the culmination of the process. The boundaries of Europe had been established: men brought up on one ocean fringe now knew that they could travel without hindrance to all the others.

Concepts of Time

The passage of time in the ancient world was variously calculated. In the literate world of the Mediterranean it was related to fixed points. The Egyptians used king lists, the Greeks began with the first Olympiad, held

1.8 The stronghold of Sarmizegethusa, high in the Orăştie Mountains of Romania, was the centre of Dacian power in the first and second centuries AD. On a plateau within the fortress, circular structures, thought to be calendars, have been excavated.

in 776 BC, while the Romans took the foundation of Rome as their starting point, relating individual years to the holders of consular office. How the communities of the rest of Europe fared in the prehistoric period is less certain, but the famous Coligny calendar found near Lyon, dating to the first or second century AD, implies a sophisticated understanding of time based on lunar months of thirty days with the year suitably adjusted by intercalary months quite possibly arranged in nineteen-year cycles. In the Dacian capital of Sarmizegethusa, in the Orăştie Mountains of Romania, a remarkable sanctuary has been found with circular settings of stones and wooden pillars representing days, seasons and years. The years were divided into twelve months, each of thirty days arranged in five weeks of six days. The sanctuary dates to about the same period as the Coligny calendar and has evident similarities in the way in which time is perceived. This is hardly surprising since the lunar month, the solstices and the rhythm of the seasons would have been readily apparent − and all-important in organizing the sowing of crops and rearing of animals upon which the wellbeing of society depended. How the passing of the years was recalled remains uncertain but genealogies and epics probably formed part of the rich oral traditions, and each community may have had time-markers embedded in the landscape to provide reference points. A line of barrows on a skyline, differing in form and size and representing the passing of individual ancestors, would undoubtedly have been endowed with chronological meaning for the community whose elite were buried there.

What is far less clear is whether time was conceived in simple linear form as we understand it today; or whether the perception was more subtle, there being different paces of time. Perhaps time was seen to be cyclical.

The concept of varying times was brilliantly expounded by the French historian Fernand Braudel, one of the most influential members of the *Annales* school of historians founded in 1929 by Lucien Febvre and Marc Bloch. Febvre's view was that history was stultifying in its narrowness. For him, 'historians [should] be geographers, be jurists too and sociologists and psychologists'. To progress to new understandings, it was necessary to break down all these compartments ('abattre les cloisons'). Braudel embraced this breadth but went much further. One of his greatest contributions to the way in which history is perceived is his concept of varying wavelengths of time.

At the base of it all is the *longue durée*, the deep rhythm of underlying forces influencing all human society, 'a history in which all change is slow, a history of constant repetition, of ever recurring cycles'. This is geographical time − a time of landscapes that enable and constrain, of stable or slow developing technologies and of deep-seated ideologies.

Above this, at a rather faster wavelength, come the medium-term cycles.

1.9 (*opposite*) A group of Bronze Age round barrows aligned on a Neolithic long barrow at Winterbourne Stoke, near Stonehenge in Wiltshire. It is tempting to see these structures, with their different sizes and shapes, as representing 'time marks' in the landscape where the ancestry and history of the tribe could be explained.

Concepts of time

1.10 Concepts of time according to the great French historian Fernand Braudel.

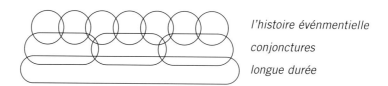

l'histoire événmentielle

conjonctures

longue durée

These Braudel refers to as *conjonctures* – a term that to French economists usually means 'trends' but to the *Annales* historians implies more specifically the changing trajectories of discrete systems, demographic, economic, agrarian and socio-political. These are essentially collective forces, impersonal and usually restricted in time to no more than a century. Together the *longue durée* and *conjonctures* provided the basic structures, largely imperceptible to the individual, against which human life was played out. These structures are the frameworks that control human action. Like the landscape itself, they constrained and enabled.

The shortest-term cycle Braudel refers to as *l'histoire événementielle* – events instigated by individuals creating diplomatic or political ripples. It is, he says, the history 'richest in human interest' yet events are little more than 'surface disturbances, crests of foam that the tides of history carry on their strong backs . . . we must learn to distrust them'. Elsewhere he is even more dismissive of the history of events, describing it as 'the actions of a few princes and rich men, the trivia of the past, bearing little relation to the slow and powerful march of history . . .. These statesmen were, despite their illusions, more acted upon than actors.'

Perhaps the best analogy one might offer of Braudel's model of 'duration' is the one he introduces himself: the sea. At the surface are the transient flecks of surf, whipped up and gone in a minute. These are carried on water enjoying a more gentle motion, that of the tide and of the swell; but further down, in the deep, are the sluggish, almost imperceptible, movements of the mass of water that bears everything.

To perceive time in this way has a real resonance with the way in which archaeologists reconstruct the past. At the base of it all is the environment, which results largely from the interaction of climate with geomorphology. It has its own dynamic of change which may be deflected or exacerbated by human intervention. The environment lays down the basic rules of behaviour, facilitating human action in some ways but constraining it in others. Within this structure societies develop their distinctive economic, social, political and religious systems. Some societies are conservative and change little; others are innovative, creating a dynamic of directional development. To a prehistorian these two levels of study – roughly equivalent to Braudel's *longue durée* and *conjonctures* – provide the very core of the study. Seldom is it possible for the effects of individuals – the *événements* – to be recognized. Only with the advent of the written record do individuals come more sharply into focus and we can begin to write what is conventionally called 'history'. But as Braudel has so cogently argued, the *longue durée* and *conjonctures* are also history. Lucien Febvre made the point well when he wrote in 1949 that the concept of prehistory is one of the most ridiculous that can be imagined. So, in this book, we are all historians.

The Peopling of Europe: Issues of Mobility

The first humans probably reached the land we would now call Europe around 800,000 years ago and, although there were periods when advancing ice sheets rendered large parts of the landmass uninhabitable, humans have remained ever since. It is a reasonable assumption that these Palaeolithic hunting communities were the direct ancestors of the Mesolithic hunter-gatherers who expanded through Europe, moving further and further north as the last cold period ended around 9600 BC. By 7000 BC these advanced foragers had established themselves in most parts of the continent, adapting their food-gathering regimes to the different ecological niches they chose to inhabit. The gene pool of the present European population is substantially that of the Palaeolithic pioneers, with a smaller component contributed by incomers from south-western Asia in the Neolithic period.

After a sedentary way of life had been established in the Neolithic period (beginning about 7000 BC), we must consider to what extent significant relocations of population took place. There were certainly recognizable changes in culture, and in the days when people naively believed, with Lord Raglan, that 'natives don't invent things' it was customary to explain change as the result of conquest or migration. The older archaeological literature is pervaded with these beliefs. We read of pioneer farmers from the east thrusting through the virgin forests of Europe and later of 'megalithic missionaries' from the enlightened Mediterranean, sailing up the Atlantic coasts of Europe to take the new religion to the benighted savages of ocean-facing Europe. Then come the Beaker Folk aimlessly (it would seem) engaged in pan-European folk wandering while sturdy horse-riding 'Kurgan folk' from the steppes galloped in to establish themselves across the North European Plain. Later still, in the mid-first millennium, marauding Celts from west central Europe hacked their way west to Ireland and Iberia and east to Anatolia. And so on.

It is all too easy now to make fun of early interpretations of European prehistory. They were, at best, an honest attempt to explain archaeological data and in doing so to create a history of events. But these were models born of their time. Scholars of the nineteenth and early twentieth centuries were trained in a classical tradition: Greeks colonized while their Roman successors conquered. Later, traditional accounts of Saxons, Vikings and Normans offered different models of the way in which cultural change could be brought about by migration and the sword. And one had only to look at the British Empire to see dramatic social and economic change imposed by the will of conquerors. It was in this cultural atmosphere that invasionist interpretations flourished, underpinned by the one big idea that innovation and enlightenment ultimately came from 'the cradle of civilization' in the east. This *ex oriente lux* hypothesis, as it was called, provided the structure for much late nineteenth- and early twentieth-century prehistory.

The 1960s saw a major change in archaeological thinking – rather grandly called a paradigm shift. This was exacerbated by two developments: radiocarbon dating was providing a new series of near-absolute dates which could offer an independent chronological framework free from preconceptions; and a new generation of archaeologists was growing up in a post-colonial world.

Before the advent of radiocarbon dating in 1947, prehistoric European chronologies were relative. Cultural change could be observed in the sequence of layers built up on archaeological sites, which allowed sets of artefacts and structures to be arranged in chronological order. From these it was possible to develop typological sequences, which showed how an object or a structure had changed over time. These could be compared between different regions to offer synchronisms. If artefacts could be correlated with finds in Egypt or the Near East, it was possible to suggest absolute dates using king lists or other documentary evidence. Thus, outward cultural diffusion from the east provided a structure for ordering the European prehistoric record.

To give one example: the megalithic monuments, and in particular the passage graves found extensively along the Atlantic façade of Europe from south-western Portugal to Orkney, were thought to have evolved from Mediterranean prototypes. The earliest megalithic tombs were believed to be the tholos tombs of Minoan Crete, dating to about 3000 BC. Thus, the scenario goes, the concepts of collective burial and the associated architecture 'diffused' westwards, carried, some believed, by 'missionaries'. The theory was based on an interpretation of a typological sequence and the belief that cultural innovation always developed in the east and 'diffused' outwards from there. By the 1960s sufficient radiocarbon dates had become available to show quite conclusively that the Atlantic passage graves predated their supposed Mediterranean 'ancestors' by up to two millennia. In a single stroke the whole tissue of preconceptions collapsed, allowing space and air for radical new thoughts, not least the realization that a highly sophisticated system of beliefs, cosmologies and architecture had developed independently on the Atlantic seaboard: by comparison, the contemporary Mediterranean was something of a backwater.

New revelations of this kind coincided with the end of empire, heralding an increasing degree of circumspection in archaeological interpretation. Diffusionism was widely rejected while belief in migrations and other large-scale folk movements was quickly dropped from the explanatory repertoire. Some prehistorians went into a state of denial, implicitly refusing to accept that population movements had ever been a significant feature of European prehistory. It was a sudden and decisive swing of the interpretative pendulum. In the new orthodoxy, change was explored through other mechanisms such as indigenous innovation, the spread of ideas through networks of exchange, and the copying of elite behaviour. Any suggestions of there having been significant movements of population were considered to be hopelessly old-fashioned.

Yet those archaeologists working in the protohistoric period have had to keep a more open mind since there are many tolerably convincing accounts of folk movements on a large scale. Celts from west central Europe moved south-wards and eastwards to settle in the Po valley and the middle Danube valley in the fourth century BC. Some went on to attack Delphi in 279 BC, and in the aftermath whole communities, and not just fighting men, migrated into Asia Minor to create new settlements. Later, in the last decades of the second century BC, the Cimbri and Teutones, whose homeland seems to have been in or near Jutland, wandered through western Europe as far as Iberia leaving chaos in their wake, while from the third to fifth centuries AD successive waves of Germanic peoples swept through the Roman frontier to carve out settlements for themselves in the old Roman provinces. While it is true that the historical accounts may have been oversimplified, and may have exaggerated the numbers involved, there can be little doubt that these movements happened and that they were the instigators of change. Why not, then, also in the more distant prehistoric period?

In recent years there has been a new willingness to look afresh at questions of folk movements in prehistory, though in a more subtle and considered way than before, using a newly available array of scientific evidence as a starting point.

The advent of DNA testing has opened up new possibilities for characterizing European populations and addressing questions of their origins and movements. In the pioneering years of these studies there were high hopes that ancient DNA could be extracted from human bones and would therefore allow prehistoric populations to be characterized. While there have been some successes, many technical difficulties, such as degradation and contamination, have yet to be overcome if sample sizes are not to remain too small to be reliable.

Meanwhile geneticists have turned to modern populations, hoping to use these as a surrogate and arguing that the modern gene pool is likely to reflect past populations living in the same regions. By restricting sampling to individuals whose grandparents lived in the area, some of the distortions caused by modern mobility can be overcome. Given a large enough sample, it is possible to arrive at useful generalizations about the different population groups represented, though the chronology of their arrival has to remain approximate since it rests on untested hypotheses.

Another technique of considerable promise to demographic studies is the analysis of the isotopes of oxygen and strontium found in human teeth. The percentages of the different isotopes of each element in teeth directly reflect the ratio in the ground water where the individual spent his or her early life and, since these ground-water ratios differ from one area to another, it is in theory possible to say whether an individual was buried in the area of his/her childhood. In one example of such a study, a second-millennium interment of a man aged 35–45, buried with a rich array of equipment near Amesbury in Wiltshire, produced results suggesting that he had grown up on the mainland of Europe. While there is still much work to be done in testing the validity of the method-ology and exploring its limitations, it is tempting to believe that here we may have a direct way of examining whether an individual, buried at a particular spot, had been brought up locally. If its application is extended to a whole cemetery or, better, to all the cemeteries of a region, the vitally important question of population mobility is, potentially at least, within reach of solution.

What prompted the journey of the Amesbury traveller we will never know, but there are many reasons why an individual or a community might choose to migrate and settle in a new territory. Herodotus tells the story of the inhabitants of Thera – the modern Greek island of Santorini – who, after seven years of disastrous harvests, decided that all they could do was to draw lots to select a proportion of the population to be sent overseas to found a new colony. When the spirit of the frightened exiles failed and they turned their ship back to the island, stones were thrown at them to keep them from landing. The approach of famine was one compelling reason for emigration. But there were many other reasons for mobility. The Phoenicians from Tyre who set up a trading colony on the island of Gadir (Cadiz) just off the coast of Andalucía around 800 BC were most likely motivated by a desire to benefit from the proceeds of trade with the metal-rich Tartessians living on the adjacent mainland, while the Irish Christian monks who sailed to Iceland in the eighth century AD did so simply to seek solitude in a deserted place, the better to commune with their god.

Many anecdotes can be told about human mobility, reflecting a bewildering variety of motives – religious calling, an innate desire to explore, trade for financial gain: all are familiar in the modern world. But the overriding imperative, then as now, was the desire for adequate personal space and the resources to support a desired lifestyle.

All animal populations are governed by basic biological rules, as Thomas Malthus long ago recognized. A population occupying a defined environment, left to breed in an uninhibited fashion, is likely at first to increase in size exponentially. But as the population reaches the holding capacity of the environment they inhabit, the rate of growth will rapidly decrease until the numbers remain steady below that holding capacity. In practice, the holding capacity may at first be exceeded resulting in stress and disruption to the social fabric before the level is adjusted.

To control the growth of population societies may introduce a number of constraints. Birth rate can be reduced in a variety of ways, from raising the age of marriage to infanticide. Warfare is another effective way to reduce surplus population, and since warfare seems to be endemic it has probably served as one of the principal regulators throughout time. Another mechanism, reflected in Herodotus's story of Thera, is emigration and colonization in which a segment of the population moves off to find a new ecological niche to settle.

The holding capacity of a particular environment may also change. The introduction of more effective means of production and distribution through improved technology allows for a larger population. In Britain in the seventeenth and eighteenth centuries, a rapidly increasing population was accommodated through a range of agricultural improvements, including the more efficient overwintering of livestock made possible by the introduction of the turnip. Later it was new technology heralding the Industrial Revolution – inventions such as the blast furnace and steam power – that enabled population growth to be sustained.

Conversely, holding capacity can be reduced, temporarily or permanently, by natural catastrophe or long-term

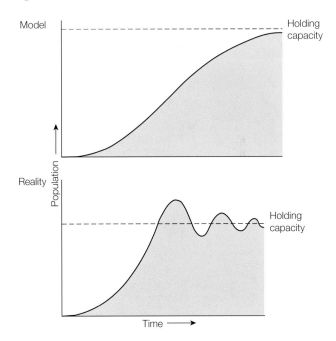

1.11 Populations have a natural tendency to increase exponentially unless constrained. One constraint is the 'holding capacity' of the environment (upper diagram). In reality the holding capacity may be breached many times, causing social stress, before the population levels out or the holding capacity is raised allowing further growth.

environmental decline. The potato famine in Ireland in the early nineteenth century caused not only a high death rate through disease and malnutrition but also mass emigration. In 1841 the Irish population was over eight million. Ten years later a million had died and another million had emigrated, mainly to America. Thereafter the momentum of emigration continued over the course of a hundred years, reducing the Irish population to about half its pre-famine level.

1.12 Societies adopt many methods to control population growth.

Methods of controlling population growth

Colonization Migration	Part of the population moves to new geological niche
Warfare Contests	Decimation of population
Marriage rules Sexual behaviour	Lower birth rate
Infanticide Fratricide Senilicide Homicide	Socially controlled culling

There are ample examples, in more recent history, to show that demographic growth can be a major cause of social dislocation and folk movement. In the prehistoric period it was probably no less significant, but discovering tangible and reliably quantifiable proof of population pressure is difficult. It is equally difficult to distinguish between short-term and long-term rhythms in population dynamics. There are, however, two long-term population trends that can be discerned in Europe – these are population gradients, one from east to west, the other from north to south. Both will be explored at various stages in the following chapters but some broad generalities can be sketched here.

The open steppe of the North Pontic region provides a corridor, constrained by the Black Sea and the dense forests of Russia, along which, over thousands of years, groups of people have moved westwards into the heart of Europe. It is almost as if there was a pulse beating somewhere deep in Asia, pumping successive waves of people outwards along various arteries, one of them being the steppe corridor. The earliest movements traceable archaeologically took place about 3000 BC. Later in the protohistoric period we can recognize peoples by name – Cimmerians, Scythians and Sarmatians came in succession, to be followed later by Alans, Avars, Huns, Bulgars and Magyars.

Most of the incomers found the Middle Danube region, and in particular the Great Hungarian Plain, to be a congenial new home, but some moved on to explore regions beyond, usually as raiders.

The North European Plain also seems to have been a place of population growth from which waves of people spilt out moving southwards. This is manifest in the migration of the Cimbri and Teutones late in the second century BC and the pressure of the advancing Germanic tribes who were confronted by Caesar in the middle of the first century BC. Rome's northern frontier later briefly contained the pressure until it broke and allowed a large number of disparate groups, Frisians, Franks, Vandals, Burgundians, Alamanni, Suebi, Lombardi, Goths and others, to flood into the provinces of the old empire. A little later it was Scandinavians from Denmark, Norway and Sweden who made their way by sea and river to south and east. Norse DNA is recognizable in the modern populations of Ireland and Scotland as well as in Iceland, where it is mixed with that of the Irish whom they took with them as slaves and wives.

That there were folk movements throughout Europe in prehistoric and early historic times there can be no doubt. DNA sampling of modern populations is beginning to show broad patterns compatible with the archaeological data and has the added advantage of allowing a level of quantification to be offered. But the very complexity of folk movements, involving the intricate mixing of populations, should not be forgotten. The many thousands of settlers, known to the classical writers as Celts, who moved from west central Europe to settle in the Po valley and Transdanubia in the fourth century BC will

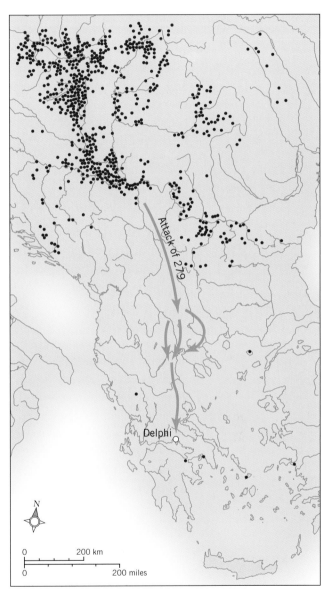

1.13 Migrations did take place in Europe during prehistory, but it is often difficult to find positive evidence for them in the archaeological record. The map shows the distribution of La Tène artefacts (brown dots) associated with the 'Celts' living in what is now Hungary and Serbia. It is known, historically, that in 279 BC a substantial Celtic army thrust southwards through Greece to pillage the sanctuary of Apollo at Delphi. The invasion is archaeologically invisible.

have left their genetic signature as well as their readily recognizable material culture, while the war bands of Celts who attacked Greece in 279 BC and then quickly retreated are archaeologically unrecognizable and are likely to have had comparatively little time or inclination greatly to enhance the gene pool of Greece.

What we can reasonably say of Old Europe is that people were always on the move – settlers, raiders, traders, pilgrims and explorers. The direction and intensity of these movements will have varied over the millennia but, viewed in the long perspective of deep time, there was always an underlying turbulence made up of varied surges, from sizeable waves to minor eddies and imperceptible trickles, as the populations of the peninsula flowed into and among each other.

Ways of Interaction

Human behaviour may be varied but cross-cultural studies have shown that, at a level of generalization, human beings across the world and through time share certain basic characteristics. They are individually territorial and aggressive but since they are also gregarious they develop systems of social behaviour that allow groups of various sizes to live together and work cooperatively. These groups, be they lineages, clans, tribes or states, establish relationships with each other, frequently through the medium of gift exchange. Gifts may be actual commodities – stone axes, glass beads, slaves or wives – but they might equally involve feasting or the offer of group labour as a contribution to some great communal enterprise. In this way networks of interaction are created, binding disparate peoples through accepted patterns of behaviour.

The constraints of the natural environment have a significant part to play in these interactions since geography determines that natural resources are not evenly distributed. Fernand Braudel summed it up in a memorable phrase. Reflecting on the Mediterranean, he wrote, 'so we find that our sea was from the very dawn of its prehistory a witness to those imbalances productive of change which would set the rhythm of its entire life'. In that phrase 'imbalances productive of change' Braudel encapsulated the essence of the dynamic driving social networks. So varied is the structure of Europe and so uneven is the spread of its desirable commodities that intricate networks of exchange have come into being to enable materials to be redistributed. An example from the modern world, familiar to us all, is oil, a rare commodity with a restricted distribution, upon which the motor-power of the world is at present dependent. The mechanisms of production and exchange, now heavily politicized, are immensely complex, maintaining an equilibrium that is at best unstable.

In prehistory and early history systems were much simpler. An axe produced in the Neolithic period from Alpine jadeite could, through successive exchanges embedded in systems of reciprocal gift-giving, end up in a tomb in Brittany. The axe was desirable but not essential to the wellbeing of the societies who briefly owned it, but the exchange of prestige gifts of this sort would have facilitated the movement of staples with real utilitarian value. As societies became more complex, so the networks became more directly commercial. The Greek city-states that needed corn to feed their growing populations could offer the producers of the Pontic steppe an abundance of wine and consumer durables like fine pottery and metalwork. Later, the Roman need constantly to top up its slave population encouraged entrepreneurs to transship huge quantities of wine from the overproducing north Italian vineyards to Gaul where slaves were to be had in plenty – and at a very good rate.

The jadeite axes will no doubt have passed from hand to hand at highly formalized social events, feasts and the like held in prearranged places and structured by delicate protocols. The bulk trade of the Greeks and Romans would have required more complex mechanisms involving specialist entrepreneurs and shippers, systems of tolls and duties and established markets. While these types of exchange could have taken place in the settlements of the barbarian producers, specialist trading centres also sprang up, often at the interface between two different communities. These places, variously referred to as 'ports-of-trade' or 'gateway communities', often seem to have been located on neutral territory, such as offshore islands, where both parties could exchange their goods in safety. The island of Ictis, off the coast of south-west Britain, was, according to the Greek writer Diodorus Siculus, the designated place where foreign traders could acquire tin from friendly Britons. Somewhat earlier, around 800 BC, the Phoenicians had established the port of Gadir (Cadiz) on an offshore island within easy reach of the kingdom of Tartessos whence came silver and other metals. Once established, these ports and markets could become large population centres and influential cities in their own right. More recent examples include Macao and Hong Kong, both originally established on islands to facilitate trade between China and the west.

In a continent as structurally diverse as Europe, where communities developed at different rates and to different levels of complexity, interactions between them will have taken many forms. One popular model used to explore these relationships is the core-periphery model derived from World Systems Theory propounded by Immanuel Wallerstein. Simply stated, this sees developments in all parts of the world as being interdependent, and articulated through a highly complex matrix of social, economic and political systems. Some parts of the world, experiencing periods of intense innovation, will drive the trajectories of change for brief periods, but feed-back mechanisms in the system will provide checks and balances.

Such a model cannot be wholly applicable to the ancient world, not least since the interactions were partial for most of the period, but there is much in the model that helps to put pre- and early historic social interactions into a helpful perspective. At a simple level it would be possible to see the Mediterranean world – a centre of innovation from the third millennium BC – as a core for which the rest of Europe served as a periphery. There is a degree of validity in this simple generalization. Extending the argument, one could say that things only began to change in the seventh and eighth centuries AD when the focus of innovation started to shift to the Atlantic fringes of Europe where it remained until the end of the nineteenth century.

But over-simple applications of core-periphery models can obscure the real situations, not least because the tacit assumption is often made that the periphery is subservient to, and manipulated by, the core. This is not necessarily the case. A charming foundation myth, told about the Phocaean Greeks who established the colony at Massalia (Marseille) on the Mediterranean coast of Gaul around 600 BC, records how, when the Greeks landed, they were invited by the local Celts to a party at which a Celtic princess was due to choose a husband. To the delight of all she chose the leader of the Greeks. Whatever the reality of the moment of contact, the myth embodies the understanding that the foundation of the Greek colony was beneficial to both the incoming community and the indigenous natives. Indeed, it is highly unlikely that networks of interaction involving trade and exchange could have survived unless they satisfied the needs of all partners.

The Roman wine trade with Gaul in the first century BC is an example of this. To a Roman entrepreneur the idea that a Gaul would exchange a slave for an amphora of wine – 'Thus exchanging the cup for the cupbearer' – seemed like an exceptional bargain since a slave would have been worth six times more in the Roman marketplace. But to a Gaul, whose systems of maintaining social status and hierarchy involved providing elaborate feasts for his peers lavishly supplied with exotic goods, to find a trader who would willingly give him an amphora of wine for a worthless captive must have seemed like manna from heaven. Who was duping whom? Which was the core and which the periphery? To the Gaul the core was where he was – it was all a matter of cognitive geography.

Face-to-face encounters of this kind would have been rare in the pre-historic world outside the Mediterranean before the Roman Empire expanded beyond its Mediterranean niche. The more usual mechanism by which commodities moved would have been down-the-line trade: that is, the movement of goods through the hands of a succession of middlemen. The Britons, who used Hengistbury Head overlooking Christchurch Harbour as a port-of-trade in the first century BC, received exotic Mediterranean goods such as wine, metal drinking cups, lumps of raw coloured glass and figs from Armorican shippers who carried the goods from their home ports in northern Brittany, bringing with them commodities of their own making. They in turn would have got the Mediterranean exotics from middlemen further back down the chain of distribution.

Encounters of this kind, pervading all corners of the European peninsula, brought people into contact and through such contact knowledge and ideas would have flowed. It was in this way that Herodotus, or his informants, heard of the mysterious Tin Islands in the Atlantic.

In Europe distances are not great and knowledge could spread rapidly. The networks of communication pulsated with the flow of information – stories of exotic lands and people, technological know-how, systems of values and beliefs. At the nodes where the exchanges took place, be they cities like Miletos or isolated promontories like Hengistbury Head, the excitement of the new would have been palpable. Even the most remote communities would not have been totally immune from the flow of information. So it was that the disparate peoples of Europe, from the most innovative to the most conservative, became enmeshed in networks of contact that inexorably drove change.

CHAPTER TWO

The Land between the Oceans

A Peninsula in Outline

One of the great attributes of the straggling peninsula of Europe, with its deeply convoluted coasts and its island fragments scattered all around, is the sheer length of the interface between land and sea. Estimated to be 37,000 km (23,000 miles), it is equivalent to the circumference of the world. It was no accident that Europe's first civilization – the culture named by archaeologists as Minoan – began in the Aegean, where the ratio of coast to land was at its greatest. Perhaps it was a folk memory of this and an awareness of the importance of the sea that lay behind the Greek myth of Europa. Europa was a princess, daughter of a Phoenician king, whose great beauty captivated Zeus. The god assumed the form of a bull and joined a herd on the sea shore, showing such tameness that Europa was persuaded to climb on to his back. Thereupon Zeus rushed with her into the sea and swam to Crete, where in due course she gave birth to his son Minos – a reminder, if one were needed, that the seashore is a liminal place where unexpected things can happen! Though why the continent should be named after a Phoenician princess the sober Herodotus found it difficult to understand.

To visualize Europe for what it is – the most westerly protuberance of the landmass of Asia – it is convenient to turn the map so that west is at the top, a simple device that helps to readjust our cognitive geography. The skeleton of the peninsula is created by mountains folded in later geological times – the Tertiary period – and is flanked on either side by depressions now flooded by the sea. On the southern side the mountain ranges present a sharp shoulder to the ocean while to the north the slope is far more gradual. South of the peninsula the Mediterranean and the Black Sea together extend for about 4000 km (2500 miles), from Gibraltar to Georgia, or from 'the Pillars of Hercules to Tanis' as the Greeks would say when expressing the immensity of the subcontinent. Both are inland seas with one common outlet to the outer ocean. The north side is more complex – a complexity compounded by the continuing readjustments of land and sea as the ice sheet has receded over the last twenty thousand years. But the Baltic–North Sea could be envisioned as another inland sea (overlooking the fact that there is something of a gap between

2.1 The myth of Europa being carried away by a bull was widely known in the ancient world. Here it is depicted on a mosaic floor in the Roman villa found at Lullingstone in Kent.

Scotland and Norway which the Orkneys and Shetlands scarcely fill!), the journey from Dover to St Petersburg being some 2500 km (1500 miles).

The root of the peninsula, between the Baltic and the Black Sea, is barely 1100 km (700 miles) across. Where Europe ends and Asia begins has for long been a matter of debate. For those who favour a mountain barrier, the Urals have their attraction. The idea of 'Europe from the Atlantic to the Urals' was formally proposed as long ago as 1833 by the German geographer Wilhelm Friedrich Volger, though others have preferred a river boundary, suggesting the Don or the Volga. There is little consensus nor need there be one: peninsulas by their very nature grade imperceptibly into continents.

The many disparate factors that together contribute to the personality of peninsular Europe defy easy definition. But what underlies it all is the inter-action between the geological skeleton of the land and the climate, which together create the many varied natural environments so characteristic of the landmass. Nothing, however, is static. Long-term climatic amelioration following the last Ice Age has led to the gradual shift of vegetational zones. Melting ice caps take the pressure off land, allowing it to rise, at the same time pouring quantities of melt-water into the oceans, causing the sea level to rise. The delicate balance between the two opposing factors is still being played out in parts of northern Europe today. Over and above these gradual changes there has been a succession of minor climatic oscillations, causing cold snaps like the sharp downturn about 6200 BC or periods of increased precipitation encouraging the growth of extensive areas of continuous bog in parts of Atlantic Europe noticeable around 1000 BC. Geofactors of this kind create the ecozones within which the human communities choose to live.

Human populations have always had an effect on their environments, often initiating long-term change. Hunter-gatherers who cut clearings into forests to increase new growth and so encourage animals to congregate and browse, the more easily to be captured, affected the removal of water by plants through transpiration which, in marginal conditions, led to the formation of blanket bog. Increased herding of sheep and goats in the mountainous fringes of the Aegean damaged vegetation cover, causing massive erosion, while in the Midlands of England intensification of agriculture in the first millennium BC led to large-scale deposition of alluvium in the river valleys. With growing populations these human-generated effects on landscape have increased to the extent that humans have now, for the first time, begun to have a direct, and potentially devastating, effect on the all-controlling climate.

The most sharply drawn of Europe's ecological zones is the Mediterranean, divided from the rest of Europe by a rim of mountains. Its distinct climate of hot dry summers and cool winters, with such rain as there is falling in spring, gives rise to conditions in which grain can be grown,

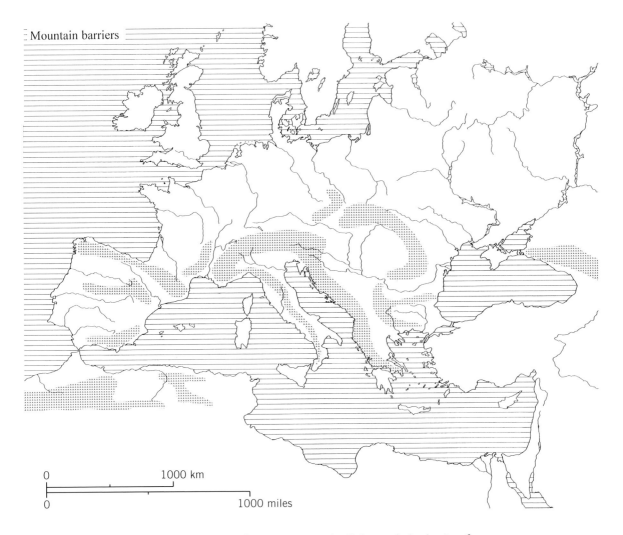

Mountain barriers

0   1000 km

0   1000 miles

vines ripen easily and olives flourish. Grain, wine and oil formed the basis of classical Mediterranean agriculture, creating a cuisine that was culturally distinctive. The point was well made by a Spanish nobleman, Alonso Vázquez, who, visiting Flanders in the sixteenth century, wrote disparagingly of the north, describing it as a 'land where there grows neither thyme nor lavender, figs, olives, melons or almonds; and where parsley, onions and lettuce have neither juice nor taste, with butter from cows instead of oil'.

Travel north from the Mediterranean fringes and one rapidly enters an entirely different ecozone dominated by mixed oak forest, but with considerable variation dependent on altitude. Forest once covered the Great European Plain, extending northwards as far as Bergen, Stockholm and Helsinki in southern Scandinavia, giving way, beyond about 62°N, to the Boreal forest of conifers stretching to the tundra. The mixed oak forest zone was quickly

2.2 Europe is best seen as a sinuous peninsula almost surrounded by sea, with a mountainous spine to give it strength.

33

colonized by hunter-gatherers and later by agricultural-based communities who began the process of clearance. These first farmers introduced the basic farm-yard animals, cattle, sheep, goats and pigs, which have remained the staple sources of protein and fat ever since. Thus, while the Mediterraneans got their fat and light from the olive, the temperate Europeans were dependent on their cows and sheep for milk, butter, cheese and tallow. Carbohydrates were derived from a variety of cereals, the production of which varied with soil and micro-climate, but in a general the southern part of temperate Europe relied heavily on wheat bread while those living on the North European Plain were more dependent on rye bread, differences that still remain despite globalization.

To the east, the southern limit of the forest zone sweeps northwards, leaving a wide swathe of grassy steppe stretching from the Lower Danube around the north shores of the Black Sea, across the valley of the Volga, to skirt the southern end of the Urals, eventually reaching deep into Asia as far as the Altai Mountains. The grassy steppe provided a wide corridor between the southern edge of the forest steppe and the northern edge of a huge arid zone, facilitating the movement of successive waves of people. Although agriculture was practised within this zone, the maintenance of flocks and herds, greatly aided by use of the horse, was a defining characteristic.

Europe Emerges

Europe, in the form familiar to us today, began to emerge during the early stages of the Holocene period around 6000 BC; before that, the configuration of the land and sea was very different. A convenient time to begin this account is during the height of the last glaciation (*c*.20,000–18,000 BC) when the temperature was about 10°C lower than it is today. Contrasts in temperature between summer and winter were greater than at present, with bitterly cold winter winds keeping temperatures to -10°C for extended periods. At this time Europe was gripped by icy ocean currents flowing south from the polar regions along the Atlantic façade. Heavy snowfall, particularly in the mountainous regions, led to the development of extensive ice sheets that covered Scandinavia and parts of northern Europe and spread westwards, over north-ern parts of Britain and Ireland to the ocean's edge. Lesser glaciers engulfed the Alps, Pyrenees and the Caucasian Mountains.

With so much water tied up in the ice sheets, the sea level dropped to 100 m (330 ft) below present levels, leaving vast expanses of land along the Atlantic and Mediterranean shores exposed. At this stage the Black Sea was land-locked, as was the greatly extended Caspian. Both seas received the melt-waters from the ice cap, by way of the great rivers, flowing from the tundra that covered much of north Europe. The Mediterranean, though less extensive

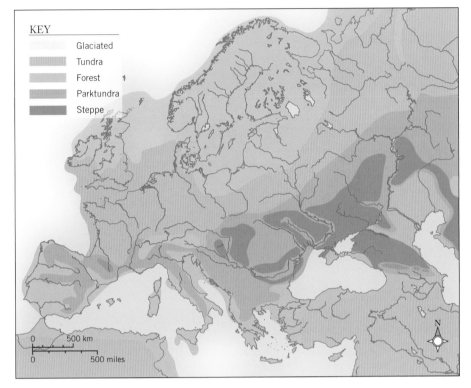

KEY

- Glaciated
- Tundra
- Forest
- Parktundra
- Steppe

0   500 km

0   500 miles

N

2.3 During the period of the last maximum glaciation, 20,000–18,000 years ago, Europe differed considerably from its present state. The sea-levels were generally lower, though the Caspian, which received melt-waters from the ice cap, was far more extensive. Ice sheets covered most of the northern lands while to the south the vegetation was mostly park tundra or steppe with forests found mainly around the Mediterranean.

than it now is, was recognizable in its main outlines with a narrow outlet, today known as the Straits of Gibraltar, leading to the Atlantic.

Around 18,000 BC the climate began to warm up and, apart from a sudden cold interlude between 10,800 and 9600 BC, reached a warm optimum around 7500 BC, which has continued with minor fluctuations ever since. One of the contributory factors to the warming process was the re-establishment of the Gulf Stream, an Atlantic current that channels warm water from the tropics to the ocean-facing regions of north-west Europe. The Gulf Stream is crucial in helping to maintain the mild oceanic climate that Europe enjoys. Without it, northern France might experience the same extremes of temperature as Newfoundland, which occupies the same latitude.

The rapid warming, over a period of less than two thousand years, caused the ice caps to melt and in consequence sea levels to rise. Meanwhile those areas of land that had lain depressed under the ice caps began to rise as the weight of the ice was reduced. For much of Europe the eustatic rise in sea level was the dominant force, but in the north from Scandinavia to Scotland the iso-static rise in land is the greater: Scotland and Scandinavia are still today rising faster than the sea level. The delicacy of the adjustment is well demonstrated by the early history of the Baltic Sea, which has fluctuated between being a

35

2.4 Satellite image of Scandinavia and the North European Plain. The great rivers of northern Europe empty into the Baltic Sea with its narrow openings to the Atlantic. The rise of land, following the melting of the ice cap over Scandinavia, continuing at a rate outstripping the rise of sea-levels, means that the Baltic is decreasing in size.

freshwater lake and an arm of the sea as the relative land and sea levels have outpaced each other.

While these changes were taking place, the north-western extremity of Europe, now the islands of Ireland and Britain, was gradually being reshaped. Two river systems developed. The precursor of the Elbe and most of the rivers of eastern Britain flowed northwards into the Norwegian Trench – a deep water channel hugging the coast of Norway – while the Thames, Rhine and Seine flowed south into the river Channel which drained the water south-westwards into the Atlantic, forming a wide estuary between Cornwall and Brittany. The remnants of the Scottish ice cap drained southwards through what is now the Irish Sea. Relative sea level continued to rise and by 8000 BC Ireland had become separated from the mainland. By c.6500 BC Britain itself had become an island, though there were still large stretches of dry land remaining for several more millennia in what was eventually to become the North Sea.

36

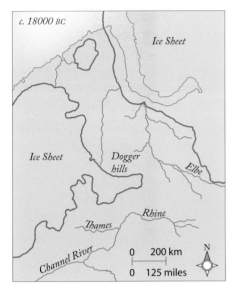

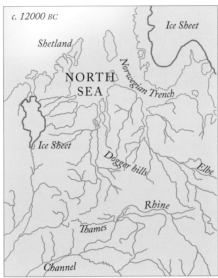

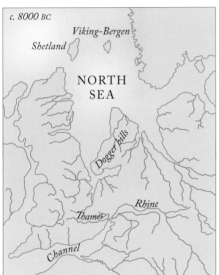

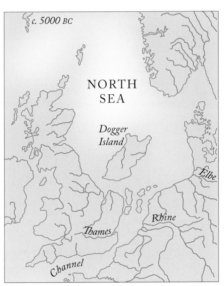

2.5 With the melting of the ice sheet, the area between what is now Britain and the Continent became a great marshy lowland. As the sea-levels rose, following the melting of the ice, this lowland became gradually inundated until *c.*6500 BC when Britain became an island.

The Black Sea also has a complex history. Throughout the glacial episode and the Early Holocene, the three great inland seas, the Aral, the Caspian and the Black Sea, were vast freshwater lakes, receiving melt-water from the Scandinavian Ice Sheet through the precursors of the great rivers of Russia. The lakes were backed to the south by mountain ranges. Much of the water draining into them evaporated, but an overflow slipway allowed excess fresh water to spill over the Bosphorus sill into the Mediterranean. So it was to remain until about 5500 BC, when the level of the Mediterranean had reached such a height that salt water began to flow in the reverse direction, drowning large areas of low-lying coast land around the north and west sides of the Black Sea lake and turning it salt in a matter of centuries. The Black Sea catastrophe – for such it would have been to the many foraging communities enjoying the rich resources of its congenial shores – is the last major episode in the creation of the subcontinent. Sea levels continued to readjust but the broad outline of the peninsula was now established: familiar Europe had emerged.

The Anatomy of the Land

In its immense variety the European landscape defies easy definition. In no equivalent area of the earth's surface is it possible to find so many different ecozones so closely packed together: it is a variety rich in opportunity, encouraging human communities to venture and to adapt, and by so doing to develop a flexibility conducive to survival.

2.6 The European peninsula was criss-crossed by natural routes following the great rivers. Where the transpeninsular (north–south) routes crossed the east–west spinal corridor nodes of interaction grew up where energetic innovating societies emerged.

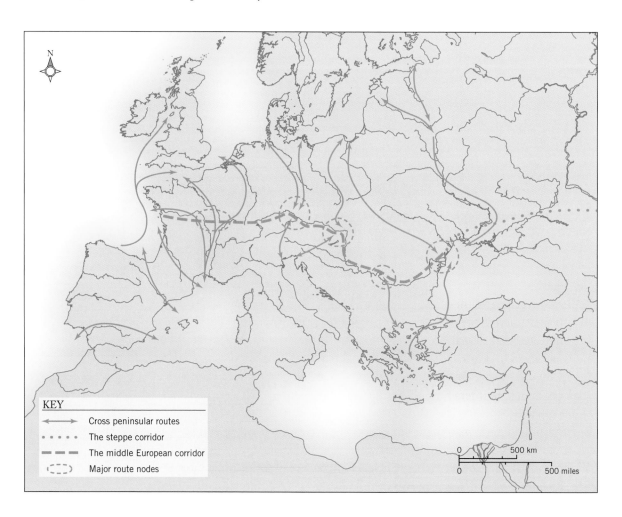

KEY

⟵——⟶ Cross peninsular routes

• • • • • The steppe corridor

– – – The middle European corridor

⟨ ⁻⁻⁻ ⟩ Major route nodes

0 ——— 500 km

0 ——— 500 miles

Dominant is the mountain skeleton commanded by the great sweep of the Alps, forming a protection for the Italian peninsula stiffened with its own mountain spine – the Apennines. No less massive in their footprint are the mountains of the Balkans, stretching down the length of the Adriatic from Slovenia to the Peloponnese and on through Crete – a great corrugation of ridges and troughs difficult to find a way across – with their extensions splaying eastwards through Bulgaria as the Stara Planina and Rodopi Planina, reaching almost to the shores of the Black Sea. The line is picked up again beyond the Crimea with the massive bulk of the Caucasian Mountains.

Westwards from the rightward sweep of the Alps, the Cevennes and Montagne Noire help block Europe from the Mediterranean. Another spine – the Pyrenees and the Cantabrian Cordillera – effectively divide off the Iberian extremity from the rest of the peninsula, while the Mesetas of the centre and the sierras of Andalucía further enforce Iberia's remoteness. From the tip of the Peloponnese to the Straits of Gibraltar the great arc of mountains isolates the communities of the Mediterranean from what lies beyond.

Within the heart of the peninsula other mountain ranges offer protective barriers for smaller territories. The Transylvanian Alps and Carpathian Mountains wrap themselves around Transylvania, the Great Hungarian Plain and Transdanubia, while the Sudeten Mountains, Erzgebirge and the Böhmerwald enclose Bohemia and Moravia. These are all lesser ranges but still present formidable barriers.

Finally, there are the two flanking ranges. The Kiølen Mountains, running the length of the Scandinavian peninsula and briefly reappearing as the Highlands of Scotland, offer Europe shelter from the worst of the weather emanating from the icy north-west, while the multiple ranges that divide up modern Turkey – the Pontic Mountains of the north and Taurus Mountains of the south – separate Europe from the endless deserts of the south-east.

Mountains may be formidable and restricting but they can provide congenial ecological niches for small communities reliant on the upland pastures for their livelihoods. These summer pastures with their lush grazing are also an attraction for other communities living in the surrounding lowlands – peoples prepared to make long seasonal journeys of transhumance with their flocks and herds. Thus, the mountain landscapes are an encouragement to long-distance movements governed by the seasonal cycle, and with these movements people interact and information flows.

The Mediterranean landscape is perhaps best characterized as a narrow rim of habitable land, backed by mountains to the north and mountains and deserts to the south and east. It faces the inner ocean and is of the ocean, depending on the sea for a range of essential resources and for communications. The land of this ocean rim is often new land, built up as alluvial fans by rivers eroding the surrounding mountains and by longshore drift creating coastal barriers of sand and shingle behind which lakes and marshes form. But while processes are similar, scales can vary. The deltas of the Nile and Rhône are huge, providing ample space and resources for large numbers of people, while along the south coast of Iberia the rivers rising in the flanking sierras produce tiny deltas of rich alluvium, used briefly by Phoenician settlers for their precarious trading towns and not much afterwards, except little fishing villages, until the quest for sun and profit spawned the concrete horror of holiday development that today engulfs everything.

The Mediterranean is also a landscape of islands. Again there are extremes of scale. Some are so large as to reflect the landward rim of the sea in miniature and in reverse. Corsica, Sardinia, Sicily, Crete and Cyprus all have mountainous centres with narrow coastal zones supporting scattered population centres. Others, like many of the islands of the Cyclades, are so small as to allow for only one or two clustered communities.

The landscapes of the Mediterranean, with their comparatively small parcels of habitable land well separated from each other, encouraged the growth of isolated communities, some of which grew to become city-states. By harnessing the sea, certain favoured places flourished, making a bid for power and ultimately empire.

One of the greatest natural attributes of the European peninsula is the Middle European Corridor leading from the Atlantic to the Black Sea. An enterprising traveller could have made the journey along it comfortably in six months. For two-thirds of its length the corridor coincides with the course of the river Danube. Beginning on the Black Sea, the lower reaches of the river could be followed with ease across the wide plain of Wallacia between the Transylvanian Alps and the Stara Planina, to the point where the two ranges converge and where the river has cut a spectacular gorge known as the Iron Gates. Beyond the latter the middle course of the Danube winds its way along the edge of the Great Hungarian Plain, separating it from the more hilly lands of Transdanubia to the west, before negotiating another pinch-point at Bratislava where the outlying flanks of the Carpathian Mountains attempt to link to the dying remnants of the Alps. In later history the crucial importance of this route, joining western and eastern Europe, was symbolized by the power of Vienna. In its upper reaches the river flanks the Alpine Foreland to its source in the Black Forest, barely 70 km (45 miles) from the valley of the Rhine and the great nexus of routes that lies in the heart of west central Europe. Here, by travelling comparatively short distances across the Vosges, it was possible to reach the valleys of the Moselle, the Seine and the Saône and, with a little further hill walking, the Loire, which could be followed to the Atlantic.

It is unlikely that at any time in the prehistoric or early historic past people used the Middle European Corridor to make epic journeys from the Atlantic to the Black Sea, but very many people will have used parts of the corridor, entering it at one point and exiting at another.

The Middle European Corridor was the axis of a broadly defined ecozone that we might call Middle Europe, a zone that embraces the entire Atlantic façade, from Portugal to Britain, and further east includes the swathe of land between the Alps and the southern edge of the blanket of Quaternary deposits that constitute the North European Lowlands. Thus defined, it incorporates a formidable variety of different landscapes, mostly very productive and capable of sustaining high population densities. The richness of the individual ecological niches has meant that, once settled by farming communities, there has been a tendency to sedentism. Over the *longue durée* this has been a landscape of peasant farmers, living in individual holdings, hamlets or small villages scattered through the utilized landscape, and owing an allegiance to an elite who variously displayed their power through rich burials, or by building hillforts, castles or grand country houses. It is, above all, the landscape of feudalism.

Beyond Middle Europe lie the North European Lowlands – a new landscape created in the Late Glacial and Early Holocene periods as the Scandinavian Ice Sheet began its final retreat. The huge blanket of outwash material was sorted and re-sorted by river action. It is a chaotic landscape, in some parts comprising large sandy outwashes – or *Geest* – giving way to ill-drained boulder clays and higher ridges of moraine (glacial gravels) dotted with lakes. The entire region is criss-crossed by a network of wide trench-like melt-water channels (*Urstromtäler*), formed by water trapped between the ice front and the uplands to the south. Some were later followed by today's great rivers, but in general lack of drainage led to the development of fen peat which began to clog the channels as the temperature warmed up, creating impassable barriers. This *Jungmorän* landscape is an uninviting region. But to the south of it lies the *Bördeland*, a zone covered with a thick accumulation of loëss – a fine, light, loamy clay formed from the very lightest particles carried south by winds blowing off the ice cap. Deposits of loëss also extended well to the south of the plain, penetrating deep into the lower-lying parts of Middle Europe. The loëss lands provide dark-brown or black soils that are well drained and highly fertile – soils sought out by the pioneer farmers of the Neolithic.

The Middle European Corridor is continued to the east by a wide zone of grassland steppe offering easy passage for horse-riding nomads, groups of whom from time to time have moved westwards to penetrate Europe. The steppe zone is comparatively narrow, delimited on the north by the southern edge of the forest steppe and on the south by the Black Sea, the Caspian Sea and the Aral Sea (the last two formerly far more extensive than they are at

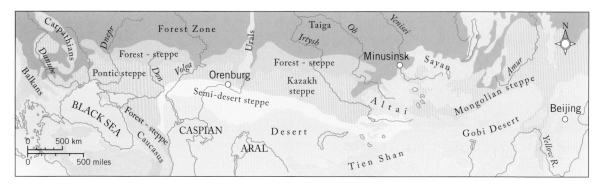

2.7 The spinal route through peninsular Europe, dominated by the Danube valley, is continued eastwards by the steppe corridor – a vast swathe of gently undulating open grassland stretching around the south end of the Urals and eventually leading to China. It was along the steppe corridor that successive waves of people, mainly pastoralists, migrated. The western extremity of the steppe corridor was the Great Hungarian Plain, nestling in the Carpathian arc.

present) and the desert regions beyond. A rider beginning his journey in the Dobrudja at the mouth of the Danube could travel eastwards through the Pontic steppe across the Volga and beneath the southern flank of the Urals, continuing on through Kazakhstan to the Altai Mountains and eventually to Mongolia, without being aware of any significant change. Indeed, it is the very monotony of the endless rolling grasslands that most impressed visitors in the past, before, that is, Soviet agriculture cleared the land for wheat, maize and sunflowers. The German travel writer J.G. Kohl, who visited the Ukraine in 1841, vividly describes the enormity of it all:

> One sees nothing but wormwood and more wormwood, then nothing but vetch and vetch . . . then a mile of mullein and another half of melilot, then an expanse of swaying milkweed, a thousand million nodding heads, then sage and lavender for the duration of an afternoon doze, then tulips as far as the eye can see, a bed of mignonette two miles across, whole valleys of caraway and curled mint, endless hills covered by resurrection plant and six days' journey with nothing but dried-up grass. This is the way vegetation is more or less distributed in the steppe, with a complete lack of charm, beauty or attractive feature of any kind.

Hesiod describes the inhabitants of the Pontic steppe as 'mare-milkers', but Herodotus is careful to stress that some groups living near the Black Sea coasts practised agriculture, while allowing that those who were more remote 'neither plough nor sow'. Archaeology suggests that in the first millennium BC agriculture was quite widely practised across the Pontic steppe to the Volga, but not necessarily on an intensive scale. The material culture and the art of the period leave little doubt that the horse dominated all. The movement of herders and warriors, and sometimes of whole families, was a feature of every-day life.

When Kohl was writing in the early nineteenth century he was aware that cultivators existed among the nomadic groups, but he considered cultivation to be an alien practice in such a landscape:

42

It is a mystery how a man could think of settling as a farmer in the steppe whose whole nature cries out against this abuse, whose whole law is movement, whose soil abhors deep-rooted plants, favouring instead mobile cattle breeding, whose winds carry everything before them far and wide and whose flatness invites everything to cross it in haste.

At its westernmost extent the Pontic steppe wraps itself around the western shores of the Black Sea to include the Dobrudja at the Danube mouth. The valley of the Lower Danube also retains a steppe-like character, but far more impressive is the Great Hungarian Plain, reached through the Iron Gates, a vast expanse of rich, black soil on either side of the river Tisza, tightly circumscribed by the Danube on one side and the mountains of Transylvania on the other. Here is the westernmost enclave of the steppe, providing a reassuring familiarity for horsemen from the east who ventured beyond the Iron Gates to confront Middle Europe. Many eastern nomads came here to settle, Cimmerians and Scythians in the first millennium BC, followed by Sarmatians, Alans, Huns and Avars and eventually the Magyars arriving in the ninth century AD. The plain was a holding-ground – a place where many stayed but from which others moved on.

Together the Middle European Corridor and the steppe corridor gave easy access from the Atlantic Ocean to the Yellow Sea. Along some such route the silks enjoyed by the Hallstatt elites of west central Europe in the sixth century BC must have come, perhaps accompanied by domestic fowl, which began to make their appearance in the west at about this time, and would, in their early rarity, have been an acceptable exotic gift. It is a reminder that Europe is merely an excrescence of Asia.

Crossing the Peninsula

Nowhere is the European peninsula too wide to cross with comparative ease for those with the will to do so. Although the journey would have cut across the grain of the landscape, it was greatly facilitated by rivers, both north- and south-flowing, cutting through hills and providing swift passage in their direction of flow. The ways were many, as the map (on p. 38) shows.

Among the best-attested are the routes through France. The shortest, using the river Aude, the Carcassonne Gap and the Garonne to the Gironde estuary, joined the Mediterranean to the Atlantic, cutting out the tortuous sea route round the Iberian peninsula. It was used to bring tin from south-west Britain and Brittany to the Mediterranean after the sixth century BC, and by the first century BC it provided a convenient route to transport amphorae of north Italian wine to the Atlantic for local traders to distribute.

The Rhône provided another way through the mountains, to the north. Once past Lyon at the confluence of the Rhône and Saône, there were options to join one of three rivers, the Loire, the Seine or the Rhine. In the early years of Romanization, *c.*50 BC–AD 20, all three routes were in active use, to be gradually replaced by a network of roads radiating out from Lyon and allowing easy access to the Channel ports and the military bases on the Rhine. A not dissimilar geography determined the distribution of major European fairs in the thirteenth century. The concentration in the upper reaches of the Seine valley reflects the convenience of the location to the major trading states of the time. Even as late as the sixteenth century spices reaching the Mediterranean ports of Genoa and Marseille were transported to Lyon for forward shipment to the redistribution centres of Nantes, Rouen and Antwerp.

The Alps created a major barrier, but from the Po valley a number of passes could be found leading west to reach the Rhône valley or north to provide access to the Rhine or the Upper Danube. The first of these was famously used by Hannibal and his elephants en route to attack Rome. Earlier, in the fifth century BC, it is likely that all three routes were used by Celts moving south to settle in the Po valley. Another route of some importance lay eastwards from the Po valley, skirting the head of the Adriatic and passing through Slovenia to Transdanubia and thence to the Danube, from where it would be possible to reach tributaries such as the Morava, providing a way northwards to join the rivers of the North European Plain to reach the amber-producing shores of the Baltic. The amber route, via the Morava and Transdanubia to the head of the Adriatic, was of great antiquity and gave rise to the myth that amber was found in the rivers flowing into the Adriatic. By the second century AD the Roman town of Scarbantia, now Sopron in north-western Hungary, was a centre for the importation of amber where craftsmen and traders congregated. Much later, in the ninth century AD, the volume of trade along the Morava contributed to the growth of the powerful Moravian Empire.

All the great rivers crossing the North European Plain – the Wester, Elbe, Oder and Vistula – at one time or another provided routes northwards to the North Sea and Baltic, and along them we can imagine a variety of products, dominated by amber and furs, flowing to the south.

Further east the Baltic-flowing rivers offered access to the Black Sea, which grew in importance in the tenth and eleventh centuries AD as the enterprising Swedes began to develop their trade with the east. The Vistula–Dnestr route was the shortest and most direct. But others chose a longer route, either via the West Dvina to the Dnepr or by sailing through the Gulf of Finland and on to Lake Ladoga before taking to the river Volkhov, eventually, after several portages, to join up with the Dnepr. We know something of the dangers of the journey from Byzantine sources. The voyage down the Dnepr could only be taken in June after the ice had melted and even then it was necessary to carry the ships by land around a succession of seven fierce rapids before the Black Sea could be reached for the onward journey to Constantinople and Trebizond.

After making journeys like this, which involved fighting off raiders at every point, it is not surprising that the Scandinavians earned a reputation as fierce, determined warriors. So famous did they become that by the late tenth century the personal guard of the emperor of Byzantium was composed entirely of mercenaries from Scandinavia. The Varangian Guard, as they were known, were recognized for their drunkenness and the massive battle-axes that they wielded, in lethal combination. It may have been one of their number who scratched his name, Halfdan, in runic script on a marble balustrade in the church of Hagia Sophia.

It could be argued that not all rivers were easily navigable and to sail against the current of fast-flowing rivers was seldom possible, but this underestimates human ingenuity. Willingness to haul even quite large vessels overland between rivers and around rapids is amply demonstrated by the actions of the Swedes in their endeavour to reach Constantinople and, much earlier, Greeks were regularly dragging large vessels 6 km (4 miles) across the isthmus of Corinth on a specially engineered track – the *diolcos*. Long overland portages between navigable waterways are likely to have been quite normal. Indeed, the Greek geographer Strabo is quite explicit. Writing of the rivers of Gaul he describes how cargoes passed up the Rhône and then overland to the Seine, while 'from Narbo [Narbonne] traffic goes inland for a short distance by the river Atax [Aude] and then a greater distance by land to the river Garonne'. From this point the flow of the river would have carried the cargoes to the Atlantic. Another Greek writer, Diodorus Siculus, describes the trade in tin, which was trans-shipped from south-west Britain to Gaul 'and after travelling overland for about thirty days, they finally bring their loads on horses to the mouth of the Rhône'. What Diodorus does not record is the route taken, but the probability is that the course of either the river Seine or the Loire was followed to gain the Rhône.

Travel against the current is by no means unthinkable, particularly for a vessel equipped with a sail using the slack water of the river's edge in a favourable wind. Nor should we overlook shallow draught vessels or even rafts being manually drawn by someone wading through the shallows. The importance of rafts on the Rhône is amply demonstrated by a guild of rafts-men (*utricularii*) who were well established at Arles in Roman times.

The great rivers that criss-crossed the European peninsula provided a network of routes linking the ocean interfaces together. They encouraged mobility and were a crucial influence on European history.

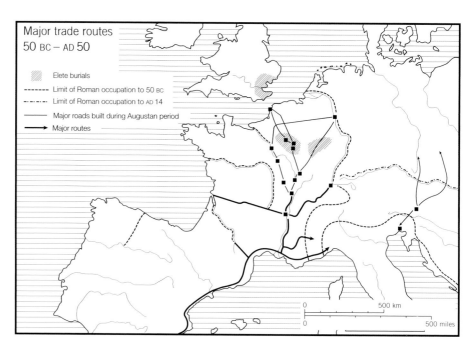

Major trade routes
50 BC – AD 50

Elete burials
Limit of Roman occupation to 50 BC
Limit of Roman occupation to AD 14
Major roads built during Augustan period
Major routes

0   500 km
0   500 miles

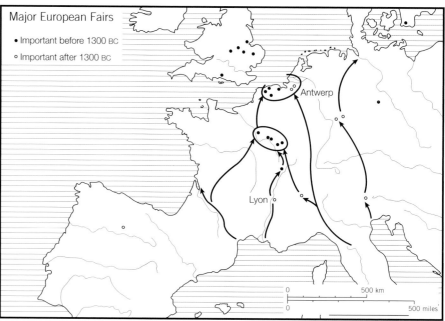

Major European Fairs

• Important before 1300 BC
○ Important after 1300 BC

Antwerp

Lyon

0   500 km
0   500 miles

2.8–10 The three maps illustrate the importance of the cross-peninsular route via the Rhône valley at various points in time. A major route transcends cultures and chronologies.

46

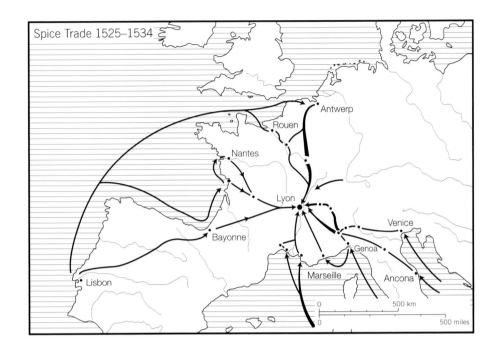

Spice Trade 1525–1534

Another Way to Look at Rivers

Above all, rivers provide access to and from the sea, while the sea itself offers the means by which the rivers themselves may be linked. Longshore cabotage linking port with port and estuary with estuary is a common enough aspect of maritime life in historic times. Thus, there is likely to be a coherence within territories bound together by rivers and oceans. One simple way of examining this is by plotting the watersheds of the major river systems of Europe. The map (on p. 48) is revealing not least in showing the great disparity in the watershed territories commanded by each of Europe's surrounding seas. These 'territories' are, of course, a purely geographical construct but they can help to reflect on broad cultural continua. To take the idea a little further, we have indicated very approximately the cultural zones that, using a variety of archaeological evidence, may be regarded as having direct or close links with their oceans. The sketch is of necessity crude, but it offers another perspective on the cognitive geography of the peninsula. Two things stand out: the comparative narrowness of the Mediterranean and Black Sea cultural zones in contrast to the Atlantic, North Sea and Baltic zones; and the very considerable area of the landmass of Europe that lies beyond direct maritime influence. The relationship between these maritime zones and the core of Europe is a recurring theme.

The Character of the Seas

Each of the seas surrounding the European peninsula has its own distinctive character. The best-known is the Mediterranean, more appropriately to be seen as a series of six interlocking seas, partially separated by intervening landmasses. The large surface area, of 2.5 million sq km (1 million square miles), and the hot climate ensure a high evaporation rate which, in turn, creates a sea of high salinity. With comparatively few major rivers entering the sea – except the Ebro, Rhône, Po and Nile – the loss of water through evaporation is made good by inflow from the Atlantic and the Black Sea. The force of water through these narrows, intensified by following winds, creates the predominant pattern of currents within the sea itself. The basic flow is anticlockwise, hugging the shore. One continuous current would carry a vessel the full length of the North African coast from Gibraltar to Port Said with little interruption, but along the European side the projecting land-masses and islands deflect the east-to-west flow, at intervals setting up crosscurrents that would take a ship out across the width of the ocean. Thus, though each of the individual seas that make up the Mediterranean has its own simple rotary

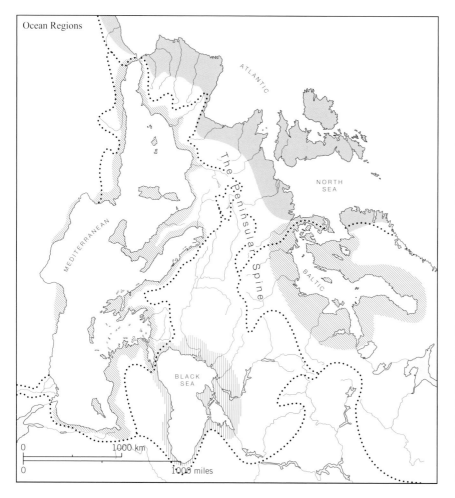

2.11 The map shows the Oceanic regions of Europe. Europe looks outwards to its surrounding oceans. The sea provides ready communications binding the ocean regions together. The rivers link the coastal regions to their hinterlands. The dotted line denotes the interfluves dividing the river systems which flow into the different oceans.

current, by careful inshore sailing it was possible to travel with ease from one to another.

Important though the currents are in providing the underlying rhythm of the ocean, their power, only one to two knots, is often overshadowed by the winds, sometimes as fierce as 30 knots. The wind patterns are complicated and varied since they are determined largely by depressions that may form within the Mediterranean basin itself or may move in from the Atlantic or the Sahara. The overall effect is that winds tend to be offshore. The individual winds have been given names, like the hot, dusty Scirocco blowing from the deserts of North Africa, the icy Bora from the north-east hitting the head of the Adriatic and the humid Mistral which sweeps in from the Atlantic, bringing discomfort to those living around the north-western shore. Seasonal variations and the different wind strengths create distinct microclimates. The fiercest winds are those blowing offshore into the Golfe du Lion, the head of the Adriatic and the north Aegean, while the coast of North Africa, especially the extreme east end, tends to be the calmest region.

The combination of winds and tides conditioned sailing routes in the time before steam power. Sailing would begin once the gales of March and April had abated and would last until September, although by Roman times out-of-season journeys were not uncommon. For most ships' masters it was sensible to stay in the waters they knew well, which usually meant remaining in one of the local seas. The little trading vessel of the fifteenth century BC that sank in deep water off the southern Turkish coast near Kaş was, judging from its cargo, engaged in coastal sailing around the east end of the Mediterranean, following the currents that took it anticlockwise from the Nile delta up the coast of the Levant, across to Cyprus and thence, by way of the Turkish coasts, to the Cyclades and Crete. From here the vessel would have struck out southwards, making use of the local winds and currents to gain the North African coast before turning eastwards to the Nile. At ports along the way goods were exchanged. Such round trips of limited duration must have been typical in the Mediterranean throughout time – there was much reassurance to be gained from the familiar.

Some centuries later more entrepreneurial sailors from the Phoenician towns of the Levant, particularly Tyre and Sidon, engaged in long-distance journeys, travelling the length of the Mediterranean to acquire silver, tin and copper from western Iberia. Vessels set out using a northern route via Cyprus, the southern coast of Turkey and Crete, to Sicily where Phoenician settlements had been established. From here the outward journey led to southern Sardinia, Ibiza and the Andalucían coast from where, in favourable conditions, passage could be made westwards, through the Straits of Gibraltar to the Atlantic trading port of Gadir (Cadiz). The return trip eastwards hugged the

2.12 The Mediterranean Sea was a challenging environment for early navigators. They would have preferred to stay within sight of land and were helped by coastal currents, but the offshore winds had to be contended with.

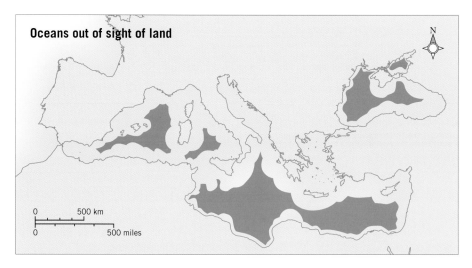

Oceans out of sight of land

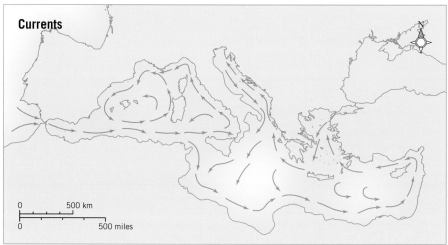

Currents

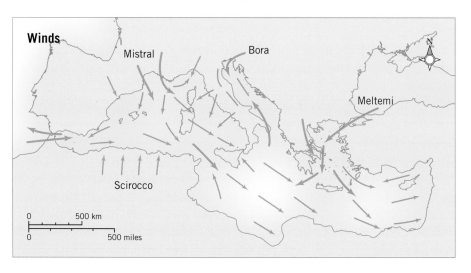

Winds

Mistral

Bora

Meltemi

Scirocco

coast of North Africa, relying on the constant, if slow, current for a safe journey home. The round trip could have been completed within a single sailing season.

The seas would have been alive with adventurers. Herodotus writes of the Phocaeans, whose home city was on an island just off the Aegean coast of Turkey, who sailed in their fast sleek warships (penteconters) to explore the Adriatic and the northern shores of the west Mediterranean. It was they who eventually founded the colony of Massalia (Marseille) around 600 BC. These exploratory ventures differed little from the activities of pirates – not unlike those of the Portuguese in opening up the Indian Ocean in the sixteenth century.

Herodotus also tells a somewhat unlikely story about a ship's captain, Kolaios, who set out from the Aegean island of Samos about 630 BC, bound for the Nile delta. He was blown off course, eventually ending up in Tartessos in southern Iberia. Here he was able to take on board quantities of goods sufficient to make him a wealthy man. For Kolaios to have been such a disastrous navigator, or the winds so fearsome, seems unlikely: it sounds more like an adventurer's expedition, carried out in secret and making use of intelligence of distant lands overheard, perhaps, in the market of Naucratis in the Nile delta, where traders of all nationalities gathered.

The Mediterranean was not without its dangers. Storms could blow up with little warning and winds could veer, forcing vessels on to a lee shore, as was presumably the case with the ship that went down at Kaş. Even the comparatively safe Golfe du Lion is littered with wrecks from the second century BC to the second century AD. A vivid first-hand description of the perils facing a voyager is given in the Acts of the Apostles in the account of St Paul's sea journey through the central Mediterranean and his shipwreck off Malta.

The Black Sea is in many ways a miniature Mediterranean, though significantly smaller, covering only 423,000 sq km (163,000 sq miles). The sea began its life as a freshwater lake (the Neoeuxine Lake), as did the Caspian Sea, with which it was probably once connected, the two receiving water from the receding Scandinavian Ice Sheet. The Greeks believed that the Black Sea had increased in depth to such an extent that it eventually overflowed into the Mediterranean, joining the two by the narrow waterways of the Bosphorus and Dardanelles. In fact, the reverse was true, the rapidly rising Mediterranean overflowing into the freshwater Black Sea lake some time around 5500 BC. At that stage the level of the lake lay at about 150 m (500 ft) below present sea level, and although the Mediterranean was also at a lower level than it is today the differential between the two was still great. As the Mediterranean rose the spill washing over the Bosphorus bar became a torrent, cutting deeply into the rock. The deep sea cores taken of sediments in the Black Sea suggest that the change from freshwater to saltwater conditions was sudden. It has been argued that the inflow of water could have been such that the level of the Black Sea rose by as much as 15 cm (6 ins) a day. If so, this would have meant that the advance of the water over the low-lying northern shores could have reached a kilometre (over half a mile) a day. Such a rate would have totally transformed the geography of the littoral zone in a single generation leaving an abiding impression of catastrophe in the folk memory.

The influx of water from the great rivers of eastern Europe and the high rate of evaporation of the Mediterranean mean that the Black Sea is now the net provider of water to the Mediterranean, but the exact relationship is not straightforward, as the sixth-century AD historian Procopius realized. He reported that when fishing nets were cast into the Bosphorus the upper part floated towards the Mediterranean while the lower part was caught by a deep countercurrent dragging it back towards the Black Sea. The explanation is

2.13 Between Europe and Asia and between the Mediterranean and the Black Sea, the Dardanelles and the Bosphorus create a crossroads of vital importance to European history.

2.14 *Opposite:* It is easy to appreciate from this satellite photograph of the Aegean with its dense scatter of islands and sinuous peninsulas that the sea was to play a major part in the life of the people. From the north-east corner of the Aegean, via the Dardanelles, the Sea of Marmara and the Bosphorus it was possible to reach the Black Sea. Anyone commanding the two very narrow waterways linking the three seas was able to control the flow of shipping. The Dardanelles and the Bosphorus have featured large throughout history.

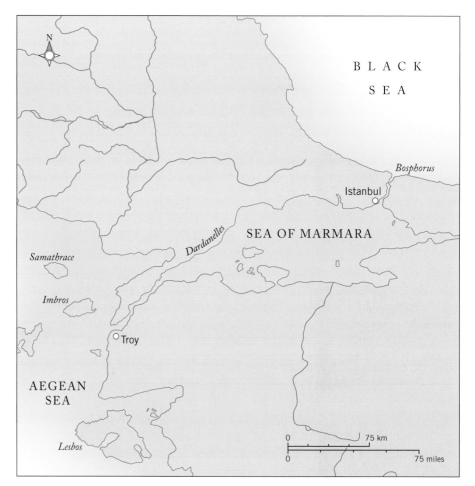

simple: the upper level of water flowing out from the Black Sea is cold and brackish and therefore floats on the lower current of denser, warm salt water flowing inwards from the Mediterranean.

This separation in salinity continues into the sea itself, with quite dramatic consequences. The upper 200 m (650 ft) is well oxygenated and carries a normal biomass of aquatic life, but below this depth 90 per cent of the sea's volume is anoxic (that is, it is without oxygen) and therefore supports no life apart from a few types of simple bacteria. Here organic material washed in by the rivers and raining down from the live sea above settles as a black sludge which can only partially decompose, giving off the poisonous gas hydrogen sulphide, which remains held in the depths and creates a lethal reservoir. The one advantage of this sinister environment is that the many ancient ships that foundered in the deep waters will have remained well preserved.

The earliest name for the sea, *Axeinos*, came from a Greek word originally

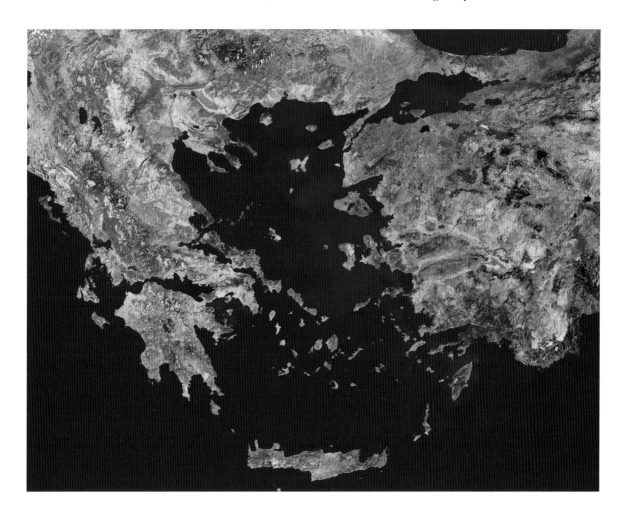

2.15 The Bosphorus – the narrow waterway
joining the Black Sea (top) to the Mediterranean
(bottom). Constantinople (now Istanbul) occupies
the promontory at the Mediterranean end, defined
on the north by the much narrower waterway the
Golden Horn. The Bosphorus divides Asia from
Europe.

meaning 'sombre' and soon took on the connotation of 'unfriendly', a reference perhaps to the sudden storms and fogs. It is tempting to see this as an early value judgment by those unfamiliar with the place, rather as the Arabs, many centuries later, referred to the Atlantic as the 'Sea of Perpetual Gloom'. Once the Greek colonists had begun to settle around the ocean by the fifth century, and to develop its trading potential, attitudes changed. It now became the *Pontus Euxinus* or 'Hospitable Sea', a change perhaps encouraged by the huge supplies of grain and excellent timber that the neighbouring land provided and the plentiful shoals of anchovy, tuna and herring there for the taking.

While the sea was, from time to time, fog-bound and susceptible to sudden changes in weather, congenial currents and offshore winds facilitated navigation. Like the Mediterranean, the Black Sea enjoyed a coastal current that flowed anticlockwise, enabling the maritime colonies to remain in easy contact, while the projecting promontory of the Crimea deflected currents both south and north across the centre, creating two separate circulatory systems in a single ocean.

2.16 The ruins of the Byzantine fortress of Anadolu Kavaği dominated the northern end of the Bosphorus and the entrance to the Black Sea. It served as a toll and customs control point, and, in the fourteenth century was taken over by Genoese traders.

Access between the Mediterranean and the Black Sea required the navigation of the Dardanelles, 70 km (44 miles) long and only 1.8 km (1⅛ miles) wide at its narrowest point, then the crossing of the Sea of Marmara, and finally passage along the Bosphorus, a winding canyon 32 km (20 miles) long and about 2.5 km (1½ miles) wide at its southern end, narrowing to about 0.5 km (⅓ mile) before opening to the Black Sea. With the current flowing constantly to the Mediterranean, and with favourable winds from the Mediterranean, passage through the two straits was not unduly hazardous, but when an icy blast of up to 50 knots blew from the north the journey was impossible and all a vessel could do was to heave-to and wait for favourable conditions. At the mouth of the Dardanelles a convenient, well-protected bay existed on the Asian shore, once extending 4 km (2½ miles) inland to Troy. Ships would have sheltered here for days or weeks on end while waiting for the wind to change. The fame of early Troy owed much to its command of this favoured location. The southern approach to the Bosphorus was also well provided for by the comparatively sheltered roadstead of the Golden Horn in the lee of that long-lived city Byzantium/Constantinople/Istanbul. Here ships could lie at anchor until the winds became favourable, though it was not always the congenial haven its name, Golden, might imply. The French writer Pierre Loti, who knew Istanbul well, wrote of it in his novel *Les désenchantées* as 'the sinister corridor where there are engulfed, under a leaden sky, all the icy squalls of Russia and all the dangerous currents by which the two seas are joined'.

At the far end of the Mediterranean, giving access to the Atlantic, were the Pillars of Hercules, so named after the sea-marks Mons Calpe (Gibraltar) and Mons Abyla (Apes Hill) on the Moroccan coast opposite. Together these created a portal marking the beginning of the narrow straits we now know as the Straits of Gibraltar, giving on to the Outer Ocean. Although the Phoenicians may have sailed into the Atlantic as early as 1000 BC, had certainly settled the offshore island of Gadir (Cadiz) by 800 BC and were exploring the coasts of Europe and Africa to north and south, the Outer Ocean was still held in awe by many in the Greek and Roman worlds. The Pillars of Hercules marked the entrance to the unknown. The Greek poet Pindar, writing in the fifth century BC, warned: 'what lies beyond cannot be trodden by the wise or the unwise. One cannot cross from Gadir towards the dark west. Turn again the sails towards the dry land of Europe.'

The straits themselves are wide – some 9 nautical miles (14 km) – but what determines the ease or otherwise of the passage is the winds and the currents. The winds are straightforward since they either blow from the east or from the west and tend to follow a pattern, with easterlies dominating in the months of March, July–September and December and the westerlies for the rest of the year. In a normal year a ship's master, knowing the pattern, could plan his

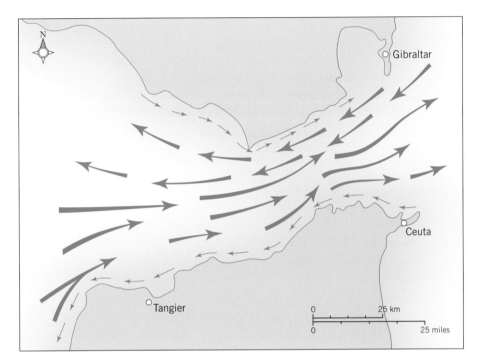

2.17 The Straits of Gibraltar are comparatively wide but the currents shown on the map and winds are complex and constrain the movement of sailing vessels.

transit but weather patterns could be unpredictable and it might be necessary to wait at Gadir (Cadiz) for a favourable westerly, or at Malaga on the coast of Andalucía for an easterly. One classical source advises that if contrary winds set in, one could make the journey overland, from Malaga to Tartessos, in only nine days – after, of course, having first sacrificed to the gods.

Currents were more complex but posed less of a problem. Here, as at the Bosphorus, the water was stratified, with cold water flowing at the rate of 5 or 6 knots from the Atlantic in a surface current 100 m (330 ft) deep below while warm, dense salt water from the Mediterranean flowed out. But to a sailor only the surface current was of consequence and the width of the straits allowed a complex pattern to exist. The main current, that flowing into the Mediterranean, occupied most of the width of the straits but immediately to the north was a countercurrent streaming out of the Mediterranean, providing a convenient route to the Atlantic so long as the wind was favourable. There were also two lesser, coast-hugging currents, one along the Spanish coast flow-ing into the Mediterranean, and the other along the African coast to the Atlantic, but these were best avoided given the immediate proximity of the dangerous rocky coastlines. The currents, then, permitted the passage to be made in either direction at all times, yet making a safe journey was entirely dependent on the strength and direction of the wind. With a following wind the passage was safe and quick but there were many times during the year when fierce contrary winds created dangerous turmoil. Then it was wise to heave-to in the shelter of a friendly coast and wait on the gods.

Once out into the Atlantic, the vessel was at the mercy of forces unknown to Mediterranean sailors. Most dramatic were the tides. Although there are tides in the Mediterranean they are slight and barely noticeable. Along the Atlantic coast of Europe no one could fail to be aware of the rhythm of the ocean with its dramatic displacements of water reaching as much as 14 m (46 ft) along parts of the north Breton coast. With the turning of the tides came quite sudden changes in the direction of the currents. To anyone familiar with these phenomena, the sea would have provided a very convenient mode of travel. With a little knowledge, based on observation, journeys could be planned in practically any direction. The variable was the wind. Frequent onshore winds could pose the hazard of driving ships on to a lee shore. An experienced sailor would take this into account by staying well out to sea, but there were always the difficult headlands to round where the unpredictable could happen.

To penetrate further, to the north-west Atlantic, two sea routes were possible. The westerly route led between Britain and Ireland using St George's Channel, between Carnsore Point and St David's Head, and the North Channel, narrowing to 20 km (12½ miles) between Fair Head and Kintyre, thereafter opening out into the difficult waters surrounding the Hebrides and the west coast of Scotland. The second route was the English Channel, gradually narrowing to the Straits of Dover, some 30 km (19 miles) wide, before giving access to the expansive North Sea. Both routes, with their changing tidal flows, were easily navigable by those familiar with the waters.

The island of Britain marks a significant divide. Its western coast is of the Atlantic. Not only does it face the oncoming Atlantic weather systems, but its deeply indented coastline and that of Ireland, which partially protects it, carved out of old hard rocks, are closely similar to the coasts of Armorica (Brittany) and Iberia. This is a rugged, blustery coast of squalls and storms. The eastern side of Britain facing the North Sea is altogether different and shares many of its characteristics with the opposite coastal lands – northern France, the Low Countries, Germany and Denmark – all of which look in towards the sea. Apart from the northern mountains of Scotland and Norway, it is a low-lying landscape of river estuaries, coastal sand bars and marshland. While the coast of Britain offers convenient sea-marks to guide sailors, the coasts of mainland Europe are far less forthcoming, presenting a low monotony, and can only be distinguished from one another on close inspection. The great attraction of the European coast lies in ease of access to the interior, along rivers like the Rhine, Meuse and Sheldt and a more northerly cluster, the Ems, Weser and Elbe, and a ready supply of amber to be found on

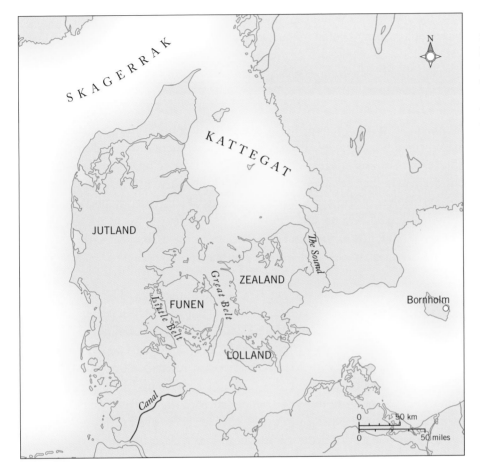

2.18 Passage between the Baltic and the North Sea was constrained by islands, shallows, tides and winds. It was comparatively easy for the coastal communities to control the sea traffic.

the beaches around the German Bight. The sea itself was also productive of an array of fish, not least the herring, which was to provide the mainstay of the medieval diet.

Finally to the Baltic, a name first used by Adam of Bremen in the eleventh century AD. The approach from the North Sea has to be made via the Skagerrak and Kattegat, a wide, continuous waterway that leads between the low-lying peninsula of Jutland and the more impressive indented coasts of southern Norway and Sweden. Once through, and facing south, the sailor is confronted by a confusion of islands (some 474 of them) through which there are three usable channels, the Sound, the Great Belt and the Little Belt. All are navigable but the last two are beset with shallows. Though only 8 m (26 ft) deep, the Sound is much the safest option. At its narrowest point, barely 5 km (3 miles) separate the fortresses of Helsingborg in Swedish Scania from Helsingar on the Danish island of Zealand. The flow of water through the Danish Straits is complex, with the brackish water of the surface discharging into the North Sea while the more saline water below flows in the opposite direction, creating overall a counterclockwise circulation. But in spite of the inflow tides are negligible.

The Baltic is a comparatively small sea with a surface area of 377,000 sq km (145,500 sq miles), fed with silt from its many rivers and diminishing in size as the land continues to rise. During the winter about 45 per cent of the area is frozen but this lies mainly in the north, in the gulfs of Bothnia, Finland and Riga. For the sparse population of these regions there is some advantage since the frozen sea encourages seals, a valuable source of oil, to breed on the ice surface where they are easily caught. The comparative calmness of the waters, the narrowness of the seas and the scattering of conveniently placed islands – Åland, Gotland, Öland and Bornholm – encouraged maritime endeavour. For the inhabitants of the coastal regions, from the earliest time, the sea was a natural extension of the land and the southern Baltic became a forcing ground for maritime technology.

The sea and its surrounding land are resource-rich. The amber of the south Baltic coast has always been greatly in demand and in prehistoric times was traded widely throughout Europe. Forests of beechwood in the south-east and deciduous forests with spruce in the north provided ample timber for shipbuilding together with the necessary pitch to caulk ships' planking. The forests were also a source of the furs and skins much in demand in the south: these came from the more remote areas of the north through networks of exchange. In the ninth century AD a Norwegian called Ottar described to the English king Alfred the tribute he received from the northern hunter-gatherers – the Saami – who lived at the extremity of the habitable world. The tribute, he said,

> consists of skins of beasts, the feathers of birds, whale-bone, and ship-rope made from walrus hide and seal skin . . . .The highest rank has to pay fifteen marten skins, five reindeer skins, one bear skin, ten measures of feathers, and a jacket of bear skin or otter skin, and two ships' ropes. Each of these must be sixty ells long, one of walrus hide, the other from seal.

Much of this tribute would have been sold in the markets of southern Scandinavia and England. Many of the commodities would have featured large in the trading systems of the prehistoric period linking deep into the heart of Europe.

The four oceans of Europe, five if we distinguish the North Sea from the Atlantic, were discrete geographical entities, each of which had a rhythm of life that would have bound its coastal and riverine communities closely together. The littoral zones were highly favoured locations rich in a wide range of natural resources and easy of access. They were also healthy places to live, where salt was easily accessible and iodine and fish oils would, for many, have formed a natural part of the diet. It is little wonder that human populations through time have favoured the sea coasts, clustering, as Socrates put it, like 'ants or frogs around a pond'.

CHAPTER THREE

Food for the Gathering

In the three thousand years from the end of the last Ice Age (*c.* 12,700 BC) to the establishment of a mild climate similar to today's around 9600 BC, the face and, indeed, the shape of Europe changed dramatically. To survive in the new habitats that emerged, human communities, whose ancestors had managed to cope with the extremes of the last glaciation by migrating to the more congenial parts of southern Europe, had to adapt their lifestyles, and in some areas to adapt very rapidly. Climate forced the pace of social change.

Large-scale changes in global temperature are the result of cyclic variations in the earth's orbit and tilt, altering its relation to the sun. Every 95,800 years or so the orbit veers from being almost circular to something more elliptical. As a result the Northern Hemisphere develops a more intensely seasonal weather pattern, leading to the growth of the northern ice sheet. Another cycle, at an interval of about 41,000 years, sees the earth's tilt change by almost 3°. This, too, exacerbates the differences between the seasons. And, to add further to the complexity, every 21,700 years the earth wobbles on its axis, varying the distance of the Northern Hemisphere from the sun and again having a direct effect on climate. These phenomena would not in themselves be enough to cause the rapid changes evident in the fossil record, but they set

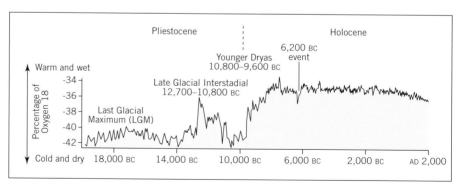

3.1 By studying the ratios of oxygen isotopes found in cores bored through the Greenland ice cap, it is possible to chart minute changes in air temperature over the last 20,000 years. The diagram shows warming during the Late Glacial Interstadial, the return to cold conditions during the Younger Dryas and the sudden establishment of stable warm conditions at the beginning of the Holocene.

off other changes in the system that amplify their effects. The result of all this is that every 100,000 years there is a cycle of climate change from intense cold to comparative warmth and back to intense cold again.

At the height of the Last Glacial Maximum, around 20,000 BC, land temperatures were about 20°C lower than they are today, and over large parts of northern Europe, stretching from Ireland to Russia, and much of North America, there were ice sheets more than 4 km (2½ miles) thick locking up so much of the earth's water that sea levels fell to 100 m (330 ft) below present levels and desert conditions prevailed over much of the globe. By about 13,000 BC the process of gradual warming was well under way.

The Changing Coast Lands of Europe

The retreat of the ice was by no means a uniform process. By 12,700 BC the temperature was increasing rapidly and within a thousand years it had already reached levels not far below those of today, but then a rapid decline set in and temperatures plummeted to a new low about 10,000 BC. The sudden plunge in temperature shows just how finely balanced the climatic readjustment really was. It seems that, as the climate began to improve and the Atlantic currents readjusted themselves to create the warming Gulf Stream, huge volumes of icy melt-water suddenly began to pour into the ocean at such a rate as to destabilize the Gulf Stream, possibly halting it altogether. The result was that Europe began to freeze. This final cold spell, known as the Younger Dryas, was short-lived, lasting only about 1200 years, and as the Gulf Stream re-established itself once more, the climate began to warm up again. By 9600 BC the cold spell was over and by 8000 BC temperatures had reached much the same range as today. The effect of the Younger Dryas interlude was to drive human communities south, but recolonization followed quickly on climatic amelioration.

With the melting of the ice cap sea levels began to rise. This eustatic readjustment applied evenly to all the oceans receiving the melt-water and to begin with proceeded at a rapid and regular rate of about one metre (3ft) every five hundred years. The effect was that large tracts of the Atlantic coasts were inundated. The rising sea level also affected the Mediterranean. Here it was the coastal lowlands around the mouths of the rivers Ebro, Rhône, Po and Nile that suffered the greatest loss of land. The Corsica/Sardinia landmass became two islands and in the Aegean the inundation led to the separation of many of the smaller islands. Around 5600 BC the level of the Mediterranean had risen sufficiently to flood over the land barrier into the Black Sea, inundating, as we have seen, vast areas of fertile Pontic lowlands over a very short period of time.

In the north another, counter, process was in operation. The massive ice

63

3.2 During the Glacial
Maximum, sea-levels in the
Mediterranean were about
120 m (395 ft) below their
present level (upper map).
The rapid rise in sea-level
during the Early Holocene
to about 35 m (115 ft)
below the present level
(lower map) produced a
coastline not very
different from today's.

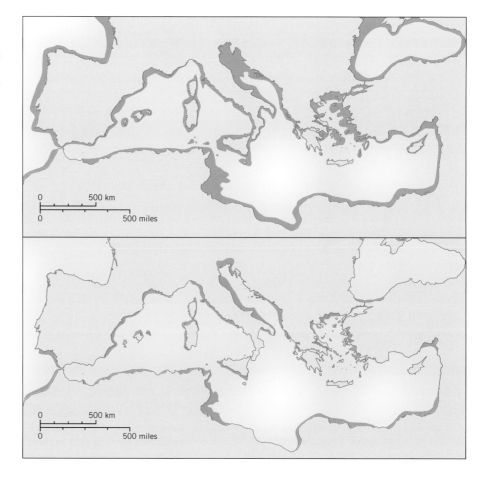

sheet had depressed the land by its sheer weight, distorting the earth's crust by
more than 200 m (650 ft) where it was at its thickest over what is now the Gulf
of Bothnia. As the ice began to melt the earth's crust rose to reassume its
original shape. This isostatic readjustment, localized to the regions that are
now Scandinavia and Scotland, worked in opposition to the rise in sea level.
The two processes continue today. Where the ice was at its thickest, at the
north end of the Gulf of Bothnia, the land is rising at the rate of 9 mm (⅓ in)
per year, while in the Highlands of Scotland, above which the ice cap had been
much thinner, the increase in height is 3 mm (⅛ in) per year.

It was in the Scandinavian region that the interplay of land- and sea-level
rises was at its most complex. At times the Baltic was an ice-dammed lake, at
others it became a sea linked to the outer ocean. Eventually, around 5000 BC,
the land bridge was finally broken, creating the Baltic much as we know it
today. But the Baltic is not stable and with readjustment still continuing, the
northern part grows ever smaller.

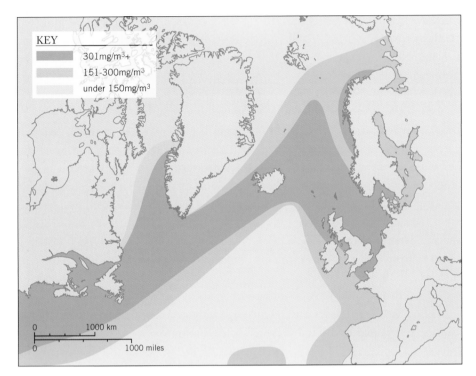

KEY

- 301mg/m³+
- 151-300mg/m³
- under 150mg/m³

0   1000 km

0   1000 miles

3.3 The plankton biomass in the Atlantic provides nutrients for fish and therefore charts the richest fishing grounds. The map shows the contrast between the rich Atlantic coasts of Europe and the Mediterranean where the biomass is low.

While this complex interplay of land and sea was taking place around the margins of the fast-diminishing ice sheet, similar processes were at work to the west where eventually Ireland and Britain were to emerge. By about 15,000 BC, as the Scandinavian ice receded and the British ice sheet shrank to a small patch over the Scottish Highlands and Islands, an extensive, low-lying land-mass extended as far north as the latitude of Shetland and Bergen. A wide, deep-water inlet, known as the Norwegian Trench, channelled the outflow of the rivers draining this land mass into the Atlantic. Its estuary was not far west of Bergen. The eustatic rise in sea level soon outstripped the isostatic rise of the land, except beneath the Scottish ice cap, with the result that large areas of land gradually disappeared beneath the encroaching ocean and created the North Sea. By 8000 BC Ireland was separate from the rest of Europe and by 6500 BC Britain had become an island. Remnants of the former land remained as islands in the North Sea but by c.4000 BC it is likely that most had disappeared beneath the waves. The Dogger Bank is all that remains.

There is one further factor that needs to be taken into account. Western Europe benefits from the ameliorating effects of ocean currents circulating in a clockwise direction around the North Atlantic. The warm current, known as the Gulf Stream, originates in the Gulf of Mexico and passes through the Florida Canal flowing northwards along the coast of America. In the vicinity

65

of Newfoundland it encounters the cold Labrador Current and is deflected eastwards towards continental Europe, where it divides into two – the north-flowing Norwegian Current and the south-flowing Canary Current. At the point where the Gulf Stream emerges from the Florida Channel it is a recognizable current only some 40 km (25 miles) wide, but beyond Newfoundland it becomes a swathe of slow-moving warm water more usually referred to as the North Atlantic Drift Current. Its great importance lies in the fact that it carries warm water to latitudes higher than in any other ocean, and since the current is significantly warmer than the surrounding sea – in March it is 8°C, compared with a surrounding sea temperature of 2–6°C – it is responsible for creating the mild oceanic climate that much of western Europe enjoys. Britain is on the same latitude as Labrador and without the Gulf Stream would suffer the same bitter climate. The sudden cold spell of the Younger Dryas probably resulted from a disruption to the Gulf Stream caused by the sudden release of melt-water from the thawing ice cap. The concern among some that today's global warming could have a similar effect is not without good cause.

The North Atlantic Drift Current brings another benefit to Atlantic Europe – it is plankton-rich, having a high biomass of over 300 mg/m³ (0.01 ounces/1.3 cu yards) This is partly due to its warmth and partly to the upwelling of nutrients from the sea bed caused by the mixing of currents. The nutrient level is further raised when the current, approaching Europe, flows above the wide continental shelf. Nutrients mixing with the warm surface water encourage the growth of phytoplankton and the zooplankton that feed off them. These in turn provide nutrition for fish. The zone of high plankton biomass generated by the North Atlantic Drift Current has created some of the world's most famous fishing grounds, among them the Newfoundland Banks, the seas around Iceland and the North Sea.

At times when the Baltic was joined to the North Sea by a wide channel, the plankton-rich water surged well into its western reaches. But even when the passage was restricted, as it is now, rivers carrying nutrients from the melting snows encouraged plankton growth and nurtured fish supplies.

The benefits of the North Atlantic Drift Current were enjoyed by communities stretching from Bergen to Finistère and the coasts of Britain and Ireland. The seas in these favoured regions far exceeded the Mediterranean and the Black Sea in the sheer variety of their bounty.

The Mediterranean and the Black Sea were well known in classical times for their shoals of tuna and anchovy, but in the Mediterranean the narrow coastal shelf and the lack of significant tides discouraged the growth of phytoplankton and the higher life forms that fed on them, with the result that the marine life of the littoral zone is poor in comparison with the Atlantic. In the period immediately following the end of the Ice Age the extensive deltas

66

of the Ebro, Rhône and Po provided highly favourable conditions for the growth of a wide range of foodstuffs, but with the rising sea level the productive lowlands were rapidly inundated and greatly reduced. The Black Sea was in many ways comparable. Around much of its perimeter mountains plunge steeply into the sea but to the west was the once-extensive Danube delta. The inundation of the mid-sixth millennium suddenly removed tens of thousands of square kilometres of these highly productive alluvial flatlands.

As they emerged from the grip of the last Ice Age, the coastal lands of the European peninsula were transformed, in some cases quite rapidly, by the land/sea readjustments. This transformation tilted the balance. The hitherto inhospitable north – the shores of the Baltic and the North Sea – became congenial, welcoming environments for the hunter-gatherers now colonizing the more northerly parts of the continent, while to the south, in the Mediterranean and the Black Sea, the productive coastal environments became successively more restricted with rapidly rising sea levels. The Atlantic coasts, particularly the coasts of France and Iberia from Ushant to Cape St Vincent, sat comfortably in between. Benefiting from the North Atlantic Drift Current, the generally warmer weather of the more southerly latitudes and the deltaic outpourings of the great rivers from the Loire to the Guadalquivir, this Atlantic face provided optimum conditions for the early hunter-gatherer-fishers to develop a comfortable and sustainable lifestyle.

The Face of Europe Transformed

With the change in climate between 10,000 and 6000 BC came the progressive advance northwards of the vegetational zones, the different species inching forwards to colonize new landscapes as, year by year, the climate became warmer, creating new environments for the changing fauna. Human communities, only a minor component of the ecosystems, had to learn to adapt if they were to survive.

During the Last Glacial Maximum, c.18,000–16,000 BC, with temperatures more than 10°C lower than they are today, with ice sheets covering a great swathe of Europe from Ireland to northern Scandinavia as well as the Alps and Pyrenees, and with no North Atlantic Drift Current to ameliorate the harshness of the Atlantic zone, Europe was at its most inhospitable. During the long winters temperatures could plunge to -10°C for many weeks, bringing heavy snowfalls, but in the summer temperatures would rise to not far below those of the present day. It was a climate of extremes. Much of Europe at this stage was open country, ranging from tundra, around the edge of the ice, to parktundra and steppe further south – treeless landscapes supporting rich growths of mosses, grasses and herbaceous plants. It was only around the

Mediterranean, the southern shores of the Black Sea and Atlantic Iberia that forests managed to maintain a tenuous grip. The open landscape supported large herds of reindeer, horse and steppe bison as well as woolly rhinoceros and mammoth who migrated with the seasons along well-established routes and were thus easy prey to the Upper Palaeolithic communities inhabiting the more congenial zone of Europe stretching from the coasts of Cantabria into southern Russia. It was these big-game hunters who produced the stunning three-dimensional carvings of the female form and the cave paintings for which the period is justly famous.

With the onset of neothermal conditions all this changed as forest began to extend northwards, creeping out from its Mediterranean refuge gradually to colonize the open steppe and tundra. The earliest colonizers were cold-tolerant trees like birch, willow, juniper and aspen, followed by pine and later by hazel. With increasing warmth the broad-leaved forest dominated by elm, lime, oak and alder moved in. So, as the ice retreated the different forest zones moved progressively northwards until, by 4000 BC, they had reached all but

3.4 The colonizing birch forest, in this example in Siberia. Birch, along with willow, juniper and aspen are cold-tolerant trees and were the first to colonize the tundra as the temperature began to rise at the end of the Ice Age.

the extreme north of Europe. Around the Mediterranean, where pockets of forest had survived the glacial extremes, the woodlands expanded, with pine dominating the higher regions and deciduous oak taking over much of the rest of the landscape.

The new vegetation cover brought with it a different fauna. Some of the herbivores of the Late Glacial period, like the reindeer and elk, were driven northwards, while others – the mammoth and woolly rhinoceros – became extinct, to be replaced by smaller beasts, red deer, roe deer, elk, pig and aurochs. In their comfortable woodland environment human communities had cause to move much less than their predecessors and inhabited their territory in much smaller and more widely dispersed groups. This forest fauna amounted to only about 20–30 per cent of the total biomass of the herbivores that had roamed the tundra before them. Such a dramatic change forced the human communities to develop new food-gathering strategies. Some groups moved forwards in advance of the forest and continued to hunt reindeer and wild horse across the North European Plain, while others remained, adapting themselves to their new environments; but the number of known inhabited sites was many fewer, implying that the overall population had drastically declined.

It would be wrong to think of the forest as entirely uniform. Tree cover would have varied considerably with geology and altitude, while rivers, lakes and bogs created openings in the canopy, each with its own localized micro-environment. One important characteristic of forest was that, by exposing a huge leaf area, it was able to capture a maximum amount of sunlight, which, through photosynthesis, it converted into carbohydrates. These carbohydrates were available for creatures at a higher trophic level to use as foods: but investment diminishes as one moves up the trophic ladder. Humans, as omnivores, can benefit from both plant and animal calories and are therefore able to make an efficient use of resources by varying their diet depending upon availability.

Different types of forest offer different volumes of resource. Temperate deciduous forests are the most productive, yielding up to 3000 dry grams of food per square metre per year (6.6 lbs/1.2 sq yds), while Mediterranean mixed woodland is the least, offering no more than 2000 dry grams of food. The one great disadvantage of the forest zone, especially of the deciduous forests, is that it is dormant through many months of the year: during this time food resources are difficult to find. Adaptation to the forest environment, then, required human communities to maximize their use of plant resources to augment the sparsely distributed animals, and to adopt a storage regime, creating stocks of nuts, dried berries and grasses, smoked fish, etc., which could tide the group over the lean months of winter. These constraints, and the fact that even at the best of times the total biomass of the forests was relatively low, meant that hunter-gatherer groups remained small and were widely dispersed throughout the landscape. Numbers are unlikely to have exceeded 0.50 persons per square kilometre (6¼ sq miles) and may, in some parts, have been a hundred times lower.

The more varied the potential food resources, the greater the chances of survival. Expanses of uninterrupted forest lacked variety, but along river banks and around the many lakes, swamps and bogs that formed in the pock-marked surface of the north European moraines there was great diversity – fish and eels, migrating birds and a formidable array of nutritious plants there for the gathering, watercress, water chestnut, water lily, and various rushes and reeds. A plant like club rush (*Scirpus lacustris*) was particularly nutritious, its large tubers, stems and seeds all being edible. It grew in prodigious quantities in its natural state, producing a greater yield than the most productive of cereals.

The deltas of all the major rivers would have been even richer in fauna and flora because of the sluggishness of the water in the subsidiary streams, the high level of nutrients brought down from the surrounding land, and the salt-rich environment of the delta fringe. The wide expanses of marshland and open fresh water with their abundance of grasses, reeds and floating flora also attracted migrating birds in great numbers; their presence provided an added benefit to human predators eager to extend the range of their diet.

And then there were the sea coasts themselves. Some shorelines like the northern Baltic and the coasts of northern Scotland were rising in relation to the sea but for the most part the European littoral zone was experiencing regression. What all had in common was their great biodiversity. The marshy fringes, estuaries and deltas have already been mentioned but then there was the littoral itself – the interface of land and sea with its hugely varied fauna and flora providing, at the highest reaches of the tide, the edible roots of sea kales, sea turnips, sea parsnips and sea cabbages. Further down the shore, especially if it was an Atlantic shore with a considerable tidal reach, were a succession of ecozones producing crustaceans and molluscs – limpets, mussels, periwinkles and cockles – as well as a range of edible seaweeds such as carragheen (*Chondrus crispus*) and dillisk (*Palmaria palmata*), which still feature in the Welsh and Irish diet today. Then there is the sea itself, offering an abundance of fish and, in some more northern parts, sea mammals like the walrus and seal and even the occasional stranded whale. Add all this to what could be gathered from the nests of birds on the flanking cliffs and the wooded hinterland beyond and the attraction of the coastal zone to the early hunter-gatherers can readily be appreciated.

The coast offered not only a variety of fauna and flora in abundance to stimulate the taste buds and counter the monotony of an unmitigated diet of reindeer, it also provided food throughout the year. There were always reserves to fall back on and sources that even the young or the frail could be sent to gather. One further advantage that may not have been evident to the shore-gleaners was that their diet was rich in iodine (related to increased human fertility) and in fish oils essential to general health. The quality and abundance of the maritime diet encouraged a rapid increase in population and led to a more sedentary lifestyle.

Some Coastal Lifestyles

The Mediterranean

While the Mediterranean might at first sight seem to be a highly congenial landscape for hunter-gatherers, it has disadvantages as well as advantages. On the plus side is the benefit of latitude, the many hours of sunshine and lack of frosts encouraging variety of plant growth. The geomorphology too has much to offer, with the characteristic mountainous or hilly interior rising abruptly from the narrow coastal plain providing a variety of ecozones that changed quite rapidly over short distances. The disadvantage of the north Mediterranean shore was the narrowness of the littoral zone which, together with the lack of tidal range and the low energy of the sea, created a comparatively low-yield ecology.

Given the extent of the north Mediterranean coastline, Mesolithic hunter-gatherer sites are surprisingly rare. Part of the reason is that the rise in sea level would have inundated earlier coastal sites, but even so the implication is that the population was thinly spread. There were, however, favoured locations. One of the best known is the Franchthi cave on the Gulf of Argos in the Peloponnese. Here, excavations have shown that the cave was used from the Late Palaeolithic (c.18,000 BC) to the Neolithic. During this time the sea level rose, bringing the shore ever closer to the cave: by 7500 BC the sea was only a couple of hours' walk away. The successive deposits in the cave show an increasing reliance on food from the littoral: first shellfish, especially limpets and periwinkles, and later deep-sea fish like tuna brought in from the open water. The diet was balanced by a very wide range of plant foods. As the community became more confident in taking to the sea to catch fish they also became more adventurous. By 11,000 BC they were making sea journeys to the island of Melos 120 km (75 miles) away to bring back the much-sought-after shiny black obsidian (a volcanic glass) from which to fashion tools. The voyages would probably have been made by island-hopping but even this required open sea crossings of up to 15 km (9 miles). Coastal communities of hunter-gatherers, drawn to the open sea by the lure of plentiful fish, soon became explorers, traders and eventually colonizers.

The colonization of Mediterranean islands must have involved sea voyages. The two Tyrrhenian islands of Corsica and Sardinia provide evidence of this. Even at the time of the Glacial Maximum the islands, then joined, were separated from the Italian mainland by a channel in excess of 50 km (31 miles) wide. By the Early Holocene they were discrete islands with coastlines not unlike those of the present day. The earliest firmly dated human occupation (9000–8000 BC) is represented by a scatter of occupation sites in rock shelters and small caves usually close to the coast. The settlements were occupied over a long period of time, up to five hundred years in one case, but not continuously, implying that the communities were probably nomadic. Demonstrating the abandonment of a site is not always easy but one convenient indicator of human absence is the colonization of the shelter by the endemic small eagle owl (*Bubo insularis*) whose pellets form a distinct layer. Such are the intricacies of archaeological interpretation.

The Mesolithic gatherer communities lived by collecting, trapping and fishing in the immediate vicinity of their home bases along the coastal zone. Particularly abundant were the remains of a now-extinct hare-like creature, *Prolagus sardus*. One site produced remains of about 100,000 animals during five hundred years of occupation. Other meat sources included species of large mice and voles, occasional great bustards, geese, ducks, monk seals and dolphins. Shellfish were collected and small fish, like eels and sardines, were caught. Although fish provided a smaller quantity of protein to the diet than small game, they were an important staple since they could be stored for long periods, either dried or smoked. That this was actually done is suggested by the fact that fish heads were very rare in the occupation debris, the implication being that preparation was carried out at another site.

These early colonists had presumably sailed to the islands from the Italian mainland some time around 9000 BC and had established themselves in the coastal regions, developing their very distinctive economy. Whether they felt any need to maintain a mobility at sea is unclear but their very restricted material culture suggests that long-distance contacts were not a significant part of their lifestyle.

The Atlantic

Once through the Straits of Gibraltar, we enter an entirely different environment – that of the Atlantic with its wide, shelving littoral zone. The upwelling of nutrient-rich deep ocean waters, the warming Gulf Stream and the abundance of river estuaries combine together to create one of the most varied and welcoming coastal regions in the world. That the Atlantic littoral extends across many degrees of latitude from 36° at Gibraltar to 61° to the north of Shetland means that there is a significant temperature variation from south to north. The coast of Portugal combines the best of two worlds – an Atlantic environment and a Mediterranean climate. It is hardly surprising, therefore, that the Later Mesolithic communities chose to concentrate in the valleys of three of its major southern rivers, the Tagus, the Sado and the Mira.

In the Tagus valley settlement sites are distributed over a distance of some 30 km (19 miles) in the vicinity of the town of Muge. Each is marked by a large shell midden (*concheiro*), several metres high and up to 100 m (330 ft) across, representing the accumulation of debris, largely estuarine shells, built up over a period of extended occupation spanning hundreds of years. For the most part the middens occupy the margins of small east-flowing tributaries of the Tagus just above the alluvial valley floor – the tidal zone in the Mesolithic period. The sheer size of the middens, and the fact that they also served as burial grounds, producing some three hundred inhumations, suggest that they were the permanent bases of the community, though this does not necessarily mean that they were occupied by the entire social group continuously throughout the year. The location of the settlements was carefully chosen to provide access to a range of resources, the freshwater zone of the river valley, the saltwater marshes beyond and the lightly wooded hinterland. Together these ecozones

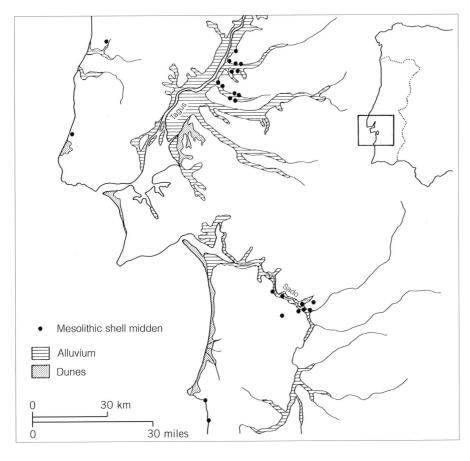

3.5 The valleys of the Tagus and the Sado provided a rich and varied environment where the settlements of Mesolithic hunter-gatherers concentrated.

• Mesolithic shell midden

Alluvium

Dunes

0   30 km

0   30 miles

produced an abundance of food, shellfish, fish, crustaceans, migratory birds, wild boar, red deer and aurochs.

One of the smaller of the middens – Moita do Sebastião – which has been extensively excavated began life as a carefully organized living space, probably for a single family. It was divided into a habitation zone and a zone set aside for the adult burials – altogether fifty-nine individuals. Eight children between the ages of one and seven were all buried within the habitation zone, as if to imply that they continued to play a part in the world of the living. Moita do Sebastião was a comparatively simple structure.

These Muge shell middens reflect a stability in the settlement systems and it is tempting to see them as statements of permanency – places invested with the spirits of ancestors – and as such visible claims to the territorial rights of the group. Long-lived home bases of this kind could only have come into being in places where the varied environment provided the assurance of a stable all-year-round food supply.

A second group of shell-midden settlements are known further to the south, concentrated in the lower reaches of the river Sado. Each community seems to have had two bases, one occupied during the autumn and winter, the other during the spring and summer. Thus, a base, downriver towards the estuary, produced an abundance of fish, particularly meagre and gilthead, which are present in the estuary between April and August and so implying spring and summer occupation; while at another site, further from the river mouth, the age of kill of the wild pig found there suggests occupation between September and February. Seasonal mobility can be taken as a sign of stability, with the various communities respecting an accepted pattern of territoriality. It is quite possible that food-gathering regimes of this kind brought disparate communities together at certain times during the year when exchanges, competitions and marriage arrangements could have taken place.

Sea-level changes around the coasts of north-western France and southern Britain have inundated large expanses of the littoral zone, leaving a very incomplete pattern of Mesolithic settlement, but there are many indications of a heavy dependence on coastal resources and hints that the coastal communities were only one element in complex patterns of interaction linking them to a deep hinterland. On the south coast of Britain, perched on the high limestone promontory of Portland, the hunter-gatherer community who built shelters out of limestone slabs at Culverwell in the sixth millennium BC and collected shellfish from the nearby beaches also spent time extracting chert (a siliceous stone) from the limestone. Portland chert became an item of exchange and was found far inland, many hundreds of kilometres from the source. Mobility is clearly indicated but this does not necessarily imply that the Portland community moved seasonally. Their environment was varied enough to allow year-round occupation. It could be that bands living in the inland regions made seasonal visits to the coast.

Issues of this kind are difficult to resolve using the very partial archaeological evidence alone but recent advances in scientific analysis are providing a valuable tool that can throw new light on the problem in those rare cases where human bones are available for study. The southern coast of Brittany is one such area. In the 1920s and 1930s extensive shell middens were located and excavated on the islands of Téviec and Hoëdic, sited just off the coast of Morbihan. They can be dated to between 5500 and 4500 BC and are a remnant of what must once have been an extensive pattern of coastal settlement. Both shell middens contained the graves of ancestors dug down into them – ten graves containing twenty-three individuals were found at Téviec while at Hoëdic fourteen individuals were found in nine graves. Bone collagen extracted from them was subjected to stable isotope analysis focusing on carbon isotope ^{13}C and nitrogen isotope ^{15}N, which are considered to be indicators of the protein diet ingested in early life. The proportions of the two enable a distinction to be made between an intake of protein from seafood and that

3.6 The island of Hoëdic in the bay of Quiberon on the south coast of Brittany was the site of a Mesolithic cemetery dating to the mid-fifth millennium BC. This reconstruction is of a burial of a female with a child. The head of the adult is surrounded by red deer antlers and the body is covered with sea shells.

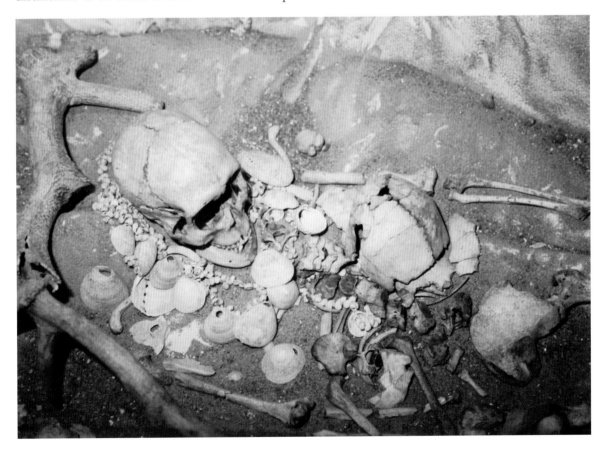

from terrestrial sources. Not surprisingly, they showed a heavy reliance on maritime resources – 70–80 per cent for the Hoëdic population and 50–70 per cent for the people of Téviec – but of particular interest was the observation that the females had relied far less on marine foods. While this could have been the result of locally applied taboos, a more likely explanation is that a proportion of the women came from the terrestrial hinterland and married into the coastal group. Marriage alliances would have helped to maintain friendly relations between coastal and inland groups sharing certain resources.

The Baltic

The partial patterns of coastal settlement that result from the rising sea level around much of the southern and western European coastline are compensated for by the very high quality of the evidence that comes from Denmark and southern Sweden where the rise in sea level is balanced against the isostatic rise of the land following the melting of the ice. By the later part of the Mesolithic period, known by the name of the famous shell midden at Ertebølle (4600–3800 BC), the overall size of the population had increased and settlements of a more permanent nature had become established, supported by networks of temporary camp sites specializing in a specific resource. These camps were worked by segments of the community who would have returned to the large coastal midden sites which were probably occupied throughout the year.

The coastal middens were always sited where the fishing potential was high and it was this maritime resource, in all its variety, that provided an assured all-year-round food source sufficient to support a permanent occupation. Many of the midden sites grew to considerable proportions. At the type site of Ertebølle, on Limfjord in northern Jutland, the shell midden, up to 2 m (6½ ft) thick, stretches along the line of the contemporary shore for 140 m (460 ft) and averages 20 m (66 ft) in width. The neighbouring site of Bjørnsholm is even larger, extending for 250 m (820 ft) and is up to 50 m (164 ft) wide. Radiocarbon dating suggests that these sites were probably in continuous use for 800–1000 years.

The remarkable stability of the Ertebølle settlement pattern was based upon a reliable and predictable source of food obtainable from the maritime environment. Most evident are the oysters, limpets, cockles, mussels and periwinkles which feature so large in the shell middens. However, the actual return in calorific value for the effort expended in collecting is comparatively small. A single red deer would be worth fifty thousand oysters! That said, the value of shellfish is that they are always available and can be substituted when other food sources run short.

Fishing was of considerable importance. Here, the emphasis was on catching small inshore species by hook, net or trap. The catch depended on local conditions and preferences. In the Limsfjord region eel was dominant and the presence of roach suggests that both were obtained from freshwater rivers. In eastern Jutland flounder was the main catch, on Fynen it was cod, while in eastern Zealand cod, whiting, pollack, coalfish, plaice, flounder and dab were caught.

Sea mammals were everywhere hunted, especially the grey seal, but other types of seal are also recorded together with killer whale, porpoise, bottlenose dolphin and white-beaked dolphin. Stranded whales were also in evidence. The numbers of sea mammals were never large but the persistence of grey seal suggests that the animal was widely targeted as a valuable source of blubber.

Sea birds and other migrating birds were also caught. Swans, ducks and geese are frequently found, with herring gulls, cormorants, great auks, guillemots, gannets and white-tailed eagles occurring in lesser numbers. To catch such a varied bag would have required focused hunting strategies and the use of specialized base camps at the appropriate season. Finally, we should remember the other things that could be gathered with ease from the maritime environment: birds' eggs, edible seaweeds and a wide variety of roots, seeds, berries and nuts.

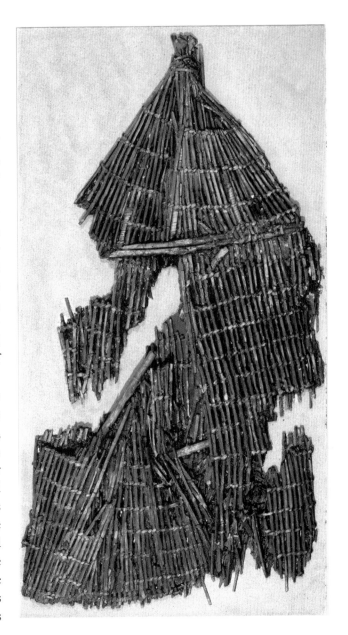

3.7 A fish trap made from small wood bound by reeds from the Ertebølle period site of Lille Knabstrup, Zealand, Denmark.

The technology necessary to capture such a variety of animal resources was well developed, using materials readily at hand, principally bone, antler, wood and fibre. From these were manufactured fish traps and nets, fish hooks, spears, leisters and harpoons as well as canoes, paddles and fishing platforms. One site that has produced a spectacular range of equipment is Tybrind Vig on the west side of the Danish island of Fynen. The settlement had originally occupied the dry land along the edge of the coast and debris was thrown from

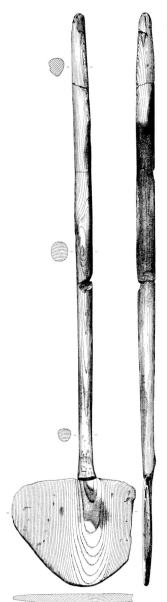

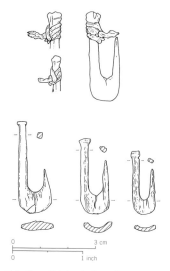

3.8 Bone fish hooks from the Danish Mesolithic site of Tybrind Vig indicate not only the importance of fishing but the size of the potential catch.

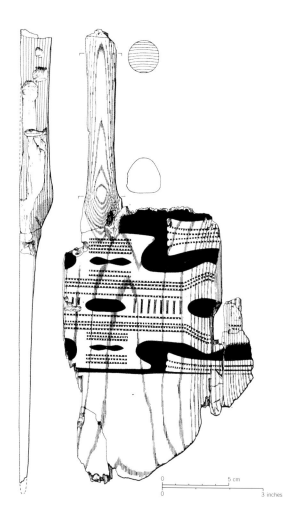

3.9 The Danish Late Mesolithic site Tybrind Vig has produced a wide range of organic material preserved in waterlogged deposits. These two paddles, both made from split ash trunks, reflect the skills of the boat-builders and their desire to decorate artefacts, even those in daily use.

it into the reed zone along the edge of the water. The subsequent rise in sea level swamped the settlement which now lies 3 m (10 ft) below sea level. Since the rubbish thrown out from the settlement has always been waterlogged the organic component is extremely well preserved. Bone fish-hooks are well represented, including some with lines attached. There is also a fish trap made of wooden rods, remains of a fish weir, fishing nets of plant fibre with wooden net floats and bone points from leisters and fish spears. More remarkable are three dugout canoes, all of lime wood, one of which is more than 9.5 m (30 ft) long. Two have clay-based 'fireplaces' in the stern, which might suggest that the boats were on the water for many hours at a time and perhaps at night. Also recovered were between ten and fifteen paddles made of ash, with heart-shaped blades and shafts over 1 metre (3 ft) long.

By the end of the fifth millennium BC the Mesolithic communities of Denmark and southern Sweden were firmly focused on the exploitation of their maritime environment. The variety and consistency of the resource base enabled stable communities to be established in well-defined social territories in conditions that favoured population growth. Their canoes were well suited to the fjords and coastal waters, but there is as yet no positive evidence to suggest that longer voyages in the open sea were being undertaken.

In the Heart of the Peninsula

So far we have concentrated on hunter-gatherer communities of the coast lands of Europe. But what of the vast inland expanses – the monotonous forests enlivened only by rivers and lakes – where successive communities lived in total ignorance of the sea? While bands of hunter-gatherers roamed most parts of Europe, the population density was generally sparse, with groups showing much greater mobility than in the coastal regions. There were, however, exceptions, not least where communities clustered along the great rivers, the river itself offering an invaluable resource base, adding stability to the fragile subsistence economy.

3.10 The Iron Gates – the point at which the river Danube cuts a deep gorge through the southern extremity of the Carpathian Mountains – creates a major constriction between the Lower Danube Plain and the Carpathian Basin.

3.11 The settlement of Lepenski Vir, Serbia, on the banks of the Danube at the Iron Gates commands the river passage. The prolific environment, not least the plentiful supplies of river fish, allowed the hunter-gatherer communities to maintain permanent settlements.

One cluster of sites that illustrates this well is a series of settlements commanding the Iron Gates – the dramatic gorge cut by the river Danube through the Carpathian Mountains in what is now Serbia. The river, wide and forceful, entirely dominates the scene: along the river flanks hunter-gatherer settlements like Lepenski Vir developed. The environment was particularly favourable. Even during the Last Glacial Maximum woodland managed to survive here, providing hunting grounds for migrant Palaeolithic bands, and as the climate improved so the vegetation became denser and more varied, harbouring an increasing range of animal life. What had been summer camps took on a more permanent appearance and by about 6500 BC substantial villages had come into being along the river banks.

At Lepenski Vir families occupied well-built houses of trapezoidal plan with compacted floors supporting central hearths. The floors were edged with stone slabs and the structures were roofed with timbers leaning inwards towards a central ridge pole. The houses were arranged with paths between them leading to a central open space fronting the river. The implication is of an imposed social order maintained over generations as the houses were successively rebuilt.

The long-term stability of the settlement was possible because of the rich and varied ecological niche it occupied. The forests covering the hills beyond the gorge produced an abundance of game – red deer, boar and aurochs as well as otter and beaver, duck and goose. There were also ample plant foods to be had and, most important, there was the river itself offering fish in plenty. The great swarms of giant beluga forcing their way upstream to spawn each spring must have been an eagerly awaited event, offering the prospect of days of feasting after the meagre diet of winter. The power of the river over people's lives is vividly captured in stone sculptures found throughout the settlement. These were usually boulders carved into animate forms incorporating characteristics that are both human and fish-like. It is tempting to see them as icons binding humanity to the surges of fish so essential to sustaining the community: perhaps the scuptures were there to ensure that the fish would return each year.

3.12 Sculptured head from the settlement of Lepenski Vir. Such heads have reminded some observers of the fish upon which the economy of the site was based. Others have considered them to be portraits. They are always associated with houses, often embedded in foundations. These remarkable heads can fairly be claimed to be Europe's first monumental sculptures.

The hunter-gatherer settlements of the Iron Gorge were exceptional in inland Europe. More normally the camps were seasonal and the shelters far less substantial. A high level of mobility and a thinly spread population over much of the peninsula prevented society from developing to the level of complexity we see at Lepenski Vir and around the Atlantic, North Sea and Baltic shores.

Populations, Complexity and Aggression

For much of Europe during the Upper Palaeolithic and Mesolithic periods the sparseness of the population was a potential threat to survival. A group had to sustain a breeding population to reproduce itself and since marriage is most likely to have been exogamous – that is, mates, usually female, coming from an outside group – it was necessary for the mating network to be large enough to allow members reaching maturity to find breeding partners. In areas where the human density fell below a certain level, because the environment could not sustain a sufficient number of bands in close enough proximity to maintain a viable exogamous mating network, total depopulation would quickly have followed. It is quite probable that large tracts of unrelieved forest were people-less, but where the natural resources were varied populations could grow and growth would lead to the development of more complex social structures.

One form of complexity is sedentism – the choice made by the community to settle at one location and for most of the group to remain there throughout the year. The Ertebølle settlements of Denmark and southern Sweden, the shell middens of the Tagus and Sado and of the Morbihan and the settlements of the Iron Gates are examples of this. Sedentism does not preclude segments of the group making visits to more distant hunting grounds at certain times during the year, but the catch would be brought 'home' for consumption or storage. Indeed, storage may have been one of the more important functions of the home base. Here, fish and meat could be smoked or dried, nuts and dried fruits cached, and edible roots stacked away in underground silos. A sedentary community storing its own food develops more complex behaviour patterns that strengthen social inequalities. It is not surprising, therefore, that graves found at the sedentary settlements often show signs of a status differential reflected in the associated grave goods.

At Skateholm on the extreme south coast of Sweden two cemeteries of differing dates have been excavated. Both exhibit a variety of burial rituals. Two examples from Cemetery II will suffice to give some idea of the behaviours involved. Grave XI contained the body of a young male laid in a supine position. Across his lower legs had been placed a number of intertwined red deer antlers, possibly reflecting his status as a hunter. Another of the graves, Grave VIII, contained a woman laid in sitting position. She wore a belt ornamented with a hundred teeth of red deer and at her feet had been placed the body of a dog. The use of teeth to decorate dress or headgear was a comparatively common occurrence in both male and female burials at Skateholm, as was the burial of dogs. A good hunting dog may well have been a prized possession. Indeed, the status of dogs was sufficiently high for some to be buried separately from humans. One dog was found accompanied by red deer antlers: could this too reflect hunting prowess? Other grave goods found with human interments include bone points, flint blades and perforated lumps of amber. If grave goods indicate status, then the evidence from Skateholm and elsewhere implies that some level of social inequality was prevalent. This can also be seen in the burials at Téviec and Hoëdic, where children were also buried with grave goods. Since it is highly unlikely that these infants earned status during their short lives we may conclude that status could now be inherited.

The differing and sometimes quite elaborate patterns of burial rituals are themselves an indication of an emerging complexity in society. At Lepenski Vir the bodies of young children were buried beneath the floors of houses or within the central stone hearth, while adults were usually buried between the houses aligned so that their heads pointed downstream: a reflection, perhaps, of the humans' relation to the all-dominant river. We have already noted a similar phenomenon with children's burials restricted to the house area at Moita do Sebastião in the Tagus valley. At Téviec and Hoëdic a number of the graves had multiple interments, the later burials often disturbing the earlier. One of the Téviec tombs was associated with a hearth that was used on a succession of occasions, possibly when each of the six bodies in the grave was laid to rest. This surprisingly sophisticated practice of collective burial lies at the beginning of a tradition that was to flourish in the region over the next two thousand years, later manifesting itself in monumental megalithic tombs.

The belief patterns underlying burial practices are an indication of growing social complexity. Along with this we might expect to be able to identify other developments in ritual behaviour which might appear as 'art' or as monumental structures of a non-domestic kind. The remarkable boulder sculptures of Lepenski Vir with their evident associations to fish are one such example. The village also has one building, larger than any of the others and centrally located, within which were found some bone armlets and a flute. It is tempting to regard this as a 'ritual' structure, but it could equally well have been the residence of a village leader or a communal meeting place.

3.13 Oak figurine (12.5 cm (5 in) high) dating to c.5300 BC found during the construction of a lock near Willemstad, Holland.

Far more impressive is a highly enigmatic structure identified beneath the car park at Stonehenge, only part of which has so far been uncovered. It consists of a row of three large pits 1.5–2 m (5–6½ ft) in diameter and up to 1.3 m (4¼ ft) in depth. In each had been placed a substantial vertical timber c.0.7 m (2⅓ ft) in diameter, which probably stood to a considerable height. Radiocarbon evidence dates the structure to the second half of the eighth millennium BC and a study of the associated pollen shows that the surrounding area at the time was blanketed with a forest of birch and pine. The exact nature of this remarkable monument – its extent and whether or not the timbers were carved like totem poles – is far from understood, but its very existence suggests a high degree of sophistication and coordination among the hunter-gatherer communities of Wessex.

The Lepenski Vir boulder statues and the Stonehenge car-park monument are reminders of how little we know of the ritual systems of the Mesolithic populations. Timber monuments may have been widespread in woodland clearings in areas where more stable complex communities were emerging. Wooden statuettes were probably commonplace. One small oak figurine dating to c.5300 BC was found during the construction of a loch at Willemstad in Holland. It owes its survival to the waterlogged conditions in which it was buried. To forest-living communities wood was the natural material to use. Others no doubt await discovery but most will long since have rotted.

Social complexity brings with it other consequences. Populations tend to increase in size, so requiring the systems of community interaction to become more refined, not least to reduce the risk of hostility. Such interactions would have included reciprocal exchanges involving a range of commodities, most of them no longer recognizable in the archaeological record. However, a reflection of these networks is to be found in the distribution of stone items. At the Iron Gates settlements a range of exotic materials have been found – obsidian from Hungary, igneous rocks and brown flint from areas north and west of the gorge and yellow flint from Bulgaria. From even further afield, from the shores of the Mediterranean, came seashells. Clearly the focal position of the Iron Gorge, commanding a major route node, made it possible for the resident population to benefit from exchange networks extending in all directions. Examples of the exchange of stone over great distances are to be found almost everywhere in Europe. A Cretaceous flint extracted from Lithuania was exchanged in the form of blades and cores over distances of 600 km (375 miles) reaching deep into Latvia, Estonia and Finland, while finished tools of the same flint got as far as the Upper Volga region. In southern Britain articles of slate and pebbles, possibly used for grinding, were transported from Devon and Cornwall eastwards for similar distances. Even more impressive is the distribution of blades of southern Scandinavian flint which reached northern Sweden 1000 km (625 miles) away.

There were many social mechanisms by which these materials could have been moved. They could have been gathered by mobile foraging parties during cyclical seasonal movements or could even have been collected by task forces sent specifically for the purpose, but the most widespread system is likely to have been reciprocal down-the-line exchange by groups engaging with neighbours at the borders of their agreed territories. Exchanges of this kind would have helped to maintain a degree of harmony. As populations grew and some groups took on a sedentary mode of existence, the intensity of exchange would have increased, driven forward by the need to interact with neighbours on a more frequent basis. Yet inherent in all this also lay the preconditions for conflict.

Warfare was widespread in the Mesolithic period. Forty-four per cent of the burials found in Denmark displayed evidence of traumatic injuries on their skulls. In Sweden and France the figure was lower at 20 per cent, but even so these are surprisingly high percentages and must imply that warfare was endemic. Alongside these bludgeoning injuries there is also widespread evidence of arrow wounds. At Téviec in the Morbihan one young man was found with two arrowheads embedded in his backbone. His body had been given special treatment: the grave had been lined with stone slabs and care had been taken not to disturb his remains when later interments were made. At

Cemetery II in Skateholm in Sweden one body was found with an arrowhead in the stomach, and another with an arrowhead in its chest. The same site also produced four individuals with depressed fractures in their skulls which could have been fatal. A rather different insight into violence comes from Ofnet in Bavaria where, in 1908, two close-packed clusters of skulls were found in pits: there were six in one group and thirty-one in the other. Men, women and children were represented: most of them had been bludgeoned to death before having their heads severed. The incident took place some time around 6400 BC.

Although it would be possible to explain away each example in terms of accident or ritual, the simplest interpretation is that by the Late Mesolithic period warfare had become a common reality. Perhaps aggression was exacerbated by increased competition for resources. As the hunter-gatherer communities grew, population in some areas may have reached the holding capacity of the land. In coastal regions, particularly around the North Sea and the Baltic, the problem would have been made more acute by a rapid rise in sea levels driving people from traditional foraging grounds. Another factor could have been social tensions resulting from communities deeper in the heart of Europe beginning to adopt a sedentary way of life associated with the Neolithic food-producing economy. Whatever the reasons, for the foraging societies of the Late Mesolithic world warfare was now an everyday reality.

Engagement with the Ocean

In offering this overview of Mesolithic society in Europe we have emphasized communities occupying coastal regions. This is partly because the significance of the ocean interfaces of Europe is one of the themes of this book, but it is in large part a reflection of the availability of the data. Much of the best evidence we have comes from coastal regions because it is here, in the highly favoured resource-rich zone of the European littoral, where hunter-gatherers chose to settle and to congregate, developing sedentary societies of some complexity.

While we will never be able to get into the minds of the early foraging bands, it is worth wondering how they might have conceived of their worlds. Communities existing for their entire lives in the perpetual gloom of the European forest will have had a very different view of the world from those who looked outwards across the shimmering light of the oceans. Inland communities will have been well aware of the cyclical dynamics of the seasons and of the vicissitudes of weather, but those at the ocean face had a more complex perspective that required them to absorb into their conceptual frame-work different rhythms – that of the tide with its link to the phases of the moon and, for some, an awareness that the sea was relentlessly gaining on the land. These coastal groups will also have been all too well aware of the ferocity of the ocean, and of the violence of the storms that could appear from nowhere. Some would have experienced catastrophes like the tsunami that broke on the coast of the North Sea about 7000 BC with waves 8 m (26 ft) high, flinging huge volumes of sediment across the east coast of Scotland and inundating many square kilometres of the lowlands of Doggerland – the region now beneath the North Sea. In the traditional stories of drowned land-scapes preserved in the folklore of north-western Europe, there may have been some distant memory of the event.

How people conceived of the sea at this time is beyond recovery. That they were able and willing to take to sea in boats and to make long journeys is clear from the discovery of obsidian from Melos in the Franchthi cave on the Greek mainland, but we know nothing of the vessels used. The log boats of north-western Europe, well suited to navigating the coastal waters, were hardly able to stand up to open sea ventures unless they were equipped with outriggers, but there is no evidence of this. It remains, however, a strong possibility that skin boats, built around a light wattle framework, were used: the foraging communities of the Atlantic and North Sea region certainly had the technical capability to build vessels of this kind and the skin boat is known to have been a feature of the Atlantic from the Iron Age until the present day. Currachs, still in use on the Aran Islands off the west coast of Ireland, daily prove themselves to be masters of the ocean.

How far did Mesolithic foragers venture into the open sea? We don't know. Vessels may have followed shoals of fish into open waters, much as hunters followed herds of deer, remaining away from home for extended periods, even spending some nights at sea. Journeys of this sort would have brought distant communities into contact with each other. They required navigational skills based on an understanding of the stars, but such knowledge would have been commonplace among people whose ancestors had habitually foraged and hunted the forests of Europe. Maritime foraging would invariably have led to social networks being established and, through these, ideas and belief systems would have spread. Within such networks contacts may have become institutionalized, perhaps on an annual basis. There is ample ethno-graphic evidence of this kind of practice among the Indians of the north-west coast of North America. In the early nineteenth century ceremonial visits are recorded between exchange partners requiring coastal journeys of up to 500 km (300 miles). There is no reason to suppose that the inhabitants of Europe's coasts were any less adventurous.

Proximity to the sea, then, opened up many opportunities denied to the inhabitants of the inland regions. But did it create a different world view? Could it be that the huge middens skirting the high-water mark around the coasts and estuaries of Denmark, Brittany and Portugal, their monumentality enhanced by ancestral burial, were deliberate statements of a direct relationship to the sea – a defiance perhaps of the incoming water? There is no answer but those who inhabited the littoral will not have been unaware of the power and possibilities of the ocean spread out before them.

CHAPTER FOUR

The First Farmers:
From the Fertile Crescent to
the Danube Valley: 7500–5000 BC

By 7000 BC Europe was peopled by communities whose basic subsistence depended solely upon collecting food. Those inhabiting the forests of Europe were mobile hunter-gatherers following their food sources as the seasons determined: others living in the lusher and more varied environments of the major river valleys, the estuaries and around the coasts were foragers with a more sedentary lifestyle. By 4000 BC all this had changed. In all but the most northern and eastern reaches of Europe communities had become food producers, cultivating crops of grain and herding domesticated animals – activities that called for a far more sedentary mode of existence based on village settlements occupied over many generations. It was a dramatic transformation. Mesolithic hunter-gatherers were replaced by Neolithic food producers and with the new regime came the 'Neolithic package' – ground stone tools, pottery and rectangular timber buildings, together with domesticated sheep, goats, cattle and pigs, and cultivated cereals.

Archaeologists in the mid-twentieth century referred to the transformation as the 'Neolithic revolution' and interpreted the phenomenon in Europe in terms of waves of people – pioneer agriculturalists from Anatolia or the Near East – thrusting through the subcontinent, carrying the benefits of food production to all regions as the indigenous hunter-gatherers withered away or were absorbed. This model argued for a substantial replacement of population and some saw it as the occasion when the Indo-European language was introduced into Europe. Other archaeologists took a more cautious line, even going so far as to argue that the 'Neolithic package' was adopted by the indigenous Mesolithic population without significant inward movement of new people. As more evidence accumulates, from excavation and from genetic studies, a far more nuanced picture is beginning to emerge. While the debate continues, most commentators now accept that the situation was so complex that in reality both processes are likely to have been involved, though in different degrees, in most parts of Europe.

The genetic make-up of modern European populations has been used to try to model population flows in prehistory. Interpretation of these data is by no means easy but the present consensus is that while mitochondrial DNA, inherited through the female line, shows that the inflow of females from the east amounted to no more than 20 per cent of the population, Y-chromosome DNA, inherited through the male line, presents a more complex picture. In Greece and south-east Europe up to 85 per cent of the male population bear genetic markers indicating an origin further east. The percentage falls rapidly to 15–30 per cent in France, Germany and north-eastern Spain. These results could be seen to support the argument that the Neolithic way of life was introduced into Greece by a predominantly male-led immigration bringing some females with it but also taking wives from the indigenous population. The interpretation is consistent with the archaeological evidence but many uncertainties remain. A far more powerful tool is the study of ancient DNA. This is still in its infancy, but early results from Neolithic burials in Germany dating to the sixth millennium suggest that the Neolithic population there was largely descended from indigenous hunter-gatherers.

The Neolithic economy in the Old World was predicated on the domestication of sheep, goats, cattle and pigs and the cultivation of wheat and barley. While cattle and pigs existed in the wild in Europe, the other domesticates and cultivates did not. Their natural habitat was the Near East (the region from Turkey to Iraq) and it was there that the wild forms were transformed through human manipulation, later to be introduced into Europe. Since much of Europe was on the same latitude as the Near Eastern zone of origin and offered much the same range of climatic conditions, the introduction was biologically unproblematic.

The indigenous Mesolithic populations were already manipulating their animal and plant resources. Dogs had long been domesticated, as their careful burial at cemeteries like those at Skateholm amply demonstrates. Domestication was not difficult since the wolves from which dogs were descended could be induced over generations to accept humans as pack leaders. Omnivores and herbivores were less easy to control but foragers deliberately improved the vegetation on which they fed, burning woodland to encourage new young growth in order to attract herds of deer to particular places and so facilitating their capture. Similarly limited control over wild pigs could be gained by providing food, in the form of offal and other animal waste, at fixed locations. The production of selected food plants could also have been enhanced by clearing away competing vegetation. Hazel, an early recolonizer, could be given a head start by burning tracts of woodland. Hazelnuts, a highly nutritious food source well attested in the archaeological record, are likely to have provided a major food reserve. By 7000 BC, therefore, the Mesolithic communities of Europe were already manipulating animals and plants in the interests of productivity. Thus, the introduction of new domesticates and cultivates will not have been an entirely alien concept.

Beginnings: In the Hilly Flanks

The cultivation of cereals and the domestication of animals began in south-west Asia within a broad arc of territory stretching from the southern Levant to southern Turkey and eastwards from there to the foothills of the Taurus and beyond to the Zagros Mountains of Iraq. This zone, which fringes the Fertile Crescent where the civilizations of Egypt and Mesopotamia were later to flourish, is known as the hilly flanks of the Fertile Crescent. It was here that the wild ancestors of the domesticated animals and cultivated cereals were to be found in their natural habitats.

The end of the Last Glacial Maximum around 18,000 BC marks the transition from the Upper Palaeolithic to what in south-west Asia is referred to as the Epipalaeolithic – a period that continues to around 9600 BC. The Epipalaeolithic is itself divided into an Early and a Late phase, with the transition coming about 12,000 BC. It was during the Epipalaeolithic that a

4.1 The maps cover the crucial zone of the Near East where the cultivation of grain crops and the domestication of animals began showing the changing environment from the end of the Last Glacial Maximum c.13,000 BC to the beginning of the Early Holocene c.7500 BC.

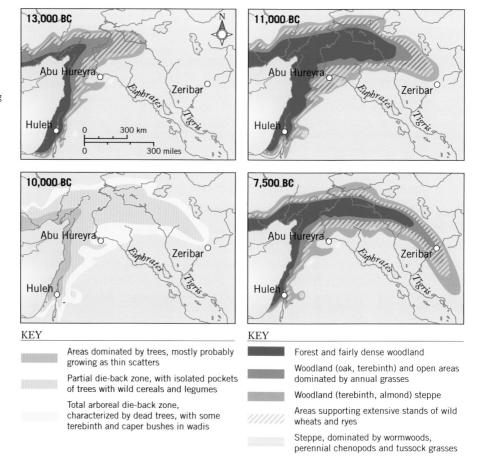

KEY

Areas dominated by trees, mostly probably growing as thin scatters

Partial die-back zone, with isolated pockets of trees with wild cereals and legumes

Total arboreal die-back zone, characterized by dead trees, with some terebinth and caper bushes in wadis

KEY

Forest and fairly dense woodland

Woodland (oak, terebinth) and open areas dominated by annual grasses

Woodland (terebinth, almond) steppe

Areas supporting extensive stands of wild wheats and ryes

Steppe, dominated by wormwoods, perennial chenopods and tussock grasses number of crucial changes occurred that paved the way for the emergence of settled food-producing economies.

The climate had been gradually improving after 18,000 BC. By about 12,000 BC dense forest covered much of the western part of the hilly flanks region, giving way, around its borders, to more open areas where extensive stands of wild wheats and ryes could flourish. Then came the sudden downturn in temperature – the Younger Dryas – which lasted from about 10,800 to 9600 BC. In the Near East this was a period of far drier, cooler weather. Tree cover thinned out and over much of the region many trees died, leaving isolated pockets of trees with areas of wild cereals and legumes spreading between them. After 9600 the climate quickly recovered: the forest spread out once more, with the zone of light woodland and wild cereals extending now into the Zagros Mountains.

In the Early Epipalaeolithic period (18,000–12,000 BC) a move towards larger, more sedentary communities was well under way in the Near East. The groups were probably transhumant, moving between uplands and lowlands as the seasons demanded. A wide range of plants was now exploited including wild emmer wheat and barley, legumes and acorns, while small game was hunted, with gazelle, fallow deer and hare dominating the catch. In order to maintain the larger community, food was now carefully stored – a strategy that required forward-planning and a high degree of communal consent which further implies some kind of coercive authority.

Settled communities and a more complex form of social organization developed further during the Late Epipalaeolithic (12,000–9600 BC), most spectacularly in the Levant where the contemporary culture is called Natufian. Permanent settlements for all-year-round occupation were now fairly widespread and extensive exchange networks were operating, bringing obsidian from central Turkey to make flaked tools, black basalt for mortars to grind seeds and seashells from the Mediterranean for personal decoration. Further east, in the Zagros Mountains, villages of stone-built huts developed, supported by an economy based on collecting hard seeds from wild cereals and pulses and exploiting wild sheep.

By 9600 BC, then, in spite of the stress caused by the climatic downturn of the Younger Dryas, the hilly flanks were occupied by communities who had established a high degree of sedentism and were now exploiting a variety of natural resources including the wild versions of those that were soon to become domesticated and cultivated staples.

The crucial step into full food production took place in the Aceramic Neolithic period (9600–6900 BC), which may be divided into an Early and a Late phase around the date 8800 BC. During this period the gathering of wild cereals intensified, the methods of cultivation and harvesting creating

4.2 The area where the domestication of sheep first took place.

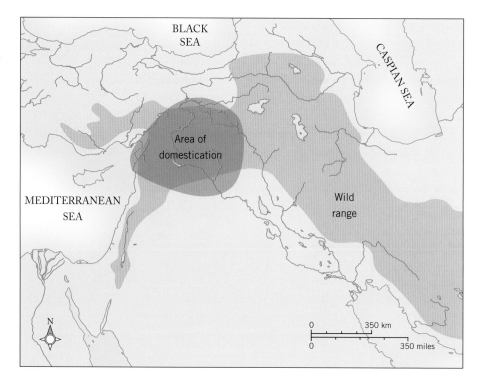

conditions of selection that favoured genetic modifications leading to the creation of domesticated species. By the Late Aceramic Neolithic fully domesticated cereals are found throughout the hilly flanks zone. Einkorn and chickpea occurred mainly in the north, with barley predominating in the Levant. In parallel with this, selected animal species, once intensively hunted, were now domesticated. Indigenous sheep and goat are found throughout the hilly flanks region, with domesticated pig and cattle appearing in more localized areas.

What triggered the change to a fully domesticated mode of subsistence is a matter of debate. The transition coincided with the improvement of climate following the Younger Dryas and is associated with a significant increase in population. One scenario would be to argue that with the ameliorating climate, allowing a return to a more sedentary existence in larger communities, birth rates increased and population began to rise sharply. The move to food production could then be seen as a result of the pressure to raise the holding capacity of the environment by intensifying food yield. This has a neat logic about it. But there are other possibilities. Perhaps the move to domestication was the result of processes already well established in the Early Epipalaeolithic period and the more assured food supply, encouraging larger clusters of people to settle together, provided the spur to the population explosion. These are the

two extreme explanations – in reality it was probably the combination of the two that created the new dynamics.

The most striking characteristic of the Aceramic Neolithic period is the dramatic growth of elaborate settlements, some of considerable size. At Jericho, in the Levant, the early settlement, c.8000 BC, reached an extent of 2.5 ha (6 acres) and was enclosed with a wall of stones set in mud, fronted by a rock-cut ditch. At one point a circular tower had been built against the inside of the wall. Even more impressive was the settlement of Çatalhöyük in central Turkey which extended over an area of 13 ha (32 acres) and comprised a large number of closely packed rectangular houses. Many villages are also known scattered throughout the region, displaying differing degrees of sophistication in their architecture. The appearance of ritual buildings and religious art in the form of figurines and wall paintings is evidence of a fast-growing social complexity. By the Late Aceramic Neolithic the exchange networks, which had begun to emerge in the Natufian period, bound the whole of the hilly flanks zone in a web of interactions through which spread not only items such as obsidian and seashells, but also ideas and beliefs.

But it was not to last: the few hundred years from c.6900 to 6000 BC saw changes caused, or at least exacerbated, by environmental degeneration brought on by overexploitation. The constant tilling of land for cultivation led

4.3 In the Early Aceramic Neolithic period the oasis settlement of Jericho was surrounded by a defensive wall. Attached to the inside of the wall was a tower built of stone set in mud, seen here at the bottom of a deep archaeological excavation cut through the tell. The tower represents a major investment by the community in monumental architecture.

to a loss of fertility and erosion, while the cutting down of trees to provide timber and fuel, combined with the intensive herding of goats, further escalated the scale of the environmental disaster. Thus, demands created by the rapid growth of population destabilized the fragile ecosystem to the point where large sedentary communities could no longer be sustained. In some areas like the Levant and northern Jordan large settlements came to an end and communities dispersed into smaller villages, some relying now more on nomadic pastoralism than cultivation. Similarly, in central Turkey, Çatalhöyük was abandoned about 6200 BC and thereafter only small scattered sites are found. Groups of farmers were now moving out to new ecological niches that could sustain their agricultural systems. In Iraq as the settlements in the Taurus Mountains were abandoned, so new settlements appeared further south on the plains between the Euphrates and the Tigris. Further east, in south-west Iran, new villages sprang up at this time along the eastern edge of the alluvial plain, while in Syria there seems to have been a similar migration from the hills around the Upper Euphrates westwards towards the Mediterranean coast.

The seventh millennium, then, was a time of change in south-west Asia – a time when farming communities were on the move, seeking new lands to provide sustenance and space for their rapidly growing populations.

Taking to the Sea

Around 7000 BC a Neolithic economy was established on the island of Crete. Five hundred years later the plain of Thessaly, on the Greek mainland, was fast being colonized by farming communities. While the evidence from these settlements is clear enough, the processes by which these dramatic changes took place remain obscure. What is beyond doubt, however, is that voyages by sea must have played a significant part.

We have already seen that, as early as 10,000 BC, the inhabitants of the Franchthi cave, on the Argolid, had access to obsidian from the island of Melos and tuna fish, probably caught off the east coast of northern Greece. Evidently a maritime capability existed by this early date in the Aegean. Travel by sea probably took on an increasing importance among the foraging communities of the coastal regions as the sea level rose, fragmenting the larger landmasses in the Aegean and creating ever more islands.

The island of Cyprus occupied a crucial position in the development of these early maritime networks. Lying only 80 km (50 miles) from the coast of Asia Minor and 100 km (60 miles) from the Levant, it was within comparatively easy reach of the heartland where the Neolithic economy developed. Around 10,500 BC hunter-gatherers living on the island were slaughtering herds of indigenous pigmy hippopotamus. They can only have got there by boat. Some time later, in the mid-ninth to eighth millennia, early farmers had established themselves on the island. The community grew cereals and pulses and had access to domesticated sheep, goats, cattle and pigs and to herds of wild fallow deer. That all of these animals had to be transported to the island by sea in large enough numbers to sustain breeding populations implies the existence of sturdy vessels and assured seamanship. Once established, the pioneer farmers maintained their contacts with the mainland.

Farming was introduced to the island of Crete around 7000 BC. The crucial data come from a deep trench dug down to bedrock in the centre of the court-yard of the Bronze Age palace at Knossos. The lowest layer of occupation debris which accumulated on the natural bedrock was without pottery, but it was decidedly Neolithic producing bones of domesticated sheep or goats, pigs and cattle together with grains of cultivated bread wheat (*Triticum aestivum*). That the pioneer farmers of Crete brought with them the full 'Neolithic package' implies a well-planned colonizing movement, employing flotillas of boats presumably setting out from the mainland of Asia Minor, an origin supported by the fact that bread wheat was a favoured crop in Anatolia. If the starting point had been somewhere in the vicinity of the Knidos peninsula, an island-hopping route could have been taken incorporating Rhodes, Karpathos and Kasos to facilitate the 185-km (115-mile) journey from the mainland to Knossos.

Any estimate of the scale of the colonizing movement is little better than guesswork but the minimum size of population that could have sustained itself would have been a group of about forty individuals. Allowing for between ten and twenty pigs, cattle and sheep/goats and an adequate supply of seed grain, the total minimum load would have been somewhere between 15,000 and 20,000 kg (33,000 and 44,000 lbs) which, allowing for 1 or 2 tonnes of cargo per boat, would imply a flotilla of ten to fifteen vessels. Calculations of this kind can only be very approximate but they give some idea of the magnitude of the venture.

The settlement of Cyprus and Crete by pioneer farmers by 7000 BC was the first step in a process that, over the next five hundred years or so, was to lead to the establishment of farmers on the Greek mainland, in particular in the plain of Thessaly – a region that provided optimal conditions for settlement.

Maritime networks already existing in the Aegean could have facilitated the movement of farming communities coming from Asia Minor and the Levant. The settlement of Crete was part of the initial phase of exploration but the fact that it does not appear to have been followed up may be explained by the rival attraction of the congenial ecological niches offered by the eastern Greek seaboard once the potential of the Greek mainland had become known.

Radiocarbon dates for the earliest Neolithic sites in Greece concentrate in the period 7500–6500 BC. This is broadly coincident with the latest phase of the Aceramic Neolithic in south-west Asia (dated *c.*7600–6900 BC), a period of mobility when the initial farming communities began to move out of their original homelands to establish settlements in the Taurus Mountains in central Anatolia and the Mediterranean coastal regions of the Levant. The initial colonization of Crete and the eastern Greek mainland may be seen as part of this general exodus.

The First European Farmers

The Initial phase of Neolithic settlement in Greece took place in the late eighth and early seventh millennia BC. At this stage communities were largely aceramic but by about 6500 BC pottery-making had become widespread, heralding the period that archaeologists distinguish as the Early Neolithic, which lasted until about 6000 BC. During the Early Neolithic settlements proliferated. Some 250–300 have been identified in the eastern parts of Greece and there must be many more yet to be discovered. The normal settlement type at this time was the village, comprising a number of close-spaced rectangular houses covering an area of 1–3 ha (2½–7½ acres). Population estimates

4.4 The valley of the river Pinios, here passing through the dramatic landscape of the Meteora, near Kalambáka, leads from the Pindhos mountains – the backbone of Greece – to the fertile plain of Thessaly beyond.

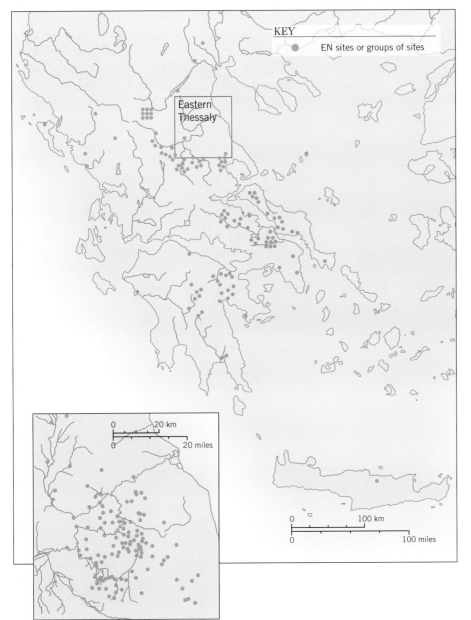

KEY

● EN sites or groups of sites

Eastern
Thessaly

0   20 km

0   20 miles

0   100 km

0   100 miles

4.5 Greece and the southern Balkans showing the extent of the known Early Neolithic settlements. The great density in the plain of Thessaly and the other plains facing the Aegean hints at the importance of the Aegean sea routes in the early phase of colonization.

are notoriously difficult to make but an average of about a hundred people per hectare (or 2½ acres) is probably in the right order of magnitude. The individual houses were normally one-roomed structures built of wattle and daub or mudbrick, often on drystone foundations. At one of the more fully explored villages, Neo Nikomedia in the Macedonian Plain, three distinct phases of building have been recognized; in the first two the houses seem to

97

have been clustered around a larger building that may have been a communal structure of some kind.

The density of the Early Neolithic settlements varies considerably throughout eastern Greece. The early farmers chose ecozones best suited to the mixed farming strategies upon which life depended. One of the most congenial of these regions is eastern Thessaly, where 117 villages have been identified in an area of 1150 sq km (450 sq miles), averaging one village for every 10 sq km (4 sq miles). Close spacing of comparatively large permanent settlements implies that social networks were sufficiently robust to maintain peaceful relations and to allow for inter-village cooperation.

The subsistence economy of the Early Neolithic settlers was based on cultivated crops and domesticated animals, with hunting playing a very minor part. The favoured crops were emmer wheat (*Triticum dicoccum*) and, to a lesser extent, einkorn (*Triticum monococcum*) and six-row barley (*Hordeum vulgare*). The bread wheat so common in the early levels at Knossos is very rare in Greece, suggesting that the pioneer farmers settling in these two regions may well have come from different parts of south-west Asia. Legumes were also important, particularly lentils, peas and bitter vetch. To sustain one person would have required one hectare (2½ acres) of land. With villages of 200–300 inhabitants there would have been ample arable land around each village, given what is known of settlement density.

Systems of food production based on domesticated animals and plants were firmly in place from the initial settlement phase and led to the rapid establishment of stable sedentary communities who placed little reliance on wild resources. The implication must be that the pioneer population arrived with their domesticated animals and seed corn and the generations of experience needed to set themselves up in the alien environments. That they chose ecological niches suitable for the direct implantation of their established practices suggests an awareness of geography that could only have come from knowledge based on reconnaissance.

The pioneer farmers brought with them a range of technological skills that successor communities continued to develop in their new homeland. The manufacture of chipped stone tools, the grinding and polishing of hard stone, spinning and weaving, pottery manufacture and the creation of figurines and 'stamps' from baked clay are among the more apparent in the archaeological record. Together with farming and the permanent settlements, these artefacts typify the 'Neolithic package' which, once introduced into Europe, spread to all parts of the continent.

The procurement of raw materials such as obsidian from Melos, favoured for chipped stone tools, raises interesting questions. Obsidian is found in considerable quantity on Early Neolithic sites in the Peloponnese and

Thessaly, but is unknown in western Greece and Macedonia at this stage. This very specific distribution would suggest that the needs of the eastern Greek communities were being met by middlemen willing and able to make the hazardous journey of several hundred kilometres over land and by sea to and from the source on Melos. Who, then, were these maritime specialists? Could it be that they were the descendants of the indigenous Mesolithic population who had been making journeys of this kind for centuries and were well used to fishing for tuna in the offshore waters? The supposition is reasonable and raises the intriguing possibility that these indigenous maritime communities may have been the carriers of the original pioneer farmers.

4.6 Volcanic glass, known as obsidian, was acquired from the island of Milos to make tools and was widely distributed in eastern Greece. Long, narrow flakes (above right) were struck from cores (left) and were finely worked by pressure flaking to make knives and other tools.

A further link with the sea is the popularity of seashells for making bracelets and beads, and in particular the *Spondylus* shell, originating in the Aegean, which is found extensively among inland communities. It is quite possible that beads and other shell ornaments were one of the commodities produced by the coastal communities for trade inland along with obsidian. The popularity of seashells may even reflect a reverence for the sea remaining deep in the folk memory of the early farmers.

Apart from obsidian and marine shells there is little evidence of extensive networks of exchange between communities, although it is possible that such exchanges took place in materials that leave no archaeological trace such as woven fabrics or live animals. What evidence there is suggests that the villages were largely self-contained with limited networks linking only to immediate neighbours.

Among the more distinctive of the village-based products was pottery. Some limited knowledge of pottery may have arrived with the pioneer settlers. However, it was not until the Early Neolithic period that pottery-making became widespread. Vessels were hand-made from local clays and were fired usually in small clamps, but production was never on a large scale. Throughout the Early Neolithic vessel forms were restricted to simple bowls and jars and occasionally handled jugs. Most were monochrome but some were painted with white slip or with red iron oxide usually in a zigzag design, and there were some regional preferences in decoration and form, more evident as time proceeded. Simple, even crude, though this pottery was, it holds a deep

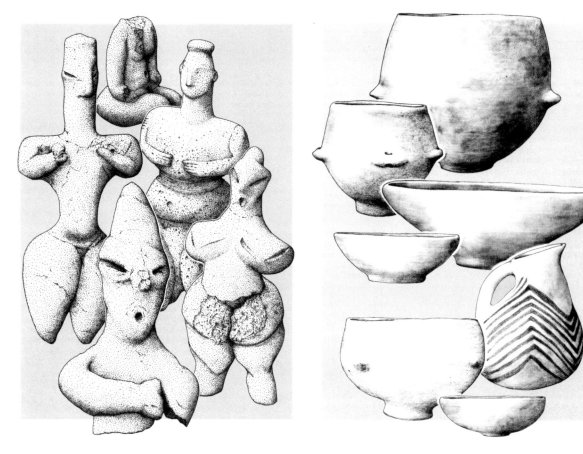

4.7 *Above:* Figures of clay and marble from Early Neolithic sites in Greece.

4.8 *Above right:* Pottery from Early Neolithic sites in Greece – Europe's first pottery.

fascination as it represents the first attempt by a European community to create an entirely new material using fire.

Another home product of potential importance to the community was woven fabric, evidenced by spindle whorls and loom weights. It is uncertain whether, at this early stage of domestication, sheep were capable of producing wool but goat hair, flax and other plant fibres could well have been used to form a thread. Flax was used to make fabrics in south-west Asia in the eighth millennium and linseeds have been found on Early Neolithic sites in Greece. Loom weights could have been used for a variety of functions and need not imply the existence of the warp-weighted loom at this early stage. Simple ground-looms were known at the time in south-west Asia and it may have been on some such structure that the Early Neolithic communities of Greece produced their fabrics.

Other aspects of material culture found on the Early Neolithic sites include small figurines usually made with clay but sometimes carved from stone. They are for the most part anthropomorphic, with a particular emphasis on the female form, but males and animal forms are also known. To these we may add pins and stone ear plugs and elaborately decorated 'seal stamps' made from clay or more rarely carved from stone. Ground and polished stone was also used to make axes, bowls and basins. These varied items, while evidently of Greek manufacture, have close similarities to objects found in Anatolia and the Levant in the context of Aceramic Neolithic dates, but in no case are the sets of material found in Greece directly comparable to assemblages found at sites in Anatolia or the Levant. This may be a factor of the incompleteness of the archaeological record, but it could also be a reflection of the nature of the pioneering group. Perhaps we are dealing with bands of adventurers from different geographical regions and with differing cultural traditions coming together to make the voyage to the west. Once settled, this heterogeneous community would draw on the pool of common cultural experience to create a new pioneer culture echoing the old but reconfigured in its new homeland, and now distinctly European.

Consolidation and Expansion

There has been much debate in the archaeological literature about the interpretation of the evidence for the Initial and Early Neolithic settlement in Greece, some observers preferring to see it as the result of the 'acculturation' of indigenous Mesolithic communities by ideas emanating from the east, others arguing for an influx of people on a large scale. The archaeological evidence is now strongly in favour of the latter and the recent DNA studies offer additional support.

If, then, we accept the general hypothesis that pioneer communities, moving out of the hilly flanks of south-west Asia at the time of the general exodus around 7500–6500 BC, established themselves in congenial ecological niches in eastern Greece, many questions arise. Were there further incomings? Did some sector of the successor generations move on to 'colonize' new parts of Europe? Indeed, how significant were folk movements in the Neolithicization of Europe? These are some of the intriguing issues to be explored in the rest of this chapter and the next.

In eastern Greece, after a rapid growth in population following the Initial Neolithic settlement, a long period of stability ensued during which the villages were rebuilt on many occasions, the accumulating layers giving rise to tells several metres high. The population was clearly sustaining itself but there is nothing to suggest stress resulting from overpopulation. In other words, there seems to have been no imperative for new pioneer communities to move out of Greece to find new homelands, yet by c.5500 BC the Neolithic way of life had been firmly established as far north as modern Hungary, over 1000 km (625 miles) north of Thessaly, and as far east as central Bulgaria.

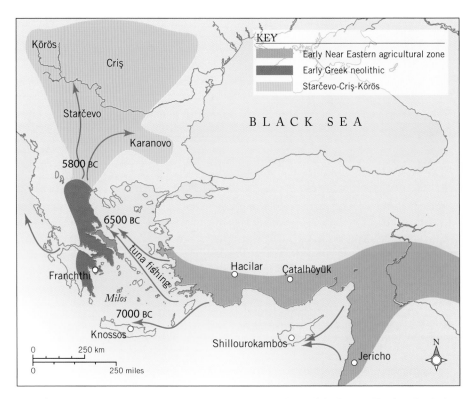

4.9 The initial spread of the Neolithic economy into Europe from the Near East and southern Anatolia would have involved sea journeys to Cyprus, Crete and Greece. It may well be that existing Mesolithic networks, known to have been involved with tuna fishing and the fetching of obsidian from the island of Melos, played some role in the transport of people, animals and grain.

Across this large and varied territory a number of different Early Neolithic cultures have been identified, each named after a typical site or a region. Thus, we have the Karanovo I culture in southern Bulgaria, the Kremikovci culture in western Bulgaria and Macedonia, the Starčevo in Serbia and Bosnia, the Körös in southern Hungary and south-west Romania, and the Criş covering the rest of Romania. We will refer to them simply as the Early South-East European Neolithic, since across this whole region there are considerable similarities in material culture – in house types, pottery and other artefacts. It is largely in the nature and location of settlements and the basic economy that regional variations appear.

Before considering the Early Neolithic communities of south-eastern Europe, it is necessary to explore the routes by which the ideas characterizing the 'Neolithic package' spread northwards from the Aegean. Of prime importance was the corridor created by the valleys of the river Vardar, which flows southwards into the Gulf of Thermaikos, and the river Morava, which flows northwards to a confluence with the Danube 100 km (60 miles) or so downriver from modern Belgrade. Together these two rivers created a convenient route, linking the north Aegean to the Danube, along which many Early Neolithic settlements clustered. From the Danube easy access could be had across the Great Hungarian Plain northwards along the Tiza and into Transylvania and westwards along the Sava and Drava. Downriver it was only a short journey to the Iron Gates and the cluster of sedentary Mesolithic villages dominated by Lepenski Vir. Other river routes led into the heart of Bulgaria.

Once out of the hinterland of the Aegean and through the mountain zone there was a significant change, from a warm Mediterranean climate enjoying long hot summers to a more rainy, temperate climate with a shorter growing season and colder winters. The differences were such that the agricultural regimes required modification as the practice of farming moved northwards.

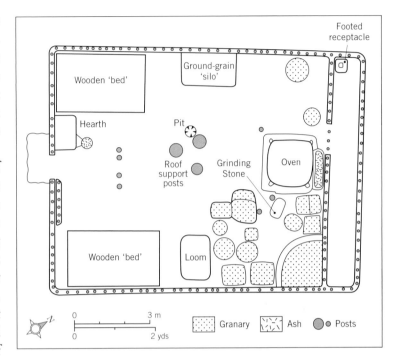

4.10 A house of Early Neolithic date from Slatina in western Bulgaria. It was built of small timber and mud.

In central southern Bulgaria, in the valley of the river Azmak near Nova Zagora, lies the type site of Karanovo. Karanovo is a tell (a settlement mound) covering an area of 4 ha (10 acres), which grew to a height of 12 m (40 ft) as successive clay-daub and timber buildings were demolished and new ones built upon the debris. The desire to remain rooted at the same spot over many generations may be seen as a deliberate expression of communal stability, the mound itself with the village perched on top symbolizing the community's longevity and legitimacy. The early houses are single-roomed structures, each with its own internal hearth and storage space, with walls built of mud and clay-daub around a framework of small vertical posts. They were clustered closely together, with narrow alleyways between. The stable economy supporting these villages was based on the cultivation of emmer wheat with lesser amounts of einkorn, and the maintenance of herds of sheep/goats, cattle and pigs. In the nearby mountains of the Stara Planina contemporary cave sites have been found where half the animal bone debris recovered came from wild species, the catch particularly favouring red deer. It may be that these sites represent temporary summer camps used by herders looking after flocks and herds as they roamed the upland summer pastures. At such times there would have been ample opportunity for hunting to supplement the diet.

Further to the north-west, in Serbia and southern Hungary, the settlements did not develop into tells, but this does not mean that they were short-lived. In a number of examples the settlement spread laterally, often along the edge of terraces, extending for hundreds of metres, which suggests that successive rebuildings took place next to the earlier settlement. The houses themselves are not well recorded but they tended to be square or rectangular, with mud walls structured on a framework of posts or stakes and often with floors sunk below ground level.

One characteristic of these more northerly sites was their reliance on wild resources. At the type site of Starčevo, in addition to the usual domesticates, there were also red and roe deer, wild cattle, pig and horse, together with beaver, fox, wolf, bear, badger, otter and wild cat. Ducks, geese, swans and birds of prey were caught as well as plentiful river fish reflecting their chosen locations close to major rivers. Among the plant foods represented, einkorn and emmer wheat dominate but millet is also recorded together with acorns and beech nuts. Domesticated animals accounted for around three-quarters of the bones represented in occupation deposits, with sheep and goats being by far the most numerous, although both were found to be considerably reduced in size compared with specimens from the Greek sites. This is probably because the riverside, and often waterlogged, conditions around the settlements were generally unfavourable for the growth and breeding of ovicaprids.

What stands out is the variety of locations chosen for settlement and the way in which the very different ecological niches were thoroughly exploited. The contrast to the Early Neolithic settlement of eastern Greece is quite dramatic. In Greece the 'Neolithic package' of the south-western Asian homeland was adopted in full without selection, though with some rearrangement. In south-eastern Europe, although cultivated cereals and domesticated animals became part of the food-producing regime, allowing a sedentary mode of settlement to be established, and pottery-making, ground stonework and clay figurines became part of the material culture, there was far more cultural selection and local variation. The implication of all this is that the processes by which the 'Neolithic package' were transmitted must have been more complex than simple colonization.

There was no single relentless advance of pioneer farming colonists marching northwards and eastwards from the primary settlement areas in eastern Greece. There may have been some limited pioneering movements setting out along the main corridors such as the Vardar/Morava valleys, but at each stage there would have been interaction with indigenous foragers. At first these interactions are likely to have been cooperative, maintained by exchanges within simple systems of reciprocity. Thus, items of polished stone or perhaps domesticated cattle and sheep may have been exchanged for furs, amber or honey. But it is possible to envisage other situations where relationships became more competitive and confrontational, the farmers taking land or women from the foraging societies. In such situations conflict could have ensued and some foraging groups might have begun to adopt a more 'Neolithic' lifestyle as a way of retaining their womenfolk. In this way elements of the 'Neolithic package' would have been selectively taken up. The reverse processes may also have been at work. As farming communities spread into new ecological niches where wild resources were abundant, there might have been a tendency to moderate the effort put into generating food by placing greater reliance on hunting.

By these disparate processes of colonization and acculturation the Neolithic way of life spread through south-east Europe and across the Great Hungarian Plain over the thousand years from *c.*6500 to 5500 BC. Wild Europe was being tamed.

Into the Temperate Forests of Europe

In contrast to the varied farming communities of south-eastern Europe, the earliest farmers to spread into the temperate forests of Middle Europe in a broad band stretching from western Hungary to the valley of the Seine display a remarkable cultural similarity. The deciding factor for settlement seems to have been a distinct preference for the light and easily worked loëss – a fine, silty clay of wind-blown origin. These early farmers are called the *Linearbandkeramik* group or culture (LBK) – a reference to the linear incised decoration that characterizes their pottery.

The Earliest LBK sites are found fairly widely spread from northern Hungary and Austria, through Slovakia and the Czech Republic, to about the

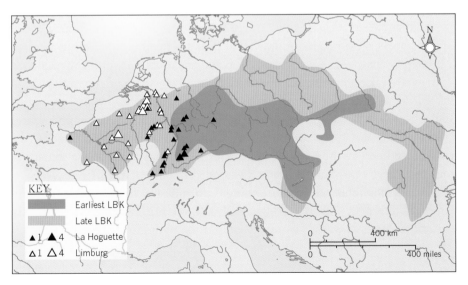

4.11 The extent of the Early Neolithic *Bandkeramik* culture in Europe at about 5300 BC. The 'Western Neolithic', characterized by pottery from La Hoguette and Limburg, which appears to be broadly contemporary, may well have developed from a separate movement coming from the west Mediterranean.

KEY

Earliest LBK
Late LBK
▲1 ▲4 La Hoguette
△1 △4 Limburg

0   400 km
0   400 miles

4.12 *Opposite:* The plan
of an early *Bandkeramik*
settlement at
Janskamperveld, Geleen,
Holland, exposed in the
excavation of 1991.
Almost the entire
settlement, covering three
or four generations of
occupation, has been
examined.

Middle Rhine. This settlement took place roughly between 5500 and 5300 BC. The Middle phase saw a consolidation and infilling of this area lasting about two centuries before a final extension in the Late phase, *c.*5100–5000 BC or a little later, took settlers westwards into eastern Belgium and the Paris Basin and northwards into central Poland. In the following millennium or so a number of regional groups developed, recognizable by their distinctive pottery styles and house forms, but there was no significant extension of the territory occupied. That Neolithic communities could colonize the forests of Europe, at the rate of some 1500 km (940 miles) in five hundred years, has excited the imagination of archaeologists. We will return to some of the possible explanations later.

The early farmers restricted their colonization to a very distinct ecological zone. The favoured settlement area was the band of deciduous forest stretching across Middle Europe between the foothills of the Alps and the less fertile glacial outwash of the North European Plain. In their chosen environment the early farmers favoured the valleys of the smaller streams that flowed through patches of loëss, but settlements did extend northwards across the plain where similar well-watered habitats with fertile soils could be found. For the most part they were located, not on the stream banks, but set back along the edge of the flood plain where they could benefit from land constantly refertilized by flood waters and nutrient-rich ground water.

The LBK settlements often give the impression that they were large villages, but when plans are separated into their different phases it is usually found that only a few buildings were occupied at any one time. In other words, what might appear to have been villages were in reality a few large farm-houses clustered together, rebuilt many times over.

The LBK houses were very distinctive. They were massive long-houses 30-40 m (100–130 ft) long and 5 m (16 ft) wide, built around a framework of upright posts set vertically in individual post-holes or, more rarely, wall slots. The walls were made of wattle and daub and the roofs were probably thatched with reeds. The internal space was divided usually by three rows of posts which served as supports for the roof. These were not rough shacks but highly sophisticated structures involving considerable skill in carpentry and established concepts of space. Long-house architecture of this kind, requiring the coordinated activity of a significant labour force, suggests that the structures may have been built by, and housed, extended families.

Basic subsistence rested on farming. Crops included emmer and einkorn wheat, barley, peas and flax. Poppy seeds also seem to have been deliberately cultivated, but this was a feature specific to the westernmost settlements. Of the domesticated animals cattle predominate, with fewer sheep and goats and surprisingly few pigs. The cattle herds would have been carefully managed to

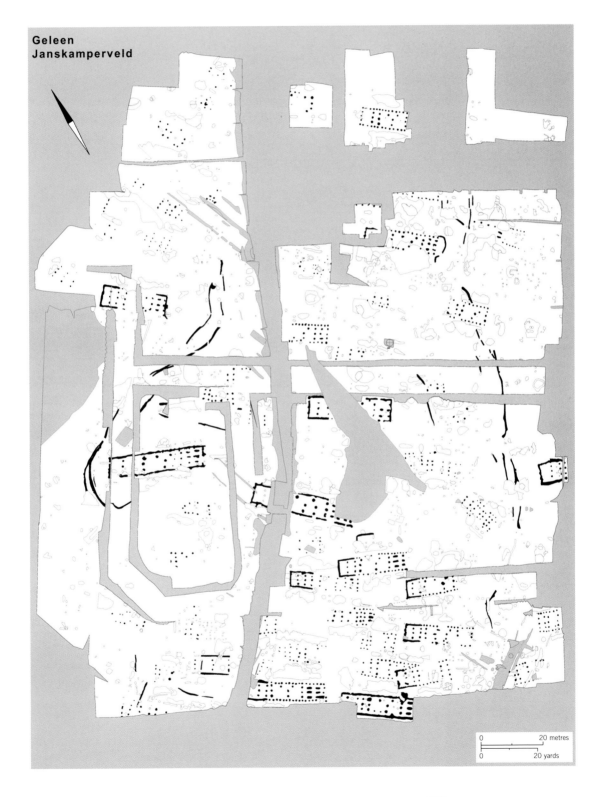

Geleen
Janskamperveld

0　　　　　　　　　20 metres
0　　　　　　　　　20 yards

4.13 *Linearbandkeramik* pottery from settlements in the Merzbach valley, Germany.

provide milk, butter, cheese and perhaps blood, which could be taken by tapping into a vein without detriment to the beast. At the appropriate time, when the herd had to be culled, meat would have been available together with valuable byproducts such as hides, horns and bones (for making implements and glue). Since cattle are by nature forest-browsers they would have fared well in the forest landscape.

The material culture of the LBK sites is similar over the entire area. Most characteristic is the linear decorated pottery, which consists of simple bowls with narrowing mouths ornamented overall with incised linear decoration.

Stone tools were made both by chipping, to make blade tools and projectile points, and by grinding, to create the various axes and adzes including the characteristic 'shoe last celt', which is an elongated chisel-like tool with a squarish cross section probably used in woodworking. Raw materials were carefully chosen, with certain types of favoured stone being transported over considerable distances of up to 200 km (125 miles). Although isolated in their woodland clearings the LBK communities were evidently linked by exchange networks extending over wide areas.

Was the dramatically rapid spread of the LBK phenomenon the result of colonization or of the acculturation of indigenous foragers? The strongest support for the colonization model comes from the fact that the complete

'Neolithic package' was adopted over a wide area in a comparatively short period of time, with the dispersed groups nonetheless retaining a distinct identity. The highly characteristic long-house that typifies the LBK has no known antecedents in the region, pottery and ground stone tools appear for the first time, while cereals and sheep and goats did not occur in their wild forms in the LBK zone. Of further relevance is the apparent sparsity of indigenous Mesolithic groups in the forested zone; indeed, there is some evidence to suggest that the foraging population was already in decline. Hunting seems to have played only an insignificant role in the LBK economy and the chipped stone tool assemblage derived little from Mesolithic tool kits. Thus, it is argued, the colonists moved easily and quickly through the forest zone, encountering no opposition and coming into contact with few indigenous people.

Those favouring the local adoption model point to the sophisticated exchange networks already in operation among the foraging groups, which provided a mechanism by which desirable commodities and innovations could quickly spread. It is also argued that the apparent mobility of small settlements in the Earliest LBK is more akin to the behaviour of foragers and that in the earliest sites there is a greater reliance on wild animals. Moreover, some archaeologists claim that there are distinct traces of Mesolithic technology in Earliest LBK flintworking. A further point that may be relevant is that sheep and goats together with pottery-making appear very early in the west, where they are characteristic of the La Hoguette culture thought to represent local foragers selectively adopting Neolithic attributes spreading from the Mediterranean via the Rhône valley (see below, p. 125).

On balance the colonization hypothesis seems to be the more convincing, but the relationship of the incoming groups with the indigenous population should not be underestimated. There is now evidence in Germany to show that some Late Mesolithic groups coexisted with Neolithic farming groups and acquired polished stone axes and grinding stones from them, presumably through exchange. In return one can imagine hunted meat and furs being well received by the farmers. It is quite possible that there was a flow of foragers, particularly women, willing – even anxious – to join what might have been perceived to be the more elite society of the farming group. How long the two communities could have existed side by side is unclear but there is no reason to suppose that assimilation was rapid.

The Earliest LBK culture developed in western Hungary out of the Starčevo–Körös subgroup of the south-east European Neolithic. From there the farming communities spread westwards along the Danube, and from the Danube valley they penetrated the forested hills to the north. This much is reasonably clear. The question that remains, however, is: what drove the

4.14 Excavations at the *Bandkeramik* site of Talheim in south-west Germany exposed a 'death pit' containing thirty-four individuals of whom sixteen were children. Most of the bodies showed signs of violence mainly resulting from axe blows to the back of the head. Three of the adults had been shot from behind with flint-tipped arrows. There can be little doubt that the bodies dumped in the pit had been massacred.

movement? One view is that the intensive cultivation around the settlements quickly exhausted the fertility of the land, forcing the community to move on. This, however, will not do. Not only has it been shown that the rich, well-watered soils of the central European valleys can sustain crops for very long periods but it is now known that many of the LBK sites were occupied over many generations, perhaps for several centuries. Another view is that a sedentary lifestyle encouraged population growth. This is, indeed, likely, but whether population growth alone was sufficient to set off the rapid spread of pioneer farmers remains doubtful. Recent surveys have shown that much fertile land remained after the initial thrust forward and only later was there infilling.

We are left, then, to accept that there was a social imperative to move on into the unknown. How might this have worked? If we allow that population increase was a real force, then in each generation there would have been a need for young men to move away from the household and set up on their own. All it requires was for society to create value systems making it socially desirable for new settlements to be established at a distance from the home base in order to set up a momentum favouring forward colonization. This imperative could then be strengthened if, in the interests of gaining enhanced status in a competitive situation, distance became a measure of prowess. This is, of course, purely speculative, but there is no reason to suppose that the 'pioneer spirit' is a characteristic only of recent societies. To put some figures on the speculation:

allowing a generation to be twenty years, it would need new settlements to be established at an average distance of 60 km (37 miles) from the home base for the LBK communities to have extended across the 1500 km (950 miles) in five hundred years. Three days' trek from the ancestral home would still have allowed social networks to be maintained.

Once the limit of colonization had been reached, inner colonization became the only strategy available to cope with population growth. With it would have come readjustments in the social system. The development of distinct regional groupings with characteristic pottery styles and the appearance of defended enclosures seem to herald a heightened sense of identity and an attachment to place. It is likely that social tension, even the periodic outbreak of hostilities, may have become more commonplace. One discovery, dating to the end of the LBK period, may be a reflection of this. At Telheim, in the Neckar valley, a pit some 3 m (10 ft) long had been dug to contain over thirty bodies of men, women and children dumped together without ceremony. Two of the adults had been shot in the head with flint-tipped arrows, while a further twenty, including children, had been dispatched with blows to the head made with stone axes, adzes and other heavy instruments. While various explanations of this gruesome discovery are possible, the level of violence suggests a society under stress. Perhaps here we are witnessing the result of a rout following inter-village conflict.

From Hilly Flanks to Temperate Forests

The initial spread of the Neolithic way of life, from its place of origin in the hilly flanks of south-west Asia to almost within sight of the North Sea and the Baltic, took place at lightning speed between 7000 and 5000 BC. It was clearly a complex process, only dimly discernible within the mass of detritus that comprises the archaeological record. The movement began with the pioneering settlement of boatloads of farmers from Asia Minor and the Levant seeking out ecological niches on Crete and in the east of Greece comparable to those of their homeland, where their traditional farming methods could be implanted. Then followed a period of consolidation and a general diffusion of the farming package eastwards into Bulgaria and northwards into the Great Hungarian Plain. It is a fair assumption that, in these rather different environments, the new farming communities that developed owed much to the indigenous foraging populations, and it may well be that the actual genetic contribution from the pioneer settlers of eastern Greece was comparatively slight. Finally, among these new farming groups in the western part of Hungary there developed a dynamic pioneering spirit that saw the rapid spread of a highly distinctive assemblage of cultural beliefs and practices throughout the forests of northern central Europe. The magnitude of the changes over these two millennia cannot be overestimated. The spread of farming through the middle of Europe involved the movement of people: it is the scale of this mobility that is the most remarkable part of the story. At some times and in some places it is almost as if there were a competition to move on and see what lay beyond. Perhaps, in a sparsely populated landscape, this was a natural human reaction.

But this is only part of the story. In the maritime regions of Europe comparable changes were in progress that had a dynamic of their own. These will be the subject of the next chapter.

CHAPTER FIVE

Assimilation in the Maritime Regions: 6000–3800 BC

The spread of the Neolithic way of life through the European peninsula from the initial settlements of sedentary farming communities on the plains of eastern Greece around 7000 BC to the colonization of the dense deciduous forests as far west as the Paris Basin less than two thousand years later is a phenomenon that justifiably causes much excitement, the discussion hinging on whether the spread was the result of 'demic diffusion' – that is, the movement of groups of people – or of 'acculturation' – the adoption of elements of the Neolithic way of life by indigenous foraging communities. Since the two processes are not mutually exclusive the argument becomes one of emphasis. The line we have taken is that actual movements of people were involved – not deep thrusting treks of discovery and exploitation but incremental moves, built generation upon generation, driven by a pioneering ethic embedded in the psyche. Along the advancing Neolithic frontier, intermarriage with indigenous people will constantly have added to the gene pool, diluting the genes of the settlers from south-west Asia who had made the initial landings on the eastern shores of Greece.

What is perhaps most remarkable about the progress of central European Neolithicization is the way in which communities adapted the Neolithic lifestyle to new environments, from the plains of Greece to the well-watered steppe land of the Great Hungarian Plain and then into the dense European forest. Now we must trace the spread of the 'Neolithic package' to even more varied ecological niches along the maritime peripheries of the peninsula.

The ocean-facing zones may be divided into two: the Mediterranean together with southern Portugal, which climatically is essentially part of the Mediterranean zone; and the Atlantic/North Sea/Baltic littoral, from Galicia to the bay of Gdańsk, including Britain and Ireland. Neolithic economies had spread throughout the southern zone by 5400 BC but in the northern zone the process of Neolithicization did not begin until about 4100 BC. The mobility of the pioneering communities in the Mediterranean, where Mesolithic settlement was at best patchy, and the stability of the Mesolithic coastal foragers in the north were what made a difference, but there were also other factors to be taken into account, not least significant climatic fluctuations around 4000 BC that may have triggered changes in the north. And, as ever, behind the major dynamics lay an intricate mosaic of local scenarios, each contributing variety to the broad picture.

The Mediterranean: Some Generalizations

From the eastern shores of the Adriatic to the Atlantic coast of southern Portugal, it took only six hundred years (6000–5400 BC) for the Neolithic lifestyle to take root. A number of possible explanations have been offered for this remarkable phenomenon. The simplest view is that pioneering groups of farmers, leapfrogging along the coasts, set up farming enclaves in regions where the indigenous Mesolithic population was sparse, and from these advance bases the Neolithic ideas spread to local indigenous populations who quickly embraced the new lifestyle. Alternatively, it is possible that the indigenous Mesolithic communities were the dominant element and that they simply adopted elements of the 'Neolithic package' through established maritime networks. One could imagine how, for example, the availability of domesticated sheep opened up the option of presenting prestigious mutton at times of feasting while a polished stone axe may have become a desirable item for exchange between elites. In this way domesticated sheep and cattle, cultivated cereals and the technology of pottery-making and stone-grinding came to be widely adopted. Whichever explanation is preferred, it is evident that the sea must have played a crucial role.

Long-distance travel by sea is well in evidence in the early fifth millennium, by which time west Mediterranean obsidian from four sources, on Sardinia, Lipari, Pantelleria and Palmarola, was being traded over considerable distances. Exactly how these distributions came about we can only guess. While it is possible that people acquired the stone direct from its source as the result of expeditions, it is more likely that it entered the complex networks of gift exchange that linked the coastal communities of the central Mediterranean together, eventually ending up in use in some distant village. The widespread distribution of obsidian is a feature of the Early Neolithic period, but the networks of interaction through which it was transported were most likely developing centuries earlier at the time when the Mesolithic foragers were beginning to explore the seas and were colonizing the larger islands. It was through these networks that the ideas and the accompanying raw materials of the 'Neolithic package' spread.

One of the most characteristic artefacts of the Neolithic culture was pottery, and throughout the central and west Mediterranean the earliest Neolithic pottery was of a very distinctive kind known as Impressed Ware.

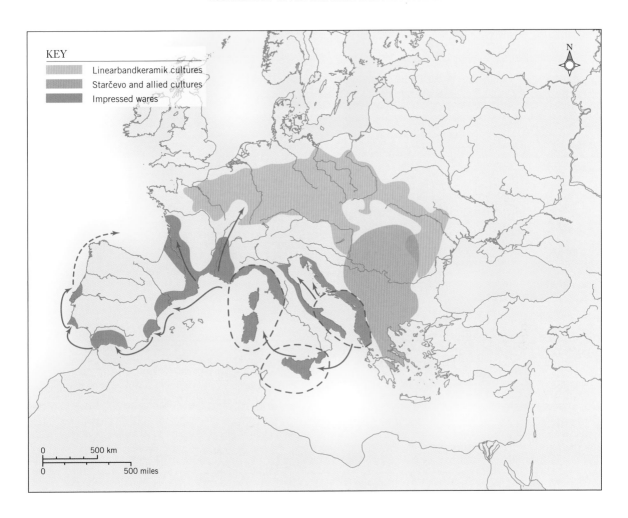

0   500 km

0   500 miles

Typically, the outer surfaces of the vessels were decorated before firing, when the clay was leather-hard, with zoned patterns impressed with a variety of implements, including the shell of the Mediterranean cockle, *Cardium*. This special type is distinguished as Cardial Ware.

Alongside the pottery and tools of polished stone are found cultivated wheat and barley and domesticated sheep/goats, cattle and pigs. Not all sites, however, have produced the full range of cultivates and domesticates. Something of this variety must be explored before we return to the broader picture.

The Adriatic, Southern Italy and Sicily

Radiocarbon chronologies for Early Neolithic sites producing Impressed Ware enable us to chart the spread of the Neolithic in the southern and middle Adriatic. The earliest sites, dating to 6400–6200 BC, are in Epirus and Corfu.

5.1 Europe in the period *c.*5500 to 4100 BC showing the two principal routes by which the Neolithic way of life spread to Europe from the southern Balkans, the overland spread via the Danube and the North European Plain and the Mediterranean route by sea ultimately to the Atlantic coast of Iberia.

115

5.2 The earliest Neolithic maritime network in the central Mediterranean c.6000–5700 BC. The desire for obsidian encouraged the use of sea routes because obsidian was found mainly on small islands.

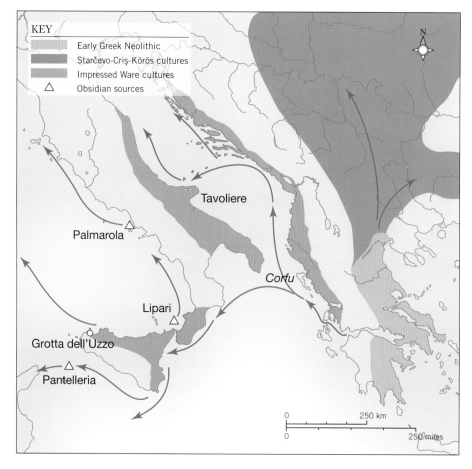

Thereafter settlements are known in Albania and Dalmatia dating to between 6100 and 5900 BC and in south-eastern Italy at around 6000 BC. This pattern suggests a spread from the west coast of Greece by sea, northwards up the Adriatic and westwards to the Italian peninsula. Within a century or two Impressed Ware settlements had spread to the northern end of the Adriatic, extending throughout Umbria and into the Po valley and along the northern coasts of Croatia.

The Tavoliere in south-eastern Italy is a region of undulating tableland between the upland massif of Gargano (which creates the 'spur' above the heel of Italy) and the Apennines. Within this comparatively restricted region of some 50 by 80 km (30 by 50 miles), over five hundred enclosed settlements have been found, the earliest established in the period 6000–5750 BC when the 'Neolithic package' was first introduced into the region.

While there can be no doubt that the essential elements of the Neolithic economy – the domesticates and cultivates and the associated technologies –

5.3 Aerial view of the Neolithic settlement of Passo di Corvo in the plain of Tavoliere, Apulia in southern Italy.

were introduced into the Tavoliere by sea from the Greek mainland, the extent to which this involved the settlement of colonists is less clear. It is conceivable that local foragers, making sea journeys to the Balkan coasts, brought back with them new ideas which they incorporated into their own systems. But the speed with which fully fledged Neolithic systems spread throughout the length of the central and west Mediterranean would seem to argue that a process of 'colonization', or demic diffusion if a less emotive phrase is preferred, was involved.

The westward spread of the Neolithic economy reached Calabria (the toe of Italy) and eastern Sicily soon after 6000 BC. In Sicily, where there existed a well-established foraging lifestyle, the Neolithic innovations were quickly taken up by the indigenous population and integrated to create new regimes of mixed and mobile farming. One of the clearest manifestations of this is found in the deep accumulation of occupation deposits preserved in the Uzzo cave at the north-western corner of the island. Here, above a succession of

Mesolithic layers, evidence of the Neolithic economy appears around 5700 BC. Various sorts of wheat are found, together with barley, lentils, vetchlings, beans and peas. Fish and wild animals, notably deer, continued to be hunted, but cattle, sheep/goat and domesticated pig make their appearance and rapidly increase in number relative to wild animals. Not long after this shift in economic base, local Impressed Ware pottery begins to be introduced into the cave deposits.

5.4 The cave of Grotta dell'Uzzo in Sicily was occupied from the eighth to the fifth millennia BC, during which time the population moved from being hunters and gatherers to being pastoralists dependent on domesticated sheep and cattle.

5.5 Animal bones and sea shells from stratified layers in the Uzzo cave provide dramatic evidence of the change in the economic base of the community over 3,000 years.

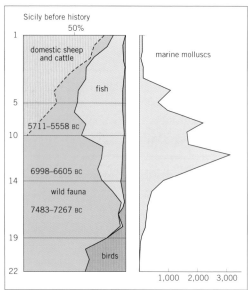

The transmission of the Neolithic lifestyle to Sicily required only a short sea journey of a couple of kilometres across the Straits of Messina from Calabria, but the predominantly coastal distribution of Early Neolithic settlements shows that the sea routes around the island were actively in use. This was a time of exploration, seafaring and island colonization. Lipari, in the centre of the Aeolian Islands, was first settled in this period. The island, easily visible from the northeastern coasts of Sicily, was already known to Mesolithic foragers who made visits to bring back obsidian. More impressive were the journeys southwards that led to the discovery and settlement of Malta, Pantelleria and Lampedusa probably towards the end of the sixth millennium. Pantelleria was a source of

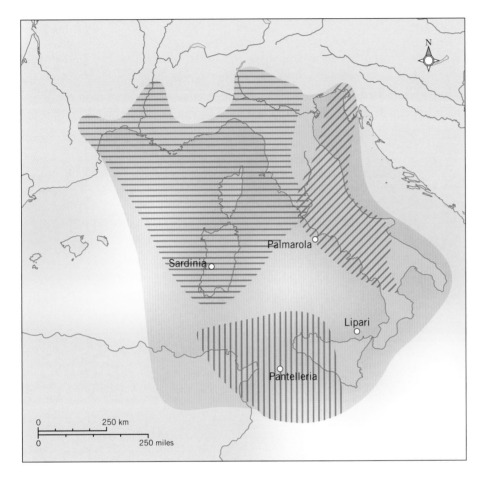

5.6 The volcanic glass, obsidian, was in great demand for making tools in the central Mediterranean. Because each source of obsidian has a distinct chemical composition, it is possible to trace exchange networks through which the stone was distributed covering very considerable distances.

obsidian, which was widely distributed throughout the Neolithic. It was probably from Pantelleria that the coasts of Tunisia were explored and perhaps settled. The initial explorations and the subsequent maintenance of the extensive maritime networks, which bound the island to the mainland of Europe and North Africa, are sure witness to the seafaring skills and zest for exploration of the Early Neolithic settlers.

Sardinia and Corsica and the Coasts of North-Western Italy

It was probably along the sea routes from Calabria and Sicily that the lands and islands of the north Tyrrhenian Sea were settled. Sardinia and Corsica were probably the first to be reached. Both islands were already inhabited by Mesolithic foragers, but the local population seems to have been sparse and it was into these almost empty landscapes that the Neolithic settlers penetrated around 6000 BC. On Sardinia – an island with little game apart from an indigenous hare-like creature, *Prolagus sardus* – the new settlers introduced not only domesticated cattle, sheep, goats and pigs, but also red deer, presumably to provide a source of game to supplement the diet. The situation on Corsica is less well understood. Sheep and pigs are recorded but, on present evidence, cattle appear to be lacking in the earliest settlements. The Neolithic settlers also introduced the ubiquitous Impressed Ware, now known from a number of sites on both islands.

On Sardinia the obsidian sources on Monte Arci were exploited and from here the sought-after stone was exported to Corsica, to the coasts of central and northern Italy and northwards to Liguria and southern France. This distribution network most likely reflects the extent of the social interactions that bound the wider community together.

Although the archaeological evidence for this region is sparse and chronologies are not yet firmly established, the spread of the Neolithic economies from the southern Adriatic via Sicily to the Tyrrhenian Sea and north to the Ligurian Sea took place with remarkable rapidity, probably within a period of no more than two hundred years. The speed alone argues that we are dealing with movements of people, a sector of the population moving on in each generation to found new agricultural colonies, leaving the inhabitants of the home base to expand within their original territory. It was the sea that set the pace.

From the Golfe du Lion to the Mondego Estuary

The initial expansion of the Neolithic economy along the northern coast of the Mediterranean, between the estuary of the Rhône and the Straits of Gibraltar, can be charted by plotting the distribution of Impressed Ware pottery. Four main concentrations of sites can be recognized – in the Languedoc, Catalonia, Valencia and Andalucía – with large areas in between where no trace of the distinctive pottery has yet been recorded. This pattern has been interpreted as an example of enclave colonization: that is, the result of the movements of small groups of Neolithic farmers leapfrogging along the coast to find suitable niches in which to establish themselves. If this explanation is correct one would expect to find colonial settlements with structures and economies quite distinct from indigenous Mesolithic systems, and this is, indeed, the case. Such a site is the lakeside settlement of La Draga near Banyoles in Catalonia. Here, stone-built platforms and timber structures associated with hearths represent a long-lived settlement that, radiocarbon dates suggest, began *c.*5900 BC and continued in use for a thousand years. An analysis of the animal bones shows that 93 per cent were domesticated (sheep/goats, cattle and pigs). Large quantities of cultivated cereals were also found, mostly wheat and barley, but with some legumes, while among the artefacts recovered were polished stone adzes and a finely polished cylindrical marble vessel. The entire assemblage marks such a dramatic break with the local Mesolithic culture that it is difficult not to accept La Draga as an example of a pioneer farming settlement.

Open sites like La Draga are rare: most of the known early Impressed Ware sites in the coastal zone are caves, some of them at high altitudes well beyond the main settlement areas where the agricultural and pastoral activities were centred. Many of these peripheral sites might have been seasonal shelters for those engaged in herding and hunting. If so, the food remains and artefacts in the rubbish deposits would be biased towards seasonality and specialist functions.

Beyond the Straits of Gibraltar one enters a different world where the sea dominates and the tides give a new rhythm to life, but landscape and latitude conspire to create environments very similar to those of the Mediterranean. It is in this region, between the Algarve and the estuary of the Mondego, that an elegant demonstration of enclave colonization has been proposed.

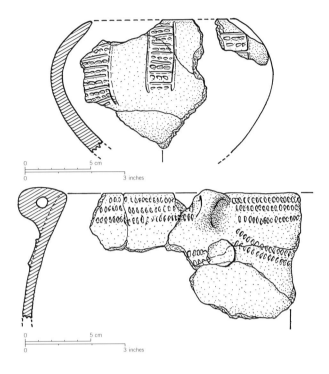

5.7 Cardial decorated vessels from the cave of Gruta do Caldeirão, Tomar, Portugal.

5.8 A pottery vessel, from Cova de l'Or, Alicante, Spain, decorated in Cardial Style.

121

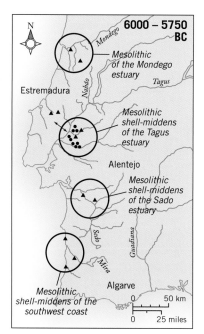

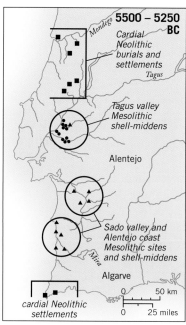

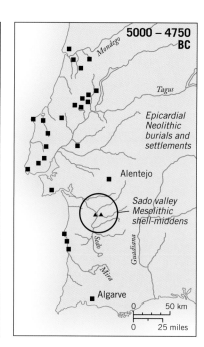

5.9 The three maps show southern Portugal in the crucial 2,000 years when the Mesolithic hunter-gatherer economy was being replaced by a Neolithic economy. In the period 5500–5250 it would appear that settlers from the Mediterranean established two enclaves on the Atlantic coast from which the Neolithic way of life subsequently spread.

We have already considered the sedentary hunter-gatherer communities who had established themselves in the valleys of the Tagus, Sado and Mira, enjoying the rich resources of the river flood plains and estuaries and creating massive shell middens around their permanent settlements (see pp. 72–4). Radiocarbon dates for these sites suggest that the middens in the Mira and Sado valleys continued in use until c.4850 BC, while those in the Tagus valley came to an end somewhat earlier, about 5300 BC. In the period 5500–5250 two clusters of Neolithic settlements appear in the region. One group extended over the limestone massif of the Estremadura, between the Tagus and the Mondego; the other occupied the extreme south-western tip of the Algarve. Over the next five hundred years or so, the 'Neolithic package' spread across much of south-western Portugal and the long-established shell middens were abandoned. Protagonists of the enclave-colonization theory argue that the evidence is best interpreted as showing a seaborne immigration of Neolithic farmers coming from south-eastern Spain and settling in the Estremadura, with later incomers taking over intervening regions in the Alentejo.

It is likely that the people here enjoyed a terrestrial diet. This contrasted with that of the people buried in the Mesolithic shell middens in the Tagus valley, whose diet was substantially based on aquatic resources. Since the two populations were contemporary we are dealing with two very different subsistence economies. The difference is further supported by stark contrasts in burial rites. While the Mesolithic community buried its dead individually with few grave goods apart from shell beads, the Neolithic community practised communal burial and included polished stone tools and pottery as offerings with its dead.

Taken together, the evidence makes a compelling case for arrival by sea of groups of Neolithic farmers settling in unoccupied territory in Atlantic-facing Iberia some time about 5500 BC, and over the next seven hundred years or so gradually merging with the indigenous Mesolithic foragers.

A Brief Mediterranean Perspective

What, then, can we conclude about the introduction of food-producing regimes throughout the Mediterranean? One inescapable fact is that the 'Neolithic package' spread from Greece to Portugal in little more than five hundred years. The spread was as rapid as the broadly contemporary advance of the LBK through the deciduous forest zone of central Europe, but the distance covered was almost twice as great, some 2,500 km (1,500 miles) as the crow flies. The rapidity of the advance is a factor of its essentially seaborne nature.

The model that best fits the totality of the evidence is, I believe, that of enclave colonization. This supposes that there was a budding-off of small groups from each settlement to found new agricultural colonies. How this was driven socially is a matter of speculation, but such forward advances are likely to have been the preserve of each generation of offspring. Perhaps the young were required as part of their entry into adulthood to set out on navigational enterprises: in this way the pioneering ethic would have become socially embedded. If, as seems likely, these undertakings were male-driven, there would have been an imperative to find wives from among the indigenous populations of the new territories, a practice that would have encouraged the rapid development of social and economic interaction with the native foraging communities. Different degrees of assimilation created a complex mosaic of economic regimes. What survived, and came to dominate, were farming practices and the technologies of potting and stone-polishing. In this way the populations of the Mediterranean region became Neolithic.

Into the Hinterland: the Garonne and the Rhône

The lands stretching around the Golfe du Lion – now Provence and the Languedoc – provided a rich array of resources for foragers and farmers alike, and it was here that the early farming communities became quickly established in the opening centuries of the sixth millennium. From this favoured zone two major routes led deep into the hinterland: one along the valleys of the Rhône and Saône, giving access northwards to the heart of west central Europe; the other via the Aude and the Carcassonne Gap, leading to the valley of the Garonne and to the Atlantic beyond. In the Mesolithic period there is evidence to show that along both corridors social networks linked the hunter-gatherer communities, creating systems through which ideas and materials could be transmitted. These networks also provided the systems by which elements of the Neolithic lifestyle were transmitted.

Impressed Ware has been found on a number of sites in western France, particularly clustering around the coasts and islands north of the Charente

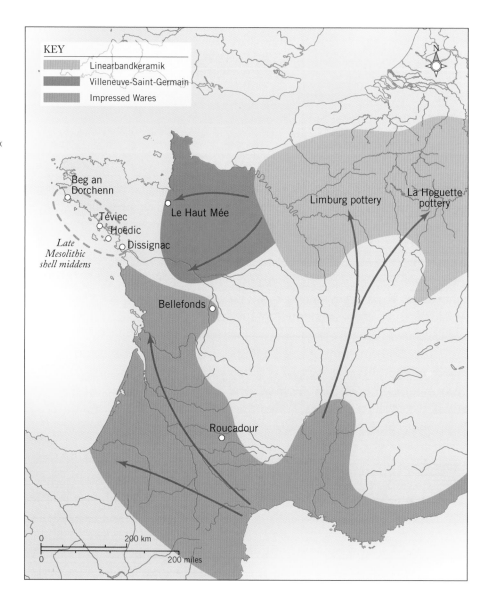

5.10 The spread of the Neolithic way of life into France is still a much debated issue, but two principal routes seem to have been in operation – the overland *Linearbandkeramik* route and an influx from the Mediterranean coast from Cardial Ware enclaves.

KEY
Linearbandkeramik
Villeneuve-Saint-Germain
Impressed Wares

Beg an Dorchenn
Le Haut Mée
Téviec
Hoëdic
Dissignac
Late Mesolithic shell middens
Limburg pottery
La Hoguette pottery
Bellefonds
Roucadour

0   200 km
0   200 miles

estuary. While it is likely that the Neolithicization of western France resulted from the acculturation of Mesolithic foraging groups, the impetus coming from the Mediterranean coast, it remains a possibility that there may have been a seaborne colonization emanating from Portugal.

Whatever the means of transmission, all the principal elements of the 'Neolithic package' were being adopted by the local hunter-gatherers who had access to commodities finding their way into the exchange networks of the Aude–Garonne route.

Much the same explanation can be given for a distinctive decorated pottery that had appeared in west central Europe by 5500 BC and is named after the type site of La Hoguette. The pottery has similarities in both decoration and fabric to the Impressed Ware of southern France and is quite unlike the LBK ware found in much the same area. At several sites in north-eastern France La Hoguette Ware has been found together with Late Mesolithic flintwork and domesticated sheep/goats. The simplest explanation for all this is that local Mesolithic groups were adopting selected elements from the 'Neolithic package' that was becoming available to them through the exchange networks operating along the Saône/Rhône corridor. It was via this route that seashells of west Mediterranean origin reached Late Mesolithic communities along the Upper Danube, and it may have been through the same networks that the culinary benefits of poppy seeds were introduced to western LBK farmers.

If these examples do, indeed, reflect the acculturation of west European hunter-gatherer communities from the Neolithic fringe of the Mediterranean, they demonstrate the strength of the existing Mesolithic exchange networks. As we will see later, these networks provided the channels along which raw materials, luxury goods and ideas continued to flow for many centuries.

From Galicia to the Bay of Gdańsk

For a variety of reasons, ranging from physical remoteness to the strength of their socio-economic systems, the coastal foragers of the Atlantic, North Sea and Baltic coasts resisted the lure of the Neolithic lifestyle for centuries. This is particularly striking in the North Sea and Baltic zones, where a distinct frontier existed between the farmers and the foragers from the establishment of the farming communities on the loëss soils c.5100 BC until about 3900 BC, when the foragers finally accepted the full 'Neolithic package'. During this interlude the two communities existed side by side. Further west in Brittany the situation was more fluid, with a gradual infiltration of Neolithic characteristics affecting different areas at different times, while on the comparatively isolated north coast of Iberia the very remoteness of the coastal plain kept the inhabitants in foraging mode until as late as 4100 BC. Britain and Ireland, equally remote, finally embraced the Neolithic lifestyle at about the same time.

Each of these regions deserves attention if only to explore the fascinating interplay of factors – geographical, ecological, environmental and social – that tipped the balance from foraging to farming.

Ertebølle and Beyond

In southern Scandinavia the Late Mesolithic period is generally known as the Ertebølle culture. Ertebølle settlements are found around the coasts of Denmark and northern Germany, and at Scania and Hålland in the southern part of Sweden. They emerged from earlier hunter-gatherer groups some time around 5400 BC and remained largely unaffected by the Neolithic culture of the south until 3900 BC when, with surprising suddenness, the entire area adopted a Neolithic way of life.

Ertebølle communities were sedentary foragers. Their territory was separated from the LBK settlement zone 200 km (125 miles) to the south by the glacial clays, sands and gravels of the North European Plain which formed something of a barrier between the two but not sufficient to prevent exchanges taking place. Through such networks it is probable that the Ertebølle communities learnt how to grind stone to make axes, adzes and other tools. They may also have acquired the art of potting, since from about 4600 BC pottery cooking vessels with pointed bases and small open bowls, perhaps serving as oil lamps, began to be made. But what is most remarkable is that little else of the 'Neolithic package' was accepted into the Ertebølle zone over the millennium and a half during which the two groups were neighbours. The implication must be that the coastal foragers made a deliberate choice not to adopt farming practices. Why we can only guess. It may simply have been that their economy was so stable that there was no advantage to be had, in nutritional or prestige terms, by investing effort in cultivation and husbandry. A few objects like LBK polished stone axes and adzes might be acceptable in return for furs or amber or seal fat, but there matters ended. All the more remarkable, therefore, is that in little more than a century, around 3900 BC, the practice of settled farming spread across the entire region to as far north as the areas of Stockholm and Bergen – a distance of 800 km (500 miles).

The introduction of food-producing regimes, known as the TRB (*Trichterrandbecher*) or Funnel Beaker Culture, saw a decline in importance of coastal settlements and the opening up of new inland locations, usually close to lakes or streams, where there would have been plenty of fresh water for flocks and herds. Nonetheless, many of the established Ertebølle settlements continued in use. At the beginning of the Neolithic two modes of agriculture were practised: the clearance of small areas of lime forest to provide pasture, and the clearance by burning of birchwood to create space for cereal cultivation. The clearances were at first small and scattered throughout the forest, but gradually they coalesced as the farming regime became more firmly established.

But why was the change from hunting to farming so rapid? It is well established that there were environmental changes around 4000 BC which may have increased the salinity of the water and affected fish stocks and shellfish, while rising sea levels would have depleted the rich coastal environments. These factors, together with an increasing population, caused stresses that might have resulted in greater competition among leaders. The equilibrium of a socio-economic system is delicate and a small dislocation at a single point can trigger change throughout. At any event, in the period of transition one can trace the rise of an elite and the development of more extensive networks of exchange. The benefits of farming may now have been seen to offer new opportunities for the emerging elites. And so a society that had for so long been resistant to change at last embraced the joys and tribulations of food production.

The Fringes of the North Sea: The Netherlands

The dynamic landscape of the Netherlands, dominated by the interaction of the rivers and the sea, presents a distinctive case of farmer–forager interaction. The region is geomorphologically very varied. To the south lie the river terraces and low hills of the Ardennes–Eifel–Sauerland Mountains covered with discontinuous expanses of fertile, well-drained loëss. These give way in the north to the flat landscape of the western extremity of the North European Plain – an expanse of glacial outwash sands and gravels blanketed by a spread of Late Glacial sands. Beyond that lie the varied sediments of the Dutch delta – a zone of fen peats, salt marshes and tidal flats transected by the wide flood plain of the Rhine/Meuse estuary – all protected from the North Sea by a discontinuous barrier of ever-moving coastal dunes perforated at intervals by river channels. These varied coastal landscapes with their range of habitats, together with the wooded sandy lowlands further inland, provided a rich environment well suited to foragers, while the loëss fringing the hills offered the friendly fertile soils sought by LBK farmers.

The first farmers of the loëss lands belong to the La Hoguette group and may have been local foragers who had adopted farming practices from the south, but they were soon replaced, around 5300 BC, by LBK groups moving in from the east and colonizing a broad swathe of land between the sandy low-lands and the more hilly areas to the south. These farming communities evolved over the centuries.

5.11 In the Netherlands around 4200 BC Mesolithic hunter-gatherers were still occupying islands in the Rhine delta, while *Bandkeramik* farmers were establishing themselves on the boulder clays and loëss to the south.

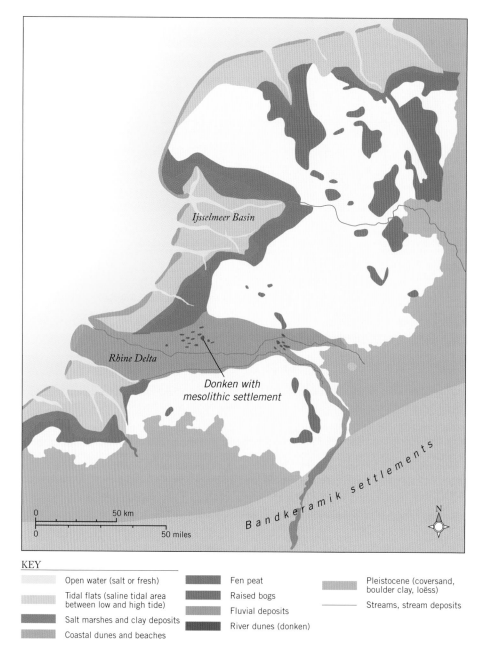

Ijsselmeer Basin

Rhine Delta

Donken with mesolithic settlement

Bandkeramik settlements

0   50 km

0   50 miles

N

KEY

Open water (salt or fresh)		Fen peat		Pleistocene (coversand, boulder clay, loëss)	
Tidal flats (saline tidal area between low and high tide)		Raised bogs		Streams, stream deposits	
Salt marshes and clay deposits		Fluvial deposits			
Coastal dunes and beaches		River dunes (donken)			

Meanwhile on the sands, marshes and estuaries, coastal foragers went about their lives largely unaffected by their farming neighbours, though the two communities interacted through the developing exchange networks.

The relationships between the two very different worlds are vividly illustrated by recent excavations at Hardinxveld in the Rhine/Meuse delta.

128

Here, two Mesolithic settlements beginning about 5500 BC were examined. They occupied the tops of Late Glacial dunes, called *donken*, projecting above the bed of the river, here some 12 km (7½ miles) wide. The main settlement areas were on the highest part of the *donken* but rubbish was thrown out into the reeds and open water fringing the dry land. The fact that the entire site became waterlogged and was later sealed by several metres of alluvial clay has meant that the archaeological evidence – in particular the organic remains – is excellently preserved.

High-quality preservation and meticulous excavation have combined to give us an exceptionally detailed view of the life of the foragers living on the *donk*. Their principal activity was fishing. Pike was the prime catch, supplemented by roach, bream, tench, eel and others. Otter and beaver were trapped in some numbers and from the woodlands of the sandy lowlands came wild boar, red deer, roe deer, elk and aurochs as well as many different types of small fur-bearing mammals. Fowling was mainly focused on duck and other water fowl, and the diet was varied by the occasional seal that had ventured into the intracoastal zone.

Contact with the farming communities to the south is well documented.

5.12 The river dunes (*donken*) in the Rhine delta provided ideal locations for Mesolithic hunter-gatherers to settle. At Hardinxveld-Polderweg the excavators had to remove many metres of clay and silt to reach the occupation level on the surface of the dune.

Alongside the appearance of pottery, *c.*5000 BC, the foragers were acquiring long flint blades from flint mines at Rijckholt some 150 km (95 miles) to the south-east, and by *c.*4600 BC the first domesticated animals began to appear in small numbers. What is particularly interesting is that, apart from pig, only limb bones are represented, suggesting that herbivore meat was brought to the site as selected joints, perhaps as gifts acquired through exchange. No trace of cereals has been found.

The site at Hardinxveld, then, provides a fascinating insight into the relationship between the foragers and farmers. In return for joints of meat and high-quality flint, the foragers would have been able to offer furs, dried or smoked fish and seal fat among the many products of their marshland environment.

The Neolithicization of the coastal inhabitants of the Netherlands was an incremental process lasting 1400 years (5000–3600 BC), the foragers coming gradually to accept domesticated animals and cereal-growing into their economy. The contrast with the Ertebølle group to the north, where the Neolithic system was rejected until 3900 BC, suggests that the two foraging societies held different beliefs and attitudes. Perhaps geography had a part to play. The Ertebølle communities faced a congenial sea with a multitude of inlets and islands stretching northwards into infinity: the north was an open world to which they were drawn, their backs to the inhospitable sandy moraine of the south. The foragers of the Dutch rivers and estuaries had a very different cognitive geography. For them the world ended on the coastal dunes and the violent North Sea beyond. It looked inwards to the hills of Europe where their immediate neighbours were farmers. Cognitive geographies are, perhaps, more important than archaeologists have hitherto allowed.

Armorica: Confronting the Ocean

The Armorican peninsula (now Brittany) is of the ocean. Surrounded on three sides by the sea, its coastline deeply indented with sheltered rias, the littoral zone has always provided a congenial habitat for human settlement. Throughout prehistory the population favoured the coastal areas, leaving the moors and forests of the interior empty or little used.

In the Mesolithic period, the south coast was the preserve of coastal foragers whose sedentary or semi-sedentary lifestyle led to the creation of large shell middens. Radiocarbon dates from the Morbihan region suggest that the main phase of use covered the thousand years from 5500 to 4500 BC, but the latest dates from Téviec and Hoëdic suggest that the sites continued to be used up to about 4000 BC or a little after. This is particularly interesting because Neolithic tombs were by now being built on the nearby mainland. If the late dates are reliable, the implication must be that some of the more remote middens were still being used for burial in the traditional mode long after new lifestyles and belief systems had become established nearby.

The bearers of the 'Neolithic package' approached the Armorican peninsula from the south and the east. Neolithic communities using Impressed Ware were settled in the coastal regions of western France between the Gironde and the Loire in the period 5500–4500 BC; that is, contemporary with the use of the Morbihan shell middens. From here, knowledge of domestication and cultivation may have spread northwards, through coastal maritime networks, to the southern shores of Brittany.

The Neolithicization of the eastern approaches of Armorica is rather better known. The initial thrust westwards of the LBK reached the eastern and southern parts of the Paris Basin by c.5300 BC, the westernmost boundary roughly approximating to the vicinity of Paris. Thereafter internal development led gradually to changes in material culture, house type and settlement morphology.

In the three or four centuries after c.5000 pioneer groups of farmers fanned out westwards from the Paris Basin, establishing scattered enclaves of their distinctive culture from the Channel coast to the Loire valley, reaching as far west as the vicinity of Saumur on the Loire and the present boundary between Brittany and Normandy, where, at Le Haut Mée, an isolated farmstead spearheading the western advance has been discovered. Radiocarbon dates place it firmly in the period 5000–4700 BC. Recent work on the island of Guernsey suggests that the pioneer settlers were also beginning to explore the offshore islands at this time.

The farming communities were thin on the ground. Living in their small scattered settlements established among the indigenous hunter-gatherers, they would have begun to engage in the local networks of interaction. Polished stone rings made from a schist found only in Brittany in the region settled by the farmers represents one facet of a system of reciprocal exchange that may well have involved farming products finding their way into the households of the indigenous foragers. Over the centuries the farmers and foragers merged, each group losing its distinctive identity to create a more diversified culture now firmly based on food production. By c.4700 the landward approaches of the Amorican peninsula were fast becoming Neolithic through pioneering settlement and acculturation. What followed on the peninsula, or more precisely around its maritime fringes, seems to have happened very quickly. Not only was the 'Neolithic package' suddenly accepted, but almost coincident with this a new ideology becomes apparent in the form of standing stones and monumental tombs.

The exact chronology of this dramatic development has still to be defined

a

b

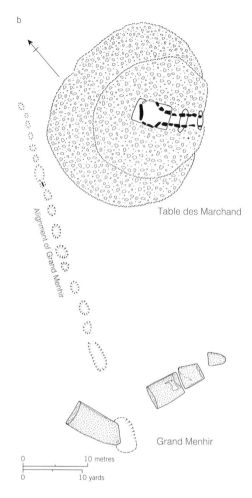

Table des Marchand

Alignment of Grand Menhir

Grand Menhir

0   10 metres
0   10 yards

5.13a+b At Locmariaquer, Morbihan, on the south coast of Brittany, a massive menhir – the Grand Menhir Brisé – now fallen and broken, probably represents the largest menhir in a menhir row, the holes of which have been identified in excavation. Nearby, and built later, is a passage grave, the Table des Marchand.

but in the south, in the Morbihan, two distinct phases can be recognized. In the first, the new monumentality involves the erection of standing stones (menhirs), sometimes singly and sometimes in groups. These menhirs varied in size. The largest is the famous Grand Menhir Brisé at Locmariaquer, now lying broken in four parts. It weighs 348 tonnes and would once have stood to a height of over 20 m (66 ft). This enormous stone had been dragged 4 km (2½ miles) from the place where the particular rock of which it was made outcropped. Excavation has shown that the Grand Menhir was probably the terminal *pièce de résistance* in a row of menhirs of gradually increasing size. Eighteen socket holes have been found in excavation. Had all eighteen had stones erected in them, the cost in terms of labour would have been huge: the implication is that this was a society that was able to mobilize itself, under some kind of coercive leadership, on an unprecedented scale. Not only were the menhirs of the Carnac region dressed but a significant number of them were also decorated with a variety of motifs pecked into the surfaces with stone mauls. Some are recognizable as bovines, others are hafted axes and crooks, but there are also enigmatic depictions referred to, rather helplessly, as 'axe-ploughs' or 'whales'. What this symbolism meant is sadly beyond recovery, though this has not prevented lively speculation.

Menhirs appear to be the earliest monumental structures in Armorica. Four were found stratified beneath a long burial mound at Lannec er Gadouer that was constructed around 4600–4500 BC. Sites for two other long mounds, Mané Ty Ec and Le Manio II, both in the Carnac region, are known to have hosted small menhirs preceding their construction. This raises questions about the origins of the menhir tradition – could it be that menhirs date back to the Mesolithic period and that what we are seeing at these sites is continuity of ritual use? In this context it may be relevant that one of the Mesolithic burials at Hoëdic was marked by a small standing stone.

The second class of monumental structures of the initial Neolithic phase are the

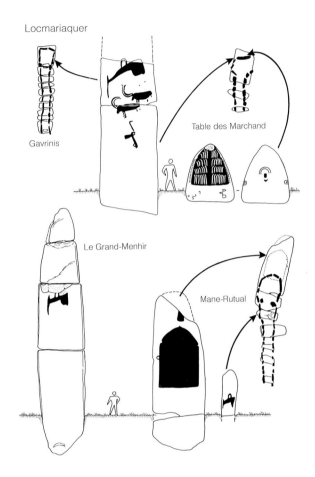

5.14 Several large menhirs, many of them carved, once stood in the Morbihan but were later broken up and incorporated in the walls and roofs of the passage graves.

long mounds (*tertres tumulaires*). These are rectangular or trapezoidal mounds of earth and rubble bounded by ditches, stone curbing or walling. Within the mounds themselves were embedded a variety of structures including stone-built cists (*coffres*) often containing burials, hearths and settings of posts and sometimes menhirs. The mounds were being constructed in the period around 4500 BC. There has been much speculation about their origin – whether the idea was introduced from outside the region or whether they developed locally around the Baie de Quiberon where they cluster. In support of the latter it is worth remembering that the Mesolithic shell middens, artificial mound-like structures, also contained burial cists and hearths associated with them. It could be argued that the long mounds, like the menhirs, may have been a local development with roots in the Mesolithic period.

If, then, the first monuments of the Morbihan, built in the period 4700–4500 BC, are an indigenous phenomenon, it remains to be asked what stimulated their construction. Was it the result of incoming farming

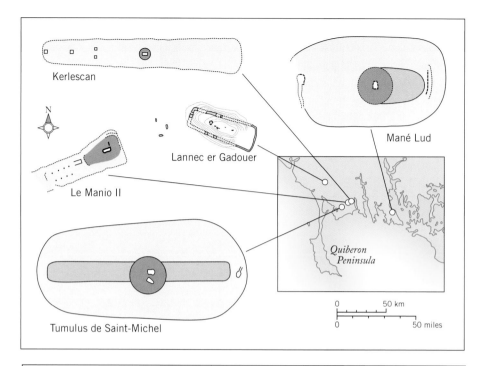

5.15 The Neolithic long mounds of the Morbihan frequently incorporate earlier cists embedded in circular or oval mounds. Others incorporate earlier menhirs suggesting a long continuity of use.

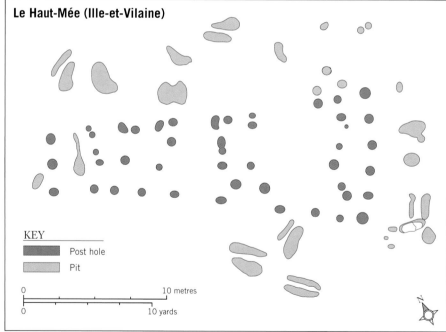

5.16 The plan of a Neolithic house at Le Haut Mée, Ille et Vilaine, in eastern Brittany. The house plan resembles the plan of *Bandkeramik* houses found in the Paris Basin and beyond.

communities or simply the accessibility of the 'Neolithic package' from the Impressed Ware settlements south of the Loire or the Paris Basin farmers who were moving westwards into Amorica?

5.17 The northern coast of Iberia facing the Bay of Biscay is an 'unfriendly' coast in that the mountains descend rapidly to the sea hindering easy communications. For hunter gatherers the landscape provided a range of different ecological zones to exploit over a limited distance which was an advantage but to the later farmers good agricultural land was limited.

The Cantabrian Coast

The mountains of Cantabria stand as a great divide between the mesetas of the Iberian peninsula and the comparatively narrow coastal strip that looks northwards across the Bay of Biscay. Over a comparatively short distance of some 50 km (30 miles) a journey southwards would take a traveller from the sea, through fast-changing ecozones each offering a distinctive range of resources, to a wall of mountain peaks over 2000 m (6500 ft) high. The coastal region supported bands of Mesolithic foragers well used to exploiting what the countryside had to offer.

The introduction of a Neolithic economy into the region cannot yet be traced in any detail. The Mesolithic foragers had some limited access to pottery early in the fifth millennium but it is not until some time later that there is any convincing evidence of domesticated animals. At present the earliest appearance of sheep/goats is in the cave of Arenaza in a context dated to 4100 BC. Nearly 80 per cent of the animal bones found here were sheep or goats, showing that the inhabitants had by now become herders as well as foragers, augmenting their traditional diet of forest game and seafood with domesticated flocks. It was only later that cereals begin to be cultivated.

The picture that emerges in this Cantabrian coastal fringe is of well-established foraging communities gradually adapting over time. Their lives were circumscribed by the mountains behind them and the sea in front – it was an inward-looking world content to maintain traditional ways.

The Offshore Islands: Britain and Ireland

The spread of Neolithic ideas to Britain and Ireland must have involved sea journeys and the transportation, on a comparatively extensive scale, of domesticated breeding stock – cattle, sheep, goats and pigs – as well as the seed corn necessary to establish a sustainable agriculture. Whether we are dealing with pioneer farmers establishing themselves on the islands or indigenous Mesolithic foragers bringing back the novelties of farming on their maritime expeditions is difficult to say – the archaeological evidence is too ill-focused – but in all probability a variety of processes led to the introduction and spread of the 'Neolithic package'. What is perhaps most dramatic is the apparent rate of progress through the islands. The Neolithic economy is first attested in the east of England, in Cambridgeshire, by c.4300 BC. By 4000 BC it had reached Wales. A hundred years later it is found in Northern Ireland and by 3800 BC many parts of Scotland had been reached, including the islands of Orkney and Shetland in the far north. By any standards the spread was rapid – so rapid that we must suppose that the new ideas, and their necessary material back-up, were transmitted principally by sea. This would allow that a number of different routes were used. One would have been the short Channel crossing from Normandy to the loëss-covered coastal plains of Sussex; another from the coast of northern France and Belgium to the ports of East Anglia with their easy access to the light but fertile soils of Norfolk. These routes may have attracted pioneering farmers to settle and it is perhaps significant that the earliest Neolithic dates are for settlements in the east of Britain. But other routes were also possible, not least the Atlantic route leading northwards from the Armorican peninsula linking Ireland with the west coasts of England, Wales and Scotland. It is highly probable that maritime networks already bound these coasts, providing well-established channels for the new ideas to spread along. It may have been in this way that the foragers of south-western Ireland, living on the remote tip of the Dingle peninsula, were able to acquire cattle and a polished stone axe about 4100 BC. The western maritime route would also have been the way by which Neolithic concepts reached the western coasts of Scotland, the Western Isles and finally Orkney and Shetland.

Leaving aside the late fifth-millennium settlements in East Anglia, the rest of Britain and Ireland, including the remote Northern Isles, began to adopt a Neolithic way of life within the brief period 4100–3800 BC, at the same time that the Ertebølle communities of Denmark and southern Sweden and the foragers of the Cantabrian coast embraced food-producing regimes. While this synchronism may be little more than coincidence, the question of whether there was a single cause deserves to be considered.

One idea recently put forward is that the surge of Neolithicization across these regions may have been a response to a significant change in climate observable in a range of scientific data, beginning about 4100 BC, peaking around 3800 BC and lasting to 3200 BC. During this time there was a marked increase in the annual temperature range, with warmer summers and colder winters. This corresponded with a stronger meridional atmospheric circulation over the North Atlantic which would have decreased the western air flow, causing a reduction in winter rainfall. Taken together, these factors would have enhanced the agricultural potential of large tracts of north-western Europe by extending the length of the growing season and thus ensuring a greater cereal yield.

While the scientific facts are not in dispute, and a significant rise in the cereal-growing capacity of Britain and southern Scandinavia may have facilitated the spread of a Neolithic economy, what actually kick-started the movement is still unclear. It may simply be that a long period of consolidation was required to allow the early farmers, occupying the coastal regions from Amorica to the Rhine estuary, to establish stable and sustainable systems before venturing to explore the lands across the sea. Another factor that cannot be neglected is the willingness of the Mesolithic foragers in Britain and Ireland to open themselves to change. The change in climate and the continued rise in sea level may have so decimated the traditional foraging environments that indigenous communities were forced to be more innovative and more receptive to new modes of production. Cultural change is seldom monocausal and we must accept that the Neolithicization of Britain and Ireland came about as a result of a myriad of local decisions creating the complex mosaic of differing socio-economic systems dimly visible to us in the very incomplete archaeological record.

Talking to Each Other

The major language groups spoken in Europe are closely related and derive from a single root which has been called Indo-European. The study of the origin and spread of Indo-European has largely been the preserve of linguists, but in recent years the discussion has been greatly enlivened and given a new direction by archaeologists who have attempted to bring linguistic theories into contact with the realities of the material evidence. While it is only fair to say that large areas remain unresolved, there is a growing consensus, at least among a significant group of archaeologists, that the most appropriate context for the introduction of the Indo-European language into Europe is the spread of the Neolithic way of life. In other words, the language originated among the early food producers of south-west Asia and thereafter spread through Europe, one branch following the route through the Balkans to the Great Hungarian Plain and then westwards through the deciduous forest zone of Middle Europe, the other spreading westwards through the Mediterranean to the Atlantic shores of Iberia. In both of these zones Indo-European was swept quickly forwards in the fifth millennium as the language of the colonizing farmers. Around the frontiers of this early advance lay the regions where Mesolithic populations were numerous and where elements of the 'Neolithic package' were gradually being adopted by the indigenous peoples. In these peripheral zones, it is argued, Indo-European became the accepted language through a process of contact-induced language shift, eventually giving rise, by creolization, to the distinctive forms of Indo-European that we call Slavic, Baltic, Germanic and Celtic. This process should broadly be dated to the period 4000–2500 BC. The theory has considerable attractions, not the least of them being that it fits well with the archaeological evidence.

And So . . .

It can fairly be said that in the two thousand years or so, from the time that the pioneer farmers from south-western Asia unloaded their animals and seed corn on the flower-decked coasts of eastern Greece until a very different crew made a precarious landfall on the remote islands of Shetland, to set up their homesteads in what by any standards was a marginal environment verging on the hostile, the very foundations of European society were established. Throughout the peninsula and its islands, farming now underpinned human existence, offering a new stability. Communities became sedentary, enmeshed in networks of gift exchange that were soon to drive technology and lead society to greater heights of complexity.

The rapidity of the spread of the Neolithic way of life was remarkable. While there can be no doubt that the indigenous Mesolithic populations played an active role, contributing massively to the gene pool of the emerging farming societies and providing an ambience of mobility, there was also an inbuilt ethic of pioneering that drove the early farmers inexorably forwards to the limits of Europe, by land, through the deciduous forests of the north, and by sea, land-hopping through the Mediterranean to the Atlantic. We have suggested that this dynamic may have been embedded in a system of social values enshrining the belief that young men could gain status only by leading colonizing expeditions. This may well be, but perhaps behind it all lay an innate desire to explore the unknown, drawn on westwards by a curiosity to discover the wonder of the setting sun. All speculation, of course – but then we are dealing not just with settlement plans and pottery distributions but with real people with aspirations and hopes.

CHAPTER SIX

Europe in Her Infinite Variety: *c.*4500–2800 BC

After the initial rapid spread of farming, which must have involved the movement of people in small but frequent increments, two broad processes began to get under way. In the areas of initial settlement – the loëss soils of the deciduous forest zone, and the islands and coasts of the Mediterranean – indigenous hunter-gatherer populations were quickly assimilated and settlements increased in number, gradually filling up the available spaces between the original pioneer holdings. But beyond the limits of the initial Neolithic settlement zone the processes of change were more complex, varying from localized population advances to the assimilation of Neolithic ways by indigenous foragers. The overall result was the opening up of more and more land to agriculture and the creation of a thoroughly mixed gene pool. As the communities settled into their ecological niches and established their territories, cultural differences became more evident and social networks developed to bind disparate communities together. Thus, a kaleidoscope of different 'cultures' crystallized out across the face of the European peninsula.

At one level there was considerable similarity from one end of Europe to the other. Most communities cultivated wheat and barley and ran herds and flocks of cattle, sheep/goats and pigs, though the balance betwen crops and domesticates varied. Land was cleared using axes of polished stone and the soil was broken first with hoes but later with ards drawn by oxen which scratched furrows through the ground but did not turn the soil in the manner of a plough. All communities now made pottery – humankind's first artificial material – and for many the plasticity of unfired clay provided a freedom for expressing identity by favouring particular shapes and kinds of 'decoration'. In the structure of buildings and the arrangement of settlements there is a general sameness – the houses were usually rectangular and timber-built and were grouped together in hamlets or villages – but different social systems led to variation and distinct regional vernaculars began to appear.

It used to be thought that the east was instrumental in introducing new technologies and new belief systems into Europe: this was the *ex oriente lux* hypothesis. More recently, as the complexity of European development has become known and a reliable absolute chronology has been established, principally through radiocarbon dating and dendrochronology, it has become clear that many of the significant advances seen in Europe resulted from indigenous energies and inventiveness. Yet the fast-developing communities of south-west Asia are likely to have had some impact on their peripheries. The centre of the urban development in south-west Asia lay in Mesopotamia, in the valleys of the Tigris and Euphrates. It was here, *c.*5900 BC in the Ubaid period, that irrigation agriculture began leading to permanent settle-

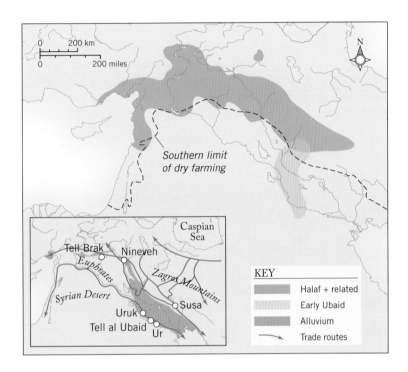

ments and an increasingly complex society controlled through some kind of theocratic power. In the succeeding Uruk period (4200–3000 BC) the first towns emerged, some of them growing to considerable size: around 3200 BC Uruk itself was 100 ha (250 acres) in extent and later, by about 2900 BC, had quadrupled in area. The spectacular growth of an urban civilization in what was a highly fertile but otherwise resource-poor region created a massive demand for materials such as metals, timber, precious stones and other luxury goods, and to meet this demand a huge hinterland came to be exploited. It is not at all unlikely that some of the commodities consumed by Mesopotamian urban societies came from Europe through developing trade networks. The demands of the core could well have stimulated production in the periphery, but, that said, it would be quite wrong to see Mesopotamian urbanization as the principal driver of European social and economic change. Those European communities that, stimulated by the new demands, may have increased production, chose to do so. The innovative surges apparent in Europe were largely self-generated.

6.1 The Near East at the time of the emergence of city states. The Halaf culture (*c.*6000–5400 BC) spread in a broad arc from the Mediterranean coast to the Gulf. The Ubaid culture (*c.*5900–4200 BC) emerged during this time in Upper Mesopotamia. By the Early Dynastic Period (2900–2350 BC) the centre of gravity had shifted slightly but still focused on the rich alluvial lands between the Tigris and Euphrates.

Diversification: Places to Live

The great diversity apparent in European society at this time can best be seen through settlements. In south-east Europe, in modern Bulgaria, the tell settlements first established in the early stages of Neolithic pioneering in the sixth millennium continued to grow. The best-known of the tells is Karanovo in south central Bulgaria. During the two thousand years of its occupation, it covered an area of some 10 ha (25 acres) and grew to a height of 12 m (40 ft) as a result of successive houses being built on the debris of their predecessors. While the houses differ in detail and spacing through time, they are all either square or rectangular and built with walls of vertical posts. Sometimes they were divided into two or three rooms. Each house was provided with a hearth. From the comparatively small sample excavated, the overall impression is of a large village of closely packed houses showing little significant social differentiation. The impressive height to which the tells grew was a result of a deliberate choice made by the occupants to build on the debris of the past with the intention, perhaps, of demonstrating the permanence and longevity of their village, in this way stressing their deep ancestral roots.

Further to the east, in the broad zone of lightly wooded land between the steppe flanking the north shores of the Black Sea and the Russian forests, pioneer farmers had established a network of farming villages which exploited the thick, rich black soils of the region. This group, known archaeologically as the Cucuteni-Tripolye culture, colonized a swathe of land from the eastern foothills of the Carpathians as far as the valley of the river Dnepr. In the early fourth millennium some of these villages, centred on the valley of the southern Bug, grew to colossal sizes – up to 400 ha (1000 acres) in extent – capable of housing, it is claimed, a population of up to ten thousand! Such staggering concentrations may have been a defensive measure against internal or external threat, or perhaps they represent a stage in the transformation from an egalitarian tribal system towards a more ranked society or chiefdom. Whatever the reason, these super-centres were by far the largest anywhere in Europe at the time and from what we know of their plan they were carefully laid out, with zones of houses separated by

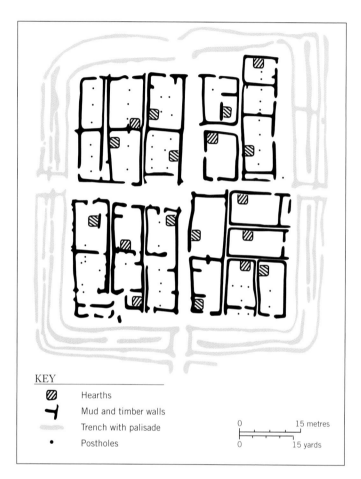

KEY

▨	Hearths
⅂	Mud and timber walls
～	Trench with palisade
•	Postholes

0   15 metres
0   15 yards

6.2 The settlement of Polyanista in north-eastern Bulgaria as it was first laid out about 4500 BC. The four compact blocks of houses, perhaps each representing a lineage, were protected within a multiple palisade.

streets. Clearly some kind of coercive power was at work to maintain such a high level of order.

Over much of the region settled by the first farmers of the LBK, small villages continued to be built but, instead of the long-houses so characteristic of the LBK, the later houses tended to be smaller and there was greater variety reflecting the different regional cultures that had crystallized out. The overall decrease in the size of houses shows the emergence of a rather different social structure, with more emphasis now being placed on the individual family and less on the extended families or lineages who had occupied the earlier long-houses.

The use of timber to build houses was widespread in central and northern Europe from south Russia to Brittany. In southern Europe, while timber was still employed in many parts, extensive use was also made of stone. This is nowhere better demonstrated than in the impressive stone-built 'fortifications' of Portugal, south-eastern Spain and southern France. In Portugal the sites are assigned to a cultural group usually referred to as Vilanovan, after

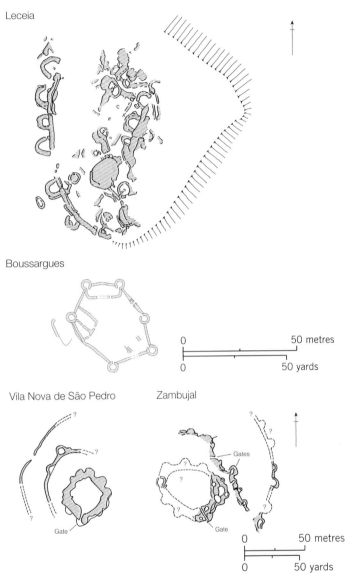

6.3 Settlements with stone-built fortifications were a feature of the Early Bronze Age in many parts of southern Europe. Leceia, Vila Nova de São Pedro and Zambujal are from the Tagus region of Portugal; Boussargues is in southern France.

the type site of Vila Nova de São Pedro, near Santarém. Vila Nova comprises a central, roughly circular, enclosure about 35 m (115 ft) across built of a thick drystone wall with forward-projecting bastions and a single, long, narrow entrance. Outside were two further arcs of walling, the inner one having hollow cells set within bastions.

Similar stone-built fortifications are known in Almería in south-eastern Spain, most famously at Los Millares. Here, a promontory between two rivers, the Andarax and the Rambla de Huéchar, was defended by three lines of walling, the outer being the most extensive, running for more than 200 m (650

6.4 The fortified settlement of Zambujal in Portugal has undergone extensive excavation. The aerial photograph shows successive walls strengthened with circular bastions.

ft), emboldened by nineteen forward-projecting 'bastions' and a gate flanked by foreworks. The approach to the site was 'guarded' by four smaller stone forts. Beyond the outer wall and overlooked by the smaller forts was an extensive cemetery of about eighty passage graves. The complex and the graves were in use from the end of the fourth millennium to the end of the second millennium.

While it is easy to describe these stone-built structures it is more difficult to offer a convincing explanation for their function. Everything about them – the massiveness of the walls, the 'bastions' and the narrow, well-protected entrances – argues that they were built with defence very much to the fore. But the size and elaboration may also have been designed to impress – to demonstrate the might of the polity responsible for their construction. Places of such visual prominence might also have served as foci for assemblies, perhaps for seasonal meetings associated with feasting and worship of the gods. In other words, sites of this kind, representing the consolidated effort of the community working under some kind of coercive leadership, are likely to have performed a range of functions.

This brief review has done scant justice to the range of constructional work under way in all parts of Europe at this time. Timber, drystone, wattle and daub, and *pisé* (tightly packed mud) had all been mastered, and in the variety of the individual buildings, their arrangement one with another and the ways in which the settlements were separated from the world around, we can begin to glimpse the many different identities that contributed to the patchwork of Europe.

Pottery: A Medium for Self-Expression

Pottery is of central interest since it is usually prolific – sometimes inconveniently so – and, after the Mesolithic period, pretty well ubiquitous. More to the point, the plastic clay was used by societies to transmit messages about themselves and their beliefs. Mastery of the medium was rapidly acquired. The choice of the right kind of clays, the creation of the vessel forms by hand usually using a coil-building technique, the application of various forms of decoration by impression, modelling and painting with slip, and the control of heat and oxygen during firing were all practices well established early in the Neolithic period in Greece, where the technology was introduced from southwest Asia around 7000 BC, spreading to the rest of Europe by around 4000 BC.

Local inventiveness soon takes over, creating a stunning array of vessels often of high artistic merit. Some, like the simple round-bottomed bowls found in many parts of western Europe at the beginning of the Neolithic, were shapes determined by the clay medium itself. This thread runs through the rest of this period, but because of its wonderfully flexible nature clay can be used to copy containers made of other materials – a phenomenon referred to as skeuomorphism. In some assemblages it is possible to recognize the organic prototypes – basketry or leather – that the potters chose to copy with great attention to detail. Other vessels are evidently inspired by metal prototypes. More intriguing are pottery vessels in human form – a frequently recurring phenomenon in the Balkans. This is presumably far more than playful inventiveness. Perhaps these anthropoid pots were meant to represent individual people. If so, their manipulation in the social space in which people lived and died would be redolent with meanings well understood by the initiated. We know from modern ethnographic examples that the grouping and placing of pots within the living space could convey a variety of messages. In one African community the way in which a woman placed her own pot (that which represented her) could inform her sexual partner of her availability or otherwise. In prehistory, interpretations of this kind are beyond the reach of even the most imaginative archaeologist.

Pottery was, for many societies, a way to express their identities. Thus, the

6.5 Anthropomorphic pottery vessel, *c*.4000 BC, from Hotnica, near Veliko Turnova in Bulgaria. It is possible that pots of this kind were directly identified with individuals living or ancestral.

reproduction of a set of motifs on the body of a pot was a reaffirmation of group coherence and a way to distinguish 'us' from 'them'. At another level the adoption of a particular vessel form associated with a belief system was a demonstration of one's adherence to that belief.

Not all societies expressed their identities through pottery. In many regions of Europe it is possible to recognize a change to much simpler and less highly decorated ceramics in the Early Bronze Age after *c*.2500 BC. A possible reason for this is that bronze, in the form of weapons and ornaments, may

146

now have provided the means of demonstrating group identity, with pottery receding from view and now restricted to a more limited utilitarian role.

Europe's early potters were brilliantly inventive. Their sense of form, space and colour was often stunning, and in sheer creativity they could hold their own with the best of modern craft potters. Diversity in pottery form and decoration is a direct reflection of the many different cultural groups that were now identifying themselves across the face of Europe.

Commodities and Networks: Hard Stone

The exploitation of select commodities and their movement, often over great distances, is as old as mankind, but it is not until the period 4500–2500 BC that the exploitation of rare resources begins to take on a momentum sufficient to create interlocking networks of exchange robust enough to be clearly visible in the archaeological record.

By definition, the material that dominates the Neolithic period is stone. Different kinds of stone contributed in different ways. Siliceous stones – flint, chert and obsidian – that would easily take a concoidal fracture when struck were particularly useful for making tools worked from flakes and blades. Hard, more granular stones of igneous and metamorphic origin could be roughly chipped, pecked and then ground and polished to make robust axes and adzes, while stones of exceptional colour or texture could be polished to create items of high prestige. Throughout Europe there are many examples of the exploitation of stone.

Obsidian, a black, shiny volcanic glass, was a popular commodity in the Mediterranean and its hinterland. Obsidian from the Cycladic island of Melos was already being extracted and distributed in the Late Palaeolithic period, while obsidian from central Mediterranean sources was first used in the Mesolithic period and came to be heavily exploited and widely distributed in the period around 5000 BC when it is found across the width of the Mediterranean from Liguria to Tunisia. Sources in eastern Slovakia and northern Hungary were also exploited on a lesser scale. Obsidian owed its attraction partly to the ease with which it could be worked into long, regular blades, but it was its striking black, shiny appearance that pleased the eye and made it the more desirable.

The visual appearance of flint, as well as its mechanical qualities, made the products of certain sources particularly sought after. Chocolate flint, honey flint, spotted flint and banded flint were all exploited in different regions in north central Europe. Of these, banded flint from Krzemionki in the Holy Cross hills of Poland was one of the most widely distributed, reaching distances of up to 400 km (250 miles) from the source. Banded flint, with its flowing streaks of light and dark colour, has a particular attraction, especially

6.6 Banded flint was mined on a large scale at Krzemionki in Poland and was distributed widely across the North European Plain.

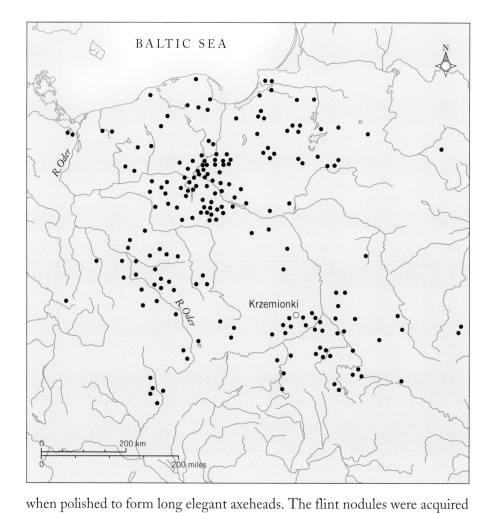

6.7 *Opposite:* The flint mines at Rijckholt in Holland. The depth at which good flint lay required the miners to dig deep shafts to find the seam before digging a dense network of interlocking galleries to maximize the extraction of workable flint.

when polished to form long elegant axeheads. The flint nodules were acquired by digging pits or shafts down through the chalk to the level of the nodule bed. When the bed was close to the surface the open cast digging of pits would suffice, but as the layer sloped away and became deeper it was necessary to dig shafts and open up galleries radiating from the bottom. The source was exploited for a considerable period of time throughout the Funnel Beaker Culture (TRB) (3900–3100 BC) and the subsequent Globular Amphora culture (3100–2700 BC). In the earlier period the mined flint was taken to a single large production site at Cmieló nearby and there worked into finished axes which were distributed over distances of up to 100 km (60 miles). In the later period the manner of production changed, with the axe-manufacturing sites now being located close to the shafts, the products reaching sites of up to 400 km (250 miles) away. One explanation offered to account for these differences is that during the TRB period, when production was centralized, the axes were fed directly into the exchange networks, while in the Globular

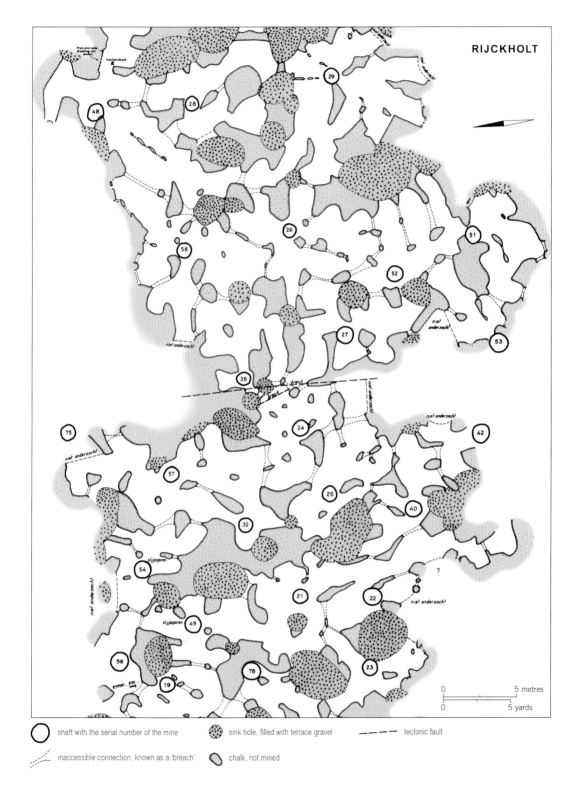

RIJCKHOLT

○ shaft with the serial number of the mine

⋰ inaccessible connection, known as a 'breach'

⬤ sink hole, filled with terrace gravel

◗ chalk, not mined

– – – tectonic fault

6.8 *Opposite:* The two
maps show the distribution
of two different types of
stone used to make axes in
Brittany. The dolerite was
used to manufacture simple
axes while the hornblendite
was used for more complex
shaft-hole axes. Both maps
show the extensive network
of distributions with the
rivers, particularly the Loire,
featuring large.

Amphora period people travelled to the mines from distant parts and worked for a limited period, extracting and shaping the stone they required, before leaving for home with their new stock of axes. At their home bases the axes would then have entered the local distribution networks.

There is nothing at all unreasonable in supposing that production in the later period was by direct access. Indeed, one could go so far as to suggest that this method may have been the norm, with the resource being regarded as belonging to the people at large rather than to the locality. It is quite possible that the mining season brought disparate communities together for feasting, games, worship and the like. At such times allegiances could be reaffirmed, marriages agreed and gifts exchanged, giving strength to a wide-flung network. In other words, the source of the commodity may have become the centre of the social network.

Flint mining became widespread in the chalklands of western Europe, in southern Britain, Belgium, Holland and Denmark. The mines of Rijckholt in southern Holland give a good idea of the skill of the miners. Because of the thickness of the overburden and depth of the desired flint band within the chalk the miners had to dig shafts 1–1.5 m (3–5 ft) in diameter to a depth of between 4 and 12 m (13 and 40 ft) depending on the slope. There are estimated to have been two thousand shafts altogether.

An average mine would have taken three men about a month to exploit, during which time they could have extracted 8000 kg (17,600 lbs) of flint. Given that there were two thousand individual shafts, the total yield would have been enormous, but since the mines were probably in use throughout much of the fourth millennium the annual yield was relatively modest. Rijckholt flint was much favoured and widely distributed throughout Holland, Belgium and western parts of Germany.

In areas where flint did not naturally occur, hard stone of igneous or metamorphic origin was chosen to make axes which were usually carefully polished before use. Of the large number of sources identified as production centres, the most extensively studied is the quarry at Sélédin near Plussulien in the centre of Brittany, where a fine-grained dolerite was easily accessible. The quarry seems to have been in use from just before 4000 BC until as late as *c.*2200 BC. During this time extraction was on a very large scale, extending over an area of 100 ha (250 acres) with the nucleus concentrated within about a hectare. Between 80–100,000 tonnes of raw material was extracted, which, allowing for the inefficiencies of the production methods used, would have yielded about two million rough-out axes. If the quarry had been in use for the full two thousand years, the average output per year would have been about a thousand rough-outs or three per day.

Again we are faced with the question of how the quarries were managed –

whether by local specialists, or by groups coming from far and wide to make axes for a short period every year before returning home. The latter seems the more reasonable explanation since axe production as part of a seasonal assembly would explain why this one source was favoured above all others. The compulsion to use Sélédin dolerite may have come from its direct association with a prestigious meeting place rather than from any special quality of the stone itself or monopoly on production.

What stands out, besides the huge production, is the considerable area over which the axes were distributed, stretching from the Pyrenees to the west Midlands of Britain. It is a vivid demonstration of the mobility of artefacts passing from hand to hand through the networks of exchange.

While it may have been the significance of 'place' that gave Sélédin axes their particular value in the minds of those who acquired them, other types of stone may have been valued more for their unusual qualities. This would seem to be true of jadeite – a highly distinctive, greenish-coloured, fine-grained rock that could take a very high polish. The general term 'jadeite' is frequently used to cover a variety of metamorphic rocks including true jadeite, chloromelanite, nephrite, etc., but analysis has suggested that the great majority of the so-called 'jadeite' axes found in Europe are likely to have come from deposits in the Alpine area, more particularly in the Italian Piedmont and Liguria.

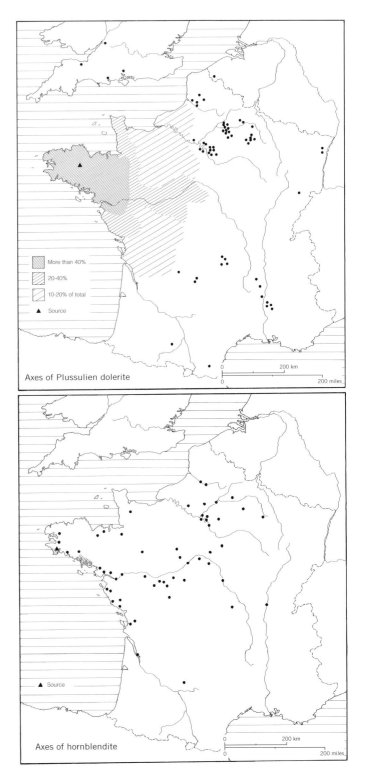

More than 40%
20-40%
10-20% of total
▲ Source

Axes of Plussulien dolerite

0 — 200 km
0 — 200 miles

▲ Source

Axes of hornblendite

0 — 200 km
0 — 200 miles

6.9 The distribution of jadeite axes from their source in the western Alps across Europe. The distribution vividly displays the exchange networks then in operation.

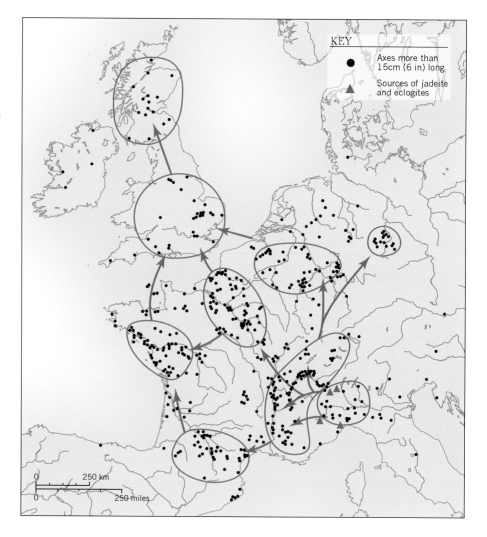

Jadeite was used to make axes and, more rarely, rings. The axes were widely distributed in Europe in the period 4700–3800 BC and most prolifically in the centuries from 4500 to 4300 BC. Several thousands of jadeite axes have been found in western Europe but the distribution is far from even. Small axes, presumably utilitarian examples, are found in some number in the Alpine region close to the sources, while larger, more fragile and highly finished examples tend to be found in more distant parts, extending from southern Italy to the north of Scotland, implying that these were more prestigious items distributed through networks of elite exchange. Many have been found in 'watery' contexts where they were probably deposited as gifts to the spirits of the places, while others were deposited in burials, particularly in the *grands tumuli* of the Carnac region of Brittany. Clearly jadeite axes were items greatly to be revered.

6.10 Finely finished jadeite axes were made in the western Alps and transported via the exchange networks across western Europe, some reaching as far afield as Scotland. The axes were items of considerable value and many were deposited in ritual contexts. These two fine examples were found in Scotland.

The Europe-wide distribution of the large prestigious jadeite axes is particularly revealing since it reflects the exchange networks then in operation. From the Alpine sources two main routes seem to have been followed. One passed through the Lower Rhône valley and the Languedoc, and by way of the Carcassonne Gap–Garonne–Gironde route to the Atlantic. Thence the axes were carried, most probably by sea, to the Loire valley and southern Amorica (Brittany) The second main route led up the Rhône–Saône valley and then bifurcated, with one branch leading to the Seine valley, and the other to the Rhine–Moselle valleys and beyond to Thuringia. From Amorica, the Seine valley and possibly the Rhine mouth, axes were carried to most parts of Britain, with a few reaching Ireland. This astonishing distribution pattern is the first full reflection of a network of exchange routes that is to recur many times.

By the mid- to late fifth millennium BC disparate communities, scattered across hundreds of kilometres, were linked, albeit loosely, in systems of reciprocal exchange through which commodities, and with them ideas and beliefs, could quickly spread. We will see later in this chapter and the next how these systems were further consolidated, leading to convergent developments in culture across extensive regions.

Glittering Metals

Humans find coloured stones attractive. Among the stones that stand out from the usual dun-coloured rocks, copper minerals – the bright green of malachite and the vivid blue of azurite – are among the most striking. It is easy to understand how such minerals, picked up as pebbles or chipped out of the living rock, may have been taken home and, by accident or design, may have been heated in an open hearth. In such circumstances, the minerals would, comparatively easily, have been reduced to metallic copper, itself a substance endowed with remarkable properties – it is shiny, reflective and malleable, and can be changed from solid to liquid and back again simply by the application and removal of extremes of heat.

While there is some evidence to show that copper was first being extracted in small quantities in Anatolia in the sixth millennium BC, the first large-scale production took place in the Balkans. The earliest mines so far discovered are at Aibunar near the town of Nova Zagora in north-western Bulgaria. Here the copper ore was dug out of the rock, leaving long, narrow trenches as much as 80 m (260 ft) long, from 3 to 10 m (10–33 ft) wide and up to 20 m (66 ft) deep. This was mining on a large scale involving a massive expenditure of labour. The Aibunar mines are dated to around 5100 BC and since the technology involved in casting the shaft-hole tools in two- or three-piece moulds was already quite advanced here, it is likely that even earlier workings remain to be discovered.

The copper tools found at Aibunar had been used in the mining process, but similar artefacts found elsewhere, particularly in graves, show little or no evidence of wear. Simple axes and chisels have also been found, again usually in burial contexts – in fact, the full range of common tools, previously made of stone, was now being made in copper. Yet, at this early stage, most copper implements were probably not meant to be used but were prestige goods symbolic of the power to command raw materials and the 'consolidated work' required to produce them.

The fifth-millennium copper production in the Carpatho-Balkan region was a remarkable phenomenon. While it is possible that some knowledge of the properties of brightly coloured copper ores had spread to Europe from

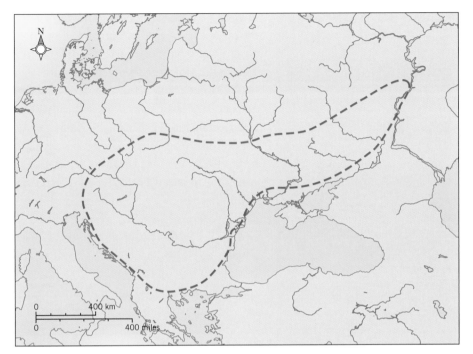

6.11 The extent of the Carpatho-Balkan metallurgical province showing areas maintaining contact with each other through exchange networks in the fifth millennium BC.

Anatolia in the late sixth millennium, the developments in the Balkans, both in the range of items made and the sheer volume of production, owed little to outside influence – we seem to be witnessing here an entirely indigenous development. What gave impetus to all this is a matter of guesswork. Most likely it was related to the rise of elites demanding new ways to display their power and the exalted status of their lineages. Yet this precocious production was short-lived, lasting only until about 3800 BC, after which output declined very rapidly and metallurgy all but disappeared for several centuries before it eventually got under way again, the specialist craftsmen now generating a different range of tools and weapons owing little to the fifth-millennium types.

In the period of their floruit the Carpatho-Balkan mines produced huge quantities of copper that was distributed through exchange networks over considerable territories reaching westwards to the flanks of the Alps and eastwards across the steppe, through Moldavia and Ukraine, as far east as the Volga. No doubt the metal was used in the reciprocal exchanges that served to give a degree of unity to this vast territory. In many ways the distribution of this early copper in eastern Europe was equivalent to the distribution of Alpine jadeite in the west.

The sudden development of copper production in the Balkans by indigenous communities may not be unique. Recently some evidence has been put forward from the site of Cerro Virtud in Almería in south-eastern Spain that

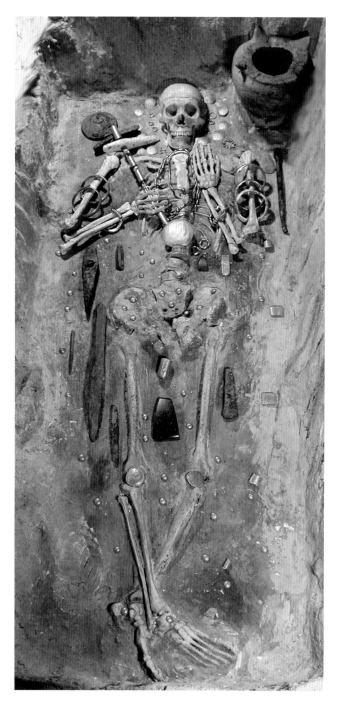

6.12 An elite burial from the cemetery at Varna on the Black Sea coast of Bulgaria. The burial, of a man in his mid-40s, is adorned with 990 separate gold objects as well as an impressive array of copper tools and weapons. The burial dates to about 4000 BC.

suggests copper was being extracted here as early as the early fifth millennium BC. It would not be at all surprising if the metal-rich regions of Iberia proved to be the centres of other autonomous copper industries, the necessary skills developing locally without reference to events in the Balkans.

The second metal to make a dramatic appearance in the Balkans in the fifth millennium BC was gold – a metal that would have been found in its native form in alluvial deposits and as veins exposed in bedrock. For the most part gold was used for small objects such as beads and bracelets or, in sheet form, as coverings for other objects or as attachments for clothing. The most dramatic example of the use of gold comes from a cemetery of some 280 burials excavated at Varna on the Black Sea coast of Bulgaria. More than half of the burials were accompanied by grave goods and of these eighteen were particularly rich. The most elaborate grave, that of a male 40–50 years old, produced nearly a thousand gold objects, mostly beads but also including rings, bracelets and a number of applied decorations for the hair, clothing and body, including a penis sheath. He was also provided with copper axes and other tools and a sceptre in the form of a perforated stone axe. The lavish use of gold was focused almost entirely on enhancing the body and its dress, but in two cases even the accompanying pottery was enlivened with gold sheet. The consumption of gold in the Varna cemetery was colossal: in all some three thousand items are recorded, weighing over 6 kg (13 lbs)! No sources are known in the immediate vicinity, the nearest being in south central Bulgaria.

Inventive Minds and New Technologies

The fifth millennium saw the development of many new technologies. The most dramatic was pyrotechnics – the skilful control of fire – to release copper from its ore and to transform its shape, and to create high-quality ceramics with carefully controlled surface colouration. These were specialist skills, though those involved may well not have worked full time at these crafts.

Equally far-reaching developments lay in the field of land transport with the appearance of the wheeled vehicle and the domestication of the horse. The earliest evidence for wheeled vehicles appears simultaneously in south-west Asia and in northern Europe about 3500 BC. In Mesopotamia pictographs representing four-wheeled wagons are found on tablets of the Late Uruk period while models of solid wheels, made from chalk and from clay, have been found in Syria and Turkey dating to a century or two later. The earliest European evidence consists of parallel wheel ruts from beneath a megalithic long barrow at Flintbek, near Kiel, and a pot from Bronocice near Cracow in Poland which is decorated with a schematic picture of a four-wheeled wagon. Both European finds are broadly contemporary with the Uruk pictographs. The likelihood is that the wheel was a Mesopotamian invention but new finds could well change our perception. By the beginning of the third millennium the idea had spread widely throughout Europe and the Pontic steppe. The earliest wheels were single-piece discs but these were soon augmented by composite wheels built of two or three pieces.

Wheeled vehicles soon spread across Europe and in the third millennium many clay models of high-sided four-wheeled carts are found throughout the Great Hungarian Plain and Transdanubia. Thereafter four-wheeled vehicles are found as a recurring motif in rock-art depictions in many regions. Mobility was important. The ability of a community to harness its ox-drawn carts and to transport goods opened up new opportunities for interaction and, where the terrain was open enough to permit passage, bulk commodities could now be moved over great distances. Mobility was becoming a feature of life.

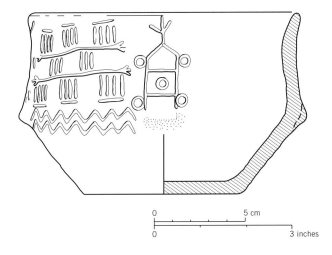

6.13 Early wheeled vehicles illustrated as pictographs (below) from the Late Uruk (mid-fourth millennium BC) in Mesopotamia and (above) on a pottery vessel of c.3500 BC from Bronocice, near Cracow, Poland.

6.14 Pottery cup in the form of a four-wheeled vehicle from Szigetszentmárton, Hungary dating to the early third millennium BC.

Parallel with these changes came the domestication of the horse. Wild horses roamed the steppe in large numbers and it was in this region that domestication, and later horse-riding, first took place. During the fifth millennium BC a distinctive culture – the Sredny Stog culture – emerged in the region between the Lower Dnepr and Lower Don valleys, spreading across a broad zone from the open steppe to the forest steppe. Sheep/goats, cattle and pigs were domesticated but horses were also vital to the community's well-being. Wild horses were hunted but there is also evidence that they were herded and that some were becoming sufficiently tame to be ridden. At one site, Dereivka, located above a tributary of the river Dnepr, perforated strips of antler have been found that are thought to have been the cheek pieces of simple bridles. At the same site the teeth of a stallion show a pattern of wear that probably resulted from chafing against a solid bit. These scraps of evidence, pointing towards the beginnings of horse-riding, date to c.4000 BC. Thereafter the successive peoples of the steppe became the most proficient horse-riders in Europe.

The advantages of horse-riding are obvious – speed of movement was greatly increased, probably as much as tenfold, and this new manoeuvrability allowed flocks and herds to be managed with much greater ease. When, later, horses were used for traction in place of paired oxen to pull vehicles, speed of transport also improved from around 25 km (16 miles) per day to between 50 and 60 km (31 and 37 miles). The trained, domesticated horse, therefore, offered many benefits and it is hardly surprising that horse-riding spread rapidly throughout Europe, reaching most parts by the end of the third millennium. The well-trained horse may itself have become a valuable item of exchange. It was probably in this way that riding horses were introduced into the Great Hungarian Plain and Transdanubia, in exchange for items of Balkan copper. In the more westerly parts of Europe indigenous wild horses – the successors of herds that had colonized Europe in Upper Palaeolithic times – were the stock from which domesticated horses arose. It was, therefore, the knowledge of horse-breaking, training and riding that spread to these parts rather than the beasts themselves.

One final 'technological advance' may be mentioned – the woolly sheep. The earliest sheep were hairy, rather than woolly. Wool-bearing sheep were first introduced into Europe from the Near East in the early part of the fourth millennium. These beasts could be plucked to remove the woolly undercoat, providing a fine fibre that could be beaten into a felt or spun into thread for weaving, opening up an 'industry' that has provided wealth for European communities ever since.

The Emergence of Europe-Wide Networks

With the increase in the production of 'rare commodities' such as easily worked flint, fine polished stone, copper, gold, trained horses, etc., exchange intensified and as a result networks of interaction became more far-reaching. In this way ideas and beliefs spread, creating the appearance of cultural similarity over very considerable regions. The flow of ideas and the acceptance of value systems were clearly a consequence of contact through the various exchange networks rather than folk movement. This is not to say that there was no mobility – ideas and commodities cannot move without the agency of people – but there is no need to call up mass migrations to explain change.

The Atlantic-Facing West

Many of the communities of the Atlantic-facing part of Europe, from south-west Portugal to southern Sweden, and including Britain and Ireland, adopted the practice of collective burial in chambers built of large stone slabs (hence *mega-lithic*). The earliest manifestations of this practice in the Upper Alentejo in Portugal and in Brittany date to the period 4700–4500 BC, while in some parts of the broader region megalithic tombs were still in active use up to the mid-third millennium.

The earliest megalithic tombs, known as passage graves, dating to *c.*4700–3500 BC, developed in regions where indigenous Mesolithic popula-tions were dense and had begun to adopt a more sedentary way of life. In the

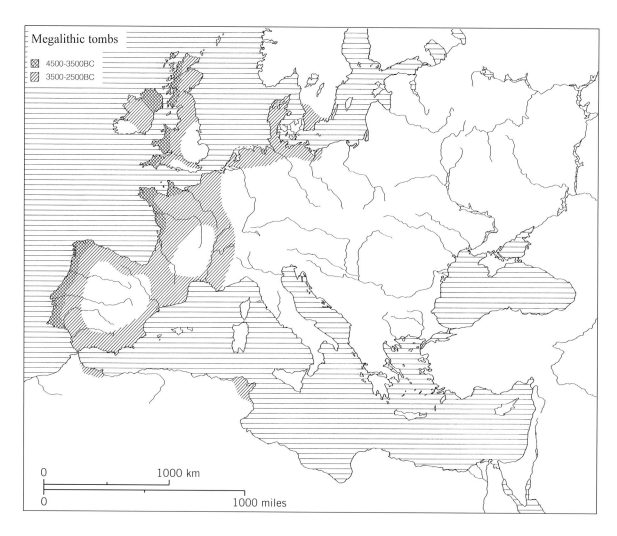

6.15 The distribution of megalithic tombs shows them to be essentially an Atlantic phenomenon. The earliest of the tombs – passage graves dating *c.*4500–3500 BC – have a maritime distribution, suggesting that the beliefs and technologies behind their construction were communicated along the Atlantic seaways.

following millennium megalithic tombs, now in the form of gallery graves, spread inland to cover much of Iberia and France as well as the Low Countries and northern Germany. In origin, therefore, the megalithic idea was inspired and developed among Atlantic coastal communities.

In addition to the megalithic tomb itself, long mounds associated with collective burial feature prominently in funerary ritual in the western parts of Europe. These mounds occur at least as early as megalithic architecture in areas like Brittany and western France, and are found throughout the megalithic zone as well as in areas beyond it. One view, which has much to commend it, is that the long mounds echo the shape of Early Neolithic longhouses of the LBK tradition and can therefore be considered as 'houses for the dead'. An alternative view is that the long mounds were a construct designed to replicate the elongated shell middens of the Mesolithic foragers. In Portugal and Brittany shell middens were places where the ancestors were interred and in the Téviec middens collective burial in stone-lined cists was also practised, lending some weight to the argument. The two interpretations are not necessarily mutually exclusive. The different manifestations of megalithic burial rites along the length of the Atlantic interface reflect the different patterns of interaction between indigenous belief systems and new ideas reaching the area as part of the 'Neolithic package'. Each region, indeed each micro-region,

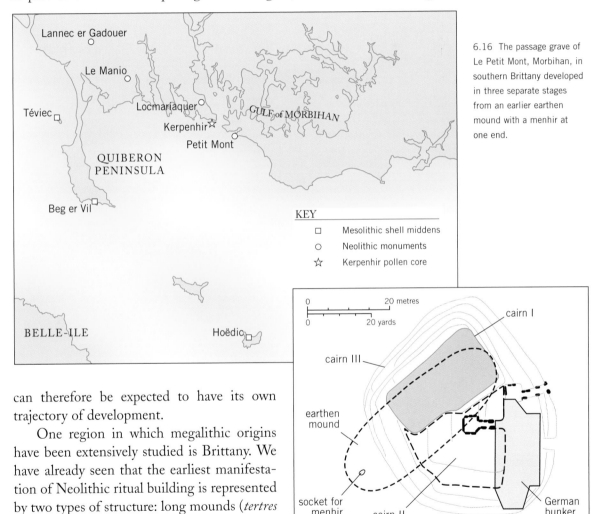

6.16 The passage grave of Le Petit Mont, Morbihan, in southern Brittany developed in three separate stages from an earlier earthen mound with a menhir at one end.

can therefore be expected to have its own trajectory of development.

One region in which megalithic origins have been extensively studied is Brittany. We have already seen that the earliest manifestation of Neolithic ritual building is represented by two types of structure: long mounds (*tertres tumulaires*) and menhirs. The long mounds were rectangular or trapezoidal constructions containing a variety of structures including hearths, settings of posts or stones and small stone-built cists (*coffres*) often containing human burials. Thus, they combine the stone-cist burial tradition and the idea of the long mound. However, in cases where it has been possible to observe carefully the

6.17 The distribution of megalithic tombs in Brittany clearly demonstrates that the earlier passage tombs have a very distinctive coastal distribution. The later gallery graves are more evenly spread which may reflect the expansion of communities into more inland areas.

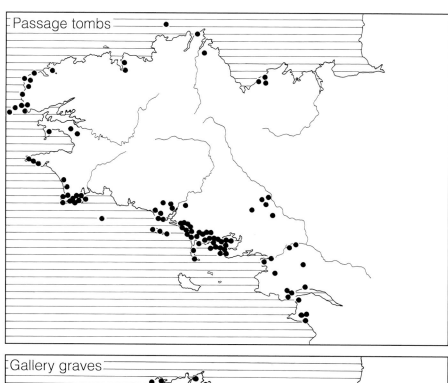

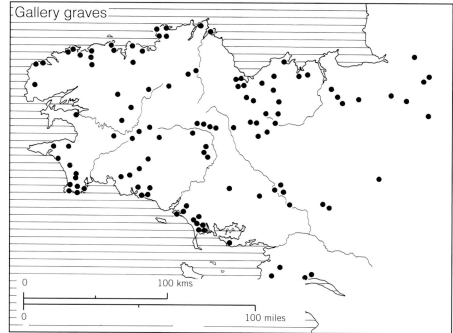

relationship of the mound and the burials within, it can be shown that the cists, often set within small circular mounds, predate the construction of the long mounds. Where dating evidence is available, most mounds fall within the period 4700–4400 BC. They are found exclusively in the Morbihan, overlooking the Baie de Quiberon and therefore represent a distinctive regional development. It was in much the same area that the menhirs, many of them decorated, were also found.

At some stage between 4000 and 3800 BC it is possible to identify a significant change in the burial architecture of the Morbihan. This is neatly exemplified by the tomb of Le Petit Mont which occupies a prominent position overlooking the entrance to the Gulf of Morbihan. The construction began as an earthen mound with at least one menhir placed at one end. The mound was then partially overlain by a stone-built cairn (Cairn I), which was later enlarged (Cairn II), this new structure containing a passage grave. In a final stage the cairn was again enlarged (Cairn III) to contain two separate passage graves. The original earthen mound probably dates to the mid-fifth millennium BC while the first of the passage graves dates to early in the fourth millennium. What is particularly interesting is that the passage graves incorporate three decorated menhirs. This same phenomenon is also recorded at three other passage graves in the Morbihan, Locmariaquer, Table des Marchands and Mané-Rutual, at all of which decorated menhirs are found to have been reused. The evidence, then, is clear enough. After a fifth-millennium phase of long mounds and menhirs, the menhirs (or at least some of them) were pulled down and incorporated into an entirely new form of burial monument – the passage grave. While the sequence could be interpreted as one of local development, it could equally well be seen to be the replacement of one ideological system with another.

To place the Morbihan sequence in its context it is necessary to look at the north-west coast of Brittany where radiocarbon dating suggests that passage graves were being erected before the middle of the fifth millennium, that is, several hundred years earlier than the passage graves of the Morbihan. The classic site here is Barnenez on the bay of Térénez, not far from Morlaix. The long stone cairn contains eleven passage graves, but is clearly a composite structure that has been extended over time. The core of the monument contained only three tombs, with radiocarbon dates suggesting construction around 4700–4500, while later extensions yield dates in the second half of the fifth millennium. Barnenez is not alone. At several other sites, also on the north coast of Finistère, passage tombs have produced dates indicating construction in the period 4500–4300.

Taken at face value, the evidence would seem to suggest that initially, in the fifth millennium BC, two very different mortuary traditions were practised in Brittany, and only by the turn of the millennium did the passage-grave tradition of the north-west spread to other coastal regions around the peninsula. This pattern – of many different regional traditions converging into one

6.18 The passage grave of Barnenez, near Morlaix in northern Brittany was discovered when a farmer began to dig a quarry into it for stone. Subsequent excavation showed it to be a complex of 11 separate passage graves set within a single mound extended over time. The monument occupies a prominent position visible from the sea.

– may well have been widespread along the Atlantic coastal zone; it is only when the evidence is of sufficient quality that such complexity can begin to be recognized.

In Portugal less can be said about the sequence of development. Megalithic tombs exist in some number, clustering in the Algarve, the Tagus estuary and the coastal regions of the Alentejo. There is much variation but most fall into three basic types: rock-cut tombs, simple dolmens and passage graves. Reliable construction dates are few but thermoluminescent dates of around 4500 BC for passage graves in the valley of the Guadiana suggest a broad contemporaneity with developments in Brittany.

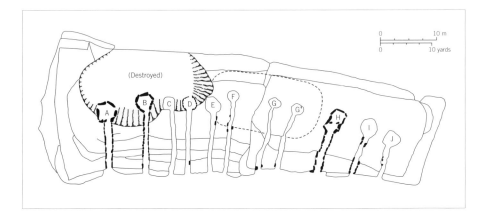

0   10 m
0   10 yards

(Destroyed)

6.19 Plan of Barnenez showing stages in the development of the tomb.

In Britain and Ireland, the 'Neolithic package' is not in evidence before *c.*4300 BC; megalithic tombs appear a few centuries later. Of the many types of tomb found in the islands, the earliest seems to be simple portal dolmens, comprising a single chamber flanked by a pair of monoliths, and the more complex passage tombs, characterized by a corridor leading to a central chamber. Both types have similar distributions in Cornwall, Wales, northern and eastern Ireland, and the west coast of Scotland and Orkney – a pattern that strongly suggests maritime introduction via the Irish Sea. The earliest dates for the construction of portal dolmens lie in the first half of the fourth millennium; before the end of the millennium the passage grave had developed to its most elaborate form with the great monuments of New Grange, Knowth and Dowth in the Boyne valley, Barclodiad-y-Gawres and Bryn Celli Ddu in north-west Wales, and Maeshowe in Orkney. These monuments represent the pinnacle of passage-grave development – embodying not only a massive expenditure of effort but also refined architectural technique, a sophisticated cosmology and, in some cases, highly complex pictorial expression in the form of rock engravings.

The North Sea and Baltic megaliths differ in many respects from those of the Atlantic. The first megaliths emerge in the Funnel Beaker Culture (TRB), resulting from the acculturation of the indigenous foraging groups and early farming communities. Within the broad zone of the TRB, which stretches across

6.20 Portal dolmens, like this example from Ballykeel, Co. Armagh, Ireland, are very simple structures which may be among the earliest megalithic monuments to be built in Britain and Ireland. The excavation of Ballykeel produced material of Early Neolithic date.

the North European Plain from Poland to the Low Countries, two distinct burial traditions emerge: burial beneath long earthen mounds and burial in stone-built chambers embedded in mounds. The long earthen mounds cover much of the TRB territory, while the stone-built chambers are restricted to Holland, the coast of north-eastern Germany, Jutland and the Danish islands and southern Sweden – a zone never far from the sea. The earliest of the northern megaliths are found on Zealand and were built about 3700 BC, while those in Holland (the *hunebedden*) are somewhat later, dating from 3400 to 3000 BC. In terms of the Atlantic sequence this northern group is late.

The use of the single term 'megalithic' for both the Atlantic and the northern groups of stone-built collective tombs implies that the phenomena are related. While it is quite possible that physical contacts were maintained between the two zones by way of the sea, there is no direct evidence to suggest that this was so. TRB burial rites were varied and differed from region to region. Collective burial was being practised beneath the long mounds, which suggests that, at least among some communities, the bones of ancestors were being collected together after exposure for final disposal. In such circumstances it would be quite natural for communities to develop accessible stone-built chambers within their long mounds so that the bodies of the dead could be deposited at any time. In other words, the rite of collective burial was the driver, the megalithic tomb the result.

The belief system manifest in the construction of the passage grave developed in the Atlantic zone, in Iberia and Brittany, in the first half of the fifth millennium. It embodied a complex cosmology that required some of the tombs to be set out so as to 'capture' the setting or rising sun on the midwinter or midsummer solstice. As part of this cosmology, linear and circular settings of standing stones were erected, the former most spectacularly in the Carnac region, and an intricate art developed involving the 'carving' and painting of the surfaces of the standing stones. This sophisticated complex of beliefs and practices was transported northwards, along the Atlantic sea routes, to Ireland and to western coastal regions of Britain in the last decades of the fourth millennium. Although there is much regional variation between the territories making up this Atlantic megalithic zone, the similarities are such that direct contact by sea must have been maintained over a period of time and in all probability these disparate regions remained in contact on a continuous basis. It is tempting to see cycles of exchange now being geared to religious ceremonies associated with the major monuments drawing people from considerable distances.

From the beginning of the fourth millennium BC the concept of collective burial in megalithic tombs and the associated belief systems spread eastwards, deeper into Europe. In Iberia collective burial was quickly adopted around the

Mediterranean coast as far as Catalonia, while in France it was by the rivers – the Garonne, Loire and Seine – that ideas spread, reaching the Rhône valley and the western flanks of the Alps. What we are seeing here is a flow complementary to that of the jadeite axes from the eastern Alps, which suggests that the Atlantic beliefs and the Alpine commodities used the same networks of exchange following the natural routeways across the peninsula. When discussing the distribution of jadeite axes, we noted that the network linked northwards to the Rhine valley and beyond. Perhaps it was in this way, as well as along the coastal routes, that knowledge of Atlantic concepts of collective burial quickened the development of megalithic tombs among the coastal TRB groups.

The patterns of interaction, sketched out here for the period 4500–2500 BC, are intricate. But the various strands of evidence tell much the same story: by the mid-third millennium the Atlantic zone of Europe had become linked by corridors of communication, by sea and by way of the great rivers, along which many commodities freely passed, and with them flowed knowledge, belief systems and values. The varied cultures of western Europe were now beginning to share many things.

The Corded Ware/Single Grave Culture

This somewhat cumbersome piece of archaeological terminology refers to a broad cultural continuum recognizable across a vast area of northern Europe, stretching from the Alpine Foreland to the vicinity of Oslo and from the Rhine valley to the Ukraine in the region of Kiev, with its influence spreading much further east through Russia to the Ural Mountains. The cultural continuum originates around 2900 BC and lasts, little changed, for about five hundred years. As the name implies, it is typified by a tradition of single burial with the body placed crouched in single graves or cists, sometimes enhanced with small circular mounds (or barrows) often arranged in groups. Men, women and children are buried in this way, the sexes sometimes being distinguished by different sets of grave goods. Most are accompanied by large beaker-shaped pots, often with their surfaces decorated with impressions of twisted cord applied when the pot was leather-hard before firing. Male graves often contained stone battle-axes and mace heads perforated in the centre to take a handle. These may have been symbolic of the status of the grave's occupant and are evidently copies in stone of the copper and bronze axes originating in the Carpathian region.

What are the origins of the Corded Ware/Single Grave culture? Most persistent has been the view that the culture represents an intrusion by people migrating from the Pontic steppe region; some have argued that it was by this

6.21 The distribution of Corded Ware in northern Europe in relation to the contemporary Yamnaya culture of the steppes.

6.22 Pottery drinking vessels and their associated stone battle-axes from Denmark belonging to the Corded Ware culture. From left to right the examples represent the Early, Middle and Late phases, spanning 3000–2400 BC.

means that the Indo-European language was introduced into peninsular Europe. Others have suggested that the culture developed in a core zone stretching from the mid-Rhine to southern Scandinavia and northern Poland, and that it spread out from there. But it may simply be that what we are observing in the Corded Ware/Single Grave culture is a unifying change adopted by a variety of different indigenous cultures giving the impression of cultural uniformity over a huge area of northern Europe.

Single burial and the symbolism of the beaker and the battle-axe represent a new set of values, widely adopted across northern Europe. The emphasis is no longer on ancestral tombs reflecting long lineages, but is now very much on the individual or the kin group. This could show a shift in values reflecting changes in landholding. The wooded landscape was fast being opened up and land was now being ploughed on a regular basis using the ox-drawn ards that were coming into use. With the open land came an increased use of wheeled vehicles, creating enhanced mobility. Perhaps land was now regarded as the property of the kin group, in recognition of the input of their labour in maintaining its productivity. The siting of burial mounds on tracts of abandoned arable (plough marks can be recognized under some of the barrows) may symbolize the close link between the individual and agrarian productivity. The other commonly found symbols of the burial – the beaker and the battle-axe – were no doubt redolent with meaning, the one perhaps reflecting hospitality (assuming the vessel to have held an alcoholic drink), the other denoting authority.

However one may view the origins and spread of the Corded Ware/Single Grave continuum, it represents the acceptance of a set of common values over a huge stretch of northern Europe in much the same way that the use of megalithic tombs did for western Europe. The megalithic tradition was, of course, much older in origin but for a brief period, in the first half of the third millennium, these two entirely different systems confronted each other. The dramatic changes that brought the old practice of collective burial in megaliths to an end and saw the further spread of the single-grave tradition will be considered in the next chapter.

The Balkans and the Steppe

The spectacular development of copper technology in the later part of the fifth millennium in the Balkans – rather grandly referred to as the Carpatho-Balkan Metallurgical Province – embraces a number of different regional cultures within the Carpathian arc. In parallel with its development, the great expanse of grassy steppe land extending from the Danube's mouth, around the north side of the Black Sea and eastwards to the Volga and beyond, was colonized by

communities of pastoral horse-herders. It was here that horses were domesticated not only for food but for riding. The open grassy landscape was ideal for travel on horseback while four-wheeled wagons pulled by paired oxen transported families and baggage at times of seasonal movement. Thus, there developed a very distinctive steppe culture. One defining characteristic was the pit-grave covered by wooden beams and marked by a large mound or kurgan. In some of these burials the wagon, whole or dismantled, was buried with the dead. In this early phase the complex is known as the Pit-grave, or Yamnaya, culture and is the beginning of a very long-lived steppe tradition.

Exchange networks developed between the copper-producing region and the steppe zone. This is most clearly shown by the distribution of copper items of Balkan origin in pit-graves: horses trained for riding may have been given in exchange. Relations between the two regions were active and probably involved the movement of groups of people migrating from the steppe, along the Lower Danube valley and into the Great Hungarian Plain. This is not particularly surprising since the plain is ecologically an extension of the steppe and would have supported a very similar lifestyle.

Compelling evidence for the westward movement of some steppe communities comes from burials. At Plachidol, in northern Bulgaria, a pit-grave 5 m (16 ft) deep had been set beneath a massive barrow 7 m (23 ft) high and 55 m (180 ft) in diameter. The skeleton, sprinkled with ochre pigment, lay upon what may have been a felt blanket in a lower pit with planks placed over the top. Two solid wooden wheels were then laid in two corners of the upper pit, presumably matched by another pair at the other end which were later destroyed. The burial, quite alien to the local burial tradition, closely resembles pit-graves from the steppe.

6.23 A silver bowl from a mid-third millennium BC burial at Maikop, Kuban, in south Russia. The craftsman depicts the two animals vital to the well-being of the community, long-horned cattle (seen on the side) and wild horses (on the opposite side), probably the *Equus przewalski*.

6.24
The gold bull, which formed part of the frame of a canopy in the Maikop burial, is a brilliantly observed model coming from daily familiarity with the animals.

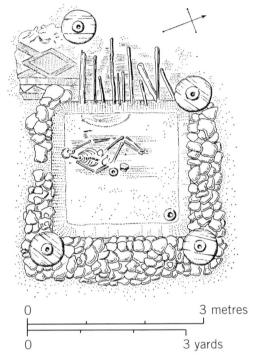

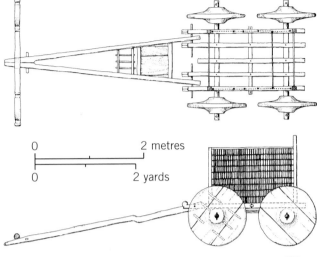

0   2 metres

0   2 yards

6.25 Vehicle burial from the pit grave of Tri Brata, Elista, Kalmyk, ASSR, dating to the third millennium BC. And, above, reconstruction of a four-wheeled wagon from a second millennium burial at Lchashen in Armenia.

6.26 Pit grave burial from Plachidol in northern Bulgaria, dating to about 3000 BC. The similarity to Tri Brata is striking.

0   3 metres

0   3 yards

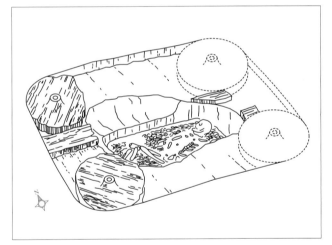

Other burials of a similar kind are found in Hungary, in the flood plain of the Tisza and Körös rivers. Dating evidence for the movement is imprecise but the Plachidol burial dates to around 3000 BC.

The close links between the steppe and the Great Hungarian Plain, and the westward movements of people from the steppe, is a recurring theme in the prehistory and early history of Europe. This steppe axis is one of the formative structures underlying European development.

The Mediterranean

In the Mediterranean region individual localities developed their own distinctive cultures in relative isolation. It is almost as if the sea and exploration no longer presented a challenge; status was now to be achieved in other ways.

Malta presents an extreme case. Malta and Gozo were colonized towards the end of the sixth millennium, most probably from Sicily, and thereafter maritime contact was maintained, no doubt as part of the exchange networks

associated with the movement of obsidian and stone axes. But after about 3600 BC links with the outside world waned and a period of isolation set in. Over the next thousand years or so Malta experienced a remarkable cultural development with the construction and subsequent elaboration of seventeen monumental stone-built temples. Although they differed in detail, they were all symmetrically built about a long axis and comprised pairs of lobes, sometimes with a terminal chamber giving rise to four-,

6.27 The distribution of Neolithic temples on Malta, dating to c.3500–2500 BC.

6.28 *Below:* The temple of Ħaġar Qim on the southern coast of Malta.

172

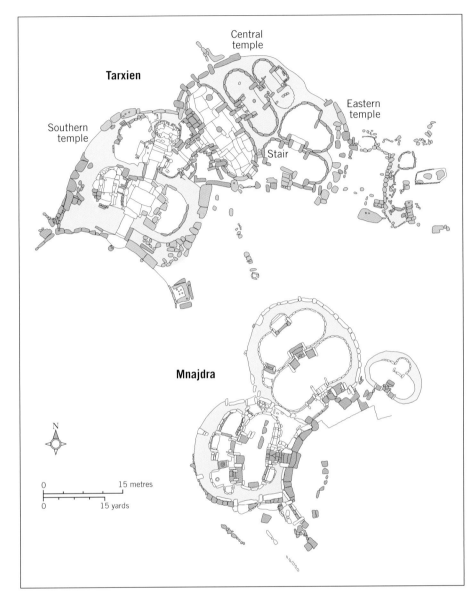

6.29 (Above) Plan of the Neolithic temple of Tarxien, Malta showing three conjoined buildings of broadly similar plan which had developed over time. (Below) The temple of Mnajdra is another composite structure that has grown over time, reflecting the longevity of these religious sites.

five- or six-lobed structures. Construction involved large orthostats of limestone with drystone walling between. Associated with the temples were massive sculptures of steatopygous (very fat) females, variously interpreted as mother goddesses or priestesses.

The Maltese temples are, by any standards, remarkable: they are unique and owe little to outside inspiration. It is tempting to explain them as the result of indigenous inventiveness, self-nurtured in a period of isolation. It could be that the increasing elaboration of the buildings reflected a competitiveness between different communities, but a more likely explanation is that the gradual environmental depletion of the islands drew the people to make ever-greater investments in religious worship. In the end their expectations were not met and a crisis ensued from which it took centuries to recover.

A quite different story can be told of another group of Mediterranean islands – the Cyclades in the south Aegean. Here, over the period 4500–2500 BC, the islands became increasingly enmeshed in a maritime network. The earliest evidence of maritime activity begins in the Mesolithic period with the exploitation of obsidian from the island of Melos and the fishing of tuna by the inhabitants of the Franchthi cave in the Argolid, but there is no suggestion that any of the islands were occupied at this time. Crete, to the south of the Cyclades and separated from the group by more than 150 km (94 miles) of open sea, was settled around 6000 BC by migrants, probably from Anatolia, and it may well be that Rhodes was settled at the same time – but of this there is as yet no evidence.

Communities began to establish themselves on the Cyclades in the fifth millennium (Late Neolithic). Most of the major islands in the Aegean were settled by c.3200 BC, with all but the smallest being occupied by c.2600 BC. Besides the generally benign character of the islands which favoured mixed farming, there were also other commodities to be had. The obsidian of Melos was an obvious attraction. Good marble was easily accessible on Naxos and Greater Paros. Naxos also had sources of emery for grinding stone. By the Early Bronze Age Kythnos was producing copper, while on Siphnos silver and lead were available and maybe a little copper. Finally, good potting clay was fairly widely distributed, with the best coming from the volcanic islands of Melos and Thera. Taken together, the Cyclades had much to offer.

The process of colonization still has to be reconstructed in detail, but on present evidence the first islands to be settled were not those closest to the Greek mainland but a group of medium to large islands at the south-east extremity of the group clustering around Naxos, which was evidently of central importance throughout. This might suggest that the original colonizers set off from the coasts and islands of Asia Minor, but the question is best left open pending more evidence.

Mastery of the sea was of crucial importance to the wellbeing of the island communities. Such was the combination of winds and currents that at most times during the year inter-island travel would have been possible, although most of the sailing probably took place in the period from May to September when conditions were at their best. Even then there would have been times when the weather conspired to make sailing inadvisable. Shorter island-hopping trips could have been made at any time provided conditions permitted, but for the longer voyages embedded in social systems of ceremonial

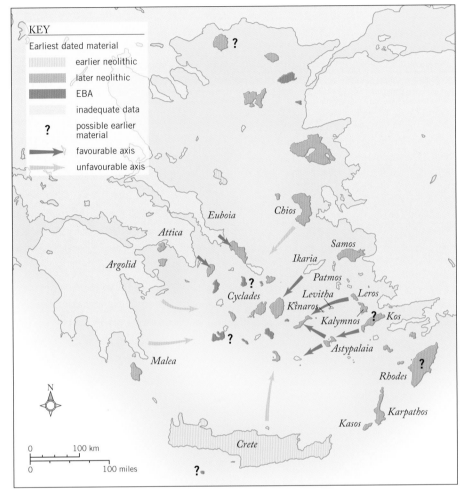

KEY

Earliest dated material

- earlier neolithic
- later neolithic
- EBA
- inadequate data
- ? possible earlier material
- favourable axis
- unfavourable axis

6.30 The Aegean islands seem to have been gradually colonized over a period of about 4000 years, starting with the settlement of Crete in the Early Neolithic period. The islands were more easily approached from the coasts of Asia Minor than from the Greek mainland.

exchange it is likely that set times were adhered to during the late summer months when the farming cycle allowed men to leave the land.

While the existence of sturdy seagoing vessels from as early as the Mesolithic period is not in doubt, there is no direct evidence for the form of the vessels until after 2600 BC, when a series of images inscribed on pottery and carved on rock become available. These artefacts strictly date to the developments described in the next chapter, but the boat-building traditions depicted are likely to have been rooted in the much earlier period. Two types of vessel have been identified: small canoes and more elegant long boats. The small canoes probably represent vessels used for local everyday activities such as fishing trips or hauling cargoes. One rock carving from Naxos actually shows what appears to be the loading of an animal. The long boats are often depicted on flat pottery vessels (inaccurately referred to as frying pans)

and are far more sophisticated structures, with a raised stem and a high stern post surmounted by a fish emblem. They would have been about 15–20 m (50–65 ft) in length, sufficient to accommodate twenty-five or so rowers whose presence is indicated by schematic oars. Sophisticated long boats of this kind may well have been developed for the ceremonial interactions between the islands characteristic of the more complex social systems that were to flourish in the latter part of the third millennium. For the communities of the Cyclades the period 4500–2500 BC was a time when their maritime culture was fast evolving – this was a prelude to the spectacular cultural developments of the full Aegean Bronze Age, to be considered in the next chapter.

6.31 Cycladic boats of the Early Bronze Age are frequently depicted on pottery 'frying pans'. The above example is from the Chalandriani cemetery on Syros. The illustrated vessels are clearly narrow-bodied rowing boats with high decorated prows.

The Transformation of Early Europe

The eighteen hundred years or so covered by this chapter were a time of dramatic transformation across the face of Europe. Populations expanded, new landscapes were occupied and new technologies were developed and disseminated. The extraction and working of copper and gold, and the introduction of woolly sheep and ox-drawn ards contributed to the greatly increased productivity of the times, while four-wheeled carts, horse-riding and sophisticated boat-building and navigation enhanced mobility, enabling commodities, people and ideas to move with rapidity over long distances.

The European landscape now supported a bewildering number of different communities, each with its own distinctive package of material culture, belief systems and social practices. But over and above these local variations it is now possible to discern more widespread configurations reflecting a greater level of interaction and leading to the adoption of patterns of behaviour and belief across extensive territories. The megalithic zone of the Atlantic seaboard, the Corded Ware/Single Burial zone of northern Europe, the precocious copper users of the Carpatho-Balkan zone and the horse-herding pastoralists of the steppe are among the more significant of the new configurations. But nothing was static: it was a time of change. The rise of the Corded Ware/Single Burial zone overlapped with the end of the megalithic tradition. By the end of the third millennium the western collective-burial tradition had been replaced by single burial similar to that of the Corded Ware zone but characterized by the bell beaker. Meanwhile, in the southern part of the Aegean, a new island culture was forming that was soon to blossom into Europe's first 'civilization'.

Within these broad cultural patterns and trajectories we can see the social fabric of Europe beginning to take shape. It was conditioned, as always, by the nature of the landscape, which determined the lines of communication, and by the uneven distribution of rare resources such as stone and metal, but these geographical 'givens' were now an essential part of the emerging social landscapes. The Europeans of the third millennium had achieved a new level of equilibrium with their environment.

Finally, how much had developments in south-west Asia influenced Europe at this time? The answer would seem to be very little. Woolly sheep are one possible benefit and it may be that solid-wheeled vehicles were first developed in the Trigris and Euphrates valleys and that some knowledge of the benefits of copper may have been learnt from Anatolia. But, that said, the development of European culture was *sui generis*: there is nothing to suggest that its creative energies and trajectories were in any way driven from the east. Europe at this time had a momentum of its own.

CHAPTER SEVEN

Taking to the Sea – Crossing the Peninsula: 2800–1300 BC

The period before us, c.2800–1300 BC, saw the pace of change intensify. At the beginning, a kaleidoscope of different cultural groups were scattered across the face of the peninsula. All were rooted in the past, intent on maintaining their distinct cultural identities. But already networks of interaction linked them loosely together, facilitating the flow of desirable commodities such as copper, gold, amber and finely polished stone. The degree of interconnectedness varied, but no community could be said to be completely isolated. By the end of the period Europe's first 'civilization', centred on Crete and named Minoan by archaeologists after the mythical figure King Minos, had come and gone and the face of European society had changed for ever. A rigorously hierarchical system now prevailed across much of the peninsula, evident in the burial record with its emphasis on the elite, while the exchange networks saw a flood of varied commodities transported over very considerable distances. It was almost as though the natural routeways of Europe had coalesced into one great system of intercommunications. And with the new connectedness came individual mobility on an ever-increasing scale. The continent was diversifying and pulling together at the same time.

7.1 *Opposite:* The sacred enclosure of Stonehenge, situated on Salisbury Plain in the centre of Wessex, was first laid out in the Neolithic period about 3000 BC, but the stones which now dominate the site were put up several centuries later. Bluestones were brought from south-west Wales c.2600 BC but these were rearranged when the Sarsan circle and the great trilithons were erected c.2500 BC. Thereafter Stonehenge remained in active use as a religious centre for 800 years.

Bronze Age Dynamics: An Outline

What characterizes the development of Europe in the third and second millennia BC is the speed of change evident in virtually every region. There is a feeling of energy, of vigour and of a real enthusiasm for innovation and change. It is almost as if the old – that which is traditional and ancestral – is deliberately put aside as communities embrace a pan-European spirit, not because of any political desire for unity, but rather for the excitement of the new. The European world was beginning to open up. This was not a sudden development. Already in the fourth millennium connections along the Atlantic seaways were allowing belief systems to spread rapidly over great distances and at the beginning of the third millennium the Corded Ware/Single Grave culture saw the practice of single burial, and with it a new attitude to the significance of the individual, extend across large parts of the North European Plain. What happens now, towards the middle of the third millennium, is an escalation in these processes of change.

Behind it all lies a stable economic base founded on food production. Livestock were now playing a more significant part, not just for their eventual meat yield but for a variety of ancillary products: wool, milk and its derivatives, and also blood, a useful source of salt that could be tapped from a living beast. It was probably in this period that the European population finally developed lactose tolerance and woollen fabrics became a commodity capable of being produced in surplus and traded in bulk. The beasts, when finally slaughtered, contributed to the all-important feast, which was central to the workings of society.

A stable economic base, allowing the holding capacity of the land to rise, favoured a growth in population and, where the land was especially fertile, could have allowed segments of the population to spend less time engaged in the daily tasks of food production. One of the results of all this was that society now had more energy to invest in social pursuits – feasting and cere-monial – and on creative tasks such as developing technologies and adding value to products by finessing their form and finish. These two strands, each enhancing the other, led to hot spots of innovation springing up across the face of Europe. The most spectacular of these was the palace-centred society that emerged in Crete in the second millennium – the 'Minoan civilization' – but many other communities throughout Europe enjoyed a creative momentum of their own.

Over much of Europe it is possible to distinguish elites through their distinctive, well-furnished burials, often given added prominence by large barrows built over them to create a monument ever-present in the group consciousness. These barrows would have served as time-markers, enabling societies to demonstrate – and to declaim – their history in terms of promi-nent ancestors and tales of their heroic pursuits.

It is likely that the paramount leaders were regarded as semi-supernatural beings, serving both secular and religious functions. But in complex societies, like those of the Egyptians or the Near Eastern states, a more developed hier-archy existed, with a king at the top exercising divine powers and a separate theocracy performing other functions below him. In the Minoan world, power was vested in a theocratic chiefdom comparable to those evident in other parts of Europe at the time; but with power more centralized and systems more complex, it is possible that some separation of functions had begun.

One of the characteristics of more hierarchical societies is the imperative for the elite to distinguish themselves from lesser beings by their ability to control the flow of desirable goods, their command of knowledge and their

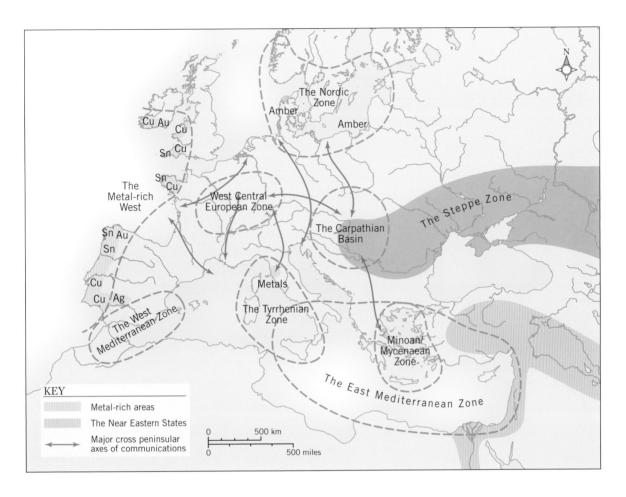

7.2 Europe in the period 2800–1300 BC. The ocean interfaces now support very distinct cultural zones, bound together by maritime exchange networks. These zones are variously linked to centres of innovation occupying route nodes in the heart of Europe.

physical prowess in leadership and battle. This imperative in turn led to a far greater flow of commodities and encouraged mobility among the elite.

Networks of exchange had long been in operation. What changed now was the extent of those networks and the sheer volume of materials that flowed through the arteries of Europe. Most important was bronze – the alloy of copper and tin – an attractive metal, gold-like in colour when untarnished and capable of taking a fine polish. In Europe, once full tin-bronze (*c.*90 per cent copper and 10 per cent tin) had been developed, it was adopted universally, replacing unalloyed copper and the arsenical alloys. The earliest appearance of a regular bronze-using economy is to be found in Britain and Ireland in the period 2200–2000 BC, after which it spread eastwards and southwards through Europe, reaching all parts by 1400–1300 BC. Since the constituents of bronze were not widely found, and tin was (and is) exceedingly rare, bronze took on value as a prestige commodity. Once established, it became highly desirable and the movement of the metal as ingots or as scrap or finished items became widespread. Many other commodities now entered into the exchange networks in quantity: gold, silver, amber, furs, horses, textiles, oils and exotic stones like lapis and amethyst are all evident in the archaeological record.

The movement of materials in bulk required efficient modes of transport. Bullock-carts were already widely in use and we may suppose that packhorses and donkeys had by now become common. Transport by water was easier and river routes would have begun to come into their own. Maritime networks were also enhanced and seagoing ships become more visible in the archaeological record. In pictorial form, they occur inscribed on pottery vessels in the Cyclades, painted on pottery and in frescoes in Minoan contexts, and carved into hard rock along the coastline of southern Scandinavia. Actual vessels have been found in estuarine mud at various locations around the coasts of Britain, most spectacularly at Ferriby on the Humber estuary and at Dover, while wreck sites, largely devoid of their timberwork, have been identified at Cape Gelidonya and Uluburun off the southern coast of Turkey, and off Sozopol on the Black Sea coast of Bulgaria. The dramatic increase in evidence for seagoing vessels no doubt reflects both the heightened awareness that communities now had of maritime travel and an actual increased commonness of the vessels themselves. There were notable improvements in shipbuilding technology, not least with the introduction of the sail in the east Mediterranean by about 2000 BC – a technique developed in Egypt and quickly adopted by Levantine shipping.

Knowledge, particularly knowledge of distant places and people, became a desirable attribute for those who aspired to power. An overseas expedition mounted by the Greek elite provides the storyline for Homer's *Iliad*, while in the *Odyssey* the hero, Odysseus, attains greatness through his tireless adventures and his survival skills. He returns home not only with honour, but with new knowledge of the alien, awe-inspiring world beyond. That these stories could be told shows that there were audiences who revered the nobility achieved from undertaking voyages into the unknown.

Emerging elites, competition for luxury goods and a new socially determined mobility created a world in which innate aggression could easily flare up into outright warfare. Of this there is ample evidence in the huge quantities of arms and armour found throughout Europe. Short daggers give way to swords suitably weighted for thrusting and for slashing blows; the battle-axe is everywhere present while body armour becomes increasingly common. Although the full panoply of arms and armour developed in the centuries after 1300 BC, the archaeological record is already redolent with signs of aggression.

Mobility begins to break down the earlier cultural isolation. In the west, for example, the 'bell beaker' – a highly distinctive ceramic vessel type – gains wide popularity. It is one of the items accompanying single inhumation burials together with bronze daggers and archers' gear. While some limited movement of people may well have been involved in the spread of the so-called 'beaker package', what we are seeing is the uptake of a value-system by local societies in accordance with their own needs and beliefs. Thus, over a wide area of western Europe, 'beaker' culture traits are shared by diverse groups. Much the same can be said of the Corded Ware/Single Grave culture that emerged in the North European Plain at the beginning of the third millennium (see pp. 167–9) and was adopted by indigenous cultures in a swathe from Holland to Russia. Another broad cultural zone stretched from the Carpathian Basin eastwards to the Urals, characterized by distinctive single-bladed bronze battle-axes made in a variety of regional styles, and the use of horses for riding and for pulling two-wheeled vehicles with spoked wheels. It would be wrong to suggest that these zones represented single ethnic or political entities, or even thought of themselves as a unified people. At best they are zones of interaction, selectively sharing aspects of culture, linked by networks along which goods and ideas were exchanged: they reflect the inter-connectedness that now characterized Europe.

Meanwhile in the East . . .

How far were the changes taking place in Europe the direct result of developments in south-west Asia and Egypt? The Minoan world had developed links with Anatolia and Egypt and by 1300 BC maritime systems were linking the coastal regions of the east Mediterranean in cycles of exchange. This much is not in doubt. But what effect, if any, the enhanced 'trade' with the east had on Aegean developments is less clear. Few would now argue that the impetus for the spectacular Minoan civilization came from outside, though it is quite likely that becoming part of an enlarged trading system helped stimulate the Minoan economy. Beyond that, in 'barbarian' Europe, there is no need to see the various innovative changes in economy, technology and social structure as anything other than the result of indigenous energies.

South-west Asian and Egyptian societies underwent a period of rapid change. In Mesopotamia the third millennium saw the emergence of the Sumerian city-states, culminating in the Akkadian Empire, while in Egypt, in its relative isolation, the pharaonic system of the Old Kingdom flourished. During this time trading systems were established, extending eastwards and down the Persian Gulf to the Indus valley civilization, and westwards across Asia Minor. The Levantine coast of the Mediterranean now became an important route linking Egypt into the broader network.

The centuries 2300–1900 BC saw widespread social disruption. In Mesopotamia the Akkadian Empire came to a sudden end about 2200 BC. In

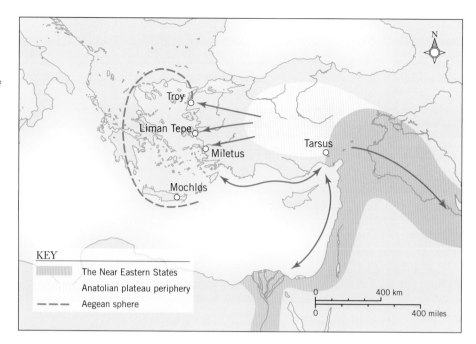

7.3 Anatolia served as a link between the Near Eastern states and the Aegean sphere. A number of trading ports developed through which trade and exchange were articulated.

Egypt the Old Kingdom ended in 2125 BC and a century and a half of instability ensued, while in the Levant many cities were abandoned at this time. What caused the crisis is uncertain but there is growing evidence to indicate a severe and sudden change in the climate, heralding a period of greater aridity. By 1900 BC, however, recovery was well under way. In Egypt the New Kingdom was established in 1975 BC, and in Mesopotamia new people – the Amorites – established many cities in the south, among which Babylon, under its king, Hammurabi (1792–1750 BC), became dominant. In northern Mesopotamia the city of Assur, commanding the routes between southern Mesopotamia and Anatolia, rose in importance, by the middle of the millennium becoming the centre of growing Assyrian power, while in Anatolia the fast-developing trade networks gave increasing prominence to the city of Hattusa which had become the centre of the Hittite Empire by 1650 BC.

The names of the different polities and their rulers abound and the inter-relationships between them, political, economic and military, are intricate in the extreme. What is significant for us is that, in the period of recovery, c.1900–1300 BC, the three great centres of innovation – Mesopotamia, Egypt and Anatolia – became consuming societies on a gigantic scale, needing to be fuelled by commodities from far and wide. The lands around the eastern end of the Mediterranean had now been gathered into their sphere to create a single, linked maritime interface stretching from the Dardanelles in the north-west to the Nile delta to the south-east. It was through the many ports along this sinuous littoral that exchanges with the maritime communities of Europe were to be articulated.

The Eastern Mediterranean: Minoans and Mycenaeans

The Cyclades

The Cycladic Islands had the advantage when it came to developing competence to cross the seas. In the earlier period, *c.*3100–2700 BC, long boats powered by many rowers were already actively in use for inter-island journeys, facilitating cycles of reciprocal exchange interspersed with periodic bouts of raiding.

In the period that followed, *c.*2700–2200 BC, a new internationalism becomes apparent, manifest in the growth of settlements within and around the Aegean at nodal points on the mainland coast where land routes reached the sea and on the islands where maritime routes coalesced. The best-known example of such a site is Troy, guarding the Dardanelles. Here, in the phase designated Troy II, a defended citadel, comprising a row of well-built megaron-style houses, rises above a settlement spread at its base. The style and quality of the buildings and the surprising amount of gold vessels and jewellery found in the ruins leave little doubt that the city was in the hands of an elite with access to conspicuous wealth. So too at Lerna, on the Argolid, where a substantial rectangular house – known as 'The House of Tiles' and comparable in size to the megarons at Troy – has been found. From its ruins were recovered a number of clay seals, the detritus from the process of registering, recording and securing goods in transit. Some of these new 'international' sites grew to considerable proportions: Manika, controlling the seas between the Greek mainland of Attica and the island of Euboea, covered 50–80 ha (125–200 acres).

That there was now much greater mobility within the Aegean is apparent from the distribution of artefacts. People were also on the move. At Agia Photia, close to the north-west extremity of the island of Crete, a cemetery has been found embodying practices and materials quite alien to the rest of Crete but closely similar to those of sites in the Cyclades. Here, surely, is evidence for a colony of Cycladic traders who had established themselves in a convenient location to exploit the maritime systems linking Crete and the Anatolian coast.

Later, in *c.*2500–2200 BC, a significant change can be recognized in the Cyclades represented by the appearance of a distinctive array of pottery known as the Kastri group (after a fortified settlement on the island of Naxos) found spread widely across the islands, extending to the mainland of Attica. These vessels, designed for pouring and drinking, were made with a mono-chrome black or brown burnished surface in imitation of metal vessels and are clearly derived from Anatolian prototypes. At broadly the same time many

185

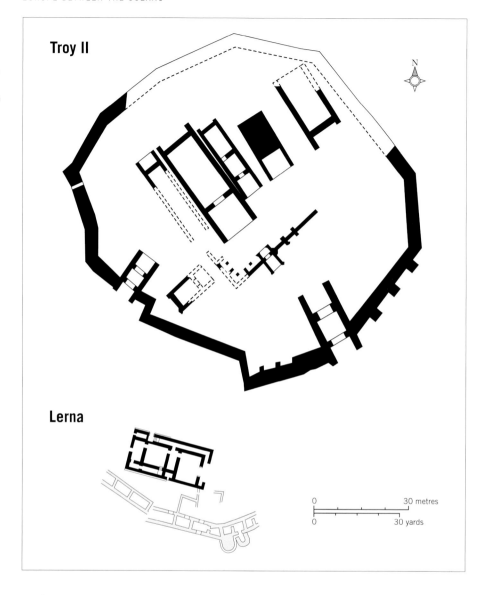

7.4 Elite enclaves of this period, like Troy and Lerna, are now fortified by strong defensive walls. Within, the prime house, or megaron, dominates the settlement.

settlements were abandoned and a wholly new type of settlement with strong fortifications makes an appearance; Kastri is one of the best-known examples. These changes have been interpreted by some archaeologists as evidence of an intrusion of alien groups from the Anatolian coast lands. This is possible but it could equally be that greater access to Anatolia through the exchange networks led to the adoption of Anatolian drinking rituals, while the dislocation in settlement pattern may have been a result of internally generated social stress; the changes need not have been related.

At about this time the maritime interactions between the Cyclades and Crete change significantly. While Crete is still in receipt of Cycladic copper

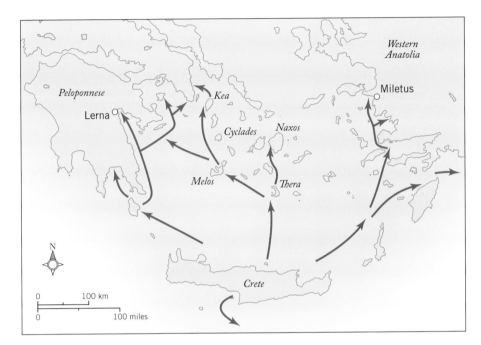

7.5 By the end of the third millennium Crete has begun to dominate the Aegean maritime trade networks, benefiting from its central position and productivity to engage directly with the islands and the Greek and Anatolian mainlands.

and obsidian, no other Cycladic goods are found at Cretan sites in contrast to the preceding period. The implication would seem to be that the Cretans were making voyages to the Cyclades in search of raw materials but were no longer prepared to receive Cycladic shipping. In other words, the Cretans were beginning to develop their own exclusive maritime networks. The establishment of a strong Cretan presence, possibly even a colony, on the island of Kythera off the coast of the Peloponnese is a further indication of the newly emerging maritime aspirations of the Cretans. The Cretan challenge to the southern part of the Cycladic maritime network may explain the settlement changes apparent on the Cyclades. With their cycles of voyaging now curtailed, the elite systems of the islands would have been put under stress, creating severe inter-island rivalries. The emergence of strongly fortified settlements thus becomes more understandable.

The following period, 2200–1900 BC, saw a collapse in the dispersed settlement system of the Cyclades and the emergence of a few large centres. This coincides with widespread dislocations in Egypt and south-west Asia, there ascribed to a sudden climatic change to more arid conditions. Whether or not climatic fluctuations were a significant factor in the Cyclades is less clear. It could be that the changes were simply a continuation of trends already under way in the preceding period as the traditional canoe-based maritime systems came under increasing stress. Another factor that had a profound impact was the introduction into Aegean waters of the deep-hulled sailing

7.6 Cast of a Minoan seal stone showing a sailing vessel with a central mast. Vessels of this kind would have been capable of making longer journeys and carrying more bulky cargoes than the earlier rowing boats.

ship. The depiction of these sailing vessels on Cretan seals around 2000 BC shows that the islanders had adopted the technology of the so-called 'Byblos ships' that had been active in the sea lanes linking the Nile delta and the Levantine coast from the middle of the third millennium. These vessels, with their centrally placed, square-rigged sails and deep plank-built hulls, were greatly superior to the traditional Cycladic canoes. In fair weather they could travel at speed over much greater distances, and since the ships' crews were far fewer in number than a full complement of rowers, and the vessels were anyway of increased capacity, they could carry a greater bulk of cargo and stay at sea longer. The Cycladic canoe was no match for these revolutionary vessels.

The appearance of deep-hulled sailing vessels in the Aegean was a death blow to the long-established social systems of the Cyclades based on prowess gained by taking part in canoe flotillas to distant islands. The new ships needed proper anchorages at deep-water harbours. This in turn encouraged the nucleation of settlements around ports, and as greater quantities of supplies could be transported with ease, so the population of the port settlements grew, increasing security in the event of attack. The changes set in train by the advent of the sailing ship were profound indeed.

The Cycladic network continued for a while, though in a modified form, linking the islands and the adjacent mainland to the east and west. This was the situation around 2000 BC as the Aegean world was poised on the brink of dramatic change. For the next half-millennium, Minoan Crete was to assume hegemony of the southern Aegean – an interlude remembered in the later Greek tradition as the 'Thalassocracy of Minos'.

Crete and the Minoans

The discovery of an advanced Bronze Age culture on Crete, which could justifiably be called a 'civilization', began with the excavations of Sir Arthur Evans at Knossos in 1900. Since then numerous expeditions have expanded our understanding of the spectacular world of the Minoans – a name chosen with insight and panache by Evans though with little basis other than in mythology. A detailed discussion of Minoan Palatial society is not possible within the limits of the present book, but a brief sketch must be given before we can consider its place in the development of the Aegean Bronze Age.

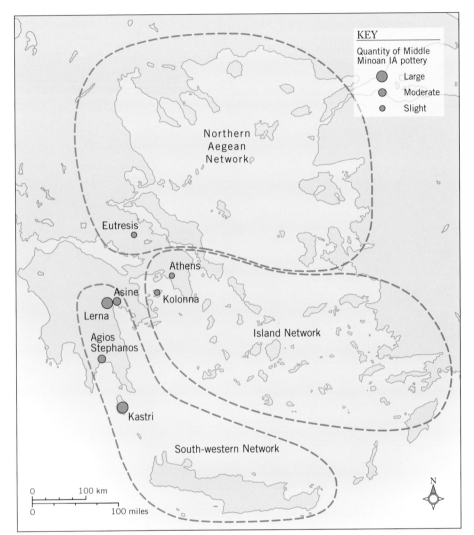

7.7 By the beginning of the Middle Bronze Age, *c*.2000 BC, three distinct trading networks had emerged in the Aegean and are clearly reflected in the archaeological evidence.

Until *c*.2000 BC Crete played a relatively minor role in regional developments, not least because of its comparative isolation. But with the advent of the deep-hulled sailing ship, able to make longer journeys at greater speeds, the position of the island, conveniently placed between the Aegean, Anatolia and Egypt, began to give it an advantage in the more adventurous long-haul journeys now becoming the norm. The island soon began to assume a central position in the trading networks. The period 1950–1700 BC saw the development of a series of monumental regional centres, usually referred to as 'palaces', at Knossos and Mallia on the north coast of the island and at Phaistos on the south coast. These palaces were surrounded by much larger settlements. Some time around 1700 BC there was a devastating earthquake that caused extensive

7.8 The palace of Knossos has been extensively excavated and is now displayed to the public. The aerial photograph gives a clear idea of the extent of the palace and the way in which it is arranged around a large central court.

destruction, but such was the stability of the society that the palaces were immediately rebuilt and new ones were erected at a number of other sites, including Kato Zakros at the eastern end of the island and probably at Chania in the north-west. These sites continued to flourish until *c*.1450 BC when they were destroyed in what appears to have been a single phase of conflagration, though whether through a natural catastrophe or as a result of human activity is unclear. Only Knossos was rebuilt after the destruction. The historical sequence is, therefore, comparatively simple, with two Palatial phases, Old and New, followed by a Post-Palatial phase to accommodate the last stage of the occupation at Knossos lasting to *c*.1050 BC.

The palaces are generally similar in form and comprise a number of different functional areas. Focal to them all is a large, open central court around which are rooms for residential, ceremonial, performance, manufacturing and

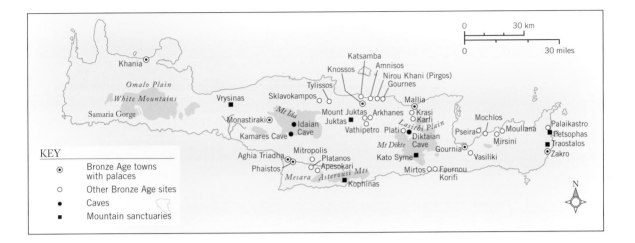

7.9 Crete in the Bronze Age showing the distribution of the palace centres and the mountain sanctuaries.

storage use. Storage facilities are particularly impressive, providing space for ranks of large storage jars (*pithoi*) and rows of below-ground silos and granaries. At Knossos the silos in the west court could hold sufficient grain to feed eight hundred people for a year. The discovery of stamped seals together with lists written in various scripts (hieroglyphic, Linear A and Linear B) shows that complex systems of control and accounting were in operation. Evans was probably correct in his assumption that the palaces were the residences of the elite – the kings and sub-kings – but they were also centres of communal storage and redistribution: places where commodities in the form of tithes or gifts could be assembled and controlled, later to be redistributed by means of direct gifts to equals or in recognition of services, or more indirectly by the provision of feasts. In the palace workshops, raw materials were converted by resident craftsmen into commodities of enhanced value. In the great courtyards performances and religious ceremonies could be staged in the presence of the elite and here, or in the secondary courtyards attached to some palaces, emissaries and subordinates could be given audiences. In other words, the palaces were central sites where all the functions necessary to the maintenance of the state could be enacted.

The palaces, and the cities that grew up around

7.10 *Below:* The Linear A script inscribed on a clay tablet found in Aghia Triada, on the southern coast of Crete.

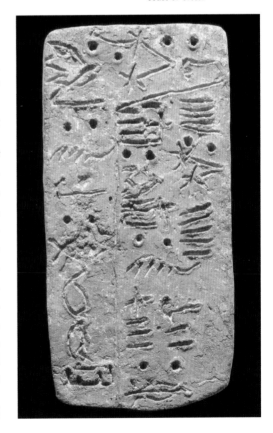

them, were only one element of the settlement system. There were also small towns like Gournia, Palaikastro and Myrtos, each clustered around a central courtyard house, most likely the residence of a local community leader who perhaps served as an administrator answering to the palace authority. And in the surrounding countryside were many isolated farms like the small establishment at Vathypetro with its storeroom full of *pithoi*, its olive and grape presses, and cluster of sheds and barns. The landscape was settled, ordered and productive, and well able to support the complex state system that had emerged with its many groups of full-time specialists – priests, scribes and recordkeepers, wall painters, stonecarvers, potters, bronzeworkers, seal-stone engravers, jewellers and many others. Each of the palace centres would have been self-contained under its own ruler, but it is quite probable that all were subservient to the king in residence at Knossos.

Overseas trade seems to have intensified over time. Already in the Pre-Palatial period an enclave of Minoan traders lived on Kythera and in the mid-sixteenth century it seems that another group settled in the Nile delta at Tell el Dab'a, where wall paintings in Minoan style have been found. Other enclaves may well have gained a foothold on the coasts of western Anatolia. Minoan pottery has been found at several sites, including the ports of Miletus, Iasos and Knidos.

Imports to Crete abound. Large oxhide ingots of copper have been found at Aghia Triadha, Tylissos and Zakros which isotopic analysis shows probably came from south Russia or Afghanistan. Afghanistan was also the source of the lapis lazuli and quite possibly the tin arriving on the island. These commodities would have travelled over land by well-established routes through Anatolia to one of the west-coast ports and thence by ship to Crete. Silver came from the Laurion mines in Attica and from the island of Siphnos. Fine stone for making vessels arrived from Greece and from Egypt: Egypt may also have been the source of the gold used in small quantities in the palace workshops and of elephant ivory, as well as of finished items including stone vessels, statues, scarabs and other small trinkets.

In return Crete had much to offer: woollen fabrics, wine, olive oil, scented oils dispatched in distinctive stirrup jars, ointments packaged in fine stone vessels, medicinal herbs and good timber. All were desirable products welcomed in Egypt, a major consumer with few natural resources of its own. Egyptian texts also refer to lichens to make embalming fluid brought in from 'Keftiu' – the name used at this time by the Egyptians for Crete. In the reign of Tuthmosis III (1479–1425 BC) tomb engravings depict men from Keftiu in the ranks of tribute-bearers carrying Cretan vases of gold or silver. The annals of Tuthmosis also record the presence of ships from Keftiu in Levantine ports loaded with cargoes of poles, masts and great trees destined for Egypt, though it is not clear whether

7.11 *Opposite:* The citadel of Mycenae from the air. The defensive wall was extended in the thirteenth century to include the early shaft graves of Grave Circle A (bottom centre). In the centre of the site at the highest point lies the palace (megaron). Mycenae dominates the route from the Gulf of Argos to the Gulf of Corinth.

7.12 The settlement of Thera on the island of Santorini was buried in ash at the time of a devastating volcanic eruption which altered the shape of the island. The houses of the Bronze Age settlement are exceptionally well preserved including the West House where the walls of one room were found to be decorated with a frieze depicting a naval expedition. The frieze provides incomparable details of sailing ships of the period in all their variety as well as the architecture of the settlement and the lush land around.

the Cretan ships had picked up their cargo of timber in the Levant or were simply stopping off there on a circuitous route down to Egypt.

Who were the carriers of all these goods? The simplest explanation would be to suppose that there was now a seafaring class resident on Crete and under the control of the Cretan overlords. These men would set out on their maritime expeditions as the spring sailing season opened, carrying tribute for their masters to prearranged ports to establish diplomatic relations or to repay obligations. On their return journeys they might bring back gifts for the Cretan elite. How much true trade there was is impossible to judge, but trusted ships' masters might have been given some leeway to acquire goods in foreign ports on an entrepreneurial basis. Once back in the home port at the end of the sailing season, there would have been ample work to occupy the men in repairing their vessels and building new ones. In addition to the Cretan 'merchant navy' it is

7.13 Mycenaean Greece in the fourteenth and thirteenth centuries BC. All known sites are plotted, giving an idea of where the main centres of population were clustered.

highly likely that ships from Egypt, the Levant and the southern coasts of Anatolia bringing tribute and merchandise visited the ports of Crete.

Our knowledge of Minoan vessels is limited to seal engravings of deep-hulled sailing vessels dating to *c*.2000 BC and a remarkable series of painted reliefs found at Akrotiri on the island of Thera in a building destroyed by the eruption of the volcano probably some time in the sixteenth century BC. Some of the vessels appear to have been decked out for a festival or maritime parade, while others seem to be involved in a naval expedition. The size and style of vessels varies. One is shown in full sail with steering oars slung aft, others are depicted as being propelled by paddlers while the vessels involved in the naval expedition appear much sleeker and less cluttered. The Thera paintings are ample demonstration that there now existed an established and assured tradition of shipbuilding.

Enter Mycenaeans

Minoan civilization was flourishing when, early in the fifteenth century BC, palaces, towns and villas, with the exception of Knossos, were devastated by fire, leaving most of the sites abandoned. The cause of the destruction continues to excite: natural catastrophe, internal strife or external attack have all been suggested, with the weight of opinion favouring the last. After the destruction influences from mainland Greece greatly increase. Mycenaean material culture replaces Minoan, mainland-style chamber tombs with weapon burials are introduced, and the language of administration, recorded in Linear B script, is now Greek, replacing the earlier non-Greek of Linear A. Crete had evidently been incorporated in the Mycenaean sphere though whether by armed invasion or peaceful annexation remains unclear.

The name 'Mycenaean' is an archaeologically imposed term used to describe cultural developments centred on the Greek mainland dating from the seventeenth century BC until towards the end of the millennium. During this period a number of centres of power emerged under the control of elite rulers. They shared a broadly common culture and may have owed allegiance to an over-king living at Mycenae in the Peloponnese.

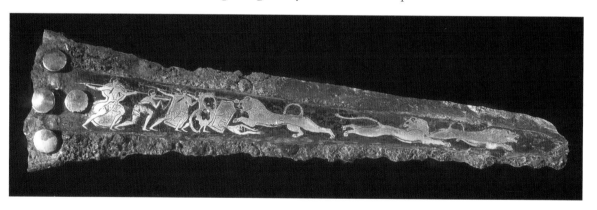

7.14 A bronze dagger blade of *c.*1550 BC from Shaft Grave Circle A at Mycenae inlaid with gold and silver to depict an animal hunt. The large shields are of types described by Homer.

Mycenaean society was a world of warrior heroes – a world hauntingly echoed in Homer's *Iliad*. The leaders lived in 'palaces' based on the megaron house and buried their dead first in shaft graves typified by the famous Grave Circles at Mycenae and later in huge tholos tombs (corbelled structures shaped like beehives) like those clustering outside the citadel of Mycenae and close to the palace at Pylos. It was this culture that spread to Crete, establishing its power base at Knossos.

The Mycenaean palaces of mainland Greece developed apace after about 1400 BC. Clusters of buildings spread out around them and many were surrounded by massive walls built of Cyclopean masonry, using huge stone blocks redolent with power. The entrance to the citadel of Mycenae, with its corridor approach and four-square gate surmounted by a pediment depicting a pair of heraldic lions, proclaims the might of the resident king and, even today, awes the visitor.

The heroic warrior society of the time is well demonstrated by contemporary depictions of warriors in wall paintings, seals and metalwork. Weapons and armour abound, most famously the sophisticated suit of bronze body armour and the boars'-tusks helmet found in the chamber tomb of Dendra in the Argolid. And if any further proof were needed, chariots, armour, weapons and fighting men, amassed in preparation for military adventures, are listed in the Linear B texts.

The emergence of an elite in Greece whose authority was based on heroic prowess echoes what was happening in many other parts of Europe at about this time, the only significant difference being the facility of the Mycenaean leaders to manipulate resources – a power reflected in their profligate use of gold, silver, ivory, amber and the like. While their personal authority would have attracted exotic gifts, it was their locations, set in highly fertile regions astride major routes, that allowed them to command the flow of commodi-

7.15 A suit of bronze body armour from the Mycenaean chambered tomb at Dendra in the Argolid. The cuirass is made of telescoping plates of bronze with hinged shoulder pieces and a separate neck guard to provide a degree of flexibility. The helmet is made of boars' tusks.

ties. The Mycenaean world lies at the interface between the consuming zone of the east Mediterranean, feeding the states and empires of the east, and the highly productive expanse of peninsular Europe. The key node in this system was the Plain of Argos at the head of the Gulf of Argos – easy to approach by ship and from where, by a comparatively short overland portage, it was possible to reach the Saronic Gulf which provided access to the north Aegean, and the Gulf of Corinth and thence to the Adriatic and Italy.

Barely 10 km (6 miles) from the head of the gulf the early inhabitants chose the hill of Mycenae as their base. A rich and fertile landscape and full command of the overland route ensured that Mycenae rose to a position of

7.16 Clay tablet inscribed
in Linear B text from the
palace at Pylos.

7.16 Clay tablet inscribed in Linear B text from the palace at Pylos.

supreme dominance. The other palatial centres elsewhere in Greece were also located so as to control sufficient fertile land to support large populations, and to oversee communications by land or by sea. The importance of local production is well illustrated by the Linear B tablets found at Pylos, which give detailed accounts of the manufacture of woollen and linen fabrics and perfume. To these must be added wine, oil and grain – the staple products of the Aegean world.

Mycenaean pottery is found around the shores of the east Mediterranean and as far west as the Tyrrhenian Sea. But pottery distributions do not necessarily mean that the exchange networks were dominated exclusively by Mycenaean overlords or even by Mycenaean shipping. Coastal communities from other regions of the east Mediterranean must by now have been heavily involved in the trans-shipment of goods and it remains a possibility that the mainland Greek polities played little direct role in these matters themselves.

Something of the complexity of the problem is well illustrated by the cargoes of two ships wrecked off the southern coasts of Anatolia – the Uluburun wreck, which went down in the fourteenth century BC, and the Cape Gelidonya wreck, which met its fate a century or so later. The Uluburun wreck carried a mixed cargo dominated by 354 oxhide ingots of copper weighing in total 10 tons (10.16 tonnes), 120 bun-shaped copper ingots, *pithoi* packed with Cypriot pottery, and Canaanite amphorae containing about 1 ton (1.016 tonnes) of terebinth resin. Packed around this bulk cargo were ingots of tin weighing 1 ton (1.016 tonnes) and coloured raw glass, scrap gold and silver, an

7.17 Diver excavating the shipwreck of Uluburun. He is stepping on a pile of oxhide ingots of bronze and carries an amphora.

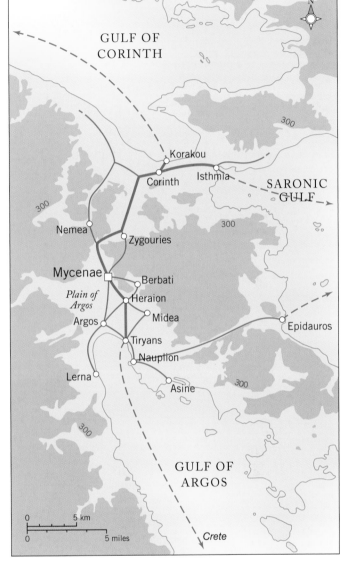

7.18 *Right:* Mycenae commanded the crucial cross-peninsular route which led from the Gulf of Argos to the Gulf of Corinth, and the Saronic Gulf and was the focus for a number of roads. The plain of Argos was quite densely settled in this period with another fortified palace at Tiryns nearer to the coast.

elephant tusk cut into sections, twelve hippopotamus teeth, logs of Egyptian ebony and ostrich shells. Additional items which may have belonged to the crew included two swords, one Syrian and one Mycenaean, Syrian pendants, a Mesopotamian cylinder seal, an Egyptian scarab and various Mycenaean pots. Something of the organization of the operation is hinted at by two wooden writing tablets with ivory hinges and a pair of weighing scales with sets of weights. The cargo was clearly of very considerable value and may indeed have been a tribute in transit to a king. The most likely point of departure for the

199

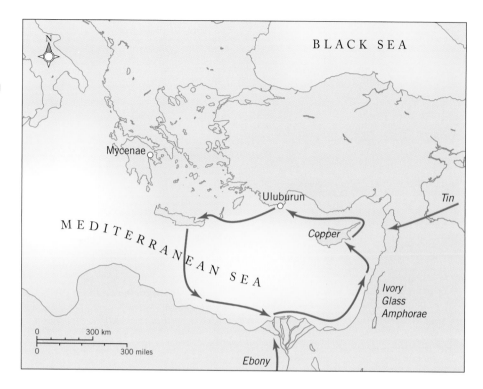

7.19 The Bronze Age ship which was wrecked at Uluburun on the Turkish coast was probably engaged in a circular voyage circumnavigating the eastern Mediterranean picking up rare raw materials en route. Which was its port of origin is unclear but it may have been a Cypriot vessel.

vessel was Cyprus or, perhaps, one of the Levantine ports. Who the intended recipient of the cargo was we can only guess – perhaps it was one of the Mycenaean overlords. But even if these speculations are correct they provide no clue as to where the vessel was built or the ethnicity of its master.

The Cape Gelidonya cargo was altogether different, comprising copper ingots and copper scrap from Cyprus and tin ingots from an unknown source, perhaps the stock of a merchant or bronzeworker. Together the wrecks offer an incomparable insight into the complexities of maritime exchange in the east Mediterranean in the late second millennium BC, linking the European kingdoms to the empires of the east.

The Tyrrhenian Sea and Beyond

The discovery of Mycenaean pottery and bronzework in Italy, Sicily, Malta and Sardinia shows that communications had been established between the east Mediterranean and the Tyrrhenian Sea after about 1600 BC, but to interpret this as evidence of Mycenaean exploration of the west is to force the material remains beyond their reasonable limits. All that can safely be said is that voyages took place between the two seas.

Maritime networks were already well established in the central

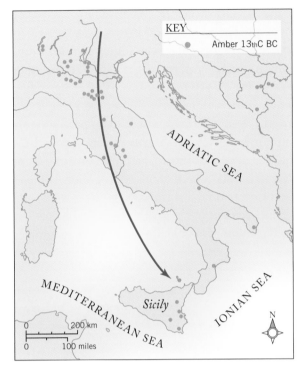

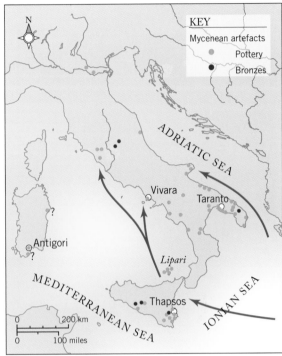

Mediterranean (see p. 119). These networks, linking the central Mediterranean islands to North Africa, Italy and Liguria, continued to develop throughout the third and second millennia, providing the structure for the distribution of Mycenaean and Cypriot finds around the Tyrrhenian Sea. Lipari in the Aeolian Islands, the principal source of obsidian and focus of the Neolithic network, was chosen by east Mediterranean entrepreneurs as their earliest entrepôt. It lay conveniently sited in relation to the main shipping routes and could boast a maritime tradition going back for centuries. At about the same time another landfall was established on the tiny island of Vivaria close to Ischia in the Bay of Naples, whence it would have been possible to access the northern coasts of the Tyrrhenian. Contact between the two seas continued to develop. By the fourteenth century BC a major port of call had been established at Scoglio del Tonno, near Tarento in the instep of southern Italy, and by the thirteenth century a port near Antigori on the Gulf of Cagliari was providing direct access to southern Sardinia. On Sicily, Thapsos on the east coast provided entry to the island. The east Mediterranean ships' masters probably chose one of the five major ports as their favoured *emporium* (market) and it was there that the major exchanges took place, with local shipping transporting goods to and from the more distant regional ports.

The Mycenaean and Cypriot pottery arrived presumably as containers for

7.20 The Italian peninsula was closely linked to the east Mediterranean trade network in the Mycenaean period as the distribution of objects of Mycenaean origin demonstrates. One of the commodities which it may have been trading is amber from the Baltic which was transported across the Alps to the Po valley and thence to the south.

7.21 A rich burial of the Argaric culture from Cerro de la Encina, near Granada, in Andalucía. The status of the burial is indicated by its two gold earrings, a copper dagger and four fine pottery vessels.

oils, unguents and other desirable luxuries. Cypriot copper, in the form of oxhide ingots, was carried in some quantity. Ingots have been found on Lipari and in southern Sicily and more than fifty have been recorded scattered across Sardinia. There are a few clues as to what commodities may have been taken back to the east Mediterranean. One possibility is alum, important in many activities including leather-working, the dyeing of textiles and in the manufacture of pharmaceuticals. The importation of alum is mentioned on Linear B tablets from Pylos and Tiryns; one of the prime sources in classical times was the Aeolian Islands. Another possible commodity was amber. Baltic amber was transported across Europe to the Po valley and scattered distributions throughout Italy hint that it may have passed, via Etruria, to the Tyrrhenian Sea and thence to eastern Sicily where it would have been available to traders.

It is difficult to gauge the intensity of the interaction between the two seas. It was probably on a modest scale but by the thirteenth century BC pottery and metalwork in Mycenaean style were being made on Sicily, possibly by artisans who had arrived with the traders and stayed to serve the local markets.

The extent to which east Mediterranean entrepreneurs were able to trade in the Tyrrhenian Sea was determined by the existence of local maritime networks with which they could articulate. The virtual absence of Mycenaean finds to the west of Sardinia is a strong indication that, at this time, the west Mediterranean was a world apart, but the occasional ship's master would surely have been tempted to venture west, lured on by curiosity. The only evidence that this might have happened is two sherds of Mycenaean pottery found in southern Spain, at Montoro in the valley of the Guadalquivir, upriver from Cordoba. The west Mediterranean was to remain largely unknown to the emerging civilized world for a few more centuries.

Yet the west was not without its own cultural developments. In Iberia one well-defined cultural group, called the Argaric culture after the settlement of El Argar, developed in south-eastern Spain between Granada and Murcia. The region is semi-arid but the river valleys provided ample cultivatable land, and extensive upland pastures were available for flocks and herds during the summer months. The region was also metal-rich, with ample supplies of copper and significant, but more restricted, deposits of silver.

Here, single burial was practised in stone cists or very large pottery vessels, with the dead now treated as individuals, decked out in their own personal finery and accompanied by weapons and pottery. Status was indicated by the quality of the grave goods, the richer individuals being accompanied by items of silver (which was quite abundant), gold, faience and ivory. The dead were buried within settlements beneath floors or behind walls to remain close to the living.

Everything about the Argaric culture suggests that it developed locally with very little external stimulus: inland there were endless mountains and barren mesetas and, although the Argaric zone had an extensive interface with the sea, there is very little evidence of maritime contact except with the adjacent coast of North Africa, whence came the coveted elephant ivory and rare ostrich eggs used to make personal ornaments. At this end of the Mediterranean the maritime networks were still little more than parochial.

The Atlantic and the North Sea

In the third and second millennia BC many parts of western and central Europe were caught up in the beaker phenomenon. From Portugal to Hungary and from Provence to Scotland the rite of single burial was widely adopted. In many zones within this broader region the burials were accompanied by highly distinctive grave sets including a ceramic beaker and items redolent with status such as archers' equipment (arrows, wrist guards and presumably bows), daggers of copper or bronze, stone battle-axes, and personal adornments such as amber beads and gold earrings. In western Europe archers' equipment is preferred while in northern Europe battle-axes occur more frequently. So widespread is the beaker phenomenon and so distinctive are the grave sets that early observers came to look upon it as evidence of a rapid and pan-European folk movement. But interpretations change and the consensus now is that the phenomenon represents the acceptance of a set of beliefs and values that spread rapidly along networks of exchange. While there may have been some level of mobility, significant migrations of population are unlikely. One of the confusions to have arisen in the past was over the significance of the beaker itself. So long as the form was believed to have a single origin, arguments focused on the direction in which the idea of the beaker moved, but if we accept that the basic form is sufficiently generalized to have developed in more than one place, it becomes much easier to give proper emphasis to regional sequences and local inventiveness and to tease out the threads that come together to give the impression of widespread cultural unity.

We have already seen, in Chapter 6, how a distinctive cultural grouping – the Corded Ware/Single Grave culture – emerged in the North European

7.22 The third millennium trading networks of Atlantic Europe were complex. Their extent is best exemplified by the distribution of a distinctive pottery type – the Maritime Bell Beaker. The crucial nodes in this network were the Tagus valley and the Morbihan, but major hinterland routes existed along the major rivers.

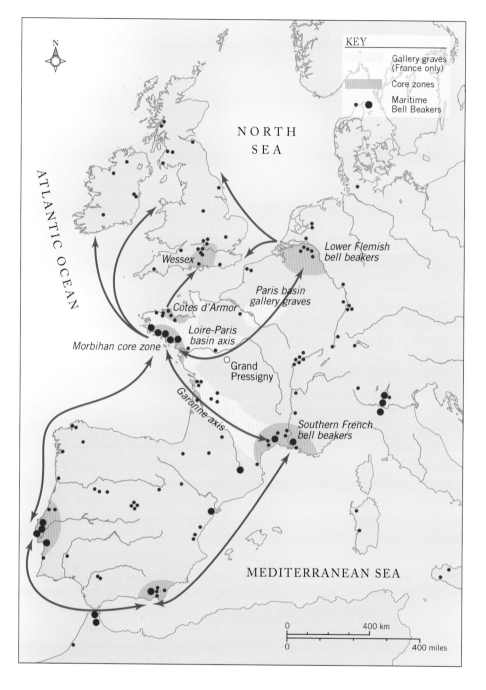

Plain some time around 3000 BC, and over the next hundred years or so spread into adjacent areas, into Denmark, Netherlands and Switzerland in the west and eastwards deep into Russia. The characteristics of the culture were single burial usually accompanied by a cord-decorated beaker and often by a stone

battle-axe. The western extent of this
Corded Ware complex roughly coincided
with the valley of the Upper and Middle
Rhine.

A quite separate thread is the development of a highly distinctive decorated bell
beaker – known as the Maritime bell
beaker – in the Tagus region of Portugal
some time around 2800–2700 BC. These
vessels were fired to a red or red-brown
colour and decorated with horizontal
bands of comb decoration covering the
entire outer surface. The vessel form
and decoration clearly emerge from the
indigenous ceramic tradition and the bow-
and-arrow grave set of the hunter may also
have originated in this same region.

The initial spread of the Maritime
bell beaker took place along the Atlantic
seaways in the middle centuries of the third
millennium, using the well-established
routes between the Tagus and Morbihan/
Loire estuary regions that had been in
operation at least since the initial spread of
the megalithic passage graves two millennia previously. From Armorica (Brittany)

7.23 A Beaker grave
group from Culduthel,
Inverness-shire, Scotland.
The wrist-guard and the
arrow heads show that
the deceased was provided
with the equipment of an
archer.

the beliefs inherent in the Maritime bell-beaker package spread out across
western Europe using long-established exchange networks, one southwards
along the western coast of France to the Gironde estuary and thence via the
Garonne and Aude to the Mediterranean coast and the Rhône estuary, the
other along the Loire to the vicinity of Orléans and across the Gâtinais to the
Seine valley, thence northwards to the Lower Rhine. These major axes were
well attested in previous periods and can be traced in the distributions of other
artefacts throughout the third millennium. One example is the stone shaft-
hole axe made from hornblendite in the vicinity of Quimper in western
Brittany. The distribution of axes from this source neatly charts the two
routes. Another commodity much favoured in exchange at this time was the
attractive honey-coloured flint from Grand Pressigny, found in the valleys of
the Claise and Creuse not far from Poitiers. It was distributed in various forms,
from large cores or long, narrow blades, to finely flaked daggers and lance
heads. Grand Pressigny flint is found in many burials in the Paris Basin and

accompanies beakers in the Netherlands. It was also exported in considerable quantities eastwards to the Rhône–Saône valleys, to be used in many west Alpine settlements of the period 2800–2400 BC.

It was along these same active exchange routes that the beaker package spread across western Europe, to be adopted and adapted by many of the communities who encountered it. In the Rhine valley it was introduced into regions where the single-grave traditions of the Corded Ware complex were already established. Here the fusion of the two created a rich mixture of beliefs and a bewildering variety of beaker types. The Loire/Seine/Rhine corridor opened up northern France to influences from both the Atlantic and the Corded Ware complex; and it was from here, across the English Channel and the southern North Sea, that the beaker package was introduced into southern and eastern Britain in the last two centuries of the third millennium BC, to be incorporated into the already vigorous indigenous cultures. To what extent this involved the movement of significant numbers of people it is difficult to say, but the very widespread introduction of the single-burial tradition might indicate some inflow of people – a suggestion given support by the discovery that oxygen isotope analysis of the teeth of a beaker burial found at Amesbury near Stonehenge in Wessex showed that the individual had probably grown up in mainland Europe.

If we are correct in seeing the Morbihan–Loire estuary as the core zone from which the Maritime bell-beaker package spread through the networks of western Europe, we need to consider whether the long-established maritime routes, leading onwards to western Britain and Ireland, also enabled beaker ideologies and technologies to reach these regions. Until recently the evidence has been ambivalent, but new work in the south-west of Ireland is beginning to clarify the situation. Survey and excavation on Ross Island, on the eastern side of Lough Leane in Co. Kerry, have revealed evidence of copperworking associated with early beaker pottery in contexts dating to 2400–2200 BC. The copper produced here from sulpharsenide ores, principally tennantite, was of a distinctive low-arsenic composition; it was used to make flat axes that were distributed throughout Ireland and into Britain. That the choice of ore type and the methods used to smelt it are characteristic of a specialized technology practised in Atlantic Europe in the mid-third millennium BC suggests that individuals with a knowledge of copper production arrived in south-western Ireland, from Brittany or further south, along the established seaways.

The initial discovery of copper in Ireland probably dates to 2500–2400 BC and the Ross Island works were still being exploited as late as 1900 BC, the metal being fashioned into flat axes and halberds – the traditional products of the earliest Atlantic copper industry. Once the technology was established, other copper sources came on stream, the best-known being from Mount

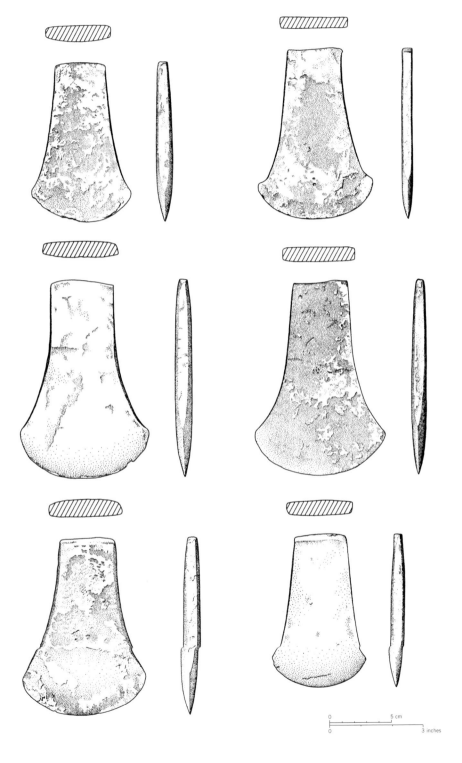

7.24 Early Irish copper axes from the Cappeen hoard, Co. Cork. Axes of this kind are the earliest copper tools to be made in Ireland and circulated to Britain.

0 _____ 5 cm

0 _____ 3 inches

Gabriel some 54 km (34 miles) to the south where surface workings have been identified producing copper from *c.*1700–1500 BC.

The Irish 'copper age' ended about 2100 BC with the rapid transition to the use of tin-bronze, the tin most likely coming from Cornwall, a peninsula that lies conveniently astride the maritime routes between Brittany and south-west Ireland. It is easy to envisage how travellers practised in metal technology could have learnt of Cornish tin and decided to experiment with the new metal. The highly innovative nature of these interactions led to Britain and Ireland being the first regions in Europe to develop a regular tin-bronze metallurgy.

At about the same time gold was being extracted from the Wicklow Mountains in south-eastern Ireland. Much of it was fashioned into magnificent collars known as *lunulae* in the period 2200–2000 BC. These elite items entered into the Atlantic distribution networks. More than eighty-five have been found in Ireland, five sites have produced *lunulae* in Cornwall and six in Normandy and Brittany. The distributions neatly reflect the western maritime route used by the metal specialists.

Crossing the Seas

A willingness to face the Atlantic Ocean, making long-haul trips across the open sea as well as hopping along coasts, implies not only a tradition of seamanship but also the availability of sturdy vessels. The coastal waters of Britain have produced remains of eight vessels of the second millennium BC: from the Humber estuary, Dover, Southampton Water and the Severn estuary. The two best-preserved examples come from Ferriby on the Humber and from Dover: both are masterpieces of carpentry and demonstrate the existence of a well-established shipbuilding tradition. The vessels were built plank first; that is, their coherence and strength as structures came from the planks of the hull and the way in which they were attached rather than from an inner frame or from transverse timbers. The thick oak planks of the hull were fastened together by sewing with twisted yew withies and were caulked with moss held in place with laths. In the Dover boat additional waterproofing was provided with a stopping made of beeswax and animal fat. To give added rigidity to the bottom planking, transverse timbers were used which passed through cleats integral with the upper surfaces of the planks. In shape the vessels were long boats – Ferriby 1 was 13 m (43 ft) long and Dover about 11 m (36 ft) – with flat bottoms making them easy to beach. None had keels, though in the case of Ferriby 1 the central base plank was thicker than the others. The means of propulsion is not immediately apparent but was probably paddling, though it has been suggested that some of the projections on the central base plank of

7.25 The remarkably-preserved Dover Bronze Age boat *in situ* during excavation. The cleats to hold strengthening bars and the bindings of the laths covering the plank joins can be clearly seen.

7.26 Conjectural reconstruction of the Dover boat. The left end of the boat (?the bow) was recovered within the excavation, but the right-hand end (?stern) with the square transom is hypothetical since it still remains to be excavated.

the Ferriby 1 vessel could have supported a movable mast. Sea trials carried out with a half-size replica showed that this was entirely feasible and offered a highly efficient form of propulsion.

The British second-millennium sewn-plank boats demonstrate the carpenter's intimate knowledge of timber and deftness with the bronze axe and adze. They show too that a series of solutions to constructional problems had been tried and tested. This is a mature boat-building tradition, the antecedents of which must have stretched back for centuries, even before the advent of metal tools increased the speed and precision of construction.

There has been much discussion about the capability of these vessels: whether they were restricted to coasts and estuaries or whether they were regularly used on open sea expeditions. Recent sea trials have suggested that, under appropriate conditions, such vessels would have been able to cross the Channel or the southern North Sea in comparative safety. In the context of the time, journeys of this kind would have endowed those who led them with well-earned prestige.

The sewn-plank boat tradition was well established in British waters by the second millennium BC, but what of other vessel forms? The contemporary Nordic tradition (see pp. 217–9) is based on the long boat with well-defined keels and high stems and sterns, while the strong possibility remains that skin boats, constructed of a light wattle framework covered in cows' hides, were widespread. Such a comparatively simple form of construction, very well suited to the buffeting waves and swells of the Atlantic, has long been used in western waters. For the coastal communities, then, mobility at sea employing a variety of craft would have been commonplace.

Emerging Local Elites

Throughout western Europe the third and second millennia BC saw the emergence of elites. They appear in the archaeological record as individuals endowed at their time of death with rich grave goods. Although the phenomenon is widespread, three distinct clusters stand out – in the Tagus region of Portugal, in Armorica (Brittany) and in Wessex.

The Tagus region was developing a very distinctive culture of its own by the beginning of the early third millennium BC. This was characterized by settlements with massive stone-built 'fortifications' – sites like Vila Nova de São Pedro after which the culture is generally named (see p. 143). It was very probably in this region that the form of the Maritime bell beaker first developed c.2800 BC and spread along the Atlantic seaways together with knowledge of copper-producing technologies. The next stage in the Portuguese development, known as the Palmela complex, begins in the middle of the third millennium BC. The fortified settlements continued in use, as did the tradition of burying the dead in collective tombs, but there is now an increase in the desire to display the elite status of the dead through a range of exotic grave goods. Local copper was widely used to make tools, but only rarely weapons. Gold, probably from Galicia, but perhaps from as far afield as Ireland, was plentiful in the form of personal jewellery and small sheet attachments for dress, while fastenings for dress and other trinkets were made of ivory imported from North Africa. Another favoured commodity was callaïs – a fine-textured stone, usually greenish-blue in colour, used to fashion beads. Much of the callaïs probably came by sea from Armorica where it was also popular in contemporary burials.

In Armorica the elite burials of the second millennium are concentrated in the west of the peninsula, west of the rivers Blavet and Trieux, with a particularly dense cluster on the southern flank of the Monts d'Arrée – a distribution contrasting with that of the earlier megalithic tombs which focused on the southern Morbihan. The burials were usually individual and were placed in stone-built cists beneath barrows. Bronze daggers and short swords, flat axes, and flint-barbed-and-tanged arrows are frequently included. The daggers were provided with wooden handles which in some cases were ornamented with closely spaced gold pins. Other luxury goods include the silver beakers, and items of amber and gold, like the small decorated gold box from La Motta near Lannion and the large amber plaque accompanying the burial at Saint-Fiacre in the Morbihan. The distribution of the Armorican barrow burials, away from the traditional megalithic focus in the Morbihan, suggests that a new political geography was emerging, with the elite now choosing to distance themselves from the past. This view is further supported by the fact that the Armorican barrow burials owed little to the beaker package: here was a community able to benefit from local resources of copper, tin and some gold, and from their favoured location at the end of a peninsula, thrusting into the middle of a vibrant maritime network. Maybe they saw themselves as new men carrying little from their past.

Across the Channel in Wessex lay another centre of power. In the earlier part of the third millennium BC the Wessex chalkland saw the emergence of massive ceremonial sites referred to by archaeologists as 'henge monuments', but by the middle of the millennium most had declined in significance, with the notable exception of Stonehenge where, some time before 2600 BC, a number of bluestone monoliths imported from the Preseli Mountains in south-west Wales were set up. Within a century the famous circle of sarsen stones enclosing five towering trilithons had been erected, creating a monument without parallel in Europe. Thereafter Stonehenge remained in active use, remodelled on a number of occasions during the course of the next eight centuries or so.

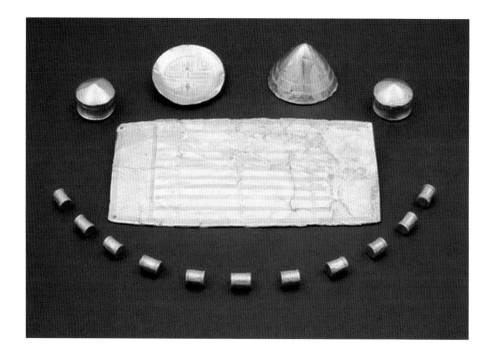

7.27 The array of gold objects found with a mid-second millennium BC burial in a tomb at Upton Lovell, Wiltshire. The collection well displays the craft of the sheet gold worker.

The rich burials, clustering in Wessex in the period *c.*2000–1400 BC, belong to an indigenous tradition developing from the single inhumations of the Beaker period. The richest are lavishly provided with exotic goods. One of the most famous is the burial beneath Bush Barrow, a prominent mound within sight of Stonehenge. The chieftain buried here was accompanied by three bronze daggers, an axe, a stone mace head attached to a staff decorated with bone fittings, two decorated gold plaques and a gold belt hook. One of the daggers had a wooden handle decorated with gold pins which may well have been made in an Armorican workshop. Not far away, at Upon Lovell in the valley of the river Wylye, a female had been buried wearing an elaborate multi-strand necklace of amber beads, the strands separated from each other by large amber spacer plates. Among her other grave goods were a bronze knife and an awl, gold beads, a decorated gold plaque and a gold-coated cone of Kimmeridge shale. Other exotic materials enjoyed by the Wessex elite included jet from the Yorkshire coast and beads of bright blue faience probably made in Britain. One of the most spectacular items from a grave of this period was a handled cup carved from a solid lump of amber, found with a burial at Hove in Sussex – an outlier to the main distribution.

The chalklands of Wessex were able to sustain a stable agricultural economy but commanded few other resources. The reason for the prominence of the region lay in its central position with regard to routes from the southern coasts of Britain to other parts of the country. The chalk uplands converging on Salisbury Plain together with the rivers flowing into the Solent provided the natural lines of communication along which most other parts of southern Britain could easily be accessed. An added attraction was Stonehenge itself, which must have been a sight of wonder and veneration worthy of pilgrimage.

Finally, we must consider Ireland. We have already seen that it was highly productive of bronze, used to make axes, daggers, halberds and spears, and of gold, most dramatically displayed in the spectacular *lunulae* found throughout the island. But no clusters of rich burials proclaim centres of power. It may simply be that the Irish elite chose to demonstrate their access to wealth by dedicating it to the gods and consigning it to bogs or to pits in the ground rather than using it in sumptuous burials. Such is the variety in human behaviour.

The Nordic Realms

In Denmark the Late Neolithic period continued until *c.*1730 BC, after which comes the Bronze Age. This is divided into six periods, the first two of which, Bronze I (1730–1500) and Bronze II (1500–1250), are of direct concern to us in this chapter.

During the Late Neolithic the single-grave burial traditions continued little changed, the only significant difference being that the battle-axes, buried with the dead as a symbol of status, were now replaced by flint daggers laboriously flaked to replicate metal prototypes. These daggers, and also the long barbed arrowheads that now appear alongside them, represent the apogee of the flintworker's craft. An intimate knowledge of the material and consummate skill in the flint-flaking technique created artefacts of beauty and wonder in a land with no copper supplies of its own.

Around 1700 BC metal begins to flow in in some quantity – copper, tin and gold – becoming abundant by the middle of the millennium, by which time local metalsmiths were producing a range of items equal to or excelling in quality those of neighbouring regions. The Scandinavian Bronze Age was a period of stunning technical and artistic achievements, nurtured under the patronage of chieftains who dominated an increasingly hierarchical social structure.

The elite were now buried with equipment appropriate to their rank, including, in the cases of the most prestigious individuals, items of gold. In a number of cases burials, monumentalized by large barrows, were made in waterlogged conditions that have preserved much of the organic component of the grave, providing a wealth of detail seldom available elsewhere in Europe. At Egtved in Jutland the grave of a young woman of 18–20 was excavated in

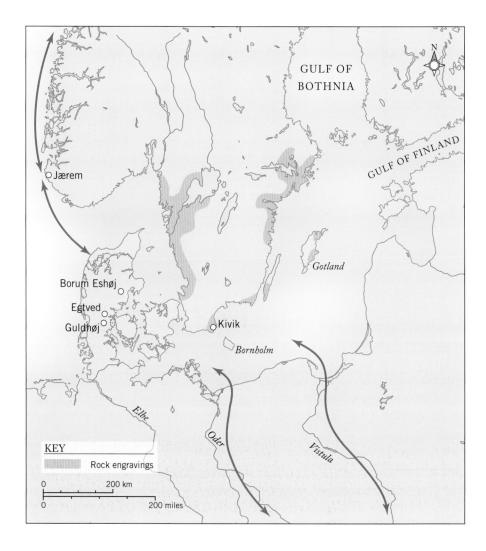

7.28 The Nordic region in the second millennium BC showing some of the major sites and routes.

1921. She had been buried in an oak coffin carved out of a solid trunk, and was lying on a cow's hide dressed in a shirt of brown sheep's wool with elbow-length sleeves and a string skirt also of wool. Across her stomach she was wearing a bronze disc with a substantial protruding spike of sufficient prominence to deter an over-ardent admirer. She wore bracelets on each wrist. At her head was a birch-bark box containing woollen cord and an awl, and at her feet was a birch-bark pail once filled with beer or fruit wine. The cremated remains of a child of six or seven were placed in the coffin before she was laid to rest. The Egtved woman was buried in the second half of the second millennium BC. At about the same date a young man of about twenty was interred at Borum Eshøj in eastern Jutland. He too had been laid on a cow's hide in an oak coffin. He was dressed in a loincloth held by a leather belt and

7.30 The burial of a young woman from Egtved in south Jutland, Denmark. She was clothed in a woollen shirt and string skirt. The body, together with a birch bark container, lay on a cow's hide and was covered with a woollen blanket. It had been placed in an oak coffin beneath a barrow around 1370 BC.

7.29 Flint dagger from Hindsgavl, Denmark, dating to about 2000 BC. By using a technique of carefully controlled pressure flaking, the highly skilled craftsman has been able to imitate the shape of contemporary bronze axes to produce this masterpiece.

7.31 An exposed face of granite carved with a flotilla of boats at Hornnes, Skjeborg, Norway. The rock face once overlooked the sea. The red pigment is a modern application to accentuate the carving.

was covered with a woollen cloak. Buried with him was the scabbard of a long sword surprisingly containing only a short dagger. These well-preserved burials, just two of a number found in Denmark, offer a fascinating insight into life and death in the Bronze Age. They were young people of moderate status belonging to a hierarchical system that used the ceremony of burial to display both the social rank of the deceased and the status of his or her lineage.

While the countryside of Denmark and southern Sweden was fertile enough to sustain its population and to meet its basic needs, it was totally deficient in copper, tin and gold, all of which had to be imported from the south. In return the region could offer furs, hides, woollen fabrics, seal oil, resin and the much-sought-after amber found in quantity along the eastern shores of Jutland and the Baltic coasts of what are now Poland and Russia. To sustain the constant inflow of metal (much of which was taken out of circulation by the social customs that required it to be buried in graves or consigned to ritual deposits) it would have been necessary to husband the local products and channel them into the exchange networks.

The pattern of exchanges that developed between the Thy district of northern Jutland and the western coast of Norway, between Stavanger and Trondheim, provides an insight into the local networks in operation. A detailed survey of the artefacts found here shows that during the Late Neolithic and Early Bronze ages the Norwegian communities received flint daggers and items of bronze and gold from Denmark. In all, 1800 imported

216

artefacts have been found. Most were flint daggers but there were also 172 bronze and seven gold objects. While the distribution of flint daggers no doubt reflected the density of population, the more prestigious metal objects were concentrated in two areas, Jæren and North Karmøy, where local elites were able to control the incoming exotics. What the Norwegian communities offered in return were most likely products derived from pastoralism and hunting. Some hint of this comes from one maritime rock shelter in the region of Sogn, where the faunal remains show that squirrel, hare, bear, marten and wild cat were being trapped, presumably for their skins. Another product that would have been easily accessible to the coastal communities of this region was seal oil which was widely valued. The coniferous forests also offered a ready supply of resin. It is not at all impossible that the wealth of the elite of the Thy district of Jutland was in no small part the result of their ability to acquire these rare commodities from western Norway for further transmission south. This example illustrates but one of the many maritime routes linking Norway and Sweden, and Jutland and the Danish islands. Control of the sea was of crucial importance.

The maritime nature of Scandinavian society in the second millennium BC is amply demonstrated by the ship imagery that pervades the cultural record. Most prolific are the rock engravings of the coastal regions of southern Sweden, where engravers had been at work over centuries, laboriously pecking images into the exposed surface of the igneous bedrock. The symbols are rich and varied but everywhere the ship dominates, sometimes appearing in scenes recording flotillas of vessels.

Ship images also enhance the surfaces of

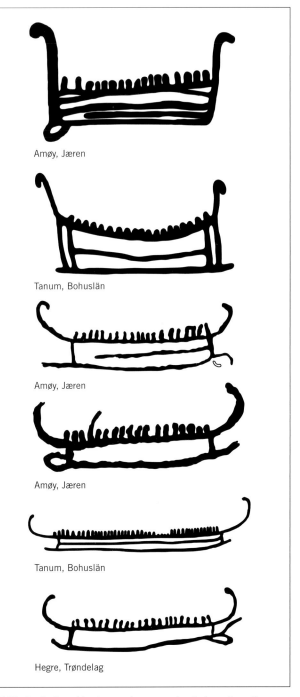

Amøy, Jæren

Tanum, Bohuslän

Amøy, Jæren

Amøy, Jæren

Tanum, Bohuslän

Hegre, Trøndelag

7.32 A selection of boats carved on exposed rocks in southern Norway. All share the same high prows and sterns. If the stick figures represent people then the vessels were long sleek rowing boats with upwards of twenty rowers.

217

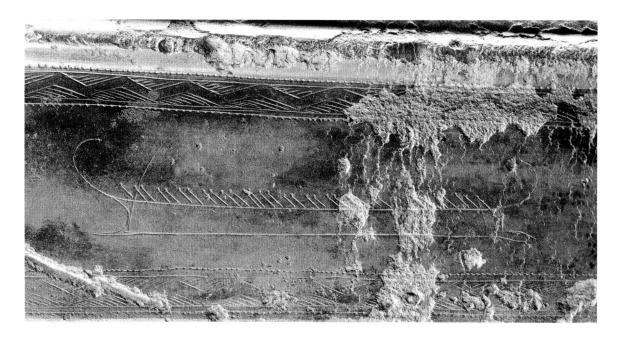

bronze implements. The earliest known example is engraved on the blade of one of a pair of elegant bronze single-edged swords (or scimitars) found at Rørby in western Zealand. The image of the vessel is precisely drawn, the hull outlined with two thin lines representing the keel and the gunwale. The gunwale-line sweeps up at both ends to create a high incurved prow and stern, while the keel-line is extended fore and aft, the aft extension being expanded perhaps to depict some kind of stabilizer. Above the gunwale were thirty-four or thirty-five strokes, each representing a crew member. This is an assured drawing by someone who fully understood the essence of a ship. The Rørby ship, dating to 1600–1500 BC, represents a tradition of boat-building that was already well established. It incorporates the basic elements that are to be found time and time again on the Swedish and Norwegian rock carvings.

So extensive is the rock-carving iconography that it allows huge scope for discussion about both ship construction and changing styles of vessels over time. There are also indications of different regional styles in the carvings which might reflect local variations in construction. Opinions differ as to how the actual vessels were constructed. In most cases a keel is indicated and no example is known to depict a mast or sail. The lengths of the vessels vary but the great majority can be classed as long boats. This much is clear; what is debatable is the actual form of construction. Some commentators favour hides stretched over a light timber skeleton, others prefer a plank-built construction, basing their argument on the fact that some carvings appear to indicate distinct side strakes. Both options remain possible, but given the contemporary

English Channel/North Sea tradition of sewn-plank construction and also the assured plank-built tradition represented by actual vessels found in the Nordic area dating from the first millennium BC, it seems likely that the Bronze Age vessels were also plank-built; we can but await the discovery of an actual wreck.

The prevalence of ship images on rock carvings and bronzes underlines the importance assigned to maritime journeys in Nordic society and carries with it the implication that to command a ship and lead it on an expedition was a mark of high status. But how ambitious were these voyages? Most journeys would have been essentially local, between Jutland and the Danish islands and the coasts of southern Norway and Sweden, in pursuit of profitable exchanges. But it is perfectly possible to conceive of a situation in which competition to gain prestige encouraged voyages to be undertaken over greater distances, thrusting deep into the unknown. Returning successfully from such expeditions with cargoes of exotics and with knowledge of distant lands previously shrouded in mystery would have endowed the successful leader with an aura of the supernatural. Voyaging would have become a measure of status and legitimacy to rule – much as it was in the same Nordic region more than two thousand years later when the wayfarers were called Vikings.

The more ambitious might have directed their vessels northwards up the Baltic to the Gulf of Finland or past Åland to explore the Gulf of Bothnia, or they might have chosen the less arduous journey across the North Sea to Scotland. Another possibility is that they may have explored the great rivers of the North European Plain, the Vistula, Oder, Elbe and Weser, to seek out the sources of the metals and to establish diplomatic relationships with the distant chiefs who controlled the throughput of supplies. The Oder and Elbe were the routes by which many cultural influences reached Scandinavia from the south-east. The Carpathian Basin had a flourishing bronze industry that produced finely cast shaft-hole axes and elaborately decorated, solid-hilted swords named after the Hungarian type site of Hajdúsámson and the Romanian site of Apa. These elite weapons were being produced in the period 2100–1700 BC and the distribution map shows them extending northwards towards Denmark. It was probably along this route that knowledge of the spoked wheel and the two-wheeled chariot, together with well-trained pairs of horses, reached the north. With a flood of such desirable goods flowing from the south-east, it would not have been surprising if one or more of the Nordic voyagers had taken his ship up the Oder, reaching deep inland via the Odra to the northern foothills of the Carpathians. A determined band of voyagers, firmly led, could have made the overland portages to the headwaters of the Morava, from where it was downriver to the Danube and thence to the Carpathian Basin. Whether such a voyage was ever made we cannot know,

but compared to the great journeys made across Europe by the Swedish Vikings two millennia later it would not have been a particularly outstanding achievement.

The idea of voyages of discovery penetrating deep into the heart of Europe is by no means as far-fetched as it may at first appear. One site in particular throws fascinating light on all this – a Bronze Age cist burial set in the great mound of Bredarör (broad cairn) near Kivik on the south coast of Sweden. The walls of the cist, discovered in 1748 and dating to the period 1700–1500 BC, were composed of eight decorated stone slabs. The scenes are virtually without parallel. They depict pairs of spoked wheels, pairs of horses, a figure riding a two-wheeled chariot pulled by a pair of horses, long boats, two axes facing each other on either side of a triangular monolith, and parades of human figures, two of whom blow horns, all evidently taking part in group ceremonials. The subject matter and the sophistication of the imagery leave little doubt that the scenes were inspired from beyond the Nordic realm. Some have argued for the Aegean but there is no need to go further south than the Carpathian Basin.

What was the immediate inspiration for the carvers, for whom was the tomb built, and are the scenes illustrative of an epic story? The questions must remain unanswered. But a possible scenario is that in the sixteenth century BC the lord of Kivik led his warriors on an epic journey, sailing south from home via the island of Bornholm to the mouth of the Oder, and thence by river and overland portage to the Carpathian Basin. On their return, scenes from the adventure and the mysteries they had witnessed were painted on cloth to adorn the lord's residence, thereby endowing him with great power in the eyes of all. On his death the scenes were carved on the stones of his burial chamber and a huge mound of boulders – the Bredarör – was piled up over it, dominating the view across the sea to the south and visible to all sailors approaching the coast: a fitting memorial to a great voyager. Fantasy perhaps, but that voyages of exploration were made at this time is not in doubt. The Kivik lord may have been one of many such explorers.

The Carpathian Basin and the Steppes

In the period from *c.*2300 to 1400 BC, the Carpathian Basin saw the development of a spectacular bronze industry producing an array of elaborate weapons and ornaments for the elite. Prominent among these were the solid-hilted swords and shaft-hole axes, many of them elaborately decorated, of the types represented in the hoards from Apa and Hajdúsámson – types that are found concentrated in the northern part of the Carpathian Basin (now Romania, Hungary and Slovakia). This distinctive Early Bronze Age culture is known by

7.34 *Opposite:* One of the engraved slabs from the wall of the Kivik tomb dating to *c.*1300 BC, showing a vigorous scene including a fast-driven two-wheeled chariot. The meaning of the scene is unrecoverable but the lower line of figures looks like a procession in prayer.

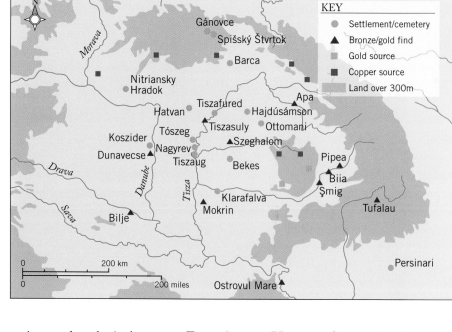

7.35 By the middle of the second millennium BC the Carpathian Basin had developed as a vital route node in the Bronze Age trading networks of central Europe. Many fortified settlements had been built to guard the major routes.

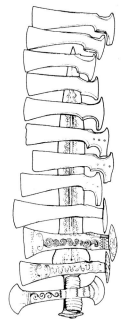

7.36 A hoard of bronze weapons (one sword and 12 battleaxes) found at Hajdúsámson near Debrecen in Hungary dating to the second half of the second millennium. The high quality of the work reflects the refined skills of bronzesmiths working in the Carpathian Basin.

various archaeological names – Füzesabony in Hungary, Otomani in Romania, Madarovce in Slovakia – but these are all local manifestations of one broadly similar cultural group. Something of the richness of the culture is indicated by objects in everyday use that were buried in debris when the fortified settlement of Barca in Slovakia was burnt down. In addition to tools and weapons, the finds included three necklaces of gold beads, one of amber and twenty sheet-gold hair-rings.

Many factors will have contributed to the wealth of the Carpathian communities, not least the fertility of the land and the ample deposits of copper and gold in the Carpathians and in Transylvania. But of vital importance was command of the routes leading from east to west and north to south – the Carpathian Basin was one of the great route nodes of the European peninsula. With an escalation in the flow of commodities in the second millennium, those living astride network interchanges of this kind were able to flourish. It is a reflection of this that the valleys and passes reaching northwards through the Carpathians were guarded by strongly fortified settlements surrounded by timber-laced earthen ramparts fronted by wide ditches – these were Europe's first true hillforts. Even on the lowlands to the south the long-established villages were now fortified, enabling local leaders to maintain a firm hold on the land.

The Carpathian Basin from a very early date shared many aspects of its culture with the steppe region to the east, and it was from here that horse-riding

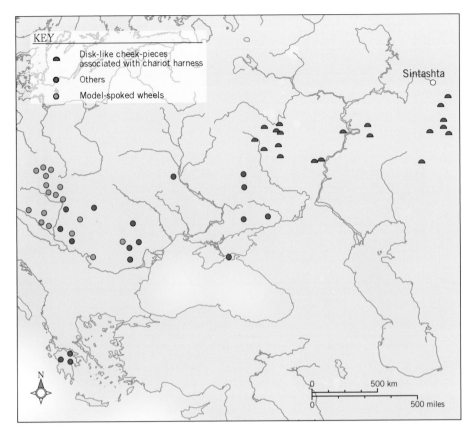

7.37 The distribution of cheek-pieces from horse harnesses and of model-spoked wheels, in the latter part of the second millennium, shows the zone in which horse-drawn chariots were in use. The Mycenaean world is an outlier of the main distribution.

and the use of four-wheeled bullock-carts were learnt. In the second millennium these Pontic links continued with the introduction of the chariot – a vehicle with two spoked wheels pulled by a pair of horses. No actual examples of chariots are known in the Carpathian Basin region, but many models of spoked wheels have been found and there is a very clear illustration of two chariots pulled by horses on a pot of this period from Vel'ke Raskovce in Slovakia. The origin of the two-wheeled chariot has been much discussed, many writers favouring the Near East, but recent work has shown that the earliest chariots so far known are to be found in burials in the forest steppe region of Russia between the Urals and the river Volga, in contexts dating to as early as 2800 BC. The steppe region, with its long tradition of horse breeding and training and an even longer tradition of using wheeled vehicles, is a likely location for the emergence of light vehicles with spoked wheels that could travel at speed across the open terrain. From here the advanced technology spread south to the Near East in the period around 2000 BC and westwards into the Carpathian Basin, a region that had maintained close cultural relations with the steppe since the fourth millennium. By the sixteenth

7.38 Reconstruction of the chariot burial found at Sintashta, in northern Kazakhstan just east of the Urals, dating to the period 2000–1800 BC.

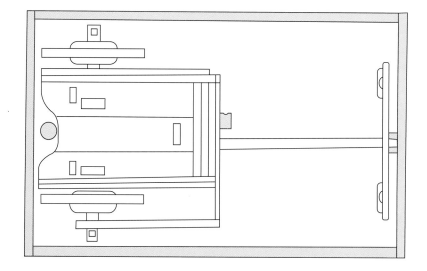

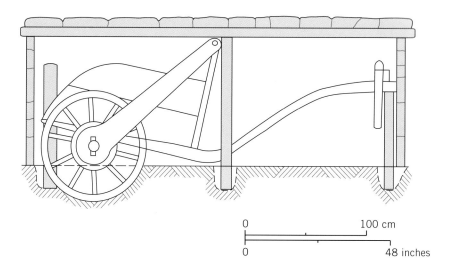

century BC horse-driven chariots, clearly vehicles of prestige, are depicted on reliefs in Mycenaean shaft graves.

It has long been recognized that there were a number of marked cultural similarities between Mycenaean culture and that of the inhabitants of the Carpathian Basin – not only the use of the spoked wheel but also in curvilinear styles of decoration applied to bonework and other kinds of horse gear. This used to be interpreted as a result of Mycenaean influence spreading north, but with the advent of radiocarbon dating it has become clear that these cultural elements had emerged in the Carpathian Basin centuries before they

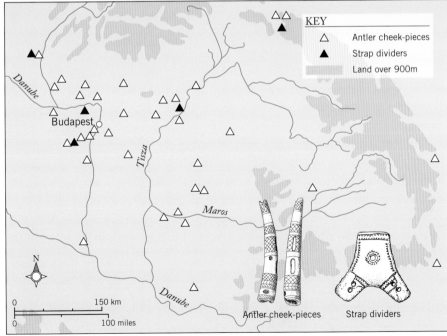

7.39 One of the decorated stone slabs from Shaft Grave V in Grave Circle A at Mycenae, depicting a two-wheeled chariot in action. The carving dates to c.1600 BC.

7.40 The Carpathian Basin in the mid-second millennium BC showing the distribution of antler cheek-pieces and bone strap dividers of the types illustrated.

are found in Greece. The inescapable conclusion is that the Mycenaean elites were drawing some of their inspiration, including perhaps knowledge of the chariot, from the north: it remains a possibility that there may even have been some limited movement of northerners into Greece at this time. The idea is unproven but merits consideration.

Adventurers and Heroes

It is abundantly clear that the period 2800–1300 BC was one of innovative energy and mobility in Europe. It was a time when the peninsula was opening up, allowing commodities, ideas, beliefs and values to be shared over wide areas, leading not to a sameness but to a vivid variety as the individual communities reinterpreted what was new to meet their own particular needs.

The emergence of hierarchical societies throughout Europe created demand for commodities. Copper, tin, gold, silver, amber, marble, lapis lazuli, ivory, ostrich eggs, textiles, furs, oils, perfumes, wine, trained horses and wives were among the enormous range of goods moved from one place to another along the networks of interaction that enmeshed all parts of the peninsular.

In the east Mediterranean ships linked the states of Egypt, the Levant and Anatolia with the emerging polities of the Minoan–Mycenaean world. Overland routes through Anatolia led deep into the east, while a short sea journey westwards linked to the maritime systems of the Tyrrhenian Sea. From the Aegean ships could easily access the south and west shores of the Black Sea, or overland routes, like the Varda–Morava corridor, could be taken to reach the *carrefour* of the Carpathian Basin linking the great expanse of the steppe to peninsular Europe. From here routes led northwards through the Carpathians and across the North European Plain to the Nordic realms of the Baltic, or westwards along the Danube to Middle Europe and the other great route node where the Danube, Rhine and Saône/Rhône converged.

Two of the routes to the north, following the Oder and the Elbe, pass through an area, now south-eastern Germany, the Czech Republic and south-western Poland, where there was a spectacular cultural development called the Aunjetitz or Únětice culture (depending on whether it is on German or Czech soil). The elites of this area benefited not only from the routes that they commanded but also from the rich supplies of copper and tin on hand in the Erzgebirge Mountains. The Únětice culture reflected a brilliant development in bronzeworking in the period 2300–1800 BC that was to influence much of north-western Europe.

Finally, the western parts of Europe were linked by systems of their own based on the Atlantic seaways and the transpeninsular routes following for the most part the major rivers. The network was all-embracing: all parts of Europe were interconnected.

What all this means in terms of mobility is difficult to quantify. The movement of commodities by land is likely to have been short-haul, with consignments changing hands many times as they were transported along the traditional routes. But the sea was altogether different. True, short-haul cabotage would have been practised but the sea encouraged longer journeys and there is ample evidence of this in the east Mediterranean and along the Atlantic façade. Journeys between the Tagus and Armorica (Brittany) and from Armorica to southern Ireland are quite likely to have been made, though with what frequency we can only guess.

Comparative ease of travel by sea would have encouraged the more adventurous to explore. The ethos of heroic travel that pervades the works of Homer is captured well by King Menelaus's boast:

> But when it comes to men, I feel that few or none can rival me in
> wealth, considering all the hardships I endured and journeys I made in
> the seven years it took me to amass this fortune and to get it home in
> my ships. My travels took me to Cyprus, to Phoenicia and to Egypt.
> Ethiopians, Sidonians, Erembi, I visited them all: and I saw Libya too.
> (The *Odyssey* IV, 75–85)

Here, admittedly, his exertions seem to have been motivated more by personal gain than by a quest for knowledge; but fame, fortune and self-fulfilment are frequently intricately linked and travellers' tales of far-flung places will have enhanced the wanderer's reputation. In such a context the Kivik lord may have set out on his journey to the south. How many others made comparable journeys, driven by a curiosity to know what lay beyond? The archaeological record holds many tantalizing clues; just one example will suffice. In Wessex craftsmen developed a particular technique to perforate amber spacer plates used to separate the threads in multi-strand necklaces. Since perforated amber spacers of this kind are known only in southern Britain and in Mycenaean Greece, and are totally absent from the rest of Europe even though amber objects are comparatively plentiful, the simplest explanation is that a consignment of amber containing perforated spacers was somehow transported from Wessex to Mycenae. Was it the result of a single journey – carried perhaps on a Mycenaean boat that had ventured into the Atlantic, or by an enterprising Wessex warrior exploring the wider world? Or could the carrier have been a Wessex woman wearing her finery as she left home as a gift to a Mycenaean prince? While possibilities are many, certainties are few. But what is certain is that the corridors of Europe were now resounding with whispers from far and wide. For those able to hear them, the excitement must have been palpable.

CHAPTER EIGHT

Emerging Eurozones:
1300–800 BC

In the east Mediterranean the period 1300–800 BC was a time of massive transformation. Complex social systems collapsed and, after a phase of deep and widespread social disruption, new configurations emerged. But for most of Europe, continuity and sustained development were the overriding characteristics. These different trajectories neatly demonstrate the independence of the European peninsula from events in the east. True, some of the ripples caused by the collapse of the states around the east Mediterranean were felt in far-flung parts, but their effects were minimal compared to the energies driving the peninsula at large.

By the end of the fourteenth century the individual power centres of the Mycenaean world were able to hold their own in their dealings with the two great powers – the Egyptians and the Hittites – and with the smaller states on the interface between them in Palestine, Syria and Cyprus. Relations between the elites were articulated by gift exchanges on an increasingly elaborate scale and, on the back of this, bulk trade in lesser goods flourished. Power was maintained by the ability of the leaders to command the movement of rare raw materials, and was supported by state-financed armies. In the fourteenth century the system was flourishing, with the disparate polities linked together in a network of exchanges by land and sea. The scale of the operation is vividly brought to life by the cargo of the Uluburun wreck, by Egyptian tomb engravings illustrating the arrival of foreign tribute and by Hittite texts listing goods in transit. But it was not to last for long. In the brief period from 1250 to 1150 the entire edifice of centralized, bureaucratic, palace-based exchange fell apart. Glimpses of what was happening come from Egyptian sources. In the reign of the pharaoh Merneptah, about 1224, Egypt faced a concerted attack from without. Libyans poured into the delta region from the Western Desert supported by 'northerners coming from all lands'. The attack was weathered but a generation later the pharaoh Ramesses III faced an even greater threat: 'The foreign countries . . . made a conspiracy in their islands. All at once the lands were on the move, scattered in war. No country could stand before their arms.' Scenes from these momentous events, carved on

8.1 *Opposite:* Ramesses III (1187–1156 BC) in triumph over captive raiders from the east Mediterranean – the Sea Peoples. Relief carved on the first pylon of the temple of Ramesses III at Medinet Habu, Thebes.

monuments at Karnak and Luxor, show the pharaoh triumphant, but for all the bombast Egypt had been seriously weakened. Other states fared worse. The Hittites were extinguished while the smaller polities in Cyprus, Syria and Palestine suffered varying degrees of devastation. Further away, at the western extremity of the system, the power of the Mycenaean lords was broken and a long period of decline set in. People were now on the move. On more than one occasion there is reference to seaborne attacks, and mysterious 'Sea Peoples' make fleeting but devastating appearances.

The events in the east had little effect on Europe outside the Aegean. Here, there was steady development that led to regional complexes representing a consolidation borne of increasing connectivity. It is rather like a crystallizing-out of European society into broad Eurozones – the mega-regions that underlie much that will follow. The central group of culture complexes – Nordic, Lusatian, North-West Alpine, Italian and Iberian – have much in common, while the more peripheral – the Atlantic, the Carpathians/steppe and the Aegean – develop along separate trajectories, the Aegean complex soon becoming a focus for the emergence of a cluster of city-states collectively known as Greek.

Viewing Europe as a whole allows a number of broad generalizations to be made. Perhaps the most significant factor is population growth. In many regions where detailed surveys have been carried out, the number of settlements markedly increases over time, suggesting a steady, and in some places rapid, expansion in population. To accommodate this, it would have been necessary for more land to be brought into cultivation while at the same time an increase in productivity was achieved through improved methods of husbandry and the introduction of a greater range of crops. While most communities relied to differing degrees on the basic farmyard animals, cattle, sheep/goats and pigs, there was now far more specialization to make better use of the available land. A greater variety of crops now appear alongside the ubiquitous wheat and barley. Legumes such as lentils and peas become increasingly popular and the celtic bean (*Vicia faba*) is now introduced as a regular crop for the first time. Oil-bearing plants like flax and poppy are grown in greater quantities than before while the cereals millet and rye, both able to grow in poorer soils, enabled marginal land to be brought into cultivation. The ox-drawn ard which tore furrows through the soil had long been used, and ard marks have been found beneath barrows of the late third/mid-second millennium, but it was not until the thirteenth century BC or thereabouts that permanent fields with well-defined boundaries make their appearance in north-western Europe. Extensive field systems imply deliberate acts of land apportionment. The individual fields were ploughed over long periods of time, giving rise to distinct banks (lynchets) around the edges. Long-term use implies that a sophisticated system of

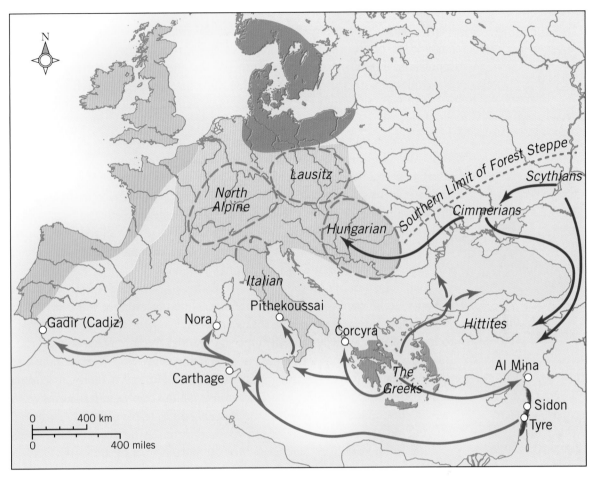

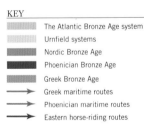

fallowing and manuring was now in operation – another indication of the revolution in agriculture that was under way.

It was during this period, *c.*1300–800 BC, conventionally called the Late Bronze Age, that bronzeworking technology was refined to a peak of perfection. The alloy used was now a regular tin-bronze but sometimes lead was added to improve the metal's casting characteristics. Two-piece moulds had been in use for centuries but the Late Bronze Age saw the introduction of multiple-piece moulds and of casting using the lost-wax (*cire perdue*) technique. This involved fashioning a beeswax model of the item to be made and investing it with clay. The object was then heated so that the wax could be poured away, leaving a cavity in the now-baked clay mould into which molten bronze could be introduced. The skill of the casters is amply demonstrated by the magnificent curved bronze trumpets (*luren*) found in Denmark and the lively figurines from Sardinia. In sheet metalwork, too, the bronzesmith excelled, producing sets of repoussé-decorated body armour – greaves, corslets, helmets and shields – to adorn warriors. To be able to produce such masterpieces without weakening or cracking the sheet required an intricate knowledge of the physical qualities of the metal and of the techniques of annealing. The European bronzesmith of the late second millennium BC had a complete mastery of his material, his skills having been honed by the elite's demand for fine bronzework to satisfy their constant desire for display.

Much of the effort of the bronzesmith was focused on the production of weapons – socketed spearheads and wide-bladed swords suitable for cut-and-thrust fighting. Palstaves, socketed axes and shaft-hole axes also made effective weapons when needed. The warrior armed with sword, spear, shield and helmet was a favourite subject for depiction. The warrior motif is found throughout Europe, from the memorial slabs of south-western Iberia to the rock engravings of southern Sweden. He is also immortalised on bronze, depicted in repoussé work and engraving and as cast figurines. The warrior was an ever-present figure in Late Bronze Age society.

The huge number of weapons in circulation in Europe at this time and the ubiquity of the warrior image give the impression that warfare was everywhere in evidence. But while it is true that warfare was endemic, it would be wrong to think of it in terms of the all-out mass conflict of more recent times. Late Bronze Age society was dominated by warrior elites who were required to display their prowess both in appearance and in deeds, particularly by leading raids against distant neighbours to establish claims over new territories or to redefine boundaries. There would have been gain in terms of booty, cattle and women, but the real aim was to provide opportunities for the aspiring young to show their worth in defence of the homeland and to allow the leaders regularly to redisplay their prowess in the eyes of the people. Existence was dominated by the fearless energy of the individual, displayed in single combat, rather than in the confrontation of armies.

Echoes of such a world resound through the works of Homer. The motley band of prima donnas who sailed against the Trojans in the *Iliad* provide an unforgettable image of the times. The arming of Patroclus in preparation for his fatal single combat against Hector before the walls of Troy brilliantly captures the macho arrogance of it all.

> Patroclus put on the shimmering bronze. He began by tying round his legs the splendid greaves, which were fitted with silver clips for the ankles. Next he put on his breast Achilles' beautiful cuirass, scintillating like the stars. Over his shoulders he slung the bronze sword, with its silver-studded hilt, and then the great thick shield. On his sturdy head he set the well-made helmet. It had a horsehair crest, and the plume nodded grimly from on top. Last, he picked up two powerful spears which suited his grip. (Homer, The *Iliad*, XVI.)

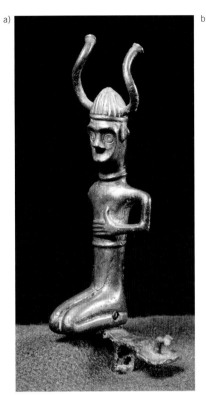

8.3 A gallery of Bronze Age warriors: a) from Grevensvaenge, Denmark b) from Abini (Teti), Sardinia and c) carved on a rock at Tanum, Bohuslän, Sweden.

Overseas expeditions on this scale may have been uncommon but martial prowess and adventure drove ambitious young men throughout Europe to explore the wider world. They are made especially vivid for us in the Aegean world through the writings of Homer and the material culture of the Mycenaean palatial centres, but even in rural Devon in the south-west of Britain, or on remote islands like the Aran Islands off the west coast of Ireland and Shetland, well north of mainland Scotland, the detritus of bronzecasters' moulds shows that the local elites were being freshly supplied with the weapons that signified status. In the Late Bronze Age aspiring leaders throughout Europe all subscribed to the culture of the warrior lord. It was the universal acceptance of these social values, and the material culture that supported them, that gave the European Late Bronze Age its appearance of unity.

There is no conflict between the vision of communities rooted in their ancestral territories maximizing the productivity of the land and the existence of footloose warrior lords; they could have functioned well together, the home base providing the stability and resources for the elite who, in turn, by virtue of their prowess attracted other resources through gifts and the spoils of successful raids. There was a tightness of interdependence that gave a degree of stability to the system. With raid an ever-present threat, defence became a preoccupation and from about 1300 BC fortified settlements begin to appear in most regions – stone-built towers (*nuraghi*) in Sardinia, defended ridge-end settlements in the Alpine Foreland, lake settlements surrounded by log-built ramparts in Poland and hillforts throughout Britain. These constructions show great variety but the aim was always the same: to defend the community while at the same time proclaiming in architecture the physical might of the residents.

In spiritual life, too, a uniformity of beliefs can be discerned across Europe. Perhaps most dramatic is the change from inhumation to cremation, which gathers force in the years after 1300 BC. In most areas of Europe bodies were now burnt on funeral pyres and the ashes collected for burial, usually in cremation urns which were grouped together in cemeteries or 'urnfields'. In fact, so common and widespread was the procedure that the Late Bronze Age has also traditionally been referred to as the Urnfield period. The change to cremation must signify a change in attitudes towards the dead. Perhaps the transience of life was now being acknowledged and the prowess of ancestors celebrated more in oral tradition than in monuments devoted to their physical remains. Another possibility is that there was a major shift in belief systems that separated concepts of earth from concepts of sky. Previously the earth had been the receptor of the whole person and the deceased's material wealth expressed in the form of grave goods, in recognition of the fact, perhaps, that the earth provided the essential sustenance for the community. In cremation

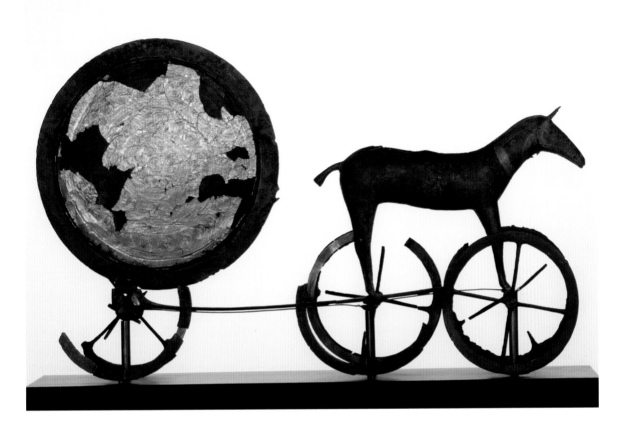

8.4 The cult vehicle from Trundholm in north-west Zealand, Denmark. The gold-plated disc, drawn by the horse, represents the sun. The sun features large in the religious iconography of the period.

the spirit of the deceased was set free into the sky, which realm the spirits now inhabited. But the earth was not forgotten. The power of the chthonic deities was now acknowledged by offerings, often of bronzework, buried in pits dug into the rock or thrown into lakes, rivers and bogs. This practice was particularly well developed in the Atlantic and Nordic regions, where deposition increased dramatically as the Late Bronze Age proceeded. These belief systems, which appeared for the first time towards the end of the second millennium BC, can be traced in many parts of Europe over the next millennium and a half, continuing in some regions throughout the Roman period.

In generalizing about the Late Bronze Age, we have underplayed the regional variations. But generalization has its value in stressing what a remarkable period 1300–800 BC was in European history. It was a time of change, socially, economically and politically when something approaching a pan-European culture begins to appear. The beliefs, values and behaviours, all so clearly reflected in the archaeological record of the Late Bronze Age, resonate throughout much of Europe's subsequent history.

Systems Collapse in the Aegean, 1250–1150 BC

The collapse of the state systems that had emerged around the east Mediterranean in the third and second millennia BC was, from the European point of view, of marginal significance. It has often been implied that demand from the east Mediterranean states for commodities was the motor that drove production and distribution in Europe and was, therefore, a major formative influence on European progress, but in reality there is little evidence for this. By far the greatest part of the raw materials consumed in the east Mediterranean region came either from the region itself or from North Africa and south-west Asia. Europe contributed a few sacks of amber and bundles of furs, and probably some tin and gold, though this is by no means proven. The only clearly defined link to European systems was the sea route that allowed east Mediterranean ships to engage with the Tyrrhenian maritime network and, later, the Adriatic. While these contacts would have been a stimulus to trade they had little impact on the development of the recipient communities. The links northwards to the Carpathian Basin are more tenuous. This region may have been the source of well-trained horses and possibly of two-wheeled chariots, but the dynamics of Carpathian Basin culture was little influenced by the contact, except perhaps in acquiring a taste for flashy bronze body armour. The evidence strongly implies that the rise and fall of the east Mediterranean states in the second millennium BC would have passed little noticed in Europe outside the Aegean.

The spectacular collapse of the palace-based economies of the east Mediterranean was probably due to a combination of factors interacting in a way that amplified the total effect. Contemporary texts, though frustratingly vague in their geographical detail, tell of the movements of peoples both by land and by sea. Many are named but their origins are obscure. Some were evidently desert-fringe or mountain nomads in search of new lands to settle; others were freebooters prepared to join together to raid easy targets or to sell their services as mercenaries to states in need of defence. Mobility was to the fore and the sea was alive with vessels carrying men in search of adventure and plunder, many of them venturing out from ports along the tortuous southern coast of Anatolia, the home of pirates for many centuries to come.

Some flavour of the times can be gleaned from contemporary texts. We have already mentioned the raids on Egypt in 1224 and 1186 BC when attackers descended from the western deserts and the northern sea. In a fiercely energetic scene depicted on the north wall of the Great Temple at Medinet Habu we see the ships of raiders coming under attack from Egyptian archers, some lined up on the shore, others going to meet the aggressors on board their own vessels. Two different groups of raiders are depicted, one wearing horned helmets and carrying long swords and round shields, others similarly armed but with high feathered headdresses – the careful separation encourages us to read them as ethnically different foes.

Another vivid insight into the worsening situation comes from cuneiform texts found at the Hittite capital of Hattusas and in the city-state of Ugarit on the Syrian coast. In one telling letter, from the king of Alashiya (Cyprus) to King Hammurabi of Ugarit, the Cypriot ruler gives advice:

> You have written to me that 'enemy shipping has been sighted at sea'. Well now, even if it is true that enemy ships have been sighted, be firm. Indeed then, what of your troops, your chariots, where are they stationed? Are they stationed close at hand or are they not? Who presses you behind the enemy? Fortify your towns, bring the troops and the chariots into them and wait for the enemy with feet firm.

The reply, probably never sent, is desperate:

> The enemy ships are already here, they have set fire to my towns and have done great damage in the country. Did you not know that all my troops were stationed in the Hittite country and that all my ships are still stationed in Lycia and have not yet returned? So that the country is abandoned to itself. . . . There are seven enemy ships that have come and done very great damage.

No one can doubt from this exchange that the situation was fast deteriorating into anarchy.

On the fringes of this tumultuous world the Mycenaean polities were drawn into the chaos. There are no texts to tell us of the end, no carvings to depict the battles, only mute archaeological evidence of defence, destruction and depopulation. Mycenae and Tiryns were strengthened, so too was the palace on the acropolis of Athens at or soon after 1300 BC when the troubles began. It was at about this time that a wall was built across the Isthmus of Corinth to protect the Peloponnese. Over the next 150 years many of the palace centres were destroyed. In the Argolid, Mycenae, Tiryns and Dendra were burnt. In Laconia, the Menelaion near Sparta was destroyed; so too was Pylos in Messenia; while further north Thebes and Gla in Boeotia and Iolkos in Thessaly all met violent ends. Whether the destructions were part of a single phase of widespread violence it is difficult to say. Most likely the end came gradually, extending over many decades as, one by one, the great palace centres fell. By c.1150 BC the Mycenaean world was at an end.

Some have argued that the prime cause of the collapse lay in environmental decline, creating social dislocation in the marginal regions. This may have been a contributory factor but it was hardly sufficient to topple polities

8.5 The heavily fortified
citadels of Mycenae, Tiryns
and Gla reached their final
form in the thirteenth
century BC at a time of
increased tension before
the collapse of Mycenaean
culture.

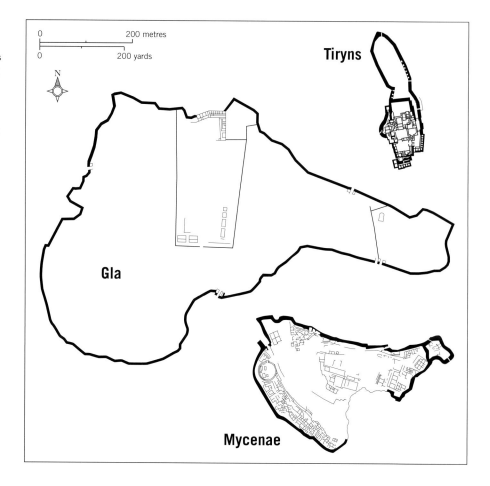

commanding highly fertile lands. The real cause must surely have lain within: the east Mediterranean states were essentially unstable. They were controlled by elites who owed their power to their ability to sustain a high level of production in order to support burgeoning bureaucracies and to maintain a constant flow of the rare or exotic commodities used in diplomacy and trade. Failure in any part of that system would have caused the entire edifice to crumble.

Systems had a built-in trajectory of growth. Local productivity had not only to be maintained but had to be increased; failure to do so would have created instability. But natural constraints limited production. Under bureaucratic pressure to increase yield, the peasantry would despair and move away to fend for themselves, leaving the palace-dominated territory depopulated, much as the archaeological evidence suggests. Collapse from within would follow quickly.

Another factor contributing to the general instability was the vulnerability of the commodity flows upon which interstate diplomacy depended. Supplies

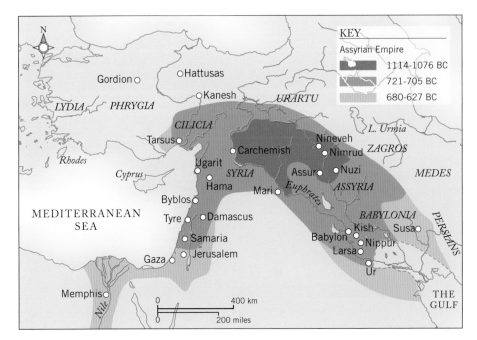

8.6 The Phoenician cities occupying the coast of the Levant came under the influence of the expanding Assyrian Empire, which reached the peak of its power in the seventh century BC.

of goods depended on the safety of overland routes and the willingness of those who controlled them to cooperate, as well as the assurance of reliable shipping lanes free from predators. Both means of transmission could easily be disrupted by peripheral groups. Once raiding of caravans on land and piracy at sea had begun, the entire system would quickly disintegrate. Peripheral middlemen who had once been facilitators would soon become predators, turning on the cities and palaces they had once supplied.

The situation was infinitely complex and no set of simple explanations can contain the variety of actions and interactions there must have been in this century of systems collapse. Some states and palace centres were totally destroyed, complex systems of exchange were disrupted, and people in large numbers were on the move by land and sea. This mobility created a new political geography. But amid the turmoil some fragments of the old world survived. The Egyptians were still a force to be reckoned with and somehow the long-distance shipping lanes between Alashiya (Cyprus) and the Tyrrhenian Sea remained open, providing a network around which new systems were to grow.

Re-emergence in the East: 1150–800 BC

While Egypt survived the chaos of the systems collapse largely intact, elsewhere in the region mobility and resettlement led to new political

8.7 Part of a wall-relief from the palace of the Assyrian king Sargon II (722–705 BC) at Khorsabad in Iraq. It depicts Phoenician river craft with horse-head prows (*hippos*) transporting logs.

configurations. The Philistines who took control of the southern coastal plain of the Levant (now Israel and Palestine) around 1200 BC were probably a small warrior elite who set themselves up over the existing populations, developing five cities – Gaza, Ashkelon, Ashdod, Gath and Ekron – as their principal centres. That they were one of the 'Sea Peoples' from the north is made explicit in various historical sources and there is a suggestion that they may have come from the Aegean region – an idea that gains some support from their pottery, which derives many of its characteristics from Late Mycenaean styles. Once settled in the Levant, they turned their back on the ocean and played no part

240

in the development of maritime commerce, being content to leave these matters to their northern neighbours, the Phoenicians.

Phoenicia is the name given to the northern coastal zone of the Levant extending from Mount Carmel in the south to Arvad in the north – a territory more or less coincident with modern Lebanon. Along the coast a series of great harbour towns developed, many of them, such as Byblos and Sidon, originating long before in the Canaanite period. Tyre, which with Sidon was to rise to dominance, was probably refounded some time in the twelfth century. Whether people from abroad were involved in the renaissance of Phoenicia is difficult to say; everything about the culture and language of the region suggests strong roots in the Canaanite past.

The narrow coastal territory of Phoenicia occupied a crucial position between the Mediterranean and the growing might of the landlocked Assyrian Empire. As order began to be re-established in the twelfth century BC, the elite of the port cities of the Phoenician coast became the great entrepreneurs linking east to west. They greatly extended the old maritime networks, eventually, after c.800 BC, pushing westwards beyond the Mediterranean and out into the Atlantic. The land of Phoenicia also benefited from resources of its own, most notably the famous 'cedars of Lebanon' which were in huge demand for shipbuilding and other works, especially by the Egyptians whose land offered little usable timber. Another marketable commodity was the purple dye made from the murex shell, its importance hinted at in the name Phoenicia, which means 'land of purple'.

A rare insight into commercial activity in the region in the eleventh century is provided by the account of an Egyptian envoy, Wen-Amon, who visited Phoenicia between 1075 and 1060 BC to acquire supplies of cedar wood for the pharaoh. At this time Byblos seems to have been the principal centre. The life of an envoy was not easy. Wen-Amon found the seas infested with pirates and had to contend with the arrogant disdain of the Phoenician elite. In one passage he tells how he was summoned by Zakar-Baal, prince of Byblos:

> When morning arrived he sent for me and bade me go up, but [he] stayed in the tent where he was on the seashore. And I found him seated [in] his high room, with his back turned to a window, so that the waves of the great Syrian sea were [seen] breaking against the back of his head.

This was a neatly contrived setting to put the envoy at a disadvantage!

Eventually the deal was done. Seven great cedar logs were sent to Egypt. In return, the Egyptians sent a mixed cargo containing: '4 crocks and 1 *kak-men* of gold; 5 silver jugs; 10 garments of royal linen; 10 *kherd* of good linen from Upper Egypt; 500 rolls of finished papyrus; 500 cows' hides; 500 ropes; 20 bags of lentils and 30 baskets of fish.'

The prince of Byblos was pleased with the deal and immediately gave the order for more trees to be cut down.

The exchange throws an interesting light on the range of commodities in transit at the time – mostly commodities that would leave little or no archaeological trace. Centuries later Byblos had become the centre for the distribution of Egyptian papyrus, much of it by this time providing for the needs of the Greek world. Indeed, the name by which the city became known comes directly from the Greek word for papyrus – *biblos*: its original Canaanite name had been Gabal.

Wen-Amon's adventures were not quite over. Setting off home from Phoenicia, his ship was driven by a contrary wind to the shores of Alashiya (Cyprus) where he met a hostile mob but he was able to throw himself on the mercy of Heteb 'princess of the city', offering a persuasive argument for his life to be spared.

> Hear me, as for me, they will seek me to assassinate me. As for this crew of the Prince of Byblos, whom they are preparing to kill, shall not their lord find ten of your crews which he will kill.
>
> She [Heteb] summoned the people, who came together. And she said to me 'Spend the night . . .'

At this crucial moment the account breaks off. All we know of the outcome is that Wen-Amon lived to tell the story.

Byblos declined in importance soon after Wen-Amon's visit, giving way to Tyre which, by the late tenth century, had become the dominant Phoenician city and one of the most important ports in the Mediterranean. By the end of the ninth century the Phoenicians had annexed the south-east coast of Cyprus and had founded the trading post of Kition. Their maritime exploits soon extended throughout the Aegean. Inspired by the need to keep records of their fast-expanding mercantile activity, the Phoenicians had, by about 1000 BC, developed an alphabetic writing system which was rapidly adopted by neighbouring communities and soon became the basis of the systems used to write Greek, Hebrew and Aramaic, and hence all modern alphabetic scripts.

The island of Alashiya (Cyprus) occupied a crucial position in maritime exchange networks, being conveniently located in the major sea lanes. It was also a major source of copper as well as having large tracts of fertile land. In the period *c.*1200–1050 BC the island's communities suffered attacks followed by economic decline: settlements were destroyed and abandoned and the population shrank. The two principal harbour towns, Kition and Enkomi, both succumbed, but commercial life continued, though on a more restricted scale. Towards the end of the twelfth and again in the early eleventh century BC there seems to have been an influx of people from the Mycenaean world sufficiently large, or powerful, to introduce the Greek language, which was widely adopted throughout the island.

Throughout this period of turmoil and mobility the Cypriot communities managed to maintain lively trading contacts with partners around the Tyrrhenian Sea. The expansion of Phoenician influence to the island in the tenth century and the foundation of a colony by the city of Tyre at the old port of Kition around 850 BC brought Cyprus firmly into the Phoenician ambit. It is hardly surprising, therefore, that at about this time we find the Phoenicians infiltrating the Cypriot sea lanes to the Tyrrhenian Sea. A generation or two later the Phoenicians were establishing mercantile colonies on Sicily and Sardinia, and along the coast of North Africa.

On the mainland of Greece and the Aegean islands, though the palace-centred economy had collapsed and the population had shrunk, life continued and a pale reflection of Mycenaean culture was kept alive in some areas well into the eleventh century. Yet in the twelfth century changes in material culture can already be detected. New styles of dress appear and there are widespread changes in pottery manufacture. It has been conventional to interpret these innovations as evidence of the Dorian migration from the north recorded in classical tradition. This may indeed be the case, but considerable caution is needed in dealing with evidence of this kind – stylistic changes can come about by means other than mass migration.

One of the most thoroughly studied of the Greek 'Dark Age' sites is Lefkandi on the southern coast of the island of Euboea. Here, a small town developed around which several cemeteries grew up. The settlement began about 2000 BC and was occupied more or less continuously until around 700 BC. In the cemetery area burials began soon after 1100 BC. At first the graves were fairly modest but around 1000 BC exotic grave goods begin to appear. The earliest contained a pot imported from the Levant while a slightly later burial was accompanied by a necklace from the same region. But more remarkable is a large rectangular structure built of mudbrick and timber which the excavators call a heroon – a sanctuary or shrine commemorating the death of a great hero. It was constructed in the tenth century BC and consisted of two

8.8 Cast bronze statue of a warrior god from Enkomi, Cyprus dating to the twelfth century BC. The figure stands on an ox-hide copper ingot typical of those traded widely in the east and central Mediterranean at this time.

243

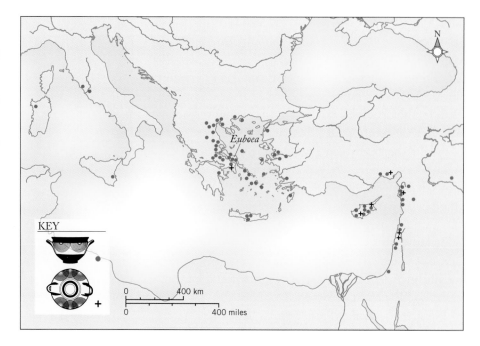

8.9 The inhabitants of the island of Euboea played a crucial role in maritime trade networks in the ninth century BC. The distribution of their distinctive painted pottery (known as pendent-semicircle skyphoi) gives an idea of the possible extent of their trading activities.

shafts, one containing the skeletons of four horses, the other the cremated remains of the 'hero' placed in a bronze vessel of Cypriot manufacture with the body of a woman laid alongside. The woman's body was decked out with a lavish display of jewellery, much of it gold, including an antique gold necklace and pendant, probably of Babylonian origin. In front of the heroon a small cemetery developed, largely comprising rich burials containing fine pottery from nearby Attica as well as a range of grave goods from Syria, Palestine, Cyprus and Egypt.

The evidence from Lefkandi leaves little doubt that the inhabitants of Euboea were closely linked, by networks of exchange, to the east Mediterranean during the period 1000–800 BC. The simplest explanation for this is that Phoenicians, or perhaps Alashiyans (Cypriots), were now exploring the mercantile possibilities of the Aegean and were seeking to establish diplomatic relations with the natives. But there are other alternatives. Could it be that the Lefkandi 'hero' visited Phoenicia some time in the tenth century to meet the king of Tyre and returned laden with gifts, including antiques, and that in the wake of this propitious encounter Phoenician ships were thereafter welcomed in Euboea? We will never know, but it is at least a possibility. One thing, however, is clear: during the ninth century, but perhaps starting a little earlier, highly distinctive Euboean pottery – skyphoi and plates painted with pendent circles – was being widely distributed around the Aegean to Cyprus and the Levant. Such a distribution is most likely to represent Euboean

244

enterprise. At the Syrian port of Al Mina in the estuary of the Orontes, a considerable Euboean presence, perhaps a group of resident traders, is apparent in the last decades of the ninth century. By the ninth century, then, the Euboeans were developing their own maritime networks and in the early decades of the eighth century they had expanded their activities to the Tyrrhenian Sea, where they were instrumental in founding the first of the Greek overseas colonies at Pithekoussai on the island of Ischia in the Bay of Naples. Their maritime prowess is unacknowledged in the classical texts except by the poet of the Delian Hymn to Apollo, who writes of Euboea as being 'famous for its ships' – a fleeting memory, perhaps, of 'Dark Age' achievements.

Iron

It was during the Greek 'Dark Ages' that iron came into regular use, quickly replacing bronze as the metal favoured for weapons and tools. The rapidity with which it was adopted was more a feature of its relative commonness than of any superiority over bronze – until, that is, carburization created a tougher, steel-like metal. Iron oxides occur widely and can be reduced under suitable conditions at temperatures of around 800°C to a spongy mass of iron called a bloom. By constant reheating and beating of the bloom remnant slag can be driven out, leaving serviceable iron that may then be combined with other blooms to create ingots for forging into usable items.

Iron, usually in the form of small trinkets, was in use in parts of Europe and south-west Asia throughout the second millennium BC but it was not until the fifteenth century that the metal was produced on any scale by the Hittites in Anatolia. To begin with, iron was a luxury product suitable as gifts for kings. In the tomb of Tutankhamun (*c*.1327 BC) a fine iron dagger blade and two iron armlets were among the pharaoh's possessions. These may well have been gifts from the Hittites. A little later, in the thirteenth century BC, the Hittite king Hattusilis III wrote to the king of Assyria:

> [A]s for the iron which you wrote to me about, good iron is not available . . . that it is a bad time for producing iron I have written. They will produce good iron but as yet they will not have finished. When they have finished I shall send it to you. Today I am dispatching an iron dagger blade to you.

The scarcity and value of iron is clearly implied and there may at this stage have been some kind of monopoly in bulk production, but by the twelfth and eleventh centuries BC iron was being regularly produced in northern Syria and Cyprus, and from here the technology was introduced to Greece.

By about 900 BC the use of iron was widespread in most regions of the east Mediterranean.

The comparatively rapid adoption of iron has been ascribed to falling supplies of bronze. It is unlikely that copper was in short supply given the rich deposits available on Cyprus, but there could have been a genuine lack of tin caused by the collapse of the Hittite Empire which oversaw the safety of supplies coming from distant Afghanistan. Perhaps it was a desire to find new supplies of tin that drove the Cypriots and Phoenicians to explore the potential of the Tyrrhenian region and beyond.

Cyprus and the West

That maritime interaction took place between the east Mediterranean and the Tyrrhenian Sea from the middle centuries of the second millennium is amply demonstrated by the Mycenaean pottery found in Italy, Sicily and Sardinia. Besides pottery, and a few metal items, the other major 'export' to the west was copper in the form of oxhide ingots. These are found in spectacular quantity on Sardinia and those that have been analysed can be ascribed to a Cypriot source. Chronologically they come from contexts dating from the fifteenth to ninth century BC. The vibrant Cypriot bronze industry was also the source of other luxury items that were carried west along the maritime trade routes – bronze basins of the thirteenth century, mirrors of the twelfth to eleventh centuries and tripod stands of the late eleventh century. To this list of elite items may be added sets of smithy tools, implying that during this period Cypriot smiths visited Sardinia, where they introduced skills that were taken up by local craftsmen and that are reflected in Sardinian copies of Cypriot tripod stands of the eleventh century or later.

Taken together, the evidence suggests that in the fourteenth and thirteenth centuries BC a limited quantity of Cypriot material, including some early copper ingots, a few bronze objects and some pottery, entered the Tyrrhenian maritime system in the context of the general trade with the Aegean which also saw the inflow of Mycenaean pottery. In the twelfth and eleventh centuries Cypriot involvement in the west, particularly with Sardinia, increased dramatically and a group of bronzesmiths arrived on the island, perhaps to settle. Thus, it seems that during the chaos of the twelfth and eleventh centuries the Cypriots maintained and strengthened their links with Sardinia. Why this should have been the case raises a number of interesting issues. One plausible suggestion is that the attraction was Sardinian iron. Sardinia may also have had access to the resources of Tuscany, rich in copper, iron and tin. Another possibility is that tin from the Atlantic region, particularly from Galicia in north-western Iberia, may have been accessible to the

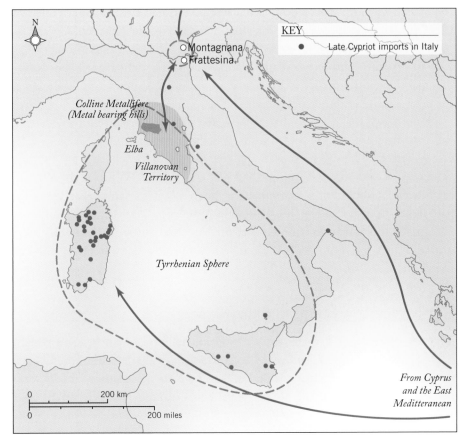

8.10 In the period c.1200–900 BC Cypriot entrepreneurs developed active trading contacts with the communities around the Tyrrhenian Sea and in particular with Sardinia and Sicily. One of the attractions may have been iron and other metals readily available in the region. Trading links were also established with the Po valley communities who commanded trans-Alpine trade.

Sardinians through the Atlantic maritime network. The other commodity always in demand in the east was amber. In the twelfth and eleventh centuries BC quantities of amber from the Baltic and possibly from Jutland were reaching Sardinia via the Po valley and Etruria. Sardinia was now emerging as the focus of exchange networks linking to the east Mediterranean, the Atlantic and the Baltic. Small wonder that the Cypriots, whose market included the newly emerging states of the east, should have taken such an active interest in the island.

There is a related matter to be addressed – the relationship of one of the 'Sea Peoples', the Shardana, to Sardinia, the island known to the Phoenicians as Shardan. The issue has, not surprisingly, been enthusiastically debated, some arguing that the Shardana sailed from Sardinia to become raiders and mercenaries in the east Mediterranean; others preferring to see them as natives of the coastal region of Anatolia who, after the events of 1250–1150, sailed west to settle in Sardinia. On balance, the latter seems the more likely and may be reflected in the much closer links that developed with Cyprus at this time.

A possible scenario would be to see a few boatloads of warriors, attended by their craftsmen, piggybacking on the maritime route between Cyprus to Sardinia to seek out a new home. It would not have been difficult for a skilled elite to establish authority on the island. The subsequent Phoenician settlement of the southern part of the island in the ninth century could be seen as simply a continuation of the same process.

Another of the 'Sea Peoples', the Shekelesh, may also have travelled westwards to find a home on Sicily, whose inhabitants were called Sikels by later Greek writers. There is no convincing archaeological evidence for this but the similarity of name must be more than just coincidence. While archaeologists are reticent in identifying movements of peoples whose names crop up in the half-light of protohistory, the different groups of 'Sea Peoples' were real enough to those who encountered them, and that some of them may have settled in the west at landfalls well known to maritime entrepreneurs is not an unreasonable suggestion.

The Tyrrhenian Systems and the North

The Mycenaean and Cypriot involvement in the Tyrrhenian Sea instituted a link between the central and east Mediterranean in the late second and early first millennia that was soon to be built on by Phoenicians and Greeks seeking niches for their new colonies. The lands around the Tyrrhenian were bound together in a long-established local maritime network, and the period 1300–800 BC was to see a spectacular internal development that owed little or nothing to influences coming from the east. Two regions stand out: Sardinia and Etruria.

In Sardinia, the archaeology of the period is dominated by stone-built settlements – the nuraghi – of which more than seven thousand are known. The nuraghi, at their simplest, are towers up to 18 m (59 ft) high built of large stone blocks. Some are enclosed within outer walls while others form the central focus of larger stone-built settlements that grew up around them. The earliest date to the early second millennium BC but the tradition is long-lived and continued well into the first millennium, even after Phoenician settlements had been established in the south. Although attempts have been made to see Mycenaean inspiration behind the architecture of the nuraghi, it is now widely agreed that the phenomenon is entirely indigenous, the result of local inventiveness developing undisturbed in relative isolation. The one contribution that the east offered was an improved bronzeworking technology. This may have inspired local smiths to experiment with lost-wax casting, which enabled them to create a range of highly original bronze figurines, mostly of humans, giving a unique insight into peoples and their lives. Warriors

dominate but there are shepherds offering sacrifices, musicians and wrestlers, and women carrying water pots or nursing children, as well as animals and boats. In spite of all the swords, shields and bows and arrows depicted, there is a gentle innocence about these figurines.

In Etruria it is customary to divide the cultural sequence into a Late Bronze Age dating to *c*.1350–1020 BC and an Early Iron Age, referred to as the Villanovan culture, which spanned the period from 1020 to 780 BC. After this came the Etruscans. This gives the impression that there were major changes,

8.11 The nuraghe of S. Antine in northwest Sardinia. The central tower dates to the ninth century BC with the enclosing wall added a century or two later. The site continued to be in use into the Roman period.

249

but it is now generally accepted that development was continuous, with no influxes of new people. There were, however, significant changes reflecting growing social and economic complexity.

In the Late Bronze Age populations were widely scattered across the generally congenial and productive landscape with the main settlements averaging 4–5 ha (10–12½ acres) in area, suggesting agglomerations of one or two hundred people. Population was growing and there are signs of increased agricultural production. By this stage cremation had become widespread and social differentiation was beginning to be reflected in grave goods. The ninth century saw profound changes in settlement structure, particularly in southern Etruria where the number of nucleated settlements declines and a few very large conglomerations, covering 100–200 ha (250–500 acres), emerge. The largest of these, Caere (Cerveteri), Tarquinia, Veii, Volsinii (Orvieto) and Vulci, continued in use eventually to become Etruscan towns.

Clearly, in the ninth century we are witnessing the emergence of a more complex system with sufficient stability, both economic and political, to allow settlement nucleation to occur, presumably under the 'patronage' of a few paramount leaders whose authority was underpinned by a stable hierarchical system. Similar processes were at work in Greece at about this time.

For such a system to maintain itself, and to develop a century or two later into a fully urban structure, implies an underlying economy that was both sound and capable of growing. Etruria had much to offer: the land was highly productive and the climate congenial and not subject to extremes. There were also rich metal supplies. The Colline Metallifere (Ore Mountains)

8.12 Warriors, wearing horned helmets, dating to the eighth–seventh century BC. From the nuraghe of Albi (Teti), Sardinia.

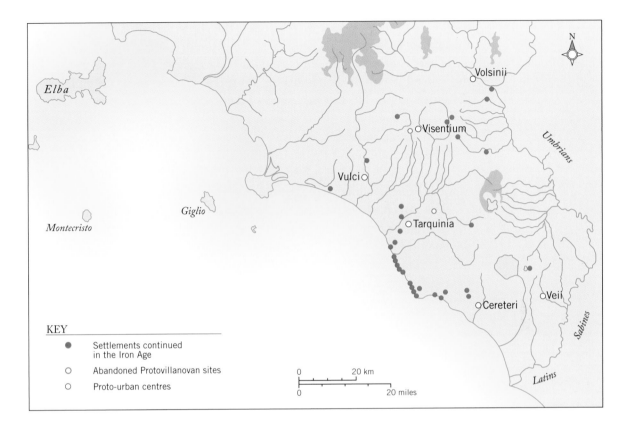

KEY

● Settlements continued
  in the Iron Age

○ Abandoned Protovillanovan sites

○ Proto-urban centres

0   20 km

0   20 miles

in the north produced copper and some tin, while the offshore island of Elba became famous for its high-quality iron ore. These factors were important, but so too was the location of Etruria, looking south to the Tyrrhenian Sea with its flourishing mercantile activity, and north, through the passes of the Apennines, to the Po valley – a region fast becoming a focus of dynamic growth in its own right through its command of major routes to northern Europe and the Adriatic.

By the fourteenth century BC a range of commodities were being moved southwards along these routes, with Etruria providing the interface with the maritime networks of the Tyrrhenian Sea and beyond. Northern amber was transported this way in some quantity from the fourteenth to tenth centuries together with weapons and trinkets, all of European type. The European weapons, with their novel 'foreign' forms and lavish use of metal, would have been highly valued in the Mediterranean world, the swords in particular since they represented a more flamboyant style of fighting. Not surprisingly, we find them being trans-shipped from the Tyrrhenian to the Aegean. Judging by the number of European bronzes reaching the east Mediterranean at the end of the second millennium, the shipments passing through the Tyrrhenian Sea

8.13 In southern Etruria, in the tenth–eighth centuries, large proto-urban settlements emerged as the central places for their discrete regions. These later developed as Etruscan towns.

251

must have been considerable. As a result the elites of Etruria, who controlled the exchanges, flourished.

There is evidence, too, of local trade. Grave goods from the cemeteries of the coastal town of Populonia in northern Etruria included bronzes of Sardinian origin. The fact that many of these exotic items accompanied female burials is a reminder that the exchange of women, given in marriage to establish bonds between peers, was an accepted practice.

The communities of the Po controlled the flow of goods coming from the north through the Alpine passes and from the Middle Danube region through Slovenia. The inhabitants of Etruria were dependent on them.

The Po valley communities were also developing direct links to the east Mediterranean through the maritime networks of the Adriatic. Several sites in the Po valley have yielded pottery of east Mediterranean type dating to the late twelfth to mid-eleventh centuries BC. This raises the intriguing possibility that the Cypriot carriers who were so active in Sardinia were beginning to explore the Adriatic. Could it be that they were attempting to establish more direct routes to northern Europe, not least to acquire the all-important amber? Two trading bases of this period have been found: one at Frattesina on the Po, the other at Montagnana on the Adige to the north. At both there was extensive evidence of craft activity using exotic materials – amber, elephant ivory and ostrich eggshell. The extent of trading links is vividly demonstrated by an ivory comb, made at Frattesina, which eventually ended up in a tomb on Cyprus.

Two processes, then, were at work: a major exchange network was developing, linking territories from north of the Alps to the Tyrrhenian Sea and passing through the Po valley and Etruria, while at the same time entrepreneurs from the east Mediterranean, most likely from Cyprus, were accessing networks both in Sardinia and at the head of the Adriatic. Within this matrix of communications Etruria occupied a focal position; it was a region also blessed with rich resources of its own.

For the moment we must leave the story here at the end of the ninth century, but, looking forward, the Tyrrhenian Sea was soon to become a crucial theatre of development in the Mediterranean and the eventual successor of Etruria – Rome – the principal actor.

The West Mediterranean

Compared to the Tyrrhenian Sea, the nature of maritime activity in the west Mediterranean in the period 1300–800 BC is surprisingly little known but this may be more a result of a lack of focused research than of evidence. There are strong hints, in the scattered distributions of artefacts, that the west

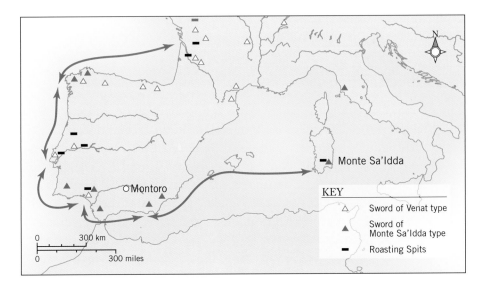

8.14 Links between the central and western Mediterranean are demonstrated by the occurrences of Iberian bronze swords and roasting spits on Sardinia and in Etruria. Mycenaean pottery has been found in Spain at Montoro in the valley of the Guadalquivir.

Mediterranean region was connected with the more vigorous Atlantic exchange network. This is shown by a number of items of Atlantic bronze-work, notably long slashing swords (of types called carp's tongue, Vénat and Monte-Sa-Idda) which are found along the south-east coast of Iberia, in southern Sardinia and northern Etruria. The hoard found at Monte Sa Idda in Sardinia, in addition to the swords, contained a roasting spit of a type well known along the Atlantic coasts of Europe. Finds of this kind reflect, albeit rather faintly, what might have been a well-established local system of maritime exchange. To what extent east Mediterranean entrepreneurs penetrated this system is difficult to say but sherds of Mycenaean pottery found at Montoro in southern Iberia hint at contact.

Classical sources record the tradition that Phoenician entrepreneurs were active in the west Mediterranean in the twelfth century BC, founding settlements at Utica on the coast of Tunisia and then sailing through the Straits of Gibraltar to establish trading ports at Gadir (Cadiz) on an island off the coast of Andalucía and Lixus (Larache) on the Atlantic coast of Morocco. There is no archaeological evidence for these early settlements and most archaeologists believe that Phoenician expansion to the Tyrrhenian Sea and the west Mediterranean did not get under way until the last decades of the ninth century at the earliest. The traditions are nonetheless interesting in that they may reflect a memory of journeys of exploration made by east Mediterranean ships in the twelfth or eleventh centuries BC at a time when, as we have seen, Cypriot maritime activity in the Adriatic and the waters around Sardinia was at its most intense. The inhabitants of Sardinia will have heard much of the far west from the Iberian ships that visited the island. This knowledge, and the

253

expectations it engendered, were soon to inspire Phoenician ships' masters from Tyre to set out on remarkable journeys to open up the west.

Atlantic-Facing Europe

The Atlantic sea routes, linking the ocean-facing communities of Europe from Neolithic times, became increasingly important in the second millennium BC as the consumption of metal intensified. The old hard rocks of southern Ireland, Wales, Cornwall, Brittany and the western coastal regions of Iberia were metal-rich, producing abundant copper to service regional needs and tin and gold for export to other parts of Europe. The scale of metal production during this period can be gauged from the huge number of bronze items pre-served in museum collections – axes, swords, spears, a variety of tools and lux-ury gear. Axes alone number in the tens of thousands. Quantifying objects by period gives the impression that the volume of bronze in circulation increased over time, particularly after 1000 BC. But there are inherent difficulties in deal-ing with crude numbers of discoveries because the great majority of surviving objects come from hoards – that is, deposits that were deliberately buried in the earth – or from watery contexts such as rivers, lakes and bogs where they were presumably thrown as votive offerings to the gods. Comparatively few bronzes have been found in the occupation debris of settlements. Thus, the increase in the number of bronze items recovered may be more a reflection of society's need to placate the deities by placing social wealth in the realms of the chthonic deities than of the quantity of metal in circulation as a whole.

Ritual deposition frequently involved the deposition of offerings in water. The various bogs of Ireland were favoured locations, as were the east-flowing rivers of Britain. The Thames has produced a formidable quantity of fine metalwork, mostly swords and spears, and the tradition continued throughout the subsequent Iron Age with the deposition of shields and helmets as well. Given the importance of the sea to the networks of exchange, we might expect offerings to have been made to the gods of the ocean. One deposit of this kind was found in south-western Iberia in the estuary of the river Odiel, close to the Tartessian port settlement now beneath the modern city of Huelva. Among the 400 or so objects dredged from the river were 78 swords (55 of the distinctive carp's-tongue kind), 22 short swords or daggers, 88 spearheads (some of Irish type), fragments of a helmet and a brooch.

The distribution of the various types of bronze objects found along the Atlantic coasts of Europe provides a proxy for the innumerable journeys made and the exchanges subsequently enacted. They speak of intense maritime and riverine mobility and of the flow of ideas and values to every part of the region, however remote. The deposit in the Odiel estuary near Huelva contained

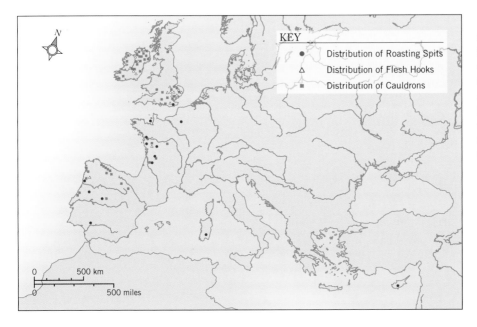

KEY

- Distribution of Roasting Spits
△ Distribution of Flesh Hooks
■ Distribution of Cauldrons

8.15 Distributions of elite feasting gear, such as cauldrons, flesh hooks and roasting spits, along the Atlantic seaways indicate the maritime networks along which ideas and value systems were communicated and exchanged in the period 1200–800 BC.

distinctive lunate spearheads from Ireland and carp's-tongue swords from Armorica (Brittany). This much is clear – but it doesn't tell us how these items travelled. Were they collected by one enterprising ship's master from Huelva who made the 2000 km (1250-mile) journey to Ireland and picked up a consignment of Armorican swords and other items en route, or were the items assembled and carried by a succession of vessels making short-haul journeys, exchanging parts of their cargoes as they moved from port to port? The latter option is likely to have been the norm but longer journeys were probably made from time to time.

Two things stand out from a review of the tons of metal on the move: first, how many local types there were, particularly of axes, which had limited distributions reflecting restricted exchange within a prescribed area; and second, the universal acceptance of elite war gear – swords, shields and spears – and the equipment of the feast – cauldrons to cook in, flesh hooks to lift out stewed joints, and spits to roast the carcass before the fire. The distribution of these items neatly highlights the disparate regions extending the length of Atlantic Europe where elite feasting was prevalent in the tenth and ninth centuries BC, embodying complex social values of hospitality and hierarchy.

A rare glimpse of the world of the Atlantic Bronze Age hero is provided by a series of carved stone stelae found in south-western Iberia dating from the tenth to the eighth century BC. Their exact function is unclear: they are markers of some kind, but whether of graves, territories or routes remains obscure. The depictions, however, memorialize the warrior hero – quite

255

8.16 Leather shield of V-notched type, like that depicted on the stela from Solance de Cabañas, from Clonbrin, Co. Longford, Ireland.

8.17 A group of carved stelae found in south-western Iberia dating from the ninth to seventh centuries BC depict elite items appropriate to the status of the individual commemorated by the monument. This example from Solance de Cabañas shows a warrior with sword, shield and spear, mirror and brooch with a four-wheeled wagon. The shield is of the V-notched type found widely along the Atlantic seaways.

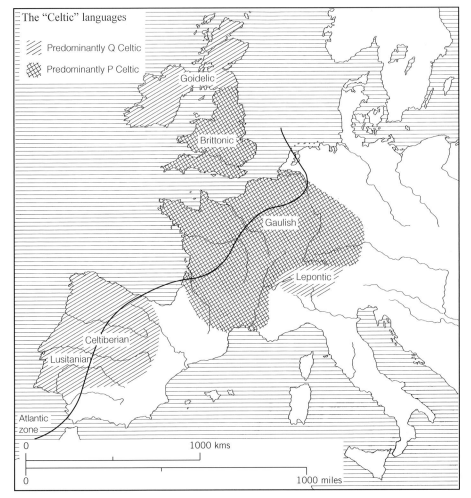

The "Celtic" languages

/// Predominantly Q Celtic
Predominantly P Celtic

Goidelic

Brittonic

Gaulish

Lepontic

Celtiberian

Lusitanian

Atlantic zone

0   1000 kms

0   1000 miles

8.18 The map shows the extent of spoken Celtic in its various dialects in relation to the area of distribution of artefacts of the Atlantic Late Bronze Age. It could be argued that Celtic developed as an Atlantic facade lingua franca which spread along riverine exchange networks into the European hinterland.

possibly individual warriors. The stela from Solance de Cabañas in Cáceres, Spain, is a good example: here the depiction of the person is surrounded by symbols of rank, a four-wheeled vehicle, a large circular V-notched shield of a type known throughout the Atlantic region, a long slashing sword, a spear and two other items less certain in type (perhaps a mirror and a cloak fastening). A man commanding all these things was a man of status in the Late Bronze Age.

The Cáceres warrior probably never travelled far from his native territory, but had he gone to the centre of Ireland, to Co. Longford, he might have seen a warrior carrying a leather shield identical to his own (it was later thrown into a bog), and had he travelled on to the settlement of Jarlshof on remote Shetland far to the north of the Scottish mainland, he could have watched a bronzesmith cast a flange-hilted sword like the one he was carrying. The similarity between cultures brought about by intensive contact along the Atlantic seaways was quite remarkable.

By the Late Bronze Age the communities of the Atlantic zone had been bound to each other by networks of interaction and exchange for more than three thousand years, and the period from *c*.1300 to 800 BC saw an intensification of these contacts. In such circumstances it would not be surprising to find the development of broadly similar languages evolving out of the common Indo-European that had probably been introduced in the Neolithic period. This language group would be the one we now call Celtic, which is still spoken in different forms in Brittany, Wales and Ireland and on the western coasts and isles of Scotland. Celtic probably evolved in the Atlantic zone during the Bronze Age. There is some textual evidence to suggest that Celtic names were in use in the region by the sixth century BC and thereafter there is ample material in proper names and inscriptions to suggest that forms of Celtic were spoken in most regions of Atlantic Europe. The one exception is the Basque region, spanning the Pyrenees in northern Spain and south-west France. The Basque language is quite different and is thought to have originated earlier than the introduction of Indo-European. Interestingly, this region, facing the Golfe de Gascogne, seems to have been remote from the Atlantic maritime networks of the Late Bronze Age. Ships seldom, if ever, penetrated this cul-de-sac; the mountainous coasts of northern Spain and the monotonous and uninviting sand bar of the Landes offered little attraction. The Basques were left in isolation to nurture their language until the early Middle Ages, when they began to embrace the sea with enthusiasm.

The Nordic World and its Neighbours

In the Nordic zone the traditions of the preceding period continued but the burial rite changed from inhumation to cremation, accompanied by changes in the deposition of metalwork. Previously, bronze, and occasionally gold, items were buried with the dead, but with the widespread adoption of cremation the deposition of personal wealth was now made in bogs. This change in the belief system and the ritual associated with it is part of a Europe-wide phenomenon and is accompanied by the widespread use of the 'sunship bird' motif (*sonnenbarkenvogel*) which represents a sun disc being carried on board a boat, the prow and stern of which are fashioned to represent the heads of swans. Motifs of this kind were popular on repoussé bronzework and were inscribed on bronze knives and razors. This imagery of sun and birds represents an increasing emphasis on the sky where gods and the spirits of the departed were thought to reside. There may also be some concept embedded in these images of the sun, having set in the west, being transported back to the east to rise again.

8.19 Repoussé decoration on bronze vessels found in central and northern Europe frequently adopted a motif incorporating a sun disc and two birds' heads, which is usually interpreted as a ship carrying the sun on its journey through the underworld.

The boat is a dominant symbol among the huge number of rock engravings found in southern Sweden and Norway. The carvings were already under way by the middle of the second millennium BC and continued to be added to and expanded over the next thousand years. A recent assessment of the extent of rock carving found in one of the more prolific zones, along the west-facing coast of southern Sweden in the Østfold and Bohuslän regions, estimates a

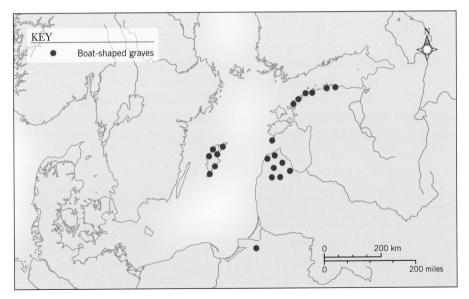

8.20 The distribution of boat-shaped graves in the Baltic.

8.21 Boat-shaped grave of the Late Bronze Age at Boge on the Baltic island of Gotland.

total of five thousand individual sites accounting for 75,000 individual images – and the number rises yearly as fieldwork continues. The most common motifs are boats, humans and other animals, with discs, feet and wheeled vehicles occurring less often. Boats are represented by more than seven thousand images in Bohuslän alone.

Boat imagery was also incorporated into the burial ritual among communities around the Baltic. In parts of southern Sweden and on the Baltic island of Gotland and along the coast of the Baltic States, boat-shaped stone settings were created to enclose grave mounds. In the more elaborate examples, stone blocks, standing on end, are so arranged that the sheer-line rises to a high prow. Sometimes the stern is squared off with a transverse stone, giving the appearance of a transom-sterned vessel. Among the coastal communities and the islanders of Gotland, where more than three hundred of the boat-shaped graves have been found, the seagoing ship must have dominated their lives.

The Nordic zone continued to depend for its metals, copper and gold on regions far to the south – the Carpathian Basin and the Alpine zone – while tin and possibly some copper could have been got from nearer to home in the Ore Mountains on the border between modern Germany and the Czech

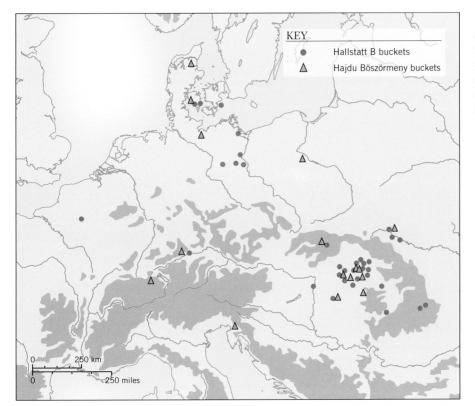

8.22 The distributions of buckets of the ninth and eighth centuries BC indicate an axis of exchange extending from the Carpathian Basin to the Baltic.

Republic. But supply was by no means constant. By the twelfth century imports of new metal from southern Germany and the Alps had almost dried up and the Nordic communities were forced to recycle old bronze, but by about 1000 BC a new exchange route had been established with the Carpathian Basin, probably via the river Oder. This lasted until some time in the ninth century when all links with the region ceased. Why this should have happened is not clear. It could be that the elites who occupied Poland blocked the passage of goods across their territory, but a more likely explanation is that the Carpathian Basin communities were in disarray in the face of new settlers arriving from the steppes, a matter to which we will return (see pp. 264–5). The effect of all this was that the Nordic zone now began to rely on the north-western Alps for its bronze. From the distribution of traded bronze objects it is possible to trace the interregional route northwards across the Middle Rhine, the central Elbe and the Lower Odra to the Baltic coast, and from there to the Danish islands and eastern Jutland.

Along this route lie a succession of centres where luxury goods are concentrated, many in burials and in hoards. These must have been the territories of local elites who maintained their power by controlling the passage of

261

8.23 The distributions of sword types of the eighth century BC indicate the exchange networks linking communities from the Po valley to the Baltic.

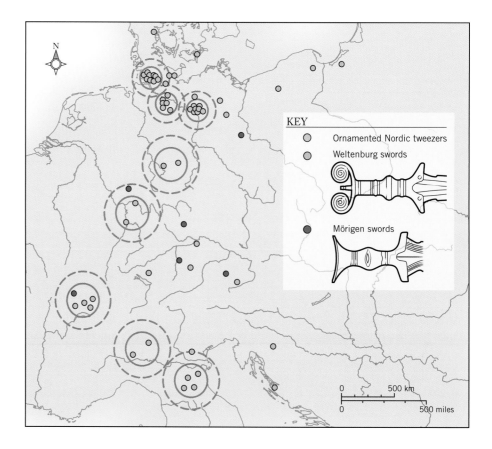

KEY

Ornamented Nordic tweezers

Weltenburg swords

Mörigen swords

commodities. Concentrations of antennae-hilted swords – weapons of high prestige – are a good indicator of these elite centres. One of the best-known is at Seddin on the river Elbe, a region producing some 320 rich burials in 240 barrows. The largest of the 'royal' barrows was a colossal structure, 80 m (260 ft) in diameter and 11 m (36 ft) high. Within was a stone-built chamber with a corbelled roof. The walls were plastered and painted in white, black and red. The chieftain afforded this glory had been cremated and his bones put in a bronze amphora accompanied by swords, metal vessels, other small bronzes and a set of unique pots. Nearby were buried two women, probably his wives, each with her own ornaments.

Another of the elite centres has been identified in the region of Voldtofte on the Danish island of Funen. At the 'royal' cemetery of Lusehøj the principal barrow was 40 m (130 ft) in diameter and 7 m (23 ft) high; it had been built of large turves, which would have required the stripping of more than 7 ha (17 acres) of grassland. The primary burial comprised a cremation. Sufficient survived of the grave goods to show that they included a complete wagon of central European type, various fittings usually associated with

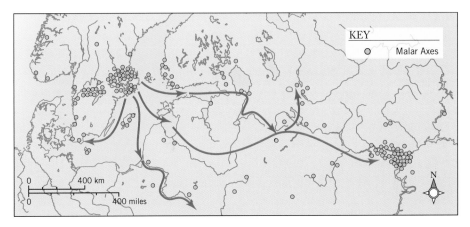

KEY

○ Malar Axes

8.24 The distribution of a particular type of bronze axe, made in the region of Mälar in Sweden, demonstrating the extensive trading systems linking Sweden with the river Volga.

musical horns (lurs), a sword or dagger, and pieces of iron and gold. The burials at Seddin and Lusehøj are quite exceptional. The quality of the grave goods, access to rare foreign luxuries and massive input of labour in constructing the mounds signify men of considerable prestige. Here, we are surely glimpsing the chieftains who exercised total control over the movement of goods on one of Europe's busiest transpeninsular routes. While the demand for bronze lasted, their power was unshakeable.

The boat-shaped burials found in the coastal areas of Sweden and on the island of Gotland are a reminder of the importance of the sea to those living around the shores of the Baltic. Similar boat-shaped burials are also known along the eastern shore, in Latvia, along the north coast of Estonia, overlooking the Gulf of Finland and on the island of Saaremaa at the mouth of the Gulf of Riga. The burials on Saaremaa used sandstone of a type that does not occur on the island and that therefore has to have been brought by sea. These are tantalizing glimpses of the rich coastal culture that must have bound the inhabitants of the shores and islands of the Baltic together in a maritime comradeship.

The eastern Baltic coast land offers an interface with the intricate river systems that interlace their ways across the vast expanse of the forest zone of northern Europe as far east as the Urals. That these rivers were used as routes penetrating deep into Russia is shown by the distribution of a particular kind of bronze axe, known as the Mälar axe, that was produced in large quantities in central Sweden, in the vicinity of the Mälaren Lake, and traded widely around the Baltic. They are found on the islands of Bornholm, Gotland and Åland, in the coastal regions of Finland and in the Baltic states, and from here the distribution extends eastwards for some 1600 km (1000 miles) almost to the Urals. Although axes of this kind were essentially an everyday tool, in the middle of Russia they seem to have been treated as a prestige item,

263

elevated to the status of symbols of authority by their foreignness and the great distances they had to travel. What other Scandinavian products were carried eastwards along the Russian rivers is a matter of guesswork. Nor do we know what kind of goods made the return journey though it may have been ingots of bronze. The people of the Kama–Middle Volga region had access to ample supplies of metal from the Caucasus. Could it be that the Baltic entrepreneurs were attempting to find alternative sources when, in the period around 1100 BC, bronze from Europe was suddenly in short supply? Whatever the reason, those making the great eastward journey in the Late Bronze Age were exploring a route that their successors would make their own two thousand years later.

Enter the Cimmerians – Horsemen from the Steppe

The first of the peoples to inhabit the steppe for whom a name is recorded are the Cimmerians. In a brief passage in Homer's *Odyssey* we encounter them when the hero's ships in the Black Sea are driven to 'the frontiers of the world, where the fog-bound Cimmerians live in the City of Perpetual Mist'. Not much helpful geographical detail there, but a few centuries later Herodotus adds a little precision. Writing of the Scythians, he describes how, under pressure from warlike neighbours, they 'gutted their homes, crossed the Araxes [Volga] and entered the land of Cimmeria. For the land which is now inhabited by the Scyths was formerly the country of the Cimmerians' (*Hist.* IV, 11). He goes on to explain that, hearing of the threat of the Scythian advance, there was dissent among the Cimmerians, which led to fighting between the diverent factions: 'All of the Royal tribe was slain and their people buried them near the Tyras [Dnestr], where their grave is still to be seen. Then the rest of the Cimmerians departed, and the Scythians, on their coming, took possession of a deserted land' (*Hist.* IV, 11).

Finally, we are told, some of the Cimmerians fled southwards, following the east coast of the Black Sea into Asia Minor, hotly pursued by Scythians who took a more easterly route. These bands, both Cimmerians and Scythians, reappear in history in Assyrian texts as mercenaries in the long-drawn-out battles fought between the kings of Uratu and the Assyrians over control of Anatolia in the seventh century. Other bands took no interest in Asia Minor and moved further south into the Levant where they appear in the Old Testament as the children of Gomer. The south-moving Cimmerians are known to us because they are caught on the fringes of history. Those who travelled westwards and buried their kings near the Dnestr are anonymous, but they can be glimpsed in the archaeological record as they move into the Great Hungarian Plain.

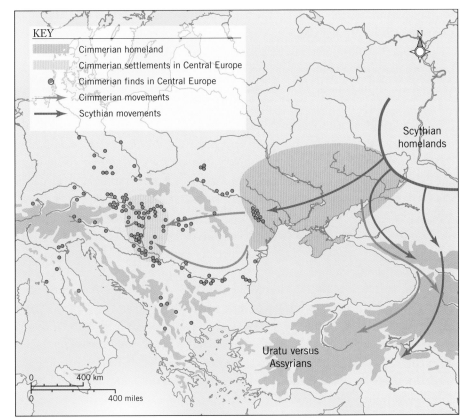

8.25 The map indicates the mobility of steppe pastoralists in the eighth century BC.

But, first, to return to the steppes. In the period from the fourteenth to the twelfth century BC, a large area of steppe around the north side of the Black Sea experienced a period of stability and population growth based on a settled agricultural regime (referred to archaeologically as the Sabatinovka culture). At the end of the thirteenth century there is clear evidence of a sharp climatic change bringing colder and much drier weather conditions, which disrupted stability by undermining the subsistence base. What followed (known as the Belozerka culture) saw the abandonment of settlements in what had become the more arid regions, and a readjustment of the farming systems with a much greater emphasis on animal husbandry, especially the rearing of large herds of cattle. The horse became even more important. In the period 1100–900 BC the first truly nomadic groups emerged in the central part of the east European steppe and a new mobility began with whole communities moving out of this central zone into more peripheral areas like the northern flanks of the Caucasus, the Krim peninsula and the Middle Dnepr and Middle Volga valleys. The reverberations of these events were also felt in the east, east of the Altai Mountains and in Manchuria, where migrating bands of semi-nomadic peoples had to be restrained by the kings of the Western Chan dynasty in the twelfth–eighth centuries BC.

The archaeology of this period is redolent with the warrior horseman: large numbers of weapons were buried in the richer graves and horse gear was everywhere to be found. These disparate and sometimes warring groups were the peoples known to the literate world as Cimmerians.

In the valley of the Lower Danube and the Carpathian Basin beyond, the ninth and eighth centuries BC were a period of dislocation and change. It is difficult to disentangle the complex of causes, but prominent among them was a greatly enhanced contact with the steppe zone which seems to have involved the inward migration of nomadic bands arriving over an extended period. This was probably related to the general outward movement of nomads from the central part of the east European steppe to the more peripheral areas beginning in the eleventh century BC, the mood of which is captured in the over-simplified vignette of the migrating Cimmerians provided by Herodotus. In archaeological terms the arrival of steppe communities in the Carpathian Basin is represented by a completely new set of artefact types relating to warrior horsemen – short, narrow-bladed swords and daggers of iron (with whetstones to sharpen them), spears of iron as well as of bronze, a range of horse gear including highly distinctive bits and side pieces, and bronze sceptre beads often with animal-headed terminals. These items, all closely related to the material culture of the steppe, are found distributed throughout the Carpathian Basin, with isolated examples occurring beyond as far as the Po valley, the eastern Alps and Poland.

While there can be little doubt that there was intense interaction with the steppe region in the ninth and eighth centuries BC, the nature of that contact is difficult to specify. But it is not impossible that bands of warrior nomads were able to establish themselves in enclaves within the region, to be strengthened as other clan members joined them. One such enclave settled in the Eger region of northern Hungary where a distinctive cultural group, known as the Mezöcsát culture, has been identified. Their metal artefacts and the inhumation burial rite are quite alien to the indigenous traditions and the economy is heavily dependent on animal husbandry: all this relates closely to steppe culture, yet the pottery is in the local tradition. Here, perhaps, we are seeing a mixing of populations as incomers intermarry with the local people.

The influx of nomads from the steppe had a profound effect on the long-established trading networks of Europe. Links between the Carpathian Basin, North Alpine and Nordic regions came to an end in the ninth century, leaving the western route between the Baltic and the Mediterranean to carry the bulk of the commodity flow. Threat of attack from the south may have been one of the reasons why the Lausitz cultural zone of Poland developed strongly fortified settlements. But it would be wrong to assume that a kind of

266

pre-historic Iron Curtain descended across Europe; the interface between east and west was permeable, and ideas and beliefs flowed freely in each direction even though cultural identities were maintained.

Middle Europe

We turn finally to the heartland of Middle Europe – the North Alpine cultural complex – which typifies the Late Bronze Age Urnfield culture as we characterized it at the beginning of this chapter. This broad region is the most favoured of Europe: not only does it command the northern approaches to all the passes through the Alps but it also incorporates the headwaters of the major rivers, the Rhône/Saône, Garonne, Loire, Seine, Rhine, Weser, Elbe and Oder. All the cross-peninsular routes between the Atlantic, North Sea and Baltic, and the Mediterranean passed through this single zone. By the Late Bronze Age, when commodities were being transported on a massive scale, movement through the North Alpine zone reached a crescendo. This fluidity helped to create a unified culture which expanded outwards from the core following the main axes of communication. The phenomenon used to be described as 'the expansion of the Urnfielders' – the concept being of Middle Europeans who moved out from their homeland to conquer neighbouring areas – when what we are really seeing is the progressive adoption of central values by peripheral exchange partners – a precocious manifestation of European 'globalization'.

Over the half-millennium from 1300 to 800 BC the disparate communities of the North Alpine zone developed a homogeneous culture with a rich ritual symbolism and a distinctive style of elite display. Central to both was the idea of the journey symbolized by a four-wheeled carriage pulled by two yoked horses represented by actual ceremonial vehicles and by models used for rituals. The functional ceremonial carriages were elegant affairs with small wheels 50–75 cm (20–30 ins) in diameter assembled from cast- and sheet-bronze elements. In the thirteenth and twelfth centuries BC they were used to take the dead body to the funeral pyre and were burnt with the body. Later, in the ninth century, similar vehicles, possibly for use in religious processions, are found throughout a broad zone stretching from the Rhône and Rhine. Bronze cult models used in rituals also occur throughout the North Alpine zone. They are usually in the form of four-wheeled vehicles carrying urns, often protected by symbolic birds, and were carefully deposited at the end of their ritual lives. Sturdy workaday carts must have existed alongside the delicate ceremonial version but there is much less evidence for them.

While it is likely that working carts were pulled by oxen, the light cere-monial vehicles were horse-drawn – a point demonstrated by the discovery of horse gear, usually the mouth bars and side pieces of bits, now made in bronze.

8.26 These two bronze vessels are masterpieces of the bronze-smith's art dating to the late Bronze Age. They participated in the passage of the dead (as cremated remains) to the afterlife and clearly incorporate representations of funerary vehicles which may well have been symbols of high status. Above: from Peckatel, Mecklenburg, Germany; below: from Bujoru, Teleorman, Romania.

In the earlier period the bits were made with side pieces of antler while the mouth piece was usually a twisted thong of leather. In the thirteenth century BC both elements began to be made of bronze. In these early examples the mouth pieces were direct copies in bronze of twisted leather bars while the curved form of the side piece echoes the shape of the antler predecessor, providing a convincing example of skeuomorphism. From the horse gear it is possible to show that the mouth widths of these North Alpine horses were 8–10 cm (3–4 ins) (compared with an average of 15 cm [6 ins] for a modern horse). The beasts were therefore small and ponylike, and were probably the indigenous west European type rather than the sturdier steppe breed employed in the east.

The use of the horse and the carriage, well established at an elite and ceremonial level in the North Alpine zone in the Late Bronze Age, continues a tradition that goes back into the third millennium. Though the technology changed, the funeral cart was to become a potent symbol of authority in many parts of Europe throughout the rest of the millennium, in some parts lasting until the Roman invasion.

A Brief Epilogue

Europe in the period 1300–800 BC was a vibrant place – a place of energy and assurance, interconnected as never before. Commodities were moving across the continent and around the coasts at a rate previously unknown and with them flowed ideas, so creating a remarkable degree of similarity across huge territories. Slashing swords, spears and socketed axes, bronze body armour and round shields were in use almost everywhere and the religious iconography of the bird/boat/sun suggests a universality of belief, as does the widespread adoption of the rite of cremation. The symbolism of the horse-drawn ceremonial cart could be seen on the stelae of south-west Iberia or carved on the living rock in the passes of northern Italy and on the shores of southern Sweden in familiar simplification. Bronze figurines of warriors wearing horned helmets are found in Sardinia and Scandinavia and, in the guise of sea raiders from the north, are carved on the walls of Egyptian temples. The overriding impression is of cultural fluidity borne of mobility.

True, in one corner of Europe a precocious political system collapsed, but hardly a ripple affected the spectacular developments in the rest of the peninsula where the established trajectories continued unmoved. But by the ninth century BC change was in the air. In two separate regions of the Mediterranean – Greece and Etruria – large agglomerations of population were coming together as early states began to form. Meanwhile, on the Pontic steppe and in the Carpathian Basin nomadism was becoming an alternative lifestyle. The stage was now set: Europe was poised for a period of unprecedented change.

269

CHAPTER NINE

The Three Hundred Years That Changed the World: 800–500 BC

'The three hundred years that changed the world' is perhaps a somewhat exaggerated claim but it rather depends on one's viewpoint. To a classicist focused on the Mediterranean, this was a period of phenomenal change during which all those who were to become big players on the world stage emerged from prehistoric obscurity – Greeks, Phoenicians, Etruscans, Carthaginians and Romans – and serious 'history' begins, with texts providing the names of the key actors and stories of political intrigue spiced with set-piece battles – presented of course through the eyes of the victors. For them, it was as though the fog had lifted, allowing the glories of Greece and the might of Rome to burst through. An archaeologist might approach the period from a different perspective. This was a time when many of the social and economic trajectories already under way in the preceding centuries escalated and collided. The desire to control resources led to political entanglements that created new imperatives. It was a time, too, when tens of thousands of people were leaving their homes to set up enclaves in distant territories, creating new interfaces with *barbarians* (the general phrase used by the Greeks and Romans to describe other people) and from these contact zones ripples of change spread deep into the hinterland of Europe. The nature of exchange was also transformed: at the beginning of the period the movement of commodities was still embedded within systems of tribute and gift-giving between elites; by the end we can at last talk of trade in the sense of the purchase of commodities without further obligation. The real fascination of the period lies in being able to trace the exponential growth in interconnectedness between the developing polities in the Mediterranean and the interactions between the Mediterranean states and the chiefdoms of the European peninsula.

The information base becomes much richer. In addition to the mute archaeological evidence there is now a body of textual data. By its very nature all written evidence is selected and distorted by its authors, but among the more reliable sources are the histories of Herodotus written in the mid-fifth century BC and of Thucydides written later in the same century. Both writers were close to the events they described and, while by no means free from bias,

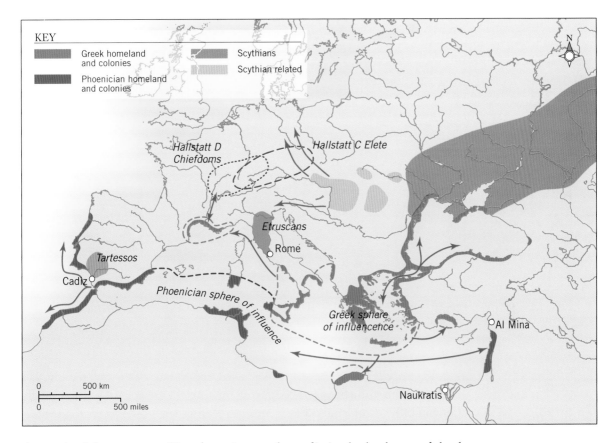

9.1 Europe 800–500 BC. The cities of the two Mediterranean powers, Phoenicia and Greece, were now beginning to carve up the Mediterranean into spheres of influence, the Greeks making the Black Sea their own while the Phoenicians expanded into the Atlantic. In Eastern Europe the Scythians from the steppes established enclaves as far as the Great Hungarian Plain.

they strived for accuracy. Herodotus is encyclopaedic in the background, both historical and geographical, that he provides for his story of the struggles between the Greeks and the Persians, while Thucydides offers a detailed account of much of the Peloponnesian War between Athens and Sparta (431–404 BC), an event that he lived through and took part in. Other scraps gleaned from later writers help to sketch in some of the background and to create a tolerably robust chronological skeleton.

The archaeological evidence is much richer for this period than for earlier times, not least because generations of scholars working on the stylistic niceties of Greek pottery, fine metalwork and statuary have been able to develop tightly dated sequences that give reasonably accurate dates to the contexts in which they are found. In addition, coins minted by many of the states, lawcodes inscribed on stone, and graffiti scratched on pots all add to the varied database. For barbarian Europe, apart from a few generalized insights gleaned from Herodotus, we are still reliant on material evidence preserved in the archaeological record, though a few datable Mediterranean imports help in constructing chronologies and offer some insight into social interactions.

The disparity in the data base between the Mediterranean zone and the

9.2 The Greeks in the Mediterranean and the Black Sea. Over a brief two centuries, 750–550, the Greeks had established cities and trading posts throughout the Black Sea and the central Mediterranean, extending as far west as Emporion in north-eastern Iberia. These western colonies were a direct threat to the trading activities of the Etruscan city states.

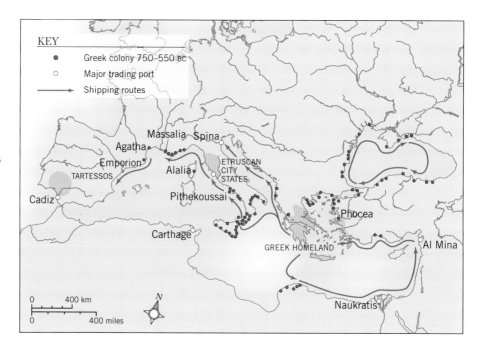

KEY

●   Greek colony 750–550 BC
○   Major trading port
→   Shipping routes

Massalia   Spina
Agatha
Emporion
TARTESSOS   Alalia
ETRUSCAN CITY STATES
Cadiz
Pithekoussai
Carthage
GREEK HOMELAND
Phocea
Al Mina
Naukratis

0   400 km
0   400 miles

N

rest of Europe tends to distort the perceived importance of the two regions and has led to the unfortunate tendency of treating them separately when really they can only be understood in relation to each other. In the pages that follow we will make some effort to restore a balance and to resist the temptation of being drawn into too many of the intriguing sidelines of classical archaeology.

The Big Players: A Very Brief Sketch of the Mediterranean, 800–500 BC

Since we are concerned in this book with the broad processes of change that underlie the development of Europe, rather than the events and the personalities flitting on the surface, conventional history will not feature large. But to set the scene it will be helpful, first, to give a very brief sketch of geopolitical events in terms of the big players – the main ethnic configurations as they were perceived by the classical writers.

The two most active of the Mediterranean peoples in this period were the Phoenicians and the Greeks. The Phoenicians occupied the narrow coastal strip of the Levant (Lebanon and Syria) dominated by the cities of Tyre and Sidon, while the homeland of the Greeks lay in the lands surrounding the Aegean. While they may have begun as partners in exploring the Mediterranean, they were soon to become competitors as they set up colonies the better to exploit the potential of the barbarian world. The Phoenicians

272

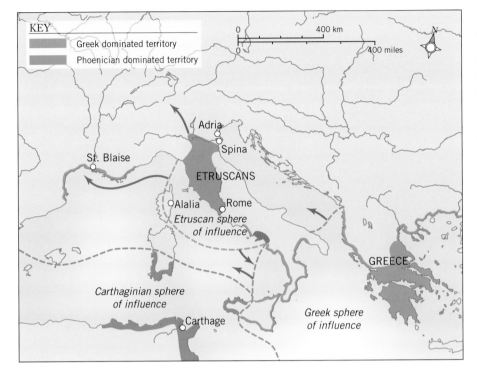

9.3 The Etruscans maintained a sphere of influence, extending from Campagna to the Rhône delta, which was complementary to the Carthaginian sphere in the south Mediterranean. The two maritime powers existed in harmony but the expansion of Greek influence into the west Mediterranean upset the balance.

concentrated on the North African coast, western Sicily and Sardinia, and were soon thrusting through the Straits of Gibraltar to explore the Atlantic regions, while the Greeks focused mainly on southern Italy and eastern Sicily, later extending to the northern shores of the west Mediterranean. This brought them into direct conflict with the Etruscans who had previously commanded the trade routes in the region.

Beyond the immediate confines of Europe were the Assyrians and the Persians, both of whom played a significant part in European history. The Assyrians – inland neighbours of the Phoenicians of the Levant – were a consuming people who relied on the seagoing Phoenicians to supply their material needs, thus galvanizing Phoenician entrepreneurs in their efforts to explore the Mediterranean. The Persians, whose homeland lay in what is now Iran, were a more distant power but for a brief period they turned their attention westwards. Under King Cyrus (557–530 BC) the Persian armies embarked on a series of spectacular campaigns, annexing Greek cities on the Aegean coast of Anatolia. Under Darius (522–486 BC) Persian generals pushed westwards along the north coast of Africa and into Europe, taking control of Thrace and Macedonia before turning their attention to Greece.

The resilience of the Greeks and their famous victories at Marathon (490 BC), Salamis (480) and Platea (479) stemmed the Persian advance and the

273

9.4 In the Near East the rise of, first, the Assyrians and, later, the Persians began to impact on Europe. The presence of the Persian army in the Balkans greatly influenced the development of Thracian art.

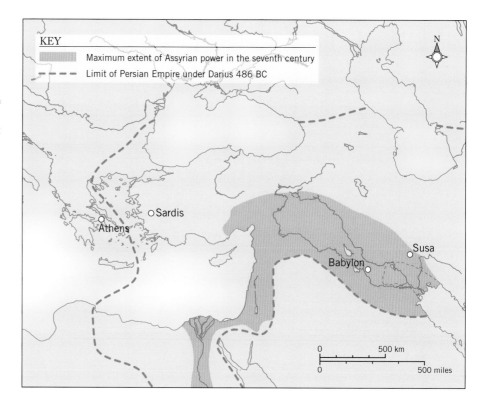

threat rapidly receded. While understandably featuring large in Greek history, however, these events had little lasting impact on the course of European development. Greek unity soon collapsed into a squabble of city-states.

What lay behind this broad sweep of events was a fast-developing network of intricate interactions driven by the desire to command commodities. The only way to compete in such a changing world was to become entrepreneurial and aggressive.

The East Mediterranean: The Phoenician Sphere

By the beginning of the eighth century Tyre had emerged as the most power-ful of the commercial maritime powers operating in the shadow of the Assyrians. It had two principal strengths: its merchant fleet, which had a long tradition of overseas trading; and its resident craftsmen, renowned for creating luxury and prestige items designed to satisfy the elites, mainly in the east. The one fed on the other. The ships could bring exotic materials from far-flung parts, adding considerably to the value of items made by the craft schools, while the promise of luxury consumer goods could entice distant kings to arrange for stockpiles of rare raw materials to be ready for exchange and trans-shipment. Thus, sets of ritual bronze vessels and elaborate jewellery were welcomed in Iberia by the kings of Tartessos in exchange for raw silver which was to be had in plenty.

The Assyrian demand for tribute was a spur to international trade and manufacturing. Tribute lists exist. In the early ninth century Tyre was supplying gold, silver, tin, linen, monkeys, ebonite, and chests of wood and ivory. Later in the century gold, silver, lead and bronze are mentioned along with wool dyed purple, metal vessels and ivory, while early in the eighth century huge quantities of iron are added to the staples of purple cloth and ivory. On the back of the tribute, trade goods flowed eastwards to satisfy the growing consumer market.

Tyre's relationship with its other neighbour, Israel, presents a rather different picture. In the tenth century the king of Tyre Hiram I agreed a deal with King Solomon to supply luxury goods, building materials, including cedar wood, and technical assistance in return for silver, wheat, olive oil and 'food for the Royal household'. The emphasis here, on staple food supplies, is a reminder that Phoenicia was a comparatively infertile and restricted land which struggled to supply its growing population.

The tenth-century accounts of exchanges refer specifically to relationships at the highest level, king to king, implying systems of tribute and reciprocity, but a separate class of traders was already in existence, making deals in the interests of profit. Yet these should not be seen as two separate systems since each was reliant on the other the two, working closely in harmony, supporting each other's interests. In the ninth century the texts specifically refer to independent merchants from Tyre who were now managing the long-distance overland movement of goods, presumably including royal exchanges, and a seventh-century document refers to both 'the ships of Baal' (the king) and the ships of 'the people of Tyre', the implication being that the royal house and the merchant oligarchy were running separate enterprises. We have now moved firmly into a commercial world – a world of supply and demand, price fluctuations and private speculation. Above all, it was a world in which there were big profits to be made. With these the merchant oligarchy could grow their businesses by reinvesting in the ships so necessary to keep trade booming.

The foundation of Kition on the east coast of Cyprus around 830 BC was a crucial first step in the Phoenician opening up of the west Mediterranean, since not only was the port a vital link in the long chain of watering places en route, it was also the home of a people with a long tradition of successful maritime trade in the central Mediterranean going back for centuries. As a repository of geographical knowledge and sea lore it was invaluable.

Beyond Cyprus, for a ship's master wanting to make rapid headway west

9.5 The Phoenicians focused their colonial attention at first on the southern part of the Mediterranean on the islands of Sicily and Sardinia and along the north African coast, but the foundation of Gadir (Cadiz) brought them into the Atlantic sphere.

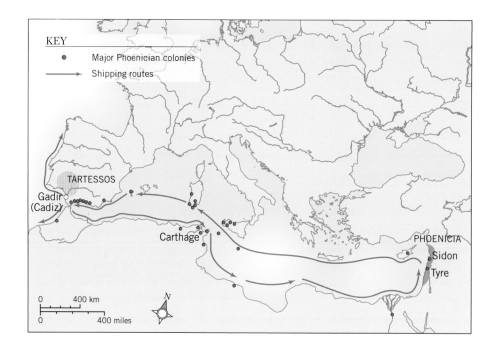

there was much to be said for open-sea sailing. From Cape Drepanum at the western end of Cyprus he could have sailed along the latitude to the south coast of Crete using the port of Kommos where excavation has exposed a shrine built in Phoenician fashion. Travelling the same distance again from north-eastern Crete, once more following the latitude, would have brought him to Malta, the point at which the Tyrrhenian system was engaged and the west Mediterranean came into view. Kommos in southern Crete was also a convenient place from which to sail south to Cyrenaica and from Cyrenaica the current along the north coast of Africa would take the vessel on an easterly course back to Tyre.

Egypt was an important trading partner for the Phoenician world. Herodotus writes of a Phoenician enclave at the Egyptian capital of Memphis clustered around the temple of Ashtart: 'Phoenicians from the city of Tyre dwell all around this precinct, and the whole place is known by the name of "the camp of the Tyrians".' This was evidently not a colony but a Phoenician ghetto where the resident merchants lived.

Phoenician traders also penetrated the Aegean. In the tenth and ninth centuries they were in direct contact with the Euboeans, as we saw from the elite items buried in the cemetery at Lefkandi. It is possible that a close alliance was established at the time that saw both Euboeans and Phoenicians working together in the early eighth century, exploring the Tyrrhenian Sea and setting up the colony at Pithekoussai. But in general the Greek opinion of

276

the Phoenician merchants was not very flattering. The *Odyssey* and the *Iliad*, probably written in the eighth–seventh centuries, give a decidedly deprecating view. The Phoenicians are portrayed as pirates and slave raiders, greedy and always prepared to cut a sharp deal. In the ports of the Aegean they trade fine metal vessels, gold and ivory work, and high-quality multi-coloured cloth for *biotos* (necessities for life) such as cattle, sheep, wine and wheat – another reminder of the ever-present need to feed Phoenicia's growing population. In one story we learn that a ship's crew spent a whole year on one island, probably Syros, while bartering their goods and reloading their ships: when they left they kidnapped the king's son. Another account involves a ship's master who had a home in Tyre and traded in slaves. In the summer season he set out on the round route, sailing from Phoenicia to Crete, then to Libya and Egypt, before returning home.

The Phoenicians we encounter in Homer are all entrepreneurs trading in their own right to make a profit. The caricature of the Phoenicians is succinctly summed up by Homer when he describes an incident in which Odysseus is mocked for his travel-worn appearance. He doesn't look, the observer says, like a warrior or an athlete but more like 'some captain of a merchant crew, who spends his life on a hulking tramp, worrying about his outward freight, or keeping a sharp eye on the cargo when he comes home with his extortionate profits' (*Odyssey* 8.161–64). Here is Greek disdain for those who specialized in trade (*emporós*). In Homer's world this was alien to the aristocratic ideal. And yet some semblance of 'proper' behaviour shone through from time to time, as when a great silver krater – 'a masterpiece of Sidonian craftsmanship' – was 'shipped by Phoenician traders across the misty seas' to the island of Lemnos there to be offered as a present to the king. A noble gift in the true heroic tradition perhaps, but to an astute merchant it was also an effective way to open up a new market.

The East Mediterranean: The Greek Sphere

The spread of Greeks to the western coast of Anatolia at the beginning of the first millennium BC turned the Aegean into a Greek sea but, although people were tied by speaking the same language and some will have held deep filial feelings for what was perceived to be their motherland, Greece was far from united – it was a collection of separate citizen-states, each for the most part focused on a single city that commanded the population's unquestioning allegiance. States could work together in times of need, as they did to some extent during the Persian Wars, but, as the Peloponnese War of the fifth century vividly showed, antagonism between them could lead to destructive and long-drawn-out conflict.

Each citizen-state had its own distinctive ethos, and pace of change varied from one to another. Before 500 BC the most spectacular developments in the Greek world took place in the cities of the western Anatolian coast and islands, most particularly in the Ionian cities stretching from Phocaea in the north to Miletos in the south. Art and architecture flourished, developing new and highly original styles, and it was here that philosophy and science were born. Miletos in the sixth century was home to a succession of brilliantly original thinkers, Thales, Anaximander and Anaximenes, men who thought about the world rationally and tried to understand it from first principles. The mathematician Pythagoras was a native of Samos, Heraclitus the philosopher came from Ephesus, Hecataeus, historian and geographer, was a Miletian, as was the townplanner Hippodamus, while the poet, or poets, we know as Homer may have come from Smyrna. The Dorian cities to the south were home to the fifth-century giants – Hippocrates, the physician who was born on the island of Cos, and Herodotus, fairly called the father of history, whose town of birth was Halicarnassus. And these are only the better-known names: it was a stunning cast, encompassing the greatest minds who created the basis of western civilization. The world in which they lived was energized by mobility facilitated by the sea: travellers flocked to their cities and many of them made journeys of discovery of their own. It was a unique interlude in history.

On the Greek mainland a number of separate states developed. For the most part they were focused on cities, like Athens, Argos, Corinth, etc., where the *polis* – that is, the political community comprising state and citizens – was centred. But not all of the states were dependent upon a single city. In western Greece the polity was of a different kind. Here we find federal states embracing several small towns and villages. These constituted the *ethnos*, whose decisions were usually made in the major religious centre of the region.

The emergence of the *polis* is a much-debated issue, though most would agree that it originated in the eighth or seventh century. An early indication of centralization was the creation of a focal sanctuary adorned with monumental temples. Another sign taken to reflect the *polis* was the hoplite army comprising groups of citizens fighting together in close formation units, each man depending on his neighbour. Such a system would have fostered a sense of common purpose and equality, and would leave no place for the individual heroics that had been the cornerstone of the old aristocratic system. Evidence from burials and vase paintings suggests that the hoplite phalanx was in existence by the mid-seventh century but could have originated a little earlier. Finally, we have the creation of constitutions, lawcodes and magistracies which for many of the *poleis* were in place by about 700 BC. Clearly, crucial changes were taking place throughout the eighth century but the process may not have been complete until the end of the seventh.

By this time urban centres were growing rapidly. In Athens, for example, estimates based on cemetery evidence suggest that in 700 BC there were seven thousand inhabitants, but within a hundred years the population had grown to twenty thousand. Towns like Athens and Corinth grew up in a haphazard fashion around their central sanctuaries. Gradually, however, throughout the seventh and sixth centuries BC, this was rationalized. In Athens the site of the agora – a large open communal space – was being cleared of old buildings in the mid-sixth century and defined by boundary stones proclaiming 'I am the boundary of the agora'. Around the edges of the open space public buildings were now constructed including lawcourts, the council house, shrines and *stoas* (public walks). The creation of such a space, where the population could assemble and where the institutions of the state were now formalized in public buildings, can be seen as the final act in the long process that led to the fully functioning citizen-state.

The eighth and seventh centuries saw a remarkable mobility among the Greek population as tens of thousands of people sailed away from their homes

9.6 The Greek army – hoplites – in action as depicted on the Protocorinthian Chigi Vase (*c*.650 BC) found at Veii.

279

to found colonies in distant lands around the Mediterranean and the Black Sea. The Greeks had two words for colonies – *apoikia* and *emporion*. An *apoikia*, which means literally a 'home away from home', was a fully fledged citizen colony, with an urban centre and surrounding territory, which recognized a mother city as its place of origin and usually maintained close links with that homeland. An *emporion* was a settlement set up as a trading centre to articulate exchanges between the Greek world and the barbarian hinterland. In practice the difference was much less clear-cut: an *apoikia* would indulge in trade while an *emporion* could quickly assume the attributes of a citizen colony.

But what drove this remarkable diaspora? One possibility is overpopulation in the homeland. Statistics derived from cemeteries, and in particular the cemeteries of Athens, suggest that there was a dramatic growth in population in the eighth century BC. It is quite possible that such a rapid rise simply could not be accommodated within the holding capacity of the land and that the only option was for a segment of the population to seek a new ecological niche. This was certainly true of the colonists from Thera who set off for North Africa after their island had suffered successive harvest failures, but it cannot be the whole story since Attica and the Argolid, where the evidence for population growth can be demonstrated archaelogically, sent out no colonists in the early period. There must have been other factors involved. Perhaps one was the desire of the young for freedom and opportunity, wishing to escape from a home undergoing the traumas generated by the rapid social changes that accompanied the emergence of the citizen-state. For many of the young it must have seemed a tediously slow process as the forces of conservatism reacted against beneficial change. Nor should we overlook the pure spirit of adventure as a motivator. There were new worlds beyond the home seas crying out to be explored by those with the spirit to accept the challenge. The desire to engage in profitable trade must have been an ever-present inducement, too.

The east Mediterranean offers two examples of Greek trading colonies embedded in foreign territory: Naucratis on the Nile delta and Al Mina on the coast of Syria. The small town of Naucratis was built on the eastern bank of the Canopic branch of the Nile about 80 km (50 miles) from the sea. Archaeological evidence suggests that it was founded some time between 640 and 620 BC but was not given formal recognition until the reign of pharoah Amasis (570–526), an event recorded in some detail by Herodotus:

> [Amasis] gave them Naucratis as a commercial headquarters for any who wished to settle in the country. He also made grants of land upon which Greek traders, who did not want to live permanently in Egypt, might erect altars and sanctuaries. Of the latter the best known and most used – and also the largest – is the Hellenion.

Excavations over a century ago were poorly recorded but the general layout of a large part of the settlement has been recovered and the Hellenion (a shrine to the deities of Greece) and temples dedicated to Hera and to Apollo have been identified. Two other temples have also been found, dedicated to Aphrodite and the Dioscuri, as well as a factory for making faience scarabs and a fort or large storage building.

Naucratis was an important port-of-trade and Herodotus makes it clear that all ships visiting Egypt were required to report there; if contrary winds prevented them from entering the Canopic branch of the Nile, they were compelled to transport their freight on barges through the delta waterways to the port where the appropriate officials (*prostatai*) dealt with the necessary bureaucracy.

The principal function of Naucratis was as a trading entrepôt, allowing the Greek states direct access to Egyptian markets. Prominent among those exploiting the facility were east Greeks from the coastal cities of Asia Minor and also Aeginetans (from the island of Aegina) who seem at this time to have managed the trade of the mainland Greek cities. What commodities were exchanged we can only guess, but grain was always in great demand in Greece and Egypt was a bulk supplier; in return the Greeks could offer wine, oil and silver.

The Syrian port of Al Mina lies on the delta of the river Orontes. The area has since been subject to much silting but it would originally have been a port town directly accessible from the sea. The early buildings were of timber and mudbrick erected on low stone foundations. Little can be said of their function but later structures resemble warehouses and storerooms. Greek pottery is present in quantity from the beginning, suggesting that the settlement may well have been founded by Greek traders wishing to establish a foothold in the lucrative eastern market sometime towards the end of the ninth century. Prominent among the earliest pottery are distinctive vessels made on Euboea. Given the widespread distribution of Euboean pottery at this time, it is not unreasonable to suggest that Al Mina may have been, at least in origin, a Euboean trading enclave. The initial settlement flourished until around 700 BC when it appears to have come briefly to an end, perhaps as the result of disruption caused by Assyrian campaigns in the region. But the port facilities were quickly rebuilt and the settlement continued for another century or so. By this time Euboean interest had waned and instead eastern Greeks from Rhodes, Samos, Miletos and Chios seem to have taken over. The presence of Corinthian pottery also suggests interest from mainland Greece.

It seems that Al Mina housed a permanent group of Greek merchants who, together with other nationalities including Cypriots and Phoenicians, facilitated trade with the hinterland. To that extent they were not unlike their kinsmen who later lived at Naucratis, though Al Mina seems to have been less organized and more cosmopolitan as befits a frontier post.

The Ships

Efficient and safe movement at sea was central to life around the east Mediterranean. Since communities had been sailing for at least six thousand years it is fair to assume that the technology of boat-building and the skills of seamanship were now well honed. Little survives of actual vessels of the period, but illustrations on ceramics and metalwork and references in contemporary texts give details of sailing patterns and of the vessels themselves. The Greek poet Hesiod tells us, in his *Works and Days*, that the period from 5 May to 25 October was the appropriate time for taking to the sea but recommends that journeys should focus on the fifty days following the midsummer solstice at the end of June. As to the performance of the vessels, Herodotus records that an average of about 120 km (75 miles) could be covered in a day and night of sailing, while Thucydides gives the average speed of a merchant ship as about 6 knots, which is roughly in agreement.

Three types of vessel were in use by the Phoenicians. For inshore waters there were small craft rowed by two or three men. Their raised prows and sterns were similarly decorated with figureheads in the form of horses' heads, giving rise to the name *hippoi* for such vessels. Boats of this kind would have been used for local transportation and fishing. For long sea journeys deep-hulled vessels with large square rigged sails set amidships were in operation. These broad, tub-shaped vessels were called *gaulos* by the Greeks – an appropriate word meaning 'bathtub'. The reliefs show them as equal-ended with high prows and sterns, the stern carrying two steering oars. There was provision for rowers when required, but most important was their capacity to carry bulky cargoes, at this time probably ranging from 100 to 500 tons. The third type of vessel was the warship propelled by oars and distinguished by having a long, forward-projecting prow at water level, sharpened to form a ram that was used to disable enemy shipping. Since the effectiveness of this method of attack depended on speed of approach it was necessary to ship as many oarsmen as possible. This led to arranging them in two tiers, creating a vessel that the Greeks called a bireme.

The Phoenician vessels were the direct descendants of the 'ships of Byblos' that had traded with Egypt two thousand years before and no doubt inherited much from the Egyptian 'ships of the Punt' – trading vessels depicted on Eighteenth Dynasty Egyptian reliefs. The sturdy Phoenician vessels, modified over the centuries to suit the vagaries of Mediterranean sailing conditions, provided the basic stock from which other Mediterranean shipping was to develop.

a)

b)

9.7 Mediterranean vessels of the eighth and seventh centuries BC: a) a Greek double-decked war galley, sixth century. b) a Phoenician war galley shown on a relief from the palace of Sennacherib, Iraq. c) a Greek merchant vessel being chased by pirates, sixth century. d) a two-level war galley of the eighth century.

c)

d)

Greek vessels are well recorded in paintings on contemporary pottery and in the classical literary sources. While the basic structure remained largely unchanged over time, oar power was increased from the crew of twenty oarsmen recorded by Homer to larger ships with thirty (triconters) and fifty oarsmen (penteconters); further decks were also added to create the bireme and the trireme. These improvements, driven largely by the exigencies of warfare, were adopted by both Greeks and Phoenicians, but large vessels like the penteconters were also used in expeditions to set up colonies because of their impressive carrying capacities. When the Therans set out to found the colony in Cyrenaica, Herodotus tells us that two penteconters were used to carry the 200–300 colonists. One of the most useful vessels would have been the bireme penteconter – a short vessel with its fifty rowers split between two decks. The great advantage was that it combined the speed provided by fifty oarsmen with greater seaworthiness, since shorter vessels were less susceptible to stress caused by longitudinal bending. Vessels of this kind were designed to have sufficient storage capacity to make them useful for carrying cargoes, their speed enabling them to evade the ever-present menace of pirates.

The volume of shipping plying the seas must have been enormous. No figures are available but some hint is given by the fact that at the Battle of Salamis in 480 BC the Persians were able to commandeer a total of 1207 triremes to oppose the Greeks.

The Tyrrhenian Sea

Classical historians and some archaeologists have tended to treat the Phoenician and Greek colonizations of the Tyrrhenian area as separate and largely unrelated phenomena, giving the accolade of first to arrive to one or the other according to personal preference. A growing body of archaeological evidence is, however, showing the situation to have been far more complex – and far more interesting. The Tyrrhenian region, and Sardinia in particular, was actively trading with Cyprus up to the eleventh century BC and the probability is that contact was maintained throughout the tenth and into the ninth century. In the latter part of the ninth century the appearance of Phoenician and Euboean pottery on a number of sites implies a revitalization of the maritime contacts. While we may be witnessing two distinct and competing explorations, it is quite possible that, at this early stage, Euboeans and Phoenicians were working cooperatively. Phoenician pottery found at the Euboean settlement of Pithekoussai and Euboean pottery recovered from early layers at Carthage and Phoenician settlements on Sardinia suggest that there was much interaction. In the pre- and early colonial phase of the late ninth and early eighth centuries the rules of separate engagement were not rigorously enforced.

The earliest historical date we have for a colonial foundation is 814 BC when the Phoenicians from Tyre established a daughter colony at Carthage on a congenial site looking out over the Bay of Tunis. It is not impossible that enclaves of traders had already settled in Tunisia, Sicily and Sardinia. According to tradition, Utica, not far from Carthage, had been established two centuries earlier, while at Nora on Sardinia an early Phoenician inscription has been claimed to be of the ninth century or earlier. The formal foundation of the colony at Carthage is likely to have been the culmination of a long process of exploration and experiment that may have lasted several generations. Thereafter, in the eighth century a firm hold was established on the coasts of Tunisia, Sicily and Sardinia as successive colonies were set up, all at coastal locations with good harbour facilities.

In parallel with the Phoenician activities, the Euboeans were exploring the

9.8 The Tyrrhenian Sea in the sixth and fifth centuries BC at the time of Etruscan expansion.

west coast of Italy. Their distinctive pottery – particularly a type known as chevron skyphoi – has been found in various native cemeteries in Campania and as far north as the Etruscan town of Veii in southern Etruria. The distribution of these vessels suggests that there was an active phase of pre-colonial exploration in the late ninth and early eighth centuries. This was followed, some time around 770 BC, by the establishment of the colony of Pithekoussai on the little island of Ischia on the north side of the Bay of Naples. The choice of an offshore island is the tentative act of a group not wishing to offend the indigenous population. The early pioneers would have come to appreciate the riches of the Campanian countryside and the fabulous metal resources of Etruria. Both were actively exploited by traders now settled at Pithekoussai; at an early stage there is evidence that iron ore from the island of Elba was being trans-shipped to the colony for smelting.

The first Euboean settlers were most likely predominantly men. This is

285

supported by evidence from the cemetery of the colony where a high percentage of the female burials were accompanied by indigenous-style jewellery, the implication being that they were local women. Some may have come from families already living on the island, others from the mainland. Through intermarriages of this kind good relations were established with the adjacent region of Campania, and within a generation – about 740 BC – a new colony had been established on the adjacent coast at Kyme (Cumae). This event coincides with an influx of colonists into the region, some making for the new mainland site, others choosing to settle at Pithekoussai, swelling the pioneer population already in residence. But the situation was fluid and by about 700 BC Kyme was flourishing while Pithekoussai was fast declining. This may have been the lure of the prosperous mainland attracting manpower away from the island but the possibility of volcanic activity on Ischia cannot be ruled out.

After the initial phase of Phoenician and Greek colonization, c.830–740 BC, two different strategies emerged. The Phoenicians were content to maintain their original holdings in the Tyrrhenian and to put their further efforts into developing the opportunities offered in the west, particularly in Iberia and the Atlantic coast of Africa, while the Greeks chose to focus on intensifying their hold on Italy and Sicily. The explanation for this striking difference was probably economic: the Phoenicians wanted metals, particularly silver, to satisfy the demands of the Assyrian market, while for the Greeks corn and other agricultural products were needed to provide for the growing populations of the Aegean. Not surprisingly, the new Greek colonies in Magna Graecia occupied the most productive agricultural land available within easy reach of the Aegean homeland.

For the indigenous populations the colonies brought many advantages, not least in opening up new markets and introducing new technologies and skills to satisfy the aspirations of local elites. This is demonstrated to a spectacular degree by Etruria, where urbanization was now well under way and competitive elites were vying for status. Society was wide open to the new and the exotic. The result was that foreign goods, notably Greek flowed in in enormous quantities. Until the middle of the sixth century supplies came mainly from Corinth and eastern Greece but thereafter Athens became the main supplier. Etruscan demand was such that Greek craftsmen settled in some of the main urban centres and inscriptions record the presence of resident Greek and Phoenician traders in Etruscan ports. A glimpse of the trade is provided by a wreck dating to around 600 BC found off the island of Giglio: its cargo included Etruscan goods, Phoenician amphorae, pottery from Corinth and Sparta, and a magnificent bronze Corinthian helmet. So long as Etruscan interests were not under threat, international trade could flourish and at ports like Alalia on the eastern coast of Corsica,

Phoenician, Greek and Etruscan merchants and sailors could live together in harmony.

While the Etruscan merchants appear to have been content at first to share the Tyrrhenian Sea with others, they were busy exploring the northern coasts of the west Mediterranean, and by the middle of the seventh century had developed close trading ties with communities around the Golfe du Lion. They were also expanding in Italy and by as early as 800 BC had established a degree of control over large parts of Campania, maintaining contact possibly by overland routes but certainly by sea, using the Gulf of Salerno, sandwiched uncomfortably between two Greek enclaves, as the main entry point.

Towards the end of the seventh century the commercial interests of the three main powers began to come into conflict. Carthage was now flexing its muscles by assuming territorial control over Sardinia and the eastern part of Sicily, while expanding Etruscan interests in western Italy were bringing it into confrontation with Kyme and the Greek enclave in the Bay of Naples. The rising tension was further exacerbated when, in about 600 BC, the Greeks from Phocaea established their colony at Massalia (Marseille) in the middle of a flourishing Etruscan enterprise zone. Matters came to a head sixty years later when another group of Phocaeans, under threat from the Persian advance, decided to leave their home town on the west coast of Asia Minor and settle at the international port site of Alalia, directly challenging long-established Phoenician and Etruscan commercial interests in the northern Tyrrhenian. The move was vehemently opposed, resulting in a major naval engagement in the Sardinian Sea in about 535. Although the Phocaeans decided to move off and settle elsewhere the Etruscans were now being increasingly constricted. Their unsuccessful attacks on Cumae in 525 and 474 effectively marked the end of the Etruscans as a serious power in the Tyrrhenian Sea. It was now the preserve of the Greeks and Carthaginians. The repulse of the Carthaginian navy at Himera by the Syracusans was the opening of a new story.

The Ionian Sea and the Adriatic

The island of Corcyra (Corfu) occupies a crucial position between Greece and the heel of Italy, and between the Ionian Sea and the Adriatic. It is hardly surprising, therefore, that the earliest Greek explorers, the Euboeans from Eritrea, established a colony on the island as a staging post on their journey to the west. A little later, Corinth appropriated the island as a stepping stone on the way to Syracuse. The power of Corinth, which commanded the isthmus between the Peloponnese and the rest of Greece, was considerable. According to Thucydides, they were the first of the Greeks:

to adopt more or less modern methods of shipbuilding and it is said that the first triremes ever built in Greece were laid down in Corinth.... and when the Greeks began to take more to seafaring, the Corinthians acquired a fleet, put down piracy, and, being able to provide trading facilities on both the land and the sea routes, made their city powerful from the rewards which came to it by both these ways. (Thucydides I, 13)

The city of Corcyra flourished. In 627 BC Corcyra in partnership with Corinth founded a colony at Epidamnus on the mainland coast; later Corinth established another colony at Apollonia further to the south. In the early sixth century, Corcyra played a part in setting up new settlements on the island of Korčula and other islands off the Dalmatian coast. Meanwhile, at the northern end of the Adriatic the indigenous communities of the Po valley began to come into direct contact with the Greek world through traders who were prepared to make the long sea journey north.

Etruscan influence in the Po valley was now already considerable and by the end of the sixth century Etruscan political control had been established. Etruscan sources record a confederacy of twelve cities, which probably included Marzabotto (Misa), Bologna (Felsina), Mantua, Moderna and Ravenna as well as two ports, Spina and Adria, at the head of the Adriatic. This deliberate attempt to take a firm hold on the Po valley and thus control the vital trading links northwards through the Alpine passes into the heart of Europe, as well as the outlets to the Adriatic, was probably a direct consequence of the Battle of the Sardonian Sea in *c.*535 BC and the failure to take Kyme (Cumae) ten years later. It must have been all too evident to the Etruscans that their time as a power in the Tyrrhenian Sea was over and that it was in their interests to develop new markets to the north. As a consequence the old ports on the west coast of the peninsula fell into decline while Etruscan involvement in the Po valley began to be pursued with greater energy.

The two Adriatic ports of Spina and Adria were probably Etruscan foundations, although there seems to have been a considerable Greek involvement from the outset. Spina lies on the Adriatic coast some 65 km (40 miles) south of Venice on the south side of the Po delta. Aerial photographs show the plan of the city represented now by a network of canals and waterways linking to a grand canal that emptied into a branch of the Po, long since silted up. The resemblance to Venice is striking. Excavations of the town's extensive cemeteries have yielded quantities of Greek Attic pottery, the earliest dating to around 530 BC – by which time there must have been regular trade with Greece. The presence of graffiti in both Greek and Etruscan indicates a mixed population living in mutually beneficial harmony. The town of Adria, lying between Spina and Venice, is less well known since it is now buried deep beneath the alluvial deposits of the delta. On present evidence Adria seems to have been founded a generation or so before Spina, and like Spina it too is likely to have supported a highly cosmopolitan population, with Greek and Etruscan settlers living and working alongside an indigenous population.

The extension of Etruscan influence over the Po valley and the increasing Greek involvement after the mid-sixth century are a continuation of processes that were already under way in the preceding centuries. The Po valley continued to be an important interface between the Mediterranean world and the barbarian north, and from the beginning of the fifth century lively exchange networks grew up between the Etruscan world and the communities of the North Alpine zone (see p. 314).

The West Mediterranean

Phoenician colonization in the west Mediterranean began about 800 BC with the foundation of Gadir (Cadiz) on an island off the Atlantic coast of Iberia 'beyond the Pillars of Hercules'. An account of the foundation derived from local sources is preserved in Strabo's *Geography*. The essence of the story is that Tyrians were directed to found the settlement at the Pillars of Hercules by an oracle. Anchoring off the Andalucían coast, they offered a sacrifice to the gods but since the omens were not propitious they returned home. In a second attempt they sailed through the straits and landed on an island off Huelva, but again the omens were unfavourable and again they returned home. They tried once more, this time landing on the island in the estuary of the Guadalete, and there successfully founded Gadir. The account is interesting in that it implies that the choice of the site for the colony was the result of a process of exploration taking place over a period of time. Perhaps the legend embodies memories of a long-drawn-out period of exploration and trading extending back centuries before the decision was finally made to found a permanent colony.

The site was well chosen. The main settlement was established on the small island of Erytheia, which was separated by a narrow channel from a much larger island – a narrow spit of land some 12 km (7½ miles) long – known as Kotinousa which was used as the burial ground of the colony. The channel between the two became the main harbour, the approach to which was dominated by two temples, one on each side of the harbour mouth. At the southern end of the island of Kotinousa a temple to Herakles was set up to mark the approach to the colony. Although there has been a slight rise in sea level and much silting between the islands and the mainland, modern Gadir – Cadiz – still retains much of the form of the original colonial settlement.

As an offshore island Gadir was in a good position to defend itself if necessary, and since it made no real territorial claims it was of no threat to the

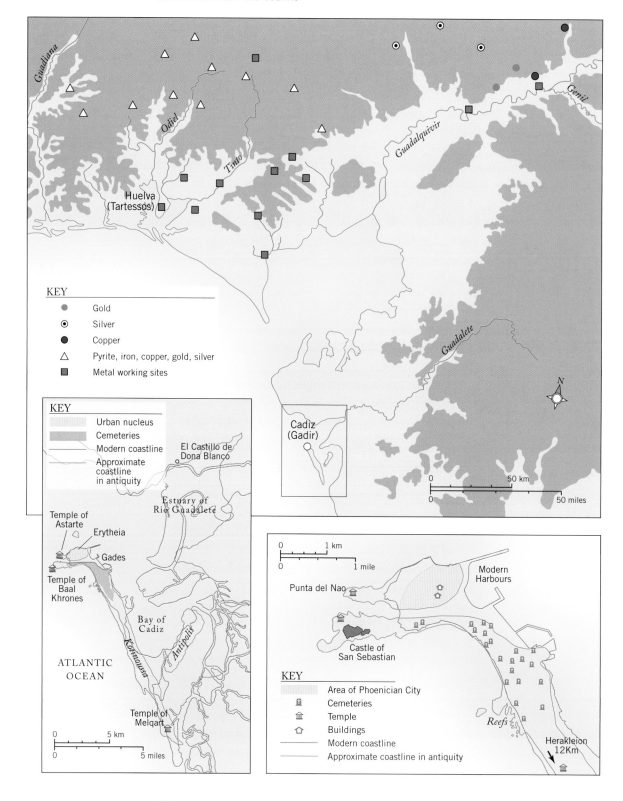

KEY

- Gold ●
- Silver ◉
- Copper ●
- Pyrite, iron, copper, gold, silver △
- Metal working sites ◼

KEY

- Urban nucleus
- Cemeteries
- Modern coastline
- Approximate coastline in antiquity

KEY

- Area of Phoenician City
- Cemeteries
- Temple
- Buildings
- Modern coastline
- Approximate coastline in antiquity

indigenous population. It was also very well sited to trade with the mainland, having access, via the rivers Guadalete and Guadalquivir, to a huge and highly fertile hinterland. More to the point, by sailing 100 km (62 miles), across the estuary, it was possible to reach the principal Tartessian port on a promontory between the estuaries of the river Odiel and river Tinto. This may well have been the ancient city of Tartessos, eventually to become the modern port city of Huelva. It was here that the Phoenicians from Gadir would have been able to take on their cargoes of silver so much in demand by the Assyrian neighbours of their mother city Tyre.

Tartessos was renowned throughout the ancient world for providing an inexhaustible supply of silver. Stories of the immensely rich deposits in the Rio Tinto region and the Sierra Morena abounded. One ancient writer, Diodorus Siculus, tells of a great forest fire that burned for many days:

> Much silver trickled away from the fiery ground and, as they melted, the silver-bearing ores formed countless rivulets of pure silver. The natives did not know how to exploit it but once the Phoenicians heard of the affair, they bought the silver in exchange for objects of negligible value. The Phoenicians took the silver to Greece, to Asia and to all the other countries they knew, thus obtaining great riches. It is said that such was the cupidity of the traders that they replaced the lead anchors of their ships with silver ones after there was no more room for silver in the vessels, and there was still a great quantity of the metal left over. (Diodorus 5:35, 4–5)

While we need not believe the details, it is a lively story that fairly reflects the abundance of silver in the region and its importance to Phoenician commerce.

At this stage the silver, together with gold and copper, came mainly from the Rio Tinto region to the north of Huelva/Tartessos. The principal mining centre was at Cerro Salomón, Tejada, while silver was being worked at a number of sites including the port settlement at Huelva. The Tartessians would have been thoroughly conversant with the technology needed to extract the metal long before the arrival of the Phoenicians, but extraction increased dramatically only after the initial Phoenician contact provided new market opportunities. In return for their silver the Tartessians received oil, wine, unguents and jewellery. Poseidonius (via Strabo) gives a glimpse of the organization of the trade when he says that in Gadir there were great transport ships commissioned by the rich traders of the place. These men would have been agents working under orders from Tyre.

The effect of the burgeoning trade on Tartessos is evident in the archaeological record with the sudden appearance, in the eighth and seventh centuries, of rich graves adorned with exotic luxuries like sets of bronze jugs, bowls and incense-burners, made in Phoenician style, as well as jewellery, some of which

9.9 *Opposite:* The foundation of Gadir (Cadiz) by the Phoenicians c.800 BC marked the beginning of the Phoenician exploration and settlement of the Atlantic coasts of North Africa and Iberia. The site chosen for the city was a small island conveniently close to the Tartessian kingdom of south-western Andalucía which was known to be rich in metals, particularly silver.

9.10 The city of Cadiz
occupies the site of the
Phoenician colony of Gadir.
Although the sea-level has
risen slightly it is possible
to make out the entrance to
the original channel which
separated the small island
of Erytheia where the main
settlement lay, from the
larger island of Kotinousa,
used as a cemetery.

was imported from the east Mediterranean region. One of the most spectacular cemeteries was found at La Joya on the summit of a steep hill at the edge of the settlement beneath modern Huelva. About twenty tombs have so far been excavated. One of the richest, Tomb 17, was the grave of an adult male. The body was accompanied by a two-wheeled vehicle of walnut wood adorned with lion-headed hubcaps in bronze and a silver boss fitted to the end of the draught pole. A bronze-sheathed wooden quiver was probably attached to the vehicle. His other possessions included a finely carved ivory box with silver hinges, iron knives with ivory handles held by silver rivets and a bronze mirror with an ivory handle. The grave also contained a libation set comprising a jug, a large-handled bowl and an incense-burner, all in bronze. The tomb dates to the second half of the seventh century.

It is likely that most of the craftsmen serving this elite market were working in Gadir, but an ivory workshop has been found at a native settlement, Doña Blanca, on the mainland opposite Gadir, showing that some at least of the craftsmen had migrated to nearby Tartessian towns. Most of the materials that these workshops used came from local sources, but the ivory must have been imported from North Africa, probably through the Phoenician ports on the Atlantic coast of Morocco. Ivory was a favourite

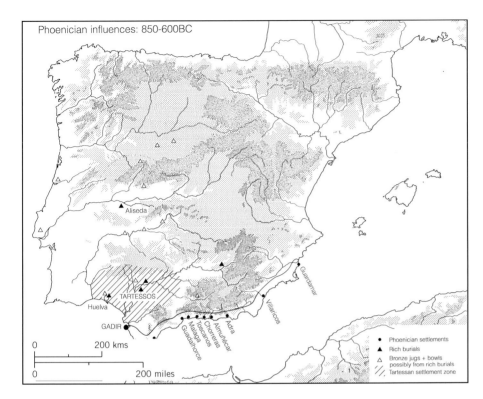

Phoenician influences: 850-600BC

9.11 Iberia in the eighth and seventh centuries BC. The Mediterranean and Atlantic coasts on either side of the Tartessian kingdom were settled with small Phoenician colonies trading with the interior. Gadir, close to the Tartessian metal deposits, was the dominant port. Luxury goods probably made in workshops in Tartessos found their way into the hands of the elites of the interior who were able to control the trading routes along which gold and tin were transported.

material among the Tartessian elite and ivory combs, probably of Iberian man-ufacture, were exported to Carthage.

Luxury goods, particularly the bronze jugs and bowls, were found in elite graves not only within Tartessian territory but also to the north, extending to the centre of Iberia. These probably represent gifts made to local chieftains in return for goods passing through their territories, particularly tin and gold coming from the north-west of the peninsula. One group of rich burials was found along the river Guadiana, while further to the north another was found at Alisada (Cáceres) on the cross-country route to the Tagus. The riverine distribution suggests that those commanding the major crossing points were able to exercise firm control over the movement of goods.

Soon after the foundation of the trading colony of Gadir, Phoenician settlement of the southern coast of Iberia began, with new settlements being established throughout the seventh century. Mostly they concentrate along what is now the Andalucían coast but they also extend eastwards to Cape Palos in the vicinity of Cartagena. The coastal zone between the Penibaetic mountain range and the Mediterranean is narrow but in places it widens where rivers from the mountains cut valleys and deposit sediment; these were the locations favoured by the Phoenician settlers whose livelihood was based on agriculture and fishing supplemented by trade. They were admirably placed to

293

9.12 *Opposite:* The
foundation of Massalia
(Marseille) *c.*600 BC by
Phocaean Greeks opened up
the southern French coast
to Greek settlers and traders
and many other Greek towns
were soon founded between
Nice and Ampurias.
Massalia dominated the
trade route northwards, via
the Rhône, to the centres of
the Hallstatt elite in west
central Europe.

command the many routes coming from the north, from the metal-rich Sierra
Morena across the fertile Guadalquivir valley and then through the sierras by
way of the high intermontaine plateaux.

The coastal Phoenician colonies were so close together that trade cannot
have been the sole motive for their establishment. The most likely explanation
is that they were set up by communities migrating from Phoenicia to find new
territory to settle and to farm as Assyrian pressure on the homeland increased.
The potential colonists will have learnt of these fertile and congenial coasts
from regular traders whose outward journeys would have taken them from
southern Sardinia across the open water to Ibiza (again by latitude sailing) and
south-westwards to Cape Palos. From there the Iberian coast would have been
followed, giving ample opportunity to stop off overnight to take on water and
to explore. It may well have been on outward journeys of this kind that groups
of settlers were dropped off to begin to carve out new lives for themselves.
Existence must have been precarious and many of the colonies were
abandoned before the end of the sixth century.

While the Phoenicians were establishing themselves in the west,
Etruscans were exploring the northern shores of the west Mediterranean.
Their activities are visible in the archaeological record through the distribution
of the distinctive black bucchero pottery – mainly jugs and cups – made in
Etruria and exported together with wine transported in large amphorae. The
fine pottery provided the barbarians with the accoutrements with which the
wine could be consumed in style in a civilized manner. Some reality has been
given to the bald archaeological distribution maps by the discovery of a shipwreck off the Cap d'Antibes which was carrying a cargo of several hundred
wine amphorae and the accompanying sets of bucchero tableware.

Etruscan trade was aimed at the Golfe du Lion and seems to have begun in
the seventh century. One of the most important sites in the region was a settlement at Saint Blaise sited on a hillock in the marshy reaches of the Rhône delta.
Occupation here was under way in the Bronze Age and by the latter part of the
seventh century the settlement seems to have been the entrepôt of Etruscan
merchants trading with native communities. It is a reasonable assumption that
the prime import was Etruscan wine and the paraphernalia required for its
consumption, together perhaps with metals and other consumer luxuries. What
the locals had to offer is less clear. Salt is one possibility, since there is evidence
that it was being produced by evaporation in the region. Salt could also have
contributed to the preservation of meat exports and to the curing of leather.
The locals were also making jewellery and working coral, but such things are not
likely to have been particularly attractive to Etruscan merchants. Another
possibility, leaving little or no archaeological trace, would have been slaves – a
highly desirable commodity among the Etruscan elite.

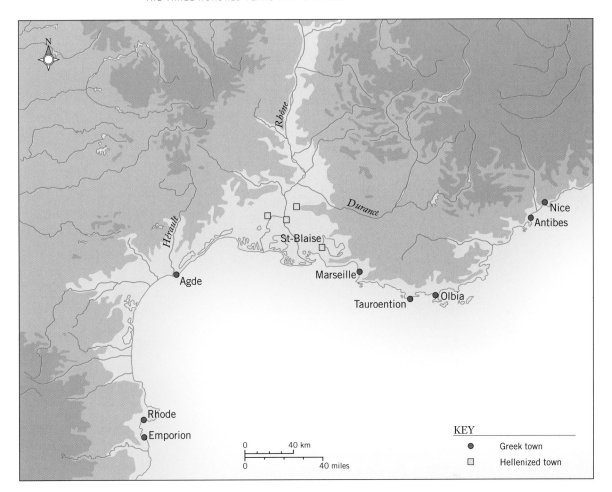

KEY

● Greek town

□ Hellenized town

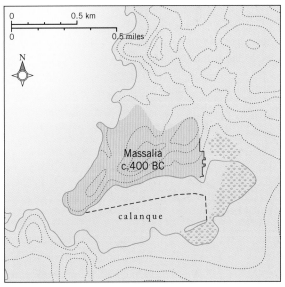

9.13 The excavation at the Bourse in Marseille exposed the inner end of the silted up ancient harbour and nearby the Greek defensive wall. Beyond the modern buildings the outer part of the harbour is still in active use leading to the open sea beyond.

The Etruscan entrepreneurs were most likely attempting to establish trading links with the barbarian elites of the North Alpine zone by sending gifts of high value through the indigenous networks. To this category belong the two bronze Rhodian flagons found at Vilsingen and Kappel in Württemberg and a griffin-headed cauldron found in a native grave at St-Colombe in Burgundy. These items are of seventh-century manufacture and could have reached the heart of Europe at this time. As it turned out, the Etruscan initiative was brought to a speedy end by the foundation of the Greek colony of Massalia (Marseille) in about 600 BC. Thereafter the Phocaean Greeks began to drive the Etruscan merchants from the west Mediterranean.

296

The earliest positive evidence we have of Greek activity in the west Mediterranean is in the voyage of Kolaios to Tartessos in about 630 BC when he claims to have found the market ripe for picking. It was probably at about this time that Phocaean explorers arrived and were enthusiastically greeted by the Tartessian king who, according to Herodotus, tried to persuade them to settle in his territory. The archaeological evidence shows that Greek material was reaching southern Spain at this time, c.640–580 BC, but how much of it came directly in Greek ships and how much was picked up in Tyrrhenian ports and transported by Phoenicians it is difficult to say. The sheer quantity of east Greek pottery from Huelva is, however, suggestive of direct east Greek activity.

After the period of exploration the Phocaeans decided to establish their first colony at Massalia on a rocky promontory overlooking a superb harbour. Once established here, the Greeks could not only dominate coastal shipping in the gulf but they had within reach the ancient route along the Rhône valley leading deep into the heart of Europe. Not long after the foundation, they secured their hold on the region by establishing two more colonies: one at Agathe (Agde), well sited to control the metal-producing Montagne Noire as well as the westward route via the river Aude and the Carcassonne Gap to the Garonne and the Atlantic; the other at Emporion (Ampurias) on the coast of Catalonia, well placed to trade with the hinterland and to provide a base for those wishing to sail further south along the Iberian coast. From the three early settlements daughter colonies soon sprang up, until the entire coast from the Alpes Maritimes to the Pyrenees was ringed with Greek ports.

Massalia remained the dominant city throughout. In the first twenty-five years of its existence its main maritime links were with its east Greek homeland and with Corinth. Following this initial phase, the port seems to have opened up to Etruscan goods, but after the middle of the sixth century there was a dramatic decline in Etruscan imports, suggesting a deliberate attempt to squeeze out the Etruscan merchants. Ten years later, around 540 BC, the city was greatly extended as more settlers arrived from the homeland. This phase marks the beginning of active trade with the barbarian north.

During the sixth century Massalia and the other Greek colonies of the gulf developed maritime trading contacts with communities along the south and east coasts of Iberia. Low-value goods such as pottery are found at the coastal sites while more exotic items such as bronze vessels or east Greek faience tend to turn up further inland, reflecting attempts to negotiate with the elites controlling the more desirable resources of the interior. But by far the greatest quantities of Greek material have been found at Huelva. Finds include fine Attic, Corinthian, Laconian, Chian and Ionian wares, and transport amphorae for wine or oil from Chios, Corinth and Samos, all dating to the period 630–530. The implication must be that following the initial contacts around 630 the Greeks had no difficulty in sailing through Phoenician-dominated waters to trade with the Tartessians. Whether this indicates a weakening of the Phoenician enterprise or simply a tolerant attitude to Greek traders it is difficult to say.

After about 540 BC, however, a marked change can be seen: Greek activity at Huelva comes to an abrupt end and there is little evidence of Greek presence along the southern coast of Iberia. It is tempting to see this as a result of the worsening political situation after the Battle of the Sardonian Sea. Greek interest in the east coast, however, continued to intensify, as a result of which the shore bases mentioned by classical authors at Alanis, Akra Leuke and Hemeroskopeion probably began to take on a more permanent appearance. This crystallizing-out of discrete spheres of economic interest characterized the later decades of the sixth century and was to set the scene for the conflicts to come.

The Atlantic System

The traditional belief that Tyre's Atlantic colonies of Gadir (Cadiz) and Lixus were established about 1000 BC may have been based on some dim folk memory that Mediterranean vessels had explored the Atlantic coasts in the distant past. That this may, indeed, have been the case gains some support from the scatter of Mediterranean artefacts of the tenth and ninth centuries found along the Atlantic coast of Iberia. There is, however, nothing to suggest that actual colonization began before about 800 BC. The first move in this process seems to have involved the foundation of Gadir and Lixus, roughly equivalent distances north and south from the Straits of Gibraltar. The site of Lixus was built on a hill overlooking the fertile delta area at the mouth of the Oued Loukkos, commanding a fine sheltered harbour facing the Atlantic and a major river route into the Atlas Mountains whence came gold, copper and ivory. It was probably from Lixus that a series of other entrepôts were established, extending southwards down the coast of Morocco to the Oued Ksob (between Casablanca and Agadir). Here, on the little island of Mogador, stood the southernmost outpost of Phoenician entrepreneurial activity – until, that is, the great exploration of the fifth century saw ships travelling southwards into the unknown.

Northwards from Gadir Phoenician entrepôts were established at intervals along the coast of Portugal as far north as Santa Olaia at the mouth of the river Mondego. Beyond this point some Mediterranean material – brooches, beads and pottery – has been found along the Galician coast, showing that Phoenician traders had developed contacts with indigenous communities and were making use of the superb harbours provided by the drowned coastline of the Rías Baixas. The attraction would have been the rich supplies of tin and gold for which Galicia was renowned.

By the seventh century BC the Phoenician Atlantic system was in full operation, embracing a coastline 1400 km (875 miles) in length. It was driven entirely by the desire to acquire commodities for the Mediterranean market – gold, silver, copper, tin, ivory and ostrich eggshells, and very probably skins and furs, exotic wild animals and slaves. The archaeological evidence is still too coarse-grained to say much about the viability of the system as a whole but by the end of the sixth century BC many of the southern Iberian entrepôts were in decay or had been abandoned, reflecting a general crisis in the western Phoenician world in the late sixth century, in the interlude before Carthage began to exert leadership.

The Phoenician expansion into the Atlantic took place at a time when the Atlantic communities were undergoing deep-rooted social and economic change linked, in part at least, to a decline in the value of bronze and the frenetic desire to consign huge quantities of bronze, usually in a debased form, to the earth as hoards. In parallel with this, there seems to have been

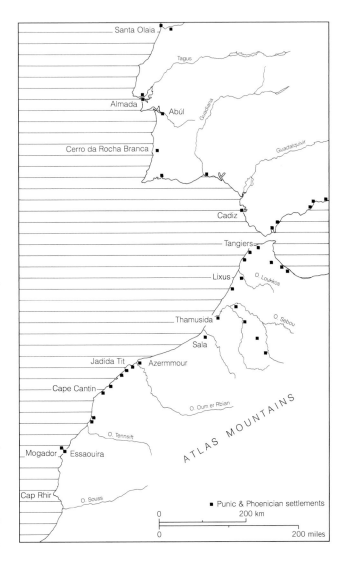

9.14 From Gadir (Cadiz) the Phoenicians established trading colonies along the Atlantic coasts. Through the African colonies rare commodities, such as gold, ostrich shell and ivory from the African hinterland, would have passed. The Iberian colonies would have overseen trade in gold, silver, copper and tin.

a greater emphasis on controlling the productive power of the land. This manifests itself in the development of field systems, boundaries and fortifications, and also in evidence of the large-scale storage of grain. At a very simplistic level it is almost as if a social system based on the control of bronze supply was being replaced by one predicated on the command of agrarian surpluses. What caused the change is difficult to say, but the widespread appearance of iron, combined with a constantly rising population, may have undermined the value of bronze while giving food surpluses a far greater prestige value.

These changes, which affected much of the Atlantic and the Nordic zone, took place in the period 800–500 BC. The immediate effect was the dislocation of the old Atlantic exchange network that had linked the entire coastal zone

299

for many centuries: in place of a single network, a series of discrete local networks emerged with little interaction between them. In the south this change coincided with the expansion of Phoenician interest which drew the Iberian Atlantic zone firmly into the Phoenician Mediterranean sphere.

Further north the situation is less clear. While there is evidence of some continued maritime contacts between north-western France, western Britain and Ireland, it in no way compares with what had gone before. However, the eighth and early seventh centuries were a time when the eastern part of Britain developed close links with northern France and the Low Countries, the two regions communicating across the southern part of the North Sea. The network is reflected archaeologically in the exchange of elite goods. The British communities received a range of continental Hallstatt horse gear, which presupposes that it was actual horses decked out in their tack that were brought into Britain, while one of the British contributions was the development of well-crafted slashing swords. Craftsmen based in the east of Britain, quite possibly in the Thames valley, had been manufacturing bronze swords for centuries, gradually improving details of the design. Their latest model, known as a Gundlingen type, became particularly popular around the southern North Sea in the early eighth century and was widely adopted in western Europe among the Hallstatt elite and in Ireland, showing that at this stage Ireland was still part of the broader exchange network.

After the middle of the seventh century the network began to break down still further. The southern North Sea system was still in operation, linking eastern Britain to northern France and the Low Countries and allowing valuable objects like daggers and cauldrons to be exchanged, but the northern and western regions of Britain as well as the whole of Ireland seem now to have become isolated: a new regionalism was beginning to take hold.

If we are correct in interpreting the distributions of archaeological material in this way, then we can trace the disintegration of the Atlantic network, first with the separation of Atlantic Iberia in the eighth century, followed by a further break-up in the northern part of the network with the isolation of Ireland in the sixth century. This scenario provides an interesting framework for modelling the later development of the Celtic language which, we have already argued (see p. 258), had probably already emerged as the lingua franca spoken along the Atlantic seaways. So long as the Atlantic networks were active one would expect a broad similarity of language throughout the contact zone, but with the gradual breakdown and the separation of the different regions after about 800 BC conditions would be ripe for divergent development. This could account for the Celtic languages spoken in Iberia being different from the rest and for the Celtic of Ireland seeming to have retained more anachronisms than the Celtic spoken in Britain and Gaul.

The Nordic Zone

The Nordic region shares many of the characteristics of the Atlantic zone during the period 800–500 BC – an expansion and intensification of agrarian production, and a greater degree of regionalization as the exchange networks of the Late Bronze Age decline in importance. Elaborate burials, like those of the elites able to control the supply of resources from the south, are no more to be seen, while the ritual deposition of metalwork in bogs once so prevalent now tails off. Exchange with the south was, however, maintained, as the flow of metalwork from the Hallstatt culture of the North Alpine region demonstrates. In parallel, the consumption of amber by the south continued and, if anything, intensified.

In the period before c.800 BC the economic and political centre of the Baltic region had focused largely on Denmark. Now there was a distinct shift to the east, to eastern Pomerania – the Baltic coastal region of Poland around the lower reaches of the Vistula. Here, an elite can be recognized, able to command Mediterranean commodities such as cowrie shells and blue glass beads, both coming via the Po valley network. At the same time new funerary traditions were introduced involving the use of cremation urns, some with faces on them, others in the form of houses. These are quite alien to local traditions but bear remarkable similarities to funerary vessels in use in northern Italy among the Etruscans. These facts have led some archaeologists to argue for an actual movement of Etruscans northwards to the Baltic. This is highly unlikely. What we are seeing in the archaeological record is almost certainly the result of a well-developed transpeninsular trade route linking the Po valley to the mouth of the Vistula. A scatter of north Italian artefacts – brooches and the like – across Europe suggests that the route probably lay through the eastern Alps, via the Vlatava or the Moravian Gap, to the North European Plain. The communities of east Pomerania were very well situated to acquire Baltic amber as well as other northern products such as furs to offer in exchange for Mediterranean trinkets. How such a system of exchange came into being remains an open question. It is tempting to suggest that it may have been the result of direct Etruscan entrepreneurial activity designed to establish control of an important resource flow. There is no inherent difficulty in supposing that Etruscan traders made the journey to the north to negotiate with the Pomeranian elites, setting in motion an exchange system that lasted for generations.

Greeks and Scythians in the Black Sea Region

There is surprisingly little firm evidence of maritime contact between the Mediterranean and the Black Sea before the eighth century BC, but given the enthusiasm that the Mycenaeans and their successors showed for maritime adventure it is inconceivable that no attempt had been made to explore the great sea that lay conveniently to the north. By the eighth century Greeks had begun to penetrate beyond the Bosphorus. The poet Hesiod, writing at this time, had some knowledge of the Black Sea, and a scatter of Greek artefacts found around the shores may have been gifts to natives. Classical sources suggest that the first colony was established by the Milesians at Sinope on the north coast of Asia Minor in the first half of the eighth century, followed, in 756 BC, by Trapezus (Trebizond) 350 km (220 miles) to the east. The earliest pottery so far found at Sinope, however, belongs to the second half of the seventh century, which throws some doubt on the traditional account.

Other Milesian colonies followed during the course of the seventh century: Apollonia (Sozopol) on the coast of Thrace, Histria on the west coast near the Danube delta, Berezan on an island between the mouths of the rivers Dnepr and Bug, and Amisos on the north coast of Asia Minor between Sinope and Trapezus. A second wave of colonization began in the sixth century, focusing on the Taman and Kerch peninsulas on the north side of the Black Sea commanding the approach to the Sea of Azov. It was probably at about this time that Olbia was founded on the mainland not far from Berezan. The final stage, c.560–530 BC, saw the infilling of the gaps with such colonies as Odessos on the Bulgarian coast, Chersonesus on the Crimea and Phasis at the easternmost extremity of the sea. The majority of the colonies were claimed to be Milesian foundations, though other eastern Greek towns no doubt contributed to the flow of settlers. Land for settlement was clearly an important factor in the migration, as was the attraction of being able to trade in the metals, furs and corn available from the hinterlands, and to have access to the famous anchovies and tuna with which the sea abounded. In the home region, on the coast of Ionia, the expansion of the powerful Lydians occupying the inland regions put constant pressure on the coastal Greek communities, preventing territorial expansion. For the rapidly growing Greek population the only option was to take to their ships and find new homes.

In the middle of the fifth century BC the historian Herodotus made a journey into the Black Sea to the colony of Olbia, located near the mouth of the river Bug. There he had ample opportunity to observe the native Scythians and to gather stories about their history and the customs of the remoter tribes. This collection of anecdotes and personal observations forms the basis of Book IV of his *Histories*. Like all compilations of this kind it is partial, highly

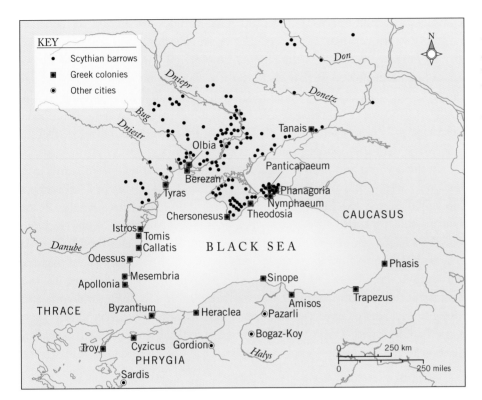

9.15 Between the seventh and fifth centuries BC, Greek colonies were established around the Black Sea and the Sea of Azov. The north Pontic colonies interfaced with the Scythians who occupied the Pontic steppe.

selective, muddled and in places probably downright wrong, but it is a source of incomparable value, full of fascinating insights – and a sheer pleasure to read.

Herodotus was well aware that the inhabitants of the Pontic steppe comprised a number of groups of varying lifestyles. 'Scythians', therefore, is an umbrella term referring more to the general nomadic culture of the region than to any tight-knit ethnic identity. Herodotus is at some pains to distinguish the different groups. The most important were the 'Royal Scythians', who occupied the region between the Dnepr and the Donetz rivers: 'here dwells the largest and bravest of the Scythian tribes, which looks upon other tribes as their slaves'. To the north-west of them were 'the wandering Scythians who neither plough nor sow: their country as a whole . . . is quite bare of trees'. Between the Dnepr and the Dnestr lived agriculturalists, a southern group who 'sow and eat corn, also onions, garlic, lentils and millet', and to the north of them were 'cultivators who grow corn, not for their own use but for sale'. Those closest to Olbia he classes as Graeco-Scythians – presumably natives who had embraced aspects of the colonial lifestyle.

The origin of Scythian culture is uncertain. It may have developed locally in the Lower Volga regions from earlier nomadic groups related to the

303

Cimmerians, or alternatively in central Asia. Whatever the truth of the matter, the seventh century was a period of considerable mobility, with nomadic groups ranging wide across the steppe. One of the bands who called themselves Scythians moved westwards to settle in the land between the Dnepr and Donetz, displacing earlier populations, while a splinter group moved southwards to become a significant mercenary force in the struggle for power in Anatolia. These events date to the seventh century and were therefore coincident with the first stage of Greek colonization.

In the seventh and sixth centuries Scythian culture spread northwards into the forest steppe and westwards into the eastern foothills of the Carpathians (now Moldavia), extending southwards from there to the Danube delta. During this time the elite centres began to focus on the Crimea and the valley of the Dnepr and the coastal region from the Dnepr to the Danube. It was in this broad zone that elites were buried with their riches under massive burial mounds (kurgans) the excavation of which, in the late nineteenth and early twentieth centuries, filled the museums of Russia with goldwork and brought the Scythians to the forefront of public attention. Herodotus gives a particularly vivid account of a Scythian burial ceremony which is worth quoting in full:

> when their king dies, they dig a great square pit. When they have prepared this they take up the corpse, its body smeared over with wax and its belly slit open, cleaned out, and filled with chopped frankincense, parsley and anise, and then sewn up again and bring it on a wagon to another tribe. These who receive the corpse when it is brought do as the Royal Scythians. They cut a piece out of their ears, cut their hair short, slash their arms, slit their foreheads and noses, and thrust arrows through their left hands. Then they convey the corpse to another tribe among their subjects, and the tribe first reached goes with them. When they have gone round all the tribes with the corpse, they are among the Gerrhi, who live farthest off of all their subjects, and among the tombs.
>
> When they have laid the corpse upon a mattress in its chamber, they stick spears into the ground on all sides. Then they lay beams across and cover these with wicker, and in the remaining space of the tomb they strangle and bury one concubine, the cupbearer, a cook, a groom, an attendant and a messenger; they also bury the pick of everything else and golden vessels. They use no silver or bronze. When they have done this, they heap up a great mound, vying with one another and full of eagerness to make it as great as they can. Then when a year has passed they do as follows. They take the most suitable of the other attendants – these are true-born Scythians and are called to attend him by the king

himself, for they have no bought slaves – and strangle fifty of them and fifty of the finest horses. They take out their entrails, clean them, fill them with chaff and sew them up. Then they put half the rim of a wheel with the hollow side upwards on two stakes, and the other half-rim on two others, fixing many such frames, drive stout stakes lengthwise through the horses to their necks and hoist them on to the rims. The front rims support the horses' shoulders and the rear ones their thighs and bellies, while both pairs of legs hang free. They put reins and bridles on the horses, draw these forward and tie them to pegs. They then hoist every one of the strangled youths on to his horse, after driving a vertical stake through him by the spine to the neck, and part of this stake that projects downward they fasten into a socket in the other stake that runs through the horse. When they have set up riders in this style round the tomb they ride off. (Herodotus *Hist.* IV 71–72)

9.16 Around the northern Pontic coast a lively art style developed as Greek craftsmen made luxury items for the Scythian elites. This silver-gilt mirror from the burial mound of Kelermes (mid-sixth century BC) incorporates Greek- and Scythian-inspired motifs.

His informant was a meticulous observer. Here we see not only the way that death was treated in a highly mobile society, but also the importance of the *rite de passage*, the process by which the community guides the soul of the departed across the dangerous liminal zone between life and death. The accuracy of the observations is amply demonstrated by the many excavations of kurgans where close matches for the recorded description can be observed.

From the seventh century onwards Greeks and Scythians were in very close contact in the coastal zone and inevitably the two communities interacted with each other. Greek luxury goods were imported for use as diplomatic gifts to pave the way for exchanges and as trade goods, while large quantities of wine – mainly from Ionia – made their way into the Greek ports en route to the Scythian hinterland. But the colonies were dealing not with primitive savages but with an indigenous population that had, over the centuries, developed a sophisticated culture, including a brilliant animal art that drew on its nomadic roots and on orientalizing concepts absorbed from contact with the

Near East. Such clients were demanding and from an early date we find Greek craftsmen, working in the colonial ports, adapting their styles to suit Scythian tastes and in doing so creating a hybrid art style of great vitality. Its floruit was to lie later in the fifth century when assured masterpieces were created but already in the sixth century lively, innovating pieces were being produced. Among the best is a collection of items from the tombs at Kelermes in the Kuban dating to the late sixth century BC. One item, a gilt silver mirror with an elaborately decorated back, was entirely Greek in concept and decoration except that the animals attending the Mistress of the Animals included beasts stylized in an entirely Scythian manner. By the same hand was a gilt silver rhyton (drinking horn) of Scythian type decorated with a winged goddess, two griffins, a centaur and a hero fighting a lion, all eastern Greek in style. One might reasonably wonder whether the craftsman was a Greek working for native clients or a Scythian metalworker content to incorporate what he had been taught of contemporary Greek styles. The Pontic interface in the seventh and sixth centuries bustled with innovative energies as two artistic traditions, not entirely alien in values and skills, eagerly explored each other.

While the Scythians of the Pontic steppe could hardly avoid the impact of Greek culture, those occupying the more northerly region of the forest steppe lay beyond the reach of Greek luxury goods. Other groups who maintained their independence were the Scythian communities who moved into the Carpathian Basin in the late seventh or early sixth centuries BC and settled in two separate areas, Transylvania (central Romania) and Alföld (north-eastern Hungary and south-western Slovakia). Much of the area had already received an influx of people from the steppe region in the eighth century as a result of disruptions within the Cimmerian homeland. The arrival of Scythian culture therefore represents a continuation of long-established links with the steppe involving exchange of goods as well as a degree of population mobility. By the sixth century communities in Transylvania and the Great Hungarian Plain had adopted the elite male-dominated material culture of the Scythian steppe, including arrows tipped with highly distinctive trilobate arrowheads and the quivers to contain them, short iron daggers, iron battle-axes, iron-headed spears and shields now represented by the gold animal totems once attached to them. In addition sets of Scythian horse gear are found throughout the region. Other items include bronze mirrors probably made in Greek work-shops in Olbia, a range of personal ornaments, mostly rings and earrings, and bronze rattles for attachment to the ends of poles or sceptres – probably a symbol of personal authority. The sheer quantity of Scythian-style items found within the Carpathians is sufficient to suggest both the arrival of new people from the east and the maintenance of strong cultural contacts between the European and Pontic zones.

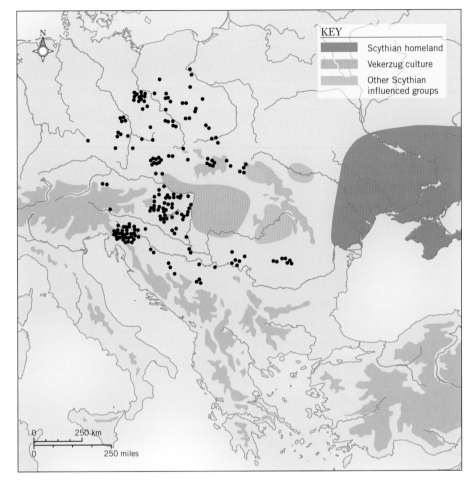

9.17 Elements of Scythian culture are found deep in central Europe particularly in the Carpathian Basin (where it is called the Vekerzug culture), suggesting that migrating bands moved westwards from the Scythian homeland on the Pontic steppe. Scythian objects found even further west – in Transdanubia, Slovenia and Poland – probably resulted from exchanges and raids.

In the Alföld the Scythian-style culture is called the Vekerzug culture, after a cemetery at Szentes-Vekerzug – one of twenty or so burial grounds found in the region. For the most part burials are modest, with none of the ostentation of the great Pontic kurgans, but one grave in the cemetery of Ártánd in the eastern part of Hungary stands out. The warrior buried here, complete with his scale armour and iron battle-axe, and the tackle and harness decoration of his horse, was also provided with two bronze vessels, a large wine container (hydria) manufactured in Greece, possibly in Sparta, about 570 BC, and a swing-handled cauldron from the Hallstatt region to the west. The grave set is a vivid reminder that the communities of the Carpathians were on the interface between the east and the west.

The Vekerzug culture dates to the sixth and fifth centuries BC. To the west the river Danube formed a very definite boundary with the Hallstatt cultures of central and western Europe, but Scythian-style material is found extending

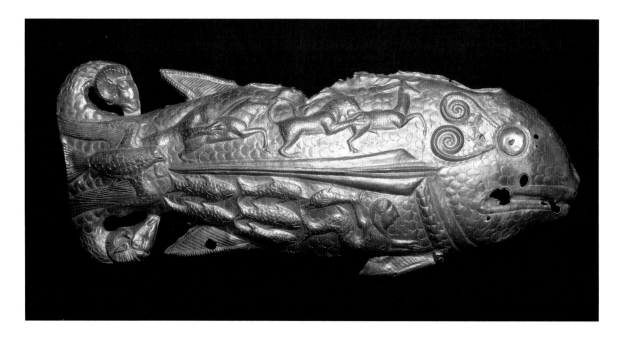

9.18 This large gold fish (41 cm/16 in long) was found with other elite items at Vettersfelde in Germany. It dates from the late sixth century BC and is of Scythian workmanship, possibly serving as a shield decoration. It probably came from the grave of a Scythian chieftain far from home who may have been engaged in raiding.

both to the west and to the north, with concentrations in the Upper Sava valley (Slovenia) and in Silesia (south-west Poland). While it is tempting to explain these distributions in terms of raids fanning out from the home-land east of the Danube, accompanied perhaps by limited land-grabbing, the spread of Scythian finds may simply reflect exchanges with the west. This is particularly true of the finds that cluster in the Upper Sava valley, which formed the major route between the Carpathian Basin and the Po valley and hence the head of the Adriatic. With the intensification of trade flowing through the Po valley, the Sava corridor would have become the way by which the eastern breed of horses could have been obtained. These were greatly superior to the more puny western horses and were therefore a highly desirable commodity.

The Scythian-style material found to the north, in southern Poland, is predominantly warrior gear – arrows, swords and battle-axes – and has tended to be seen as evidence of raiding or at least mercenary activity. One spectacular find, made at Witaszkowo (Vettersfelde) some 80 km (50 miles) east of Berlin, is the gear of a warrior chieftain comparable in status to the Pontic steppe elite. Although the burial was not properly recorded and many of the finds were dispersed, what remains is still impressive – a massive gold fish-shaped shield boss, golden armour, a sword in a golden sheath, an iron dagger, a whetstone in a gold frame and a number of other items including gold jewellery. Unique finds like this are difficult to explain. Perhaps we are glimpsing here a warrior leader who had taken his fighting force on a raiding expedition far from home into the dreary depths of Silesia. Or could it have been a set of finery acquired through the exchange network, perhaps as a gift, by a local Lusatian chieftain? Archaeological evidence is sometimes tantalizing in its vagueness.

That some Scythian groups may have raided deep into the North European Plain need not surprise us. They were by nature a warlike people as their mercenary activities in Asia Minor in the seventh century amply demonstrate. In their relations with the Greeks they showed little aggression but when, in 513 BC, Darius led his Persian army across the Danube into Scythian territory he found them a difficult enemy to pin down: they were always on the move, drawing him further and further into the steppe. In the end there was nothing he could do but turn back and leave the Scythians to themselves. Even the great Darius was no match for men born to the saddle and proud of their unfettered mobility.

In the Centre of the Peninsula

Compared to the fast-changing scenes in the Mediterranean, Middle Europe – or the North Alpine zone – exhibited a stolid stability in the period from the eighth to sixth centuries BC. This is not to deny that social and economic changes took place, but more to emphasize that the culture (which archaeologists call Hallstatt after a salt-mining settlement in Austria) was deeply rooted in the preceding Urnfield culture of the Late Bronze Age. The Hallstatt culture, or rather the many regional groups that comprise it, extended from central France to Transdanubia (western Hungary) and from the Alps to Kujavia in the centre of Poland. The broad similarities across this vast region are not the result of conquests or folk movements but of a tight network of routes through which exchanges were articulated – this was, after all, the region where the majority of the river systems of peninsular Europe converged and through which the major transpeninsular routes were forced to thread their way.

Within the Hallstatt region there were three broad sub-zones: a western zone that extended roughly from Burgundy to Bohemia; an eastern zone between the eastern Alps and the Danube bordering on to the Scythian cultures of the east; and a northern zone extending across the old Lusatian cultural area into central Poland. Each of these sub-zones derived its characteristic culture from indigenous roots in the Bronze Age past. It was in the western zone – the area at the heart of the route network – that the greatest range of innovations became archaeologically visible.

Most evident was the emergence of a rite of elite burial involving the use of a ceremonial four-wheeled vehicle to carry the body of the deceased to the grave. The vehicle and the horse gear (but not the horses) were placed in a large timber-lined grave pit together with the body and a range of equipment

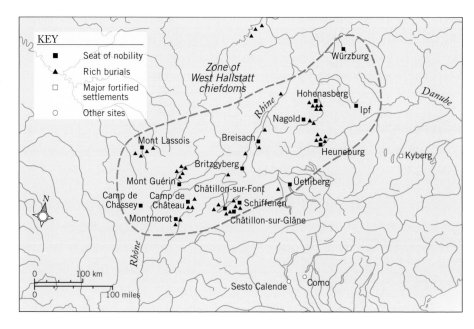

9.19 In the Late Hallstatt period (c.600–480 BC) the elite built defended hilltop settlements and buried their dead with elaborate grave goods, including items of Greek and Etruscan origin. These centres of power extended from Burgundy to southern Germany.

9.20 *Opposite:* The defended hilltop settlement of Heuneburg in southern Germany overlooking the Danube was an elite centre in the Late Hallstatt period. At one stage it was defended by a wall of mudbrick built on a drystone foundation. The corner of the defensive circuit has been reconstructed together with several close-spaced timber buildings found inside.

appropriate to the status of the person. This ritual is clearly rooted in Urnfield traditions that used small vehicles and models of vehicles in religious processions. The difference now was that inhumation became the norm for high-status burials and the four-wheeled vehicles were large, elaborate constructions with multiple-spoked wheels and iron tires attached to the felloe with large-headed iron nails. These were sophisticated constructions involving the skills of highly inventive coach-builders working under the patronage of the elite.

In the early part of the Hallstatt period (Hallstatt C), in the eighth and seventh centuries BC, burials of this kind are found over a wide territory extending from eastern France to the Czech Republic. But in the later period, Hallstatt D, which covers broadly the sixth and beginning of the fifth centuries, the focus of elite burial in the western Hallstatt region becomes more restricted to a zone of about 200 by 500 km (130 by 310 miles) extending from eastern France to southern Germany. Here, the rich burials clustered around fortified hilltop settlements, the traditional homes of the lineages of local rulers. These 'seats of nobility' (*fürstensitz*), of which some sixteen have so far been identified, occupy prominent positions and are clearly the centres of large territories over which the resident elite exercised power. One of the most extensively studied is Heuneburg in the valley of the Upper Danube. The hilltop had been occupied in the Urnfield period and continued to be refurbished from time to time thereafter. In one phase, dating to the opening decades of the sixth century, the rampart, previously of earth and timber, was rebuilt in Mediterranean style with a drystone base and mudbrick

9.21 The grave chamber found beneath a great barrow mound at Vix, Châtillon-sur-Seine, France dating to the end of the sixth century BC. The timber-lined chamber contained the body of a woman together with a disassembled funerary cart and a set of Mediterranean wine-drinking equipment.

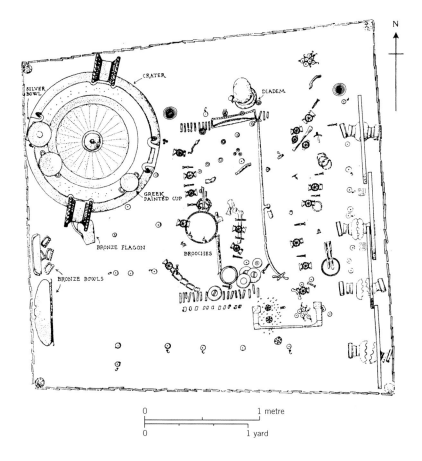

SILVER BOWL

CRATER

DIADEM

GREEK PAINTED CUP

BRONZE FLAGON

BROOCHES

BRONZE BOWLS

N

0   1 metre

0   1 yard

9.22 *Opposite:* Bronze krater from the burial chamber at Vix. It was probably made in a Greek workshop in southern Italy. Its great size (1.64 m/5¹/₂ ft high) would have required it to have been dismantled for its long journey from the Mediterranean to the barbarian north.

superstructure, the circuit aggrandized by forward-projecting square towers. The rebuilding can only have been overseen by someone thoroughly conversant with Greek construction methods. The choice of such an exotic mode of building – one totally unsuited to the local climate – must have been made deliberately to impress by its 'foreignness'. This same attitude is amply displayed in the grave goods placed in the elite graves. These usually include exotic gear of Mediterranean origin associated with wine-drinking. At Vix, near Châtillon-sur-Seine, the female, buried in a large timber-lined grave chamber some time about 510–500 BC, was accompanied by her ceremonial vehicle and personal ornaments as well as a huge Greek krater for mixing wine, basins, a beaked flagon and two Attic cups – all part of the equipment of the wine-drinking ritual. A generation or so earlier a chieftain buried at Hochdorf near Stuttgart lay on a bronze couch with his funerary wagon nearby. His drinking set included nine gold-mounted drinking horns together with a large Greek cauldron that had contained mead. Apart from the cauldron his finery was of entirely local origin.

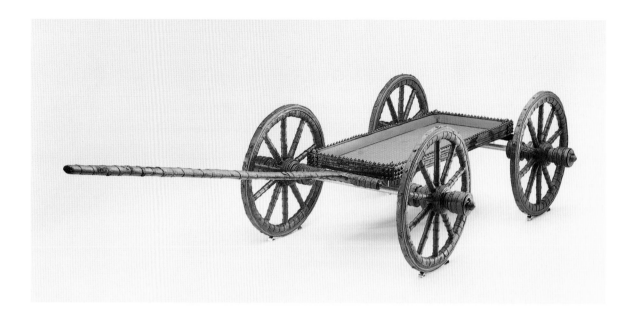

9.23 The princely burial at Hochdorf, near Stuttgart, Germany, dating to the second half of the sixth century BC, contained a four-wheeled funerary wagon sheathed in iron. The body of the chieftain lay on a bronze couch and nearby was a large bronze cauldron of Greek manufacture. A set of drinking horns was hung on the wall of the chamber.

The elite of the western Hallstatt zone had access to a range of Mediterranean goods, including wine, coming from the coastal regions of France and imported in distinctive Massaliot amphorae, as well as bronze vessels and Attic pottery. These they accepted, selecting items that best fitted into their patterns of behaviour. Much of this material will have been transported, via the Rhône, from the Greek port of Massalia (Marseille) in the second half of the sixth century BC, the bulk of the imports following the extension of the colony c.540 BC and the development of local wine production. To begin with, the imports on offer were high-grade metal vessels but in the last two decades of the sixth century quantities of cheaper Attic pottery became increasingly available.

The Rhône valley seems to have functioned as the main route to the north until about 500 BC, when Etruscan entrepreneurs, working from the Po valley, began to develop trading connections northwards through the western Alps, using as middlemen the communities of the Golasecca culture, who commanded the southern approaches to the western Alpine passes. In that way the Hallstatt elites acquired Attic Red-Figured wares (brought by sea to the ports of Spina and Adria) and the first of the highly distinctive Etruscan beaked flagons that were to become popular in the first half of the fifth century. The foundation of Massalia c.600 BC had seriously disrupted Etruscan trade with the north. It took about a century for the Etruscans to re-establish their links with the transalpine world by a neat outflanking movement that must have caused some economic distress to Massalia in the early part of the fifth century.

314

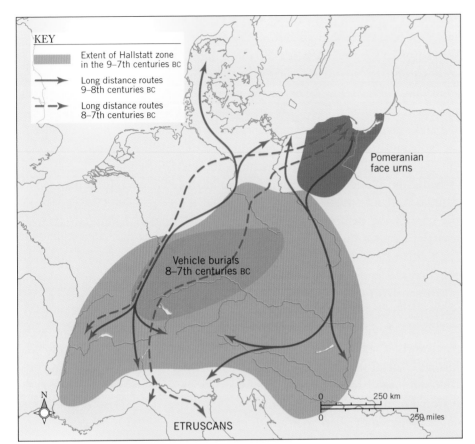

9.24 The major exchange networks across the centre of Europe in the ninth to seventh centuries BC.

The elite system in west central Europe has been described as a 'prestige goods economy' – that is, a system in which the social hierarchy was maintained by the paramount chieftains controlling the throughput of rare raw materials and distributing elite goods downwards through the social pyramid as gifts. So long as the flow of elite commodities was kept up the system remained in equilibrium, but if flow faltered the system would become unstable. In effect the system lasted for barely two generations before undergoing major readjustments in the early years of the fifth century. It is tempting to see the prime cause of the collapse as readjustments in the competing trading spheres in the Mediterranean. Those commanding the active routes might flourish, but trade was a fickle friend.

The three hundred years from 800 to 500 BC can fairly be said to mark a major turning point in European history. Many things were happening. In the Mediterranean state formation was now well under way, with distinct polities

– Greek, Phoenician and Etruscan – vying for control of the seaways, extending their territorial hold all around the Mediterranean coasts and expanding well beyond, into the Black Sea and out into the Atlantic. A sailor who wished to boast of his adventuring could now claim to have sailed from the Pillars of Hercules (Gibraltar) to Tanis (at the mouth of the river Don) without facing too much incredulity. But while the Mediterranean-wide system was expanding and intensifying, the Atlantic and Baltic sea routes were fragmenting into far more localized systems, largely because of the collapse of bronze as a prime commodity of liquidity as iron became the metal of choice. That said, the Atlantic and Baltic zones were highly productive of commodities that were in general demand and so the intercontinental routes remained active. Within the core of the peninsula the Celtiberian and Hallstatt communities maintained a tenuous stability deeply rooted in tradition, while to the east in the Carpathian Basin the steppe culture, closely related to that of the Scythians of the Pontic steppe, was now firmly established with the Danube, flowing north–south through Hungary, becoming a cultural frontier that was to remain operative for a thousand years.

At the beginning of the period, around 800 BC, most of Europe was a patchwork of communities enmeshed together in what were essentially 'prehistoric' social and economic systems. Three hundred years later the Mediterranean had become a lake of warring states vying with each other for dominance over land and commodities. A sharp divide was beginning to appear between the 'barbarian' north and the 'civilized' south. That divide was to become increasingly evident as the power struggle for the Mediterranean followed its course.

CHAPTER TEN

States in Collision: 500–140 BC

For barbarian Europe – Europe beyond the narrow Mediterranean fringe – the three and a half centuries or so that concern us in this chapter are a time of immense social upheaval and readjustment. The period opens with the continent dominated by elites that, though iron-using and having access to Mediterranean luxury goods, were still following the long-established traditions of the indigenous Bronze Age. But the system was breaking down and soon after 500 BC communities living in the swathe of territory stretching from the Marne to Bohemia were drawn into a vortex of change resulting in large-scale migrations thrusting southwards and eastwards, first into the Po valley and the Carpathian Basin and later into Greece, south Russia and Asia Minor. Since all the barbarian peoples of temperate Europe west of the Middle Danube Basin were described as Celts or Gauls by contemporary writers, these movements, settlements and raids are loosely called the 'Celtic migrations'. Meanwhile in the east there was a new influx of nomadic peoples, the Sarmatians, who moved westwards from their homeland east of the Volga into the Pontic steppe causing disruption throughout the region.

This phase of mobility, which saw the shunting of local peoples out of their traditional homelands, the mixing of populations as migrant groups swept across Europe, and an all-pervading ethos of raiding, had largely subsided by the beginning of the second century. In many parts of temperate Europe, a more stable way of life was beginning to develop, characterized by large nucleated settlements referred to as *oppida*, which were fast acquiring many of the characteristics of urban centres. It was this zone into which the Roman armies were to move in the first century BC and first century AD.

While the core of Europe was experiencing three centuries of turbulence, the Mediterranean had itself become a cockpit of conflict as the many different polities striving for dominance competed by land and sea. The rise of naval power was a major factor in the escalating violence. The importance of commanding the sea had been a lesson well learnt in the wars between Persia and the Greeks. But maritime supremacy was not only a necessity for

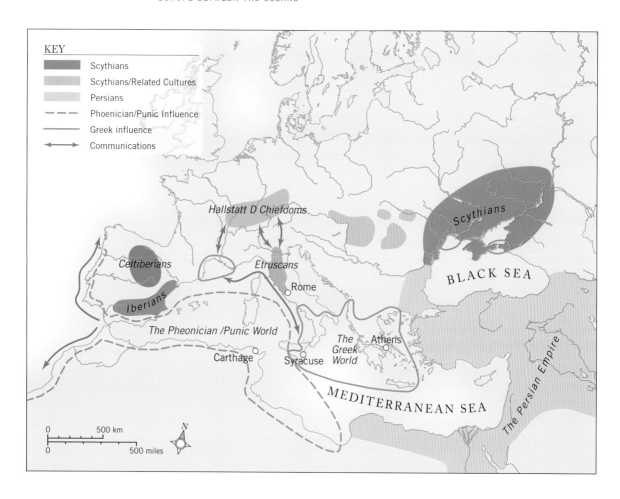

KEY

	Scythians
	Scythians/Related Cultures
	Persians
– – –	Phoenician/Punic Influence
——	Greek influence
←——→	Communications

Hallstatt D Chiefdoms

Celtiberians

Etruscans

Rome

Iberians

The Pheonician /Punic World

The Greek World

Athens

Carthage

Syracuse

BLACK SEA

Scythians

The Persian Empire

MEDITERRANEAN SEA

0   500 km

0   500 miles

N

10.1 Europe about 500 BC.

defending the homeland – it also became a means of taking the battle speedily into the territory of the enemy. It was now an instrument of escalation.

The period begins with the two decisive battles fought in 480 BC. At Salamis the Greeks defeated a massive Persian-led naval force not far from Athens while in the same year a Syracusian army mauled the Carthaginians in northern Sicily. The period ended in 146 BC with two further major engagements. In the central Mediterranean the Romans delivered the *coup de grâce* on the Carthaginian Empire by destroying Carthage at the end of the Third Punic War, while at the other end of the ocean the sacking of Corinth marked the final stage in Rome's attempt to keep the bickering Greeks under control. Carthage and Corinth had been two of the greatest centres of maritime commerce in the Mediterranean: Rome was now master of both.

The Mediterranean had changed out of all recognition in the 340 or so years between these two famous years of triumph. The historical events of this period are, to say the least, complex. The ancient historical sources provide a wealth of detail that focuses on men and their motives as theatres of conflict shift around the Mediterranean. Armies and navies of increasing size confront each other, death tolls mount to massive proportions, cities are destroyed and landscapes devastated as the desire to dominate the land and resources of others outstrips the simple need to protect home and family. The historical sources would have us believe that everything was driven by the egos of men and the honour of the state, but this was really only petulance on the surface of deeper movements.

Among the more deep-seated causes was a growing social complexity that created greater divisions of labour and greater expectations. The number of people no longer engaged in genuine production increased dramatically while society now sought to monumentalize itself with massive temples, public buildings, elegant funerary monuments and the like – all trappings of status and communal self-esteem requiring massive inputs of labour. The increasing expectations of urban societies, combined with steady overall rises in population density, placed impossible demands on the home territory and required a mobilization of resources on an unprecedented scale if systems were to be maintained at a level of equilibrium. Polities now found it increasingly necessary to expand their control both over sources of desirable commodities and over the routes along which they were procured. The parallel development of several states with similar demands, throughout the Mediterranean world, led to active competition and to the aggressive expansion of spheres of influence. The result was persistent warfare. Other factors also played a part. Degradation of land through overcropping and overgrazing created local problems, while failures of crops caused by minor fluctuations in climate contributed to the stress; but these were minor issues when seen against the prime causes of population increase and expectation inflation.

The economic imperatives, demanding increasing supplies of raw materials and labour, were embedded within a social system predicated on personal and communal display and the maintenance of an increasingly sophisticated lifestyle – someone had to provide the food and services needed to support gaggles of philosophers and droves of vase painters. But deep within the human psyche is the desire to gain honour and recognition through leadership: in the situations of stress and conflict that prevailed, military and territorial adventures provided a ready vehicle. In other words, desire to control resources met a deep-seated psychological need by offering leadership opportunities to young men intent on seeking honour. Later, in the Roman system, military prowess became an essential step in the career structure leading to high office. There was no shortage of young men prepared to join and to lead overseas wars. Thus, the desire to fight exacerbated the volume of conflict. Warfare can also have an impact on demography since slaughter in

10.2 Above, the Athenian
Empire, 460–446 BC, and,
below, the state of the
alliance in 431 at the
beginning of the
Peloponnesian War when
the Greek world was divided
between two warring
factions based on Athens
and on Sparta.

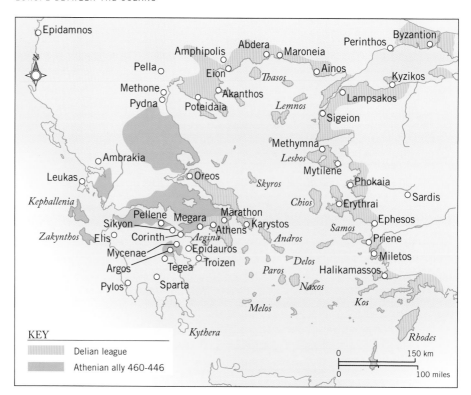

Epidamnos

Pella

Amphipolis Abdera Maroneia Perinthos Byzantion

Eion

Methone
Pydna

Akanthos

Poteidaia

Ainos

Kyzikos

Lampsakos

Sigeion

Thasos

Lemnos

Ambrakia

Leukas

Oreos

Methymna

Lesbos

Mytilene

Phokaia

Sardis

Skyros

Kephallenia

Chios

Erythrai

Ephesos

Zakynthos

Pellene Megara Marathon

Sikyon

Elis Corinth

Athens Karystos

Aegina

Andros

Samos

Priene

Mycenae

Epidauros

Troizen

Miletos

Argos

Tegea

Delos

Paros

Halikarnassos

Pylos

Sparta

Naxos

Kos

Melos

KEY

Kythera

Rhodes

| | Delian league |
| | Athenian ally 460-446 |

0   150 km

0   100 miles

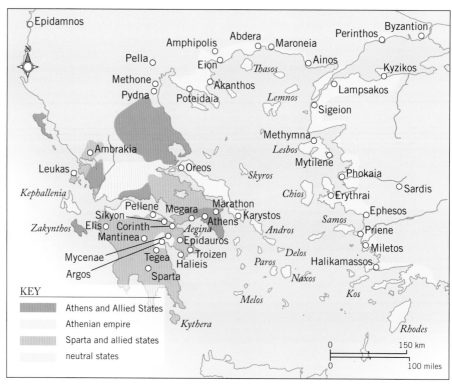

Epidamnos

Amphipolis Abdera Maroneia Perinthos Byzantion

Pella

Eion

Methone
Pydna

Akanthos

Poteidaia

Ainos

Kyzikos

Lampsakos

Sigeion

Thasos

Lemnos

Ambrakia

Leukas

Oreos

Methymna

Lesbos

Mytilene

Phokaia

Sardis

Skyros

Kephallenia

Chios

Erythrai

Ephesos

Pellene Megara Marathon

Sikyon

Elis Corinth

Athens Karystos

Mantinea

Aegina

Andros

Samos

Priene

Mycenae

Epidauros

Troizen

Miletos

Argos

Tegea Halieis

Sparta

Delos

Paros

Halikarnassos

Naxos

Kos

Melos

KEY

Kythera

Rhodes

	Athens and Allied States
	Athenian empire
	Sparta and allied states
	neutral states

0   150 km

0   100 miles

battle acts as a form of population control, though culling in this way is unlikely to have significantly affected the inexorable population increase.

These, then, were some of the forces underlying the events of the late first millennium BC, more familiar to us through the campaigns of the Peloponnesian and Punic Wars or the actions of personalities such as Alexander the Great and Hannibal.

The Mediterranean: 480–146 BC

To understand the themes developed later in this chapter it is necessary to give a brief sketch of events in the Mediterranean as the principal contenders struggled for dominance.

In the immediate aftermath of the Persian wars Athens emerged supreme. Armed for the first time with a highly successful navy, the Athenians created a confederacy of cities and states within the Aegean – the Delian League – which soon became a virtual empire. But internal dissent, spearheaded by Sparta, quickly led to the outbreak of the Peloponnesian War – a long and debilitating slog lasting from 431 to 404 BC. During the war the Athenians made an attempt to take control of Sicily, to expand their power base into the central Mediterranean, but the ill-judged campaign ended in disaster and by the time the war was at an end the Athenian navy had been destroyed and the city starved into submission. Less than a century after her triumphs at Marathon and Salamis, Athens was a spent force. Subsequent history was to confirm that the Greek city-states of the Aegean, separated from each other by mountains and the sea and imbued with a passionate sense of independence, could never really unite.

But not so Macedonia, which lay to the north of Greece. Here, a rather more backward social system (compared to Athens) allowed strong kings to emerge and to build increasingly stable power bases uninhibited by the constraints of democracy. In 359 BC Philip of Macedon took control. By the time of his death in 336 he had extended Macedonian power across Thrace (central and southern Bulgaria) and had forced the Greeks to submit. After

10.3 A small ivory head, probably Philip II of Macedon (382–336), found in a fourth-century BC tomb at Vergina, Macedonia, Greece.

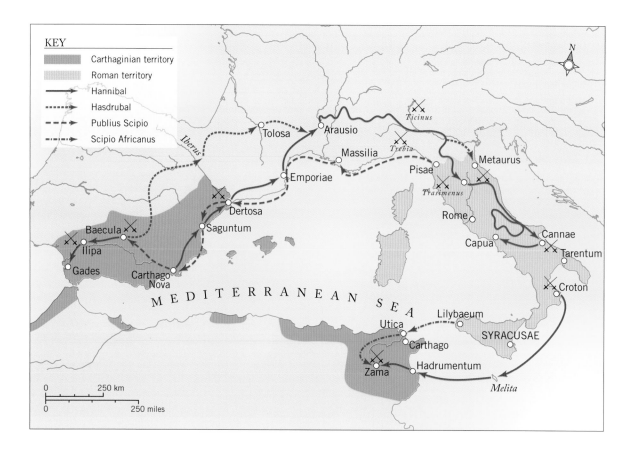

KEY
- Carthaginian territory
- Roman territory
- → Hannibal
- ⋯→ Hasdrubal
- ⟶ Publius Scipio
- ⋅—⋅→ Scipio Africanus

10.4 The Second Punic War was fought out between Rome and Carthage between 218 and 202 BC in southern Iberia, Italy and North Africa.

his murder his ultimate intention, to lead a full-scale war against the Persian Empire, was taken up by his nineteen-year-old son, Alexander, with spectacular results. Alexander's great military adventure (334–323) reached as far as Afghanistan and the Indus valley and took in Egypt for good measure. After Alexander's death his vast and unmanageable conquests were divided between his generals, and although they and their successors were constantly at each other's throats, Alexander had succeeded in embracing the whole of the east Mediterranean and the surrounding lands in a single distinctive Hellenistic culture rooted in the Greek past and Greek values.

In the central Mediterranean two power blocks were now emerging – Rome and Carthage. Rome's story conventionally begins in 509 BC, the traditional date when the city is said to have thrown off the last of its Etruscan kings. Over the next two and a half centuries Rome extended its domination over much of the rest of the Italian peninsula – a process that brought it increasingly into contact with Carthage. Carthage, founded on the Bay of Tunis by the Phoenicians at the end of the ninth century, was a maritime power whose sphere of influence included much of Sicily and Sardinia. Both

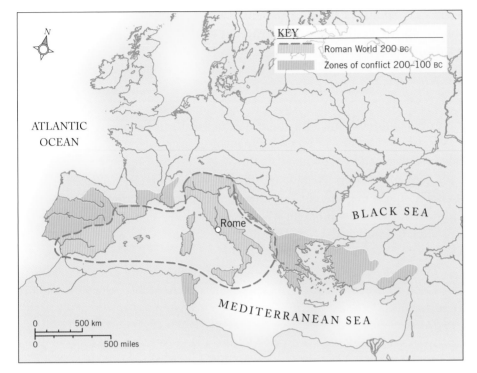

10.5 After the Second Punic War the Roman Empire was rapidly extended to encompass much of the western and central Mediterranean. Around this core was a broad periphery where Rome was in conflict with her neighbours for the next hundred years.

states, therefore, had vested interests in the control of the Tyrrhenian Sea. To begin with, equilibrium was maintained by treaties but eventually, in 264, war broke out over territorial disputes in Sicily. This long-drawn-out conflict – the First Punic War (264–241) – left Rome, the victor, in control of Sicily, to which Corsica and Sardinia were soon added, making the Tyrrhenian Sea a Roman domain.

For the Carthaginians this was a devastating blow. Squeezed out of the central Mediterranean, they now turned to the west with the intention of rebuilding their power base in the old Phoenician territory of southern Iberia. The expedition set out in 237 BC and within a few years Cartago Nova (New Carthage) – now Cartagena – had been established on a fine harbour midway along the summer sailing route between the Carthaginian base on Ibiza and the Straits of Gibraltar. With the sea lanes secure, successive Carthaginian generals set about bringing inland Iberia under control. But with Rome also in expansive mood the Mediterranean was becoming too small to contain the two superpowers, and a territorial dispute at Sagunto on the Iberian coast was used as an excuse by the Romans to open hostilities again.

The ensuing Second Punic War (218–202 BC) was a fight to the death fought out in Iberia, Italy and North Africa. Rome was again the victor. Carthage had been emasculated but it was still a danger, as the Elder Cato

323

constantly reminded the Roman Senate with his clarion call: '*Cartago delende est*' – Carthage must be destroyed. When he flung down luscious Carthaginians figs before the Senate he was dramatically reinforcing what everyone knew – Carthage was too close (only 600 km [375 miles] away). It was also an extremely desirable territory to acquire. The Third Punic War (149–146) was little more than a mopping-up operation: Carthage was destroyed and the Roman province of Africa came into being.

Rome was becoming increasingly involved in power struggles in the east Mediterranean and Asia Minor. At this stage the state preferred to manipulate Asia through its allies Pergamon and Rhodes, but unrest in Macedonia and constant squabbling among the Greek cities demanded direct intervention. Both territories were annexed: Macedonia in 148 BC and Achaea (Greece) in 146 after Corinth had been destroyed and its surviving population sold as slaves.

With the destruction of Carthage and Corinth in the same year Rome's sphere of influence extended from Andalucía to Anatolia. Almost the entire Mediterranean – *mare nostrum* – was now a Roman preserve.

Some Aegean Themes

For much of the period that concerns us in this chapter the Aegean world, and in particular Greece, was distracted by endemic conflict, the intensity of which ebbed and flowed over time. The effort needed to maintain the military machine, to build defences and, in times of peace, to aggrandize the cities and sanctuaries, was considerable. The populace had to remain productive at home and to nurture trade overseas.

The Greek countryside was not particularly productive and, as time went on, it had difficulty feeding the burgeoning populations. It was imperative to secure a reliable supply of corn and thus the security of the trade routes with the Black Sea colonies, with Egypt and with the cities of Magna Graecia became of prime concern. By the sixth century BC the major trading cities were Corinth and Aegina. Corinth commanded the isthmus linking the Peloponnese to the rest of Greece. It looked out on a long, well-protected waterway, the Gulf of Corinth, which provided direct and easy access to the Ionian Sea and to Magna Graecia and the Adriatic. Aegina, situated on an island in the middle of the Saronic Gulf, faced eastwards to the Aegean. As an island polity, favoured by virtue of its proximity to mainland cities, it fast became a maritime state, growing rich on the services it provided for its neighbours. Until the beginning of the fifth century Athens was content to

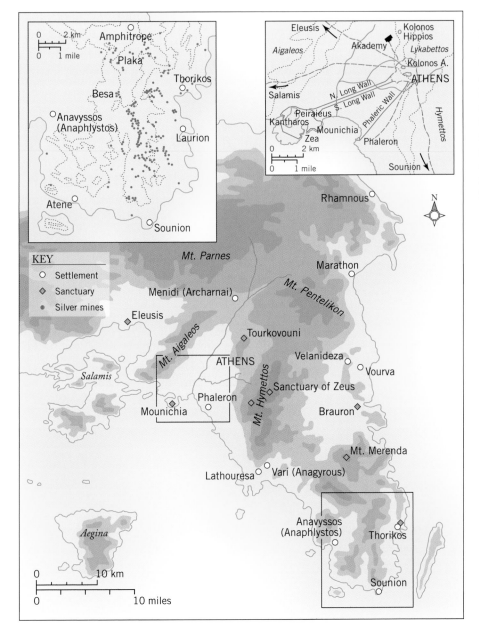

10.6 Attica in the seventh century BC was dominated by the growing city of Athens. The wealth of Attica lay in its silver mines in the south-east of the peninsula between Thorikos and Sounion. Athens, as a developing maritime power, constructed extensive naval installations at Peiraeus on the Saronic Gulf.

rely on Aegina to organize the importation of the city's corn from the Black Sea and from Egypt, and to distribute Attic pottery made for export. The Aeginetans became famous for their trading endeavours. Herodotus mentions one merchant venturer by name – Sostratos, son of Laodamas – who grew so rich that 'no one can compare with him'. One of the commodities that he transported to the Etruscans was Attic Black-Figured pottery, many examples of which have been found in Etruria inscribed 'SO . . .' – the mark of the importer. The same man or one of his family was probably responsible for a dedicatory inscription found in Gravisca, the port of Tarquinia, which reads: 'I am of Aeginetan Apollo: Sostratos had me made . . .'

The proximity of Aegina and Athens soon led to rivalry which erupted into outright hostility. In 490 BC the Aeginetans mustered seventy ships to send against Athens. Themistocles, all too aware of Athens's vulnerability, persuaded the Athenians to spend the considerable profits from the silver mines of Laurion not in hand-outs to the citizens but in shipbuilding. It was this fleet of some two hundred ships that was to come to the city's rescue when, in 480, the Persians sailed into the Bay of Salamis. By this time the Athenians had become not only competent sailors but also skilled shipbuilders with a strongly fortified port at Peiraeus. After the successful conclusion of the Persian Wars the Athenian navy emerged supreme, enabling the city to maintain a tight hold over the Delian League and to develop it, albeit briefly, into a maritime empire.

The Athenian silver mines at Laurion lay at the south-eastern extremity of Attica, a few kilometres north of the famous sanctuary of Sounion. The mines had been worked sporadically since the Bronze Age, producing copper in addition to silver, but in 483 BC a new, deeper, silver-rich level was opened and the works became massively productive, generating huge profits. It was as though the gods were providing for Athens in her time of need and had given her the wise Themistocles to guide her in the use of her new-found wealth. After the war the silver, converted into coins with the head of Athena on one side and her symbol, the Little Owl, on the other, became common currency throughout the Aegean and beyond. The 'Owls of Laurion' was how the playwright Aristophanes referred to the coins.

Another product of the Greek mainland that was widely exported was pottery made in workshops on the outskirts of the cities. In the seventh and early sixth centuries BC Corinth had by far the largest market share but by the middle of the sixth century Athens was beginning to compete with its fine Black-Figured ware and the later Red-Figured ware, which came into production about 530 BC. There was huge demand for fine Greek pottery throughout the Mediterranean. In Etruria, in the seventh and sixth centuries, the consumption of fine wares for funerary deposits reached epic proportions, but the more ordinary wares were also avidly sought and were probably mass-produced in Attica specifically for export.

Another export, which came mainly from the larger Aegean islands and the cities of the Anatolian coast, was wine. It was transported in amphorae, these bulky cargoes being mainly destined for the Black Sea market. Once

offloaded at the ports, the wine was either decanted for local distribution and drinking, or transported into the barbarian hinterlands where, eventually discarded, the amphorae provide valuable archaeological evidence of trading patterns. Amphorae from all the main wine-providers – Thassos, Samos, Chios and Rhodes – are found deep in barbarian territory, westwards from the Black Sea coast along the valleys leading far into the Carpathians, and northwards from Olbia along the Dnepr to Kiev and beyond. In return the Greek world acquired grain to feed its fast-growing population.

Another commodity of increasing importance was slaves. Greece, like most Mediterranean and Near Eastern societies, had for long been a slave-owning society, though it was not until the sixth century BC that slaves began to become a significant part of the economy. The fourth-century historian Theopompus of Chios offers a specific insight:

> The Chians were the first Greeks after the Thessalians and Spartans to use slaves, but they acquired them in a different way. For the Spartans and the Thessalians clearly constituted their slave class out of the Greeks who had earlier inhabited the land which they now possess. . . . But the Chians acquired barbarian slaves paid for by purchase.

10.7 An Athenian silver coin known as the 'Owl of Laurion' – a reference to the rich silver deposits of Laurion upon which the strength of Athens was based. The owl is a symbol of wisdom usually associated with the goddess Athena.

327

10.8 The power of Corinth lay in its command of the peninsula joining the Peloponnese to the rest of Greece. Its position also enabled it to control the *diolkos* – a paved way – along which ships were dragged overland between the Corinthian and Saronic Gulfs.

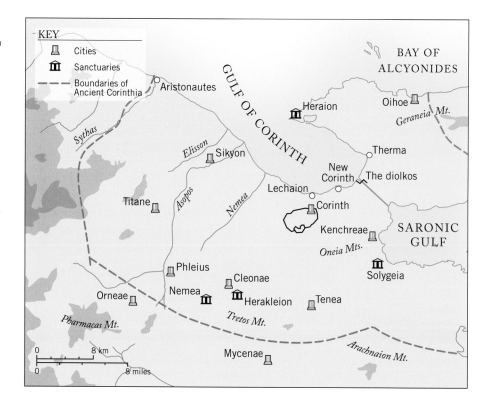

Home-grown slaves, called *helots* and *penestai*, had varying degrees of rights. Chattel slaves were altogether different: they were a commodity whose value lay entirely in their productive capacity. Chios's reputation as a slave-owning state was also confirmed by Thucydides at the end of the fifth century, when he noted that the island had the largest number of slaves after Sparta. We know of one Chian slave merchant, Panionios, who dealt in eunuchs for eastern consumers. As Herodotus records, with obvious distaste: 'Whenever he could get any boys of unusual beauty, he made them eunuchs and, carrying them to Sardis or Ephesus, sold them for large sums of money. The barbarians value eunuchs more than others since they regard them as more trustworthy.' (*Hist.* 8.40). The opening up of the slave market in the sixth and fifth centuries BC saw large numbers of slaves from Scythia, Thrace and Illyria drawn into the major Greek cities; in some, the slave population may have equalled that of adult citizens.

To facilitate trade at the greatly increased level that prevailed after the Persian Wars large fleets of ships were required, not only to carry goods but also to protect the sea lanes and the hard-contested monopolies. We have already seen how Athens used her sea power to further her own commercial interests after stifling her rival Aegina. The other great naval power at the time was Corinth, whose favourable position enabled the city's merchant venturers to open up the Ionian Sea and the southern Adriatic, establishing entrepôts along the eastern Adriatic coastline to facilitate trade with the chiefdoms of the interior. But they also had interests in the Aegean and to obviate the need to sail around the Peloponnese – a potentially dangerous voyage facing treacherous headlands – they created a stone-paved dragway (*diolkos*) across the isthmus from the Corinthian to the Saronic Gulf so that vessels could be drawn on trolleys from one gulf to the other: this was the precursor of the Corinth canal.

Another of the powerful maritime states was Rhodes, which became the natural port of call on the route from the Aegean to the Levant and Egypt. Rhodes's relationship with Egypt was particularly well developed and when the trading entrepôt was being established at Naukratis in the Nile delta in the mid-sixth century Rhodes was given privileged treatment, the pharaoh Amasis sending valuable gifts to the sanctuary of Athena at Lindos to mark the occasion. In 408 a remarkable event took place – the island's three ancient cities of Lindos, Ialyssos and Kameiros, agreed to come together in an act of synoecism to found a single city – Rhodes – at its northern end. The site was very well chosen and the port soon flourished. The Rhodians became widely known for their skill as seamen and their acumen and inventiveness as ship-builders. The historian Polybius mentions one Carthaginian sea captain who was so skilled that he was nicknamed 'the Rhodian'. As traders in their own right and as the carriers of other people's merchandise Rhodians gained a Mediterranean-wide reputation for efficiency and fairness – a reputation based on the careful laws that they developed to safeguard the rights of those engaged in maritime commerce. To give one example – the provision of general average. If merchandise had to be jettisoned in time of danger at sea to save the rest of the cargo, then the person whose goods had been lost had an entitlement to compensation from those whose cargo had been saved. The maritime code of the Rhodians became justly famous. Many of its principles are embedded in maritime law current today.

Macedonians and Thracians

The Macedonian kingdom was a peripheral region of little import until Philip II came to power in 359 BC. Hemmed in by mountains and with a comparatively restricted coastline, it was dominated by Greece in the south, the powerful Thracian kingdoms in the north and the Illyrians living in the mountain ranges to the west. Its hereditary monarchy, culled by frequent assassinations and riven by intrigue, provided a structure within which a charismatic leader could command universal allegiance. When such a man

329

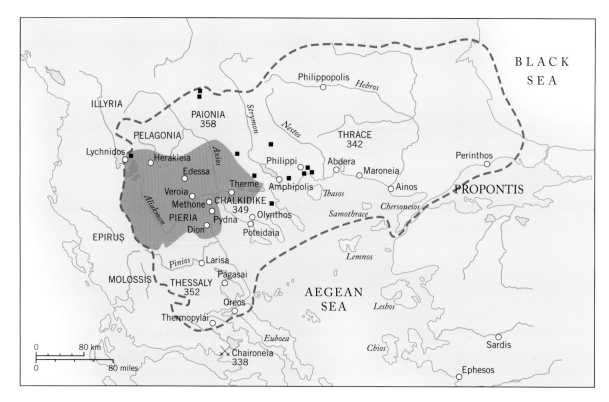

10.9 Under the strong rule of Philip II, Macedonia became a regional power of increasing importance, extending its sway from Thrace in the east to Thessaly in the south. After Philip's victory at Chaironeia in 338 he became master of the whole of Greece allowing him to turn his attention to Asia but death intervened. His Asian ambitions were realized by his son Alexander the Great.

KEY

▨	Kingdom of Macedon in 359
– – –	Expansion of Macedon to 336
THESSALY 352	Date of Macedonian invasion
■	Gold / Silver mine
✕	Site of major battle

emerged, the fragmented Greeks, constantly at each other's throats and burdened with democracy, were no match for him. In the space of twenty-three years Philip had established Macedonia as a world power. What had been a periphery had now become a centre – a centre from which Alexander was to set out to conquer the world.

To the north of Macedonia lay the region that Herodotus and subsequent writers knew as Thrace. Thrace included a large part of south-eastern Europe, from the river Morava (in modern Serbia) to the Black Sea and from the north Aegean to the arc of the Transylvanian Alps and Carpathians. According to Strabo, writing at the end of the first century BC, there were twenty-two different tribes. The most powerful – those who established strong confederacies incorporating other smaller tribes – were the Getae north of the Danube, the Triballi in north-west Bulgaria, and the Odrysai whose homeland lay in the centre of modern Bulgaria in the valley of the Maritsa between the Stara Planina and the Rodópi Mountains.

The establishment of Greek colonies along the south and east coasts of Thrace from the middle of the eighth century led inevitably to the Hellenization of the Thracian elites occupying the coastal regions. Another event of some significance was the arrival in the region of the army of Darius I in 513–512 BC, and the subsequent establishment of a Persian satrapy (governorship) in Thracian territory. During the thirty years that the Achaemenid army and its attendant bureaucracy was present in Thrace the character and values of the Achaemenid craftsmen came to be accepted into Thracian art, creating a highly original aristocratic style. As well as this, Macedonians, Scythians and Celts all contributed to Thracian culture. Thrace, then, was a melting pot – a region of many different tribes reacting in their different ways to a wide range of external influences.

The greatest impact came from the Greek world via the colonies along the north Aegean and west Pontic coasts. The distribution of wine amphorae within Thrace shows that imports were coming from Corinth, Chios, Thassos, Cnidos, Kos and Rhodes, and also from Black Sea vineyards, from Sinope and Scythian Chersonesos. Popular, too, was oil, and a range of Greek manufactured goods. In return Thrace offered corn, livestock, slaves and metals, as well as honey, beeswax, tar and timber. To facilitate these exchanges Greek coinage was used and Greek merchants settled in Thracian territory, establishing *emporia* protected by the Thracian kings.

Under this barrage of external influences Thracian culture became thoroughly Hellenized. The most advanced developments are seen in the kingdom of the Odrysai where towns adopted many of the characteristics of Greek urban planning. The most sophisticated was the capital, Seuthopolis, founded by the Odrysian king Seuthes III in *c.*320 BC. The town was laid out entirely in the style of a Hellenistic city, with a stone-built defensive wall, a regular street grid with a central agora and houses built on the peristyle plan; in one corner was an enclosed enclave separating what is thought to have been the king's palace from the rest of the town.

The most spectacular manifestations of elite Thracian culture were the tombs of the aristocracy. Xenophon gives an account of Odrysian burial rites following a battle. The ceremonies were prolonged affairs involving feasting, wine-drinking and competitive games, including horse-racing, held in honour of the deceased. Kings and priests were deified after death and were worshipped as immortal heroes.

From the sixth until the third century BC the graves of the elite were decked out with arrays of elaborate gold and silver tableware both locally made and imported, together with fine jewellery and sometimes spectacular gold

10.10 The tombs of the Thracian elite of the fourth and third centuries BC copied elements of Greek tomb-building. The small tholos tomb of Kazanluk in Bulgaria was elaborately painted inside, possibly by a Greek artist. The tomb of Maltepe, Mezek, Turkey was a massive structure approached by a long *dromos* (passage). It had later been used for the burial of a Celtic chieftain.

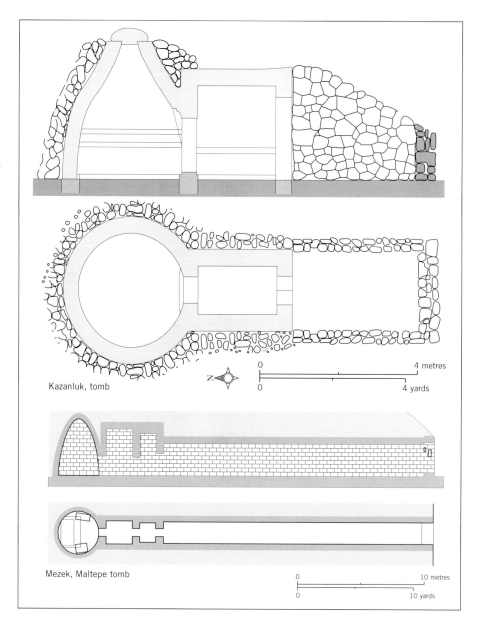

Kazanluk, tomb

0   4 metres
0   4 yards

Mezek, Maltepe tomb

0   10 metres
0   10 yards

funerary masks. In the fourth and early third centuries the tombs themselves take on a more sophisticated appearance. Beehive tholos chambers with corbelled or barrel-vaulted roofs buried within large tumuli become widespread, adopting the styles of Late Classical and Early Hellenistic architecture. Some were internally plastered and painted with funerary scenes often showing the last banquet enjoyed by the deceased hero, together with hunting and combat scenes. One of the most accomplished of these is the tholos tomb at

10.11 Details of the painting in the roof of the tholos at Kazanluk. The dead king and his wife (off picture to the left) are shown in the centre, with servants bringing gifts or their possessions to them. In this part of the scene a groom brings the king's four-horse chariot. In the crest of the dome a chariot race is in progress replicating, perhaps, funerary games and symbolizing the passage of the soul to the nether world.

10.12 Thracian craftsmen were skilled in working silver and gold. The jug (above) from a treasure hoard found at Vratsa, in Bulgaria, dates to the fourth century BC and is typical in its depiction of fabulous beasts. The cauldron (right), found at Gunderstrup in Denmark, has many of the characteristics of Thracian metalwork. One possibility is that it was made in Thrace by Thracian craftsmen as a gift for a Celtic king living in a nearby territory and eventually found its way, by gift exchange, to the north.

Kazanluk, in the Valley of the Roses, dating to the late fourth or early third century. While the composition and the detailed subject matter, including the brilliantly drawn horses, complete with their harnesses and saddles, are entirely Thracian, the execution is wholly in the spirit of Hellenistic art. It is quite likely that the painter was Greek or Greek-trained, working under contract to the royal household.

Thracian art is most vividly represented in quite stunning arrays of fine metalwork, usually gilded silver vessels of varying kinds. There is nowhere better to trace the various stylistic elements brought together and moulded into a harmonious whole by the highly skilled Thracian metalsmiths. The rich iconography frequently includes the Great Goddess in various guises and the Thracian king-hero shown as a mounted hunter, but Greek deities also make an appearance, emphasizing the eclectic range of the Thracian craftsmen. Much of this material is known from hoards – presumably votive offerings to the deities – which can reach considerable size. A hoard from Rogozan in the territory of the Triballi contained 165 silver vessels weighing nearly 20 kg (44 lbs). Several were inscribed with the names of Odrysian kings, which suggests that they were diplomatic gifts offered to the Triballi by the Odrysai.

The Macedonian and Thracian kingdoms existed on the fringes of the Greek world and to that extent they were peripheries absorbing influences from the south. But it would be wrong to think of the cultures that emerged simply as pale reflections of Greek achievements. Far from it. Focusing on its military might and inspired by successive charismatic leaders, the Macedonian state very rapidly created a culture that was unique and sufficiently energetic to absorb the crumbling Greek edifice. The Thracians present a rather different story. Throughout the first millennium BC the indigenous communities

334

were able to draw into themselves many alien traditions – Greek, Achaemenid, Scythian and Celtic – and create a highly distinctive culture, with its own political structures and belief systems, including the concept of the king as a warrior-hero god. The Thracian elite may have been receptive to Greek culture but they were nonetheless selective, taking only those aspects consistent with their own social constructs. What emerged was no faint echo of Greece but one of the most original and inventive cultures of barbarian Europe.

Conflict in the Tyrrhenian Sphere

The conflict for the control of the Tyrrhenian sphere began in the context of competition for trading rights and ended in a scramble to control territory. As early as 509 BC the two principal contenders for power – Rome and Carthage – understood that to avoid potential hostilities it was necessary to define, with care, spheres of influence through treaty arrangements. The original treaty was reaffirmed, with modifications to take into account the expansion of Carthaginian interests, in 348 BC, renewed again in 306 BC and updated once more in 279–278 BC, with additional clauses describing mutual aid. It is no mean achievement that for 244 years, from the time of the first treaty to the outbreak of the First Punic War in 264 BC, the two powers managed to coexist in moderate harmony.

The treaties defined spheres of interest and laid down protocols of behaviour for any party operating in the other's 'territory'. Thus, from the treaty of 348 BC transcribed by the historian Polybius we learn that:

> There is to be friendship on the following conditions between Romans and their allies and the Carthaginians, Tyrians and the people of Utica and their respective allies. The Romans shall not maraud or trade or found a city on the further side of the Fair Promontory and Mastia or Tarseum. . . .
>
> If a Roman gets water or provisions from any place over which the Carthaginians rule, he shall not use these provisions to wrong any member of a people with whom the Carthaginians have peace and friendship. The Carthaginians shall do likewise. . . .
>
> No Roman shall trade or found a city in Sardinia and Libya [Africa] nor remain in a Sardinian or Libyan port longer than is required for taking in provisions or repairing his ship. If he be driven there by stress of weather he shall depart within five days. In the Carthaginian province of Sicily and at Carthage he may do and sell anything that is permitted to a citizen. A Carthaginian in Rome may do likewise.

The clarity of the treaty is impressive: a notional line had been drawn through the Tyrrhenian Sea giving Rome rights to the territorial waters of Italy but nothing more.

The First Punic War ended all this. Rome had been drawn beyond the Italian peninsula into a dispute in Sicily and, in her success, had begun to glimpse new horizons. The annexation of Sardinia and Corsica was the logical next step. The advantages of having total control of overseas territories were fast becoming apparent – empire-building had begun.

With the horrors of the Second Punic War over – a traumatic time when the Roman state was under real threat of annihilation – Rome found herself in possession of a large part of the Iberian peninsula, with all its fabulous mineral riches within her grasp: territorial expansion was now firmly on the agenda. Thus it was that by the middle of the second century BC the logic of annexing what remained of the Carthaginian domain in North Africa became inescapable. This particular corner of the North African coast (modern Tunisia) was exceptionally fertile. That Rome was already experiencing corn shortages, caused by the rapid growth of a demanding urban proletariat, made action the more urgent. The historian Polybius gives a fulsome description of the attractions of the countryside around the Bay of Tunis. The land was:

> divided into gardens and plantations of every kind, since many streams of water were led in small channels and irrigated every part. There were also country houses one after another built in a luxurious manner and covered with stucco which showed the wealth of the people who owned them. The farm buildings were filled with everything that was needed for enjoyment. . . . Part of the land was planted with vines, and part yielded olives and was also thickly planted with every variety of fruit-bearing tree. On all sides herds of cattle and flocks of sheep are pastured on the plain and the neighbouring meadows were filled with grazing horses. There is manifold prosperity in the region since it is here that the leading Carthaginians have laid out their private estates and with their wealth had beautified them for their enjoyment.

Knowing of this promised land on their very doorstep, it is little wonder that the Roman Senate voted to invade in 149 BC.

The contest between Rome and Carthage, though dominated by great set-piece land battles, depended to a considerable extent on mastery of the sea. In this, Rome, a land-based state, was, at first, no match for the Carthaginians whose culture lay deeply rooted in their traditional maritime capabilities. In this difference may lie the reason why the two powers managed to coexist in the same region for so long.

Carthage maintained a sturdy fleet of over a hundred vessels known as 'fivers' (*pentereis*) powered by well-trained professional crews. Used to enjoying maritime supremacy, the Carthaginians had little incentive to improve or update their navy and were caught at a serious disadvantage when, in the winter of 261–260, the Roman Senate gave orders for the construction of a hundred quinqueremes and twenty triremes. Roman historical tradition has it that the design of the quinqueremes was based on a Carthaginian 'fiver' captured at Messina a few years before. The vessels were built, it is claimed, in sixty days, most likely in the shipyards of Ostia, and while this feat of construction was under way 33,000 rowers were trained from scratch on staging set up on dry land.

While the shipbuilding technology the Romans used was tried and tested, they were not averse to innovation. One ingenious improvement they made was a boarding device known as the *corvus* (raven) which consisted of a timber walkway about 4 m (13 ft) long which could be rotated about a short mast set in the bows. It could also be raised up or lowered down the mast by ropes and pulleys as the height of the enemy vessel required. The name of the apparatus comes from a spiked iron beak at the free end of the walkway that was designed to penetrate the deck of the enemy ship when dropped on to it and hold the two vessels fast together, allowing the Romans to board.

The contest finally came in the late summer of 260 BC when, to draw out the Roman fleet, the Carthaginian flotilla of 130 ships attacked Mylae in Sicily. From this overconfident beginning the day turned into a rout: fifty of the Carthaginian ships were lost and the rest fled in disarray. Early the next year Rome celebrated her first naval victory by erecting a column decorated with the beaks of the captured Carthaginian vessels in the Forum and by building a temple to Janus – the god of beginnings and endings. The Battle of Mylae was indeed a turning point. Rome was now a naval power with the means and confidence to break out of the constraints imposed by the long succession of treaties with Carthage. For Carthage it brought the stark realization that her naval supremacy in the central and west Mediterranean was now under serious threat. Four generations later the city of Carthage was in ruins.

In the three islands that Rome acquired as a result of the First Punic War – Sicily, Sardinia and Corsica – lay the basis of empire. The acquisition of Sicily, wrote Cicero in 70 BC, was 'the first to teach our ancestors what a fine thing it is to rule over foreign nations'. Cato was more explicit. Sicily was the 'Republic's granary, the nurse at whose breast the Roman people is fed'. The reality behind this lay in the tax system that the Romans imposed on the island. One-tenth of the annual grain crop was shipped direct to Rome. A comparable tax on wine, olives, fruit and vegetables was also probably paid in kind while that on pasture land was rendered as a cash payment. The Roman Senate could also acquire additional grain, by compulsory purchase, at a

10.13 Triumphal column set up by Caius Duilius in the Forum at Rome. It is ornamented with the prows of Carthaginian ships, commemorating Rome's defeat of the Carthaginian navy, and signals the birth of Rome's maritime supremacy.

price fixed by themselves. Duties on imports and exports were set at the rate of 5 per cent, the cash going straight to the Roman exchequer. The Sicilian communities were also responsible for the protection of the surrounding seas from piracy. While there can be no doubt that Sicilians enjoyed peace and prosperity as a result of Roman rule, Rome's gain was enormous not only in terms of cash but also in the assurance gained of a constant supply of grain and other foodstuffs to meet the needs of her increasingly non-productive citizenry.

The rewards of empire were many – assured food supplies, regular tax income and, at moments of conquest, booty and slaves. Roman authors delighted in listing the spoils of war. The quantity of riches pouring into the Roman coffers was staggering. To give just one example, the Roman triumph over the eastern ruler Antiochus in Asia Minor in 190 BC yielded: '224 military standards, 134 models of towns, 1231 ivory tusks, 234 golden crowns, 137,420 pounds of silver, 224,000 Attic tetradrachms, 321,072 cistophori [a type of tetradrachm], 140,000 Philippi [gold staters], 1423 pounds of chased silver vases, 123 pounds of gold vases.' Sudden influxes of wealth on this scale had a dramatic effect on the Roman economy.

Another outcome of imperialist wars, to effect massive changes to Roman society and its economy, was the availability of huge numbers of slaves. When in 176 BC a Roman army was sent to put down a revolt in Sardinia, the triumphant general boasted that he had killed and captured eighty thousand of the island's inhabitants. Most of the survivors would have been sold into slavery in Italy. Nine years later the suppression of a revolt in Epirus generated 150,000 slaves. As a result there must have been a glut in the market.

Much of the wealth pouring into Italy found its way into rural investment, so leading to the growth of large estates. Since the traditional peasantry could no longer provide an adequate labour force, the only way for the elite to maximize their investment was to run the estates with slave labour. This new trajectory – a direct consequence of imperialism – was to change Roman society radically.

In parallel with the growth of the city of Rome, both in power and in population, its ports developed too. There were two of particular consequence; Ostia towards the mouth of the Tiber downstream from Rome; and Puteoli on the Bay of Naples. Puteoli was the principal port of entry for goods from the east. From here cargoes for Rome were trans-shipped to local vessels and carried along the coast to Ostia. Ostia also received grain direct from Sicily, together with wine, oil and fruit. Campania contributed a similar range of agricultural products. After the Second Punic War, the acquisition of large, highly productive territories in Iberia greatly enhanced Ostia's importance and led to the expansion of its port facilities. Rome had now become the centre of a maritime empire.

Iberia: The Prize

Already by 500 BC the Mediterranean powers had staked out their claims to the coast of Iberia. In the south the Phoenician colonization stretched eastwards from the Straits of Gibraltar to Guardamar at the mouth of the river Segura, while the Greek enclave, focused around the Golfe du Lion, extended

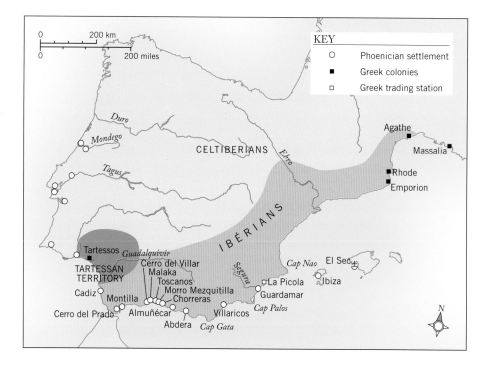

10.14 Iberia in the fifth–fourth centuries BC at a time when the Phoenicians and Greeks were beginning to compete for control of the Levantine coast and its trading opportunities.

westwards to Emporion (Ampurias) on the Costa Brava. Between the two lay 650 km (375 miles) of unclaimed coastline. That said, the Phoenician sphere of interest really began with the Cabo de la Nao 100 km (60 miles) north of the Segura estuary because it would have been for this point that vessels on their outward journeys from the east would have sailed after leaving Ibiza. From here, westwards along the coast, a succession of harbour towns provided convenient overnight ports of call on the route to Gadir (Cadiz).

The sixth century BC is generally considered to be a time of crisis for the Phoenician settlements; indeed, fewer than half of them survived into the fifth century. An account of the southern Iberian coast incorporated into a much later poem, *Ora maritima*, tells that 'On this shore frequent cities formerly stood and many Phoenicians held these lands of old. The deserted earth now extends inhospitable sands.' Greek trade with the Phoenician ports also dropped away and at Huelva imported Greek pottery, so prolific in the earlier periods, disappeared altogether until the second half of the fifth century when there was a revival. What caused the late sixth-century downturn is difficult to say: probably a combination of factors, not least the breakdown of relations with the Phoenician homeland and the rise in power of Carthage and the cities of Magna Graecia. There is also some hint that the easily accessible silver ores of Tartessos may by now have been exhausted – at just the time when the Laurion mines of Attica were suddenly becoming highly productive. Whatever the causes, the vitality of the Phoenician settlements was in decline.

For the Phocaean Greeks of the Golfe du Lion the late sixth century BC was a time of expansion. Their efforts seem first to have been focused on developing markets in the north with the elites of west central Europe, but events deep within Europe were to change all this. The old elite systems of the Hallstatt period collapsed and there followed a period of turbulence and migration (the so-called Celtic migrations) that saw serious disruption to the existing trading patterns. The result was that the Phocaean cities began to turn their backs on the north and to look increasingly to Iberia for valuable trading opportunities. This is the time when Emporion shows a dramatic rise in importance.

During the early and mid-fifth century BC the elites of Levantine Iberia were provided, in increasing quantities, with high-quality Attic wares probably from Emporion. But around the middle of the fifth century large volumes of cheaper Attic pottery begin to flood the Levantine markets, among them the ubiquitous Castulo cups mass-produced as an export ware in the late fifth and early fourth centuries. The bulk of this material seems to have come not via the trading ports of the Golfe du Lion but direct from Magna Graecia, which was at this time beginning to experience an increased involvement with Athens. A direct trading link between the towns of Magna Graecia and the Levantine coast of Iberia may explain how it was that Iberian mercenaries came to serve on the side of the Greeks at the Battle of Himera in 480 BC.

The Greek pottery found in Iberia need not, however, all have been carried by Greek ships. A large quantity of Greek pottery was reaching Etruria and it is quite possible that the Etruscans shipped pottery, along with other goods, to Phoenician ports such as Huelva and Malaka (Malaga) where it has been found in abundance. Another possibility is that Phoenician ships took Greek and other pottery on board at friendly Etruscan ports. A shipwreck dating to around 350 BC, found on the sea bed at El Sec close to the harbour mouth of Palma de Mallorca, provides an insight into the nature of trade. It was carrying a cargo of millstones, bronze ingots, bronze vessels, amphorae and pottery including Attic Red-Figured cups and kraters for wine-mixing. A number of the pots were scratched with graffiti, some in Greek, others in Punic (Carthaginian). Many of the Greek graffiti were batch numbers giving the size of the various consignments, while the Punic inscriptions were personal names indicating ownership. The implication is that the El Sec wreck was a Carthaginian merchantman tramping from port to port and picking up useful cargoes wherever possible. Its discovery shows just how complex were the processes of trade.

We can, however, be reasonably sure that many of the ships reaching the coast of the Iberian Levant were Greek and it is likely that the Greek

10.15 The remarkable sculptures from Porcuna, Jaen, in Andalucía, Spain belong to a monumental group depicting a battle between Iberian warriors and their enemies, including fabulous beasts. The massive composition, of which this is a part, dates to the early fifth century BC and, while clearly of Iberian origin, owes much to the inspiration of eastern Greek sculpture.

10.16 *Opposite:* The 'priestess' from Cerro de los Santos, Albacete, Spain, is a classic piece of mature Iberian art dating to the third century BC. It gives a finely detailed impression of the dress, jewellery and hair style of a woman of the Iberian elite.

merchants established trading bases at strategic points. One of these, La Picola, lies on the north side of what was then the estuary of the river Segura. The establishment was small – only 60 by 60 m (180 by 180 feet) – but was strongly defended by a double wall fronted by a wide, flat ditch in a style found elsewhere in the Greek world. Inside were regular rows of buildings probably used for storage. Occupation began *c.*430 BC and seems to have lasted for a century. The choice of site for the trading base of La Picola was conditioned by a detailed knowledge of geography and sound economic judgment. The site was conveniently close to La Alcudia – the most important Iberian town in the region with which, no doubt, a profitable trading relationship had been built up. An additional advantage was that the river Segura provided a direct route to the west, leading via the high mountain pass of Despeñaperros to the valley of the Guadalquivir. From here the metal resources of Tartessos and the Sierra Morena were directly accessible. The Segura route, therefore, enabled Greek traders to access the riches of the west without having to negotiate with

Phoenicians who controlled the southern coastal approach. By opening up this overland route, the Greek entrepreneurs helped further to weaken the local Phoenician economy.

Until the mid-fifth century BC the Greek imports into Iberia were mainly luxury goods used by the elite. But there were other ways in which Greek contact contributed to the development of Iberian culture, the most spectacular being its influence on monumental sculpture. One of the earliest pieces of Iberian sculpture yet discovered is an elaborately carved funerary monument found at Pozo Moro near Albacete, dating to the early fifth century. Although undoubtedly Iberian in conception the sculptor was clearly inspired by eastern 'orientalizing' styles. Dating to the second half of the fifth century is a remarkable sculptural composition from the Iberian town of Obulco (Porcuna) in Andalucía. It depicts warriors, some of them mounted, engaged in conflict with fabulous beasts. Carved in the round, it is a hugely energetic composition, designed and executed by highly skilled craftsmen thoroughly conversant with east Greek styles. But the composition itself is Iberian, depicting local warriors armed with Iberian weapons and body armour. While the sculptors, or their teachers, may have learnt from Greek masters, they were by now confidently working in their own distinctive style.

Iberian sculpture continued to develop throughout the fourth and third centuries BC, producing famous masterpieces like the Dama d'Elche, the Dama de Baza and the priestess from the sanctuary of Cerro de los Santos (Albacete), as well as emblematic carvings of elegantly stylized bulls, squatting lions and horses that may have adorned funerary monuments. It is a mature art of assured Iberian master sculptors.

By the fourth century BC Iberian society had developed a degree of sophistication that justifies the word 'civilization'. Towns were now being built, defended with city walls adopting Hellenistic building techniques, and some were issuing their own coinage. An Iberian script, owing much to Ionic prototypes, was

10.17 The crouching lion from Nueva Carteya, Cordoba, Spain is characteristic of the highly distinctive art of the Iberians. The piece dates to the fifth or fourth century BC, and was part of a monumental composition.

10.18 Painted vessel from La Alcudia, Elche, Alicante, Spain, dating to the third century BC. The hooded figure is probably a priest but the rest of the symbolism is obscure.

also widely in use. Socially, too, there had been significant changes as chiefdoms dominated by elites gave way to a more ordered state system. There are also signs that the army was being organized in a more professional way, not unlike that of the Etruscans or the Greeks with their contingents of hoplites. Iberian fighters, well known for their quality, began to be used as mercenary forces in wider Mediterranean conflicts. The mounted Iberian warrior was revered and the quality of his short single-edged sword (the *falcata*), made with skilfully refined iron, was widely admired.

344

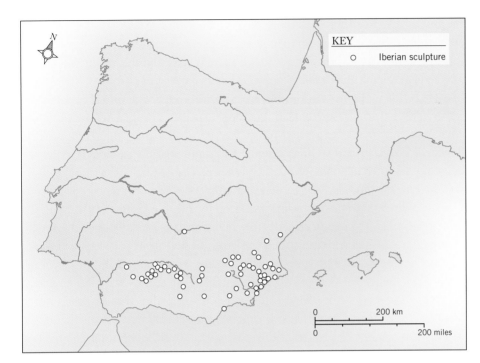

10.19 The distribution of Iberian sculpture in Spain concentrates in the two zones in which Iberian culture flourished: the valley of the Guadalquivir and the Levant.

In 237 BC the Carthaginian army landed at Gadir (Cadiz) intent on conquest. The creation of a new capital, Cartago Nova (Cartagena), sited to dominate the west Mediterranean, was a statement that the Carthaginians were here to stay. The Iberians of the south-east were quickly subdued while the army forced the frontiers of Carthaginian influence west into the Meseta and north towards the Ebro valley. The integration of Carthaginians with the Iberians was well under way (both Hasdrubal and Hannibal had married Iberian women) when, in 218 BC, hostilities with Rome led to the outbreak of the Second Punic War. With the fall of Gadir in 208 BC the Mediterranean zone of Iberia was quickly brought under Roman control. Thereafter Rome found itself engaged in almost continuous warfare in the peninsula as the frontier was slowly forced westwards to meet the Atlantic. The conquest was to take two centuries to complete.

Into the Atlantic

Gadir must have been a remarkable port – a place on the edge of the world looking out across the endless Atlantic Ocean. Sitting on the harbour side watching the sun set cannot have failed to stir the imagination. By this time Phoenicians were already exploring the coasts of Africa and Iberia and trading south as far as the island of Mogador, but towards the end of the fifth century

345

there was a new surge of activity. Some time around 425 BC a Phoenician entrepreneur, Hanno, led a maritime expedition down the west coast of Africa into the unknown. On his return he set up an inscription in the temple of Baal at Carthage giving the details, no doubt in the context of thanking the god for his safe return. The inscription has not survived but it was transcribed in the tenth century AD. It seems that Hanno's expedition began as a colonizing adventure but thereafter turned into a voyage of discovery that took him far down the coast, at least to Sierra Leone and quite possibly eastwards along the belly of Africa to the Cameroons. It was a remarkable feat not least because he returned to tell the tale.

Another Atlantic expedition, mounted by Himilco, set out at about the same time. Our main source is the poem *Ora maritima* compiled in the fourth century AD and incorporating scraps of information from earlier sources. We learn of a voyage lasting three months during which time Himilco encountered only sluggish, windless seas and masses of seaweed which impeded progress. The text is sometimes interpreted as suggesting that he sailed north to Britain and Ireland but this is wrong; it is more likely that his intention was to sail west. A later historian, Pliny, knew of Himilco's exploits but tells us nothing more than that he was sent to explore 'the parts beyond Europe' (*Nat. Hist.* 2.169).

These are the Phoenician journeys we know about but there must have been many others. Diodorus Siculus records the story of the discovery of a large Atlantic island blessed with a congenial climate: it is unnamed but is most likely to have been Madeira. When the Etruscans heard of it they wanted to found a colony but the Carthaginians refused to let them. The discovery, in AD 1749, of a small hoard of eight Carthaginian coins of the third century BC on the island of Corvo in the Azores offers a tantalizing indication that some explorers may have been making a real attempt to discover the limits of the Atlantic. Of the many, Greeks as well as Carthaginians who ventured into the Atlantic to explore its wonders we know but few of their names.

By the fourth century BC the Phoenician hold on the Straits of Gibraltar seems to have hardened, with the Atlantic ports in Morocco and Portugal remaining firmly under Phoenician control. By now there was regular trading contact with the west coast of Gallica, where tin and gold were to be had in plenty. A scatter of Phoenician pottery and other trinkets shows that traders were getting as far as the north-west extremity of Iberia. But there is no convincing evidence that they ever sailed further north to Armorica (Brittany) or to Britain. The highly mineralized zone of western Iberia would have produced all the metals they could have desired within easy reach of the comparatively safe and convenient coastal route.

The Greeks of the Golfe du Lion also had a direct interest in acquiring metals and other commodities from barbarian Europe. There were two main routes into the still-mysterious hinterland, one via the Rhône, the other along the Aude and, by an overland portage, to the river Garonne, thence to the Gironde estuary and the Atlantic. The Rhône route was in active development as a major trading axis in the late sixth and early fifth centuries BC, but the fifth-century folk movements in west central Europe – the Celtic migrations – seem to have disrupted the network, forcing the focus to shift to the Aude/Garonne route. It was along this corridor that the all-important tin was brought from Armorica (Brittany) and south-west Britain.

In about 320 BC an explorer, Pytheas of Massalia (Marseille), set out on an expedition to the north. What his motivation was we can only guess. Pytheas was evidently a scientist with a lively enquiring mind who was curious about the limits of the world, but there may also have been an economic incentive – to research the sources of the tin and amber that the Mediterranean world consumed in quantity.

Pytheas described his journey into the Atlantic in a book called *On the Ocean* which is known now only from scraps quoted by later authors. Even so, his route can be reconstructed with reasonable certainty. It seems that he followed the tin route in reverse, travelling back to the source in Britain, using local shipping to make the sea journeys. He then circumnavigated Britain. During this voyage he learned of Iceland (Thule), either second- or first-hand, and he probably also visited the source of Jutish amber in the estuary of the Elbe. His journey was a remarkable achievement, enabling him to make available accurate information about the distant Atlantic, hitherto an obscure and mysterious region. It is even possible that, as an ambassador of the Massiliots, he was able to negotiate a secure supply of tin.

In his journey around Britain Pytheas would have used the copious shipping tramping around the coasts, but little information about the vessels survives beyond a mention of skin boats – 'boats of osier covered with stitched hides' (quoted by Pliny probably from Pytheas's account). The impression given, however, is of a lively trade in tin between Cornwall and western France. There is also ample archaeological evidence to show that in the fourth century the early La Tène elites of the Marne region (see p. 356) were trading with the Atlantic regions, presumably for copper, tin and gold, along the valley of the river Loire. In this way elite items of metalwork, helmets, vessels and the like, decorated in the La Tène styles were reaching Brittany, south-west Britain and Wales by way of the western seaways. The new styles, and no doubt the values embedded in them, were accepted into indigenous cultures and reinterpreted to meet local needs. The Seine and quite possibly the Rhine were also active routes at this time, feeding the maritime networks linking the

10.20 Two masterpieces of British Celtic art. The shield was dredged from the Thames at Battersea. The other item, from Torrs, Kircudbright, Scotland, is a composite structure made up of two drinking horn terminals attached to a pony cap. It was found in a bog.

continent and Britain across the English Channel and the southern North Sea. La Tène styles and weaponry, particularly the swords and long oval shields, were introduced into Britain through these networks. There soon developed, somewhere in eastern Britain, a school of master craftsmen making an array of exquisite parade armour for the local elites.

The Nordic Realms

Crisis is perhaps too stark a word, but the years c.500–200 BC were something of a null point in the social and economic development of the Nordic region. This was a liminal period between the spectacular prestige goods economy which for two thousand years saw the elites manipulate social surpluses in the form of fine bronze and gold work, buried in their graves and later in hoards, and the emergence of a far less flamboyant society firmly based on a stable agricultural regime and the development of small villages surrounded by their fields and pastures. From the second century onwards village-based farming became the basis of a Nordic social system and was to last, with remarkably little change, until the nineteenth century AD. Seen in this perspective, the fifth to third centuries were a time of revolutionary change – a period of transformation from one socio-economic system to another.

As is so often the case, the causes of this major social upheaval were many. Climatic change will have played its part. Around 600 BC the congenial climate that the region had enjoyed changed to a wetter and colder regime. As a consequence nutrients were leached more rapidly from the fragile soils, leading to a loss of fertility and an expansion of bog land. All this caused settlements to move creating a need to develop the heavier land. These were long-term changes extending over three centuries or so but by the end of the period a new stability had emerged and in many regions the population was on the increase. Another significant factor that cannot have failed to have had an effect was the disruption of the long-established transcontinental routes caused, in west central Europe, by the turmoil of the Celtic migrations and, in east central Europe, by the mobility of 'Scythian' raiders working out of the Carpathian Basin. This zone of instability stretched right across Europe and seems to have shattered the networks of exchange that had been so active in the early part of the first millennium. Few luxury goods from the south were now penetrating as far as the Nordic zone and those that did – a few Etruscan buckets and suchlike – were being constantly recycled, eventually ending up as heirlooms in graves. A rapid decline in the use of bronze was in part a consequence of the dislocation of trade but the need for metal by the Nordic communities could now be met by local iron supplies, in particular the bog-iron widespread in the region. Thus, as the incentive to trade with the south diminished, the Nordic world increasingly looked inwards upon itself and, for a few centuries at least, developed in relative isolation.

The landscape – of islands, peninsulas and long, indented coastlines – ensured that maritime activity continued, even though the depiction of boats in rock art was now coming to an end. One spectacular discovery offers a rare insight into the maritime world. In AD 1920–21 peat-digging at Hjortspring on the small Danish island of Als brought to light the very well-preserved remains of a boat piled with artefacts. The vessel, some 19 m (62 ft)

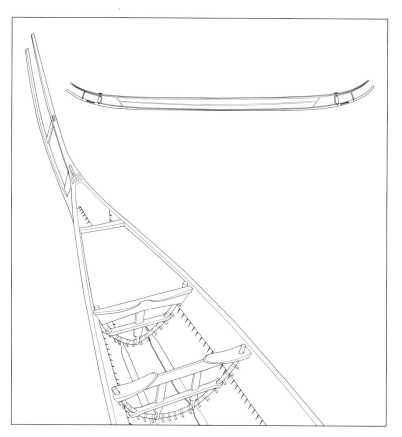

long overall – better described as a war canoe – had been dragged inland to a tiny lake, barely 50 m (164 ft) across and not much more than 1 m (3 ft) deep, and there sunk, presumably as part of a ritual to propitiate a local deity. The contents of the boat included 10 or more coats of iron ring mail, 64 wooden shields, 11 single-edged iron swords, 169 spearheads and a number of small objects mainly of bronze or wood. It is a reasonable assumption that the canoe and its contents were captured, perhaps when a raiding party was defeated, and was dedicated to the island's guardian deity as a thank offering. Radiocarbon dates suggest that the deposit was made in the second half of the fourth century BC.

10.21 The Hjortspring boat, found in a bog on the island of Als, Denmark, offers a unique insight into the technology of boat-building in the Baltic region in the late fourth century BC. It is probably the vessel of a raiding party captured and dedicated by the victors to their gods.

The canoe bears a striking resemblance to vessels depicted in the earlier rock art, leaving little doubt that the Hjortspring vessel continues a tradition of boat-building that goes back deep into the Bronze Age. It is an immensely valuable survival which provides intricate details of how these craft were constructed. The main part of the vessel was built of seven components, all of lime wood. The principal timber was a slightly hollowed bottom plank to which were attached at both ends hollowed block stems (there was no defined fore and aft). Between these ran four side strakes, two on each side. The planks, base timber and the wings of the stems were lapped and sewn together with two-ply cords made from the roots of birch or fir with the holes stopped with a mixture of animal fat and linseed. Internally the vessel was strengthened with ten ribs of bent hazel lashed to cleats integral with the side planks. The ribs were kept firm with an upper thwart of lime and lower crossbeams of ash. The thwarts would have served as seats for paddlers, two to each thwart, making a crew of twenty, with steersmen manipulating wide-bladed steering paddles in the bow and stern. With twenty paddlers at work the canoe would have skimmed through the waters at considerable speed.

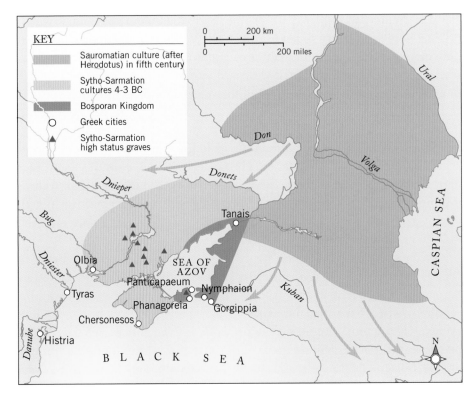

10.22 The north Pontic region in the fourth–third centuries BC. The Bosporan kingdom around the Sea of Azov managed to maintain some semblance of Greek culture in a region where Sarmatian culture was beginning to replace Scythian.

It is tempting to see the Hjortspring deposit as a war trophy reflecting a situation in which coastal raiding expeditions continued to be part of the Nordic social system. But the possibility also remains that the vessel and its weaponry now played a more symbolic part in the life of the community – an echo perhaps of a glorious heroic past remembered with nostalgia by farmers whose livelihood was now firmly rooted in the productivity of the soil and the dull slog of agrarian life.

Greeks and Nomads: The Black Sea Again

When, in the middle of the fifth century BC, Herodotus was gathering information about the peoples of the Pontic steppe, he was told that west of the river Don lived the Sauromatae whose territory stretched 'northward a distance of fifteen days' journey, inhabiting a country which is entirely bare of trees' (*Hist.* IV, 21). They 'speak the language of Scythian but have never talked it correctly'. The women were particularly warlike, 'frequently hunting on horseback with their husbands, sometimes even unaccompanied; in war taking the field; and wearing the very same dress as their men. . . . The marriage law lays it down that no girl shall wed till she has killed a man in battle' (*Hist.* IV, 116–17).

351

The Sauromatae were part of the Sarmatian nomadic group whose original homeland seems to have been on the Volga. From here they migrated both eastwards to China and westwards, eventually, in the second century AD, reaching eastern Hungary. Their westward move began at the end of the fifth or early in the fourth century BC when they crossed into Scythian territory. At about this time the archaeological record shows that there was widespread destruction among the Scythian settlements in the Lower Dnepr valley and new burial traditions were introduced including the interment of females armed in the Sauromatian manner. The evidence would seem to suggest that Sarmatians were now entering Scythian territory, though on what scale it is difficult to say – we may well be dealing only with an elite powerful enough to drive out the royal Scythians and impose themselves as rulers over the indigenous population.

In the culture of the Pontic steppe there is a noticeable change between what is referred to as the Early Scythian period, of the sixth and fifth centuries BC, and the Late Scythian or Scytho-Sarmatian period, of the fourth and third centuries, when Sarmatian influence in burial style and art becomes more evident. The animal art now shows greater Iranian influence while burial practices incorporate new elements. The famous royal tomb of Chertomlyk, on the Lower Dnepr, contains, among other sumptuous items, three cast-bronze cauldrons of Siberian type, and it is claimed that the king buried there was, anthropologically, from the east. Much of the rest of the high-quality metalwork that adorned the burial was, however, manufactured in Greek workshops serving the local market.

As the nomadic world of the Pontic region was gradually changing, so too was the Greek world: the fortunes of the various colonies fluctuated as the elites of the hinterland changed their allegiances. Once-prosperous Olbia, increasingly isolated after the beginning of the fourth century, became little more than a local trading post serving only a narrow coastal strip between the estuaries of the Dnepr and the Dnestr. Its position as an international centre trading with the Scythian elites had now been eclipsed by the rise of the Bosporan kingdom which had developed from the cluster of Greek colonies centring around the Straits of Kerch – the Cimmerian Bosporus – between the Black Sea and the Sea of Azov. In about 480 BC the thirty or so cities of this region came together as a single state under the leadership of Panticapaeum (Kerch) to create a union for mutual defence against the steppe nomads. During the fifth century the kingdom expanded to include all the Greek colonies around the Sea of Azov as well as a substantial part of the hinterland. The cities of the kingdom grew rich on trade. Corn and fish were exported to the Greek world, particularly to Athens, while wine was among the principal imports. Here, Greek craftsmen working in gold and silver were carefully

10.23 A vase of gold/silver alloy (electrum), thought to be of Greek workmanship, from Kul-Oba, near Kerch, south Russia, dating from the fourth–third centuries BC. It shows two Scythian warriors deep in conversation. The clothing and weaponry are typically Scythian and the piece may well have been made for a member of the Scythian elite.

modifying their outputs to satisfy native tastes, creating vigorous and highly original pieces with a distinctly 'barbarian' flavour.

Over the decades the populations of the old Greek cities became more and more mixed as intermarriages took place and nomadic inhabitants of the hinterlands gravitated towards the urban centres. At Tanais, the remotest of the Bosporan cities established at the mouth of the Don, the city was divided into separate sectors for the two populations. Writing of Tanais at the end of the first century BC, the Greek historian Strabo mentions its main exports as 'slaves, hides and other such things as nomads possess', in return for which they were given wine, clothing and 'things belonging to a civilized life'.

Yet for all its barbarian remoteness the Bosporan kingdom was a place where new energies were unleashed. Graeco-Scythian metalwork draws from both traditions, creating a truly original art with the power to startle. Yet little if any of it would have been seen in the Aegean homeland. Once in the hands of the indigenous elites, it disappeared with them into their graves. It was not until the nineteenth century AD that the reappearance of these exquisite items, dug out of the kurgans by an entrepreneurial peasantry and acquired by the Russian aristocracy, brought the wonders of Graeco-Scythian art to an astonished and appreciative western audience.

The Rise of the Celts

There has been much confusion about the use of the word 'Celt'. To early Greek writers like Hecataeus and Herodotus it meant peoples living in the west of Europe over against the Atlantic Ocean. But as time went on, the words 'Celt' and 'Gaul', which were often used synonymously, tended to be applied more generally to the barbarians of western Europe to distinguish them from the inhabitants of eastern Europe, who were banded together under the general name of 'Scythians'. When, therefore, the Roman and Greek worlds began to come into direct contact with migrants from west central Europe they classed them all as Celts or Gauls, though whether the migrants considered themselves to be ethnically one people is unknown. According to Julius Caesar, however, writing in the mid-first century BC, the tribes then occupying the part of France between the rivers Seine and Garonne did specifically call themselves Celts. Clearly the concept of the Celts was variously interpreted by ancient writers. We will use the word here in the same way as the historians Livy and Polybius, as a general term to refer to the tribes of west central Europe who migrated towards Mediterranean lands in the second half of the first millennium BC.

In the previous chapter we considered the Late Hallstatt elites who occupied a broad territory extending through west central Europe from north-eastern France across to southern Germany in the sixth century BC. This zone was linked to the Mediterranean by trade routes via the Rhône valley, and through the Alpine passes to the Po valley. Another transcontinental route led from the Po valley to eastern Pomerania on the Baltic. By the beginning of the fifth century these systems were in collapse and a new elite zone was beginning to develop around the outer fringe of the old Late Hallstatt zone: archaeologists call this new culture Early La Tène. A simple way to explain the shift in power is to suppose that the communities occupying key positions on the periphery of the Late Hallstatt zone were able to take control of the throughput of commodities. The inability of the Hallstatt chieftains any longer to ensure a flow of goods led their prestige-goods economy to collapse.

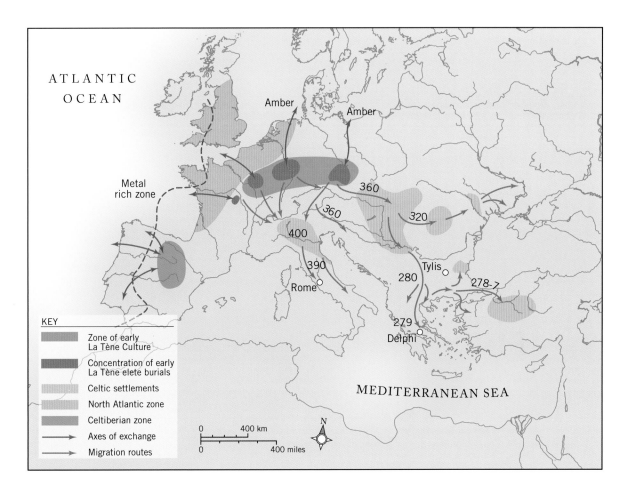

10.24 Cultural interactions in Europe in the fourth to third centuries BC.

The La Tène cultural zone of the fifth century BC occupied a wide arc stretching from the mid-Loire valley to Bohemia. Within this it is possible to identify four specific regions where there were concentrations of elite burials: the area around Bourges, the Marne valley, the Moselle valley and Bohemia. Significantly each of these regions commanded a major route: Bourges controlled the route via the Loire valley to the Atlantic and the main sources of tin from Armorica and Britain; the Marne group sat between the Seine and the Meuse which provided access to the English Channel and the southern North Sea; the Moselle group controlled the Rhône–Rhine axis; while the Bohemian group developed astride the major intercontinental route between the Po valley and the North European Plain with the amber resources of the Baltic beyond. The emergence of the La Tène elites, therefore, can most simply be explained by their favourable geographical positions, controlling the flow of commodities from western and northern Europe to the consuming Mediterranean world. In return they received a range of luxury goods from the south.

355

10.25 Two Early La Tène chariot burials from the Marne region of northern France: left from Somme-Bionne found in 1876; right from La Gorge-Meillet found in 1878. The graves were accompanied by Etruscan bronze flagons and horse gear for the pair of ponies which pulled each chariot.

Among the items traded northwards to the Early La Tène zone were Etruscan bronze vessels – beaked flagons, probably made at Vulci, and two-handled *stamnoi* (jars) used in the wine-drinking ritual. To accompany these sets, Attic Red-Figured cups, coming through the ports at the head of the Adriatic, were also trans-shipped to the north. Most of the trade seems to have been managed by the Etruscans who had by now firmly established themselves in the southern part of the Po valley. It was probably from the Etruscans, that the La Tène elites took over the idea of the fast two-wheeled chariot which they now also used as a funerary vehicle. In this way they were embracing the technology and style of the exotic Etruscan world while adapting them to suit traditional practices.

Etruscan trade with the north, passing through both the eastern and western Alpine passes, was being actively developed from the beginning of the fifth century BC. This would have required the negotiation of agreements with the communities controlling the southern approaches to the passes, but it may also have involved sending ambassadors to the north to establish friendly relationships with native elites. Already in the sixth century there are indications that this may

356

have been done with the east Pomeranians and now, in the early fifth century, the large number of Etruscan beaked flagons found in the Moselle region makes it look as though a special relationship had been established with the chieftains of the region. It is possible that the clusters of beaked flagons found in the Marne and Bohemia may also represent some kind of introductory offer.

The Early La Tène elites were receptive to Etruscan goods and ideas but quickly integrated them into their own highly distinctive culture. From the beginning local craftsmen were copying and adapting the form of the Etruscan flagon to better match their own aesthetic values, but even more spectacular was the way in which they developed a totally new art style – referred to as Early Celtic Art – from the basic concepts of classical Etruscan design by incorporating indigenous elements and aspects of animal art learned from their eastern neighbours.

One recurring theme in La Tène male burials was the deposition of weapons, usually a sword and one or more spears, with the deceased. This contrasts noticeably with Late Hallstatt burials and suggests that we may now be dealing with a more warlike society in which warrior activity and raiding had some prominence within the social system. Such a predisposition may have developed, or at least have become intensified, in response to the increasing demand for slaves by the Mediterranean world. Once it became known through contact with the south that slaves were a marketable commodity, the incentive would have been to acquire more by increasing the frequency of raiding.

Some time towards the end of the fifth century BC a massive social upheaval convulsed west central Europe. The effects can be seen in the archaeological record, while classical authors, particularly Livy and Polybius, give detailed accounts of what they believed to have been happening. Livy writes of the Celts living to the north of the Alps as having become so prosperous 'and so numerous that it seemed hardly possible to govern so great a multitude'. The king therefore decided to send his two nephews 'to find such homes as the gods might assign to them by augury and promised them that they should head as large a number of emigrants as they themselves desired'. One migrant group set out eastwards for the Black Forest and Bohemia, another took 'a far pleasanter road into Italy . . . with a vast host, some mounted, some on foot' (*Hist.* 5.34). Once in the Po valley, they defeated an Etruscan army and founded a settlement at Mediolanum (Milan). Polybius gives an outline of the Celtic settlement in the Po valley, enumerating the various tribes taking part and describing how they rapidly took over the entire region, except for the land of the Veneti who lived around the head of the Adriatic, later thrusting southwards down the Adriatic coast into Umbria. He goes on to describe their settlements and their society. They lived in open villages following 'no pursuit other than war and agriculture . . . they wandered

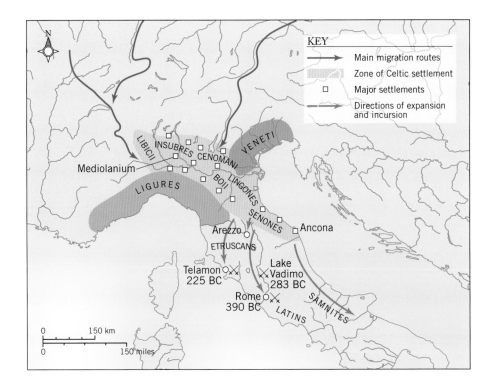

10.26 The movement of Celtic tribes into Italy in the fourth century BC and subsequent Roman response.

10.27 *Opposite:* A Celtic helmet from a burial at Canosa, Apulia, Italy decorated in distinctive Early La Tène style, fourth century BC. Helmets of this kind were developed by Celtic craftsmen in Italy and the idea was transmitted back into the Celtic homelands in Gaul.

from place to place and changed their dwellings as their fancy directed'. Wealth was measured in terms of gold and cattle, and status by the size of a man's entourage and his ability to offer hospitality.

There can be little doubt that the classical sources were describing a mass migration brought about by population pressure. The archaeological evidence is consistent with this. In the homeland in the Marne and Moselle regions there are clear signs of social disruption, with an apparent thinning-out of population, while the material culture of the early immigrants settling in the Po valley clearly derives from the Early La Tène culture zone north of the Alps. The date of the main migration lies at the end of the fifth century BC but there may have been more limited movements through the Alpine passes in the preceding centuries.

From their new homeland in the Po valley Celtic raiding parties penetrated the Apennines and descended on the cities of Etruria. Rome intervened but in 390 BC a Roman army was defeated. Large parts of Rome itself were sacked and the remainder besieged for some months before the Celts were bought off with a thousand pounds of gold. Thereafter Celtic war bands, sometimes serving as mercenaries, were active in Italy until the end of the third century BC, when the Roman army drove the remaining Celts back through the Apennines and then set about subduing and settling the Po valley with Roman colonies.

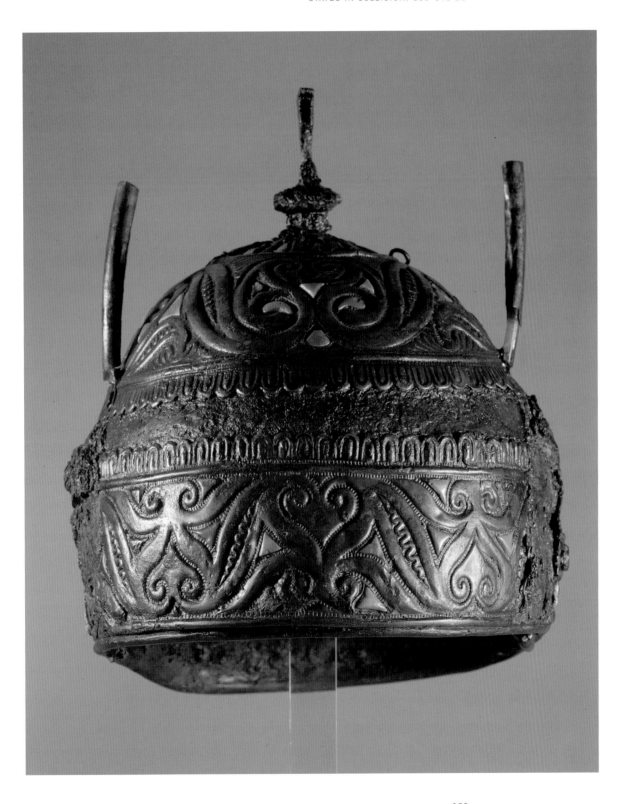

Meanwhile, the second band of migrants moved along the Danube valley into the Carpathian Basin, settling in both Transdanubia and the Great Hungarian Plain in the middle of the fourth century, some of the migrants moving into Transylvania about 320 BC. The evidence for this is largely archaeological. La Tène material culture spread throughout the region, replacing the Scythian material culture of the local inhabitants. What this means in terms of population replacement is more difficult to say. There can be no doubt that 'Celtic' immigrants moved into the area, but the probability is that they merged with the indigenous population to form a hybrid community. The material culture that emerged was predominantly La Tène in character but with a recognizable indigenous component.

From the Middle Danube valley (present-day Serbia) raids were mounted against the Illyrians and it was here that the Celts came into direct contact with the kingdoms of north-western Thrace with whom it appears they established a degree of harmony in their relations. At this time the Thracian region was fast coming under the domination of the Macedonians and in 335 BC Celtic emissaries visited the court of Alexander the Great to negotiate a treaty of friendship. Some flavour of that moment is captured by Strabo:

> The king received them kindly and asked them, when drinking, what they most feared, thinking that they would say himself, but they replied that they feared nothing except that the sky might fall on them, although, they added, they put above everything else their friendship with such a man as he. (*Geog.* 7.3.8)

So long as the Macedonians had a firm hold on Thrace the Celtic groups were constricted to the region around the confluence of the Sava and the Danube (modern Belgrade). But in the chaos that followed Alexander's death, their love of raiding was given full rein again and in 279 BC a large Celtic raiding party fought its way southwards through Thrace and Greece to the sanctuary of Apollo at Delphi. The Greek sources give us to understand that the raid was unsuccessful and that the entire force rapidly retreated. Some of the invaders returned to their homeland in Serbia while others moved eastwards, crossing the Dardanelles and the Bosphorus and entering Anatolia, where eventually they set up a kingdom near present-day Ankara. This particular enclave continued to indulge its passion for raiding, choosing the rich Greek cities of the Aegean coastal region as its prey, until, eventually, in the mid-second century BC it was decisively defeated by the rulers of Pergamum.

The continent-wide scale of the migration was unprecedented. Transcontinental trade routes were disrupted, the long-term cultural divide between the western and eastern zones of central Europe was overriden and, for the first time, the civilized Mediterranean world experienced the full

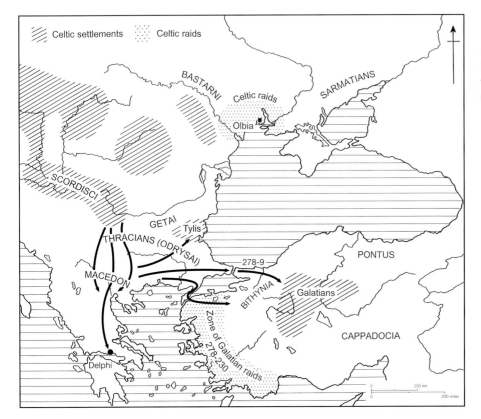

10.28 The Celts in eastern Europe and beyond, showing areas of settlement and the major thrust of the migrations of 279–277 BC.

might of its barbarian neighbours. It was a shock that Rome was never to forget.

What initiated the migrations is not entirely certain but Livy was probably right when he saw uncontainable population growth as the underlying dynamic. La Tène society was based on warrior prowess and success in the raid. With more young men wishing to compete for status and with the general population increasing, the only safety valve was to find new homelands from which successful raids could be mounted – homelands preferably within easy reach of rich pickings. The Po valley offered the wealth of Italy, the Carpathian Basin had Thrace and Macedonia on its doorstep, from Transylvania raids could be mounted into the north Pontic zone, and from central Anatolia there was a broad periphery of ripe cities to prey on. Instead of being passive recipients of luxuries from the Mediterranean, the communities of the Middle European zone now set out to acquire them for themselves. There was also a social imperative. Since status was predicated on aggressive leadership, engagement with the Mediterranean world offered not only raiding opportunities but also the chance to sell mercenary services. Dionysius of Syracuse recruited Celtic mercenaries to fight with him in

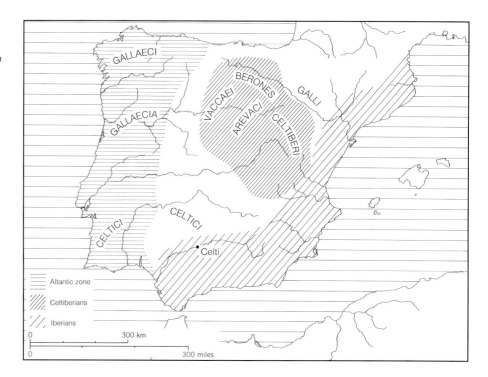

10.29 The extent of the Celtiberian culture in Iberia with the peripheral Celtic tribes named. These tribal groups may have migrated from the Celtiberian homeland.

Greece. Mercenaries also found employment in the service of Hellenistic states in Anatolia and in Egypt. Mercenary activity was little different from perpetual raiding.

The population mobility that gripped temperate Europe from the fifth to the second centuries BC is also evident in Iberia. The powerful Celtiberians, comprising a number of separately named tribes, occupied a large part of the centre of the peninsula. From such a position they were able to benefit both from the metal resources of the west coast and ease of access to Mediterranean luxuries through the Iberian states that occupied the Levantine littoral. In the fifth century there is some archaeological evidence to suggest expansion westwards into the territory of the Vettones and into the Estremadura. The historian Pliny also writes of movements of Celtiberians south into Andalucía as well as north into what is now northern Portugal. In all these regions names such as Celtici, Celti, Galli and Gallaeci are recorded, derived from general ethnic designations rather than specific tribal names. This implies the movement of mixed groups made up of a number of different tribes. The evidence hints at a considerable degree of mobility in the centre and west of the peninsula but there is no reason to suppose that peoples from Europe beyond the Pyrenees were involved. It was an indigenous Iberian phenomenon. The similarity lay in the prime causes – population growth and the need for new outlets for aggressive energy.

362

A Brief Overview

The rise of Rome from comparative obscurity in 500 BC to control much of the Mediterranean region by 140 BC was the dominant event in this period. Rome was a militaristic state from the outset, requiring its citizens to serve in the army and its elite to lead them. Only by serving with distinction in a succession of posts could a young man of senatorial rank rise in status. So it was that Rome was drawn on to conquer the disparate tribes and towns of Italy and to bind the conquered, through rights of citizenship, into a nation state. The turning point came in 261 BC when the Senate in its wisdom gave the order to build a navy. From that moment Rome became a maritime power, able to extend its field of operations across the Mediterranean. In doing so, unlimited possibilities opened up for those with military ambitions. The subjugation of Carthage was the inevitable first consequence; thereafter Rome was drawn to the east, to Greece, Asia Minor and eventually beyond. By 140 BC the Mediterranean had become virtually a Roman lake – *mare nostrum* (Our Sea).

While these processes were under way a series of spectacular cultures developed across temperate Europe – the Iberians, the Early La Tène Celts, the Thracians and the Scytho-Sarmatians. All emerged in the fifth century BC and flourished in the fourth, combining native energy and originality with ideas and values selected from the broad portfolio offered by contact with Mediterranean states. It was a flowering of creative brilliance that overshadowed anything that had gone before.

In the heart of west central Europe population growth, exacerbated by a number of other factors, led to the collapse of the traditional system, resulting in a mêlée of folk movements that reverberated across the continent for two centuries, penetrating deep into the Mediterranean world. The wide swathe of instability created across Europe severed the transcontinental routes, leaving the North European Plain and the Nordic zone to develop in relative isolation. A new configuration was beginning to emerge: in the Mediterranean the nascent Roman Empire had at last become the sole power – with the military might to extend out of its narrow ecological niche. But the inhabitants of temperate Europe had learnt that they too could cross traditional boundaries if they wished: the lines were being drawn up for a Europe-wide confrontation.

CHAPTER ELEVEN

The Interlude of Empire: 140 BC–AD 300

The rise of Rome as an imperial power totally changed the social and economic dynamics of Europe. Its impact was such that, in any description of the continent, at this time the empire inevitably dominates. Yet in the *longue durée* of history Rome's period of dominance was only an interlude – a brief period of a few centuries when the power of a single city extended beyond the Mediterranean zone to embrace temperate Europe, bringing a huge territory within a single administrative and financial system. But the empire was innately unstable. By AD 300 it had already begun to fragment and the infrastructure was showing signs of failure. Within a century it was all over and the old regional patchwork had re-established itself. What was left of the empire was now reduced to an enclave in the east Mediterranean with its capital at Constantinople.

The 'interlude of empire' can be divided into three distinct phases. In the first, *c.*140 BC–AD 100, Rome made the transition from republic to empire. As the debilitating civil wars of the late republic gave way to the relative stability of empire under its first emperor Augustus, the frontiers were pushed forwards to their natural geographical limits: the Atlantic to the west, the deserts to the south and east, and the forest zone to the north. The Rhine–Danube became the accepted frontier, weaving through the middle of the peninsula. The second period, AD 100–250, was a time of comparative peace and prosperity. Roads bound all parts of the disparate empire tightly together, a single monetary system was in use throughout and trading networks enabled commodities to flow on an unprecedented scale, spreading a material culture that differed little from one end of the empire to the other. The third period, AD 250–300, saw the monolithic system begin to break down. The province of Dacia was lost, Gaul and Britain broke away for a time, economic instability became chronic and tribes living to the north of the frontier began to break through, devastating towns to the south and causing panic. Towards the end of the century the situation was stabilized by the tough and far-sighted emperor Diocletian (284–305), but the end of the empire had already begun.

The Roman Empire embraced the temperate zone of Middle Europe. At the time of conquest these territories were home to tribes that had already developed a degree of social and economic sophistication. Large nucleated settlements – *oppida* – served as seats of local government and centres of production and exchange. Settled territories of this kind were comparatively easy to conquer. Where appropriate, the *oppida* could be taken over and developed as towns while the local elites could be won over to the Roman cause and could soon become good Romans. But beyond the temperate zone, in the North European Plain, in the north of Scotland and in Ireland, native social systems were less complex and settlements were far more dispersed. Such peoples were difficult to conquer. If beaten in battle, they could melt away into the forests suddenly to reappear in strength. In Germany the Romans quickly learned this truth and retreated behind the Rhine–Danube frontier. The general Julius Agricola may have cast a covetous eye on Ireland, saying that it could be conquered by a single legion, but his successors had the wisdom to leave it alone, finding the unruly inhabitants of Caledonia (Scotland) more than enough to contend with.

Much of Europe lay beyond the frontier, but well within reach of Roman consumer goods which were traded northwards in quantity, the more desirable items ending up in the hands of local elites. This broad barbarian region, stretching from the North Sea to the Black Sea, became increasingly turbulent as populations grew in size and tribes jostled for territory. The only way to relieve the pressure was migration and the only direction to move was southwards across the Roman frontier.

The Mediterranean Basin in Late Republican Times: 140–27 BC

By 140 BC Rome, after two centuries of near-continuous fighting, had conquered almost the whole of the Mediterranean Basin. Rome was a warrior state and the city became a theatre where elites competed for adulation and status, parading in state-sponsored triumphs and erecting monuments to their military prowess. To conquer was the imperative. As one general boasted, 'I do not negotiate for peace, except with people who have surrendered.'

Constant warfare set in train a dynamic system with its own trajectory, which totally changed the society and the economy of Rome. Endemic militarism, predicated on overseas wars of conquest, took large numbers of able-bodied young men from the land (about 130,000 at any one time), undermining the ability of many small peasant farms to maintain a livelihood. Those who returned from the army in a fit state to work often found their farms abandoned and may have felt little incentive to face the drudgery of labour on the land. The overall effect was a drift of the poor and landless into the towns and in particular to Rome, which grew dramatically, achieving a population of about one million by the end of the first century BC.

Foreign wars generated huge wealth which flowed into Rome in the form of booty. Much of it passed into the hands of the elite whose instinct, conditioned by custom, was to invest in land by buying up peasant farms or, when there was a dearth of land to buy, by taking over public land that had been acquired by the state, usually by requisition at the time of past wars. By these processes the spoils of war were transformed into huge estates – the *latifundi* – owned as investments by a comparatively small group of the elite. Wars of conquest also added overseas territories to the state's portfolio. These could be taxed, drawing into the centre a significant percentage of the annual productivity of the conquered province. Foreign taxes benefited all the citizens by enabling the state to keep its domestic taxes at a low or non-existent level, by funding new infrastructures of roads and water supplies and, in Rome, by providing an array of public amenities for entertainment and leisure purposes. Tax revenues could also be used to alleviate the plight of the urban poor. In 123 BC wheat was subsidized. After 58 BC it was provided free to citizens. Thus, the entire urban proletariat benefited from warfare: they also had ample opportunity to join the army and receive additional benefits. Finally, it was the revenue from war that funded new wars.

Rome was now inextricably caught up in the momentum of unlimited empire-building: this was to drive the state until the early second century AD when the emperor Hadrian decided to call a halt and begin to stabilize the frontiers.

Much of the new money flowing in was invested in the creation of huge estates, which in many areas began to replace the patchwork of small peasant holdings. These estates needed labour and that labour was provided by slaves – another of the byproducts of warfare. Slaves were preferred to free peasant labourers. They were an investment that, properly used and well maintained, could make the owner a profit through their labour. Columella, a writer on farming matters, noted that an arable farm of 200 *iugera* (*c*.50 ha/125 acres) could be fully cultivated by eight adult male slaves. A comparable area farmed by free colonists was said to be able to support twenty families. Clearly slaves offered considerable efficiency savings. Another treatise on farming advised that when there was hard or potentially dangerous work to be done it was sensible to hire in day labour because a good slave was too valuable to be put at risk of injury. Slaves also had another advantage in that they could breed and thus produce a fresh crop of manpower for their owners without significant additional expense.

There were, then, many reasons why the large landowners chose to run their estates as slave establishments. Another contributory factor must have been a decline in the availability of suitable free labour in the countryside as more and more people flocked into the cities. By the mid-first century BC there were more than a million slaves at work in Italy and the number was increasing. Such large numbers posed a threat and, indeed, there were slave rebellions in Sicily and Italy in 135, 104 and 73 BC. These were put down, usually with extreme brutality. After the crushing of the rebellion of 73 BC led by Spartacus, the road from Rome to Capua was lined with six thousand crucified slaves as a warning. The tension between master and slave was never very far below the surface.

Inequalities in landholding, which were to cause major social upsets in the last decades of the second century BC, began in the aftermath of the war with Hannibal. At this time, men who had provided massive loans to the state to fund the war demanded their money back. The state repaid them in kind with large tracts of land confiscated from those who had opposed the Roman cause. At the same time there was an attempt to resettle the rural poor from central Italy, moving them to more than twenty new colonies. About 100,000 men, women and children were involved. The new settlements were designed to alleviate poverty but the small size of many of the individual holdings simply exacerbated the problem. Further distress was caused by the migration of peasants from the countryside to Rome, leaving the Latin towns seriously depleted and unable to meet their obligations to provide troops. But worse still was the insidious grabbing of state land by the rich. Some of the land put up for auction by the state was bought up directly by the wealthy. The rest was made common land, which was in theory distributed to the poor on payment of a small rent, but more often than not was appropriated by the rich who offered higher rents. So it was that smallholdings disappeared while large estates were amassed in their place.

There had been several attempts to address the land problem through legislation in the earlier second century but they were ineffectual. Finally, in 133 BC, Tiberius Gracchus, a tribune of the people, decided to confront the issue head-on with a new programme of legislation. The ancient law limiting a person's holding of state land to 500 *iugera* (125 ha/310 acres) was reaffirmed and a new land commission was set up charged with surveying the state's holdings and redistributing the surplus fairly to the poor. A second law proposed that extensive revenues from Asia Minor should be distributed as subsidies to new farmers and the urban poor. The laws were deeply unpopular among the rich landowners and when Tiberius put himself up for re-election violence broke out, resulting in his assassination and the slaughter of four hundred of his followers. The land commission was, however, now operative and continued slowly to redistribute land, though its activities were severely restricted. Yet the same basic problems remained. A partial solution was to establish new

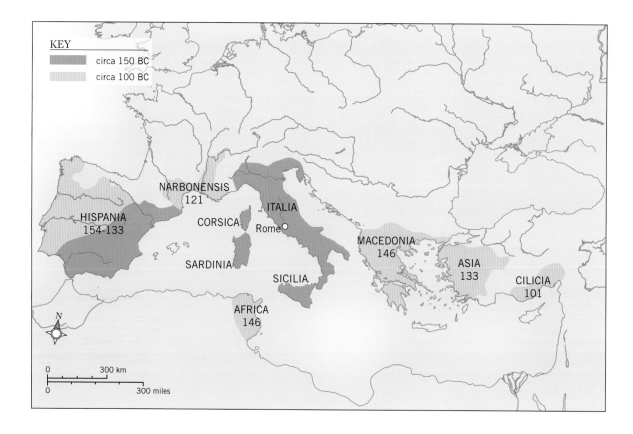

KEY

circa 150 BC

circa 100 BC

NARBONENSIS
121

HISPANIA
154-133

CORSICA

ITALIA

Rome

NARBONENSIS

SARDINIA

MACEDONIA
146

ASIA
133

CILICIA
101

SICILIA

AFRICA
146

N

0   300 km

0   300 miles

11.1 The expansion of the Roman Empire in the second century BC.

colonies in Italy, a cause championed by Gaius Gracchus (brother of Tiberius), who had become tribune of the people in 123 BC. He also strengthened the power of the land commission and passed a law preventing those who had been allocated land by the state from selling it on. The measures provoked violent opposition: Gaius was assassinated and the law formally abandoned. So great were the forces of conservatism that the social problems gripping Italy seemed insoluble.

In the next century, during a period of massive upheaval and civil war, a way out of the dilemma was found – state-organized mass migration out of Italy. It was, after all, at root a simple biological problem: if the population exceeded the holding capacity of the land (itself constrained by the expecta-tions of the resident elite), then strife would ensue until a sector of the population moved away to colonize a new ecological niche. This is precisely what happened. After a long period of civil war, about one-fifth of the Italian population was decanted to the provinces. It was a bold act of social engineer-ing, the more remarkable in that it was accomplished in a single generation between 45 and 8 BC. About a hundred overseas colonies were established, each with a core population of 2,000–3000 males. Apart from alleviating pressure on land at home, the creation of overseas colonies also provided a convenient method of dispersing the potentially dangerous mass of soldiers demobilized every year.

The century of political turmoil and military conflict that engulfed Italy and spread to its provinces in the period from 133 to 27 BC is usually explained in terms of the ambitions of the 'big men' who inspired the factions and led the armies – people like the Gracchi, Marius, Sulla, Pompey, Julius Caesar, Mark Antony and Augustus – but really they were only helpless human beings caught up on the deep swell of change set in motion by the rise of acquisitive elites vying for space in a peninsula too small to contain them. The inevitable result was territorial expansion and colonization. By the end of the first century BC the Roman Empire had grown to more than half the size of the present USA with a population of 50–60 million, accounting for about a fifth of the world's human population.

11.2 Julius Caesar, 100–44 BC, was responsible, among other things, for the conquest of Gaul. He was the first Roman commander to bridge the Rhine into Germany, and to lead an army across the English Channel into the south-east of Britain.

The German Threat

While the Roman state was undergoing its painful transformation from republic to empire, a new and terrifying threat appeared on the northern horizon. All Roman schoolchildren would have learnt of the Celtic raid on Rome in 390 BC – the image of the ferocious barbarians from the north was seared into the communal memory. Now rumours of a new threat from beyond the Alps reached Rome. Some time about 120 BC a highly mobile horde composed of warriors from two tribes, the Cimbri and the Teutones, began to move south from their homeland in Jutland and the adjacent North Sea coast. They forged southwards through Moravia to the Danube valley and then along the river, through the Carpathian Basin to the confluence of the Danube and Sava, forcing the local Celtic tribe, the Scordisci, to migrate into Macedonia. They then turned westwards along the Sava towards the Alps where, in 113 BC, they attacked the kingdom of Noricum, a valued trading

369

11.3 For about twenty years, from c.120 to 101 BC, migrating northern tribes, known to the classical writers as Cimbri and Teutones, wandered through Europe causing unrest particularly in Gaul. They posed a real threat to the Roman army but were eventually defeated in two battles in 102 and 101 BC by the Roman general Marius.

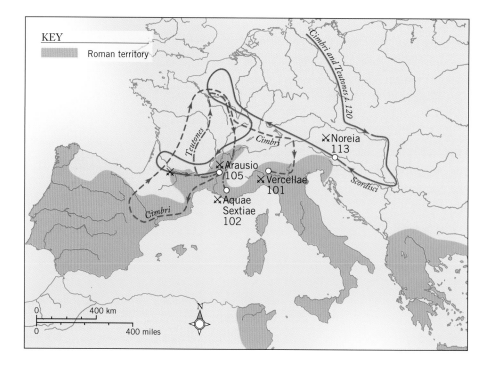

partner of Rome. A Roman army intervened but was decisively beaten. With the horde barely 100 km (60 miles) from the Po valley, a frisson of fear was felt in Rome. But instead of moving south to enjoy the rich pickings of the Roman world, the horde continued westwards, skirting the north side of the Alps, and for the next few years rampaged across Gaul, passing briefly through the Pyrenees into northern Iberia and back again into Gaul. On three separate occasions, in 109, 107 and 105 BC, Roman armies were sent to meet them in southern Gaul and on three occasions they were defeated. After the last defeat, at Arausio (Orange) in the Rhône valley, Rome was thrown into panic. Gaius Marius was immediately commissioned to overhaul the structure and organization of the army. This he did with ruthless energy, greatly improving its fighting efficiency. When the new army took to the field under his command, it defeated first the Teutones at Aquae Sextiae in Province in 102 BC and then the Cimbri at Vercellae in the Po valley in 101. The immediate terror had been contained but the threat from the ferocious Germanic barbarians from the north was now ever-present.

Our only sources for this remarkable episode are Roman historians. Their perceptions are necessarily partial and biased. They give the impression of a single confederacy of people from the Jutish peninsula moving together in a long march through western Europe until the two tribes split after the Battle of Arausio to go their separate ways. This is likely to be a gross over-simplification. In all probability we are dealing with a ragged and disorganized movement, with disparate groups joining in or breaking away at different points and time. The two armies faced by Marius in 102 and 101 BC are likely to have been composed of a very different ethnic mix from those that had started out twenty years before. Julius Caesar gives some hint of the disorder of their movements when he notes that the Aduatuci, a tribe located in Belgium between the Scheldt and Waal,

> were descendants of the Cimbri and Teutones, who, on their march to our province in Italy, had left on the west bank of the Rhine cattle and baggage they could not drive or carry with them, together with six thousand of their own people to guard it. After the destruction of the main body of the Cimbri and Teutones, these six thousand struggled for many years with neighbouring tribes [before eventually settling].
> (*BG* II, 29)

This kind of fragmentation is likely to have happened time and time again. A confident horde on the march would also have attracted many followers wanting to share in the adventure and the spoils. The Germanic threat probably originated in a migration of displaced people in search of territory. It was one of the many such movements in the later first millennium, spanning the period from the early Celtic migrations of the fifth century to the last pathetic attempt of the Helvetii whose search for a new home on the Atlantic coast of Gaul was cut short by Caesar's devastating intervention in 58 BC.

Temperate Europe: *c*.150 BC–AD 50

Around 100 BC Rome had reached a temporary lull in its forward rush for new territories. It was still essentially a Mediterranean state, though in its wars in Iberia it had been drawn westwards to the Atlantic coast. Its long European land frontier, running from Iberia to Asia Minor, more or less followed the boundary between the Mediterranean and temperate vegetational zones: it was a natural divide on which to pause. Soon after 60 BC a new forward drive was under way with the Roman armies thrusting northwards through Europe, conquering and annexing piecemeal until, by around AD 50, a new land frontier had been established along the line of the Rhine and Danube. To the west the Atlantic had been reached and Britain was in the process of being subdued, while in the east the southern part of the Black Sea and the adjacent lands were now largely under Roman control.

The absorption of much of temperate Europe into the Roman Empire was a logical consequence of the trajectory upon which Rome had embarked in the middle of the third century BC when war was declared against Carthage. To

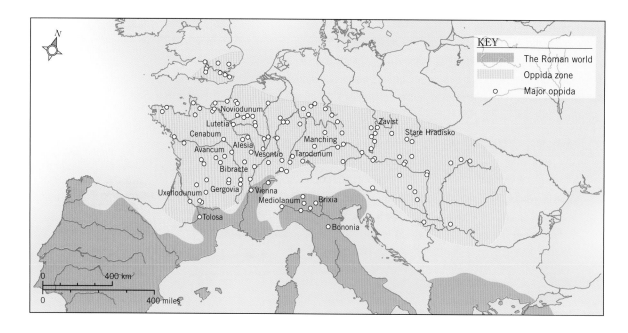

KEY

The Roman world

Oppida zone

○ Major oppida

Noviodunum
Lutetia
Cenabum
Avancum
Alesia
Vesontio
Bibracte
Uxellodunum
Gergovia
Tolosa

Manching
Tarodunum

Zavist
Stare Hradisko

Vienna
Mediolanum
Brixia
Bononia

0   400 km
0   400 miles

11.4 Beyond the Roman frontier, in a wide swathe of Europe stretching from the Atlantic to the Carpathians, large centres of population known as *oppida* developed in the latter part of the second century BC. Their appearance reflects a centralization of production and power among the tribes peripheral to the empire. The *oppida* display many of the attributes of towns.

maintain the fast-growing and largely non-productive core, new territories had to be drawn into the empire to provide an immediate injection of booty and manpower (slaves), followed by a constant drip-feed of taxes. Hovering around this essential economic imperative was the justification typical of imperialist aggressors – the need to maintain homeland security. The public could easily be persuaded that the terror threat posed by the Germans to the north justified pre-emptive military action.

By 100 BC much of barbarian temperate Europe from the Carpathian Basin to the Atlantic was experiencing a degree of social and economic security: the mobility of previous centuries had given way to a more stable pattern of tribes for the most part ruled by kings. Some of these polities were recognized as pre-eminent, serving as patrons for weaker groups prepared to acknowledge their subservience.

One of the dominant characteristics of the temperate European zone was the development of large settlement complexes to which the term *oppidum* is generally applied. The word, used specifically by Julius Caesar to describe the fortified native capitals he encountered in Gaul, is not particularly satisfactory because, even in Caesar's usage, it could embrace sites of widely differing character. But provided it is broadly defined to include the centralized foci of settled populations, and it is understood that in size and planning there may be variation, the term has a validity.

The *oppida*, which spread like a rash across temperate Europe from the late second century BC, were the locations within discrete socio-political terri-

tories where many centralizing functions were carried out. They are likely to have been the seats of authority from which the polity was governed. They were also places of production where raw materials were amassed and turned into consumer durables, and where interregional exchanges took place, and at many coins were minted. In other words, the *oppida* performed many, if not most, of the functions of towns.

The *oppidum* of Bibracte (Mont Beuvray) near Autun in eastern Gaul featured large in Caesar's account of his Gallic War. It was the capital of the Aedui and served as a seat of government from where two elected magistrates ordered the affairs of the tribe. Ambassadors from other tribes were called there to meetings and the settlement was sufficiently prestigious to be chosen by Caesar himself as a place to winter when he needed to remain in Gaul during the last stages of the conquest. Campaigns of excavation over the years have shown Bibracte to have been a massively defended hilltop location carefully laid out with areas reserved for elite residences, communal meeting

11.5 The *oppidum* of Bibracte (Mont Beuvray), now hidden by trees on the prominent hill (centre, left) was the capital of the Aedui in the middle of the first century BC. The Aedui were a pro-Roman tribe who gave support to Caesar during much of the Gallic Wars.

373

places, religious foci and artisan quarters. From the material record it was clearly a centre of manufacturing and a place where a wide range of goods, including wine and luxury goods from the Mediterranean world, were received and redistributed.

The *oppidum* of Manching in Bavaria occupied a rather different kind of location, sited in a river valley commanding a major route node. It was massive in extent, covering some 380 ha (950 acres) with an enclosing rampart 7 km (4 miles) in length. It lay in the territory of the Vindelici and was probably the tribal capital. Extensive excavations have shown an ordered layout of streets and buildings, and have produced huge quantities of finds demonstrating beyond doubt that Manching was a major centre of production, smelting and forging iron, casting bronze, minting coins, making pottery, working raw glass into beads and bracelets, and manufacturing textiles on a large scale. Among the materials imported to the site were large numbers of Roman wine amphorae and Campanian bronze vessels associated with wine-drinking, as well as exotic raw materials such as coloured glass, bronze, gold and silver.

How, then, to explain the *oppida*? They emerged during the second century BC and served as social and industrial centres. Most of them commanded significant route nodes and many were sited near to sources of raw materials. The implication is that the catalyst for their being was economic and that they developed in response to the need to regulate trade and intensify production.

There are two ways to view this phenomenon: either it was a response to the increasing Roman demand for raw materials and manpower, or it resulted from socio-economic changes generated within La Tène society. In reality both factors are likely to have played a part. In the 'classic' Celtic society of the fourth and third centuries, elite status was maintained through the mechanism of the raid which provided the successful leader with status and with enhanced resources to redistribute to his entourage. With increased social stability the opportunities for raiding were becoming limited. But as the Mediterranean market grew more demanding the La Tène elites would have found it possible to continue to acquire exotic products to redistribute to their followers by themselves controlling the flow of regional commodities. In other words, the increasing demands of the Mediterranean world provided the La Tène elites with the opportunity to transform their social system from one that had been essentially predatory to one now founded on production; the relationship that emerged between Mediterranean and temperate Europe in this brief period was, then, largely symbiotic.

The Greek historical geographer Strabo, writing of Europe at the end of the first century BC, provides detailed lists of the exports pouring into Rome from temperate Europe. These lists, compiled after the Roman conquest of the north was well advanced, probably give a fair reflection of what the north was producing throughout the earlier period of contact. As might be expected, slaves and raw materials predominate but it is interesting to see a few more specialist, manufactured products appearing such as the trained hunting dogs from Britain, salted sides of pork and woollen garments from Gaul, and cheeses from the eastern Alps: luxury goods now flowed in both directions.

Iberia

Rome had become involved in military action in Iberia in the late third century BC, at the time of the Second Punic War. It soon found itself bogged down in a long war of attrition against two powerful confederations, the Celtiberians and the Lusitanians. The Celtiberian Wars were brought to an end with the successful (for the Romans) siege of Numantia in 133 BC but Rome's civil wars spilt over into Iberia in 82–72 BC, when much of the west and north of the peninsula was still unsubdued. Various campaigns were fought against the recalcitrant Lusitanians and the tribes of the north-west in the period 61–29 BC, including Julius Caesar's first military command, but little was done to follow up the initial successes until Augustus decided to complete the conquest. Preparations began in 29 BC but it was ten years before the last outposts of resistance in the Cantabrian Mountains and Galicia were finally subdued. The conquest of Iberia had taken two hundred years but Rome was now in control of the rich metal resources of the peninsula – iron, copper, tin, silver and gold – as well as the phenomenally fertile valley of the Guadalquivir, which now supplied much of Rome's olive oil as well as grain. The three provinces into which Iberia was divided were among the most productive in the empire.

Gaul and Britain

Rome's involvement with Transalpine Gaul (that is, Gaul on the other side of the Alps as opposed to the Po valley – Cisalpine Gaul) dates back to the time of the Second Punic War, when troops and supplies used the coastal road through what are now Provence and Languedoc en route from Italy to the Spanish front. In this way the old Greek colonial cities and the local tribes grew used to the Romans and came to appreciate the benefits that friendship with the fast-growing power brought.

Gaul was of interest to Rome not just because of its strategic military importance but also because it was a populous region that offered a valuable marketplace for Roman goods, especially the wine that the large Italian estates were beginning to produce in inconvenient surplus. By 200 BC the Romans

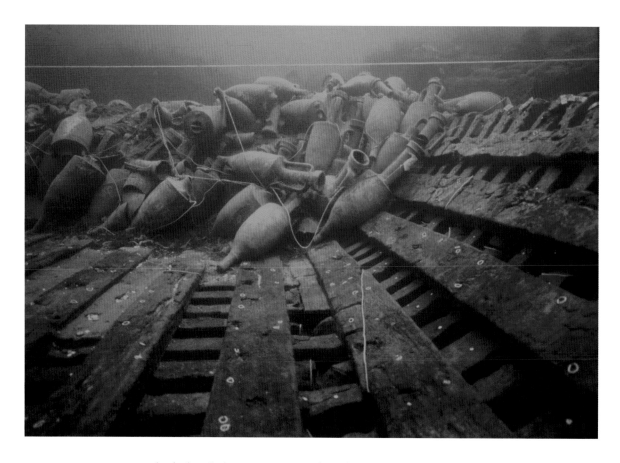

11.6 Many Roman shipwrecks are known off the south coast of France. This example, off Giens, was loaded with amphorae bringing wine from northern Italy in the first half of the first century BC. It was probably on its way to Massalia when it sank.

had already begun to trans-ship their wine to the southern Gaulish ports. At first quantities were small but during the course of the second century the volume increased dramatically: on settlement sites in the Vaunage (the region around Nîmes), Italian amphorae had completely replaced local Massiliot amphorae by about 100 BC.

Confirmatory evidence is provided by Roman shipwrecks found off the coast of southern France. One can see a dramatic increase in the number of wrecks after about 150 BC and the incidence remains high throughout the first century BC. If we make the not unreasonable assumption that the number of wrecks is directly proportional to the volume of trade, then the later second and first centuries must have been a time when maritime trade with Italy was at its peak. Most of the wrecks carried mixed cargoes but wine was dominant, usually occupying in excess of 75 per cent of the available cargo space. To give just one example: a mid-first-century BC wreck found at Madrague de Giens, off Hyères, carried about 400 tons of cargo which included 6,000–7000 wine amphorae. The volume of Italian wine imported into Gaul must have been enormous. One estimate suggests that something in the order of forty million amphorae may have been trans-shipped over the course of a century, representing an inflow of 100,000 hectolitres (two million gallons) of wine every year.

While wine was undoubtedly the main import, the wrecks give an idea of the other commodities sent as trade goods to Gaul. The wreck found off the island of Planier to the south-west of Massalia was carrying oil in amphorae made in Apulia in the region of Brindisi. En route the vessel had stopped, probably at Puteoli, to take on board a consignment of fine ceramic tableware and a range of dyestuffs before continuing on its journey northwards. From scraps of textual evidence it seems that the vessel was part of an enterprise managed by a consortium comprising a senator, C. Sempronius Rufus, a prominent citizen of Puteoli, C. Vestorius, who was involved in dye production, and a commoner, M. Tuccius Galeo, whose name was found stamped on the oil amphorae – he was presumably the supplier of the oil. The loss of the vessel off Planier could have spelt financial disaster for the entrepreneurs who had risked their capital in the venture.

As the wine trade with southern Gaul built up, so Roman involvement in the region increased. The coastal road around the Alpes Maritimes had always posed something of a problem because it was susceptible to raids from the inland hill tribes. During the course of the second century raiding increased to such an extent that eventually, in 125 BC, Rome was forced to send two legions under consular command to bring the situation under control. The operation focused first on the Saluvii who lived in the hills above Massalia and had become a very real threat to the colony, but the armies were soon drawn northwards along the Rhône valley to deal with two powerful Celtic tribes, the Allobroges and the Arverni. Some years later, during the period of the raids by Cimbri and Teutones, the Roman armies moved westwards along the Aude and through the Carcassonne Gap to take control of the old native capital of Tolosa (Toulouse), strategically sited on the Garonne. Thus, by 100 BC, Rome was not only fully in control of Transalpina, but now commanded two crucial routes, one linking the Mediterranean northwards to the heart of Europe, the other leading westwards to the Atlantic.

Much of the wine imported into southern Gaul was consumed in the region that had become the Roman province of Transalpina, but huge quantities also found their way into the barbarian territories beyond. Two major trans-shipment points have been identified: one on the outskirts of Tolosa, the other at Chalon-sur-Saône. At both, tens of thousands of amphorae had been dumped, suggesting that at these locations the wine was decanted into barrels or skins for easier onward shipment. Wine was also being carried in amphorae to *oppida* deep in the barbarian hinterland where some would have been consumed and the rest redistributed through the local networks. It is quite likely that Roman traders had established themselves in the major *oppida* in

11.7 The Provincia Romana occupied much of southern France. It was annexed by Rome in the period 123–58 BC, largely to protect the coastal road from Italy to Spain. Huge quantities of Italian wine were imported into the province for trans-shipment to the Gauls living beyond the frontier in exchange for slaves and other commodities.

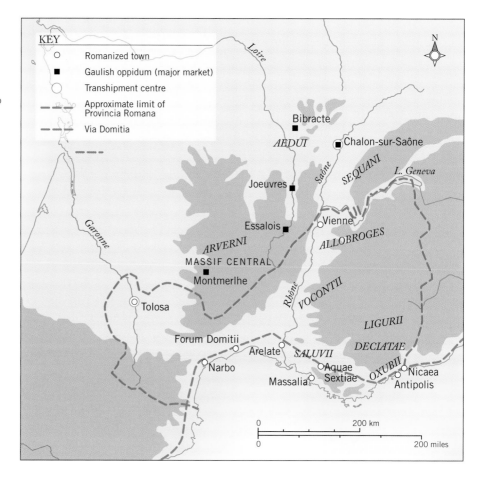

order to negotiate these exchanges. Some sense of the importance of the wine trade is given in an account of the Gauls by Diodorus Siculus:

> They are exceedingly fond of wine and sate themselves with the unmixed wine imported by merchants; their desire makes them drink it greedily and when they become drunk they fall into a stupor. . . . Therefore many Italian merchants, with their usual love of cash, look on the Gallic craving for wine as their treasure. They transport the wine by boat on the navigable rivers and by wagon through the plains and receive in return for it an incredibly high price, for one amphora of wine they get in return a slave – a servant in exchange for a drink. (*Histories* 5.26.3)

The dense distribution of Roman amphorae throughout Gaul gives ample support to Diodorus's claim that wine was popular among the Gauls. It was used lavishly in the feasts that played a crucial part in maintaining social cohesion. For this reason it was more highly valued among the Celts than among the Romans. In exchanging slaves for wine both societies were trading their surpluses to benefit themselves.

Many factors – the ragged and rather ill-defined frontier between Gallia Transalpina and Gallia Comata ('hairy Gaul'), the mercurial nature of tribal politics, the growing pressure of Germans from beyond the Rhine and the attractive productivity of the Gaulish countryside – made it inevitable that sooner or later the Romans would absorb Gaul into the empire. The moment came in 58 BC when the threatened migration of the Helvetii from their Swiss homeland to the Atlantic coast and the movement of a German army into north-eastern Gaul coincided with Julius Caesar's political and financial need for a spectacular military success. The eight-year Gallic War more than satisfied Caesar's ambition. At the end, the Roman frontier stood at the Rhine, Roman troops had marched, albeit briefly, into Germany and had crossed the Channel to campaign in Britain and, to use Caesar's own words, 'all Gaul was at peace'. The 'peace', or rather lack of organized resistance, was hardly surprising. The country was exhausted. Plutarch gives some figures – Caesar had taken by storm more than eight hundred towns and had subdued three hundred states, and of the three million Gauls who made up the total number of those engaged in the fight, he had killed one million and had captured a second million. These figures may well be an exaggeration, but the massacre of male youth over an eight-year period and the selling of hundreds of thousands of captives into slavery decimated a population that is unlikely to have numbered more than six or seven million in total at the outset. In the immediate aftermath, there were a few minor uprisings but for the most part Gaul was content to lick its wounds for a generation. The process of incorporating the devastated country into the empire, which had been begun by Augustus in 27 BC, was finally completed with the inauguration at Lugdunum (Lyon) of an altar to Rome and Augustus in 12 BC. The date chosen was Augustus's birthday, 1 August, which was also, coincidently, the Celtic feast of Lugnasad!

Julius Caesar's brief expeditions to Britain helped to demythologize the fog-bound islands, believed by some to be the home of creatures half-beast and half-human. Political links were established with the ruling households of the south-east and trade flourished. There matters rested until AD 43 when, on the pretext of supporting allies in trouble, the emperor Claudius set in train a full-scale invasion. Conquest was slow but by the end of the century most of the island, up to the Tyne–Solway line, had been brought under control and the territory beyond had been extensively explored. Britannia was now a Roman province.

Noricum and the Alps

Rome's advance into the Po valley culminated in the 180s BC with the foundation of colonies at Bologna, Modena and Aquileia (now Trieste). Thenceforth the southern flanks of the Alps marked the border of the Roman world, but it was in Rome's interest to establish friendly relationships with neighbouring tribes, if only to form a buffer against unexpected attack from the north. One of the most powerful polities was the kingdom of Noricum (roughly coincident with modern Austria), ruled from the mountain-top *oppidum* of Magdalensburg. Roman diplomacy opened the way and merchants poured in to develop the trading possibilities. Relations were amicable, apart from tensions caused by a brief gold rush, and by about 100 BC the Roman traders had set up a permanent colony on a terrace below the *oppidum*. These men were the representatives of the large business houses established in the port of Aquileia at the head of the Adriatic and a direct road was soon established to facilitate the movement of goods to and fro. The colony flourished and by about 30 BC stone buildings, constructed in the Roman manner and decorated with painted frescoes, had replaced the original timber structures. When in 17 BC the emperor Augustus began to turn his attention to the conquest of the Alps, Noricum was peacefully absorbed into the empire, its elites content to align themselves with Roman protection and prosperity.

Augustus's initial intention was to extend the Roman frontier to the Rhine and the Danube. Caesar had already reached the Rhine, so it remained for Augustus's generals to push forwards to the Danube. The Alpine region was subdued in 15 BC and in the next year the conquest of Dalmatia and Pannonia began. Only Thrace remained nominally free as a self-governing client kingdom but the arrangement eventually proved inconvenient and in AD 46 the Thracians were absorbed to become a province of the empire too.

The Rhine and Danube rivers made a convenient line to rest on while the state gathered strength but there is no suggestion that Augustus regarded it as the limit of his empire: his subsequent expedition into Germany showed as much. But the North European Plain was to prove too hard a territory to master and by the time of Augustus's death in AD 14 the two rivers had in reality become a permanent frontier.

By AD 50 the main thrust of the Roman advance was all but over. What had begun as a Mediterranean power now commanded much of the Atlantic and Black Sea regions. Only the Baltic lay beyond reach, blocked by the Germans.

Germany

Until the end of the second century BC nothing is heard of the Germans. There was a general realization that beyond the Celts more primitive peoples existed, and occasionally in the rather muddled cognitive geography of the time, the inhabitants of the north were referred to as Scythians, but it was the wanderings of the Cimbri and Teutones that really began to focus attention on the mysterious and dangerous north. It was Caesar who first confronted the issue in the field and it was he who offered the convenient generalization that Germans begin at the Rhine. The ethnic situation was, however, far more fluid, as a close reading of Caesar's text shows: there were Germans living to the south and Celts to the north of the river. But the creation of the Rhine as a frontier caused the situation to change by preventing the freedom of movement that had hitherto allowed the pressures of population growth in the north to dissipate. The establishment of the frontier, then, did two things: it made a reality of the Rhine as an ethnic divide and it created a dam that arrested the flow of migrants coming from the north, thus causing the population density to build up gradually.

11.8 The major German tribes beyond the Rhine–Danube frontier in the first century AD.

As already stated, the first serious attempt to describe the Germanic tribes was Julius Caesar's account, based partly on his own observations of the tribes he encountered on his two brief forays across the Rhine in 55 and 53 BC and partly on what he managed to glean from informers. By the time the historian Tacitus wrote his account nearly a century and a half later a great deal more was known, not least as a result of the generally unsuccessful military campaigns initiated by Augustus; information also came from Roman traders who were attempting to open up new markets in the barbarian north.

The Roman caricature of the Germans was that they were primitive, warlike and unstable. It was, in many ways, the typical stereotype of 'the barbarian' that the classical world felt comfortable with. Tacitus sums it up succinctly:

> The chiefs fight for victory, the followers for their chief. Many noble youths, if the land of their birth is stagnating in a long period of peace or inactivity, deliberately seek out other tribes which have some war on their hands. For the Germans have no taste for peace; renown is more easily won among perils and a large body of retainers cannot be kept together except by means of violence and warfare. (*Germania* 14)

The social system that Tacitus describes is one in which prowess is gained from military success. Care of the land is left to the old, the women and the weaklings, leaving the young men free to take to the field to raid and fight whenever the opportunity presents itself. Such a society was, by its very nature, mobile. Tribes migrated and resettled; some shrank into insignificance while others became the leaders of great confederacies. The tribal map sketched by Caesar in the mid-first century BC was very different from that reported by Tacitus at the end of the first century AD: the Germans were a people undergoing rapid social transformation.

In 12 BC Augustus launched a new forward policy with a military thrust into Germany. It seems that the initial intention was to advance to a new frontier along the Elbe–Vlatava–Danube line. Annual campaigns in 12–7 BC and AD 4–5 established a degree of control over free Germany up to the Elbe, but it was crucial to gain control of Bohemia which provided the vital link between the Elbe and the Danube. Bohemia was at this time occupied by the Marcomanni, who were ruled by a pro-Roman king, Maroboduus. Roman entrepreneurs were already well established here and were growing rich on the throughput of trade between northern Italy, the North European Plain and the Baltic zone. There was an unshakeable logic in the Augustan strategy – the Elbe–Danube made good military sense while Bohemia was a commercial gateway of huge potential.

However, the momentum of the advance stalled when, in AD 6, a serious

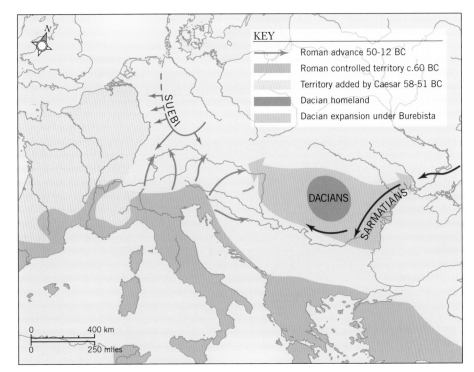

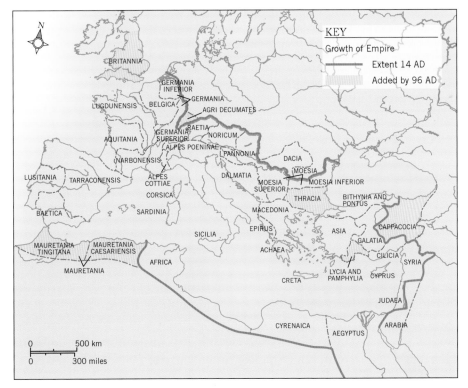

11.9 The upper map shows the dynamic situation in Europe in the middle of the first century BC immediately following Caesar's conquest of Gaul. The lower map shows the situation in the first century AD as the Roman Empire began to reach its most expansive form. Dacia and Arabia were still to be conquered.

rebellion broke out in Illyricum. With Rome distracted, the German war leader Arminius took the initiative and in AD 9 three Roman legions, commanded by Varrus, were lured deep into the Teutenburg Forest and annihilated. It was a shocking reversal and, although the military campaigns continued for a few more years, the realization finally dawned that the cost of holding Germany was too great. In AD 16, after twenty-eight years of campaigning across the North European Plain, the Roman army withdrew to the Rhine. From the security of the heavily defended frontier zone the traders could now get to work on developing the markets of Germany and beyond.

Dacians and Sarmatians

The swathe of land running eastwards from the Danube, where it flows in its long north–south course through modern Hungary to the river Don, includes a variety of landscapes – the gently rolling Great Hungarian Plain, Transylvania hedged in by the enclosing mountain ranges of the Carpathians and the Transylvanian Alps, and, beyond, the Dobroga and the Pontic steppe extending eastwards between the Black Sea and the forest zone to the north. This varied landscape was occupied by peoples of different ethnic origins. Successive nomadic tribes had moved westwards from the Pontic steppe into Transylvania and the Great Hungarian Plain while Celtic tribes from the west settled in Hungary and Transylvania, some of them crossing the Carpathians to reach the Pontic steppe. The movements created a cultural and ethnic variety that crystallized into a patchwork of different cultures. There were no new incursions from central Europe but pressures from the east continued to build in the Pontic steppe, forcing successive waves of Sarmatian peoples to seek new lands in the west. Classical writers distinguish two discrete groups, the Iazyges and the Roxolani.

The Iazyges originally lived north-west of the Sea of Azov, between the rivers Dnepr and Don, while the Roxolani occupied the adjacent region between the Don and Lower Volga. By the early second century BC both were coming under pressure from nomads to the east forcing the Iazyges westwards, first into the region of the Lower Dnestr and then down into the Danube delta area. From here the Iazyges raided Roman territory to the south of the river, unleashing, in 78–76 BC, a Roman military expedition against them. Any further expansion westwards was temporarily halted by the expanding power of the Dacians and by the formalization of the Roman frontier along the Danube, but they were eventually able to cross the Carpathians and around AD 20 began to establish themselves as a major force in the Great Hungarian Plain, confronting the Roman province of Pannonia on the other side of the Danube.

11.10 A Dacian silver cup of the first century BC from the Sîncrăieni treasure.

As the Iazyges moved west, so the Roxolani took over their abandoned territory. They eventually settled in the Walachian Plain flanking the Lower Danube south of the Transylvania Alps. It was from here, in AD 62–63, that the Roxolani and Dacians invaded the Roman province of Moesia south of the Danube and thereafter continued to be an irritation to the Romans.

The westerly movements of the Sarmatians in the first century BC and first century AD took place at the time when the Dacians, who occupied Transylvania and the surrounding mountains, were developing as a major regional power. In 60 BC, under the charismatic leadership of their king, Burebista, a huge army of 200,000 warriors marched westwards against the Celtic tribes who had settled in Hungary and Slovakia, totally devastating the region and causing some alarm in Rome. A decade later Burebista marched east to the river Bug and destroyed the old Greek city of Olbia, which though rebuilt never again attained its former status.

Burebista's decade of power almost exactly coincided with Caesar's Gallic War. Burebista understood what was going on in the Mediterranean and saw himself as a player on the world stage. Such was his ambition that he offered Caesar military support against his rival Pompey. Caesar refused but the incident was a reminder that the Dacians had now become a power to be reckoned with. Moreover, Dacia was rich and presented a respectable challenge to someone of Caesar's ambition. Once Gaul was secured, Caesar intended to conquer it, but in the event he became caught up in a civil war and

385

11.12 The Dacian fortress
of Blidaru dating to the first
century BC–first century AD.
It is one of a series of forts
which protects the
approaches to the Dacian
capital of Sarmizegethusa.

11.13 The sacred precinct
in the Dacian capital of
Sarmizegethusa. The large
circular monument is a
calendar. The flat circular
monument is a
representation of the sun.

died in Rome at the hands of conspirators in 44 BC. Burebista was assassinated at about the same time and the Dacian state he had created through forceful leadership fragmented. It took 120 years before a new war leader emerged to meld the Dacians once more into a force powerful enough to pose a serious threat to the empire.

In the intervening period Roman traders were not slow to develop the potential of the Dacian market. For the gold and slaves that Dacia produced in plenty the Roman merchants paid in cash. More than 25,000 Roman republican denarii, minted in the period 130–131 BC, have been found in Dacia. This surprisingly large sum, probably only a small fraction of the total coin used to buy Dacian commodities, gives some idea of the intensity of the exchanges now taking place across the Danube.

The European Frontier: Advances and Retreats, c.AD 50–250

The European frontier following the Rhine and the Danube served the Romans well for more than two hundred years. But still there remained a potential threat from tribes to the north. For the most part the 'enemy' was ill-organized and no match for the Romans, but the Dacian state was altogether different and when, in the early 80s AD, a new leader, Decebalus, emerged who was capable of uniting the kingdom's many factions, the frontier along the Lower Danube came under serious pressure. Raids into the Roman province of Moesia and counterattacks by the Romans brought an uneasy truce, with Decebalus receiving a handsome annual tribute from Rome as well as the assistance of Roman engineers.

Whether Decebalus posed a lasting threat to Rome is difficult to say but in AD 101 the recently appointed emperor, Trajan, moved his army into Dacia, attracted no doubt by the wealth of the kingdom. Decebalus sued for peace and agreed to accept Roman terms, including a garrison based not far from his well-defended hilltop capital of Sarmizegethusa high in the Orăştie Mountains. The treaty bought him time and by AD 105 Decebalus was strong enough to go on the offensive once more, attacking the province of Moesia. Trajan's immediate response was to contain the situation. The next year, AD 106, he invaded Dacia and rapidly conquered the whole country. The suicide of Decebalus and his nobles and the migration of a large part of the population eastwards left Rome in possession of the kingdom – its first and only Transdanubian province. The spoils of war, it was claimed, included 165,000 tonnes of gold and 300,000 tonnes of silver. Yet the new province, for all its mineral wealth, remained something of an anomalous excrescence. In the turmoil of the third century it became increasingly difficult to defend and was eventually abandoned in AD 270.

387

11.14 Trajan's Column, erected in Rome in the early second century AD, depicts scenes from Trajan's conquest of Dacia which was completed in AD 106. Here the Dacians can be seen attacking a Roman garrison. Dacia became a Roman province but lasted for only 170 years.

The German frontier remained comparatively quiet for a century and a half after the German campaigns of Augustus and Tiberius, a calm that may in no small part have been caused by the devastation and depopulation resulting from three decades of warfare. But in the peace that followed, the German population steadily grew, building up in number against the frontier line.

In AD 166, under intense pressure from tribes beyond, hordes of Marcomanni and Langobardi broke through the frontier into the province of Pannonia in search of land to settle. It was a foretaste of what was to dominate the frontier region for the next three centuries. The Roman response was simply to drive them back. Not long after, a much larger horde comprising Marcomanni, Quadi and Sarmatian Iazyges forced their way across the frontier, some groups penetrating as far as Aquileia (Trieste) at the head of the Adriatic. It was Rome's worst nightmare – the German threat from the north made real. The rapid response of the emperor Marcus Aurelius

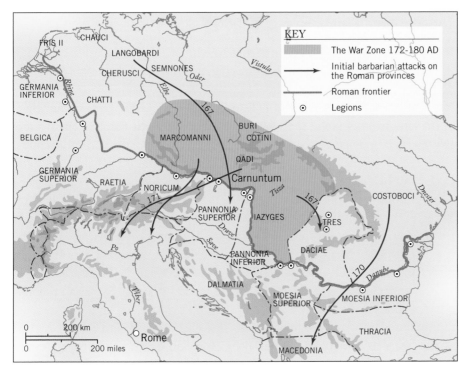

11.15 In the second half of the second century AD Germanic and Sarmatian tribes began to put pressure on the Roman northern frontier. The emperor, Marcus Aurelius, intended to create two new provinces, Marcomannia and Sarmatia, but events elsewhere in the empire distracted his efforts and the idea was abandoned.

contained the situation and drove the invaders back, but it was now clear that a more proactive course of action was needed.

To stabilize the situation and to prevent further outbreaks, a strategy was hatched to create two new provinces, Marcomannia in Bohemia and Sarmatia in the awkward re-entrant between the Danube, bounding Pannonia and the province of Dacia. To relieve the pressure from population growth, large numbers of Germans and Sarmatians were brought within the empire, some to be dispersed and settled on available land within the provinces, others to serve as auxiliaries in the army. One contingent of Sarmatian horseman, recruited at this time, ended up stationed at Ribchester in north-western Britain. Beyond the frontier large territories had been subdued and preparations to control them were well under way when a serious revolt in Syria deflected the military effort. By the time the emperor was able to return again to the problems of the northern frontier the impetus had been lost and the situation had seriously deteriorated. New efforts were made but two years later, in AD 180, Marcus Aurelius died at Vindobona. His successor, Commodus, had little stomach for northern campaigning and abandoned the scheme, leaving the problem unresolved. Eighty years later the frontier was to explode once more as population pressure from the north became uncontainable: this time it was the beginning of the end.

389

The Maritime Frontiers: AD 50–250

Rome showed a surprising indifference to its maritime boundaries created by the Black Sea and the Atlantic, an indifference for which it was to pay in the declining centuries of the empire.

The Black Sea was left in a politically uncertain state. The establishment of the land frontier along the Danube in theory brought much of the western Pontic coast under Roman control, though Thrace remained an independent client kingdom until AD 46. It was, however, something of a 'wild west', with Iazyges and Dacians mounting periodic raids from the north.

The southern Pontic coast – that is, the north coast of Asia Minor (now Turkey) – was eventually taken under Roman control when the province of Bithynia and Pontus was set up in 64 BC and Cappadocia added in AD 18. But it was a long, unfriendly coastline, isolated by the mountain ranges of the hinterland and largely undeveloped except for the original Greek colonies.

The northern part of the Black Sea remained a largely barbarian preserve but embedded within it lay the old Bosporan kingdom, which had grown out of the confederacy of a group of Greek cities clustering around the eastern side of the Sea of Azov. It was annexed by Rome in 65 BC and throughout the Roman period managed to maintain its identity, serving as one of the remotest outposts of Mediterranean civilization though it continued to be ruled by a local dynasty of mixed Sarmato-Thracian origin. Rome regarded the kingdom as a useful bulwark against the steppe nomads and was prepared to station a garrison there, but took little direct interest in its political affairs.

Under Roman protection the first two centuries AD were a time of prosperity for the Bosporan kingdom. Old craft skills were revived and the work of the Panticapaeum goldsmiths once more became famous. Efforts were made to retain the Greek cultural heritage, with Greek remaining the spoken language, but by the first century AD, owing to generations of intermarriage, the kingdom had become essentially a Sarmatian state. Economic decline in the third century, as trade wasted away, so weakened the enclave that when the Goths advanced on it in the fourth century they met no resistance and the kingdom disappeared from the map.

Viewed from a Roman perspective, the Bosporan kingdom was a useful outpost to have in one of the remotest border regions of the empire. It provided traders with access to the north Pontus, but it was never regarded as a strategic zone either militarily or economically. So long as the sea lanes were kept open Rome was content to leave this end of the world to look after itself.

The Atlantic offered different challenges: it was the end of the world in a different sense. Julius Caesar realized the importance of the Atlantic interface from the moment he first encountered it in Iberia in 61 BC. During this campaign he developed a two-pronged strategy, moving up the coast by land and by sea as successive tribes were brought under control. A few years later, during the early stages of his Gallic campaigns in 57 and 56 BC, he paid particular attention to securing the maritime regions as a preliminary to conquest and fought a major naval battle with the Venetii of Armorica (Brittany) to gain supremacy of the seas. In 55 and 54 BC he again took to the ocean to explore the potential of Britain. Some time later, in 12 BC and AD 5, during the long-drawn-out campaigns against Germany, naval expeditions were mounted along the North Sea coast to explore the estuaries of the Ems and Elbe. The subsequent conquest of Britain also involved considerable maritime activity and to complete the first stage of the conquest the governor Julius Agricola sent a fleet round the northern extremity of the island; during the course of this journey the Orkney Islands were visited.

By the time the frontiers were finally established in the early second century AD the Irish Sea and North Sea had become the limits of the empire, leaving the whole of Ireland, much of Scotland and all the north European coastline north of the Rhine estuary as unconquered barbaria. It was from these three regions that, in the late third and fourth centuries, the barbarians were to take to their ships to close in on the collapsing empire.

The Empire Within: AD 50–284

The reign of the emperor Hadrian (AD 117–38) marks an end and a beginning. It was the end of Rome as an imperial aggressor intent on forcing the frontiers of its Empire ever forward and the beginning of a period of relative stability that lasted for about a century during which the provinces flourished. Yet even during this interlude of prosperity the incursions of the Marcomanni, Quadi and Sarmatians provided a forewarning of what was to come. In his twenty-one-year reign Hadrian spent more than thirteen years touring the provinces, concerning himself largely with military dispositions and with frontier security. Unlike his predecessors, Hadrian accepted that the empire had reached the limits of its extended ecological niche and the main issue for him was how best to make it sustainable. Frontiers had to be secured, urban life encouraged and the empire-wide road system brought to a peak of efficiency to facilitate the rapid circulation of administrators, traders and armies.

The more perceptive contempories realized the delicate balance on which the new stability rested: the Germanic incursions of AD 166 had been enough to shake some people from their complacency. Marcus Aurelius, who had to face the onslaught head-on, well understood the deep rhythms underlying

11.16 Hadrian's Wall in northern Britain was begun in AD 122, the year in which the emperor visited the province. It was intended to be the northern frontier against the tribes of the north. Where possible (as in the photograph) the wall made good use of local topography.

such events when he wrote: 'Time is like a river made up of events, and the current is strong; no sooner does anything appear than it is swept away, and another comes in its place, and will be swept away too.' Some semblance of the old order was maintained until the accession of the emperor Severus Alexander in AD 235. Then followed fifty years of near-anarchy as emperors came and went with some rapidity, barbarians broke through the frontier, the province of Dacia was abandoned and the infrastructure of the empire began to come apart.

The decline of the Roman Empire has long been a subject of fascination for historians. Like all major events in history, its causes were complex and interwoven, one feeding upon another and creating a system in escalation. But for all the complexity, the underlying causes can be traced back to productivity and demography.

The empire divided into three concentric rings. In the centre lay Italy and the city of Rome where the court and government were situated. This was a highly non-productive zone that sucked in and consumed the productivity of the provinces, largely in the form of taxes. The outermost ring comprised the frontier provinces where the armies were stationed: this too was a consuming zone. Between the inner and outer rings lay a middle zone comprising the productive provinces of Spain, Gaul, Africa, Asia Minor, Syria and Egypt which generated the surpluses and the revenue required to maintain the other two. Such a system was predicated on a constant flow of tax revenues sufficient to sustain the huge body of non-producers concentrated in the consuming regions. In the productive provinces each group of producers was forced by the tax regime to maximize output, with the result that the volume of interregional trade increased at an almost exponential rate. To facilitate the now-complex networks of exchange, the money supply also increased. Reliable statistics for the period 157–50 BC suggest that the quantity of silver denarii in circulation rose tenfold during this time. Comparative figures for money supply in the different provinces show that in the first two centuries AD the monetary economy of the empire became integrated into a single system.

So long as the Empire was in an expanding or a stable state the system could be maintained in equilibrium, but with the onset of barbarian raids in the late second century AD and the increasing demands of the imperial court, the system came under considerable stress. In response the silver coinage was increasingly debased. In AD 50 silver content was at 97 per cent, by AD 250 it had fallen to 40 per cent and by AD 270 to only 4 per cent. The result was that the traditional fiscal system broke down, leading to regional fragmentation. This in turn encouraged aspiring leaders to set up breakaway states in the productive provinces.

The situation was temporarily restored by the strong centralized government imposed by Diocletian and maintained by Constantine. This now replaced taxes in cash with taxes in kind. Since, however, there was no longer any pressure to transform local food supplies into goods of higher value and lower bulk, production and trade both began to decline rapidly, and in the fourth century cities started to lose their significance as market centres.

Against this dramatic series of economic changes we have to consider the demographic dynamic. The most far-reaching change was triggered by the devastating disease that was brought to Europe by troops returning from Mesopotamia in AD 166. It swept through the continent in successive waves until about 180. The precise nature of the infection is uncertain, though in all probability it was a form of smallpox against which the European population had no immunity. The mortality rate was heavy and may well have accounted for between a quarter and a third of the population. This exacerbated a downward population spiral already under way as a result of a low birth rate. The upshot was a serious shortage of manpower. It was in the face of this problem that Marcus Aurelius brought large numbers of Germans and Sarmatians into the empire to settle abandoned land and to serve in the army. Successive emperors were to follow similar policies until not only had the army become thoroughly Germanized but large tracts of the northern provinces had been settled by communities whose fathers and grandfathers had been immigrants from distant barbaria. The policy had the advantage of relieving some of the external pressures on the frontiers while at the same time ensuring that the land within was owned and farmed by those with a vested interest in defending it from uncontrolled incursions.

Once the downturn in population had begun, the birth rate continued to decline and no counter trend can be identified until around AD 900. The decline was exacerbated by fresh epidemics. A devastating new outbreak hit Europe in AD 251 and recurred for about fifteen years. Some circumstantial evidence suggests that it may have been measles entering the continent for the first time alongside a recurrence of smallpox. So virulent was it that in Rome at the height of the outbreak five thousand people died a day.

Disease was clearly a significant factor in population decline. The volume of commercial traffic along the roads and rivers threading through the continent and the movement of troops, combined with the high densities of urban population, provided optimum conditions for disease to spread rapidly and to incubate. There may have been other contributory factors enhancing population decline too. For instance, one suggestion is that the fertility rate had been lowered by the high doses of lead ingested in normal life, by drinking water that had run through lead pipes, by cooking in metal containers with a high lead content and by drinking wine to which lead acetate had been added as a sweetener. Finally, one should not overlook the debilitating effects of living in a time of crisis. After AD 235 barbarian raids and civil disorder were an ever-present reality. The stresses brought on by such conditions cannot have failed to have an effect on the overall numbers of live births. Thus it was that from the middle of the second century the overall population of the empire began to plummet.

Declining birth rate, fragmentation of the fiscal system and a decrease in productivity and trade, together with the increasing intensity of raiding from beyond the frontiers, combined to provide a fatal mix. The fragile edifice of the empire began to fall apart.

Europe beyond the Frontiers: AD 50–250

Julius Caesar's description of the German tribes in the middle of the first century BC gives a glimpse of the barbarian north at the moment when contact was first made with the Roman world. Tacitus, in his *Germania* and *Annals*, provides a far more detailed picture after more than a century of contact between the two peoples. The social system that Caesar describes, based on the clan and the kinship group, is structured so that wealth could not easily accumulate in the hands of the few. By the first century AD things had begun to change: a new nobility was emerging that was capable of commanding large retinues and accumulating prestigious personal wealth. It could be argued that these changes were, at least in part, the result of the close proximity of the Roman market which now offered easy access to a very wide range of luxury products.

Once the turmoil of the conquest period was over, a regular system of trade developed between the barbarian north and the Roman provinces. As early as Caesar's time the Suebi, who were considered to be the largest and most warlike of the German tribes, allowed Roman traders into their country so that they would have 'purchasers for their booty rather than because they want to import anything'. There was, however, an embargo on wine which the Suebi thought would have a debilitating effect on their menfolk. The archaeological evidence suggests that it was gold and silver coinage and bronze tableware that they exchanged for their accumulated booty, which most likely comprised largely cattle and slaves. Tacitus, writing at the end of the first century AD, provides an interesting insight into the exchange process, noting:

> [T]he Germans nearest us value gold and silver for their use in trade and recognize and prefer certain types of Roman coins . . . . They like coins that are old and familiar, *denarii* with the notched edge and the type of two horsed chariot . . . they try to get silver in preference to gold . . . they find plenty of silver change more serviceable in buying cheap and common goods.

The archaeological evidence neatly supports this, showing that the astute Germans did indeed have a preference for the old coinage with a high silver content that was minted before Nero's coinage reforms of AD 64 introduced a level of debasement.

Roman coins and other low-value Roman goods are found in a broad zone extending some 200 km (125 miles) or so into the interior from the frontier – a distribution that reflects a region within easy reach of the frontier markets where commodities could be bought and sold and local German producers could dispose of their surpluses. Tacitus gives a specific example of this when he refers to the Hermunduri who had long been allies of Rome. They were 'the only Germans who trade with us not merely on the river bank but far within our borders, and indeed in the splendid colony that is the capital of Raetia. They come over when they will, and without a guard set over them.' Beyond the market zone a more restricted range of Roman goods, including bronze tableware and other luxury items, is found extending deep into barbarian

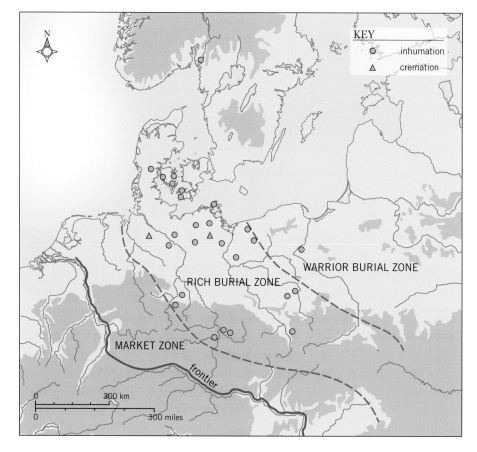

11.17 The Germanic tribes living close to the Roman frontier engaged in trade with the Roman world. Beyond the immediate market zone was a zone of rich burials where elite status was displayed by burying the dead with Roman luxury goods. Beyond that, a warrior society prevailed.

territory as far north as southern Sweden and Norway by the end of the first century AD. This represents the workings of a rather different trading system which may have begun with pioneer entrepreneurs journeying into the barbarian north to set up trading agreements with local elites, opening the way with gifts. Other groups of entrepreneurs chose to settle in German territories. We learn of one group who had attached themselves to the court of Maroboduus, king of the Marcomanni who occupied Bohemia. When the king fled in AD 18 he left behind a colony of 'businessmen and camp followers from the Roman province. They had been induced first by a trade agreement, and then by hopes of making more money, to migrate from their various homes to enemy territory. Finally they had forgotten their own country.' Not surprisingly, a large concentration of Roman luxury goods has been discovered in Bohemia. Another concentration of goods on the Danish islands, notably on Lolland, hints that there may have been other enclaves of traders serving more distant markets.

In return for the northward flow of consumer durables the Roman merchants would have acquired the usual mix of manpower and raw materials. Slaves remained a highly desirable product. Of the other commodities the north could offer, wild animals for the arena, hides for making tents and other military equipment, cattle to supply food for the army, and luxuries for the home market like furs, amber and walrus ivory would all have been eagerly sought after.

Beyond the market zone Roman luxury goods passed into the hands of local elites and the manipulation of those products helped the elites to maintain their authority. Thus, a negotiated agreement with Rome assuring a constant supply of luxury commodities would have been seen by both parties as a way of maintaining stability. In the first and probably also the second century Rome propped up many German leaders. The point is explicitly made by Tacitus when he says of the Marcomanni and Quadi: 'The power of kings depends entirely on the authority of Rome. They occasionally receive armed assistance from us, more often financial aid, which proves equally effective.'

The extent of the elite societies benefiting from Roman imports is shown by the distribution of rich burials of a specific kind named after the Pomeranian cemetery of Lübsow. The burials are mostly inhumations, with bodies placed in coffins or carefully built chambers buried beneath cairns or barrows. In each case the deceased was provided with sets of imported Roman wine-drinking or banqueting equipment including vessels of silver, glass and bronze. One of the more elaborate examples, found at Hoby on the Danish island of Lolland, is the inhumation of a male, buried in a coffin, dating to the early first century AD. His grave goods included two elaborately decorated silver cups and a silver ladle, a bronze tray, a bronze situla, patera and jug, and two bronze-mounted drinking horns. His personal equipment comprised bracelets of gold, silver and bronze, gold rings, bronze belt fittings and a knife. There were also three pots and joints of pork. The Lübsow-style burials lay in a broad zone between the Elbe and the Vistula extending from Bohemia to the Danish islands with a single northern outlier near Oslo.

The Vistula marks the eastern limit of the penetration of Roman goods in the first and second centuries AD but some items reached southern Norway and Sweden, arriving at their final destination by sea from the Danish islands of Fyn and Zealand. Finds of Roman bronze vessels on Gotland reflect the use of the sea route north to the Mälaren region of southern Sweden, while finds extending up the Norwegian coast to just south of Bergen show that the Atlantic routes remained active at this time.

We have argued (see pp. 388–9) that the explosion of the Marcomanni, Quadi and Iazyges through the Roman frontier was caused, or at least

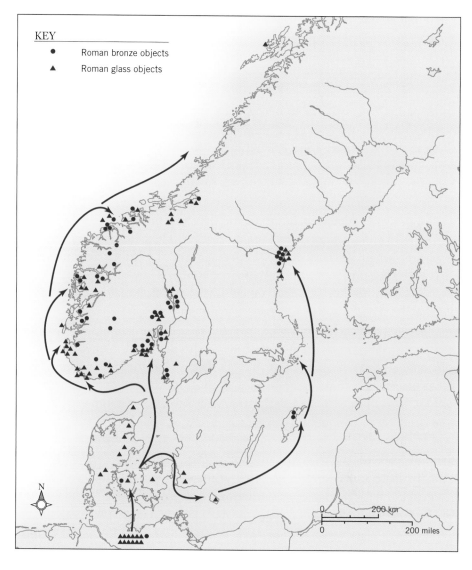

11.18 The distribution of Roman luxury goods in Scandinavia indicates the vitality of the local maritime networks then in operation.

triggered, by the build-up of tribal populations to the north-east and the pressure that they exerted on their southern neighbours. Archaeology throws some light on the situation. In the homeland zone from which the pressure came – the area to the east of the Oder – two distinct archaeological cultures can be recognized: the Oksywie, which spread throughout Pomerania and the Lower Vistula region; and the Przeworsk, which extended across a broad tract of the North European Plain from the Upper Oder valley to the Upper Vistula. The Przeworsk culture is known almost entirely from cemetery evidence. Cremation predominated and male interments were usually accompanied by their swords and shields and in some cases by spurs. The Oksywie culture presents a broadly similar array of evidence, though with typological differences in the material culture. Overall there was little social distinction between the warrior burials but occasionally elite warriors were distinguished by richer graves.

Towards the middle of the second century AD changes can be discerned in burial patterns, suggesting social change. Cremation is replaced by inhumation and weapons cease to be buried with the dead. In archaeological terminology this marks the transition from the Oksywie to the Wielbark culture. There are also signs of folk movement. The Wielbark culture begins to extend towards the south-east, impinging on territory of the Przeworsk. In the old Przeworsk zone the intensity of cemeteries thins out as people move away towards the south-west. It was this turbulence among the east German tribes in the late second and early third centuries that began to exert pressure upon their neighbours in the elite burial zone – the Marcomanni and the Quadi – forcing them up against the Roman frontier.

The Wielbark culture, as we will see later (pp. 402–3), was the archaeological manifestation of the early Goths, while the Przeworsk culture seems to have represented the Burgundiones and the Vandali. All three tribes continued their migratory movements throughout the third century AD to become significant players in the final confrontation with the Roman Empire.

In the aftermath of the Marcomannic Wars networks of exchange were re-established and in some cases saw a significant intensification. Links with Italy diminished and much of the high-volume trade seems now to have come through Gaul. The network linking to the Danish islands and the Baltic continued and intensified but now, in the third century, Zealand took over from Lolland as the main centre of redistribution. The volume and range of imports, and the fact that they were now being more widely distributed to lower social echelons, show that the basis of trade was changing. No longer was it elite exchange but rather a form of administered trade with a set of agreed values and recognized exchange rates. The sea continued to be the principal route of distribution with the Baltic islands of Öland and Gotland featuring large. Roman bronzeware is now found along the Swedish coast as far as the Gulf of Bothnia. Another major point of entry was Oslo Fjord while along the Atlantic coast of Norway Roman goods were reaching as far north as Trondheim Fjord.

The North Sea routes running northwards from the Rhine mouth also developed in the third century, enabling large quantities of low- to medium-value Roman goods to be introduced into the coastal regions of Holland, northern Germany and Jutland. Here again we seem to be observing administered trade maintained over a long period of time. Alongside these changes

399

there is evidence of enhanced production – metalworking, weaving, tanning and flax-retting – but all at a village level. This intensification of production seems to have been closely related to the increase of administered trade from the Roman world. The breakdown of the Roman economic network in the later fourth century may have been one of the destabilizing factors that forced the North Sea communities to join in with the mass migrations of the period.

Across the North Sea the province of Britannia followed the fortunes of the empire. The Scottish frontier, fluctuating between Hadrian's Wall and the Antonine Wall, provided an interface with the unconquered tribes of the north and trade in low-value goods continued, upset only by barbarian raids and follow-up campaigns. The contact seems to have had little effect on the economy or the social development of the native tribes.

Ireland remained unconquered but commercial relationships soon developed: Tacitus mentions that even as early as the end of the first century the merchants had a detailed knowledge of the harbours of Ireland and their approaches. A limited range of low-value Roman goods were trans-shipped to ports in the vicinity of Dublin and Cork and distributed to the native communities in the hinterland. In return the traders acquired slaves, hides and hunting dogs. The scant archaeological evidence suggests that trade was never at a particularly intense level and contact with the Roman world appears to have had little effect on Irish society.

Finally, to the Black Sea. The old ports along the north shore – particularly those of the kingdom of Bosporus – continued to provide an interface between the Roman world and the hinterland extending from the steppe northwards into the forest zone of the Ukraine, Belorussia and southern Russia. Quantities of Roman imports were carried along the Don to find their way into native burials while the Dnepr provided a route by which Roman goods were traded deep into the forest zone to the east of the river Vistula. It was by contact along this route that the tribes of north-eastern Europe, among them the Goths, learned of the wealth to be had on the Black Sea. The gradual movement of Goths into the richer lands of the Ukraine was already under way in the late second century AD; by the mid-third century they had become a major force in the north Pontic region.

The Failing Frontiers: AD 250–84

Population increase among the tribes to the east of the Oder was, as we have seen, the likely cause of the break-out of the Marcomanni, Quadi and Iazyges that initiated the Marcomannic Wars. By allowing large numbers of the displaced peoples to settle within the provinces and to serve as auxiliaries in the Roman army, Marcus Aurelius was relieving the immediate problem but not

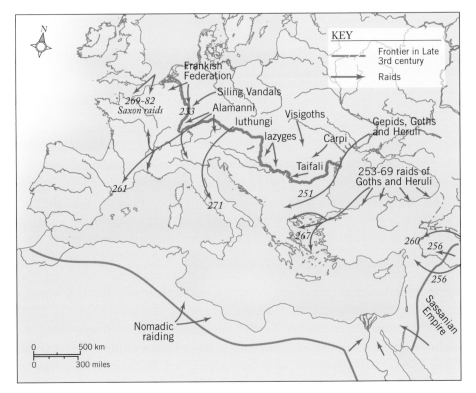

11.19 The second half of the third century AD was a time when pressures built around all the Roman frontiers. The pressures reached such a pitch that, on a number of occasions, the frontier collapsed and northern barbarians poured south into the Roman provinces.

addressing the prime cause. Population pressures among the east Germans increased, causing turbulence and instability. Old tribes disappeared from the map and new tribes – confederacies built up from existing groups – make their appearance. The Alamanni, first recorded in AD 213, were created in south-western Germany out of a confederacy of the Suebi, the Hermunduri and smaller tribes west of the Upper Elbe. Significantly their name simply means 'all people'. The Franks, who are first heard of around AD 250, emerged from a coalescence of tribes living between the Rhine and the Weser, while to the west the peoples living along the North Sea coast became known as Saxons. In the east the Goths, who were to become the dominant barbarian force, were a confederacy of many different tribes moulded into a 'people' during their migration southwards to the coast of the Black Sea. These multitribal confederacies forged what identity they had from their common purpose and unity of action.

The pressure on the European frontier built up gradually during the early third century, at first focusing on the short land frontier between the upper reaches of the Danube and the Rhine. In AD 213 Caracalla repelled a force of Alamanni and Chatti, but by 233 the Alamanni were back. This time they smashed through the frontier and rampaged across the provinces of Raetia and Noricum. The frontier was operative again two years later but the raids

401

resumed in 254 and reached a crescendo in 259–60, when the land frontier collapsed, never to be restored. Thereafter the rivers alone formed the boundaries with barbaria. The raid of 259–60 caused widespread devastation and panic. The Alamanni occupied parts of the province of Germania Superior and some raiding bands moved southwards into Gaul, to Arles and into the Auvergne, and one group reached Tarragona in north-eastern Iberia. About the same time the Franks were raiding freely into northern Gaul, breaking through the Lower Rhine frontier and attacking the coastal regions from the sea. For the inhabitants of Rome it was a reminder of the fearsome days of the Cimbri and Teutones.

In 275 even worse was to come. Alamanni, Franks, Vandals and Burgundians poured across the Rhine, sacking Trier and many other towns in northern Gaul. One contemporary source claimed that sixty Gallic towns were damaged and in need of restoration. If true, it would mean that about half the urban infrastructure of Gaul had in some way been affected. Although the emperor Probus dealt effectively with the crisis, morale within the western empire had been severely undermined.

In the southern part of the North Sea and the English Channel Frankish raiders were joined by Saxons from around the estuaries of the Weser and the Elbe. The pirates preyed not only on shipping but also raided the coasts of Gaul and Britain. So serious was the threat that late in 285 a Menapian soldier, Carausius, was appointed to rid the 'seas of Belgica and Armorica' of pirates. The appointment was not a success. Carausius was accused of being in league with the pirates and was condemned to death but escaped by seizing Britain and claiming imperial power there. The breakaway province was eventually returned to the empire in 296 after an invasion force had defeated and killed Carausius's successor, Allectus.

In the east of Europe large-scale folk movements were completely changing the geopolitics of the region. To Roman writers the peoples on the move were simply Goths but the name probably belies the complexity of the situation. Tacitus, writing at the end of the first century AD, had located the Gotones on the southern shore of the Baltic in the region of the Lower Vistula. They can be recognized archaeologically (as the Wielbark culture) and their movement can then be traced south-eastwards, using the valleys of the Dnestr and Bug, to the Black Sea coast. There they merged with the various local tribes to become the fearsome confederacy that Roman writers referred to under the ethnonym of Goths.

Once established on the Black Sea, these Goths and their Germanic allies came into direct contact with the Roman world, mounting a number of raids in the middle years of the third century, culminating in a concerted attack on Bithynia and Propontis (north-western Asia Minor) in 257. Another decade was to pass before the next onslaught got under way in 268. This time a huge fleet of some two thousand ships was employed to transport the army of Goths and Heruli. After an unsuccessful attack on Byzantium the armada forced its way through the Dardanelles and into the Aegean and there split into three flotillas. One landed near Thessalonica and attacked the Balkans, a second rampaged through Attica seizing Athens, Sparta, Corinth, Argos and Olympia, while the third group raided the coasts of Asia Minor and the islands of Rhodes and Cyprus. This devastating break-out was quickly contained: the Balkan group was defeated by the emperor Gallienus in 268; the raiders in the Aegean were driven back to the Black Sea in 269; while the Gothic army in Attica, which had moved into the mountains of Epirus, was decisively defeated by the emperor Claudius in 270.

The effectiveness of the containment was impressive but the break-out had come as a profound shock for Rome. Thereafter the policy was to block the Bosphorus to contain the Gothic threat within the Black Sea. In 270 there were further land attacks across the Danube but the next year a Roman counterattack, led by the emperor Aurelian, defeated a large Gothic force. In the aftermath the Roman province of Dacia was abandoned and large groups of people from the north-western Pontic region, among them the Bastarnae and Carpi, were brought into the Balkans and settled there. Further folk movements north of the frontier forced the loosely knit Goths to separate into two groups, the western and eastern Goths – Visigoths and Ostrogoths. Both were to become significant players on the European scene in the centuries to come.

Diocletian and Recovery: AD 284–305

The barbarian inroads of the third century, the failure of the monetary system, the disastrous decline in population, and the fragmentation of government as rival factions fought for power, brought the empire to a state of near-collapse. Yet there remained the energy and the will to reform and to rebuild, and in a practical, level-headed soldier, Diocletian, Rome found a man capable of driving the reconstruction. Diocletian was an Illyrian who had, by sheer ability, risen steadily through the ranks from humble origins. In 284 the Praetorian Guard appointed him emperor and during the twenty years of his reign he set about tackling the ills that beset the empire.

The empire was too large for one man to govern and disputed successions inevitably caused massive upheavals. To counter this Diocletian created the Tetrarchy – the rule of four. He split the empire into two, the East with a capital soon to be established at Byzantium (Constantinople) and the West with Rome as its capital. The two parts were ruled by 'Augusti' of equal rank. Diocletian took the East and appointed a fellow soldier, Maximian, to the West.

11.20 To help the unwieldy empire regain some stability the emperor Diocletian introduced a new system of leadership and succession known as the Tetrarchy. The empire was divided into an eastern and western half, each ruled by an Augustus with a younger second-in-command ready to take over after an agreed period. The four Tetrarchs are seen here in a carving of red porphyry of *c.*AD 300, originally from Constantinople but now set into the wall of St Mark's in Venice.

Answering directly to them were two Caesars, Constantius and Galerius, who served in more junior capacities. The arrangement was that after twenty years the Augusti would retire and the Caesars would take over, appointing a new pair of Caesars to replace them. Perhaps the most remarkable thing about this ambitious system is that it lasted as long as it did. In 305, after the agreed twenty years, both Diocletian and Maximian retired, leaving the empire to the two Caesars. Though violent disagreements quickly set in, causing the elegant arrangement to collapse, neither of the retired Augusti attempted to resume power.

However, to return to the beginning of Diocletian's reign: having created a degree of stability at the top, the emperor set about reforming the army, provincial administration and the fiscal system. The army was now reorganized to create two types of unit, frontier forces (*limitanei*) stationed in forts along all the land frontiers, and mobile field armies (*comitatenses*) located strategically so that they could respond rapidly to emergencies such as rebellions or sudden incursions of barbarians. Since the *limitanei* occupied their frontier forts for very long periods, and sons generally followed their fathers' profession, the frontier forces fast became sedentary militias; and since by now the army had become heavily 'Germanized', ethnic distinctions between the populations on either side of the frontier line became blurred to extinction.

To improve provincial administration the old provinces were subdivided, creating about a hundred smaller provinces which were grouped into twelve dioceses each

11.21 The emperor Diocletian (245–316 AD) whose reforms stabilized the empire. The head comes from one of Diocletian's residences at Nicomedia in Turkey.

under the authority of a *vicarius* whose task was largely to oversee taxation. Each of the Tetrarchs had control of a group of dioceses. The tax system was also reformed, becoming far more complex and prompting the gibe that there were now more tax collectors than taxpayers. One important element of the new system was the introduction of tax in kind, which meant that much of the product could be 'consumed' close to the region of production, so obviating the need to transport goods over long distances and greatly simplifying the fiscal system. An adverse effect was that it led towards a demonetarization of the economy.

Finally, to tackle the runaway inflation, Diocletian reformed the currency, creating a new gold coin of high purity backed by a new silver issue which held its value well. Although the gold was later devalued by 20 per cent by Constantine, it remained the basis of the monetary system throughout the early Byzantine period. The second fiscal measure designed to counter inflation was the introduction, in 301, of an Edict of Maximum Prices which set out in minute detail permitted prices throughout the empire, tariffs for transport by sea from port to port, wages payable to different categories of workers and the price of every commodity from grain to fish glue. Prices were set in denarii, which did something to keep the monetary economy alive, but the overall effect of the edict was that goods ceased to be offered for sale on the open market and barter became increasingly common.

The reforms also attempted to counter the problems of the declining birth rate and the increasing mobility of the population, caused by excessive taxation, which saw tenants, traders and small farmers give up their jobs and drift to the towns, or become workers on the larger estates, or, *in extremis*, join the ranks of the bandit groups now infiltrating into the countryside in increasing numbers. A series of new edicts now bound men to their professions and sons were forced to follow those of their fathers. It was an act of desperation designed to prop up the fast-decaying social fabric.

The reforms of Diocletian were a remarkable achievement. They created a peace and prosperity throughout the empire that were to last for much of the fourth century, but at best they were temporary palliatives to systemic problems. The momentum of change in Europe on both sides of the frontier could not be deflected by the dictates of one man.

CHAPTER TWELVE

The Turn of the Tide:
AD 300–800

Between the abdication of Diocletian on 1 May 305 and the coronation of Charlemagne on Christmas Day 800 Europe underwent a total reformation. The period opened with the Roman Empire, unnerved but still largely intact, dominating the entire Mediterranean and much of the European peninsula besides. It ended with a patchwork of polities, vying with each other for power, occupying territories from which the modern nation-states of Europe were to emerge. This turmoil of folk movements ended in an era of state formation.

The plethora of tribes on the move throughout the continent, the lengthy cast of war leaders and kings appearing briefly upon the stage, and the endless list of battles won and lost make this a frenetic, confusing period to follow in all its detail. The seismic shifts taking place can all too easily be obscured by the superficialities of narrative history. In essence: the Roman Empire was reduced to an opulent enclave commanding the vital eastern crossroads between Europe and Asia, the Black Sea and the Mediterranean; waves of

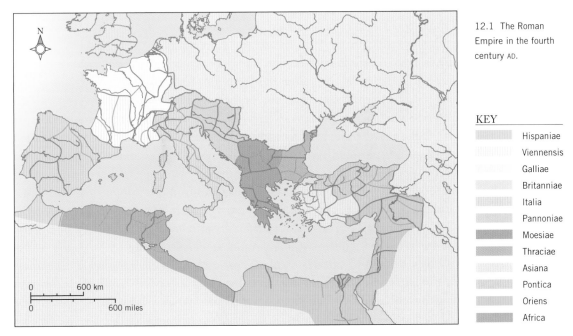

12.1 The Roman Empire in the fourth century AD.

KEY

Hispaniae
Viennensis
Galliae
Britanniae
Italia
Pannoniae
Moesiae
Thraciae
Asiana
Pontica
Oriens
Africa

nomads and semi-nomads from the steppes beat their way westwards; Germanic peoples surged across the frontier, eventually dissipating their energies by colonizing the old Western Roman Empire; while around the Baltic Sea stable, productive farming communities developed an increasingly comfortable lifestyle strengthened by their ability to articulate the fast-developing northern trading arc. It was Old Europe behaving true to form. But now an entirely new energy intruded on to the scene as the Arab armies began their spectacular advance, first into Syria, Palestine and Egypt, and then along the entire North African coast to spill across the straits into Iberia. Henceforth the world of Islam was to share the European stage.

The Empire Repackaged

The Tetrarchy as set up by Diocletian had been a sensible theoretical solution to the problems of governance and continuity faced by an overextended Empire, but it took no cognizance of human nature and was bound to fail. After the abdication of Diocletian and Maximian in 305 some semblance of the system continued, but in the clash of egos that inevitably followed, one man – Constantine – fought his way to supreme power and, in 324, once again united the empire. During his bid for power Constantine fought two major battles with far-reaching consequences. At Milvian Bridge near Rome he embraced Christianity and later, when fighting on the Bosphorus, he suddenly grasped the enormous strategic importance of Byzantium which thenceforth became the heart of the empire – New Rome – Constantinople. The new capital was formally inaugurated in 330. The move was not an idle whim. It had long been apparent that the centre of gravity of the empire was shifting to the east; from here the two frontiers, in the east and in Europe, could be quickly reached and, perhaps even more to the point, Constantinople lay in the centre of a trade network that commanded both European necessities and eastern luxuries while being within easy reach of corn shipped from Alexandria.

Although the city grew quickly in size and splendour it was not until the reign of Theodosius I (379–95) that emperors chose to make Constantinople their imperial residence. By that time the city had acquired the trappings of state officialdom, including a three hundred-strong Senate, magistrates and a prefect, giving it constitutional parity with Rome. So it was that Constantinople, Greek-speaking and Christian, took on the mantle of empire, leaving old Rome, Latin-speaking and pagan, to waste away.

The decline of the west came fast. Germanic incursions began in earnest in the late 360s. Under intense pressure along its entire length the European frontier collapsed as land-hungry migrants poured into the depleted and exhausted western province to carve out new territories for themselves. By 476,

when the last emperor of Rome, the grandly named Romulus Augustalus, was deposed, the west had become a patchwork of largely Germanic kingdoms.

As Rome withered, Constantinople grew in grandeur, assuming the leadership of the civilized world. In 527 Justinian became emperor and immediately threw the resources of the state into reconquering the lost Western Roman Empire. After strengthening the eastern frontier against the Persians, the reconquest began in 533 with a maritime assault on the Vandals who now occupied North Africa. Success was surprisingly rapid and provided the bridgehead from which to begin the reconquest of Italy, but the campaign was hard and long and it was not until 563 that the war-racked peninsula was finally secured together with the southern third of Iberia. The thirty years it had taken to win back at least some of the west had seen a huge drain on manpower and resources and it is difficult to judge what the advantages were, other than satisfying a nostalgic pride. That said, almost the entire Mediterranean had been reunited under the empire, bringing two of its most productive agricultural regions, Andalucía and Tunisia, back into the supply network.

Constantinople had now became a glittering centre, attracting scholars and artists from far and wide, and there was lavish investment in the urban infrastructure. The greatest of Justinian's achievements was the rebuilding of

12.2 The emperor Justinian spent much of his reign attempting to recover the Western Empire, which had been lost to barbarian attacks. By AD 565 he had regained Italy, much of North Africa and the south-east of Iberia.

409

410

the church of Hagia Sophia – the Divine Wisdom. The earlier church had been largely destroyed during an outbreak of mob violence in 532 which Justinian had narrowly escaped. Now in piety he set about rebuilding the church on a massive and lavish scale, 'gathering together skilled workmen from every land'. Among these were the famous mathematicians Anthemius of Tralles and Isodorus of Miletus whose calculations ensured the great structure's lasting coherence. The result was (and is) one of the most outstanding architectural achievements of all times. Even the historian Procopius, a stern critic of Justinian, would write: 'The church presents a most glorious spectacle, extra-ordinary to those who behold it and altogether incredible to those who are told of it. . . . It is distinguished by indescribable beauty, excelling both in its size and the harmony of its measures.' Justinian lived to see the project completed and was present at its dedication on Christmas Day 563. A contemporary observer, Paul the Silentiary, described the scene:

> And when the first glow of light, rosy-armed, leapt from arch to arch, driving away the dark shadows, then all the princes and people with one voice hymned their songs of praise and prayer; and as they came to the sacred courts it seemed as if the mighty arches were set in heaven.

Justinian's hard-won reconquests did not remain within the empire for long: by 700 all that was left was Sicily and the toe of Italy. Yet Constantinople and its empire of the east continued to flourish, growing rich from its total command of the trade routes. As the world changed around it, Byzantium showed a remarkable resilience. It remained a significant polity, influencing the course of European history throughout the rest of the duration of our story.

The Huns: AD 350–450

We return once more to the north Pontic steppe. Much of the region, including the Crimea and the Sea of Azov, was occupied by the Ostrogoths who had begun to move into the area in the early third century AD, while the area east of the Don was still the preserve of steppe nomads – the Alans – who had come from the east in the first century BC. This was the situation around AD 350 when yet another horde of steppe nomads – the Huns – appeared out of the east and established themselves in the steppe to the east of the Volga.

Over the next fifty years they continued their inexorable advance west-wards along the north Pontic corridor, causing massive social dislocations and attacking Constantinople in 408–09. The vigorous response of the emperor Theodosius deflected the flow of the horde, leaving them little option but to cross the Carpathians into Transylvania and the Great Hungarian Plain, where they settled. It was the old story repeating itself: why, we can only speculate.

12.3 *Opposite:* The interior of the Hagia Sophia – the Church of the Divine Wisdom – built as the crowning glory of the Eastern Roman Empire, in the centre of Constantinople in the early sixth century AD. Under the Ottomans it became a mosque, but is now a museum. The interior architecture and much of the decoration are unchanged since the sixth century.

12.4 The advent of the Huns. Raiding parties led by Attila penetrated deep into western Europe but with no lasting effect.

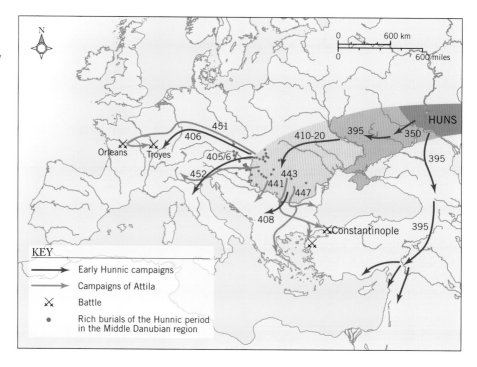

Perhaps there was some folk memory, passed among the steppe nomads, of the rich rolling plains in the west to which it was their destiny to travel.

Exactly when the final stage of the westerly migration took place it is difficult to say but Huns were already established in the Great Hungarian Plain by the 420s. Quite possibly the initial settlement began in the first few years of the fifth century and was the catalyst that drove the already-destabilized Germanic tribes and the Alans to cross the frozen Rhine on the last day of 406 to flood into the western Roman provinces.

The Hunnic Empire reached from the Carpathian Basin to the Caspian Sea, incorporating the residual population who had remained in the region. To begin with, the Huns were divided into a number of autonomous groups under their own kings but by 440 much political centralization had taken place and a single ruling dynasty had emerged, with power shared by two co-rulers. This was the position when Attila and his brother Bleda came to power, and remained so until Attila murdered Bleda to assume supreme control.

It was probably in the turmoil of the advance westwards that these essentially nomadic people reinvented themselves as a ruling class requiring a subservient indigenous population to produce the food needed for them to sustain their lifestyle. The mobile elites and their followers grew rich from raiding the surrounding lands and also by serving as mercenaries whenever the imperial regimes had need of force, but after the 430s their power had become so assured that they could now wage their own wars to generate the loot and tribute to which they had become accustomed.

The Hunnic relationship with the Eastern Roman Empire was ambivalent. The Huns had served as mercenaries for the emperor but had also raided the provinces, pushing southwards into the Balkans in 442. A negotiated settlement in 447 seems to have brought hostilities to an end. Byzantium bought them off with a massive tribute but the Huns must have appreciated the military might that the Eastern Empire still wielded: it was best left alone.

In 451 Attila led the Huns deep into western Europe but the horde was defeated by the Roman general Aetius leading a ragbag army including Visigoths and Burgundians. The next year Attila decided to try his luck in northern Italy, attacking Aquileia (Trieste) before moving into the Po valley, but illness ravaged his troops. His death, in 453 – reportedly from an excess of alcohol drunk on the last of his several wedding nights – brought the attacks to an end.

In the struggle for power that ensued the fragile Hunnic Empire fell apart. Local tribes such as the Gepids of the Carpathian Basin reasserted themselves and the Huns began to drift back eastwards to the Pontic steppe, though isolated bands continued to launch attacks on the empire across the Lower Danube until the late 460s. The pockets that remained became part of the rich ethnic mix of eastern Europe.

The Hunnic advance into the Great Hungarian Plain had been sudden and dramatic but it had had comparatively little effect on the Eastern Roman Empire with which it shared a border. Its greatest impact came in its dislocation of the many different groups of Germans as the horde moved westwards – the Goths through whose territory they rampaged and the disparate bands jostling for land north of the Danube–Rhine frontier. These people had nowhere to go except to trample down the frontiers and flood into the Western Roman Empire, so hastening its demise.

The Germans on the Move: 375–550 AD

The turbulence that can first be discerned across the North European Plain in the second and third centuries AD, and that erupted into the Roman world in the late third century, continued throughout the next two centuries. Population growth, internal warfare and folk movements, together with the creation of new confederacies, characterized the period. The population had become too large for the available territory. There were only two routes of escape: southwards across the Roman frontier into the empire, and eastwards into the Pontic steppe. Both were attempted in the late third century. The first

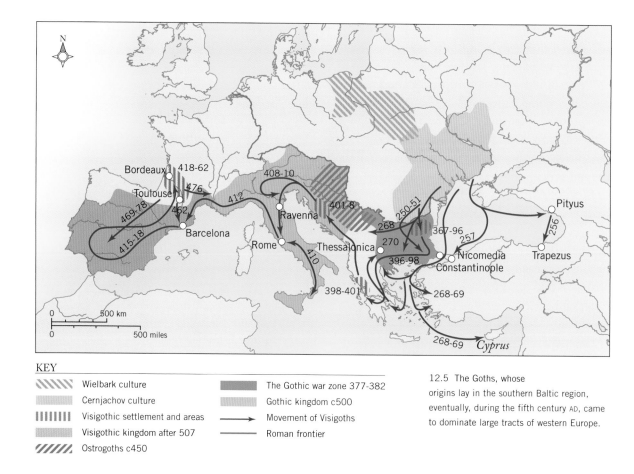

KEY

Wielbark culture	
Cernjachov culture	
Visigothic settlement and areas	
Visigothic kingdom after 507	
Ostrogoths c450	

The Gothic war zone 377-382	
Gothic kingdom c500	
→ Movement of Visigoths	
── Roman frontier	

12.5 The Goths, whose origins lay in the southern Baltic region, eventually, during the fifth century AD, came to dominate large tracts of western Europe.

led to the compromise by which the imperial authorities absorbed migrants into the army or gave them empty lands to settle, the second saw the settlement of the Goths along the north Pontic shores as far as the Don. These safety valves relieved the pressure for three or four generations, but by the middle of the fourth century it had built up again to dangerous levels just as the Huns appeared on the eastern horizon. Their westerly thrust as far as the Great Hungarian Plain exacerbated an already explosive situation and the world was tipped into chaos as huge numbers of Germans poured through the frontiers in search of land to settle. The story of the period 375–500 is the story of that readjustment.

We know little of the turbulence within the Germanic homeland during this period, but a fair amount about the movements of the Germanic bands once they had reached the Roman provinces. The surviving texts are inevitably limited to those aspects that Roman observers considered worth describing. It is a partial and often biased picture. Descriptions of, say, the wanderings of the

Visigoths, spanning a forty-year period, tell us nothing of the changes that must have taken place within Visigothic society. The mobile force would have embraced other migrants – Germans, Sarmatians and indigenous peoples; wives recruited from the local populations will have added to the gene pool, while many migrants will have chosen to opt out and settle along the way. The Visigoths establishing their kingdom in Iberia in the late fifth century would have been very different from the Visigoths who had set out to cross the Lower Danube in 376. What ethnic cohesion they had on the march lay in the authority of the leading elites and their ability to maintain the beliefs and behaviour patterns of their ancestral clans.

To detail the Germanic movements across the face of the Western Roman Empire from the late fourth to the early sixth century is beyond the scope of this book. Suffice it to say, they surged across the frontier with great rapidity, taking over the systems, structures and values of the old Roman world they found to be useful or attractive. The bishop of Constantinople could write in

12.6 Under king Theodoric, the Ostrogothic capital was established at Ravenna in AD 493. The palace church of Theodoric (now St Apollinare Nuovo) was elaborately decorated with mosaics, one of which depicts the defended harbour of Classis (Classe di Ravenna) with merchant ships riding safe inside.

12.7 The mausoleum of the Ostrogothic king Theoderic, who died in 526 AD still stands, largely intact, outside the walls of Ravenna. The roof is made of a single block of limestone weighing 300 tons.

392: 'The barbarians have left their own territory and many times have overrun huge tracts of our land, setting fire to the countryside. Instead of returning to their homes, like drunken revellers they mock us.' In the first shock of the onslaught it must have seemed like the end of the world, and yet

416

at Ravenna the Ostrogothic leader Theodoric would create a court to rival Constantinople and in 497 was formally recognized by the emperor as the ruler of the Western Roman Empire. Meanwhile in the far west, in southern Gaul and Iberia, Visigoths had begun to develop distinctive artistic and architectural styles far livelier than their purely Roman predecessors. It was not, then, a time of mindless destruction but rather a brief phase of very rapid change out of which new and highly innovative cultures emerged.

The early migrants moved into their new ecological niches in confederate waves. The Ostrogoths (eastern Goths) took over much of the Balkans and Italy while the Visigoths (western Goths) made for Gaul and Iberia. Suebi, Vandals and Alans thrust far south into Iberia, the Vandals crossing to North Africa and, with new-found maritime skills, annexed the western Mediterranean islands of the Balearics, Sardinia, Corsica and Sicily before moving on to Italy. Other groups of Germans – Franks, Alamanni and Burgundians – were content to take over northern Gaul, the Rhône valley and the Alpine Foreland, while latecomers on the scene, the Langobardi, crossed first into the old provinces of Noricum and Pannonia (roughly Austria and Hungary) before moving into Italy in the late sixth century to create the Langobardic (Lombard) state. Finally, on the Atlantic fringes of Europe, Saxons, Frisians, Jutes and Angles were settling in eastern Britain and northern Gaul as migrants from Ireland were establishing enclaves in the west of Britain. In the confusion of this mobility the New Europe was beginning to take shape.

People were on the move on a scale quite unlike anything experienced before. The frontier had inhibited the natural flow of people, but after over the four centuries or so of its existence the population pressures building up in the north could no longer be contained and the military boundary collapsed in a frenzy of mobility. But other factors besides demography may have played some part. The flow of commodities from the north on the scale demanded by the all-consuming Roman world must have distorted the productive economies of the northern lands – a distortion that may in itself have set up tensions within society. Moreover, the breakdown of the Roman fiscal system and the draconian reorderings under Diocletian may have so altered the Roman–barbarian exchange mechanism that the native economies, geared to one system, simply could not adjust to a new one. But one thing is for certain. The migrations were born of population pressures and social tensions and, once begun, they gathered a frightening momentum. A century or so later, by which time the energy had dissipated itself, reaching the remotest corners of the old Western Roman Empire, the face of Europe had been totally reconfigured.

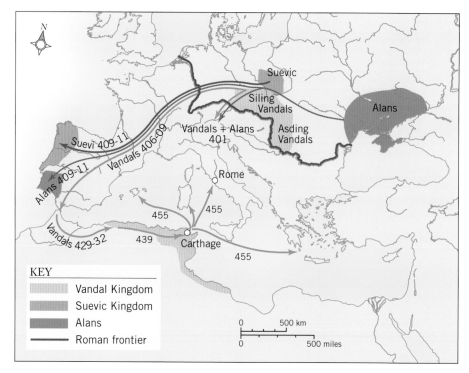

12.8 The raids of the Huns and migrations of the Goths (12.5 and 12.7) were part of a complex of folk movements which included many other peoples like the Alans, the Suevi and the Vandals who burst across the frontiers in the early years of the fifth century AD.

Beyond the Germans

The Germanic cauldron from which the folk movements emanated extended over much of the North European Plain from the North Sea coast to the valley of the Vistula. Beyond, to the north, lay the Baltic zone (see below, pp. 434–40). To the east of the Vistula, well beyond the reach of classical commentators, social re-formations were under way. This was the region from which the Slavs and the Balts were to emerge. The debates surrounding the geography of the ethnogenesis are coloured by the politics of modern nation-states, making the subject more than a little contentious. For our purposes it can be said that the Slavs emerged from the indigenous population that occupied the region between the Vistula and the Dnepr. The principal tribe in the region was, according to the earlier Roman writers of the first century AD, the Venedi who by the sixth century were called the Winidae. Around the eastern side of the Baltic, east of the Vistula, was another tribe, known to Tacitus as the Aestii. They controlled the rich amber supplies of Samland, which became a mecca for traders from the Baltic and Germanic regions and probably also from the Roman world. These tribes were to become the Balts.

By the end of the fifth century Slavic culture and language had extended eastwards towards the Don and deep into Russia, and westwards into

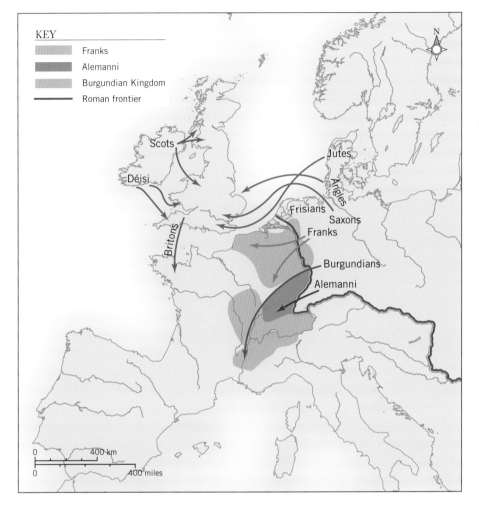

KEY

Franks
Alemanni
Burgundian Kingdom
Roman frontier

Scots
Déisi
Britons
Jutes
Angles
Frisians
Saxons
Franks
Burgundians
Alemanni

12.9 Between AD 360 and 480, far-reaching folk movements in western Europe led to the resettlement of extensive territories.

abandoned Germanic territories probably as far as the Elbe. In the south Slavs had reached the Danube. This broad cultural zone was fragmented into a very large number of small competing chiefdoms.

Horsemen from the East: Avars, Bulgars and Magyars

The memory of the Huns was just fading when another nomadic group – the Avars – swept into Europe from the east, forced westwards by the expansion of the Turkish Empire north of the Caucasus. By the mid-sixth century the Avars had established themselves in Pannonia and, in 626, a force, said to number some eighty thousand, devastated the Balkans and besieged Constantinople, though without much success; the massive walls of the city were too daunting and the attackers simply melted away. By this time the many Slavic tribes were fighting back and in the first few decades of the

419

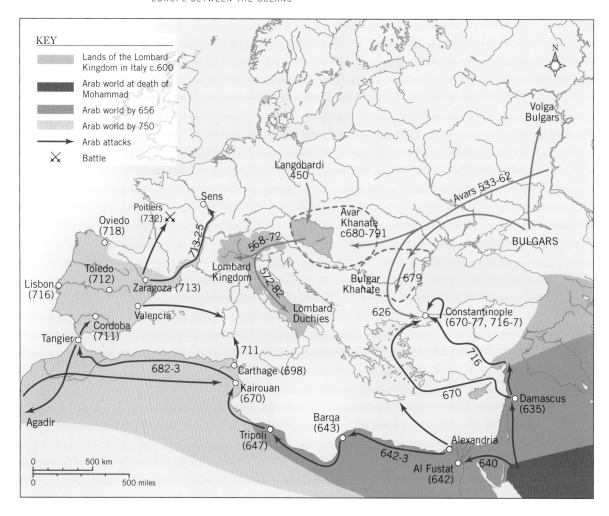

12.10 The turmoil of folk movement continued throughout the sixth and seventh centuries AD culminating, in the early eighth century, with Arab attacks on Istanbul and the Arab settlement of North Africa and Spain.

seventh century the Avar Khanate was reduced to the Carpathian Basin and Transdanubia. The Avars remained a discrete polity until the region was absorbed into the Bulgar Khanate in the early ninth century.

The Bulgars, an amalgam of many disparate ethnic groups living around the Sea of Azov, are first mentioned in the early seventh century but the expansion of yet another eastern horde – the Khazars – forced them out of their homeland. One group moved northwards to settle on the Middle Volga, while a second group moved westwards to take over the territory between the Dnestr and the Lower Danube. By the late seventh century these Danube Bulgars had become powerful enough to move south of the Danube into what is now the northern part of modern Bulgaria, and within a century had extended their power still further by absorbing the territory of the Avars.

In the early eighth century the Khazar Khanate collapsed and there emerged in the region of the steppe and forest steppe, bounded on the south and east by the Dnestr and the Don, a new ethnic configuration – the Magyars – who were probably a Finnish tribe who had migrated from the north. They were content to remain peacefully in their new homeland until, at the end of the ninth century, they were forced to migrate westwards into the Carpathian Basin and Transdanubia – the last of the major ethnic incursions that the land, eventually to become Hungary, was to receive.

The successive waves of eastern peoples sweeping westwards and ending up in the restricted territory between the Carpathian arc and the eastern Alps are a recurring theme throughout the first millennium BC and first millennium AD. It is a dynamic stimulated by the constant build-up of population on the distant steppe. Presented with such a remarkable phenomenon, it is difficult not to accept that geography is sometimes a major determinant in history.

Enter Islam

At the beginning of the seventh century the Eastern Roman Empire maintained a long eastern frontier running from the Gulf of Aqaba on the Red Sea to the Caucasus Mountains. Beyond lay the Sasanian Empire of the Persians, incorporating Mesopotamia, and to the south the huge desert tracts of Arabia, occupied by warring tribes of nomads who from time to time raided their Persian and Byzantine neighbours. The raids were an irritant rather than a threat but the unification of the Arabs under Muhammad (570–623), and the rapid acceptance of the faith of Islam, moulded them into a devastating military force.

The unification was completed by Muhammad's son-in-law Abu Bakr, the first caliph (successor), and under the next two caliphs, Umar and Uthman, the Arabs began their shattering advance: between 636 and 638 Syria and Palestine were overrun, Mesopotamia was taken, and in 642 the Sasanian army was defeated in the Zagros Mountains, opening the way to the east. In the same year Alexandria was captured and the Arab army began its advance along the coast of North Africa. In this brief span of seven years the Eastern Roman Empire had lost its three most fertile and productive provinces, Syria, Palestine and Egypt.

After the death of Caliph Uthman in 656, a period of civil war set in that saw Islam split into two factions, the Sunnis and the Shiites. But the advance continued anyway and it was not long before a substantial fleet had been constructed, opening the way for attacks on Constantinople in 669 and again in 674–80.

In North Africa the progress was spectacular. Kairouan, in Tunisia, was taken in 670 and in 682–83 the warrior Uqba ben Nafi led his forces in a furious dash to the far west. It is said that he rode his horse into the Atlantic, shouting that only the ocean had prevented his westward advance to 'preserve

421

12.11 The fortress city of Kairouan, in Tunisia, was founded in 670 AD by Uqba ibn Nafi. The great mosque which still dominates the town was built in the ninth century AD when Kairouan became the capital of the Aghlabid emirate.

the unity of Thy [Allah's] holy name and putting to the sword the rebellious natives who worship other gods but Thee'.

The early eighth century saw the final thrust. In the east the Arab armies reached the Indus valley, in the north they advanced to the Aral Sea and the Caucasus Mountains, while in the west, in 711, they crossed the Straits of Gibraltar to establish a bridgehead in Spain. Within eight years they had conquered all but the extreme mountainous north of the peninsula and had established an enclave around the Golfe du Lion. Raids along the Rhône (713–25) carried the Arab force into the heart of the Frankish kingdom. Meanwhile, in 717, at the other end of Europe, the Muslim armies advanced across Anatolia to attempt another siege of Constantinople, supported by a navy said to comprise 1800 ships. The Byzantines immediately counter-attacked using Greek Fire which caused considerable Arab losses. The besieging forces then settled down for a long, bitter winter: many died from the unaccustomed cold. In spring army and fleet reinforcements were sent but the tactics of the Byzantines and the support given by Bulgar allies wore down the Arab resolve. After thirteen months they finally abandoned the siege and returned home. It was the last attempt they were to make on Constantinople.

422

In the west raids continued against the Franks, culminating in 732 in a major thrust northwards along the Atlantic coastal region: it was met and roundly defeated near Poitiers by Charles Martel, the founder of the Carolingian dynasty.

At both ends of Europe powerful states had blocked the Arab advance. To the eighteenth-century historian Edward Gibbon the successes at Constantinople in 717–18 and at Poitiers in 732 were turning points in history – with Islam repelled, Europe was saved. Had it not been for Martel's victory, wrote Gibbon, with an evident shudder of relief, 'perhaps the interpretation of the Koran would now be taught in the Schools of Oxford and her pulpits might demonstrate to a circumcised people the sanctity and truth of the revelation of Mahomet'. He could imagine little worse. But the Mediterranean had now become a divided ocean and was to remain so for centuries to come. The Muslim world now extended from the Atlantic to the Indus: it was the largest empire the world had ever known.

12.12 The use of Greek Fire (an explosive mixture of quicklime, sulphur and petroleum) by the Byzantines proved to be a serious deterrent to the Arab attack on Istanbul. The illustration comes from the fourteenth-century edition of the *Chronicle* of John Skylitzes.

Reordering the Pieces

In AD 300 the Mediterranean lands and a wide flanking strip of temperate Europe had for generations lived under a single ruling authority. They shared the same fiscal system, accepted a single official language and enjoyed a remarkably unified material culture. Beneath this superficial unity there were, admittedly, divisions: many different local languages were spoken and from time to time in the late third century provinces broke away for a while. But what held the empire together, locking the individual pieces into a single whole, was an economic system based on the constant and massive redistribution of resources between the productive provinces and the consuming centre and frontiers. Crucial to the stability of the system was an effective method of taxation and a safe and efficient distribution mechanism by sea, river and land. Beyond the frontier, to the north, a different system was in operation – one in a state of highly unstable equilibrium structured around personal prestige and the control of luxury goods emanating from the empire. Instability was exacerbated by a rapid growth in population.

The collapse of the empire under a torrent of migrating populations spilling out of the Germanic region, and the subsequent invasions of Europe and the Mediterranean zone by steppe nomads and desert Arabs, created an entirely new political geography. The Eastern Roman Empire – Byzantium – commanded the east, controlling the routes between the Mediterranean and the Black Sea, while the reconstituted Western Roman Empire – the Frankish Empire now under the energetic leadership of the Carolingian kings – commanded the west, controlling the routes between the Mediterranean, the Atlantic and the North Sea. The two big power blocks effectively stemmed the further advances of the Arabs, who had now assumed control of the entire southern Mediterranean. Confronted by so much ocean, the Arabs had become a naval power. Remote from all this, the Baltic communities were fast developing a northern maritime system stretching from Britain in the west to Byzantium and beyond in the east. Meanwhile, between the ocean interfaces transpeninsular networks were beginning to bind the disparate worlds ever more tightly.

The Mediterranean in Transition

In the fourth century the trading network, dominated by the *annona* (corn tariff) imposed by Rome, remained in operation. As far as can be judged, maritime traffic continued, using much the same routes, throughout the fifth and sixth centuries – though now, inevitably, there was some separation between the systems serving Rome and those focusing on Constantinople. But with the arrival of the Arab presence in the early eighth century, the rhythms of commerce and exchange were totally reordered to suit the demands of the two now competing worlds of north and south.

The impetus behind maritime commerce in the fourth to sixth centuries was the need to trans-ship the huge quantities of corn, raised in annual taxes in the corn-producing regions of North Africa, Egypt and Syria, to the capitals of the empire, Rome and Constantinople. Most of the product passed

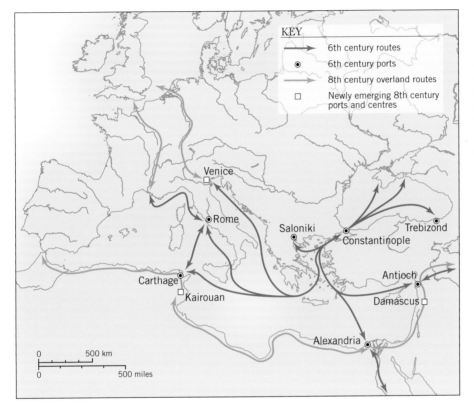

KEY

→ 6th century routes
⊙ 6th century ports
→ 8th century overland routes
□ Newly emerging 8th century ports and centres

12.13 As always, the Mediterranean provided the major routes along which commodities were transported. Many of the old route nodes continued to function, but new ones came into use as the political geography changed.

through three ports, Carthage, Alexandria and Seleucia (the port of Antioch). The quantities shipped annually were colossal. During the reign of Justinian, Constantinople received 160,000 metric tonnes of grain each year from Alexandria alone. What the total annual figure was and how it varied over time it is difficult to estimate.

Many other commodities were carried along the same sea routes, either alongside the grain or in separate cargo vessels. Next to grain, olive oil probably accounted for the greatest bulk. Most Mediterranean countries produced oil in exportable quantities. Southern Spain was the most prolific supplier for Rome and estimates based on the vast mound of amphora sherds comprising Monte Testaccio on the outskirts of the city, where the oil was decanted and the amphorae were discarded, suggest an annual importation of 22,500 metric tonnes of Spanish oil during the third century. Other bulk foodstuffs carried in amphorae included olives, wine, fish and fish sauce. Besides the necessities of life, luxury goods were trans-shipped in prolific variety. One late fifth-century text lists camels, draperies and other textiles, and silver litters stowed on a vessel leaving Africa bound for Athens. Another of about the same date records pet birds, papyrus, copper pots and a cabinet of

12.14 A detail from the Portus relief from Rome showing a large freighter arriving at the Trajanic harbour at Ostia in the early third century AD.

medicines being trans-shipped from Alexandria to Smyrna on the Aegean coast of Anatolia.

From the late third century onwards African goods began to dominate the imports that Rome received via its port of Ostia, but by the beginning of the fifth century increasing quantities of vessels from the east Mediterranean were beginning to pour into Rome and southern Gaul. With the Vandal conquest of North Africa in the 430s and the extension of Vandal maritime power throughout the western Mediterranean, Rome came to rely more and more on Alexandria for its grain, though demand must have lessened significantly as Rome's population shrank from an estimated 800,000 in the fourth century to 350,000 in 452 and 60,000 in 530.

In the Eastern Empire the population grew and increasingly the *annona* from Alexandria was deflected to Constantinople, a significantly shorter journey which allowed up to three round trips to be completed in a single sailing season. But all this must have ended in 617 when Alexandria was taken by the Persians. The following year the free distribution of bread in Constantinople came to an end and was never restored. The arrival of the Arabs in 642 removed Alexandria and the wealth of Egypt from the reach of Constantinople for ever. Carthage remained a supplier of corn for a few more years until it too succumbed to the Arabs in 698. The old Roman system of

426

supplying the non-productive centre with an annual levy of corn from the provinces, which had begun with the conquest of Sicily in 212 BC, was now finally at an end.

Maritime commerce had a rather different role to play in Mediterranean history when, in 542, bubonic plague broke upon the Mediterranean world. Since the disease was carried by black rats, which in turn were carried by ships, the pestilence spread rapidly throughout the Mediterranean and reverberated around its shores for over two hundred years. Its initial impact was devastating. Estimates vary but one contemporary observer, John of Ephesus, writes of 230,000 dying at Constantinople – a figure consistent with recent calculations which suggest a 50 per cent mortality rate. Such a loss would have had a stunning impact, undermining society's ability to adjust to what was already a fast-changing situation. Recurrences of bubonic plague continued to devastate Mediterranean populations throughout the middle of the eighth century.

The bulk of shipping in the Mediterranean was engaged in trade, but since piracy had become endemic there was a growing need to maintain naval protection forces to guard the main sea lanes. The Germanic invaders took to the sea whenever an opportunity presented itself. Visigoths reaching Barcelona in 418 were quick to build ships, the more easily to raid the nearby coasts. Later, when the Vandals took Carthage in 439 they made use of the city's excellent naval facilities, raiding widely in the west Mediterranean and extending their authority to some of the larger islands. Nor were the desert Arabs slow to appreciate the potential of the sea when they first confronted the Mediterranean in the 630s. Their maritime expeditions to Cyprus, Crete and Constantinople employed navies of increasing size. Such an investment was matched by a similar spate of shipbuilding undertaken by the Byzantine rulers. By the middle of the seventh century, as the volume of commercial shipping declined, naval vessels became an ever-more familiar sight.

The Arab presence in the Mediterranean created a new dynamic that helped to stimulate patterns of trade linking Arabs, Franks and Byzantines. Although the trading systems in their developed forms belong to the ninth and tenth centuries, their beginnings can be seen in the second half of the eighth century in the period of adjustment and consolidation following the halt of the initial Arab advance. Europe produced a range of commodities that were eagerly sought after by the Arab world – good timber for buildings and ships, furs, fine swords made by Frankish craftsmen, and slaves. In return the Arab world offered silks, spices, drugs, fabrics, and gold and silver. The demand for slaves may well have been kick-started by the last ravages of the bubonic plague which broke out in Africa in 745 and remained virulent over the next seven years. During that time mortality in the Arab cities was at between 25 and 35 per cent. The need for additional manpower was pressing,

427

not least in order to be able to service the ships whose crews would have suffered most from the pestilence. It is no coincidence that the first record of the supply of slaves to the Muslim world – by the Venetians – dates to about 748. Over the next two centuries the slave trade was to become a highly profitable business for Europeans and Arabs alike, in spite of the disapproval of the Church. In Europe crops of slaves were readily available, culled during the various frontier wars of the period and in the campaigns against the less developed Slavic chiefdoms in the east. Venice, at the head of the Adriatic, was extremely well sited to become the main commercial outlet from western Europe and began to develop as a regional power in the 730s. Once established, Venice rapidly became a major trading port with contacts extending throughout the east Mediterranean.

The opening-up of trading relations between Europe and the Arab world in the second half of the eighth century was the beginning of a process that was to revitalize the Mediterranean and its ports. The new political geography called into existence new routes which in turn encouraged the growth of new ports. Although the sea was far from safe and piracy and raiding were rife, many entrepreneurs around the Mediterranean were willing to take the chance.

The Atlantic: Endings and Beginnings

Throughout the Roman period the Atlantic seaways remained in active use as a major transport route for bulk materials and for the many traders whose livelihoods depended on the efficient workings of the maritime networks – men like Marcus Aurelius Lunaris, who in AD 237 made the journey from York to Bordeaux and set up an altar there, presumably to thank his patron deity, Tutela Boudiga (a very British-sounding name), for his safe arrival. It is tempting to think of him as a wine importer, perhaps providing for Britain's northern garrisons. Another product transported in bulk was olive oil from Baetica (Andalucía in southern Spain), carried in distinctive round-bodied amphorae. Eighty per cent of all the amphorae found in northern Britain were of this type. To sailors serving the route from Gades (Cadiz) to London and York, the great lighthouse of Brigantium (A Coruña) on the north-western extremity of the Iberian peninsula would have been a familiar landmark on their journey northwards as they faced the long and dangerous haul across the Bay of Biscay.

That few shipwrecks are known in Atlantic waters is more a reflection of the ferocity of the seas in breaking up sunken vessels than of the safety of the sea lanes. One vessel that foundered on the treacherous Les Sept Îles off the north coast of Brittany was carrying a cargo of lead ingots – about 22 tonnes

12.15 Stone relief from the fort of Housesteads on Hadrian's Wall showing three *Genii Cucullati* wearing hooded cloaks. Third century AD. This type of cloak, made of wool, was probably the *birrus Britannicus* listed as an export from Britain in the fourth century AD.

in all – some of them bearing stamps recording the British tribal names Brigantes and Iceni. The lead probably came from the Pennines (the territory of the Brigantes) and may have been shipped out of an Icenian port in East Anglia. Another wreck, which caught fire and sank in the harbour of St Peter Port in Guernsey in the late third or early fourth century, was carrying large blocks of pitch from the Landes, the coastal region of Gaul south of the Gironde. Also on board were barrels that could have contained Bordeaux wine or Armorican fish sauce. It is quite probable that the vessel was on its way to Clausentum (Southampton) or to London when the fire broke out.

Another route much used throughout the Roman period ran between the Rhine and the Thames. As a frontier zone the Rhine was a region of both production and consumption; as such it was well supplied with roads to carry commodities. The North Sea also served as a major highway, providing direct access to the eastern ports of Britain and the Channel coasts of Britain and Gaul. In the Roman period the principal route to the sea was via the Waal to the estuary of the Scheldt, where the main channel was flanked by two temples, at Colijnsplaat and Domburg, both dedicated to the goddess Nehalennia who protected the interests of traders. The temples were probably associated with harbours where goods were transferred between river boats and seagoing vessels. Dedicatory inscriptions mention a number of traders by

12.16 Portchester Castle, at the head of Portsmouth Harbour, was built initially as a 'Saxon Shore Fort' at the time of Carausius in the late AD 280s. The main (outer) enclosure wall with forward projecting bastions is still very well preserved. The exact purpose of these forts is unclear but their coastal locations suggest that they were associated with maritime activity. Portchester became the focus of later Saxon occupation and was refortified in the Norman period.

name and list principally pottery, wine and salt among their cargoes. Exports from Britain are likely to have included grain, large shipments of which are recorded to have been sent to the German frontier in the fourth century in times of shortage.

The Atlantic seaways continued to link the western Roman provinces throughout the third and fourth centuries. After the reforms introduced by Diocletian at the beginning of the fourth century, which commuted the tax burden to a tithe of production, it is likely that bulk transport increased. The corn trans-shipped from Britain to the Rhine province is a case in point. Another British product, useful to provision the army, was the heavy hooded woollen cloak (*birrus Britannicus*) for which the area was famous. But ships were also leaving Roman waters to trade with barbarians. In the North Sea region Roman pottery and trinkets were being traded along the German coast to the estuary of the Elbe, while from the western ports of Britain trade with Ireland was consistent if not prolific.

The raids mounted by Germanic sailors active in the southern part of the North Sea and the Channel in the late third century led to the construction of massively built forts along both the Gaulish and British coastlines. The siting of the forts in well-protected harbours suggests that they functioned as part of a system designed to protect both coast and sea lanes. The forts remained in use throughout the fourth century and came into their own again in the last

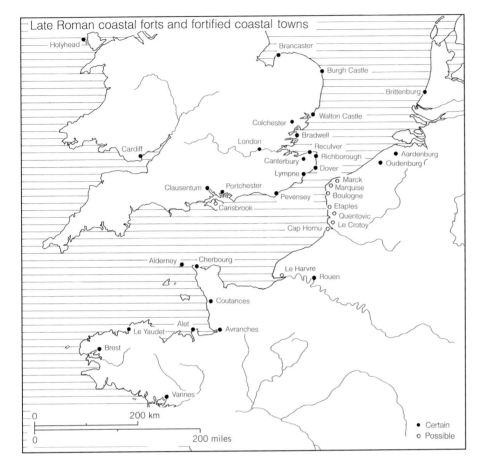

Late Roman coastal forts and fortified coastal towns

- Holyhead
- Brancaster
- Burgh Castle
- Brittenburg
- Walton Castle
- Colchester
- London
- Bradwell
- Cardiff
- Reculver
- Aardenburg
- Canterbury
- Richborough
- Oudenburg
- Lympne
- Dover
- Clausentum
- Portchester
- Marck
- Marquise
- Pevensey
- Boulogne
- Carisbrook
- Etaples
- Quentovic
- Le Crotoy
- Cap Hornu
- Alderney
- Cherbourg
- Le Harvre
- Rouen
- Coutances
- Alet
- Le Yaudet
- Avranches
- Brest
- Vannes

0   200 km

0   200 miles

● Certain
○ Possible

12.17 As the seaways between Britain and the Continent became increasingly infested with pirates, so the coastal defences on both sides of the Channel were strengthened. The fleets protecting the 'shores of Belgica' (the North Sea) and the 'shores of Armorica' (the English Channel) were under different commands in the fourth century AD.

decades of the century when sea raiding intensified and became a very serious threat. To meet the growing crisis the entire coastal system was reorganized to include now not only forts but fortified towns and other settlements. The defences were put under the command of three senior officers: the Count of the Saxon Shore looked after Britain from the Wash to the Solent and two units on the Gaulish side of the Channel, while the coast from the Rhine mouth to the Garonne estuary was divided between the *dux Belgicae secundae* and the *dux tractus Armoricani et Nervicani*. Among their tasks was the organization of sea patrols using fast forty-oared scout ships called *pictae*, painted sea-green for camouflage and sent out to spot enemy movements. The system is unlikely to have lasted far into the fifth century, by which time the Germanic raiders had given way to shiploads of settlers. By the end of the fifth century the first stage of the resettlement was over, with much of Gaul, apart from Armorica, now in the hands of the Franks while the south-east of Britain was under the control of various Saxon Germanic groups from the coastal region north of the Rhine.

431

The fifth century also saw folk movements in the west. Groups of Irish crossed the Irish Sea to settle in western Scotland, north and south Wales, and Cornwall, while from the south-west peninsula of Devon and Cornwall migrating communities moved south along the Atlantic sea lanes to establish themselves in Armorica, which henceforth can properly be called Brittany. Another group reached Galicia in the north-west corner of Iberia and installed a community that became the bishopric of Britonia and survives now as the parish of Bretoña.

These Atlantic readjustments may have involved comparatively limited movements of people. In any event the sea routes do not seem to have been seriously disrupted: commodities and people continued to be transported by sea. Around 420 St Patrick escaped from captivity in Ireland on a merchant ship carrying Irish hunting dogs to Gaul. Later, in 610, the Irish monk Columbanus, returning from Burgundy, came across an Irish trading vessel at Nantes. Another seventh-century account records Irish traders at the monastery of Noirmoutier, just south of the Loire estuary, where they off-loaded quantities of leather shoes and clothes.

The monastic communities of Ireland and Britain provided a new and potent stimulus to mobility. Their proselytizing zeal saw large numbers cross the Channel to Brittany and Gaul to spread the word and establish new monastic communities. They concentrated their efforts on Brittany in the fifth century but extended to the Frankish Empire in the sixth to eighth centuries when scores of monasteries were founded. St Columbanus reached northern Italy and founded the monastery of Bobbio in 614, while a century later St Boniface was working among the Germans. There were also movements in the other direction. In the 680s a Gaulish bishop, Arculf, was shipwrecked on the western coast of Britain, eventually finding hospitality at the monastery of Iona. These movements of the new elite led to the creation of a vibrant religious culture, most spectacularly to be seen now in the metalwork, stone sculpture and book illumination of the Irish Celtic Church.

Against this background of missionary mobility, long-distance Atlantic trade continued, at least throughout the fifth and sixth centuries. This is most clearly shown by the distribution of Mediterranean pottery along the Atlantic seaboard. The pots are of two basic types: fine bowls and dishes in red slipware made on the western coast of Asia Minor and in North Africa; and amphorae probably used to transport olive oil, and perhaps some wine, from North Africa, Asia Minor and Egypt. These cargoes were assembled by Mediterranean traders and carried through the Straits of Gibraltar to ports along the Atlantic coast of Iberia. Considerable quantities of these wares have been found at port sites in the estuaries of the Tagus, Mondego and Miño rivers and as far north as the port of Brigantium (A Coruña). We also learn in one of the *Lives of the Saints* of the visit of Greek merchants (*negotiatores*) coming from the Byzantine world by sea, and travelling, probably via the river Guadiana, to Mérida in the late sixth century. What local commodities the shippers might have received in return for their goods is not recorded but gold, tin and copper are strong possibilities.

The same assemblage of Mediterranean pottery is found further north, with a particular concentration in south-western Britain and south Wales but with smaller quantities reaching north Wales, Ireland and the west coast of Scotland. The evidence speaks of trading ships sailing north from Iberia to serve the more northerly of the Atlantic communities. These are most likely to have been Atlantic-based vessels, though it is not impossible that the occasional Mediterranean vessel braved the Bay of Biscay. For those elite communities, religious and secular, living around the bleak Irish Sea, the arrival of a trading vessel carrying Mediterranean luxuries as well as Gaulish wine must have been an eagerly awaited event. Indeed, in the *Life* of St Columba (565–97) there is a specific reference to the community of Iona anticipating 'Gaulish seamen arriving from the provinces of the Gauls' in their *barca*. There is a hint here of regular visits at fixed times during the sailing season.

The Mediterranean trade to the Atlantic came to a close towards the end of the sixth century as conditions for long-distance trade throughout the Mediterranean began to deteriorate and the volume of commercial shipping declined. However, local vessels continued to ply the Atlantic coast in the seventh and eighth centuries, carrying goods from western France to the Atlantic communities of Britain and Ireland. The network is demonstrated by the distribution of coarse grey pottery (known as E-ware) from the Gironde and Loire. The pots no doubt contained desirable commodities such as dyers' madder, coriander and dill, evidence for all of which has been found, and it is tempting to believe that they were accompanied by barrels of Bordeaux wine. And in return? One commodity now fast gaining in value was slaves. Ireland with its fragmented, warlike society would have been able to provide slaves in plenty.

Meanwhile in the North Sea maritime trading networks began to be re-established in the sixth century as the Rhine corridor regained its former levels of productivity. New ports-of-trade began to emerge at crucial route nodes to cope with the increasing flow of commodities between the Frankish-dominated territories, England and the Baltic region. One of the key locations was Dorestad, sited at the confluence of the Lek and the Rhine on what had been the frontier between the Franks and the Frisians. Towards the end of the seventh century it passed under Frankish domination and thenceforth began to develop as a major port articulating trade between all three regions. Other

Lake
Ladoga
Staraja
Ladoga

Volkhov

Kaupang

SVEALAND
Birka

NORTH

SEA

GOTALAND   Gotland
Paviken
DENMARK   Skuldevig   Köpingsvik
Ribe
HEDEBY   BALTIC
SEA

York

Wolin   Truso

Ipswich   Frisia
London   Fordwich   Dorestad
Hamwih   SAXONY   0   300 km
Quentovic   0   300 miles

KEY

▲   Early Trading Centres

12.18 By the eighth century AD new trading centres were established at ports around the Baltic and the North Sea and English Channel, reflecting the reinvigoration of trading networks as stable states began to emerge from the earlier turmoil.

ports soon developed: St Denys just outside the gates of Paris, Rouen towards the mouth of the Seine, Amiens on the Somme and Quentovic near Étaples. On the British side of the Channel the earliest ports in the sixth and seventh centuries were in Kent and on the Isle of Wight. Later, in the early eighth century, new ports developed at Hamwih at the head of Southampton Water and at London, Ipswich and York.

At the end of the eighth century the two great power blocks, the Carolingian Empire and the English kingdom of Mercia, were actively locked in trade negotiations that paid attention to such details as the approved lengths of English cloaks offered for export. The competition between the two states is neatly summed up by a gold coin minted by the Mercian king Coenwulf (796–821) some time about 807. The obverse bears an image of the king in the style of a fourth-century Roman emperor while the reverse has a legend reading *DE VICO LVNDONIAE* – 'from the wic [market] of London'. The coin is evidently meant to match that issued by Coenwulf's rival Charlemagne a few years earlier which has a reverse inscription of *VICO DORESTAMS* – 'from the wic of Dorestat'. The two states are proclaiming not their military prowess but their commercial standing in the world.

The Northern Arc

The Baltic zone continued to be in receipt of Roman consumer goods throughout the fourth century. Two principal routes were in operation: one via the Rhine and Elbe to the North Sea and then along the Atlantic seaboard of

434

Jutland to the coasts of Norway; the other by way of the Oder and Vistula to the southern Baltic coast, thence to southern Sweden, the Danish Islands and western Jutland or to the island of Gotland, and from there to the Mälaren region of western Sweden. The Roman products, everything from inexpensive pottery to elaborate silverwork and fine weapons, were drawn into the Nordic systems to be utilized for elite display or ritual deposition according to the rules of the receiving society.

Throughout the four hundred or so years of the Roman Iron Age, the agrarian economy of the region developed, farming land expanded, settlements grew and production intensified. There would have been surpluses of grain, cattle and hides to be exported to the Roman frontier, along with luxury products like amber, furs and wild animals. With growing prosperity and increasing population, social and political organization became more complex and led eventually, by the seventh and eighth centuries AD, to the development of discrete kingdoms.

Already in the fourth century clusters of rich warrior burials indicate the emergence of centres of power. One of these lay at Gudme on the Danish island of Fyn where a prosperous settlement continued in existence to the end of the sixth century. The long-houses of the community are not exceptional in any way but the discovery of a considerable amount of gold and silver suggests a site of high status. Some 5 km (3 miles) away on the coast is the contemporary site of Lundeborg which seems to have served as a seasonal market in use during the spring and summer as well as being a manufacturing centre where jewellery was made. The discovery of a large number of ships' nails implies that vessels were being repaired or possibly even built here. Lundeborg and Gudme represent high-status communities which seem to have maintained their pre-eminence by controlling maritime trade. A similar complex is known at Dankirke on the west coast of Jutland; no doubt there were others. Such sites mark the beginning of the process by which centralized markets, legitimized by the elite, began to emerge.

The Baltic communities continued to develop in comparative peace throughout the fifth century when the migrations were at their peak and by the sixth century long-distance trade was flourishing. A key site for understanding this is the small island of Helgö in Lake Mälaren in central Sweden. Here, a settlement with modest buildings was involved in the large-scale production of a range of trinkets including brooches, clasp-buttons, dress pins and dress mounts, as well as swords. Iron was imported from the north while gold and silver probably came from the Byzantine world. Among the equipment used by the craftsmen were hundreds of crucibles together with weights and scales for measuring out the metals. The settlement was occupied from the sixth to ninth centuries, during which time a remarkable array of exotic material arrived at the site. There were at least eighty gold coins including a hoard

12.19 The port of Helgö, on an island in Lake Mälaren, Sweden, became an important trading and manufacturing centre. The discovery of a bishop's crozier, probably of Irish manufacture, and a small bronze statue of a Buddha from India indicates the extent of the trading network of which Helgö was a part.

of forty-seven dating to the fifth and sixth centuries from the Eastern and Western Roman Empires, a Coptic ladle (from Egypt) of the seventh century, an ornate bishop's crozier of Irish manufacture, probably of the eighth century, and a bronze Buddha of the sixth or seventh century originating in northern India. The collection reflects the amazingly wide exchange network of which Helgö was a part.

To acquire such exotic items, and so much Mediterranean gold, implies a high volume of exports. What these were we can only guess – furs would have been important, to which we might add walrus ivory, amber and perhaps eiderdown, all items that would have been welcome in the court of Byzantium. The manufactured objects – the brooches and other dress fittings – seem to have been made for local consumption. If, as seems probable, the trading activity was controlled by the local elite, then these small items could have been used in local exchanges, to acquire the goods for export, and as gifts to clients to help maintain the stability of the social hierarchy.

The development of trade ran parallel with the emergence of an elite distinguished by elaborate burial beneath prominent mounds. 'Royal' burials of this kind characterize the Vendel period (seventh and eighth centuries), named after a royal burial site in the Uppland region of central Sweden. This is the region of the tribe identified by Tacitus in the first century AD as the Svear who have given their name to Sweden. The deceased was invariably buried in a boat which symbolized his or her authority. The earliest of the Scandinavian boat burials is that of a female found at Augerum in southern Sweden interred in the second half of the sixth century. The tradition becomes widespread in Scandinavia, culminating in the spectacular Norwegian ship burials of Gokstad and Osberg of the early ninth century and heralding the beginning of the Viking period. Vendel-period graves vary in their grandeur but in many the dead person is buried with personal armour and feasting equipment. In one particularly splendid grave in the cemetery at Valsgärde, a dead king was laid out on feather pillows and near the prow of his vessel were placed two horses and their saddles, a deer and a dog.

12.20 A nineteenth-century lithograph of Gamla Uppsala north of modern Uppsala, Sweden showing the burial mounds traditionally attributed to the kings of the Svears of the sixth century. Excavation in the nineteenth century showed them to contain the cremated burials of Vendel elite.

437

12.21 The famous ship burial at Sutton Hoo, Suffolk, as it was excavated in 1939. All the timber had rotted but the impressions of the ribs and planks remain together with the corroded nails used to clench the planks. The vessel dates to around AD 630.

In the seventh and eighth centuries ship burials are found in several places around the Baltic, in Uppland, most famously at the cemeteries of Vendel and Valsgärde, in Skåne at the extreme south of Sweden, on the island of Bornholm and in central Jutland. By the ninth century the practice has spread to the approaches to Oslo Fjord. The seventh-century ship graves at Sutton Hoo on the coast of Suffolk are so similar to the early Vendel graves that it is by no means impossible that the elite buried there were by origin Scandinavians who had begun to explore beyond the limits of their own sea.

It was through their command of the maritime routes criss-crossing the Baltic that the leaders of the scattered Scandinavian polities exercised their power. Not surprisingly the Baltic islands featured large in this. Of the 700 or so Roman gold coins reaching the area in the fifth and sixth centuries the majority came from the islands: 280 from Öland, 250 from Gotland and 150 from Bornholm. The coins from Bornholm and Öland are fifth century while most of those from Gotland are sixth century in date, indicating a gradual shift

in the focus of trade as the Uppland region of central Sweden began to emerge as a royal centre. The shift in power may to some extent have resulted from changes to the trade networks of central and eastern Europe with the decline of the Oder route and with the rise in importance of the Vistula which gave access to the Black Sea and Byzantium.

And what of the ships themselves? Fortunately there is a variety of evidence relating to Nordic boat-building of this period. At the beginning of the tradition lie three boats deposited in a lake at Nydam on the east coast of Jutland in the middle of the fourth century. All three were clinker-built, with their overlapping planking secured by iron nails driven through the lap and clenched inboard. The inner framing was inserted after the hull had been formed and was attached, by lashing, to cleats integral with the planking. This is the method we have already seen in the Hjortspring boat of the fourth century BC found only 10 km (6 miles) away. The largest of the Nydam boats was c.23.7 m (78 ft) long and 3.75 m (12 ft) wide. Cross-frames running between the top strakes would have provided seating for two oarsmen, with probably fifteen rowers ranged on either side. Steering was by means of a side rudder. Of the later vessels the best evidence is provided by the Sutton Hoo burial: the vessel, though completely rotted, was preserved as a cast in the sand together with the rows of heavily corroded iron nails that secured the lap of the strakes. Dating to c.630, the ship was about 27 m (88 ft) long and 4.5 m (15 ft) broad amidships. The number of oarsmen is uncertain but the vessel was large enough to have accommodated about twenty each side.

There is no evidence to suggest that the Nydam and Sutton Hoo vessels were provided with sails. Indeed, it could be argued that in a society in which the ship's crew doubled as a unit of fighting men, providing muscle for a raid or prestigious support for their leader on a state visit, a sail would have been

12.22 The Nydam boat found in a bog at Sundeved, Denmark in 1863 as it was exhibited at Flensburg. The vessel dates to the fourth century AD and was buried as a ritual deposit.

439

12.23 Oared vessels of the fifth and sixth centuries AD depicted on stones from the Swedish island of Gotland (above) and sailing vessels of the sixth and seventh centuries AD also from Gotland stones (below).

unnecessary. The sail, however, was more appropriate to cargo ships, and as the transport of bulk cargoes became increasingly important in the Baltic, the sail was introduced. Vivid evidence for this comes, not surprisingly, from the island of Gotland where a number of carved stones depict scenes from daily life. The first sails are shown on stones dating to the seventh century, a date that fits well with the beginnings of the development of bulk trade. The sail was later to come into more general use, advantageously facilitating the long overseas journeys of Viking raiders and traders.

In the broad perspective the seventh century marks the turning point in the development of the Baltic. Until then, society, stretching back into the second millennium BC, had been energized by the raid/expedition mounted on sleek rowing boats capable of bringing back the spoils of success. But with the intensification of trade, which got under way in the fourth century and grew as the Byzantine world became the new consuming focus, regular markets came into being. These in turn provided a stimulus for the emergence of an elite and the rise of kingdoms. The growing demands of an increasingly isolated Byzantine world, coinciding with the moment when the Frankish kingdom was beginning to take an interest in the north, further intensified the social and economic changes under way in the Baltic region, leading to the development of a full market economy and providing the leaders of society with the encouragement to embark upon ever more ambitious overseas adventures.

The Black Sea: A Backwater

The Black Sea was not much relished by the Byzantine Empire – indeed, the sixth-century historian Procopius regarded it as a place best avoided. The Ostrogoths had used the sea to good effect to attack the Eastern Roman Empire, but the peoples who replaced them on the northern Pontic shores from the fifth to eighth centuries – Huns, Avars, Slavs, Khazars and Magyars – showed little interest in taking to the water. Around the western and southern sides of the sea the ancient cities founded by the Greeks gradually decayed, and during the course of the eighth century the Bulgars absorbed much of the western coast and its hinterland into their kingdom as the border with Byzantium moved progressively southwards. Two areas remained under Byzantine control: the north coast of Asia Minor and the Crimea.

Along the Asia Minor coast the old cities of Sinope and Trebizond were now in a sorry state. Justinian made some attempts to revive them, building a new aqueduct at Trebizond, but this show of imperial concern was half-hearted and the cities were left much to their own devices. Yet Trebizond still had a function as a port at the end of an overland route extending to the east, and in the tenth century it was well known for its throughput of textiles as well as its access to rare and valuable fragrances.

In the northern Pontic region a small enclave of civilization was maintained in the southern Crimea, focused on the old city of Chersonesos, and around the entrance to the Sea of Azov guarded by Panticapaeum. Even after the expansion of the Khazar Khanate in the early seventh century Chersonesos remained a Byzantine outpost and indeed survived until the sack of Constantinople by the Christians in 1204. From this extremity of empire commodities continued to be exported: furs, hides, wax, honey and, as trade with the Arab world increased, slaves rounded up in their droves by Khazars.

One of the products much in demand by the Byzantines was naphtha which welled up to the surface on the Taman peninsula, close to the old Greek colony of Panticapaeum. Naphtha was one of the components used to make Greek Fire – a formidable weapon used at sea. The principle was simple. A long wooden tube lined with copper was arranged on board ship so that it could be pointed at enemy vessels. At the rear end an air pump was attached. A naphtha-based liquid was dripped into the tube and ignited, the air pump blowing the flame forward towards the enemy. Primitive though the appliance sounds, it proved to be highly effective, not least against the Arab flotilla besieging Constantinople in 717–18. One Arab observer wrote: 'A flame-throwing tube could cover twelve men and the flame was so sticky that no one could resist it. This was the weapon that the Muslims feared most.' Yet despite possessing this secret weapon, the Byzantines never really took to the

Black Sea. Largely surrounded by barbarians, it was an alien world not to be trusted.

Crossing the Continent

The collapse of the unified Roman Empire in the fifth century AD in the face of the Germanic folk movements and the consequent resettlement of much of Europe caused a massive disruption to the long-established communication networks that had bound much of the continent together for centuries. Perhaps the most far-reaching of the changes was the severing of communications by the intrusion of a human wedge, variously composed of Avars, Bulgars and Slavs, extending down through the Balkans and into Greece. This obstructed the Danube corridor between east and west and progressively closed other east–west routes. The old Via Egnatia, which ran from the Adriatic coast through the mountains and via Thessalonica to Constantinople, was also to suffer at the end of the sixth century. Finally, the southern route, by sea along the Gulf of Patras and over land through Corinth to join either the land or sea route to Constantinople, had withered and died by the middle of the seventh century. The safest route between Rome and Constantinople was now by sea via Carthage.

In the west the growth of the Frankish kingdom created new demands. To begin with the old Rhône route continued to provide the link with the Mediterranean world, which was greatly strengthened when the Franks occupied Arles and royal customs stations were established at Marseille and Fos-sur-Mer. From the Rhône and Saône it was an easy journey to the Rhine valley, which remained a major corridor of communication as well as providing access to other parts of the Frankish domain. But by the end of the seventh century the Rhône had lost its significance in competition with new transalpine routes linking the Po valley with the Rhine corridor. This readjustment, which was facilitated by the friendly relations developing between the Frankish royal house and kingdom of Lombardy in the early eighth century, had a number of effects. Since it replaced the river barge of the Rhône with the pack animal, it meant the decline of low-value, high-bulk trade with the Mediterranean. It also encouraged the development of hitherto insignificant places along the route, places like St Gall overlooking Lake Constantine. More significantly, it contributed to the growth of Venice after the mid-eighth century, helping to revitalize the Adriatic seaways. In 775, to encourage the development of trade with the Adriatic, the Franks exempted Italy from tolls on goods bound for the market of St Denys.

It was probably during the seventh century that the transpeninsular route between the Golfe du Lion and the Garonne–Gironde linking to the Atlantic

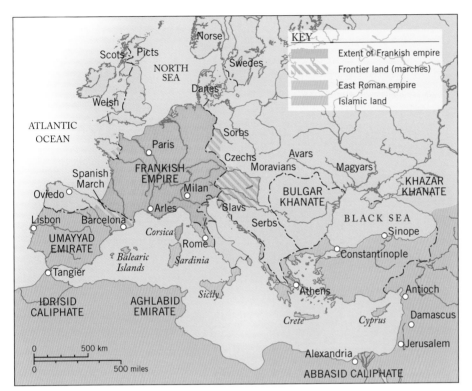

12.24 The new face of Europe emerging in AD 800. The two principal power blocks, the Frankish Empire in the west and the Eastern Roman Empire in the east, take the impact of the expanding Islamic world.

began to be re-established. The appearance of E-ware pottery from north of the Gironde estuary further north along the Atlantic seaways may be a reflection of this, though Arab raids from Spain in the first half of the eighth century are likely to have been disruptive.

To the north the Frankish Empire had access to many trading axes. The links with Britain, as we have seen, used the sea routes from the estuaries of the Seine, Somme, Canche and Rhine linking to markets at Rouen and St Denys, Amiens, Quentovic and Dorestad, and Cologne. From the Rhine mouth it was also possible to access the Scandinavian domain through markets at Ribe and Haithabu on the Jutish peninsula. Haithabu was founded by the Danish king in 808 to provide a market commanding the North Sea–Baltic route. Clearly Denmark occupied a crucial position between the Frankish kingdom and the rich resources of the Baltic. With the capture of Dorestad in c.680 the Franks began to take a serious interest in the north and from the eighth century Scandinavian traders were regularly visiting Dorestad. While many may have come by sea, it is likely that direct overland routes were now being opened up to the Baltic. At about this time a Frankish cleric, travelling northwards through Frisia, encountered a group of Northmen who 'knew the route and the harbours of the sea and the rivers that flowed into it'. They

443

sound very much like traders. Attracted by the lure of the north, the Frankish armies fought their way across Saxony in the last decades of the eighth century, reaching the Danish border in 804. By now, however, the Danes were beginning to flex their muscles and in 810 a large force of Northmen sailed down the Frisian coast, attacking as they went. A new chapter in European history had opened.

Meanwhile, in the east, Byzantium had begun to intensify trading links across eastern Europe from the Black Sea to the Baltic using the great rivers. We know little about the precise routes or even who articulated the trade but the appearance of eastern goods, and Byzantine gold coins, in quantity in the Baltic region from the fifth century AD is sufficient to show the intensity of the contact. While the process of transportation may well have involved middlemen it is quite possible that Northmen were themselves taking the initiative by exploring the two major routes, via the Vistula and Dnestr and the Dvina and Dnepr, as a prelude to their remarkable entrepreneurial activities in the tenth century.

By 800, then, Europe was beginning to become reconnected but the presence of the Arabs, from Iberia to the borders of Anatolia, introduced an entirely new imperative. Their penchant for slaves created an insatiable market which the European polities were eager to satisfy. The second half of the eighth century was a time of reinvigoration and reorientation.

CHAPTER THIRTEEN

Europe Rebalanced: AD 800–1000

On Christmas Day AD 800 in Rome, Charlemagne, king of the Franks and Lombards, was crowned *imperator et augustus* by Pope Leo III. It was an act of great symbolism designed to legitimize Charlemagne's claim to be the natural heir of old Rome – of the Latin-speaking, Christian West – an act not without its political dangers since it was done without the approval of the Byzantine emperor, who might have been expected to have views on the matter. The Byzantine rulers regarded themselves as the legitimate emperors of the Roman Empire and now the Frankish usurper was challenging their authority. It took twelve years of confrontation and bargaining before a compromise could be reached. Charlemagne was recognized as 'emperor' by Constantinople but not as *Roman* emperor. Henceforth it was publicly accepted that there were two empires which could work together against common enemies, but only one – Byzantium – was 'Roman'.

Born in 742, Charlemagne had succeeded to the Frankish throne in 768, at first sharing it jointly with his brother. His reign was characterized by a frenetic, restless energy that saw him involved in incessant campaigns along the frontiers of the empire he had inherited. In Saxony a succession of hard-fought campaigns between 772 and 803 extended his authority to the Elbe; in central Europe he fought against the Avars, absorbing Transdanubia to the banks of the Danube; Lombardy and the whole of northern Italy were taken over as far as a boundary well to the south of Rome; and in the Spanish Marches significant territories were wrested from the Muslims in a series of engagements between 778 and 806. By the end of Charlemagne's reign most of Europe west of the Elbe had been brought together under Frankish rule. Although Britain and much of Iberia were beyond his authority he had, in reality, recreated the Western Roman Empire.

Unlike the Eastern Roman Empire of Byzantium where the thread of continuity was evident, creating an inward-looking, self-congratulatory ethos, the Western Frankish Empire had been invigorated by a long interlude of Germanization. What emerged was fresh, energetic and outward-looking. The Frankish Empire, created by the Carolingian rulers, was both an end and

445

13.1 The empire of
Charlemagne AD 768–814
(above) and the division of
the Carolingian Empire in
AD 843 following the death
of Charlemagne (below).

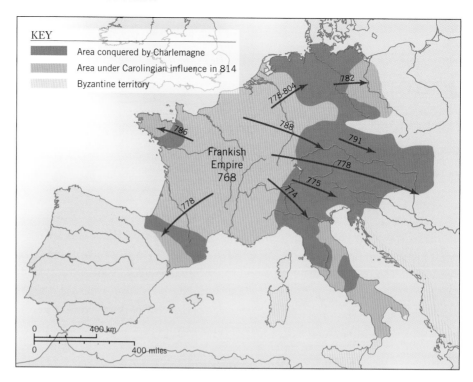

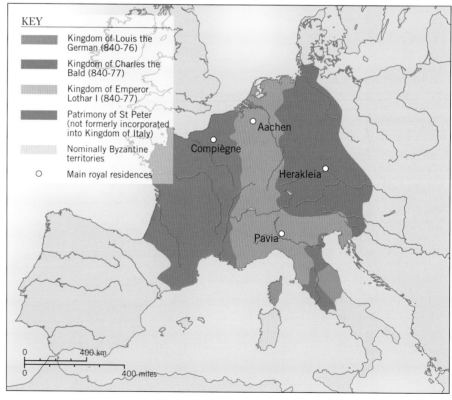

a beginning: it marked the culmination of a deeply held desire to re-establish the Roman west – hence Charlemagne's assumption of the title of *imperator et augustus* – but its subdivision in the ninth and tenth centuries gave rise to new states upon which the foundations of modern Europe were to be based. It is no exaggeration to claim that western civilization was nurtured in the ashes of Charlemagne's ambitions.

Charlemagne died in 814, leaving the empire in the hands of his sole surviving son, Louis, who managed to maintain some semblance of unity. But in 843 the empire was formally divided between Louis's three sons and over the next forty years there were further divisions, amalgamations and readjustments as successive dynasties bickered and bargained. By the last decade of the ninth century the old empire had separated into three large kingdoms – those of France, Germany and Italy – with the smaller kingdoms of Burgundy and Provence ruled by minor nobility. Peripheral regions – Brittany, the Basque country and the county of Barcelona – had once more become independent territories. The annexation of Italy by the kingdom of Germania between 951 and 961 created a new empire stretching from the North Sea and the Baltic to the Mediterranean. It was to survive largely intact for the next four hundred years. The map of western Europe was now beginning to take on a familiar appearance.

The Byzantine Empire changed surprisingly little in the period 800–1100. Unlike its two great neighbours – the Frankish Empire in the west and the Abbasid Caliphate in the east – Byzantium remained territorially compact. Moreover, the stability of its rule did not depend on dynastic continuity, nor was it driven into aggressive wars by an aristocracy bent on personal gain. The Byzantine apparatus of government was sturdy and well tried, while the co-location of centralized bureaucracy and religious authority at Constantinople meant that the entire empire, in all its manifestations, looked to a single centre for guidance and leadership.

The other great advantage enjoyed by the Byzantine Empire was the considerable length of its coastlines and the relative shortness of its land frontiers. Coasts were easier to defend and encouraged trade and exchange, while land frontiers required concentrations of troops that were expensive to maintain. The border was to some extent reduced by the agreement, reached in 812, to recognize Charlemagne as 'emperor' and thus as an equal. This brought to an end hostilities in Italy and the Adriatic. But Islam still posed a problem. It was no longer a Muslim priority to conquer Constantinople, but the Abbasid Caliphate, now based in Baghdad, actively promoted a *jihād* against the Byzantine Empire, encouraging the emirs of Syria to mount annual raids against the Asia Minor frontier. In 823 a group of political exiles from Muslim Spain captured Crete and established an emirate, while in 827 the Aghlabid Emirate in Tunisia began the conquest of Sicily. The potential loss of the two large Mediterranean islands was

447

13.2 *Opposite, above:* Detail from the Skylitzes *Chronicle* showing Arab invaders attacking and capturing the town of Taormina in Sicily.

a severe blow to Byzantine maritime commerce. However, the last Byzantine enclave on Sicily was not given up until 965, by which time the recovery of Crete, in 961, and Cyprus, in 965, had provided some compensation.

Equally troublesome neighbours were the Bulgars, with whom the Byzantines shared a long border running across the Balkans along the Hebros and Maritza valleys. The frontier was disconcertingly close to Constantinople – barely three days' march away. In the century and a half that the Bulgars had inhabited the Balkans they had grown into a formidable power. The immigrant Turkic nomads formed a warlike elite while the indigenous Slav continued to serve as a peasantry, providing a stable base that underpinned the activities of the aristocracy who were fast taking on the sophistication and the aspirations of their neighbours. The adoption of Christianity by Khan Boris in 865 was an inevitable consequence of this acculturation. Yet relations remained strained throughout the ninth and tenth centuries, episodes of outright aggression alternating with periods of uneasy peace. The stand-off came to an end at the end of the tenth century when the Byzantine emperor Basil II (976–1025) finally conquered Bulgaria, extending the empire's frontier once more to the Danube. In doing so, Basil earned himself the soubriquet 'the Bulgar-slayer'.

13.3 *Opposite, below:* The Byzantine Empire in the mid-eleventh century.

By 1000 Byzantium was still the compact state it had been two centuries earlier but on all sides it had gained territory: in the Balkans, the Crimea, the east and in the Mediterranean. The frontiers were stable and the old overland route between the Adriatic and the Aegean was once more operative. While the empire of the Franks and the Abbasid Caliphate had begun to fragment, Byzantium remained intact.

The spread of Islam across the Near East, along the coast of North Africa and throughout Iberia in the late seventh and early eighth centuries had created a vast territory unified under the Umayyad caliphs. But this unity was not to last: religious conflict arising from the Shiite–Sunni split, tribal feudings and local discontents combined to create instability and outright conflict. Rebellions in 747 and 749 led to the rise of the Sunni Abbasid family, who became caliphs in 750 after massacring most of the leaders of the Umayyad dynasty. A few of the latter had managed to flee to the west, however, to establish a breakaway Umayyad Emirate in Iberia, thus setting in train the political fragmentation of the Arab world. In 789 the Shiite Idrisid emirs, living in the Maghrib (the extreme western region of North Africa), broke away to set up a caliphate of their own and in 800 the Aghlabid emirs of Ifriqiya (Tunisia) claimed independence. The Abbasid Caliphate managed to retain its hold over the rest of the Muslim world until 868 when Libya, Egypt and Palestine became a separate province under the Tulunid emirs.

The tenth century saw further readjustments. The Abbasids reconquered Palestine and Egypt in 905 and held the region for nearly a decade but a new

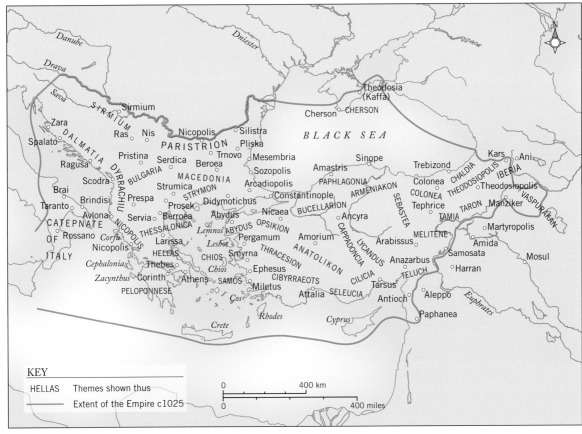

dynasty – the Fatimids – took power in Ifriqiya (Tunisia) in 909 and in 914 began to extend their control eastwards. By 1000 their caliphate included the whole of the Mediterranean coast from Tunisia to Syria as well as the island of Sicily. In the far west the Umayyad Caliphate of Iberia extended its authority over the Maghrib in 926 and now included the Balearics in its domains. For a while the revitalized emirate was a major force in the region but it collapsed into insignificance after a civil war broke out in 1008.

In the broad view of things the dynastic squabbles and readjustments among the Muslim rulers of the Mediterranean periphery had comparatively little effect upon the course of history. The strength of Muslim belief and the rich culture in which it was embedded created an overarching unity. To the Europeans interacting with them they were all Muslims – or Saracens – people to trade with where possible but of whom it was also necessary to be very wary.

Finally, in this brief overview, we must return to the steppe. Here, in the early decades of the ninth century, two culturally distinct nomadic peoples had established themselves, the Khazars living east of the Don and the Magyars occupying the region between the Don and the Dnestr – a territory they called Etelköz or 'the Country between Rivers'. This region, wedged between the Khazars, Byzantines, Danube Bulgars, eastern Slavs and Rus-Varangians, dominated a number of trade routes which the Magyars proceeded to oversee and protect. It was not long before bands were moving west through the Carpathians, exploring the potential of the region and becoming involved in the conflicts between the Franks and the Moravians. Later, in the war of 894–96 between the Bulgars and the Byzantines, they fought as allies of the empire. As a result of this alliance, the Bulgars encouraged the nomadic Patzinaks, who had insinuated themselves between the Khazars and the Volga Bulgars and were now eastern neighbours of the Magyars, to attack them. The threat was sufficient to encourage the entire Magyar confederacy – estimated to number about half a million people – to move westwards to settle in the Carpathian Basin among the remnant successors of so many other nomadic groups who had made a similar journey over the preceding two millennia. By 900 they were firmly established in their new homeland, their territory extending well to the west of the Danube into Transdanubia.

From here bands of fast-moving horsemen proceeded to raid the west, attacking Brenta in the Po valley in 899, Bavaria in 900, Saxony in 906 and in 914 cutting their way across northern Italy to ravage Burgundy and Provence. After this initial onslaught raids became increasingly frequent. At first western Europe was defenceless and resorted to buying off the raiders with rich gifts, but the turning point came in 933 when a Magyar force was defeated at Merseburg. Thereafter the western states stiffened their resistance until at Lechfeld, near Augsburg, in 955, a united German force smashed the Magyar

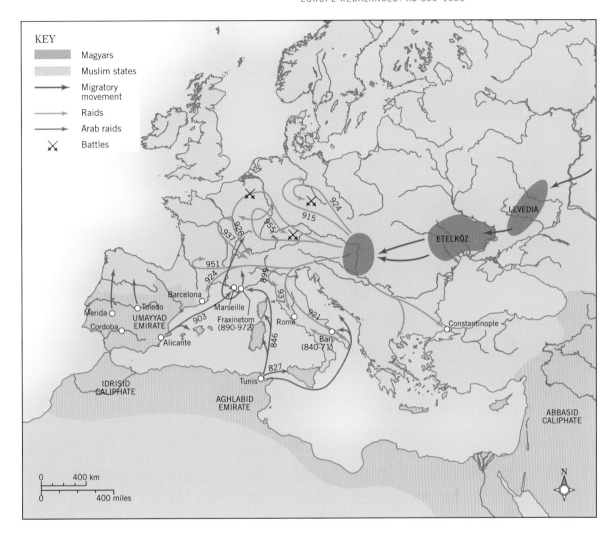

army. Raids on western Europe stopped but a few further incursions were made into the Balkans until 970 when the Magyar raids ceased altogether. By this time the Magyars were settling down to a more sedentary existence and had begun to adopt Christianity. By the beginning of the eleventh century Hungary had become an established state in the new Europe.

To complete the history so briefly outlined here we must introduce the Northmen – raiders, traders and settlers from Denmark, Norway and Sweden – who set out from their homelands on epic voyages, south-westwards along the Atlantic seaways and into the western Mediterranean, and eastwards via the great rivers to the Black Sea, the Caspian and beyond. Some took a more westerly route across the north Atlantic, settling in Iceland, Greenland and Newfoundland. So remarkable is the phenomenon of the Northmen, and so embracing of the whole of Europe, that we will consider it in greater detail later.

13.4 Muslims and Magyars and their impact on Europe in the ninth and tenth centuries AD.

451

Mare nostrum: Whose Sea?

The coastline of the Mediterranean was now shared by the three great powers – the Frankish Empire, the Byzantine Empire and the Muslim caliphates – but not in equal measure. The Muslim coast was by far the longest but a significant proportion was barren and devoid of useful ports. The Byzantine coast was shorter, but with its convoluted line, its many islands and abundance of long-established ports dating back to Greek times, it had the potential for being more maritime-active. The Frankish littoral was the shortest but was well served by the maritime entrepreneurs resident in the independent city-states of Venice, Naples and Amalfi.

The political geography of the Mediterranean neatly divided the sea into a northern, Christian half and a southern, Islamic half, the two having a highly ambivalent attitude to each other. They were in theory at war since the Islamic states were required by their faith to conquer and convert the infidel, but in practice both sides benefited from a precarious trading relationship. Looking back on the situation in the ninth century, the Arab historian Ibn Khaldun would claim that 'the Muslims gained control over the whole Mediterranean. Their power and domination over it was vast. The Christian nations could do nothing against the Muslim fleets anywhere in the Mediterranean. All the time the Muslims rode its waves for conquest.' While one might suspect an element of exaggeration here, events showed that throughout the ninth century the Muslim fleets had the initiative and were still active, and often successful, in the tenth century, even in the face of stiffened Byzantine and Frankish resistance and the divisive inter-Muslim rivalry between the Umayyads of Iberia and the Fatimids of North Africa.

The history of raiding and of naval engagements is rich in detail but cannot be treated fully here – at best we can select a few representative events. In the west Mediterranean Muslim activity, mainly emanating from al-Andalus, focused on the main islands: the Balearics, Corsica and Sardinia. The Balearics suffered a spate of raids in 798 and in 849 were subjugated by a fleet of three hundred ships although they were not finally conquered until 902–03. The more distant islands of Corsica and Sardinia proved to be a more difficult prize to claim, both by virtue of their size and by their proximity to the Frankish mainland. In 806 the king of Italy sent a fleet to drive away Andalusians who had raided the island of Corsica. This was joined in the following year by a naval force sent by Charlemagne. The Muslims retaliated in 810 by sending an even larger fleet and managed to take control of most of the island as well as making gains in Sardinia. Three years later a Muslim fleet returning from Corsica was intercepted and eight ships captured. The episode resulted in revenge attacks against Sardinia and the mainland cities of Civitavecchia and

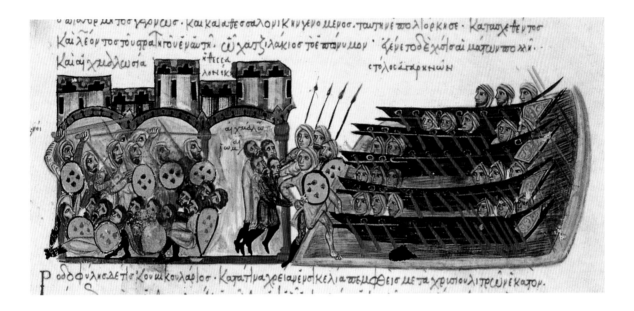

13.5 A detail from the Skylitzes *Chronicle* showing the attack on Thessalonica by a Muslim force led by Leo of Tripoli in AD 904.

Nice. The Aghlabid Emirate of Ifriqiya (Tunisia) also took a close interest in the west Mediterranean islands. In 812–13 Corsica, Sardinia, Lampedusa and Ischia were raided. Italian merchant ships returning from Sardinia were captured in 820 and the following year there were further raids on Sardinia.

Nor was France itself safe from Muslim raiders. The Andalusian attack on Nice in 813 had shown that rich pickings were to be had in the Provençal landscape. Marseille was attacked in 838 and in 842 and 850 Arles became a target. To facilitate further raids in this attractive region a permanent Muslim base was set up in the Camargue in the 860s. Some thirty years later another band of raiders landed at St-Tropez and established themselves in a nearby hilltop fortification from where they were able to mount attacks deep into Frankish territory. Marseille was threatened and raids persisted along the Rhône valley as far north as Vienne and even to the famous abbey of St Gall in Switzerland. The enclave was not finally expelled until 972.

In the central Mediterranean Sicily presented an obvious target for Muslim expansion. The conquest of the island began with a raid launched by the Aghlabids in 827 to which the Frankish Empire responded with some vigour. Pisa and Luni made a retaliatory raid on Bône on the North African coast while the governor of Corsica led an expedition to Tunisia, raiding the coast not far from the city of Tunis. But the conquest of Sicily was not deflected and town after town fell to the Muslims. Syracuse was taken in 878 and the last Byzantine stronghold, Taormina, capitulated in 902. Meanwhile Muslim attention had turned to the Italian mainland. Brindisi and Taranto were captured in 838 and 839, and in the following year a Venetian fleet sent to

453

13.6 Reconstructed drawing of a lateen rigged ship of the eleventh century AD. From a painted plate, probably of Tunisian origin now set in the wall of the church of S. Pietro in Grado, near Pisa, Italy.

relieve Taranto was defeated. In 841 Bari fell and became the capital of the emirate, providing a convenient base from which a spate of raids could be mounted along the Tyrrhenian and Adriatic coasts of Italy. Ancona was sacked in 842 and St Peter's in Rome was pillaged in 846. The situation in Italy became increasingly unstable as Muslim enclaves established themselves in coastal regions. In the Adriatic Dubrovnik was besieged in 866 but the town was relieved by Venetian intervention. In 871–72 it was the turn of Salerno and, in 875, Trieste.

To counter the growing threat, the Frankish Empire mounted several expeditions, some in alliance with the Byzantines. Bari was finally retaken in 871 and a few years later became the Byzantine capital in southern Italy. Sicily, however, remained firmly in the hands of the Muslims until the middle of the eleventh century, when the Normans began their colonization of the island.

In the east Mediterranean one of the first acts of the Muslims was to enforce the neutrality of the island of Cyprus which lay just off the coast of Asia Minor, close to the point where the land frontier between the caliphate and the empire had been established. Attention then turned to the other large islands, Rhodes and Crete, which both suffered raids early in the ninth century. Crete was strategically the most important of the islands since it provided ease of access to the Aegean and the rich lands around. It was annexed between 824 and 827 by renegades from al-Andalus and thereafter served as a base for attacks against the Aegean lands. One of the earliest encounters took place in 839 in the northern Aegean, near the island of Thassos, when a Byzantine fleet was defeated. The response of the Byzantine world was decisive. In 840–42 a Muslim force that had landed and was pillaging the countryside was destroyed. A decade later the empire took pre-emptive action when, in 853, the Byzantine fleet attacked the Egyptian port of Damietta where weapons were being stockpiled for transit to Crete. About 860 there are records of Muslim attacks against islands in the Cyclades and ships had now reached the Sea of Marmara. Later, in 872, Dalmatia suffered a seaborne attack but a squadron of Muslim ships, which had been raiding in the Ionian Sea, was destroyed by a Byzantine fleet in the Gulf of Corinth in 879.

Ports on the Muslim-held mainland harboured naval squadrons always ready to attack. Tarsus, on the south-eastern coast of Asia Minor, was an important naval base throughout the late ninth and tenth centuries and its ships were frequently in conflict with the Byzantines. In one engagement in 898 a Byzantine naval force was soundly beaten: its ships were captured and three thousand seamen were beheaded. There followed wide-ranging attacks on the Aegean as far north as Abydos and Thessalonica, sparking retaliatory action on Crete and in the Levant. Hostilities lasted until the 930s.

It will be clear from this brief but action-packed survey that the Muslim

13.7 Byzantine boat-building detailed on a ninth-century manuscript, the *Sacra Parallela*, illustrating the Life of Solomon.

caliphates and emirates maintained an aggressive attitude towards their Christian neighbours throughout the ninth and most of the tenth century. They regarded piracy, raiding and land-taking in the Mediterranean as a legitimate, and indeed God-directed, pursuit. The Frankish and Byzantine empires vigorously defended their own territories but seldom took the initiative by attacking Muslim-held lands. Ibn Khaldun's claim regarding the Mediterranean that 'All the time the Muslims rode its waves for conquest' seems entirely justified but to say, as he did, that the Christians could do nothing about it was overstating the case.

The Byzantine attitude to the sea was one of limited interest. Their naval capability was never fully developed nor was the navy considered to be a prestigious enterprise. There are several reasons for this, perhaps the most important being that the land frontiers to east and west were of prime concern: it was here that prowess could be won. Although the Muslims used the sea to attack Byzantium from time to time, the threat was sporadic and relatively insignificant compared with the continuous, and sometimes intensive, activities along the land frontiers. In the Mediterranean, the Muslim squadrons were a disincentive to maritime trade. Another factor was the high level of productivity within the Byzantine Empire. The empire was virtually self-sufficient, providing food and basic raw materials in surplus from within its own borders. Its only other needs were for spices, which came from the east via the overland caravan routes, and furs from the north by way of the Black Sea. Slaves could be got from the northern Pontic ports or from the European land frontiers by capture or purchase. Given the comparative simplicity of the empire's 'global' economy, the need for an extensive 'commercial' fleet was slight, and in developing links with the Frankish Empire the Byzantines were content to use middlemen, in particular the independent trading state of Venice which dominated the crucial maritime interface between the two Christian empires. The spectacular growth of Venice is in no small part the result of this economic interaction.

Another important interface was the Tyrrhenian coast of Campania, which at the time lay within the province of Benevento – a no-man's-land between the Frankish Empire, extending throughout northern Italy and the Byzantine Empire, and occupying the extreme south of the peninsula. The two principal trading ports to emerge on this coast were Naples and Amalfi. They articulated trade not only between the two empires but with the Muslim world as well. How extensive the maritime network of the Campanian sea cities was is difficult to judge but there is reasonable evidence to suggest that their interests extended as far north as Tuscany and Corsica and as far south as the African coast. The prime commodity traded was slaves. Captives acquired from the various conflict zones of Europe were collected together in centres such as Rome, where they could be bought and transported to the Italian ports for trans-shipment to Muslim markets in Sicily and Africa. Venturing into Muslim-dominated waters no doubt involved risks but protocols protected traders. An African jurist, Ibn Sahnun, writing in the early ninth century, gives a precise account of the ground rules:

> As to the Christian ships which come, whether they are far from port or nearby, it is not permitted to capture them, if they are merchants known for their commercial relations with the Muslims, unless they are attacked in their home country and while they are heading toward a country other than the countries of Islam.

While there seems to be some scope for misunderstanding here, the profits of the slave trade will have made the risks worthwhile.

Another interface was that between Muslim Iberia and the Frankish Empire. The land boundary to the south of the Pyrenees was highly contested and is unlikely to have been conducive to uncontrolled trade, but the sea route along the Levantine coast to the Golfe du Lion provided a ready means of access between the two polities, with ample ports of call en route where toll stations had been set up. Little is known of the coastal trade but several wrecks of Muslim origin have been found off the southern coast of France in the vicinity of Cannes, Marseille and St-Tropez, all dating to the tenth century. Their cargoes included amphorae, presumably containing oil, various other types of storage jar, millstones, bronze ingots, asphalt, glass vessels and Cordovan lamps. These were probably wrecks of Spanish merchant vessels intent on trading with the Frankish Empire, but it remains a possibility that some may have been ships providing for the Muslim enclaves established near St-Tropez and in the Camargue.

In spite of tensions along the land border, overland trading was by no means impossible. Indeed, we know of a Jewish trader named Abraham who, though serving as a court merchant for the Frankish king, actually lived in Saragossa on the Muslim side of the border. Saragossa was clearly an important trading centre and in 851 we hear of cohorts of merchants travelling to the town from the east Frankish kingdom. The evidence is fragmentary in the extreme but, taken together, it hints at a well-organized and lively overland exchange.

There can be no doubt that the Mediterranean of the ninth and tenth centuries was a divided sea – a difficult and dangerous place where piracy and raiding were endemic. But trade and profit are strong motivators. Franks traded with Byzantines and Christians traded with Muslims, the prime currencies being slaves and gold. The networks, insofar as we can judge, were short-haul, relying on local knowledge and established protocols that allowed

457

potential enemies to meet and trade for mutual benefit. But with the appearance of the maritime city-states of Naples, Amalfi and Venice, which served as specialist articulators, we are at the beginning of a new world that will see the emergence of Mediterranean-wide networks to rival those of the old Roman Empire. Soon the maritime empires of Venice, Genoa and Pisa will become a familiar part of the ocean's texture.

The Northmen: At Home

In 793 the unsuspecting monks living in the seclusion of the monastery of St Cuthbert on the island of Lindisfarne were attacked without warning by raiders coming from the sea. The Northumbrian cleric Alcuin, living in the court of Charlemagne, writes despairingly of the event:

> Never before has such terror appeared in Britain as we have now suffered from a pagan race, nor was it thought that such an inroad from the sea could be made. Behold, the church of St Cuthbert spotted with the blood of the priests of God, despoiled of all its ornaments; a place more venerable than all in Britain is given as prey to pagan people.

The next year another Northumbrian monastery, most probably Jarrow, suffered a similar fate. In 795 it was the turn of west-coast monasteries on the islands of Skye, Iona and Rathlin to succumb. But the threat from the Northerners, attacking by sea, was not limited to the northern British coasts. Three boatloads of Norwegians had landed on the Dorset coast around 790, and in 792 there was consternation in Kent which resulted in the local churches contributing to a levy to pay for defences against pagan raiders coming from the sea. In 799 the Frankish monastery of St Philibert on Noirmoutier, in the Loire estuary, was pillaged, and the next year we hear of Charlemagne organizing defences along the coast north of the Seine estuary against pirates who 'infest the Gallic sea'. Clearly the events of the last decade of the eighth century were something quite new and unexpected. So began what recent historians refer to as the 'Viking' raids.

'Viking' is a convenient term that came to prominence in the nineteenth century and refers to people whom contemporaries called Northmen or Norsemen. Its derivation is unclear – it could come from the Scandinavian word *vic* meaning 'inlet' or from Viken, the name of the land flanking Oslo Fjord. Another possibility is that *vik* refers to locations where trade was carried out, cognate with the English *wic*, as in Hamwic (Southampton) or Ipswich. The Northmen came from various regions of Scandinavia. Those who impacted on the communities of Atlantic Europe were Danes and Norwegians who came first to raid and later to settle. In their settlement phase the Danes concentrated on the east of England while the Norwegians settled in the Orkneys and Shetland, the Faroes, Iceland and Greenland. Swedes, mainly from eastern Sweden around Lake Mälaren, looked to the east, to the southern and eastern Baltic and to the great rivers of eastern Europe which provided them with access to Russia, the Black Sea and beyond. The period of 'folk wandering' that began in the last decade of the eighth century and ended in the eleventh century, by which time most of the groups had been converted to Christianity, saw the Northmen embrace the western world from the Mediterranean to Iceland and from the Caspian Sea to Newfoundland. Theirs is a remarkable story.

Why the raids began and generated such momentum is a complex issue. There was no single cause but rather a series of factors that interacted and fed each other. Beneath it all lay deep-seated social changes within Scandinavian society which during the seventh and eighth centuries had undergone an increased hierarchization with the emergence of chieftains exercising power over larger and larger regions. It was during the 'Viking Age' that the territories of Denmark, Norway and Sweden emerged as separate unified countries with single rulers. In Denmark the process of centralization probably began early in the eighth century with the foundation of the trading town of Ribe and the digging of a massive defensive earthwork, the Danevirke, across the neck of the Jutland peninsula. It is at about this time that the high king, Agantyr, is mentioned by a visiting bishop from Utrecht. A century or so later, the Danish king Godfred put up a spirited resistance to Charlemagne's advance through Saxony. At one stage he 'came with a fleet and with all the cavalry of his kingdom to Schleswig on the Danish-Saxon border' to confront Charlemagne. It was Godfred who renovated the Danevirke and established a new town at Hedeby on the Baltic coast of Jutland at the mouth of the Schlei, transferring traders there from the trading centre of Reric which he had destroyed. Clearly he was a powerful ruler, capable of organizing the defences and economic wellbeing of his kingdom and of confronting the Frankish Empire.

In Norway the topography of the country with its long, heavily convoluted coastline backed by high mountains made political unity difficult but the royal burial sites at Borre and Oseberg in the Vestfold region, on the west side of Oslo Fjord, are clear evidence of a powerful ruling dynasty in the eighth and ninth centuries. In the 880s King Harald Finehair had extended the kingdom to include much of south-west Norway but in doing so he created social tensions that may well have led to the increased rate of migration to Scotland and Iceland in the late ninth century.

In Sweden powerful leaders had already emerged in the preceding Vendel period, vividly demonstrated by their rich burial mounds in the Uppland region of eastern Sweden. Kings are mentioned from time to time in the ninth century but it was only in the tenth century that the royal house managed to establish its authority from coast to coast across the whole of central Sweden.

The development of states subject to kings, which took place in the ninth and tenth centuries, cannot have failed to create inner tensions and social dislocation. At such a time there would inevitably have been much mobility, particularly among young men with aspirations who might choose to seek their fortunes in new worlds. Raiding to increase wealth and status would have been an immediate response and, as the potentials of the wider world became known, migration to create new settlements overseas would have followed.

Another factor encouraging mobility was the very rapid growth in trade and the development of international markets which, as we have seen, were well under way in the seventh century. The expansion of the Frankish Empire and the stabilization of the English kingdoms were an added spur to trade. The north had much to offer to the luxury markets of the south. Most important were high-quality furs from the Arctic regions as well as walrus ivory, eiderdown and amber. These commodities would be gathered together at the northern markets – Kaupang on Oslo Fjord, Birka on Lake Mälar, Paviken on Gotland and Staraya Ladoga near Lake Ladoga – and trans-shipped to southern markets like Ribe and Hedeby on Jutland and Wolin and Truso on the southern Baltic coast, for onward transportation overland to the Frankish Empire or by sea to the ports of eastern England. The controllers of the Nordic trade could become rich and powerful. For those less fortunate piracy offered an attractive option, as did the possibility of opening up new markets in distant lands like Ireland.

The Baltic, then, acted as an interface between a productive north – the lands of the Saami, the Finns and the Balts – and the consuming south. A fascinating insight into the working of the system is provided by the account given by Ottar, a member of the Norwegian elite, who visited the English king Alfred in the middle of the ninth century. From his home base in the north of Norway Ottar hunted walrus for their valuable tusks and received from the neighbouring Saami an annual tribute consisting of:

> the skins of beasts, the feathers of birds, whale-bone, and ships' ropes made from walrus hide and seal skin. Each pays according to his rank. The highest in rank has to pay fifteen marten skins, five reindeer skins, one bearskin, and ten measures of feathers, and a jacket of bearskin or otter skin, and two ships' ropes. Each must be sixty ells long, one made from walrus hide, the other from seal.

The tribute he collected, together with the gains of his own hunting expeditions, was taken to the southern markets to sell.

13.8 Coin minted in the Danish port of Hedeby in the ninth century AD illustrating Nordic sailing ships.

Crucial to the Nordic trading economy was efficient transport by sea. In the early part of the first millennium AD there seem to have been two different traditions of shipbuilding in operation – one in the North Sea, the other in the Baltic. In the North Sea the sail was regularly used and indeed can be traced back to the first century BC, if not earlier. Locally built sailing ships continued to be constructed with square rigged sails throughout the Roman period, and a text of the late fifth century refers to Saxon raiders descending on the coasts of Gaul in their sailing vessels. In the Baltic ships propelled only by oars seem to have been the norm until as late as the seventh century, when depictions of sailing ships first appear carved on the picture stones of Gotland. By the early ninth century the coins issued by the trading port of Hedeby regularly feature vessels with sails, and an actual example of a sailing ship with mast intact has been found as part of a kingly burial at Oseberg on the west side of Oslo Fjord dating to about 820. The Oseberg ship also had provision for rowers but, unlike earlier vessels, which had rowlocks on the gunwale, separate oar ports were provided low down so that the oars, when in use, could strike the water at a more effective angle. When under sail the oars would be shipped and the oar ports closed. The Oseberg vessel, some 20 m (66 ft) long and 5.2 m (17 ft) in the beam, was a magnificent construction with a

461

13.9 The Oseberg ship, found near Oslo, Norway, at the time of its excavation. It was used for the burial of a high-status female in the ninth century AD. Its exceptional preservation is the result of its having been sealed beneath a mound of clay.

high, curving stem and stern. It would have made a fine ship of state but it was also highly versatile, able to carry cargo or raiders at will. The development of such vessels freed the Northmen from the constrictions of the Baltic, opening the Atlantic to those adventurous enough to accept the challenge.

Rapid social change, a steady increase in population and the intensification of trade led to a restlessness and sense of dislocation. The skill of the shipbuilder, honed over the millennia, provided the technology. So it was that in the last decade of the eighth century the Northmen burst on an unsuspecting world.

To Atlantic Europe and the Mediterranean

The attack on Lindisfarne in 793 sent shock waves through the western world, but it was by no means the first confrontation that the British Isles had had with the Northmen. The archaeological evidence suggests that contacts between Norway and Orkney were operative in the seventh century. The two

462

13.10 The raids and expeditions of the Norwegian and Danish Vikings in the first half of the ninth century AD.

KEY

→ Viking raid 793-865

→ Campaign led by Bjorn Ironside
and Hastein, 859-862

Monastery or settlement raided by Vikings

● 793-833

◉ 834-850

○ 851-865

◼ Arab fortification

areas are after all close neighbours: from the west-facing coast of Norway it takes no more than two days sailing the latitude to cross the 288 km (180 miles) of sea to the Orkneys or Shetlands. Those living in the constricted fjords of Norway would have found land in plenty in the Northern Isles. It is quite possible that the raiders who pillaged the coasts of Britain and Ireland in the late seventh and eighth centuries included among their number men whose

463

families were already settled in the Northern and Western Isles. Just such a picture is presented in the twelfth-century Orkneyinga Saga which records the lifestyle of one of Orkney's residents, Svein Asleifarson, in some bygone age:

> In the spring he had more than enough to occupy him, with a great deal of seed to sow which he saw to carefully himself. Then when the job was done, he would go off plundering in the Hebrides and in Ireland on what he called his 'spring trip', then back home just after midsummer where he stayed till the corn fields had been reaped and the grain was safely in. After that he would go off raiding again, and never come back till the first month of winter was ended. This he used to call his autumn trip.

For Svein, and no doubt many Northmen, raiding was entirely compatible with good husbandry so long as it fitted into the agricultural calendar, but for others, particularly in the later ninth century, there were different imperatives that required longer absences from home and in some cases the settlement of foreign territories.

13.11 An ivory chessman from the Isle of Lewis in the Outer Hebrides. The piece is carved to represent the popular image of a Viking raider.

Norwegians were responsible for the first attacks on the Northumbrian and Scottish monasteries and for the raiding and initial settlement of Ireland, while Danes concerned themselves with the southern shores of the North Sea and the English Channel. But by the middle of the ninth century Danes were contesting land held by Norwegians in Ireland – to the evident satisfaction of native Irish observers. By this time the ethnic identities of the Northmen were becoming confused.

In the first thirty years of the ninth century the raids were mostly coastal, picking off easy targets, especially monasteries established in remote places. Ireland suffered severely but for the most part the Frankish Empire got off lightly, though some raiders got as far as the west coast of France, striking between the Loire and the Garonne. The next twenty years, up to 850, saw a significant intensification of raiding and an extension along the entire Atlantic façade as far south as Andalucía. The raiders were now venturing further inland along the major rivers to pick off trading centres and towns. Dorestad, 80 km (50 miles) from the open sea, was raided three times, in 834, 835 and 836, Quentovic and Hamwic were sacked in 842, and in the previous year Vikings penetrated the Seine as far as Rouen, which was ravaged together with the abbey of St-Wandrille which they passed en route. In 843 it was the turn of Nantes on the Loire; Paris was threatened two years later. Further south, in Aquitania, in 844 raiders sailed up the Garonne to Toulouse and four years later Bordeaux fell after a siege.

The terror seemed never-ending. A monk in the monastery of Noirmoutier, writing about 860, paints a desperate picture:

> The number of ships grows: the endless stream of Vikings never
> ceases to increase. Everywhere the Christians are the victims of
> massacres, burnings, plunderings: the Vikings conquer all in their path,
> and no one resists them: they seize Bordeaux, Périgueux, Limoges,
> Angoulême and Toulouse. Angers, Tours and Orléans are annihilated
> and an innumerable fleet sails up the Seine and the evil grows in the
> whole region. Rouen is laid waste, plundered and burned: Paris, Beauvais
> and Meaux taken, Melun's strong fortress levelled to the ground,
> Chartres occupied, Evreux and Bayeux plundered, and every town
> besieged.

Perhaps the desire to see the wrath of God punishing sinners led the monk to exaggerate a little, but there can be no doubt that the situation was serious.

The raids did not stop with France. In 844 a force sailed along the Atlantic coast of Iberia, attacking several towns in Galicia and then Lisbon before making their way up the Guadalquivir to occupy, briefly, Seville. The Muslim response was rapid and decisive: the Northmen were beaten away and those captured were hanged on the city's palm trees. Two hundred Viking heads were sent to allies in Tangier as a reminder of the emir's authority.

An even more remarkable journey was made in 859 when a fleet of sixty-two vessels set out from the Loire under the joint command of Björn Ironside and Hastein – both battle-hardened warriors. They sailed along the Iberian coasts, sacking cities en route. Once through the Straits of Gibraltar, they raided the North African coast and the Balearics before finding a safe haven on an island in the Camargue, in the delta of the Rhône, from which to raid coastal and inland cities in southern France. Their ultimate aim, it seems, was to pillage Rome. Pisa was attacked but here their cognitive geography failed them. The next town to fall, which they believed to be Rome, was in reality Luni, some 300 km (187 miles) away to the north. On their return journey through the Straits of Gibraltar in 861, laden with treasure, they suffered at the hands of the Muslims but eventually managed to reach their home base on the Loire, though with the loss of two-thirds of their ships. While plunder was an evident motivation for the venture, the prowess gained from having led such a reckless expedition and returned would have been its own reward. Iberia was raided a third time, in 866, but by now the Muslims were prepared and the attack was driven off.

By the 860s things had begun to change. The English and the Franks were much better prepared too, but the Northmen were beginning to settle in the alien territories, at first wintering in well-defended locations and then gradually establishing enclaves in the river mouths at various points along the Frankish coast. In 865 a determined attempt at conquest was made when the 'great heathen army' invaded East Anglia and over the next five years established control over East Anglia, Mercia and Northumberland; only Wessex remained outside their grip. The occupied area became known as the Danelaw and in 879–80 a boundary was formally agreed with Wessex. Within the Danelaw a large immigrant Scandinavian population took over the land and began to farm it.

In the first half of the tenth century Wessex moved to conquer the Scandinavian-occupied regions of Britain – a process that led to the expulsion of the Norwegian king Erik Bloodaxe in 952. But in 980 raiding resumed, culminating in the conquest of England in 1013 and the establishment of the Danish king Knut as king of England three years later.

In Ireland the situation was different. Here the Viking settlement was patchy, concentrating on the major estuaries where trading posts could be set up. Dublin, Wexford, Waterford, Cork and Limerick were all established at this time and, judging by the archaeological evidence, these places flourished. But the situation was always turbulent, not least because of internal conflict between the Irish dynasts and the involvement of the Vikings on one side or the other. The arrival of hordes of Danes in 851–52 added further to the unrest. The first phase of Viking settlement in Ireland came to an end in 902 when '[t]he pagans [Vikings] were driven from Ireland [Dublin] . . . and they abandoned a good number of their ships, and escaped half-dead after they had been wounded and broken'. A new phase opened in 914 when a 'great sea-fleet' arrived in Waterford harbour from Brittany to winter there. More came the next year and in 917 members of the exiled Dublin dynasty returned. So it was that the Hiberno–Norse settlements were revived with Dublin as their centre. Across the remainder of the tenth century the Viking enclaves were drawn further and further into the struggle for kingship that raged throughout the island.

Within the Frankish Empire enclaves of Northmen had been allowed to settle in the areas of the river mouths in return for driving off further incursions. The most important of these was the settlement in the Lower Seine of a Danish contingent led by Rollo, a Norwegian warlord, following a battle fought at Chartres in 911. Under a treaty negotiated with the Franks Rollo was recognized as count of the district centred on Rouen. It was not long before the Scandinavian settlement had been extended to include the whole of the coastal region and its immediate hinterland as far west as the Cotentin. Cultural assimilation was rapid. The *Nor(d)manni* soon became a principality of Frankia, their domain, *Normannia*, becoming Normandy.

Another of the river-mouth settlements lay in the valley of the Lower Loire, which had been a favoured area for Viking penetration since as far back as the 840s. In 921 their right to settle was formally recognized by the Frankish authorities. From here raiding parties were sent deep into France along the Loire valley to the Seine valley and throughout Brittany, which for a brief period became a Viking domain (they were finally expelled from the peninsula and from their home base of Nantes in 937). Brittany suffered further raids from the Seine valley in the 940s and 960s, but with no lasting consequences. The impact of the Vikings on Brittany was minimal, a point underlined by the lack of Scandinavian place-names there, in stark contrast to Normandy where place-names suggest that Scandinavian settlement was dense.

Across the North Atlantic

The exploration of the north Atlantic began in the eighth century. In the atmosphere of religious fervour that gripped the Christian Irish community, monks began to embark upon hazardous sea journeys in search of remote places where their souls could be purified and they could commune with God away from the distractions of the secular world. The Faroes were the first islands to be settled and by the end of the eighth century journeys were being made to Iceland, even in midwinter. It was no doubt from the monks that the Northmen, settling on the Northern and Western Isles and in Ireland, heard of these distant places and learned that they were congenial for settlement. The Norse settlement of the Faroes began about 800 and of Iceland about sixty years later. Although many of the settlers will have sailed direct from Norway, making the journey via Shetland and the Faroes in as little as seven days, recent work on the DNA of the present Icelandic population shows that there must have been a substantial 'Celtic' component in the settler population. This is best explained by supposing that among the initial pioneers were Northmen who had settled in Ireland and had acquired Irish wives and slaves. The empty islands would have provided a welcome escape from the warfare that was endemic in Ireland in the mid-ninth century.

The first settlers set up home in Iceland in the 860s and 870s, and such was the rate of influx that within sixty years all the inhabitable land was taken. Once the exploration of the far north-west had begun it was inevitable that it should continue. According to tradition, a new overseas land – soon to be known as Greenland – was first reconnoitred by Eric the Red in the early 980s

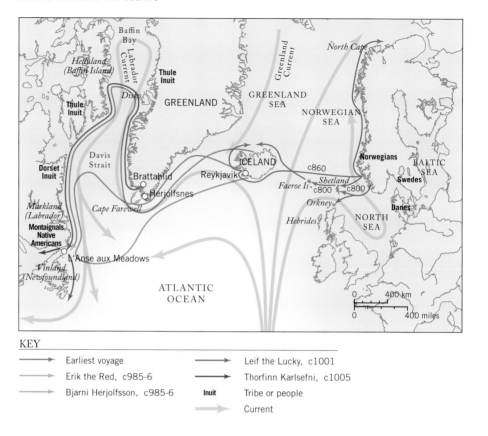

13.12 The Norwegian Vikings explored the North Atlantic in the ninth and tenth centuries AD, settling in Iceland and Greenland. Their expeditions to the Atlantic coast of America are less well known but one short-lived settlement has been found at the northern tip of Newfoundland.

KEY

→	Earliest voyage	→	Leif the Lucky, c1001
→	Erik the Red, c985-6	→	Thorfinn Karlsefni, c1005
→	Bjarni Herjolfsson, c985-6	**Inuit**	Tribe or people
		→	Current

and in 985 twenty-five ships carrying settlers set sail: fourteen survived the journey. Two colonies, totalling about three thousand people, were eventually established on the west coast, and by the early years of the eleventh century the more adventurous souls were exploring the east coast of North America. Little is known of their attempts to settle but one small community did manage to establish itself (briefly) at L'Anse-aux-Meadows at the northern extremity of Newfoundland.

Through the Forests of Europe

While geography demanded that the Danes and the Norwegians should be led to explore the west, the Swedes, facing inwards across the Baltic, were naturally drawn to the eastern shores of the sea and to the opportunities provided by the great rivers of eastern Europe. By these routes, as they were soon to discover, it was possible to gain direct access not only to the Byzantine Empire and the sumptuous markets of the Abbasid Caliphate but also to the caravan route that led directly to China. The principal route, one of the first to be developed, began directly east of central Sweden and led, via the Gulf of

468

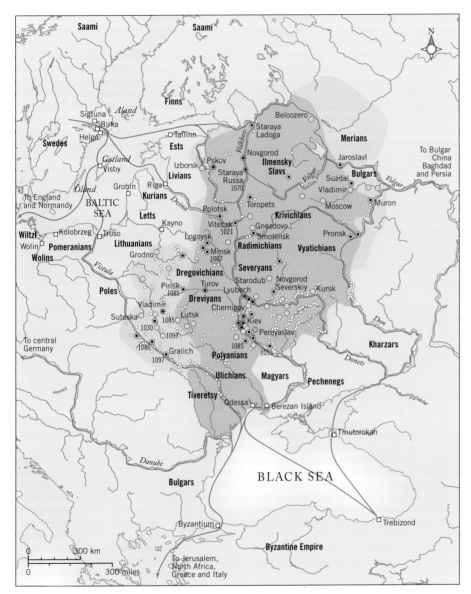

KEY

Major Viking Age settlements with
date of foundation where known

- ⬤ c900-1000
- ◕ c1000-1150
- ○ Other Viking Age settlements
  9th-11th century
- ● Excavated settlement

Bulgars Tribe or people

→ Main trade routes

Extent of the Rus state

▨ 9th-11th centuries

▨ Land gained by 12th century

13.13 The Swedish Vikings took to the great rivers of
Poland and Russia to reach the Black Sea and beyond.
The emergence of the state of Rús owes much to the Viking
activities in the region, particularly their use of the river
Dnepr as a route to the south.

Finland, to Lake Ladoga and the port of Staraya Ladoga on the Volkhov river. Here, a small market centre had begun to develop in the eighth century; by the ninth and tenth centuries it had become a major port and princely residence dominated by Scandinavian merchants and their families. From here the trade routes led south, first along the river Volkhov and then by overland portage – requiring the ships to be carried – to the Dnepr, thence direct to the Black Sea, negotiating en route a series of dangerous rapids. A rather shorter route to the Black Sea used the rivers Vistula and Dnestr.

The river network also provided access further east to the city of Bulgar at the great bend of the Volga river in the territory of the Volga Bulgars. This was a vitally important route node served by the caravan trains from the east. From Bulgar, by means of the Volga, it was also possible to reach the Caspian Sea and the markets of the Abbasid Caliphate. Other routes to the caliphate led through the territory of the Khazars. Thus, for those Scandinavians ready to face the long river journeys and arduous overland portages through the territory of the Balts and the Slavs, there were fabulous markets to be exploited. The Swedes therefore became the middlemen who articulated trade between the Baltic and Byzantium, the Abbasids, and the east.

The cross-continental trade was on such a scale that it transformed the socio-political structures of the region and led directly to the creation of the Rús state, the immediate precursor of Russia. Needless to say, there has been a long and vigorous debate about the origins of Russia and the part played by the Scandinavians in its formation. *Rús*, or *Rhos*, was the name by which the Scandinavian traders were known in the area, a name possibly deriving from the Swedish *róðr* meaning a crew of oarsmen, but all that can safely be said is that the state named after them emerged from the complex interaction between Scandinavians, Slavs and Balts at a time when intensification of trade was causing massive economic and social changes. The first capital of the Rús was at Novgorod on the Volkhov founded in about 860, but forty years later it had been transferred to Kiev on the Dnepr.

The Scandinavians had much to offer their trading partners. Furs and slaves featured large but other valuable merchandise included falcons, honey, wax, walrus ivory and fine steel swords. In return they received silver coins in enormous quantities. In Scandinavia alone a thousand coin hoards have been found totalling sixty thousand coins, which can represent only a tiny fraction of the silver that flowed towards the Baltic. Much of it was melted down and redistributed in other forms. No doubt other luxury goods were also acquired – silk, Islamic pottery and glass are all attested in the archaeological record.

So the Nordic and Muslim worlds confronted each other in contexts of mutual benefit. One such encounter took place in 922 and was recorded by the geographer Ibn Fadlan:

13.14 This ceremonial axe made of iron inlaid with silver was buried with a person of very high status in a timber grave chamber built in AD 970/1 at Mammen in Jutland. It was probably made in the Royal workshop of Harald Bluetooth. Axes were widely used as weapons of warfare. This superb example was symbolic of high status.

I have seen the Rús as they came in on their merchant journeys and encamped on the Volga. I have never seen more perfect specimens, tall as date palms, blond and ruddy; they wear neither tunics nor caftans, but the men wear a garment that covers one side of the body and leaves a hand free. Each man has an axe, a sword and a knife, and keeps each by him at all times.

He goes on to cite the Viking prayer: 'I wish that you would send me many merchants with many *dinars* and *dirhems* who will buy from me whatever I wish and will not dispute anything I say.'

The picture we have so far outlined is one of peaceful commercial activity very different from the interaction of the Danes and the Norwegians in the west. The main reason for this is that, whereas the Danes and Norwegians were coming into direct contact with rich kingdoms and well-endowed monasteries, the Swedes were engaging with simple forest-dwellers whose ability to acquire significant wealth was minimal and who were without the benefits of acquisitive Christianity: in short, since there was little worth pillaging, long-distance trade was the only option.

But in the Black Sea new opportunities opened up, for there, a few days' sailing away, was *Mikligarðr* – 'the Great City' – Constantinople, the source of huge wealth. On at least two occasions Scandinavians took part in attacks on Constantinople but for the most part they were content to enter the city as friends to trade or to offer their services in its armies. So impressed were the Byzantines by Scandinavian fighting prowess that by the late tenth century the emperor's personal armed force was made up entirely of Scandinavian mercenaries – the fearsome Varangian Guard – armed with heavy swords and great battle-axes. It may have been a member of the guard who scratched his name, Halfdan, in runes on a balcony balustrade in the church of Hagia Sophia, leaving a poignant reminder of the confrontation of two very different cultures. It is still there to be wondered at today.

The Scandinavian diaspora of the eighth to tenth centuries was a remarkable phenomenon, quite unprecedented in its magnitude. At the moment that Swedish Vikings were crossing the Caspian Sea on their way to trade in Baghdad, Norwegians were sailing down the coast of Labrador looking for suitable land to settle in America. The Scandinavians were the first Europeans to have sailed in all of Europe's seas.

The Beginnings of Modern Europe: Interconnectedness

By the early decades of the eleventh century AD the map of Europe had begun to take on something of its modern appearance, forged out of the turbulence

of the last two centuries of the first millennium. The relative stability of the two Christian power blocks – the Byzantine east and the Frankish west – provided a solid core that separated the Muslim world of the south from the turmoil of folk movement and state formation gripping the north and east of Europe during this time. As we have seen, this core absorbed blows from all sides. Take, for example, the little kingdom of Burgundy embedded safely, one might have thought, deep within the Frankish Empire. In the space of a century or so it was raided on a number of occasions by both Muslims and Northmen coming from temporary bases in the Rhône delta, and by Magyars riding out from the Carpathian Basin. No one, it would seem, was safe from the marauding bands. Yet for all its volatility Europe was being bound together ever more tightly by networks of trade as states began to crystallize out and markets developed to serve their increasing demands.

Throughout much of the period the Adriatic provided the main link

13.15 By 1150 Europe has taken on an appearance familiar to us today. The rest is history.

473

between the two empires, with Venice serving as the exchange node and growing rich and powerful in the process. In the Mediterranean the international ports of Naples and Amalfi also articulated east–west trade as well as serving as points of contact with the Muslim world, but other ports were now developing – Barcelona, Marseille, Genoa and Pisa in the Frankish realm and Ragusa (Dubrovnik), Corinth and Thessalonica on the European coast of Byzantium, not to forget the vital role of Constantinople itself. Meanwhile around the North Sea many new ports were flourishing – Hamwic (Southampton), Fordwich, London, Ipswich and York together with Quentovic, Dorestad, Ribe and Kaupang. The Baltic too was fast developing new commercial centres including Hedeby, Skuldevig, Wolin, Truso, Paviken and Birka. From the coastal ports, overland routes led deep into the hinterland to serve the aspirations of the two empires and gradually, in the comparative stability that prevailed, the routes joined up once more to become major transcontinental corridors. The Rhône re-established its former importance, linking once more to the Loire, the Seine and the Rhine. The spectacular growth of Venice and the creation of a German empire that included northern Italy encouraged the development of the central Alpine passes. The old amber route from the head of the Adriatic, around the eastern Alps to the Danube and thence to the Oder and the Baltic, was again reinvigorated, benefiting the short-lived kingdom of Moravia which commanded the central section of the route. Then to the east lay the river routes that provided direct access between the Baltic and the Black Sea and led to the emergence of the Russian state.

Beyond the confines of the peninsula were the most remarkable routes of all. In the west the Atlantic seaways enabled the Vikings of Ireland to trade with Muslim Iberia and remain in contact with their Scandinavian homeland and the new colonies of Iceland. In the east Baltic adventurers found their way to the Caspian Sea en route to the markets of Baghdad. After the turmoils of the first millennium the populations of Europe were at last settling down and geography was once more asserting itself.

CHAPTER FOURTEEN

The *Longue Durée*

A long time ago, towards the beginning of this book, we quoted with evident approval Fernand Braudel's vision of the essence of the Mediterranean: 'our sea was from the very dawn of its prehistory a witness to those imbalances productive of change which would set the rhythms of its entire life.' Braudel's brilliant insight could well be applied to any of Europe's oceans or to the peninsula itself. Imbalances have created the momentum that has driven Europe, and continues to do so – imbalances of resources and imbalances of population, all conditioned by the ageless structure of the rocks themselves which determine the continent's varied landscapes and seascapes. Landscapes are fickle in their provision of the necessities of subsistence. Many are unable to support population growth and so force mobility, while rarer resources – metals, precious stones, furs and the like – are unevenly distributed in nature, driving those who want them to develop social networks that facilitate exchange. Thus, humanity emerges willing to be mobile and forced to be sociable.

One of the underlying themes of our story has been mobility – the ceaseless movement of peoples, in vast hordes like Attila's Huns, or as individual explorers like Pytheas the Massiliot. It began with the movement of Mesolithic hunter-gatherers filtering gradually northwards as the climate ameliorated at the end of the last Ice Age and continued with the phenomenally rapid spread of farming communities drawn westwards by land and sea across the face of Europe. The first is easy to explain in simple subsistence terms – expanding populations following the migratory food sources – but the Neolithic spread seems to have had a deeper underlying dynamic. Maybe we are glimpsing here a real pioneering spirit – a desire to see what lies beyond, drawn on westwards, perhaps, by the fascination of the setting sun. We can only speculate, but the evident importance of cosmology to the Neolithic communities living in the Atlantic zone is a reminder that religious fervour can be a potent force. Five thousand years later the Arabs made a remarkable dash along the North African coast to the Atlantic, ostensibly in the name of Islam. Another seven hundred years later the Spanish were to break out of the constraints of Europe, sailing westwards to the Americas and taking with them slaughter, disease and Catholicism.

The westerly flow of populations is also deeply rooted in the steppe lands of central Asia. Our story has been permeated with tales of horsemen thrusting westwards along the Pontic steppe into the Balkans and the plains of the Alföld (western Hungary), whence they raided west and north. The first to be clearly archaeologically distinguishable were the Cimmerians, in the ninth–eighth centuries BC. Then there followed in quick succession Scythians, Sarmatians, Alans, Huns, Avars, Bulgars and Magyars, with the Turks following on later. What drove these outpourings is a fascinating problem. Population pressure building up in the homeland region and catalysing a wholly mobile population is no doubt an important factor, but is it too much to suggest that underlying it all was a folk memory, passed across the generations, that 'our people always ride into the west'? I once met an elderly traveller on a road in Sussex who told me he was making for Kent and hoped to be there by May. When asked why, he said, 'We always go there at this time.'

The other population surge that we have seen is the flow of 'Germans' from the plains of northern Europe to the south. When such movements began it is difficult to be sure but late in the second century BC the classical sources tell of the long-drawn-out wanderings of the Cimbri and Teutones. Thereafter the 'Germanic threat' is never out of the news, culminating in the mass migrations of the fifth and sixth centuries AD. While it could fairly be argued that the creation of a Roman frontier exacerbated the problem, the flow of people from north to south is probably more deeply rooted in the second millennium BC, when there are strong hints of adventurers from the Baltic region exploring the river routes to the south. Much later, towards the end of the first millennium AD, their successors – the Northmen – were travelling on the great rivers to the Black Sea and via the Atlantic coasts to the Mediterranean. The lure of the rich and fabulous south must have been irresistible.

Large-scale mobility, persistent at times, sporadic at others, was a feature of early Europe; and so it remains. The massive displacements of populations caused by the Crusades, by the flight of refugees like Jews and Huguenots in the face of religious persecution, and later by the armies of Napoleon and Hitler, are obvious manifestations of mobility, as was the constant flow of European populations westwards to America in the nineteenth and early twentieth centuries in search of new opportunities. The flow continues today: population figures issued for 2006 show that Britain received 574,000 immigrants during the year while 385,000 residents chose to leave the country. Population mobility has always been one of the defining characteristics of Europe.

476

A second characteristic that has been stressed throughout this book is connectivity – the establishment of intricate social networks by means of which commodities were exchanged and ideas and beliefs were disseminated. Peninsular Europe, with its huge stretch of coastal interface and its plethora of rivers offering cross-peninsular routes, provided ideal conditions for networks to develop. Already in the Mesolithic period regional exchange systems can be recognized and by the third millennium much of the peninsula was bound together by routes – maritime and riverine – that allowed huge quantities and varieties of commodities to flow along them. Perhaps the main achievement of the Roman Empire was that it institutionalized – by means of roads, ports, market centres and tax systems – the exchange systems of Mediterranean and temperate Europe. So important did trade become that even states locked in mutual hostilities, like the Muslim world and the Christian empires of the Franks and Byzantines, could find ways to engage with each other commercially. The 'imbalances productive of change' were also imbalances conducive to economic harmony, albeit in a somewhat unstable state of equilibrium.

Central to our story are the ocean boundaries of Europe. For the most part the littorals were congenial places, rich in a variety of food resources. The sea encouraged mobility and the many rivers provided routes to the interior. Safe havens were established which became route nodes and ports-of-trade through which information flowed and in this way the ocean interfaces developed as zones of innovation. Each had its own distinctive character, its own internal variety and its own trajectory of development.

Standing back from all the detail, it is possible to trace, in the fourth to second millennia, the emergence of very distinct innovative societies along the Atlantic seaways, in the east Mediterranean and in the southern Baltic. All used well-crafted vessels as symbols of their status, demonstrating the ability of their elites to manipulate the movement of a wide range of commodities. In the east Mediterranean the intensity of movement was such that systems of writing were developed and it is not unreasonable to refer to Minoan and Mycenaean society as state systems. How interdependent these innovating areas were is difficult to determine but the fact that the collapse of the Mycenaean system towards the end of the second millennium does not seem to have had any immediate impact on the Atlantic and Baltic systems would argue for their separate identities.

By the eighth century BC the east Mediterranean communities, notably the Phoenicians and the Greeks, were beginning to develop their maritime strengths, turning their attention first to the central Mediterranean and later to the west. It was during this time that the Greeks also began to establish themselves in the Black Sea. The battles for control in the Mediterranean saw Rome – conveniently sited in the centre of the sea – rise rapidly to dominance but, significantly, only after she had constructed her first navy in the middle of the third century BC. By the mid-first century BC Rome was supreme and was already beginning to move out of the ecological niche of the Mediterranean into the broad and productive periphery of temperate Europe – a task accomplished by the second century AD.

During this long period, the Atlantic, North Sea and Baltic zones seem to have lost their innovative energy and to have begun to fragment into smaller regional systems. While it is tempting to relate this in some way to the rise of Rome, many other factors must have been involved. The breakdown of the international trade in bronze – as iron came more widely into use – will inevitably have led to some fragmentation of the earlier networks, but there were other factors at work as well. There was now a much greater concern about controlling land and its productive output – a trend that may, in part at least, have been the result of a steady increase in population. At any event, from the Atlantic to the Baltic we see a retreat into regionalism. This does not, however, mean that this extensive maritime zone lacked inventive talent. Shipping developed apace. In the Atlantic zone and the North Sea tough square-rigged sailing vessels, so admired by Julius Caesar, were facing the open ocean, while in the Baltic sleek, fast, rowing vessels like the Hjortspring and Nydam boats were serving needs in calmer island-strewn seas. These different boat-building traditions were to give distinct characters to the later maritime enterprises of these two regions.

The rapid collapse of the Roman Empire in the period c.250–450 saw control of the Mediterranean and Black Sea fragment as Germanic invaders surged across the peninsula and took to the seas – the Vandals in the west Mediterranean and the Ostrogoths in the Black Sea and Aegean. The Byzantine Empire managed to maintain a defensive navy, but with the advent of the Muslims in the seventh century the southern and eastern shores of the Mediterranean became the preserve of an alien force that had rapidly learned the importance of naval power. Thus, the Mediterranean was split between a Christian north and a Muslim south – sworn enemies in religion, but lured to engage in trade by the vision of a quick profit. This was the context in which the great maritime cities of Venice and Pisa emerged as the mercantile power brokers of the Mediterranean.

While the Mediterranean was being reshaped the Baltic/North Sea was developing a new energy of its own, commanding trade routes that stretched out like the legs of a great spider in all directions – to the Frankish Empire via the North Sea and English Channel, along the great rivers to the Black Sea and Byzantium and beyond to Arab trading centres at Baghdad, and by way of the Caspian Sea to the caravan routes of Asia. By the end of the eighth century, the social change brought about by increased commercial activity and the emergence of states was encouraging a new mobility among the adventurous young. The Northmen, or Vikings, were on the move, raiding and settling their way southwards along the Atlantic seaways and into the west Mediterranean and making riverine expeditions through what was to become Russia to the Black Sea, some there to serve the Byzantine emperors as mercenaries. In their wide arc of advance they embraced Europe, becoming the first men to sail on all its oceans.

This counterbalancing of Europe in the tenth century AD is a convenient place to end. The Europe that was to emerge afterwards is the familiar Europe of conventional history. As the Scandinavian kingdoms lost their vigour and the circumscribed Mediterranean dissipated its energies in exhausting rivalries, the Atlantic façade came into its own again. Its skilled and well-tried boat-building traditions provided it with sturdy square-rigged cobs capable of carrying large cargoes and with lateen-rigged caravels able to sail close to the wind. And in its people the lure of the west was ever-present. It was from the ports of Spain and Portugal and later from Britain, France and the Low Countries that countless people from the peninsula of Old Europe sailed into the wider world.

Further Reading

Chapter 1: Ways of Seeing: Space, Time and People

This is not an easy chapter to provide a structured bibliography for since it touches on a wide variety of concepts and is not overly specific, but we can nonetheless offer some guidance to allow the major themes to be followed up. The subject of ancient geography is well covered in three books: E.H. Warmington, *Greek Geography* (London 1934), J.O. Thomson, *History of Ancient Geography* (Cambridge 1948) and K. Clarke, *Between Geography and History* (Oxford 1999), while the specific journey of Pytheas is explored in B. Cunliffe, *The Extraordinary Voyage of Pytheas the Greek* (London 2001). A short but up-to-date survey of Miletos can be found in A.M. Greaves, *Miletos. A History* (London 2002). For a general background to the Greeks in western Asia Minor, J.M. Cook's *The Greeks in Ionia and the East* (London 1962), though elderly, is informed and readable. The text of Herodotus's *Histories* is well worth reading and reading again. Opinions vary but I have found the translation of George Rawlinson, first published in 1858, to be the most readable. It is available in an Everyman edition (London 1964). Caesar's *Gallic Wars* (*De bello gallico*) can be read with pleasure in translation. One of the most attractive (and accurate) is A. and P. Wiseman, *Julius Caesar: The Battle for Gaul* (London 1980). For Tacitus's *On Germany* (*Germania*), A.R. Birley's translation (with copious notes) in the Oxford World's Classics series (1999) is recommended. M. Todd's *The Northern Barbarians 100 BC–AD 300* (London 1975) offers a useful commentary on Rome's encounter with the Germans.

The work of the French *Annales* School has had a significant effect on the thinking of archaeologists (the present author in particular). There is much that could be recommended but to keep it brief and not to be too carried away with enthusiasm, a thoughtful introduction to the whole movement is given by P. Burke in *The French Historical Revolution: The* Annales *School, 1929–89* (Oxford 1990), with a very useful bibliography. Some of the archaeological implications are explored in J. Bintliff (ed.), *The* Annales *School and Archaeology* (Leicester 1991). For a flavour of the method in action essential reading must include F. Braudel, *The Mediterranean and the Mediterranean World in the Age of Philip II* (revised edition, translated by S. Reynolds, London 1976, of the French edition published 1949). It is a masterpiece. Rather less successful but still to be read is F. Braudel, *The Mediterranean in the Ancient World* (translated by S. Reynolds, London 2001), which was written in the late 1960s and not published until after the author's death more than thirty years later. Inevitably the archaeology is out of date but the book is still worth reading for its brilliant insights and its verve.

We turn now to the debate over migrations and mobility in prehistoric Europe. So much of the pre-1960 literature used the paradigm of large-scale migrations to explain change in the past. One book that may stand as an example is V.G. Childe, *Prehistoric Migrations in Europe* (Oslo 1950). Migrationist views pervade much of Childe's work and provide the implicit structure for his densely packed and long-running *The Dawn of European Civilization* (London, 1st edition 1925, 6th edition 1957). *Migrations* and *Dawn* are mentioned here more for their historical interest in the development of European archaeology than as texts to be followed, but in their time they were seminal works. The first serious challenge to the migrationist paradigm was G. Clark's paper 'The Invasion Hypothesis in British Archaeology', published in *Antiquity* 40 (1966), 172–89. The whole question was more broadly explored in the light of radiocarbon chronology in C. Renfrew, *Before Civilization: The Radiocarbon Revolution and Prehistoric Europe* (London 1973). Since then our understanding of the subtleties of radiocarbon chronology has moved on and in doing so has entirely altered our perception of the past. The study of DNA in ancient and modern populations is a recent development and much of the literature is embedded in scientific journals but a highly readable and soundly informed book by one of the pioneers of the approach is B. Sykes, *The Seven Daughters of Eve* (London 2001). The application of DNA studies specifically to Britain is carefully explored in S. Oppenheimer's book *The Origins of the British: A Genetic Detective Story* (London 2006), which presents an informed and exciting read. We will return to the more specific literature in Chapter 4. The analysis of stable isotopes in human teeth is a study in its infancy but one with considerable potential. Among the highly scientific literature, a taste for the potential of the method is given in T.D. Price *et al.*, 'The Characterization of Biologically Available Strontium Isotope Ratios for the Study of Prehistoric Migration' in *Archaeometry* 44 (2002), 117–35, and T.D. Price *et al.*, 'Prehistoric Human Migration in the *Linearbandkeramik* of Central Europe' in *Antiquity* 75 (2001), 593–603.

Understanding population dynamics is of crucial importance to archaeologists. Thomas Malthus's original formulations are still well worth reading. His original *Essay on the Principle of Population* (1798) went through four editions as his ideas developed; these are conveniently brought together in his *A Summary View of the Principle of Population* (London 1830). Two useful overviews of demography from the perspective of archaeology are F. Hassan's *Demographic Archaeology* (London 1981) and A. Chamberlain's *Demography in Archaeology* (Cambridge 2006), while E.A. Wrigley, *Population and History* (New York 1969) provides a very readable account seen from the point of view of a historian. Other helpful reviews include E. Zebrow, *Prehistoric Carrying Capacity: A Model* (Menlo Park 1975) and J.W. Wood, 'A Theory of Preindustrial Population Dynamics', *Current Anthropology* 39(i) (1998), 99–135.

The themes of trade and exchange in the ancient world have been widely explored. Two of the classic papers are K. Polanyi, 'The Economy as Instituted Process', in K. Polanyi, C. Arensberg and H.W. Pearson (eds), *Trade and Market in the Early Empires* (Glencoe 1957) and Polanyi's 'Ports of Trade in Early Societies', *Journal of Economic History* 23 (1963), 30–45. Two useful collections of essays on the themes of trade and exchange are J.A. Sabloff and C.C. Lamberg-Karlovsky (eds), *Ancient Civilization and Trade* (Albuquerque 1975) and T.K. Earle and J. Ericson (eds), *Exchange Systems in Prehistory* (London 1977). The debate was usefully extended by K.G. Hirth, 'Interregional Trade and the Formation of Prehistoric Gateway Communities', *American Antiquity* 43 (1978), 35–45. World Systems Theory begins with I. Wallerstein's *The Modern World-System* (Vols 1 and 2) (New York 1974 and 1980) and his *The Politics of the World-Economy* (Cambridge 1984). The centre–periphery debate is usefully explored in E. Shils, *Center and Periphery: Essays in Macrosociology* (Chicago 1975) and T.C. Champion (ed.), *Centre and Periphery: Comparative Studies in Archaeology* (London 1989). Thereafter enthusiasm for World Systems Theory as applied to the pre-industrial world became tempered with caution, though the broad constructs remain of value.

Chapter 2: The Land between the Oceans

There is no better way to understand the structure of Europe than by leafing through the pages of a good atlas augmented with (but not replaced by) time spent scanning the satellite imagery that is fast becoming available through Google World and other sites. There are many books on the regional geography of Europe. One invaluable series – the Geographical Handbook Series – was published by the British Naval Intelligence Division during the Second World War as briefing documents for the military. They were prepared by teams of geographers culled from British universities and are a mine of carefully researched and clearly presented information. Most European countries had at least one volume devoted to them. All were published during the early 1940s and are therefore dated, but as sources for physical geography they provide excellent introductions. Other volumes that I have found useful include F. Braudel, *The Identity of France*, Vol. 1 (London 1988), P. Pinchemel, *France: A Geographical Survey* (London 1969), and A.F.A. Mutton, *Central Europe: A Regional and Human Geography* (London 1961), M. de Teran and L. Sole Sabaris (eds.), *Geografia Regional de España* (Barcelona 1968) and J.M. Houston, *The Western Mediterranean World* (London 1964).

For an inspiring vision of Europe seen through the eyes of a modern historian it is difficult to better the introduction and first chapter of N. Davies, *Europe: A History* (Oxford 1996).

We do not, in this volume, deal in any detail with Europe during the Ice Age but some background will be useful to the reader. A succinct introduction to this period will be found in two chapters, 'The Peopling of Europe 700,000–40,000 Years before the Present' by C. Gamble and 'The Upper Palaeolithic Revolution' by P. Mellars, in B. Cunliffe (ed.), *Prehistoric Europe: An Illustrated History* (Oxford 1997). For a more detailed treatment, C. Gamble, *The Palaeolithic Settlement of Europe* (Cambridge 1986) remains a standard text. Climatic change is well covered in N. Roberts, *The Holocene: An Environmental History* (Oxford 1998). More specifically, the separation of Britain from Europe is considered in B.J. Coles, 'Doggerland: A Speculative Survey', *Proceedings of the Prehistoric Society* 64 (1998), 45–81. The debate about the flooding of the Black Sea from the Mediterranean can be followed in W.B.F. Ryan *et al.*, 'An Abrupt Drowning of the Black Sea Shelf', *Marine Geology* 138 (1997), 119–26, R.D. Ballard, C.F. Coleman and G.R. Rosenberg, 'Further Evidence of Abrupt Holocene Drowning of the Black Sea Shelf', *Marine Geology* 170 (2000), 253–61, and N. Görür *et al.*, 'Is the Abrupt Drowning of the Black Sea Shelf at 7150 yr BP a myth?', *Marine Geology* 176 (2001), 65–73.

The seas that surround the European peninsula are

well treated in the archaeological/historical literature. M. Mollat du Jourdin, *Europe and the Sea* (Oxford 1993) provides a broad overview of the subject. For the Mediterranean, F. Braudel's masterpiece, *The Mediterranean and the Mediterranean World in the Age of Philip II* (revised edition, translated by S. Reynolds, London 1976) and his *The Mediterranean in the Ancient World* (translated by S. Reynolds, London 2001) are essential background reading while P. Horden and N. Purcell, *The Corrupting Sea: A Study of Mediterranean History* (Oxford 2000) introduces a wealth of up-to-date detail presented in a penetrating academic study. D. Abulafia (ed.), *The Mediterranean in History* (London 2003) is a very well-illustrated series of readable essays by specialists. The results of a wide-ranging conference debating the validity of studying the Mediterranean as an entity are presented in a stimulating volume of papers edited by W.V. Harris, *Rethinking the Mediterranean* (Oxford 2005). For the Black Sea, N. Ascherson's *Black Sea: The Birthplace of Civilization and Barbarism* (London 1995) and C. King's *The Black Sea: A History* (Oxford 2004) offer complementary approaches, the first an exploration of barbarism and civilization seen against events from the history of the region, the second a diachronic study of the sea as a bridge between the disparate communities that surrounded it. An overview of the Atlantic through history is presented by P. Butel in *The Atlantic* (London 1999). It is strongest for the period from the fifteenth century AD. For the earlier period, B. Cunliffe, *Facing the Ocean: The Atlantic and its Peoples* (Oxford 2001) examines the coastal communities and the seaways that linked them in the prehistoric and early historic period. The North Sea and the Baltic have received rather less attention from writers attempting syntheses. A series of useful specialist papers on Baltic archaeology are brought together in J. Rönnby (ed.), *By the Water: Archaeological Perspectives on Human Strategies around the Baltic Sea* (Huddinge, Sweden 2003) while P. Jordan offers a broad view of the North Sea in his *North Sea Saga* (London 2004).

Chapter 3: Food for the Gathering

There are surprisingly few general works on the Mesolithic period in Europe. The most readable overview is S.J. Mithen's chapter 'The Mesolithic Age' in B. Cunliffe (ed.), *Prehistoric Europe: An Illustrated History* (Oxford 1997). A more adventurous book by the same author (S. Mithen), *After the Ice: A Global Human History 20,000–5000 BC* (London 2003) has ten chapters covering Europe which combine imaginative storytelling with the most up-to-date archaeological evidence (fully referenced) in a highly entertaining and informative way. D. Clarke's *Mesolithic Europe: The Economic Basis* (London 1978), though now a somewhat

elderly text, offers a stimulating introduction to the natural resources available to early hunter-gatherers. Two excellent regional studies, both now rather dated, are J.G.D. Clark, *The Early Stone Age Settlement of Scandinavia* (Cambridge 1975) and R. Tringham, *Hunters, Fishers and Farmers of Eastern Europe, 6000–3000 BC* (London 1971). Clark's book has been conveniently updated by L. Larsson in his paper 'The Mesolithic in Southern Scandinavia', *Journal of World Prehistory* 4 (1990), 257–309.

Much of the new research in the period is presented in edited volumes of conference papers, among which the following contain important individual papers directly relevant to our theme: M. Zvelebil, L. Domańska and R. Dennell (eds), *Harvesting the Sea, Farming the Forest: The Emergence of Neolithic Societies in the Baltic Region* (Sheffield 1998); C. Bonsall (ed.), *The Mesolithic in Europe* (Edinburgh 1989); A. Fischer (ed.), *Man and the Sea in the Mesolithic: Coastal Settlement above and below Present Sea Level* (Oxford 1995); M. Zvelebil (ed.), *Hunter-Gatherers in Transition* (Cambridge 1986); and L. Larsson (ed.), *Mesolithic on the Move* (Oxford 2003).

We turn now to the more specific themes introduced in the chapter. For global climate change see A.G. Dawson, *Ice Age Earth* (London 1992) and J.J. Lowe and M.J.C. Walker, *Reconstructing Quaternary Environments* (Harlow 1997). The question of sea-level change has generated a huge literature but four papers conveniently sum up recent work in three key areas: T.H. van Andel and J.C. Shackleton, 'Late Palaeolithic and Mesolithic Coastlines of Greece and the Aegean', *Journal of Field Archaeology* 9 (1982), 445–54; T.H. van Andel, 'Late Quaternary Sea-Level Changes and Archaeology', *Antiquity* 63 (1989), 733–45; S. Björck, 'Late Weichselian to Early Holocene Development of the Baltic Sea – with implications for coastal settlements in the southern Baltic region' in A. Fischer (ed.), *Man and the Sea in the Mesolithic* (Oxford 1995), 23–34; and B.J. Coles, 'Doggerland: a speculative survey', *Proceedings of the Prehistoric Society* 64 (1998), 45–81. The question of the Atlantic currents and the biomass of the oceans is thoroughly covered in J.R. Coull, *The Fisheries of Europe: An Economic Geography* (London 1972).

On maritime lifestyles in the Mediterranean: for the Franchthi cave in Greece see J.M. Hansen, *The Palaeoethnobotany of Franchthi Cave* (Bloomington 1991); T.W. Jacobsen, 'Excavation in the Franchthi Cave 1969–1971: Part I', *Hesperia* 42 (1973), 45–88; and T.W. Jacobsen, 'The Franchthi Cave and the Beginning of Settled Village Life in Greece', *Hesperia* 50 (1981), 303–19. For Corsica and Sardinia, L. Costa *et al.*, 'Early Settlement on Tyrrhenian Islands (8th millennium cal BC): Mesolithic Adaptation to Local Resources in Corsica and Northern Sardinia', in L.

Larsson (ed.), *Mesolithic on the Move* (Oxford 2003), 3–10. The Atlantic sites have been more extensively studied. The Portuguese settlements have been considered in J. Roche, 'Spatial Organization in the Mesolithic of Muge, Portugal' and J.E. Morais Arnaud, 'The Mesolithic Communities of the Sado Valley, Portugal, in their Ecological Setting', both in C. Bonsall (ed.), *The Mesolithic in Europe* (Edinburgh 1989), 607–13 and 614–31, and also E. Cunha *et al.*, 'Inferences About Mesolithic Life Style on the Basis of Anthropological Data: The Case of the Portuguese Shell Middens', in L. Larsson (ed.), *Mesolithic on the Move* (Oxford 2003), 184–90. The northern Spanish coastal sites are discussed in L. Straus, 'Epipalaeolithic and Mesolithic Adaptations in Cantabrian Spain and Pyrenean France', *Journal of World Prehistory* 5 (1991), 84–104, and L. Straus and M. González Morales, 'The Mesolithic in the Cantabrian Interior: fact or fantasy?', in L. Larsson (ed.), *Mesolithic on the Move* (Oxford 2003), 359–68. Aspects of the Breton Mesolithic cemeteries are considered in R. Schulting, 'Antlers, Bone Pins and Flint Blades: Mesolithic Cemeteries of Brittany', *Antiquity* 70 (1996), 335–50, and the same author's 'The Marrying Kind: Evidence for a Patrilocal Postmarital Residence Pattern in the Mesolithic of Southern Brittany', in L. Larsson (ed.), *Mesolithic on the Move* (Oxford 2003), 431–41.

For the Baltic, the quality of the surviving evidence and the intensity of the fieldwork have generated an enormous volume of publications. We have already mentioned the overview of L. Larsson, 'The Mesolithic of Southern Scandinavia', *Journal of World Prehistory* 4 (1990), 257–309. Important site-specific publications related to our discussion include: S.H. Andersen, 'Tybrind Vig', *Journal of Danish Archaeology* 4 (1985), 52–69; S.H. Andersen, 'Ertebølle revisited' in the same journal 5 (1986), 31–86; E.E. Albrethsen and E.B. Petersen, 'Excavation of a Mesolithic Cemetery at Vedboek, Denmark', *Acta Archaeologica* 47 (1976), 1–28; and L. Larsson, 'The Skateholm Project: A Late Mesolithic Settlement and Cemetery Complex at a South Swedish Bay', *Papers of the Archaeological Institute, University of Lund* 5 (1983–84), 5–38. More thematic surveys of interest include I.B. Enghoff, 'Fishing in Denmark during the Mesolithic Period' in A. Fischer (ed.), *Man and Sea in the Mesolithic* (Oxford 1995), 67–75, and L. Larsson, 'Man and Sea in Southern Scandinavia during the Late Mesolithic: The Role of Cemeteries in the View of Society' in the same volume, 95–104.

In the heart of peninsular Europe the only site complex we have considered is in the region of the Iron Gates (Serbia), most particularly the site of Lepenski Vir. A well-illustrated popular account of this remarkable site is given in D. Srejović, *New Discoveries at Lepenski Vir* (London 1972).

Some of the complexities of the site and its chronology are explored by R. Tringham in 'Southeastern Europe in the Transition to Agriculture in Europe: Bridge, Buffer, or Mosaic' in T.D. Price (ed.), *Europe's First Farmers* (Cambridge 2000), 19–56, and in D.W. Bailey, *Balkan Prehistory: Exclusion, Incorporation and Identity* (London 2000).

On the theme of warfare, R.R. Newell *et al.* have thoroughly surveyed the human skeletal evidence in 'The Skeletal Remains of Mesolithic Man in Western Europe: An Evaluation Catalogue', *Journal of Human Evolution* 81 (1979), 1–228. Evidence of trauma on the Danish sample has been assessed by P. Bennike in *Palaeopathology of Danish Skeletons* (Copenhagen 1985). The Ofnet find of skull caches has been reassessed in D.W. Frayer, 'Ofnet: Evidence for a Mesolithic Massacre', in D.L. Martin and D.W. Frayer (eds), *Troubled Times: Violence and Warfare in the Past* (Amsterdam 1997), 181–216.

Chapter 4: The First Farmers: From the Fertile Crescent to the Danube Valley

The most accessible overview of Neolithic Europe is A. Whittle's chapter 'The First Farmers' in B. Cunliffe (ed.), *Prehistoric Europe: An Illustrated History* (Oxford 1997), 136–66, which is supported by a carefully selected bibliography. Whittle has also authored two full-length treatments of the Neolithic period, *Neolithic Europe: A Survey* (Cambridge 1985) and *Europe in the Neolithic: The Creation of New Worlds* (Cambridge 1996), both packed with relevant detail, the latter, of course, engaging in more recent debates, especially favouring the importance of the indigenous contribution to Early Neolithic communities. The theme of the introduction of the Neolithic way of life to Europe is thoroughly addressed in a series of seminal papers brought together in T.D. Price (ed.), *Europe's First Farmers* (Cambridge 2000), each dealing with a different region of Europe. L. Larsson, *Mesolithic on the Move* (Oxford 2003) contains a group of specialist papers dealing with the transition from Mesolithic to Early Neolithic. This broad theme was also the subject of an earlier work, M. Zvelebil (ed.), *Hunters in Transition: Mesolithic Societies of Temperate Eurasia and their Transition to Farming* (Cambridge 1987).

Moving on to some of the more detailed themes addressed in the chapter, the implications of new genetic studies have been widely debated in recent specialist publications. Among the copious literature the following give a flavour of the debate: M.P. Richards *et al.*, 'Tracing European Founder Lineages in the Near East mtDNA pool', *American Journal of Human Genetics* 67 (2000), 1251–76; L. Chikhi *et al.*, 'Y Genetic Data Support the Neolithic Diffusion Model', *Proceedings of the National*

Academy of Sciences 99 (2002), 11,008–13; and R. King and P.A. Underhill, 'Congruent Distribution of Neolithic Painted Pottery and Ceramic Figurines with Y-Chromosome Lineages', *Antiquity* 76 (2002), 707–14. A particularly thoughtful attempt to bring together various threads of evidence is M. Zvelebil's 'Demography and Dispersal of Early Farming Populations at the Mesolithic–Neolithic Transition: Linguistic and Genetic Implications', in P. Bellwood and C. Renfrew (eds), *Examining the Farming/Language Dispersal Hypothesis* (Cambridge 2002).

The origin of food production in the Near East is a massive subject with a specialist literature to match. A succinct summary of the current state of knowledge is provided by T. Watkins, 'From Foragers to Complex Societies in Southwest Asia', in C. Scarre (ed.), *The Human Past* (London 2005), 200–33. For a stimulating, somewhat personal overview, J. Cauvin, *The Birth of the Gods and the Beginnings of Agriculture* (Cambridge 2001) can be highly recommended. D.R. Harris (ed.), *The Origins and Spread of Agriculture and Pastoralism in Eurasia* (London 1996) and D. Zohary and M. Hopf, *The Domestication of Plants in the Old World: The Origin and Spread of Cultivated Plants in West Asia, Europe and the Nile Valley* (3rd edition, Oxford 2000) consider the broad issues of cultivation and domestication. Among the classic site-oriented works are R.J. Braidwood and B. Howe, *Prehistoric Investigations in Iraqi Kurdistan* (Chicago 1960); K.M. Kenyon, *Digging Up Jericho* (London 1957); J. Mellaart, *Çatal Hüyük: A Neolithic Town in Anatolia* (London 1967); and A.M.T. Moore, G.C. Hillman and A.J. Legge, *Village on the Euphrates* (Oxford 2001).

The colonization of Cyprus is treated in two papers: A. Simmons, 'The First Humans and the Last Pygmy Hippopotami of Cyprus' and J. Guilaine and F. Briois, 'Parekklisha Shillourokambos: an Early Neolithic Site in Cyprus', both in S. Swiny (ed.), *The Earliest Prehistory of Cyprus: From Colonization to Exploitation* (Boston 2001). For interesting thoughts on the initial Neolithic settlement of Crete, C. Broodbank and T.F. Strasser, 'Migrant Farmers and the Neolithic Colonization of Crete', *Antiquity* 65 (1991), 233–45. The earliest settlement on the Greek mainland is considered against the environmental background by T.H. van Andel and C.N. Runnels, 'The Earliest Farmers in Europe', *Antiquity* 69 (1995), 481–500. A full treatment of the archaeological record, including a careful assessment of dating evidence for the first settlements, is provided by C. Perlès, *The Early Neolithic in Greece* (Cambridge 2001). The problems of identifying Anatolian origins are explored in M. Özdogan, 'The Beginning of Neolithic Economies in Southeastern Europe: An Anatolian Perspective', *Journal of European Archaeology* 5 (1997), 1–33. One of the key sites, Nea Nikomedeia in the Macedonian Plain, is outlined in R.

Rodden, 'Excavations at the Early Neolithic Site at Nea Nikomedeia, Greek Macedonia (1961 season)', *Proceedings of the Prehistoric Society* 28 (1962), 267–88. For the Early Neolithic levels in the Franchthi cave: C. Perlès, *Les industries lithiques taillées de Franchthi (Argolide, Grèce). II: Les industries du Mésolithique et du Néolithique initial* (Bloomington 1990); S. Payne, 'Faunal Change at Franchthi Cave from 20,000 BC to 3000 BC', in A.T. Clason (ed.), *Archaeozoological Studies* (Amsterdam 1975), 120–31; and J.M. Hansen, *The Palaeoethnobotany of Franchthi Cave* (Bloomington 1991).

The spread of the Neolithic lifestyle into south-east Europe is considered with excellent summaries of the archaeological detail in A. Whittle, *Europe in the Neolithic: The Creation of New Worlds* (Cambridge 1996), chapter 3, and in D.W. Bailey, *Balkan Prehistory: Exclusion, Incorporation and Identity* (London 2000). The theme is also thoughtfully tackled in R. Tringham, 'Southeastern Europe in the Transition to Agriculture in Europe: Bridge, Buffer, or Mosaic', in T.D. Price (ed.), *Europe's First Farmers* (Cambridge 2000), 19–56.

The *Linearbandkeramik* phenomenon has generated a very considerable literature that is conveniently assessed in A. Whittle, *Europe in the Neolithic* (Cambridge 1996), chapter 6; P. Bogucki, 'How Agriculture Came to North-Central Europe', in T.D. Price (ed.), *Europe's First Farmers* (Cambridge 2000), 197–218; and D. Gronenborn, 'A Variation on a Basic Theme: The Transition to Farming in Southern Central Europe', *Journal of World Prehistory* 13 (1999), 123–210. Some classic site studies include P.J.R. Modderman, *Linearbandkeramik aus Elsloo und Stein* (Leiden 1970); J. Lüning, 'Research in the Bandkeramik Settlement on the Aldenhovener Platte in the Rhineland', *Analecta Praehistorica Leidensia* 15 (1982), 1–30; P. Stehli, 'Merzbachtal: Umwelt und Geschichte einer bandkeramischen Siedlunskammer', *Germania* 67 (1989), 51–76; and B. Soudský, 'The Neolithic Site of Bylany', *Antiquity* 36 (1962), 190–200. The multiple burial at Talheim in the Neckar valley is described in all its gory detail by J. Wahl and H.G. König, 'Anthropologisch-traumatologische Unterschung der menschlichen Skelettreste aus dem bandkeramischen Massengrab bei Talheim, Kreis Heilbronn', *Fundberichte aus Baden-Württemberg* 12 (1987), 65–193.

Chapter 5: Assimilation in the Maritime Regions: 6000–3800 BC

Since this chapter explores the same themes as Chapter 4, though covering a different geographical area, many of the general works cited in the first paragraph of the bibliographical essay for Chapter 4 are directly relevant to this chapter and serve as the introductory literature. Here we concentrate upon the publications specific to themes explored in this chapter.

Pioneering Neolithic settlements in the Mediterranean are dealt with in useful detail in A. Whittle, *Europe in the Neolithic* (Cambridge 1996), chapter 6. For the colonization of the islands of the Mediterranean, a very useful starting point, though now inevitably a little out of date, is J.F. Cherry, 'The First Colonization of the Mediterranean Islands: A Review of Recent Research', *Journal of Mediterranean Archaeology* 3 (1990), 145–221. Evidence for the Early Neolithic settlement in south-east Italy is summed up and discussed in R. Skeates, 'The Social Dynamics of Enclosure in the Neolithic of the Tavoliere, South-East Italy', *Journal of Mediterranean Archaeology* 13 (2000), 155–88, while the settlement of the string of islands between the Adriatic coast and the Tavoliere is dealt with in B. Bass, 'Early Neolithic Offshore Accounts: Remote Islands, Maritime Exploitations, and the Trans-Adriatic Cultural Network', *Journal of Mediterranean Archaeology* 11 (1998), 165–90. S. Forenbaher and P.T. Miracle take up the question of the colonization of the Adriatic coast in 'The Spread of Farming in the Eastern Adriatic', *Antiquity* 79 (2005), 514–28. The Neolithic settlement of Sicily is thoroughly treated in R. Leighton, *Sicily before History: An Archaeological Survey from the Palaeolithic to the Iron Age* (London 1999), chapter 2. For the important cave site of Grotta dell'Uzzo, S. Tusa, 'The Beginnings of Farming Communities in Sicily: The Evidence of Uzzo Cave', in C. Malone and S. Stoddart (eds), *Papers in Italian Archaeology IV Part ii, Prehistory* (Oxford 1985), 61–82, and M. Piperno, 'Some 14C Dates for the Palaeoeconomic Evidence from the Holocene Levels of Uzzo Cave, Sicily' in the same volume, 83–86. For the full report on the fauna, A. Tagliacozzo, *Archeozoologia della Grotta dell'Uzzo, Sicilia* (Rome 1993). The distribution of obsidian from sources in the Tyrrhenian Sea is discussed in some detail in R.H. Tykot, 'Obsidian Procurement and Distribution in the Central and Western Mediterranean', *Journal of Mediterranean Archaeology* 9 (1996), 39–82. Two useful papers dealing with the west Mediterranean European shore are W.K. Barnett, 'Cardial Pottery and the Agricultural Transition in Mediterranean Europe' and D. Binder, 'Mesolithic and Neolithic Interactions in Southern France and Northern Italy: New Data and Current Hypotheses', both in T.D. Price (ed.), *Europe's First Farmers* (Cambridge 2000). The debate on the origin of the Neolithic in Portugal has generated a spate of papers. The model of enclave colonization was put forward by J. Zilhão in three publications: *Gruta do Caldeirão O Neolitico Antigo* (Lisbon 1992); 'The Spread of Agro-Pastoral Economies Across Mediterranean Europe', *Journal of Mediterranean*

Archaeology 6 (1993), 5–63; and 'From the Mesolithic to the Neolithic in the Iberian Peninsula', in T.D. Price (ed.), *Europe's First Farmers* (Cambridge 2000). Contrary views have been presented in P. Arias, 'The Origins of the Neolithic Along the Atlantic coast of Continental Europe: A Survey', *Journal of World Prehistory* 13 (1999), 403–64, and M. Calado, 'Standing Stones and Natural Outcrops', in C. Scarre (ed.), *Monuments and Landscape in Atlantic Europe* (London 2002), 17–35. For some evidence from DNA studies now being brought to bear on the subject, see F. Bamforth, M. Jackes and D. Lubell, 'Mesolithic–Neolithic Population Relationships in Portugal: The Evidence from Ancient Mitochondrial DNA', in L. Larsson (ed.), *Mesolithic on the Move* (Oxford 2003), 581–87.

The question of the Neolithicization of western Europe via the Rhône valley or along the Atlantic seaways has been assessed by M. Zvelebil and P. Rowley-Conwy in their paper 'Foragers and Farmers in Atlantic Europe', in M. Zvelebil (ed.), *Hunters in Transition* (Cambridge 1987), 67–93 (especially pp. 70–73). A more detailed treatment of the pottery concerned is to be found in C. Jeunesse, 'Rapport avec le Néolithique ancien d'Alsace de la céramique "danubienne" de La Hoguette (à Fontenay-le-Marmion, Calvados)', in *Revue archéologique de l'Ouest, supplément 1* (1986), 41–50.

The spread of the Neolithic way of life into Denmark and southern Scandinavia is treated in a number of papers, among them M. Zvelebil and P. Rowley-Conwy, 'Foragers and Farmers in Atlantic Europe', in M. Zvelebil (ed.), *Hunters in Transition* (Cambridge 1987), 67–93; the same authors' more detailed treatment 'Transition to Farming in Northern Europe: A Hunter-Gatherer Perspective', *Norwegian Archaeological Review* 17 (1984), 104–28; and P. Rowley-Conwy, 'The Origins of Agriculture in Denmark: A Review of Some Theories', *Danish Journal of Archaeology* 4 (1985), 188–95. The most comprehensive overview of the TRB culture is M.S. Midgley, *TRB Culture: The First Farmers of the North European Plain* (Edinburgh 1992).

The Mesolithic–Neolithic interface in the Netherlands has been treated in general terms by L.P. Louwe Kooijmans, 'Understanding the Mesolithic/Neolithic Frontiers in the Lower Rhine Basin, 5300–4300 cal. BC' in M. Edmonds and C. Richards (eds), *Understanding the Neolithic in North-Western Europe* (Glasgow 1998), 407–26. The important Hardinxveld excavation is usefully summarized in the same author's paper, 'The Hardinxveld Sites in the Rhine/Meuse Delta, The Netherlands, 5500–4500 cal BC', in L. Larsson, *Mesolithic on the Move* (Oxford 2003), 608–24.

The fascinating issues involved in the beginnings of the Neolithic in Brittany and its approaches and the richness of the archaeological record have generated a considerable literature. Among the more recent contributions are three important papers by C. Scarre, 'The Early Neolithic of Western Europe and Megalithic Origins in Western Europe', *Oxford Journal of Archaeology* 11 (1992), 121–54; 'Contexts of Monumentalism: Regional Diversity at the Neolithic Transition in North-West France', *Oxford Journal of Archaeology* 21 (2002), 23–62; and 'Pioneer Farmers? The Neolithic Transition in Western Europe', in P. Bellwood and C. Renfrew (eds), *Examining the Farming/Language Dispersal Hypothesis* (Cambridge 2002), 395–407. Other significant contributions include S. Cassen, 'Material Culture and Chronology in the Middle Neolithic of Western France', *Oxford Journal of Archaeology* 12 (1993), 197–208; the same author's 'Le Néolithique le plus ancien de la façade atlantique de la France', *Munibe* 45 (1993), 119–29; S. Cassen *et al.*, 'L'habitat Villeneuve-Saint-Germain du Haut Mée (Saint-Etienne-en-Coglès, Ille-et-Vilaine)', *Bulletin de la Société Préhistorique Française* 95 (1998), 41–75; and S. Cassen *et al.*, 'Néolithisation de la France de l'Ouest . . .', *Gallia Préhistoire* 41 (1999), 41–75.

The introduction of food-producing regimes to Britain and Ireland was thoughtfully discussed in a classic paper some years ago by H. Case, 'Neolithic Explanations', *Antiquity* 43 (1969), 176–86, since when the dating evidence has been revised by E. Williams, 'Dating the Introduction of Food Production into Britain and Ireland', *Antiquity* 63 (1989), 510–21. More recent reviews are to be found in J. Waddell, *The Prehistoric Archaeology of Ireland* (Galway 1998) and P. Woodman, 'Getting Back to Basics: Transition to Farming in Ireland and Britain', in T.D. Price (ed.), *Europe's First Farmers* (Cambridge 2000), 219–59. A very interesting paper by C. Bonsall *et al.* considers the possible effect of climate change as a spur to the spread of agriculture to the extremities of Europe: 'Climate Change and the Adoption of Agriculture in North-West Europe', *European Journal of Archaeology* 5 (2002), 9–23.

Finally, the vexed question of the relationship between the spread of the Neolithic and the introduction of the Indo-European language is considered in the very stimulating overview by M. Zvelebil, 'Demography and Dispersal of Early Farming Populations at the Mesolithic–Neolithic Transition: Linguistic and Genetic Implications', in P. Bellwood and C. Renfrew (eds), *Examining the Farming/Language Dispersal Hypothesis* (Cambridge 2002), 379–94.

Chapter 6: Europe in Her Infinite Variety: *c.*4500–2800 BC

The best introduction to this fascinating but complex period remains A. Sherratt's 'The Transformation of Early Agrarian Europe: the Later Neolithic and Copper Ages, 4500–2500 BC', in B. Cunliffe (ed.), *Prehistoric Europe: An Illustrated History* (Oxford 1997), 167–201, which should be complemented by the relevant chapters in A. Whittle, *Europe in the Neolithic: The Creation of New Worlds* (Cambridge 1996). Useful summaries of the period are to be found in J. Lichardus and M. Lichardus-Itten, *La protohistoire de l'Europe: le néolithique et le chalcolithic entre la mer Méditerranée et la mer Baltique* (Paris 1985).

Turning now to settlement sites, a succinct overview of settlement in the Balkans is given in D.W. Bailey, *Balkan Prehistory* (London 2000). For Karanovo, see particularly S. Hiller and V. Nikolov (eds), *Karanovo: Die Ausgrabungen im Südsektor 1984–1992* (Horn 1997); and for aspects of settlement in Bulgaria, D.W. Bailey, 'The Interpretation of Settlement': An Exercise for Bronze Age Thrace', in L. Nikolova (ed.), *Early Bronze Age Settlement Patterns in the Balkans (ca. 3500–2000 BC)* (Sofia 1996, Reports of Prehistoric Research Projects 1, Part 2), 201–13, and 'What Is a Tell? Settlement in fifth-millennium BC Bulgaria', in J. Brück and M. Goodman (eds), *Making Places in the Prehistoric World: Themes in Settlement Archaeology* (London 1999), 94–111. The complex question of the Cucuteni-Tripolye culture of eastern Europe and its relations to the steppe is most conveniently introduced by I. Manzura, 'Steps to the Steppe; Or, How the North Pontic Region was Colonized', *Oxford Journal of Archaeology* 24 (2005), 313–38.

The stone 'fortifications' of Portugal, Spain and southern France have generated a rather dispersed literature. General contextual issues are discussed in R. Chapman, *Emerging Complexity: The Later Prehistory of South-East Spain, Iberia and the West Mediterranean* (Cambridge 1990). For Los Millares, A. Arribas Palau and F. Molina, 'Los Millares: Nuevas Perspectivas', in W.H. Waldren, J.A. Ensenyat and R.C. Kennard (eds), *IInd Deya International Conference of Prehistory* (Oxford 1991), 409–19. For Vila Nova de Sno Pedro, H.N. Savory, 'The Cultural Sequence at Vila Nova de S. Pedro', *Madrider Mitteilungen* 13 (1972), 23–37. For Zambujal, E. Sangmeister and H. Schubart, *Zambujal: die Grabungen 1964 bis 1973* (Mainz 1981). For the fortified enclosures in southern France, N. Mills, 'The Neolithic of Southern France', in C. Scarre (ed.), *The Neolithic of France* (Edinburgh 1983), 91–145, provides an introduction.

Although pottery is crucial to archaeological interpretation (and archaeological reports treat it ad nauseam) there are no good overviews that do justice to the technological achievements and creativity of prehistoric potters. All one can do is admire pottery in museum displays. Stone, on the other hand, has been fully explored and presented in a number of works of synthesis. The distribution of obsidian in the central Mediterranean is discussed in detail in R.H. Tykot,

'Obsidian Procurement and Distribution in the Central and Western Mediterranean', *Journal of Mediterranean Archaeology* 9 (1996), 39–82. Banded flint from Krzemionki in Poland is considered by W. Borkowski *et al.* in 'Possibilities of Investigating Neolithic Flint Economies as Exemplified by the Banded Flint Economy', *Antiquity* 65 (1991), 607–27. The flint mines of Rijckholt in the Netherlands are summarized in H.E.Th. de Grooth, 'Mines in the Marl: The flint extraction at Rijckholt', in L.P. Louwe Kooijmans *et al.* (ed.), *The Prehistory of the Netherlands, Volume 1* (Amsterdam 2005), 243–48. The same author discusses the social context of the mining activity in 'Socio-Economic Aspects of Neolithic Flint Mining: A Preliminary study', *Helinium* 31 (1991), 153–89. The famous axe factory at Sélédin near Plussulien in central Brittany is fully published in C.-T. Le Roux, *L'outillage de pierre polie en metadolerite du type A: les ateliers de Plussulien* (Rennes 1999), with a full discussion of the distribution of the axes throughout Europe. The origin and distribution of jadeite axes has generated a considerable literature – most recently, and most usefully: S. Cassen and P. Pétrequin, 'La chronologie des haches polies dites de prestige dans la moitié ouest de la France', *European Journal of Archaeology* 2 (1999), 7–33; A.-M. Pétrequin, P. Pétrequin and S. Cassen, 'Les longues lames polies des élites', *La Recherche* 312 (1998), 70–75, and E. Thirault, 'The Politics of Supply: The Neolithic Axe Industry in Alpine Europe', *Antiquity* 79 (2005), 34–50.

Early copperworking in south-eastern Europe and beyond is given a broad treatment by E.N. Chernykh in *Ancient Metallurgy in the USSR: The Early Metal Age* (Cambridge 1992). The same author published the first study of the Aibunar mines, 'Aibunar, a Balkan Copper Mine of the IVth Millennium BC', *Proceedings of the Prehistoric Society* 44 (1978), 203–18. The Rudna Glava mines in Serbia are given full treatment in B. Jovanović, *Rudna Glava: Najstarije Rudarstvo Bakra na Centralnom Balkanu* (Belgrade 1982) while N.H. Gale *et al.* provide a contextual study based on a series of metallographic analyses in 'Recent Studies of Eneolithic Copper Ores and Artefacts in Bulgaria', in J.-P. Mohen (ed.), *Découverte du métal* (Paris 1991), 49–76. Claims for very early copperworking in Almería, in south-eastern Spain, are made by A. Ruiz-Taboada and I. Ruiz Montero, 'The Oldest Metallurgy in Western Europe', *Antiquity* 73 (1999), 897–903.

The amazing cemetery of Varna on the Black Sea coast of Bulgaria is assessed in C. Renfrew, 'Varna and the Social Context of Early Metallurgy', *Antiquity* 52 (1978), 199–203. The finds are thoroughly discussed and well illustrated in the catalogue of an exhibition held at St Germain-en-Laye, *Le premier or de l'humanité en Bulgarie: 5è millénaire* (Paris 1989).

The question of the origins and development of wheeled vehicles is elegantly discussed in a wide sweep in S. Piggott, *The Earliest Wheeled Transport: From the Atlantic Coast to the Caspian Sea* (London 1983). Another seminal text is M.A. Littauer and J.H. Crouwel, *Wheeled Vehicles and Ridden Animals in the Ancient Near East* (Leiden 1979). Recent debates on origins are to be found in J.A. Bakker *et al.*, 'The Earliest Evidence of Wheeled Vehicles in Europe and the Near East', *Antiquity* 73 (1999), 778–90.

An overview of the Atlantic-facing west is given in B. Cunliffe, *Facing the Ocean: The Atlantic and its Peoples* (Oxford 2001), chapter 5. The debate about the origins of megalithic monuments in the Atlantic region can be followed in A. Sherratt, 'The Genesis of Megaliths: Monumentality, Ethnicity and Social Complexity in Neolithic North-West Europe', *World Archaeology* 22 (1990), 147–67; C. Scarre, 'The Early Neolithic of Western France and Megalithic Origins in Western Europe', *Oxford Journal of Archaeology* 11 (1992), 121–54; C. Boujot and S. Cassen, 'A Pattern of Evolution for the Neolithic Funerary Structures of the West of France', *Antiquity* 67 (1993), 477–91; M. Patton, 'Neolithisation and Megalithic Origins in North-Western France: A General Interactive Model', *Oxford Journal of Archaeology* 13 (1994), 279–93; A. Sherratt, 'Instruments of Conversion? The Role of Megaliths in the Mesolithic/Neolithic Transition in North-west Europe', *Oxford Journal of Archaeology* 14 (1995), 245–60; and C. Scarre, 'Contexts of Monumentalism: Regional Diversity at the Neolithic Transition in North-West France', *Oxford Journal of Archaeology* 21 (2002), 23–62.

Recent work on megaliths in western Iberia is summarized in a number of papers in an extremely useful compendium, A.A. Rodriguez Casal (ed.), *O Neolítico Atlántico e as orixes do Megalitismo* (Santiago de Compostela 1997). In Britain comparatively little work has been done since T. Powell (ed.), *Megalithic Enquiries in the West of Britain* (Liverpool 1969) except for C. Renfrew, *Investigations in Orkney* (London 1979). In Ireland, J. Waddell, *The Prehistoric Archaeology of Ireland* (Galway 1998) offers an up-to-date overview.

The complexities of the Corded Ware/Single Grave culture are covered in the relevant section in A. Whittle, *Europe in the Neolithic* (Cambridge 1996) and in detail in a number of more specific papers in the *Journal of Danish Archaeology*, most particularly J. Simonsen, 'Settlements from the Single Grave Culture in North-West Jutland: A Preliminary Survey' in Vol. 5 (1986), 135–51.

In eastern Europe and the steppe, the development and spread of kurgans (burial mounds) has been a favourite theme for debate. The classic paper is M. Gimbutas, 'The Beginnings of the Bronze Age in Europe and the Indo-Europeans', *Journal of Indo-European Studies* 1 (1973),

163–214. The same author has expounded her theme in *The Civilization of the Goddess* (San Francisco 1991) and these issues are further explored in J.P. Mallory, *In Search of the Indo-Europeans* (London 1989). Another useful contribution to the debate is D.W. Anthony, 'The "Kurgan Culture", Indo-European Origins and the Domestication of the Horse: A Reconsideration', *Current Anthropology* 27 (1986), 291–313. The burials from Plačidol are discussed by I. Panayotov and V. Dergačov, 'Die Ockergrabkultur in Bulgarien (Darstellung des Problems)', *Studia Praehistorica* 7 (1984), 99–111.

For the Mediterranean the literature is massive and we must be selective. Maltese issues are conveniently brought together in a paper by S. Stoddart *et al.*, 'Cult in an Island Society: Prehistoric Malta in the Tarxien Period', *Cambridge Archaeological Journal* 3 (1993), 3–19. The standard work on the archaeology of the island is J.D. Evans, *The Prehistoric Antiquities of the Maltese Islands: A Survey* (London 1971). Some of the issues of insularity are treated in A. Bonnano *et al.*, 'Monuments in an Island Society: the Maltese Context', *World Archaeology* 22 (1990), 190–205. The development of society and mobility in the Cyclades is meticulously covered in a major work, C. Broodbank, *An Island Archaeology of the Early Cyclades* (Cambridge 2000).

Chapter 7: Taking to the Sea – Crossing the Peninsula: 2800–1300 BC

This chapter covers what is traditionally called the Early and Middle Bronze Age. A readable overview of the entire period can be found in three chapters in B. Cunliffe (ed.), *Prehistoric Europe: An Illustrated History* (Oxford 1997): Chapter 5, 'The Transformation of Early Agrarian Europe: The Later Neolithic and Copper Ages, 4500–2500 BC' by A. Sherratt; Chapter 6, 'The Palace Civilizations of Minoan Crete and Mycenaean Greece, 2000–1200 BC' by K.A. Wardle; and Chapter 7, 'The Emergence of Élites: Earlier Bronze Age Europe, 2500–1300 BC' by A. Sherratt. The two standard textbooks for this period are J.M. Coles and A.F. Harding, *The Bronze Age in Europe: An Introduction to the Prehistory of Europe c.2000–700 BC* (London 1979), giving a detailed account of Europe region for region, and A.F. Harding, *European Societies in the Bronze Age* (Cambridge 2000), which has a more up-to-date thematic approach. Also to be recommended is the same author's *The Mycenaeans and Europe* (London 1984) which deals extensively with patterns of trade and exchange. Among the many compilations of conference papers relevant to our subject, useful papers are to be found in C.F.E. Pare (ed.), *Metals Make the World Go Round: The Supply and Circulation of Metals in Bronze Age Europe* (Oxford 2000); B. Hänsel (ed.), *Mensch und Umwelt in der Bronzezeit Europas* (*Man and Environment in European Bronze Age*) (Berlin 1998); and F. Nicolis (ed.), *Bell Beakers Today: Pottery, People, Culture, Symbols in Prehistoric Europe* (Trento 2001). The exhibition catalogue *L'Europe au temps d'Ulysse: dieux et héros de l'âge du bronze* (Paris 1999) is informative and beautifully illustrated. Also to be highly recommended is the elegantly produced catalogue *Symbols of Power at the Time of Stonehenge* (Edinburgh 1985), edited by D.V. Clarke, T.G. Cowie and A. Foxon, which covers mainly the British Isles though with some material from Brittany. Finally, in this introductory paragraph, A. Sherratt's stimulating paper 'What Would a Bronze-Age World System Look Like? Relations Between Temperate Europe and the Mediterranean in Later Prehistory', *Journal of European Archaeology* 1:2 (1993), 1–57, examines changing trade routes across the peninsula.

The most accessible and up-to-date short overview of developments in the Near East is R. Matthews, 'The Rise of Civilization in Southwest Asia', in C. Scarre (ed.), *The Human Past: World Prehistory and the Development of Human Societies* (London 2005), 432–71. The same author's *The Archaeology of Mesopotamia: Theories and Approaches* (London 2003) provides an in-depth guide. For the Levant T.E. Levy (ed.), *The Archaeology of Society in the Holy Land* (Leicester 1995) contains a number of useful contributions. The relationship of the Minoan/Mycenaean world to Anatolia is charted in C. Mee, 'Aegean Trade and Settlement in Anatolia in the Second Millennium', *Anatolian Studies* 28 (1978), 121–50, while the contemporary trade networks in Anatolia are considered in V. Şahoğlu, 'The Anatolian Trade Network and the Izmir Region During the Early Bronze Age', *Oxford Journal of Archaeology* 24 (2005), 339–61.

The archaeology of the Cyclades is treated fully and with great insight in C. Broodbank, *An Island Archaeology of the Early Cyclades* (Cambridge 2000). General books on Minoans and Mycenaeans abound. Most useful are P.M. Warren, *The Aegean Civilization* (2nd edition, Oxford 1990); O. Dickinson, *The Aegean Bronze Age* (Cambridge 1994); J.L. Fitton, *Minoans* (London 2002); G. Cadogan, *Palaces of Minoan Crete* (London 1976); J.T. Hooker, *Mycenaean Greece* (London 1976); and J. Chadwick, *The Mycenaean World* (Cambridge 1977). More specific studies relevant to trade and exchange are J.T. Killen, 'The Wool Industry of Crete in the Late Bronze Age', *Annual of the British School at Athens* 59 (1964), 1–15; P. Halstead, 'On Redistribution and the Origin of the Minoan-Mycenaean Palatial Economies', in E.B. French and K.A. Wardle (eds), *Problems in Greek Prehistory* (Bristol 1988), 519–30; S. Sherratt, 'Circulation of Metals and the End of the Bronze Age in the Eastern Mediterranean', in C.F.E. Pare (ed.), *Metals Make the World*

Go Round: The Supply and Circulation of Metals in Bronze Age Europe (Oxford 2000), 82–97. Two sets of conference proceedings provide many insights into maritime interconnections: E.H. Cline and D. Harris-Cline (eds), *The Aegean and the Orient in the Second Millennium: Proceedings of the 50th Anniversary Symposium, Cincinnati, 18–20 April 1997* (Liège 1998); and N.C. Stambolidis and V. Karageorghis (eds), *Sea Routes: Interconnections in the Mediterranean 16th–6th c. BC: Proceedings of the International Symposium held at Rethymnon, Crete, September 29th–October 2nd 2002* (Athens 2003). The question of ships and seafaring is explored in S. McGrail, 'Bronze Age Seafaring in the Mediterranean: A View from N.W. Europe', in N.H. Gale (ed.), *Bronze Age Trade in the Mediterranean* (Oxford 1991), 83–91. The same volume contains several other useful papers. For the Uluburun wreck, C. Pulak, 'The Uluburun Shipwreck', in S. Swiny *et al.* (eds), *Res Maritimae: Cyprus and the Eastern Mediterranean from Prehistory to Late Antiquity, Proceedings of the Second International Symposium 'Cities on the Sea', Nicosia, Cyprus, October 18–24, 1994* (Atlanta 1997), 233–62. For the Cape Gelidonya wreck, G.F. Bass, *Cape Gelidonya: A Bronze Age Shipwreck* (Philadelphia 1967). A.B. Knapp, 'Thalassocracies in Bronze Age Eastern Mediterranean Trade: Making and Breaking the Myth', *World Archaeology* 24 (1993), 332–47, provides some interesting thoughts on maritime trade.

The systems at work in the Tyrrhenian Sea in the Bronze Age have not been subject to a synthetic study but much useful material has been brought together in A.F. Harding, *The Mycenaeans and Europe* (London 1984), especially pp. 244–63. To this can be added the thought-provoking paper by D. Ridgway and F.R. Serra Ridgway, 'Sardinia and History', in R.H. Tykot and T.K. Andrews (eds), *Sardinia in the Mediterranean: A Footprint in the Sea* (Sheffield 1992), 355–63.

Atlantic systems are summarized in B. Cunliffe, *Facing the Ocean: The Atlantic and its Peoples* (Oxford 2001), Chapter 6 (with a supporting bibliography, pp. 574–75), to which can be added the many papers published in the symposium edited by F. Nicolis, *Bell Beakers Today: Pottery, People, Culture, Symbols in Prehistoric Europe* (Trento 2001) and S. Needham, 'Transforming Beaker Culture in North-West Europe: Processes of Fusion and Fission', *Proceedings of the Prehistoric Society* 71 (2005), 171–218.

The important metalworking site at Ross Island is described and fully assessed in W. O'Brien, *Ross Island: Mining, Metal and Society in Early Ireland* (Galway 2004). The origins of metallurgy in Ireland are discussed in the same author's 'La plus ancienne métallurgie du cuivre en Ireland' in *La première métallurgie en France et dans les pays limitrophes* (Mémoire XXXVII de la Société Préhistorique Française) (Paris 2005).

The ships used in the Atlantic/North Sea region in the Bronze Age are conveniently summarized in a magisterial work by S. McGrail, *Boats of the World from the Stone Age to Medieval Times* (Oxford 2001), 184–93, with full references. To this should now be added P. Clark, *The Dover Bronze Age Boat* (London 2004) and R. Van de Noort, '"The Kilnsea-Boat" and Some Implications from the Discovery of England's Oldest Plank Boat Remains', *Antiquity* 73 (1999), 131–35.

The emergence of local elites along the Atlantic seaboard have generated an extensive literature. In the Tagus region a good starting point is R. Harrison, *The Bell Beaker Culture of Spain and Portugal* (Harvard 1977), to be followed by S. Oliveira Jorge and V. Oliveira Jorge, 'The Neolithic/Chalcolithic Transition in Portugal', in M. Díaz-Andreu and S. Keay (eds), *The Archaeology of Iberia: The Dynamics of Change* (London 1997), 128–42. The Armorican peninsula is thoroughly covered in J. Briard, *Les tumulus d'Armorique* (Paris 1984) while the relationship between Armorica and Wessex is carefully assessed in S.P. Needham, 'Power Pulses Across a Cultural Divide: Cosmologically Driven Acquisition between Armorica and Wessex', *Proceedings of the Prehistoric Society* 66 (2000), 151–208. The same author's 'The Development of Embossed Goldwork in Bronze Age Europe', *Antiquaries Journal* 80 (2000), 27–65, provides an insight into one aspect of elite production, a theme that forms the main context of D.V. Clarke, T.G. Cowie and A. Foxon, *Symbols of Power at the Time of Stonehenge* (Edinburgh 1985). The papers by Needham give an up-to-date assessment of the chronology of the Wessex elite but the seminal paper by S. Piggott, 'The Early Bronze Age in Wessex', *Proceedings of the Prehistoric Society* 4 (1938), 52–106, can still be read with value.

The Nordic region can best be approached by first reading a succinct overview: J. Jensen, *The Prehistory of Denmark* (London 1982). P.V. Glob, *The Mound People: Danish Bronze-Age Man Preserved* (London 1974) is a spirited account of some of the major Bronze Age finds. The Bronze Age rock carvings of Scandinavia have generated an extensive literature but for range and insight it is difficult to better J. Coles, *Shadows of a Northern Past: Rock Carvings of Bohuslän and Østfold* (Oxford 2005). Ship imagery is fully discussed in F. Kaul, *Ships on Bronzes: A Study of Bronze Age Religion and Iconography* (Copenhagen 1998), while the remarkable tomb of Kivik is expansively considered in K. Randsborg, *Kivik: Archaeology and Iconography* (Copenhagen 1993). K. Kristiansen, 'Seafaring Voyages and Rock Art Ships', in P. Clark (ed.), *The Dover Bronze Age Boat in Context* (Oxford 2004), 112–21, discusses the possibility of long-distance voyages and this theme is extensively explored in a stimulating study by K. Kristiansen and T.B. Larsson, *The Rise of*

Bronze Age Society: Travels, Transmissions and Transformations (Cambridge 2005). Evidence for trade between Jutland and Norway is discussed in B. Solberg, 'Exchange and the Role of Import to Western Norway in the Late Neolithic and Early Bronze Age', *Norwegian Archaeological Review* 27 (1994), 112–26.

Relationships between the Nordic zone, the Carpathians, the Mycenaean world and the steppe region are variously considered in H. Thrane, 'The Mycenaean Fascination' in P. Schauer (ed.), *Spuren orientalische-ägäischen Einflüsses im Donauraum in Südwest-, West- und Nordeuropa während der Bronzezeit* (Mainz 1989); H. Thrane, 'Centres of Wealth in Northern Europe', in K. Kristiansen and J. Jensen (eds), *Europe in the First Millennium B.C.* (Sheffield 1994), 95–110; and T.B. Larsson, 'The Transmission of an Élite Ideology – Europe and the Near East in the Second Millennium BC', in J. Goldhahn (ed.), *Rock Art as Social Representation* (Oxford 1999), 49–64. The origin and spread of the chariot is a theme of recurrent interest addressed in M.A. Littauer and J.H. Crouwell, 'The Origin of the True Chariot', *Antiquity* 70 (1996), 934–39 and, more recently, P.F. Kuznetsov, 'The Emergence of Bronze Age Chariots in Eastern Europe', *Antiquity* 80 (2006), 638–45.

Chapter 8: Emerging Eurozones: 1300–800 BC

Europe in the Late Bronze Age is seldom dealt with as a whole since it is from this time that a division begins to appear between the realm of the prehistorian dealing with 'barbarian Europe' and that of the classical archaeologist whose focus lies in the Mediterranean. As a general introduction to the 'barbarian', A.F. Harding, *European Society in the Bronze Age* (Cambridge 2000) provides an excellent overview, while the paper by S. Sherratt and A. Sherratt, 'The Growth of the Mediterranean Economy in the Early First Millennium BC', *World Archaeology* 24 (1993), 361–78, offers a thoughtful view of patterns of trade and exchange. The arguments are complemented and extended in A. Sherratt, 'What Would a Bronze-Age World System Look Like?', *Journal of European Archaeology* 1:2 (1993), 1–57. The wide-ranging synthesis and overview by K. Kristiansen, *Europe Before History* (Cambridge 1998), treats the Late Bronze Age in chapters 4 and 5. A detailed consideration of the archaeological evidence for trade routes in central and eastern Europe is given in A. Pydyn, *Exchange and Cultural Interactions: A Study of Long-Distance Trade and Cross-Cultural Contacts in the Late Bronze Age and Early Iron Age in Central and Eastern Europe* (Oxford 1999).

The systems collapse in the east Mediterranean is explored in the highly readable and erudite book by

N.K. Sandars, *The Sea Peoples: Warriors of the Ancient Mediterranean* (London 1978). More specific archaeological detail is given in M. Liverani, 'The Collapse of the Near Eastern Regional System at the End of the Bronze Age: The Case of Syria', in M. Rowlands, M.T. Larsen and K. Kristiansen (eds), *Centre and Periphery in the Ancient World* (Cambridge 1987), 66–73, and L.E. Stager, 'The Impact of the Sea Peoples in Canaan (1185–1050 BCE)', in T.E. Levy (ed.), *The Archaeology of Society in the Holy Land* (Leicester 1995), 332–48. The Philistines are discussed in T. Dothan, 'The "Sea-Peoples" and the Philistines of Ancient Palestine', in J.M. Sasson (ed.), *Civilizations of the Ancient Near East* (New York 1995), 1267–79. For the Phoenicians, D.B. Harden, *The Phoenicians* (Harmondsworth 1980) and G.E. Markoe, *The Phoenicians* (London 2000) offer excellent overviews. A more detailed treatment is to be found in M.E. Aubet, *The Phoenicians and the West* (London 1987).

There is, as might be expected, extensive coverage of the period in Greece. O. Dickinson, *The Aegean Bronze Age* (Cambridge 1994) is the standard work. M. Popham, 'The Collapse of Aegean Civilization and the End of the Late Bronze Age', in B. Cunliffe, *Prehistoric Europe: An Illustrated History* (Oxford 1997), 277–303, offers a short, readable account of the period. The Greek 'Dark Age' has been the subject of several excellent volumes: A.M. Snodgrass, *The Dark Age of Greece* (Edinburgh 1971); V.R.d'A. Desborough, *The Greek Dark Ages* (London 1972); J.N. Coldstream, *Geometric Greece* (London 1977); and I. Lemos, *The Protogeometric Aegean: The Archaeology of the Late Eleventh and Tenth Centuries* BC (Oxford 2002). It is also succinctly treated in a broader context in J. Whitley, *The Archaeology of Ancient Greece* (Cambridge 2001). The vitally important Dark Age, site of Lefkandi on the island of Euboea is summarized by the excavator M. Popham in 'Lefkandi and the Greek Dark Age' in B. Cunliffe (ed.), *Origins: The Roots of European Civilization* (London 1987), 67–80.

The question of early trade between Euboea and the east Mediterranean is discussed in M. Popham, 'Precolonization: Early Greek contact with the East' in G.R. Tsetskhladze and F. De Angelis (eds), *The Archaeology of Greek Colonisation* (Oxford 1994), 11–34, and M. Popham and I.S. Lemos, 'A Euboean Warrior Trader', *Oxford Journal of Archaeology* 14 (1995), 151–58.

The standard work on iron in Old World archaeology is T.A. Westime and J.D. Muhly (eds), *The Coming of the Age of Iron* (New Haven 1980). The introduction of iron into Greece is considered in its social context in A.M. Snodgrass, 'The Coming of the Iron Age in Greece: Europe's Earliest Bronze/Iron Transition', in M.L. Stig Sørensen and R. Thomas (eds), *The Bronze Age–Iron Age Transition in Europe: Aspects of Continuity and Change in European Societies* c.*1200–500* BC (Oxford 1989), 22–35. The same volume contains many other useful papers.

The maritime relationship between Cyprus and the central Mediterranean is detailed in F. Lo Schiavo, E. Macnamara and L. Vagnetti, 'Late Cypriot Imports to Italy and their Influence on Local Bronzework', *Papers of the British School at Rome* 53 (1985), 1–71, and L. Vagnetti and F. Lo Schiavo, 'Late Bronze Age Long-Distance Trade in the Mediterranean: The Role of the Cypriots', in E. Peltenburg (ed.), *Early Society in Cyprus* (Edinburgh 1989), 217–43. A stimulating discussion of the issues of the trade connections is given in D. Ridgway and F.R. Serra Ridgway, 'Sardinia and History', in R.H. Tykot and T.K. Andrews (eds), *Sardinia in the Mediterranean: A Footprint in the Sea* (Sheffield 1992), 355–63. A paper by S. Sherratt, 'Circulation of Metals and the End of the Bronze Age in the Eastern Mediterranean', in C.F.E. Pare (ed.), *Metals Make the World Go Round: The Supply and Circulation of Metals in Bronze Age Europe* (Oxford 2000), 82–97, provides the broader context for this trade.

Aspects of Sardinian archaeology are discussed in a number of contributions in R.H. Tykot and T.K. Andrews (eds), *Sardinia in the Mediterranean: A Footprint in the Sea* (Sheffield 1992). The Bronze Age of Sardinia is given a detailed treatment in G.S. Webster, *A Prehistory of Sardinia 2300–500* BC (Sheffield 1996). Etruria and the Etruscans have generated a massive literature. Two books that can be particularly recommended are N. Spivey and S. Stoddart, *Etruscan Italy* (London 1990) and G. Barker and T. Rasmussen, *The Etruscans* (Oxford 1998). Both discuss the origins of the Etruscans using up-to-date archaeological data. The subject of the exchange systems between Italy and the Alpine region is addressed in A.-M. Bietti Sestieri, 'Italy and Europe in the Early Iron Age', *Proceedings of the Prehistoric Society* 63 (1997), 371–402. Imported materials found at the *emporium* at Frattesina in the Po valley are considered in A.-M. Bietti Sestieri and J. de Grossi Mazzoria, 'Importazione di materie prime organiche di origine esotica nell'abitato protostorico di Frattesina (Rovigo)', *Atti del Primo Convegno Nazionale di Archeozoologia Quaderni di Padusa 1* (1995), 367–70.

Little attention has been paid to the maritime systems at work in the west Mediterranean at this time but the distribution of Atlantic metalwork in the west Mediterranean, particularly on Sardinia, is referred to in A. Coffyn, *Le Bronze Final Atlantique dans la Péninsule Ibérique* (Paris 1985). The same volume provides much of the evidence for exchange systems along the Atlantic seaways. Another book stressing the focal position of Iberia in the exchange networks is R.J. Harrison's *Symbols and Warriors: Images of the European Bronze Age* (Bristol 2004). Atlantic networks are also treated in B. Cunliffe, *Facing the Ocean: The Atlantic and its Peoples* (Oxford 2001), chapter 7, with an extensive bibliography to which reference should be made for detailed works.

The rich religious symbolism of the Nordic Bronze Age has been discussed recently in K. Kristiansen, 'Cosmology and Consumption in the Bronze Age', in J. Goldhahn (ed.), *Mellan sten och järn: Rapport från det 9:e nordiska bronsålderssymposiet, Göteborg 2003-10-09/12* (Göteborg 2004), 135–47, and in R. Bradley, 'Danish Razors and Swedish Rocks: Cosmology and the Bronze Age Landscape', *Antiquity* 80 (2006), 372–89. The Swedish rock art is best appreciated through the publications of J. Coles, especially 'Chariots of the Gods? Landscape and Imagery at Frännorp, Sweden', *Proceedings of the Prehistoric Society* 68 (2002), 215–46; *Patterns in a Rocky Landscape: Rock Carvings in South-West Uppland* (Uppsala 2000); and *Shadows of a Northern Past: Rock Carvings of Bohuslän and Østfold* (Oxford 2005).

Trans-European trade with the Nordic zone is discussed in: K. Kristiansen, 'Economic Models for Bronze Age Scandinavia – Towards an Integrated Approach', in A. Sheridan and G. Bailey (eds), *Economic Archaeology: Towards an Integration of Ecological and Social Approaches* (Oxford 1981), 239–303; the same author's 'From Villanova to Seddin: The Reconstruction of an Elite Exchange Network During the Eighth Century BC', in C. Scarre and F. Healy (eds), *Trade and Exchange in Prehistoric Europe* (Oxford 1993), 143–51; and H. Thrane, 'Centres of Wealth in Northern Europe' in K. Kristiansen and J. Jensen (eds), *Europe in the First Millennium* B.C. (Sheffield 1994), 95–110. The subject is very thoroughly reviewed in A. Pydyn, *Exchange and Cultural Interactions: A Study of Long-Distance Trade and Cross-Cultural Contacts in the Late Bronze Age and Early Iron Age in Central and Eastern Europe* (Oxford 1999).

The Cimmerians are rather an intangible people but they were a significant force in the Near East and are referred to in a number of contemporary texts, conveniently summarized in E.D. Philips, 'The Scythian Domination in Western Asia: Its Record in History, Scripture and Archaeology', *World Archaeology* 4 (1972), 129–38, and A.I. Ivantchik, *Les Cimmériens au Proche-Orient* (Göttingen 1993). The classic discussion of early horse gear in the Carpathian Basin is S. Gallas and T. Horváth, *Un peuple cavalier préscythique en Hongrie* (Budapest 1939). More recent assessments include G. Gazdapusztai, 'Caucasian Relations of the Danubian Basin in the Early Iron Age', *Acta Archaeologica Hungarica* 19 (1967), 307–34, and J. Chochorowski, *Ekspansja Kimmeryjska na tereny Europy Środkowej* (Kraków 1993). There is a discussion of the types of horses used in Europe, distinguishing steppe horses from indigenous western horses, in S. Bökönyi, *Data on Iron Age Horses of Central and Eastern Europe* (Cambridge, Mass. 1968). The site of Mezöcsát is published in E. Patek, 'Präskythische Gräberfelder in Ostungarn', in *Symposium zu Problemen der jüngeren Hallstattzeit in Mitteleuropa* (Bratislava 1974), 337–62.

In the final section of the chapter were mentioned wheeled vehicles. The most accessible source is the comprehensive volume by S. Piggott, *The Earliest Wheeled Transport: From the Atlantic Coast to the Caspian Sea* (London 1983). The Late Bronze Age background to the development of wheeled vehicles is presented in Chapter 2 of C.F.E. Pare, *Wagons and Wagon-Graves of the Early Iron Age in Central Europe* (Oxford 1992).

Chapter 9: The Three Hundred Years That Changed the World: 800–500 BC

In this chapter we have of necessity been very selective, especially in dealing with the conventional history of the Mediterranean, preferring instead to focus on the broad rhythms of interaction. Those interested in following up the detailed history of the period can do no better than consult the magisterial volumes of the *Cambridge Ancient History*, aiming, wherever possible, for the most up-to-date editions.

The Phoenicians are a very underrated force, largely because of a deep-rooted classical hatred of them that has flowed through to recent scholarship. The fullest and most balanced accounts are D. Harden, *The Phoenicians* (Harmondsworth 1980) and G.E. Markoe, *The Phoenicians* (London 2000). The catalogue of a comprehensive exhibition held at the Palazzo Grassi in Venice in 1988, S. Moscati (ed.), *The Phoenicians* (Milan 1988), is lavishly illustrated and contains many excellent essays by experts. For an analytical and scholarly text dealing specifically with the Phoenicians in the west Mediterranean and Atlantic, M.E. Aubet, *The Phoenicians and the West* (Cambridge 1987) is to be recommended.

General books on the Greeks are legion. For the Greek mainland, I. Morris, *Burial and Ancient Society: The Rise of the Greek City-State* (Cambridge 1987) and J. Whitley, *The Archaeology of Ancient Greece* (Cambridge 2001) are both stimulating texts written by practising archaeologists. The standard text on the Greek colonial phenomenon is J. Boardman, *The Greeks Overseas: Their Early Colonies and Trade* (London 1980), while J.M. Cook, *The Greeks in Ionia and the East* (London 1970) is an elegant and informative essay. Another of the Palazzo Grassi's extravaganzas in 1996 led to the production of a sumptuous catalogue, G.P. Carratelli (ed.), *The Western Greeks* (Milan 1996), packed with valuable discussions and brilliant illustrations. For an overview of the emergence of cities in the Mediterranean, R. Osborne and B. Cunliffe (eds), *Mediterranean Urbanization 800–600 BC* (London 2005).

The Etruscans are no less well covered in the literature. N. Spivey and S. Stoddart, *Etruscan Italy* (London 1990); G. Barker and T. Rasmussen, *The Etruscans* (Oxford 1998); and S. Haynes, *Etruscan Civilization: A Cultural History* (London 2000) together provide incomparable coverage.

Events in the east can conveniently be followed in A. Kuhrt, *The Ancient Near East, c.3000–330 BC* (London 1995) and M. Van De Mieroop, *A History of the Ancient Near East c.3000–323 BC* (Oxford 2004), while the Persian Empire and its impact on the west are thoroughly covered in J.E. Curtis, *Ancient Persia* (2nd edition, London 2000) and J. Curtis and N. Tallis (eds), *Forgotten Empire: The World of Ancient Persia* (London 2005).

The books listed in the above paragraphs all provide background material relevant to our discussion of the east Mediterranean. In addition the following offer further detail: V. Karageorghis, *Kition: Mycenaean and Phoenician Discoveries in Cyprus* (London 1976); J.D. Muhly, 'Homer and the Phoenicians', *Berytus* 19 (1970), 19–64; A.M. Greaves, *Miletos: A History* (London 2002); A. Möller, *Naukratis: Trade in Archaic Greece* (Oxford 2000); and J. Boardman, 'Al Mina and History', *Oxford Journal of Archaeology* 9 (1990), 169–90.

The sailing vessels used at this time are well covered in a lively overview, L. Casson, *Ships and Seafaring in Ancient Times* (London 1994), and in rather more detail in the same author's *Ships and Seamanship in the Ancient World* (2nd edition, Princeton 1986), also in J. Morrison and R. Williams, *Greek Oared Ships* (Cambridge 1968) and J. Morrison and J. Coates, *The Athenian Trireme* (Cambridge 1986).

On the subject of the Tyrrhenian Sea, Chapter 3 of M. Pallottino, *A History of Earliest Italy* (London 1991) outlines the history of cultural interaction. Issues surrounding the settlement of Pithekoussai are debated in two thought-provoking papers, D. Ridgway, 'Phoenicians and Greeks in the West: A View from Pithekoussai' and J.N. Coldstream, 'Prospectors and Pioneers: Pithekoussai, Kyme and Central Italy', both in G.R. Tsetskhladze and F. De Angelis (eds), *The Archaeology of Greek Colonisation* (Oxford 1994), 35–46 and 47–60. Many of the issues are also explored in D. Ridgway, *The First Western Greeks* (Cambridge 1992). Aspects of the colonization of Sardinia are treated in a number of papers in R.H. Tykot and T.K. Andrews, *Sardinia in the Mediterranean: A Footprint in the Sea* (Sheffield 1992), notably J.M. Davison, 'Greeks in Sardinia: Myth and Reality', 384–95, and B. Peckham, 'The Phoenician Foundation of Cities and Towns in Sardinia', 410–18. Greek colonization in Sicily is considered in detail in F. De

Angelis, *Megara, Hyblaia and Selinous: The Development of Two Greek City-States in Archaic Sicily* (Oxford 2003).

For the west Mediterranean, the most convenient summary of Phoenician settlement (with a full bibliography) is in M.E. Aubet, *The Phoenicians and the West* (Cambridge 1993). Detailed studies are given in H.G. Niemeyer (ed.), *Phönizier im Westen* (Mainz 1982). Two other important considerations are H.G. Niemeyer, 'Phoenician Toscanos as a Settlement Model? Its Urbanistic Character in the Context of Phoenician Expansion and Iberian Acculturation' and M.E. Aubet, 'From Trading Post to Town in the Phoenician-Punic World', both in B. Cunliffe and S. Keay (eds), *Social Complexity and the Development of Towns in Iberia* (Oxford 1995), 67–88 and 47–66. The Greek contact with Iberia is given full treatment in: B. Shefton, 'Greeks and Greek Imports in the South of the Iberian Peninsula: The Archaeological evidence', in H.G. Niemeyer (ed.), *Phönizier im Westen* (Mainz 1982), 337–70; A.J. Domínguez, 'New Perspectives on the Greek Presence in the Iberian Peninsula', in J.M. Fossey (ed.), *Proceedings of the First International Congress on the Hellenic Diaspora. Vol I: From Antiquity to 1453* (Amsterdam 1991), 109–61; P. Rouillard, 'Les colonies grecques du Sud-Est de la Péninsule Ibérique', *Parola del Passato* 204–07, 417–29; and A.J. Domínguez Monedero, *Los griegos en la Península Ibérica* (Madrid 1996). For an overview of Greek and Phoenician activity in Iberia, B. Cunliffe, 'Core-Periphery Relationships: Iberia and the Mediterranean', in P. Bilde *et al.* (eds), *Centre and Periphery in the Hellenistic World* (Aarhus 1993), 53–85. R.J. Harrison, *Spain at the Dawn of History: Iberians, Phoenicians and Greeks* (London 1988) is by far the best available overview of the many cultural interactions in the south and east of the peninsula.

Etruscan and early Greek trade and settlement in southern France are conveniently discussed in B.B. Shefton, 'Massalia and Colonization in the North-Western Mediterranean', in G.R. Tsetskhladze and F. De Angelis, *The Archaeology of Greek Colonisation* (Oxford 1994), 61–86. Etruscan shipwrecks off the coast of southern France are summarized in L. Long, P. Pomey and J.-C. Sourisseau, *Les Étrusques en mer: épaves d'Antibes à Marseille* (Marseille 2002), while the archaeology of the colony of Massalia is attractively presented in A. Hermary, A. Hesnard and H. Tréziny, *Marseille Grecque. La cité phocéenne (600–49 av. J.-C.* (Paris 1999).

The Phoenician settlement along the Atlantic coastline is not particularly well known but evidence from Lixus is now presented in C. Aranegui Gascó, *Lixus: colonia Fenicia y cuidad Púnico-Mauritana anotaciones sobre su ocupación medieval* (Valenica 2001). A. González-Ruibal's paper 'Facing Two Seas: Mediterranean and Atlantic Contacts in the North-West of Iberia in the First Millennium BC', *Oxford Journal of Archaeology* 23 (2004), 287–317, provides a useful summary of evidence of maritime contact along the Atlantic coast of Iberia. The question of trade and exchange along the Atlantic face of Europe is treated in a broad perspective in B. Cunliffe, *Facing the Ocean: The Atlantic and its Peoples* (Oxford 2001) in chapter 7. For the developments in Britain and the relationship of the British Isles to the continent, see B. Cunliffe, *Iron Age Communities in Britain* (4th edition, London 2005).

The Nordic zone is quiescent in this period, with comparatively little happening. The situation in Denmark is well summed up in J. Jensen, *The Prehistory of Denmark* (London 1982). The broader perspective is debated in K. Kristiansen, *Europe Before History* (Cambridge 1998).

The Black Sea region sees the emergence of the Scythians and their interaction with the Greek colonies. A useful starting point is the relevant chapter in J. Boardman, *The Greeks Overseas* (London 1980), which is updated by G.R. Tsetskhladze, 'Greek Penetration of the Black Sea', in G.R. Tsetskhladze and F. De Angelis, *The Archaeology of Greek Colonisation* (Oxford 1994), 111–36. D. Braund (ed.), *Scythians and Greeks: Cultural Interactions in Scythia, Athens and the Early Roman Empire* (Exeter 2005) offers a number of interesting papers. For the Scythians as a people, the two standard approachable texts are T.T. Rice, *The Scythians* (London 1957) and R. Rolle, *The World of the Scythians* (London 1989). The literature on the Scythian penetration of Europe is assessed in A. Pydyn, *Exchange and Cultural Interactions: A Study of Long-Distance Trade and Cross-Cultural Contacts in the Late Bronze Age and Early Iron Age in Central and Eastern Europe* (Oxford 1999). A rather glossy, but nonetheless worthwhile, presentation of some of the more spectacular items from the Scythian tombs is to be found in M.I. Artamonov, *Treasures from Scythian Tombs in the Hermitage Museum, Leningrad* (London 1969). A Metropolitan Museum of Art (New York) catalogue, *From the Lands of the Scythians* (New York 1975), offers a stunning array of images of the most spectacular of the Scythian art. There are two useful critiques of Herodotus as a reliable source: F. Hartog, *The Mirror of Herodotus* (Berkeley 1988) and J. Gould, *Herodotus* (London 1989).

The situation in Middle Europe is discussed in K. Kristiansen, *Europe Before History* (Cambridge 1998). The Hallstatt elites are the subject of frequent discussion. From among the copious literature we can recommend P.S. Wells, *Culture Contact and Culture Change* (Cambridge 1980); J.-P. Mohen, A. Duval and C. Eluère, *Les princes celtes et la Méditerranée* (Paris 1988); P. Brun and B. Chaume, *Vix et les éphémères principantés celtique: Les VIe–Ve siècles avant J-C en Europe centre-occidentale* (Paris 1997); and C.F.E. Pare,

'Fürstensitze, Celts and the Mediterranean World: Developments in the West Hallstatt Culture in the Sixth and Fifth centuries BC', *Proceedings of the Prehistoric Society* 57 (1991), 183–202. For the vehicles buried with the elite, the most detailed review is C.F.E. Pare, *Wagons and Wagon-Graves of the Early Iron Age in Central Europe* (Oxford 1992).

Chapter 10: States in Collision: 500–140 BC

It goes without saying that many of the works listed in the last chapter are also relevant to this, and the grand narrative of the long march of Mediterranean civilization can be followed in the volumes of the *Cambridge Ancient History*. In what follows we will concentrate on works specific to the themes we have chosen to emphasize. To the general texts recommended we may add the lively yet meticulous account of the grand conflict between Rome and Carthage by B. Craven, *The Punic Wars* (London 1980), and three books that get deep into the economy and society of the Roman world: K. Hopkins, *Conquerors and Slaves* (Cambridge 1978); R. Duncan-Jones, *The Economy of the Roman Empire: Quantitative Studies* (2nd edition, Cambridge 1982); and P. Garnsey and R. Saller, *The Roman Empire: Economy, Society and Culture* (London 1987). All three offer brilliant insights into the substructure of the Roman edifice. Three regional studies that are essential reading are: M. Pallottino, *A History of Earliest Italy* (London 1991); M.I. Finley, *Ancient Sicily* (revised edition, London 1979); and P. Cartledge (ed.), *The Cambridge Illustrated History of Ancient Greece* (Cambridge 1998).

Turning to the Aegean, slavery in the Greek world is well covered in M.I. Finley (ed.), *Slavery in Classical Antiquity* (Cambridge 1960). The main aspects of the mines at Laurion are summed up in J.E. Jones, 'The Silver Mines of Athens', in B. Cunliffe (ed.), *Origins: The Roots of European Civilization* (London 1987), 108–20. The distribution of the mass-produced Castulo cups is explored in B.B. Shefton, 'Greek Imports at the Extremities of the Mediterranean, West and East: Reflections on the Case of Iberia in the Fifth Century BC', in B. Cunliffe and S. Keay (eds), *Social Complexity and the Development of Towns in Iberia* (Oxford 1995), 127–55.

Macedonians and Thracians are extensively covered in the specialist literature. F.W. Walbank (ed.), *The Hellenistic World* (Cambridge, Mass. 1992) offers a broad overview. More specifically for Macedonia, see N.G.L. Hammond's two books, *The Miracle That Was Macedon* (London 1991) and *Philip of Macedon* (London 1994). Thracians and Dacians are well covered in R.F. Hoddinott, *Bulgaria in Antiquity* (London 1975) and the same author's *The Thracians* (London 1981). For more detailed coverage, see A.

Fol and I. Marazov, *Thrace and the Thracians* (New York 1977); Z.H. Archibald, *The Odrysian Kingdom of Thrace* (Oxford 1998); N. Theodossiev, *North-Western Thrace from the Fifth to First Centuries BC* (Oxford 2000); and the same author's overarching survey of the recent literature in 'Ancient Thrace During the 1st Millennium BC', in G.R. Tsetskhladze (ed.), *The Black Sea, Greece, Anatolia and Europe in the 1st Millennium BC* (Leiden 2005). Aspects of Greek colonization in Thrace are addressed in C. Danov, 'Characteristics of Greek Colonization in Thrace', in J.-P. Descœudres (ed.), *Greek Colonists and Native Populations* (Oxford 1990), 151–55. A detailed study of Dacian trade is provided in I. Glodariu, *Dacian Trade with the Hellenistic and Roman World* (Oxford 1976). The exhibition catalogue *Thracian Treasures from Bulgaria* (London 1976) is a useful introduction to Thracian metalwork. The town of Seuthopolis is presented in detail in D.P. Dimitrov and M. Čičikova, *The Thracian City Seuthopolis* (Oxford 1978). The Gundestrup cauldron has generated a vast literature but most useful from our point of view is F. Kaul, 'The Gundestrup Cauldron and the Periphery of the Hellenistic world', in P. Bilde *et al.* (eds), *Centre and Periphery in the Hellenistic World* (Aarhus 1993), 39–52.

In the central Mediterranean, Phoenician urbanization is explored in H.G. Niemeyer, 'The Early Phoenician City-States on the Mediterranean: Archaeological Elements for their Description' in M.H. Hansen (ed.), *A Comparative Study of Thirty City-State Cultures: An Investigation Conducted by the Copenhagen Polis Centre* (Copenhagen 2000), 89–115. The impact of Carthaginian power is explored in D. Hoyos, *Hannibal's Dynasty: Power and Politics in the Western Mediterranean* (London 2003). The early development of Rome, providing a background for its rise to dominance in the Italian peninsula, is carefully explored in C.J. Smith, *Early Rome and Latium: Economy and Society 1000–500 BC* (Oxford 1996) and the same author's 'The Beginnings of Urbanization in Rome' in R. Osborne and B. Cunliffe (eds), *Mediterranean Urbanization 800–600 BC* (Oxford 2005), 91–111. The progress of Rome's rise to power is outlined in T. Cornell, *The Beginnings of Rome: Italy and Rome from the Bronze Age to the Punic Wars (c.1000–264 BC)* (London 1995). Carthage is thoroughly treated in an up-to-date history that takes into account the results of recent excavations by S. Lancel, *Carthage: A History* (Oxford 1995).

For Iberia, R.J. Harrison, *Spain at the Dawn of History: Iberians, Phoenicians and Greeks* (London 1988) is an excellent introduction, while M.E. Aubet, *The Phoenicians and the West: Politics, Colonies and Trade* (Cambridge 1993) provides details of the Phoenician impact. The Roman intervention in Iberia is well covered in L.A. Curchin, *Roman*

Spain: Conquest and Assimilation (London 1991). By far the best introduction to the spectacular development of Iberian culture and art is the catalogue of an international exhibition, held in Spain, Germany and France; *Les Ibères* (Paris 1997). Iberian sculpture is presented in P. León, *La sculpture des Ibères* (Paris 1998), while fortified sites are fully covered in P. Moret, *Les fortifications Ibérique de la fin de l'âge du bronze à la conquête romaine* (Madrid 1996). For religion, T. Moneo, *Religio Iberica: santuarios, ritos y divinidades (sigles VII–I A.C.)* (Madrid 2003). Other more specific studies include B. Cunliffe, 'Diversity in the Landscape: The Geographical Background to Urbanism in Iberia' and P. Moret *et al.*, 'The Fortified Settlement of La Picola (Santo Pola, Alicante) and the Greek Influence in South-East Spain', in B. Cunliffe and S. Keay (eds), *Social Complexity and the Development of Towns in Iberia* (Oxford 1995), 5–28 and 109–25.

The Atlantic coastal developments have been explored in B. Cunliffe, *Facing the Ocean: The Atlantic and its Peoples* (Oxford 2001), Chapter 8, while the activities of Pytheas are discussed in the same author's *The Extraordinary Voyage of Pytheas the Greek* (London 2001). Developments in the Nordic zone are summarized in J. Jensen, *The Prehistory of Denmark* (London 1982). More detailed studies include H. Thrane, 'Centres of Wealth in Northern Europe', in K. Kristiansen and J. Jensen (eds), *Europe in the First Millennium* B.C. (Sheffield 1994), 95–110. The Hjortspring boat was published in detail in G. Rosenberg, *Hjortspringfundet* (with an English summary) (Copenhagen 1937). The vessel has more recently been discussed in a Europe-wide social context in K. Randsborg, *Hjortspring: Warfare and Sacrifice in Early Europe* (Aarhus 1995).

Returning once more to the Black Sea and to the Greek/barbarian interaction, most of the works quoted in the last chapter are relevant to this. To these might be added K. Marčenko and Y. Vinogradov, 'The Scythians in the Black Sea Region', *Antiquity* 63 (1989), 803–13, and T. Sulimirski, *The Sarmatians* (London 1970). For the individual Greek colonies and their relations to their hinterlands, J. Boardman, *The Greeks Overseas: Their Early Colonies and Trade* (revised edition, London 1980) is still a standard work.

The Celts remain a very popular subject at both academic and popular level. By far the best visual introduction is offered by the sumptuous catalogue for the blockbuster exhibition held at the Palazzo Grassi in Venice in 1991, S. Moscati (ed.), *The Celts* (Milan 1991), which in addition to its fine photographs also contains many very useful specialist overviews. B. Cunliffe, *The Ancient Celts* (Oxford 1997) attempts a synthesis of the archaeological and documentary evidence. The confrontation between the Celts and the Mediterranean communities seen through the eyes of the classical historians is fully reviewed in H.D. Rankin, *Celts and the Classical World* (Beckenham 1987). The question of the identity of the Celts and indeed of the validity of the name has been approached in a flood of literature among which are S. James, *The Atlantic Celts: Ancient People or Modern Invention?* (London 1999); B. Cunliffe, *The Celts: A Very Short Introduction* (Oxford 2003); and J.R. Collis, *The Celts: Origins, Myths and Inventions* (Stroud 2003). Celtic settlement in Hungary is summarized in M. Szabó, *The Celtic Heritage in Hungary* (Budapest 1971), while the Celts of the Middle Danube and their movements into the Balkans and Greece are discussed in J. Todorović, *Skordisci* (Novi Sad 1974). Further movements to the east are considered in M. Treister, 'The Celts in the North Pontic Area: A reassessment', *Antiquity* 67 (1993), 789–804, and in S. Mitchell, *Anatolia: Land, Man and Gods in Asia Minor. Volume 1: The Celts and the Impact of Roman Rule* (Oxford 1993).

Finally, A. Pydyn, *Exchange and Cultural Interactions: A Study of Long-Distance Trade and Cross-Cultural Contacts in the Late Bronze Age and Early Iron Age in Central and Eastern Europe* (Oxford 1999) and K. Kristiansen, *Europe Before History* (Cambridge 1998) consider cross-peninsular interactions and social systems in fascinating detail.

Chapter 11: The Interlude of Empire: 140 BC–AD 300

It need hardly be said that there are a large number of books dealing with the Roman Empire and a plethora of journals devoted to the subject. Any selection is bound to be partial. Of the many overviews on offer aimed at the general reader one of the best in terms of content and scholarship is T. Cornell and J. Matthews, *Atlas of the Roman World* (London 1982), which has an excellent bibliography (up to its date of publication).

The themes that particularly concern us in this chapter are economy and demography. An essential book to read is M.I. Finley's inspiring *The Ancient Economy* (London 1973), if only to disagree with many of its underlying beliefs. The book began a debate that is still being pursued with enthusiasm as more and more quantifiable archaeological data become available. R. Duncan-Jones, *The Economy of the Roman Empire* (2nd edition, Cambridge 1982) provides a wealth of data and careful analysis, while a collection of essays brought together in P. Garnsey, K. Hopkins and C.R. Whittaker (eds), *Trade in the Ancient Economy* (London 1983) offers some well-worked examples. For the economy of early empire, P.A. Brunt, *Social Conflicts in the Roman Republic* (London 1971) and K. Hopkins, *Conquerors and Slaves* (Cambridge 1978) remain the essential reading, while P. Garnsey and R. Saller, *The Roman Empire: Economy,*

Society and Culture (London 1987) provides a more comprehensive review. To these should be added K. Hopkins, 'Taxes and Trade in the Roman Empire 200 BC–AD 400', in *Journal of Roman Studies* 70 (1980), 101–25. The social reforms championed by the Gracchi are detailed in D. Stockton, *The Gracchi* (Oxford 1979), with a more specific study of land reform in J.S. Richardson, 'The Ownership of Roman land: Tiberius Gracchus and the Italians', in *Journal of Roman Studies* 70 (1980), 1–11.

The situation in temperate Europe is outlined in B. Cunliffe, *The Ancient Celts* (Oxford 1997) and more specifically in relation to the Roman world in the same author's *Greeks, Romans and Barbarians: Spheres of Interaction* (London 1988). C. Ebel, *Transalpine Gaul: The Emergence of a Roman Province* (Leiden 1976) provides a detailed commentary on the increasing Roman involvement in the region. The subject of the native *oppida* is addressed in J. Collis, *Oppida: Earliest Towns North of the Alps* (Sheffield 1984) and in a well-illustrated general account, F. Audouze and O. Buchsenschutz, *Towns, Villages and Countryside of Celtic Europe, from the Beginnings of the 2nd Millennium to the End of the 1st Century* BC (London 1991). The most useful and comprehensive book for the general reader is S. Fichtl, *La ville celtique: les oppida de 150 av. J.-C. à 15 ap. J.-C.* (Paris 2000). An interesting critique about *oppida* is G. Woolf, 'Rethinking the Oppida', *Oxford Journal of Archaeology* 12 (1993), 223–34.

The conquest of Iberia is effectively covered in S.J. Keay, *Roman Spain* (London 1988) and L.A. Curchin, *Roman Spain: Conquest and Assimilation* (London 1991). The Roman wine trade has generated a considerable literature: the most comprehensive discussion is A. Tchernia, *Le vin de l'Italie romaine* (Rome 1986). Gaul is specifically considered in F. Laubenheimer, *Les temps des amphores en Gaule* (Paris 1990) and A. Tchernia, 'Italian Wine in Gaul at the End of the Republic', in P. Garnsey, K. Hopkins and C.R. Whittaker (eds), *Trade in the Ancient Economy* (London 1983), 87–104. Shipwrecks off the French coast are conveniently summarized in A.J. Parker, 'Shipwrecks and Ancient Trade in the Mediterranean', *Archaeological Review Cambridge* 3:2 (1984), 99–107. Roman trading relations with the kingdom of Noricum are outlined in G. Alföldy, *Noricum* (London 1974).

For the Germans and the Roman attitude to them, the relevant sections of Caesar's *De bello gallico* and the whole of Tacitus's *Germania* are well worth reading, together with parts of Tacitus's *Annals*. E.A. Thompson, *The Early Germans* (Oxford 1965) uses the texts in a lively discussion of Germanic social structure. The most accessible and comprehensive commentary on the subject is M. Todd, *The Early Germans* (2nd edition, Oxford 2004). Early Roman military activity in Germany is outlined in C.M. Wells, *The German Policy of Augustus: An Examination of the Archaeological Evidence* (Oxford 1972), which is now rather out of date.

There are few general books on the Dacians. D. Berciu, *Daco-Romania* (Geneva 1978) and E. Condurachi, *Romania* (London 1967) contain useful material, while F. Lepper and S. Frere, *Trajan's Column* (Gloucester 1988) is an excellent source for the war of conquest fought by Trajan against the Dacians. Trade with Dacia is explored in an important paper by M.H. Crawford, 'Republican Denarii in Romania: The Suppression of Piracy and the Slave Trade', *Journal of Roman Studies* 67 (1977), 117–24. Sarmatians are conveniently treated in T. Sulimirski, *The Sarmatians* (London 1970) and I. Lebedynsky, *Les Sarmates* (Paris 2002).

The military history of the Roman Empire is not really a theme pursued in this book but for comprehensive general reviews see S.L. Dyson, *The Creation of the Roman Frontier* (Princeton, NJ 1985) and D.S. Potter, *The Roman Empire at Bay, 180–395* (London 2004). The question of the second-century epidemics is discussed in a much broader context in W.H. McNeill, *Plagues and Peoples* (Oxford 1977).

Europe beyond the Roman frontier is covered at a general level in B. Cunliffe, *Greeks, Romans and Barbarians: Spheres of Interaction* (London 1988). Roman imports into northern Europe are discussed in detail in U.L. Hansen, *Der römische Import im Norden* (Copenhagen 1987) and J. Kunow, *Der römische Import in der Germania Libera bis zu den Marcomannenkriegen* (Neumünster 1983), while B.A. Raev, *Roman Imports in the Lower Don Basin* (Oxford 1986) and V.V. Kropotkin, *Rimskie importnye izdelija v vostocnoj Evrope* (Moscow 1970) offer an eastern perspective. For the Danish centres of redistribution, see P.O. Nielsen, K. Randsborg and H. Thrane, *The Archaeology of Gudme and Lundeborg* (Copenhagen 1994). A northern perspective is taken by L. Hedeager in two perceptive papers, 'A Quantitative Analysis of Roman Imports in Europe North of the Limes (0–400 AD) and the Question of Roman-Germanic Exchange' and 'Processes Towards State Formation in Early Iron Age Denmark', both in *Studies in Scandinavian Prehistory and Early History I* (1978), 191–216 and 217–23. The same author's book *Iron-Age Societies: From Tribe to State in Northern Europe, 500 BC to AD 700* (Oxford 1992) is an in-depth treatment to be thoroughly recommended. An exhibition catalogue, *The Spoils of Victory: The North in the Shadow of the Roman Empire* (Copenhagen 2003), edited by L. Jørgensen *et al.*, offers a well-illustrated and lively discussion of the Nordic region in the Roman Iron Age.

The cultural transformations among the northern tribes during the Roman period are also well summarized in M. Todd, *The Early Germans* (2nd edition, Oxford 2004).

The formation and early movements of the Goths are fully treated in P. Heather, *The Goths* (Oxford 1996). Roman material in Scotland is listed and discussed in A.S. Robertson, 'Roman Finds from Non-Roman Sites in Scotland', *Britannia* 1 (1970), 198–226, and from Ireland in J.D. Bateson, 'Roman Material from Ireland: A Re-Consideration', *Proceedings of the Royal Irish Academy* 73 (1973), 21–97. P. Freeman, *Ireland and the Classical World* (Austin 2001) provides a valuable overview, particularly of the relevant classical texts on the subject.

The late third-century crisis is given extensive treatment in thirty-two individual papers brought together in A. King and M. Henig, *The Roman West in the Third Century: Contributions from Archaeology and History* (Oxford 1981). The period is also well covered in M. Christol, *L'empire romain du IIIᵉ siècle* (Paris 1997). The attempted recovery that followed is carefully chronicled and assessed in S. Williams, *Diocletian and the Roman Recovery* (London 1985) and in S. Mitchell, *A History of the Later Roman Empire*, AD *284–641* (Oxford 2007).

Chapter 12: The Turn of the Tide: AD 300–800

A convenient way to prepare for this chapter is to read P. Brown's delightful overview *The World of Late Antiquity from Marcus Aurelius to Muhammad* (London 1971) and to follow it with B. Ward-Perkins' perceptive *The Fall of Rome and the End of Civilization* (Oxford 2005) and C. Mango (ed.), *The Oxford History of Byzantium* (Oxford 2002), which contains a series of first rate and highly readable essays by a number of scholars. For the western background, R. Collins, *Charlemagne* (London 1998) is excellent. On more specifically Mediterranean topics, D. Abulafia (ed.), *The Mediterranean in History* (London 2003) provides an attractively illustrated account. The history of the period is thoroughly covered in *The New Cambridge Medieval History*. *Vol. I c.500–c.700*, edited by P. Fouracre (Cambridge 2005), and *Vol. II c.700–c.900*, edited by R. McKitterick (Cambridge 1995).

The migratory groups of the fourth to sixth centuries are well introduced in M. Todd, *The Early Germans* (2nd edition, Oxford 2004) and H. Wolfram, *The Roman Empire and its Germanic Peoples* (Berkeley 1997). Good texts on specific peoples include: for the Huns, E.A. Thompson, *The Huns* (Oxford 1996); I. Bóna, *Das Hunnenreich* (Stuttgart 1991); P. Heather, 'The Huns and the End of the Roman Empire in Europe', *English Historical Review* 110 (1995), 4–41. For the Goths, P. Heather, *The Goths* (Oxford 1996); H. Wolfram, *History of the Goths* (Berkeley, Calif. 1998); M. Rouché, *L'Aquitaine des Wisigoths aux Arabes, 418–781* (Paris 1979); E.A. Thompson, *The Goths in Spain* (Oxford 1969);

R. Collins, *Visigothic Spain* (Oxford 2004); J. Moorehead, *Theoderic in Italy* (Oxford 1992). For the Suebi, E.A. Thompson, *Romans and Barbarians* (Madison, Wis. 1982), 161–87; R. Collins, *Early Medieval Spain* (London 1983), 20–24. For the Vandals, C. Courtois, *Les Vandales et l'Afrique* (Paris 1955). For the Alans, V. Kouznetsov and I. Lebedynsky, *Les Alains: cavaliers des steppes, seigneurs du Caucase* (Paris 1997). For the Franks, P. Périn and L.-C. Feffer, *Les Francs I* (Paris 1987); E. James, *The Franks* (Oxford 1988). For the Alamanni, R. Christlein, *Die Alamannen* (Stuttgart 1978) and the catalogue of an exhibition, *Die Alamannen* (Stuttgart 1994). For the Burgundians, O. Perrin, *Les Burgondes* (Neuchatel 1968). For the Langobardi, N. Christie, *The Lombards* (Oxford 1996); W. Menghin, *Die Langobarden* (Stuttgart 1985); and an exhibition catalogue, *I Longobardi* (Cividale 1990). For the Saxons, Frisians, Jutes and Angles, S. Lebecq, *Marchands et navigateurs: Frisons du haute moyen âge* (Lille 1983). The formation and early development of the Slavs is most comprehensively (and sensibly) treated in P.M. Barford, *The Early Slavs. Culture and Society in Early Medieval Eastern Europe* (London 2001). The Balts are considered in M. Gimbutas, *The Balts* (London 1963) while for the Bulgars see D.M. Lang, *The Bulgarians from Pagan times to the Ottoman Conquest* (London 1976).

Of the massive literature on Islam the following are particularly useful to our theme: M. Cook, *Muhammad* (Oxford 1983); P. Crone, *Meccan Trade and the Rise of Islam*; G. Hawting, *The Dynasty of Islam: The Umayyad Caliphate*, AD *661–750* (London 1986); and I. Shahîd, *Byzantium and the Arabs in the Sixth Century* (Washington DC 1995).

For understanding commerce in the Mediterranean during the period that concerns us, the magisterial work by M. McCormick, *Origins of European Economy: Communications and Commerce* AD *300–900* (Cambridge 2001), is incomparable. It is packed with detail. A somewhat easier read text covering part of the range is R. Hodges and D. Whitehouse, *Mohammed, Charlemagne and the Origins of Europe: Archaeology and the Pirenne Thesis* (Ithica 1983).

The maritime links along the Atlantic are considered in B. Cunliffe, *Facing the Ocean: The Atlantic and its Peoples* (Oxford 2001), Chapter 10. R. Hodges, *Dark Age Economics: The Origins of Towns and Trade*, AD *600–1000* (2nd edition, London 1989) provides a broad background to the commerce of the period. On the Roman shipwrecks, M. Rule and J. Monaghan, *A Gallo-Roman Trading Vessel from Guernsey* (St Peter Port 1993) and M. L'Hour, 'Un site sous-marin sur la côte de l'Armorique: l'épavé antique de Ploumanac'h', *Revue archéologique de l'Ouest* 4 (1987), 113–32. The Saxon Shore is well covered in S. Johnson, *The Roman Forts of the Saxon Shore* (London 1976) and V. Maxfield (ed.),

The Saxon Shore: A Handbook (Exeter 1989). For migration to Brittany, P. Galliou and M. Jones, *The Bretons* (Oxford 1991) contains a summary of the salient points, but for a more extended discussion see P.-R. Giot, P. Guigon and B. Merdrignac, *The British Settlement of Brittany: The First Bretons in Armorica* (Stroud 2003). Wandering missionaries are introduced in E. Bowen, *Saints, Seaways and Settlements* (Cardiff 1977). Commerce along the Atlantic routes is conveniently summarized in J. Wooding, *Communications and Commerce along the Western Sea Lanes AD 400–800* (Oxford 1996). For shipping, there are many relevant papers in S. McGrail (ed.), *Maritime Celts, Frisians and Saxons* (London 1990).

The best straightforward introduction to the Nordic world is provided by the early sections of J. Graham-Campbell *et al.* (eds), *Cultural Atlas of the Viking World* (Oxford 1994). The early Danish redistribution centres are detailed in P.O. Nielsen, K. Randsborg and H. Thrane, *The Archaeology of Gudme and Lundeborg* (Copenhagen 1994), while Helgö is thoroughly discussed in A. Lundström (ed.), *Thirteen Studies on Helgö* (Stockholm 1988). For the Vendel period, see J.P. Lamm and H.-Å. Nordström, *Vendel Period Studies* (Stockholm 1983). The subject of maritime activity in the region is explored in O. Crumlin-Pedersen (ed.), *Aspects of Maritime Scandinavia AD 200–1200* (Roskilde 1990). More particularly for the Nydam boats, see F. Rieck, 'Iron Age Boats from Hjortspring and Nydam', in C. Westerdahl (ed.), *Crossroads in Ancient Shipbuilding* (Oxford 1994), 45–54. The Sutton Hoo vessel is described in meticulous detail in R. Bruce-Mitford, *The Sutton Hoo Ship-Burial Vol. 1* (London 1975) and in a more accessible account, with a broader perspective, in M. Carver, *Sutton Hoo: Burial Ground of Kings?* (London 1998). The Gotland picture stones are treated in E. Nylén and J.P. Lamm, *Stones, Ships and Symbols: The Picture Stones of Gotland from the Viking Age and Before* (Stockholm 1988). Aspects of maritime exchange in the Black Sea are outlined in C. King, *The Black Sea: A History* (Oxford 2004), Chapter 3.

The development of trade networks in Europe is considered in R. Hodges, *Dark Age Economics: The Origins of Towns and Trade AD 600–1000* (2nd edition, London 1989) and in various papers in R. Hodges and W. Bowden (eds), *The Sixth Century: Production, Distribution and Demand* (Leyden 1998) and also in T. Pestell and K. Ulmschneider, *Markets in Early Medieval Europe: Trading and 'Productive' Sites, 650–850* (Macclesfield 2003). But for the interconnectedness of it all, there is nothing better than M. McCormick, *Origins of European Economy: Communications and Commerce AD 300–900* (Cambridge 2001).

Chapter 13: Europe Rebalanced: AD 800–1000

As general background reading, R. Collins, *Charlemagne* (London 1998) and C. Mango (ed.), *The Oxford History of Byzantium* (Oxford 2002) provide much of the historical framework for the Carolingian and Byzantine empires. An excellent overview of Islamic intervention in the Mediterranean is J. Pryor, 'The Mediterranean Breaks Up: 500–1000', in D. Abulafia (ed.), *The Mediterranean in History* (London 2003), 155–81. For maritime activity in the Mediterranean, two comprehensive sources are X. de Planhol, *L'Islam et la mer* (Paris 2000) and H. Ahrweiler, *Byzance et la mer* (Paris 1966). O.R. Constable, *Trade and Traders in Muslim Spain: The Commercial Realignment of the Iberian Peninsula, 900–1500* (Cambridge 1994) deals in detail with west Mediterranean interchanges.

The Magyar arrival and impact on Europe is conveniently summarized in I. Dienes, *The Hungarians Cross the Carpathians* (Budapest 1972).

The Northmen, usually in their familiar guise as Vikings, are very well covered in the general literature. One of the most accessible works is J. Graham-Campbell, *Cultural Atlas of the Viking World* (Oxford 1994), which is very well illustrated with excellent maps. Other comprehensive works to be strongly recommended are: C. Christiansen, *The Norsemen in the Viking Age* (Oxford 2002); P. Sawyer (ed.), *The Oxford Illustrated History of the Vikings* (Oxford 1997); P. Foote and D. Wilson, *The Viking Achievement* (2nd edition, London 1980); and G. Jones, *A History of the Vikings* (2nd edition, Oxford 1984). Trading centres are specifically treated in H. Clarke and B. Ambrosiani, *Towns in the Viking Age* (Leicester 1991). Viking ships and shipbuilding are fully discussed in: O. Olsen and O. Crumlin-Pedersen, 'The Skuldelev Ships', *Acta Archaeologica* 38 (1968); O. Crumlin-Pedersen, *Viking-Age Ships and Shipbuilding in Hedeby/Haithabu and Schleswig* (Schleswig and Roskilde 1997); A. Brøgger and H. Shetelig, *The Viking Ships: Their Ancestry and Evolution* (Oslo 1951); and T. Sjøvold, *The Viking Ships in Oslo* (Oslo 1985).

Viking raiding and settlement in the Atlantic zone are discussed in the general books listed above while the story of the North Atlantic adventures is explored in G.J. Marcus, *The Conquest of the North Atlantic* (Woodbridge 1980). For the eastern trade routes, there are useful papers in D. Austin and L. Alcock (eds), *From the Baltic to the Black Seas: Studies in Medieval Archaeology* (London 1990). Other useful texts are R. Milner-Gulland, *The Russians* (Oxford 1997), T.S. Noonan, 'Vikings and Russia: Some New Directions and Approaches to an Old Problem', in R. Samson (ed.), *Social Approaches to Viking Studies* (Glasgow 1991), 201–6.

Index

Sources of Illustrations

Note: where no specific source is given the illustration has been designed by the author using multiple sources.

Chapter 1: 1.1 Yann Arthus Bertrand/Corbis. 1.2 J. O. Thompson, *History of Ancient Geography* (Oxford 1948), 99. 1.3 T. Taylor in B. Cunliffe (ed.), *Prehistoric Europe* (Oxford 1994), 386, with modifications. 1.4 CNES, 1993 Distribution Spot Image/Science Photo Library. 1.5 J. O. Thompson, *History of Ancient Geography* (Oxford 1948), figs 16 and 26, with modifications. 1.6 J. O. Thompson, *History of Ancient Geography* (Oxford 1948), figs 16 and 26, with modifications. 1.7 Lauros/Giraudon/Bridgeman Art Library. 1.8 B. Cunliffe. 1.9 English Heritage/National Monuments Record. 1.13 B. Cunliffe, *The Ancient Celts* (Oxford 1997), 306.

Chapter 2: 2.1. English Heritage Photo Library. 2.3 P. Mellars in B. Cunliffe (ed.), *Prehistoric Europe* (Oxford 1994), 43. 2.4 Planetary Visions Ltd/Science Photo Library. 2.5. C. Scarre (ed.), *The Human Past* (London 2005), 108, with modifications. 2.10 Based on V. M. Masson and T. Taylor in *Antiquity* 63 (1989), fig. 1, with modifications. 2.14 M-Sat Ltd/Science Photo Library. 2.15 M-Sat Ltd/Science Photo Library 2.16 Yann Arthus Bertrand/Corbis 2.17 Based on A. T. Hodge, *Ancient Greek France* (London 1998), fig. 16.

Chapter 3: 3.1. C. Scarre (ed.), *The Human Past* (London 2005), 178. 3.2 T. H. van Andel in *Antiquity* 63 (1989), fig. 3. 3.3 J. R. Coull, *The Fisheries of Europe. An Economic Geography* (London 1972). 3.4 Wolfgang Kaehler/Corbis. 3.5 Institute of Archaeology, Oxford based on J. E. Morais Arnaud in C. Bonsall (ed.), *The Mesolithic in Europe* (Edinburgh 1989), 615. 3.6 Musée de Prehistoire, Carnac. 3.7 National Museum of Denmark. 3.8 Redrawn from S. H. Anderson in *Journal of Danish Archaeology* 4 (1985), figs 14 and 15. 3.9 Reproduced from S.H. Anderson in *Journal of Danish Archaeology* 4 (1985), figs 2.1 and 2.6. 3.10 Adam Woolfitt/Corbis. 3.11 National Museum of Belgrade. 3.12 National Museum of Belgrade. 3.13 L. P Louwe Kooijams/National Museum of Antiquities, Netherlands.

Chapter 4: 4.1 C. Scarre (ed.), *The Human Past* (London 2005), 203. 4.3 Erich Lessing/AKG. 4.4 Geoffrey Clifford/Getty Images. 4.5 C. Perles, *The Early Neolithic in Greece. The First Farming Communities in Europe* (Cambridge 2001), figs 6.4 and 7.3. 4.6 Trustees of the British Museum. 4.7 C. Perles, *The Early Neolithic in Greece. The First Farming Communities in Europe* (Cambridge 2001), fig. 12.1. 4.8 C. Perles, *The Early Neolithic in Greece. The First Farming Communities in Europe* (Cambridge 2001), fig. 10.4. 4.10 D. W. Bailey, *Balkan Prehistory* (London 2000), fig. 2.4. 4.11 L. P. Louwe Kooijmans *et al.* (eds), *The Prehistory of the Netherlands*, Vol. 1 (Amsterdam 2005), fig. 10.10. 4.12 L. P. Louwe Kooijmans *et al.* (eds), *The Prehistory of the Netherlands*, Vol. 1 (Amsterdam 2005), fig. 11.6. 4.13 Dr. Rudolph Kuper/University of Cologne. 4.14 Landesamt für Denkmalpflege Baden-Württemberg.

Chapter 5: 5.3 Pitt Rivers Museum, University of Oxford. 5.4 Robert Leighton. 5.5 R. Leighton, *Sicily Before History* (London 1999), fig. 26. 5.7 J. Zilhao in *Journal of Mediterranean Archaeology* 6 (1993), figs 4 and 5. 5.8 Museo de Prehistoria de Valencia, Spain. 5.9 Based on R. H. Tykot in *Journal of Mediterranean Archaeology* 9 (1996), fig. 10. 5.11 J. Zilhao in T. D. Price (ed.), *Europe's First Farmers* (Cambridge 2000), fig. 6.3. 5.11 Based on L. P. Louwe Kooijmans *et al.* (eds), *The Prehistory of the Netherlands*, Vol. 1 (Amsterdam 2005), pl. 3. 5.12 L. P. Louwe Kooijmans. 5.13 Editions Gisserot − Jean L'Helgouac'h. 5.14 G. Bailloud *et al.*, *Carnac* (Paris 1995), 89. 5.15 C. Scarre in *Oxford Journal of Archaeology* 21 (2002), fig. 11, with additions. 5.16 C. Scarre (ed.), *The Human Past* (London 2005), fig. 4. 5.17 Aviation Pictures. G. Bailloud *et al.*, *Carnac* (Paris 1995), 89.

Chapter 6: 6.1 C. Scarre (ed.), *The Human Past* (London 2005), figs 12.1 and 12.13, with modifications. 6.2 A. Sherrattin in B. Cunliffe (ed.), *Prehistoric Europe* (Oxford 1994), 173. 6.3 B. Cunliffe, *Facing the Ocean* (Oxford 2001), 5-28, with additions. 6.4 Deutsches Archaologisches Institut, Madrid (Hermanfrid Schubart KB 4-68-14). 6.5 Erich Lessing/akg-images. 6.6 S. Tabaczynski in *Neolithische Studien* 1. 6.7 L. P. Louwe Kooijmans *et al.* (eds), *The Prehistory of the Netherlands*, Vol. 1 (Amsterdam 2005), fig. E2. 6.8 Based on C.-T. Le Roux in T. H. McK. Clough and W. A. Cummings (eds), *Stone Axe Studies* (London 1979), fig. 3. 6.9 A.-M. Pétrequin, P. Pétrequin and S. Cassen, 'Les longues lames polies des elites', *La Recherche* 312, 70–5, fig. 6.7, with additions. 6.10 National Museums Scotland. 6.11 E. N. Chernykh, *Ancient Metallurgy in the USSR: The Early Metal Age* (Cambridge 1992), fig. 15. 6.12 Varna Regional Museum of History, Bulgaria. 6.13 Redrawn after J. A. Bakker *et al.* in *Antiquity* 73 (1999), figs 2 and 7. 6.14 Department of Archaeology/Hungarian National Museum. 6.16 (plan) J. Lecornec, *Le Petit Mont, Arzon, Morbihan* (Documents Archéologiques de l'Ouest 1994), fig. 8. 6.17 G. Daniel, *The Prehistoric Chamber Tombs of France* (London 1960), figs 23 and 24. 6.18 Philippe Beuzzen © CMN, Paris. 6.20 Department of the Environment, Heritage and Local Government Ireland, Dublin. 6.21 A. Whittle, *Europe in the Neolithic. The Creation of New Worlds* (Cambridge 1996), fig. 7.29. 6.22 National Museum of Demark. 6.23 The State Hermitage Museum. 6.24 The State Hermitage Museum. 6.25 Piggott Archive: Institute of Archaeology, University of Oxford. 6.26 I. Panayotov and V. Dergachov in *Studia Praehistorica* 7. 6.28 Hans Georg Roth/Corbis. 6.30 C. Broodbank, *An Island Archaeology of the Early Cyclades* (Cambridge 2000), figs 30 and 36. 6.31 Hellenic Ministry of Culture/Archaeological Receipts Fund.

Chapter 7: 7.1 Adam Woolfitt/Corbis. 7.5 C. Broodbank, *An Island Archaeology of the Early Cyclades* (Cambridge 2000), fig. 121. 7.6 Ashmolean Museum, Oxford. 7.7 C. Broodbank, *An Island Archaeology of the Early Cyclades* (Cambridge 2000), fig. 120. 7.8 Yann Arthus-Bertrand/Corbis. 7.10 Art Archive/Heraklion Museum/Gianni Dagli Orti. 7.11 National Geographic/Getty. 7.12 Art Archive/National Archaeological Museum, Athens/Gianni Dagli Orti. 7.14 Art Archive/National Archaeological Museum, Athens/Gianni Dagli Orti. 7.15 Art Archive/Archaeological Museum, Nafplion/Gianni Dagli Orti. 7.16 Art Archive/Archaeological Museum, Chora/Gianni Dagli Orti. 7.17 Donald A Frey/Institute of Archaeology, Texas. 7.18 A. Sherratt in B. Cunliffe (ed.), *Origins. The Roots of European Civilization* (London 1987), fig. 5.8. 7.20 A. F. Harding, *The Mycenaeans and Europe* (London 1984), figs 16 and 55. 7.21 Gonzalo Aranda/Departmento de Prehistoria y Arqueologia Universidad de Granda. 7.23 National Museums of Scotland. 7.24 W. O'Brian, *Ross Island. Mining, Metal and Society in Early Ireland* (Galway 2004), fig. 238. 7.25 Dover Museum. 7.26 P. Clark (ed.), *The Dover Bronze Age Boat* (London 2004), fig. 5.63. 7.27 Wiltshire Heritage, Museum and Gallery Library. 7.29 National Museum of Demark. 7.30 National Museum of Demark. 7.31 Professor J. M. Coles. 7.33 National Museum of Demark. 7.34 Antivarisk Topografiska/Riksantikvarieambete. 7.35 A. Sherratt in B. Cunliffe (ed.), *Origins. The Roots of European Civilization* (London 1987), fig. 5.2. 7.37 P. F. Kuznetsov in *Antiquity* 80 (2006), fig. 1 and S. Piggott, *The Earliest Wheeled Vehicles* (London 1983), fig. 52. 7.38 V. F. Genning et al, *Sintashta: Archaeological Sites of Aryan Tribes in the Ural-Kazakh Steppes* (Chelybinsk 1992), fig. 80. 7.39 R. Sheridan/Ancient Art & Architecture Collection Ltd. 7.40 S. Piggott, *The Earliest Wheeled Vehicles* (London 1983), figs 56-8.

Chapter 8: 8.1 Art Archive/Gianni Dagli Orti. 8.2 B. Cunliffe, *The Ancient Celts* (Oxford 1997), map 1. 8.3a National Museum of Demark. 8.3b Art Archive/Archaeological Museum, Cagliari/Gianni Dagli Orti. 8.3c CarlaMedia, Sweden. 8.4 National Museum of Demark. 8.6 C. Scarre (ed.), *The Human Past* (London 2005), fig. 12.40, with additions. 8.7 RMN/Herve Lewandowski. 8.8 Vassos Stylianou. 8.9 M. Popham in G. R. Tsetskhladze and F. de Angelis (eds), *The Archaeology of Greek Colonisation* (Oxford 1994), fig. 2.12. 8.11 Carlo Delfino Editore, Sardinia. 8.12 Art Archive/Archaeological Museum, Cagliari/Gianni Dagli Orti. 8.15 A. Coffyn, *Le Bronze Final Atlantique dans la Péninsule Ibérique* (Paris 1985), maps 21 and 22. 8.16 National Museum Ireland. 8.17 Oronoz Archive. 8.18 B. Cunliffe, *The Celts. A Very Short Introduction* (Oxford 2003), fig. 8, with additions. 8.20 A. Pydyn, *Exchange and Cultural Interaction* (Oxford 1999), map 31. 8.21 Antivarisk Topografiska/Riksantikvarieambete. 8.22 H. Thrane, *Europceiske Forbindelser* (Copenhagen 1975), fig. 89. 8.23 K. Kristiansen in C. Scarce and F. Healy (eds), *Trade and Exchange in Prehistoric Europe* (Oxford 1993), fig. 14.3. 8.24 A. Pydyn *Exchange and Cultural Interaction* (Oxford 1999), map 29. 8.25 Author using J. Chochorowski, *Ekspansja Kimmeryjska Na Tereny Europy Srodkowej* (Krakow 1993), map 1. 8.26a Landesant fur Kultur und Denkmalpflege, Schwerin. 8.26b National Museum of History of Romania, Bucharest.

Chapter 9: 9.2 B. Cunliffe, *The Ancient Celts* (Oxford 1997), map 6. 9.3 B. Cunliffe, *The Ancient Celts* (Oxford 1997), map 8. 9.5 B. Cunliffe, *The Ancient Celts* (Oxford 1997), map 7. 9.6 Art Archive/Museo di Villa Giulia, Rome/Gianni Dagli Orti. 9.7a Bridgeman Art Library/Giraudon. 9.7b Trustees of the British Museum. 9.7c Trustees of the British Museum. 9.7d Trustees of the British Museum. 9.11 B. Cunliffe in L. Hannestad, J. Zahle and K. Randsborg (eds), *Centre and Periphery in the Hellenistic World* (Aarhus 1993), fig. 4. 9.13 Photothèque Centre Camille Jullian/LAMM MMSH – CNRS. 9.14 B. Cunliffe, *Facing the Ocean* (Oxford 2001), fig. 7.28. 9.15 Author using V. S. Olkhovskii, *Pogrebalno-Pominalnaya Obriadnost Naseleniyo Stepnoi Skifii* (Moscow 1991), fig. 1. 9.16 Art Archive/Hermitage Museum, St Petersburg/Gianni Dagli Orti. 9.17 A. Pydyn, *Exchange and Cultural Interaction* (Oxford 1999), map 57. 9.18 BPK Berlin/Johannes Laurentius. 9.19 B. Cunliffe, *The Ancient Celts* (Oxford 1997), map 16. 9.20 Landesamt für Denkmalpflege Baden-Württemberg. 9.21 S. Piggott, *Ancient Europe* (Edinburgh 1965). 9.22 Musée

Archéologique, Châtillon sur Seine, Bridgeman Art Library/Giraudon. 9.23 Landesmuseum Wurttemberg, Stuttgart. 9.25 B. Cunliffe, *Facing the Ocean* (Oxford 2001), fig. 7.28.

Chapter 10: 10.2 P. Levi, *Atlas of the Greek World* (Oxford 1980), 140. 10.3 Art Archive/Archaeological Museum, Salonica/Gianni Dagli Orti. 10.4 B. Cunliffe, *Rome and her Empire* (London 1978), 68. 10.7 Trustees of the British Museum. 10.10 P. Levi, *Atlas of the Greek World* (Oxford 1980), 177. 10.11 Carmen Redondo/Corbis. 10.12a Julian Angelov/Travel Photo. 10.12b National Museum of Demark. 10.13 Alinari Archives. 10.16 akg-images. 10.16 Nimatallah/akg-images. 10.17 Oronoz Archive. 10.18 Fundacíon la Alcudia. 10.19 T. Chapa Brunet 1982 reproduced in B. Cunliffe in L. Hannestad, J. Zahle and K. Randsborg (eds), *Centre and Periphery in the Hellenistic World* (Aarhus 1993), fig, 8. 10.20a National Museums of Scotland. 10.20b Trustees of the British Museum. 10.21 S. Jansson in *Marinar Kceologisk Nyheds brev fra Roskilde* 2 (1994). 10.23 State Hermitage Museum. 10.25 Piggott Archive, Institute of Archaeology, Oxford. 10.27 BPK Berlin/Ingrid Geske.

Chapter 11: 11.2 Bettman/Corbis. 11.3 B. Cunliffe, *The Ancient Celts* (Oxford 1997), map 29. 11.5 Rene Gogney. 11.6 Antione Chene/CNRS Photothèque. 11.7 B. Cunliffe, *Greeks, Romans and Barbarians. Spheres of Interaction* (London 1988), fig. 36. 11.8 M. Todd, *The Northern Barbarians 100 BC–AD 300* (London 1975), fig. 2. 11.9 B. Cunliffe (ed.), *Prehistoric Europe* (Oxford 1994), 422 and 431. 11.10 National Museum of History of Romania, Bucharest. 11.12 Ioan Glodariu. 11.13 Ioan Glodariu. 11.14 Alinari Archives. 11.16 Jason Hawkes/Corbis. 11.17 B. Cunliffe, *Greeks, Romans and Barbarians. Spheres of Interaction* (London 1988), figs 70 and 71 based on Eggers 1951. 11.18 U.L. Hansen, *Der romische Import im Norden* (Copenhagen 1987), map 32. 11.20 Art Archive/Gianni Dagli Orti. 11.21 Art Archive/Archaeological Museum, Istanbul/Gianni Dagli Orti.

Chapter 12: 12.2 Based on P. Sarris in C. Mango (ed.), *The Oxford History of Byzantium* (Oxford 2002), 52. 12.3 Lawrence Manning/Corbis. 12.4 Based on P. Sarris in C. Mango (ed.), *The Oxford History of Byzantium* (Oxford 2002), 52. 12.6 Art Archive/San Apollinare Nuovo Ravenna/Alfredo Dagli Orti. 12.7 Ruggero Vanni/Corbis. 12.11 Yann Arthus-Bertrand/Corbis. 12.12 National Library, Madrid. 12.14 Museo Torlonia, Rome/Alinari Archives/Bridgeman Art Library. 12.15 English Heritage Photo Library. 12.16 English Heritage Photo Library. 12.19a State Historical Museum, Museum of Antiquities, Stockholm. 12.19b State Historical Museum, Museum of Antiquities, Stockholm. 12.20 University Library, Uppsala. 12.21 Trustees of the British Museum. 12.22 Leipziger Illustrierte Zertung 1865. 12.23 O. Crumlin-Pedersen (after Nylén 1978) in S. McGrail (ed.), *Maritime Celts, Frisians and Saxons* (London 1990), figs 14.14 and 14.18. 12.24 D. Matthew, *Atlas of Medieval Europe* (Oxford 1983), 18.

Chapter 13: 13.2 National Library, Madrid. 13.3 P. Magdalino in C. Mango (ed.), *The Oxford History of Byzantium* (Oxford 2002), 178. 13.5 National Library, Madrid. 13.7 Bibliothèque Nationale, Paris. 13.8 Royal Coin Cabinet, National Museum of Economy, Sweden. 13.9 Museum of Cultural History, University of Oslo. 13.10 J. Graham-Campbell *et al.* (eds), *Cultural Atlas of the Viking World* (Oxford 1994), 126. 13.11 National Museums of Scotland. 13.12 J. Graham-Campbell *et al.* (eds), *Cultural Atlas of the Viking World* (Oxford 1994), 117. 13.13 J. Graham-Campbell *et al.* (eds), *Cultural Atlas of the Viking World* (Oxford 1994), 189. 13.14 National Museum of Denmark.